Psychology

Preparing for the Advanced Placement® Examination

AMSCO SCHOOL PUBLICATIONS, INC.,

a division of Perfection Learning®

Reviewers

Kerri Baalman
YES Prep Pubic Schools
Houston, TX
AP Psychology Teacher and Testing
 Coordinator

Michael Berndt
Apollo Senior High
St. Cloud, MN
AP Psychology Teacher, Reader, and
 Table Leader

Andrew Christopher
Professor of Psychological Science
Editor, Teaching of Psychology
Albion College
Albion, MI
AP Psychology Reader, Table Leader,
 and Question Leader

Nancy Fenton
Adlai E. Stevenson High School
Lincolnshire, IL
AP Psychology Teacher

Lisa Jensen
Herriman High School
Herriman, UT
AP Psychology Teacher, Coach, and Reader

Kent Korek
Germantown High School
Germantown, WI
AP Psychology Teacher, Reader, Table
 Leader, and College Board Consultant

Dana C. Melone
Cedar Rapids Kennedy High School
Cedar Rapids, IA
AP Psychology Teacher, Curriculum
 Facilitator, and Table Leader

Deborah L. Firak, M.S.
Instructor of Biology, Bioethics and Human
 Anatomy & Physiology
McHenry County College
Crystal Lake, IL
Anatomy Consultant

Psychology: Preparing for the AP® Examination is one of a series of
AP® social studies texts first launched with *United States History: Preparing for the
AP® Examination.*

© 2017 Perfection Learning®

www.perfectionlearning.com

1 2 3 4 5 6 EBM 22 21 20 19 18 17

When ordering this book, please specify:

Softcover: ISBN 978-1-68240-221-4 or **1821101**

eBook edition: ISBN 978-1-68240-223-8 or **18211D**

Printed in the United States of America

Authors

Teacher Experts

Charles Schallhorn is an educator with 30 years experience, teaching psychology since the 1980s and Advanced Placement Psychology since 1992, the second year of the course. An experienced AP reader and presenter at psychology conferences, Charles was selected to place his course online for the site Educator.com. Charles is also co-founder and moderator of the *Teaching High School Psychology* blog. Charles teaches at Mountain House High School in Mountain House, California.

Laura Brandt teaches AP and IB Psychology at the College du Leman in Geneva, Switzerland. Laura has taught psychology for the past 22 years in the United States and has facilitated many conferences for instructors of psychology. Laura has served as a reader, table leader, and question leader for the AP psychology reading and has served as an examiner for the IB psychology exams. Laura has served as member coordinator and chair of the TOPSS executive board, which represents high school psychology instructors within the American Psychological Association.

Paul Hanrahan teaches AP Psychology and has taught AP U.S. History and introductory psychology for 26 years at Johnsburg High School in Johnsburg, Illinois. Johnsburg School District 12 is a member of the College Board 7th Annual AP District Honor Roll. Paul is a member of his Johnsburg, Illinois district's Academically Talented and Gifted Committee and has served as a member of his school's leadership team as Social Studies Department Chair overseeing the expansion of AP course offerings.

Academic Expert

Jeffery Scott Mio is a professor in the Psychology and Sociology Department at California State Polytechnic University, Pomona, where he also serves as the Director of the M.S. in Psychology Program. He was president of Division 45 of the American Psychological Association from 2002–2003 and president of the Western Psychological Association (WPA) from 2010–2011. During that same period he was on the advisory panel for the development of the National Standards for High School Psychology Curricula. In 2016 he was selected to be the Executive Officer of WPA.

He has published a number of books, including an undergraduate textbook on multicultural psychology from Oxford University Press, now in its fourth edition.

Contents

Unit 4 Sensation and Perception

Unit 5   States of Consciousness

Unit 6   Learning

Unit 8 Motivation and Emotion

Unit 9 Developmental Psychology

Unit 10 Personality

Unit 12 Abnormal Behavior

Unit 14 Social Psychology

Introduction

Preparing for the Advanced Placement® Examination in Psychology

Our purpose in this book is to provide the detail of a standard textbook with the readability of a review book. We have eliminated the extraneous content that makes textbooks so long and tedious. Everything in the book either explains key concepts in psychology or provides examples to help you better understand ideas in a meaningful context. The book presents the content of an introductory college psychology text but with a sharp focus on the AP Psychology course objectives and content. *We recommend that you read this introduction twice: once when you begin the course and again when the test date approaches. Some things will make more sense after you have finished the course.*

The order of the chapters reflects the College Board's course outline. Individual teachers and professors may choose to approach the content differently, depending upon their unique philosophy and individual class characteristics. There is no one "correct" way to structure an introduction to psychology course. The College Board framework is solid and gives students a broad introduction to the field of psychology.

As with almost all introductory texts, reading this book is analogous to wading in shallow water in a very big lake. Psychology as a field is deep and rich in detail; almost every chapter in this book has at least one college-level, semester-long course with its own complete textbook full of more details than this book can cover. That is part of the beauty of psychology—no matter the level you study, there is always more to discover.

Course Description

In its course description book, the College Board suggests dividing the AP Psychology course into fourteen units. The course description also indicates the relative importance to the exam of each broad subject area by assigning a percentage to it. The percentages reflect roughly the proportion of multiple-choice questions devoted to each topic. Knowing what the exam emphasizes can help you plan your study time. The chart on the next page shows the units and the percentage of multiple-choice questions devoted to each.

TOPICS	PERCENTAGE
History and Approaches	2–4 percent
Research Methods	8–10 percent
Biological Bases of Behavior	8–10 percent
Sensation and Perception	6–8 percent
States of Consciousness	2–4 percent
Learning	7–9 percent
Cognition	8–10 percent
Motivation and Emotion	6–8 percent
Developmental Psychology	7–9 percent
Personality	5–7 percent
Testing and Individual Differences	5–7 percent
Abnormal Behavior	7–9 percent
Treatment of Abnormal Behavior	5–7 percent
Social Psychology	8–10 percent

This book devotes approximately the same percentages to the topics as the exam devotes to multiple-choice questions.

The Advanced Placement Psychology Exam

The AP Psychology exam is composed of two portions. The first consists of 100 multiple-choice questions, each of which is worth one point. You will have 70 minutes to complete those. The second portion has two free-response questions (FRQs) which together are worth 50 possible points. You will have 50 minutes to complete those for a total of two hours for the entire exam. The total number of possible points is 150.

Your score on the exam will fall into one of the following five categories, which reflect the assessment of your college readiness. Since the exam is normed, the cutoff for each level changes from year to year. Different colleges have different criteria for accepting College Board scores, so be sure to check with any college of interest to you to find out its policy. The College Board considers scores of 3 and above to be passing.

> 5 = extremely well qualified
> 4 = well qualified
> 3 = qualified
> 2 = possibly qualified
> 1 = no recommendation

The Multiple-Choice Portion

Since the multiple-choice section must be completed in 70 minutes, you will have less than one minute per question. Most students finish this portion with time to spare, but be sure to keep an eye on the time. There is no penalty for guessing—scoring is done based solely on how many questions you get correct. The multiple-choice portion accounts for two-thirds of the exam's total score.

Types of Multiple-Choice Questions Every multiple-choice question has two parts: the *stem*, or problem, and the *alternatives*, the choices you have to solve the problem. On the AP exam, all of the alternatives represent genuine psychological concepts, though there will be only one clearly correct answer. The questions are written for clarity in both the stem and the alternatives. The stem can appear in many forms. You are likely to have a mix of the following four main types of multiple-choice questions.

Knowledge questions include those with stems that provide definitions. You have to select the term that best matches the definition. For example:

The study of an organism's thoughts, feelings, and behavior and how these are affected by the environment, physical states, and mental states describes which field?*

(A) Sociology

(B) Biology

(C) Physics

(D) Psychology

(E) Chemistry

*The answer is (D).

Comprehension questions are those with stems that require conceptual understanding. The answer will be a term that best fits the stem. For example:

Empirical data that supports psychological hypotheses are best derived using which research method?*

(A) Case studies

(B) Online questionnaires

(C) Experiments using the scientific method

(D) Creative thinking

(E) Intuition

* The answer is (C).

Application questions typically provide a scenario and ask which term best applies or connects to that scenario. For example:

Dr. Bharath is conducting an experiment to determine how human stress levels affect task performance. Dr. Bharath is most likely a*

(A) botanist

(B) physicist

(C) chemist

(D) psychologist

(E) sociologist

* The answer is (D).

Analysis questions often require you to see the parts within a whole and/ or recognize examples representing a psychological concept. For example:

A child is watching her mother use a credit card at the grocery store. This is an example of which type of learning?*

(A) Direct instruction

(B) Observational learning

(C) Auditory learning

(D) Inferential learning

(E) Deductive learning

* The answer is (B).

Occasionally you will have to answer a multiple-choice question that relies on a graphic. On released exams (previous AP Psychology exams you can access on the College Board website), questions with graphics have related to anatomy, statistics, various principles of psychological theories, and more.

The question on the next page is an example of a multiple-choice question with a graphic related to anatomy.

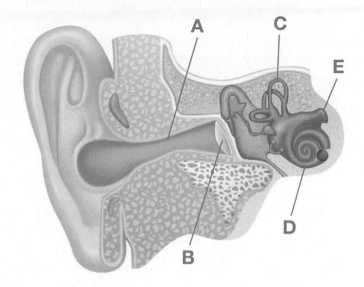

In the above diagram, which part of the ear transforms vibrations into signals the auditory nerve can carry to the brain?

(A) A

(B) B

(C) C

(D) D

(E) E

* The answer is (D).

There have also been questions with graphics related to statistics and research. Some of them asked for an interpretation of the data shown in charts. The graphics in Chapters 2 and 3 and elsewhere in this book will provide you practice in understanding these kinds of exam questions.

Many psychological theories have principles that can be clearly expressed in graphics. For example, a graph might show how many repetitions over how much time a cat needed to discover that pressing a lever led to a reward. Throughout this book, you will see graphs showing research results, and these will help prepare you for such questions.

Strategies for Answering Multiple-Choice Questions Following are strategies students have found useful for completing the multiple-choice portion of the exam.

- Although you have a limited amount of time, use it wisely by reading each question carefully.
- If you are confident of the speed of your reading, go through the multiple-choice section two times. The first time through, answer questions you are sure of, and mark questions (with a circle around the question number or an underline) that you need to read again. When you do come back to them, something in the questions you completed may have triggered your memory.
- Read the stem of the question and try to determine the answer without looking at the alternative responses. This strategy will allow you to recall an answer without getting confused by other alternatives. If you bring the answer to mind and it shows up as one of the alternatives, then you can move on to the next question. If you do not recall a response immediately, the alternative responses may help jog your memory.
- Eliminate choices you know to be incorrect right away by crossing them out or putting an X over the letter of the alternative response. You can then more clearly see the remaining alternatives.

The Free-Response Portion

The two free-response questions together are worth one-third of the overall score. Points are awarded for correct responses but not removed for incorrect material unless one part of an answer contradicts another part. Do not just write whatever comes to mind related to the question. Instead, thoughtfully provide a targeted response that shows clear understanding of the concepts in the question.

Topics of the FRQs Free-response questions are likely to include ideas from multiple units, asking about fundamental concepts in psychology that prepared students should be able to answer. Questions on perspectives of psychology and research methods have appeared many times. While some people may like to predict the FRQ topic, there is no way to know. Be prepared with material from the entire course.

Often, an FRQ is theme-based. That is, it identifies a theme and asks students to connect concepts from many different units. For example, one year, a question asked students to discuss time as it related to eight different terms. How does time connect to each of these distinct ideas? Teachers have noticed the complexity of the FRQs to be increasingly ingenious and complex but always fair.

FRQs also often ask students to apply a concept to a scenario. For example, a question about child development and personality might begin with a scenario about a couple expecting their first child who wonder how various psychological and developmental theories apply to the first year of life. Some FRQs may also ask for comparisons—how does this theory of child development compare to a different theory?

All released FRQs can be found on the College Board website along with their rubrics, or scoring guides, and samples of student work. Take the time to examine the past five years of questions to get a clear sense of what the questions, scoring rubrics, and leveled student responses look like.

Examples of Free-Response Questions Following are examples of free-response questions. Don't worry if you don't know the answers. By the time you have finished the course, you will.

Example 1

Laura arrives at home to a surprise birthday party where she is asked to put on a blindfold and play a harmless game she has never played before. She is shocked by this set of events. Explain Laura's reaction using the following terms.

- Introversion
- Yerkes-Dodson levels of arousal
- Amygdala
- Observational learning
- Cognitive dissonance
- Accommodation (related to schema)
- Procedural memory

As you will learn, each of the bulleted terms in this question comes from a different unit. The task is to apply the disparate concepts to the scenario. This kind of question assesses how well students can look at situations from a variety of perspectives.

Example 2

Raphael knew the capital cities of all 50 states when he was in fifth grade. Now he cannot recall them.

(A) Describe the concepts that might explain why Raphael forgot the information. In your answer, address the following topics.

- Decay theory
- Interference theory
- Retrograde amnesia

(B) Apply each concept as an explanation of why Raphael might be unable to recall the 50 capitals.

How to Determine Points in Free-Response Questions Each free-response question is worth a specific number of points. To be sure you are answering the question as completely as possible, try to determine the possible points. For example, in Example 1 above about Laura and the surprise party, you are asked to explain how seven different concepts apply to Laura's reaction. In that question, it is easy to see that there are seven points possible. You are given one task—to *explain*—and seven terms to explain.

In Example 2, determining possible points is not quite as clear. Obviously there are two main parts, A) and B). If you analyze the question further, you will see that each part has a separate task. The task in A) is to *describe* the theories. The task in B) is to *apply* the theories. Within each section, however, there are further subdivisions. For both A) and B), there are three concepts to either describe or apply. Together that makes a total of six possible points for that question.

The rubric the test readers will be using to score the FRQs identifies the number of possible points for each question. Determining points as you plan your answer and writing your answer to each point is one way to ensure that you are answering the questions as completely as possible.

Strategies for Answering Free-Response Questions Following are strategies to use when answering the free-response portion of the exam.

- Plan your time carefully. With two questions to answer in 50 minutes, plan for about 25 minutes per question.

- Read and reread both questions and identify exactly what is being asked before you start writing. Jot down some ideas you recall in the space around each question. You may even want to sketch out a brief outline.

- Underline the verbs that show what task(s) you are to complete: *describe, discuss, explain, compare,* and *relate,* for example.

- Write as neatly as you can. Writing in blue or black ink is required. The use of correction fluid or tape is prohibited.

- Don't be afraid to cross something out, if needed. Simply draw a line through the words you wish to remove, and they will not be considered part of your answer.

- Write in sentences—DO NOT OUTLINE OR BULLET YOUR ANSWER. To keep the response organized, skip lines between paragraphs. Readers will not score lists or answers in outline form even if the information is correct.

- Each paragraph should address the one particular point you are trying to earn. Devote a paragraph to each term or concept and clearly identify the concept the paragraph addresses.

- You do not need to write the type of essays you might write in your English classes, with an introduction stating a thesis statement or claim and a conclusion following from the evidence provided. There is no need to restate the question. The first sentence should be about the first concept in the question.

- Respond in the same order as the topics in the question so those scoring your answer can clearly align your answer to the question.
- Avoid circular definitions, those that use the terms themselves in the definitions. For example, if you are defining the term *cognitive dissonance*, do not write, "cognitive dissonance is when someone experiences dissonance in their cognition." Instead, look for synonyms. *Cognitive* relates to thinking, so use *thinking* in your response. *Dissonance* is about ideas clashing or conflicting. Use those words instead: Cognitive dissonance is the uncomfortable feeling that results when your thinking conflicts with your actions.
- Avoid contradictions. While incorrect information does not hurt your score, if you contradict a point you scored on, you lose that point. For example, if you score a point by correctly defining the id in Freud's psychoanalytic theory as following the pleasure principle but later say the id represents the reality principle, you will lose the point. (The ego represents the reality principle, as you will learn.)

To summarize:

- Read the FRQ twice to identify the tasks and plan your response.
- Anticipate the number of points in the question—write to those.
- Write legibly.
- Write following the order of the prompt, point by point. There is no need to compose a traditional essay with an introduction or conclusion.
- Use complete sentences and paragraphs—do not bullet or outline.
- Write a paragraph for each concept, skipping a line between paragraphs.
- Definitions alone do not score, but including a definition is always a good idea. Be sure to apply the terms to the scenario in the prompt.
- Address the prompt directly.
- Avoid contradictions and circular definitions.
- Show your knowledge—use psychological terms and ideas.

How This Book Can Help You Prepare

Psychology: Preparing for the Advanced Placement® Examination has a number of features to help you make the most of your preparation for the exam.

- Each unit begins with a brief overview and then a listing of the **Key Concepts** covered in the unit. The Key Concepts directly align with those identified in the AP Psychology course description and provide a quick summary of the unit's contents first to set your mind before you read and later to provide memory cues when you are reviewing for the exam.

- Each chapter begins with an **Essential Question** to help you read with a purpose and focus your thoughts on answering that question.

- At the end of each chapter, the **Reflect on the Essential Question** feature provides a suggested graphic organizer for you to complete as you take notes from each main part of the chapter to answer the essential question. Completing the graphic organizers will help you consolidate the material, and the organizers will be a helpful review tool as you study for the exam.

- A chart at the end of each chapter with **Key Terms** and **Key People** lists the important terms, concepts, and people from the chapter to help you review before the exam.

- Two features, **Think as a Psychologist** and **The Science of Psychology**, help develop critical thinking skills that will serve you well on the exam and beyond.

- **Ten multiple-choice questions** for each chapter give you practice in all the types of multiple-choice questions you will encounter on the exam.

- **Two free-response questions** for each chapter give you practice answering a variety of these types of questions.

- The **Write as a Psychologist** feature provides on-the-spot guidance for completing the free-response questions.

- Each unit ends with a **Unit Review** that recaps the essential questions from the unit's chapters and provides an **additional free-response question** that draws on concepts from multiple units.

- **A full practice exam** at the end of the book gives you a chance to complete a "trial run" of the exam and identify any areas in need of extra review.

General Tips for Preparing for the Exam

Preparing for the AP Psychology exam is like nothing else you have done (unless you have taken other AP exams). Although your teacher will likely give you quizzes and tests throughout the course on discrete topics, the AP exam itself requires comprehension and retention of a 14 units' worth of information and learning. You cannot possibly memorize all the names, dates, and facts in this book—instead, you need to create a framework in your mind for them built on important and enduring concepts. Use every possible way to make the material your own—read it, take notes on it, talk about it, create visualizations of it, and relate the ideas in this book to your prior experience and learning. In other words, think about how it connects to ideas in your other courses and to your personal life experiences. The following approaches will help you accomplish this goal.

- Start preparing for the AP Psychology exam the **first day of class**.

- Form a weekly **study group**. Use the Essential Question from each chapter as the starting point for your discussion, focusing on how the material you learned during the week helps to answer that question, or work collaboratively on the graphic organizer at the end of the chapter. Ask questions about anything you do not understand. The weekly meetings ensure that you will prepare on a regular basis, and they also give you a chance to speak about and listen to the concepts you are learning in addition to reading and writing about them.

- **Work collaboratively** in other ways, such as doing the "Practice" activities that follow each "Think as a Psychologist" or "The Science of Psychology" feature.

- Use the **techniques of the cognitive scientists** (cognitive psychologists) at *http://www.learningscientists.org/*. They offer free and more detailed information on the six strategies outlined on the next page, which have been proven in research to help people learn.

RESEARCH-BASED LEARNING STRATEGIES

Distributed Practice	**Spread out** your studying over the entire course in manageable amounts.
Retrieval	After every class, or on another regular schedule, close your book and try to recall the important points, using a practice called **retrieval**. You can use the graphic organizer that accompanies the "Reflect on the Essential Question" feature at the end of each chapter as a framework. Fill in whatever you can't retrieve from memory alone by going back into the book for the missing pieces. Whether you use sample multiple-choice questions, flashcards, or an online program such as Quizlet, take the time to test yourself with a friend or on your own.
Elaboration	When studying, **ask yourself questions** about what you are reading. How does this material connect to other material in the chapter? As you learn material, elaborate on it by connecting it to what you are experiencing in your daily life.
Interleaving	Few exams go in the order of how topics are presented in the text. The AP Psychology exam certainly does not. When you study, **interleave** the material. Switch up the order of your review. For example, when reviewing Chapters 1–3, change the order of your study. Switch it up to 2, 1, and 3. Then during your next review session, follow a different order—3, 2, and 1, for example. Use this technique only occasionally.
Concrete Examples	Write down all **concrete examples** your teacher uses in class. Note the examples given in this book. Use these examples to understand the application of the abstract concepts and ideas you are studying.
Dual Coding	Use **dual coding**, different ways of representing the information. Take notes or write reflections on a segment of text. Then create a visual representation of the same knowledge using graphic organizers, concept maps, drawings with labels, or other graphics.

Finally, have fun with psychology. Those who study psychology can develop insights into themselves and others. This field of study has given us many "Aha!" moments in our lives, and we wish the same for you.

Charles Schallhorn
Laura Brandt
Paul Hanrahan
Jeffery Mio

UNIT 1: History and Approaches

Chapter 1 *The Field of Psychology*

Unit Overview

If you were a student of psychology in the 1880s, you would no doubt have been drawn to the laboratory of Wilhelm Wundt at the University of Leipzig, the creation of which helped define psychology as a science separate from physiology and philosophy. "Young people who intend to tackle issues of experimental psychology come to the institute," wrote one observer, to learn "the specific aspects of experimental work . . . and to discuss and criticize the various methods used until now."

While Wundt's laboratory marked a turning point in the history of psychology, the roots of the field extend deep into the past—to the philosophers of antiquity. And although the idea of experimental psychology Wundt first explored has had a lasting impact on the field, psychology has undergone dramatic shifts in the 20th and 21st centuries. A number of different theoretical perspectives developed as the field branched out over time. Today, psychology encompasses a wide range of therapeutic approaches as well as subfields that have applications in many areas of life.

Key Topics

- Influence of philosophy and physiology on the field of psychology
- Variety of theoretical approaches explaining behavior
  - structuralism, functionalism, and behaviorism in the early years
  - Gestalt, psychoanalytic/ psychodynamic, and humanism emerging later
  - evolutionary, biological, cognitive, and biopsychosocial as more contemporary approaches
- Strengths and limitations of applying theories to explain behavior

- Different domains of psychology (e.g., biological, clinical, cognitive, counseling, developmental, educational, experimental, human factors, industrial–organizational, personality, psychometric, social)
- Key historical figures in psychology (e.g., Mary Whiton Calkins, Charles Darwin, Dorothea Dix, Sigmund Freud, G. Stanley Hall, William James, Ivan Pavlov, Jean Piaget, Carl Rogers, B. F. Skinner, Margaret Floy Washburn, John B. Watson, Wilhelm Wundt)

Source: *AP® Psychology Course and Exam Description*

1

The Field of Psychology

"For it all depends on how we look at things, and not on how they are themselves."

—Carl Jung, *Modern Man in Search of a Soul*

Essential Question: How has the field of psychology been influenced by other disciplines, and how has the field changed over time?

Many myths persist about the field of psychology and those who work within it. People often view a psychologist as a professional who listens while a client talks about personal problems or as someone who does testing to gather information about a client's thoughts and feelings. While there is an element of truth to each of these perceptions, the field of psychology is much more dynamic and diverse than these snapshots suggest. One aspect of psychology focuses on providing tools to allow people to lead healthy and productive lives. Another aspect raises and seeks to answer basic questions about the mind: What is the memory process? What pathways do neurochemical transmitters follow, and what is their role?

At its core, **psychology** (from the Greek words *psykhe*, meaning "mind, soul," or "spirit," and *logia*, meaning "the study of") is the scientific study of human thought and human and animal behavior. The field of psychology seeks to improve understanding of self and others and explores both biological and environmental influences on personality and behavior. This chapter will examine the historical roots of psychology and the modern approaches used to evaluate human thought and human and animal behavior. It will also explore the areas of study in which psychologists are engaged and careers in the field of psychology.

Historical Origins of Psychology

The field of psychology is a relatively new science, but its roots are in the older arenas of philosophy and physiology. Many of the questions psychologists ask today originated with the questions of the ancient philosophers. The differences in the disciplines lie in how they go about answering these questions.

Psychology's Roots

Plato (424–348 B.C.E.) proposed the idea that each of us has our own perception of the world which is unique to our life experiences. Plato showed that what people think of as reality is shaped by their experiences and that philosophers can arrive at the "truth" by looking beyond the physically observable. You may sit in the same class as thirty other students, and yet each of you takes away different experiences and interpretations from the course. Each of you perceives your own experience as the truth. Plato believed that experiences create a subjective reality. Today, psychology recognizes that perception is influenced by previous experiences that act as a filter for incoming sensory data and that shape our expectations of the world.

Aristotle (384–322 B.C.E.) was a student of Plato's. While Plato believed that the essence of a thing existed beyond observable nature, Aristotle believed the way to understand the essence of something was to study specific examples of it in nature, to gain knowledge from observation and data. Today, experimental psychology is built on the process underlying Aristotle's views: drawing conclusions based on specific observations. Aristotle also drew a distinction between knowing, which he argued was the result of experience, and the process of thinking, and he studied motivation, linguistics, and perception, key topics in psychology today.

French philosopher René Descartes (1596-1650) refined a theory known as dualism, which recognizes a duality or a two-part quality to human existence: the body, which is physical and includes the brain, and the mind, which is nonphysical. He believed further that the two parts interact in a cause-and-effect relationship. His idea contrasts with monism, the belief that nothing exists except physical matter—the mind is a function of the brain.

English philosopher and physician John Locke (1632–1704) posited that all individuals are born a "blank slate," or *tabula rasa* in Latin, and experience in the world shapes the person, filling up the blank slate. Locke formed the basic ideas that would later make up the theory of **behaviorism**. Locke, like Aristotle as well as future behaviorists, believed in **empiricism**, an approach to understanding subjects, including human behavior, by examining data rather than using intuition or reason alone. Locke's ideas are also important in an ongoing debate between the influences of **nature** (genetics) **vs. nurture** (environment), a key theme in many aspects of psychology.

The Birth of Psychology as a Science

The German philosopher, physician, and professor **Wilhelm Wundt** (1832–1920) is known as "the father of psychology" because he is the first person to study humans in a laboratory setting. As you read, Wundt began studying people in his laboratory in Leipzig, Germany, in 1879, an occasion now often referred to as "the birth of psychology." Wundt wanted to move the field of psychology away from philosophy and make it a discipline that was more measurable and scientific (empirical). Chemicals and other elements were being studied in laboratories, and Wundt believed that humans could be studied in much the same way. To study them, Wundt used a process he called **introspection,** which required people to report their conscious experiences (sensations, perceptions, and first reactions) in relation to a number of different objects. Unfortunately, the process of introspection was unsuccessful in achieving his goal because people's responses were too subjective and, unlike chemicals, they changed from trial to trial.

Edward Titchener (1867–1927) brought Wundt's ideas to the United States. Titchener worked at Cornell University and promoted the study of conscious experience by attempting to break it down into its most basic components or "structures" using Wundt's introspective techniques, examining them carefully, and then putting the pieces of the "human puzzle" back together to understand the whole. He coined the term *structuralism* to identify this approach. Because it was so closely related to the work of Wundt, structuralism is sometimes thought of as the first "school" of psychology.

William James (1842–1910), an American philosopher, physician, and professor at Harvard University, was one of many who were critical of structuralism. James believed it made more sense to examine the *function* of consciousness—what purpose did it serve? Just as Wundt had been influenced by the objective measurement of other scientific fields, James had been influenced by the work of **Charles Darwin** (1809–1882) and his **theory of evolution**—the view that organisms change over time as they adapt to their environment, and that adaptations that serve the function of promoting survival are passed on to offspring. Rather than seeing consciousness as made up of "structures," James saw it as a continuous flow; he coined the term *stream of consciousness* to describe it. Unlike the structuralists, he did not see individual puzzle pieces and wonder what big picture they make when put together—instead he saw the big picture and asked what its *function* was. James saw the function of consciousness as an evolutionary adaptation to environment that made it possible for humans to thrive and continue to adapt. His approach became known as **functionalism**. James also wrote the first comprehensive textbook of psychology, *Principles of Psychology.*

Mary Whiton Calkins (1863–1930) received one-on-one lessons in psychology from James. The reason for her individualized instruction was that all the males who had been enrolled in James's class un-enrolled when Calkins began attending as a way of protesting the presence of a woman in the class. Administrators at Harvard determined she could not be recognized as an official student. She completed all the necessary work for a Ph.D. in her "unofficial" capacity, but Harvard refused to grant her the degree. Calkins nonetheless went on to have a distinguished career in psychology. She conducted early studies on memory and served as the first woman president of the American Psychological Association. She founded one of the first psychology laboratories at Wellesley

College. Today, more than half of all undergraduate and graduate degrees in psychology at all universities are granted to women.

Margaret Floy Washburn (1871–1939) was the first woman to receive her Ph.D. in psychology from Cornell University. Earlier at Columbia University, she had studied under Raymond Cattell, a psychologist who had identified 16 discrete personality traits. Washburn was interested in animal behavior and wrote a book titled *The Animal Mind*. She would later have an impact on behaviorists (see page 6), who conducted much of their research with animals. Washburn also served as the president of the American Psychological Association and taught psychology for many years at Vassar.

While women entered the field of professional psychology later than men, they had long been on the frontline of reform for people with mental illness. In the 1840s, **Dorothea Dix** (1802–1887) undertook an investigation of the living conditions of poor people with mental illness, finding some of them kept in cages, stalls, and pens. Her investigations and tireless advocacy led to the first mental asylums in the United States.

G. Stanley Hall (1844–1924) was the first president of the American Psychological Association. He also founded the first journal for research in psychology and created the first psychological laboratory in the United States at Johns Hopkins University. He spent most of his career at Clark University in Massachusetts and helped spread the field of psychology in the United States.

Max Wertheimer (1880–1943) took the field in another direction in Germany. His approach became known as **Gestalt psychology** (*gestalt* translates to "shape" or "form"). To understand this approach, look at the picture below. It is actually made of hundreds of photos, but our focus is drawn to the larger figures of the mother and daughter. While structuralists wanted to examine each small picture, metaphorically, Gestalt psychologists, like functionalists, encouraged looking at the shape or form of the whole.

Figure 1.1

Like humans, this collage can be examined by looking at its smallest parts (as structuralists might do) or by seeing the whole entity (as Gestalt psychologists would do).

Modern Approaches to Psychology

Structuralism and functionalism are foundational theories for understanding the origins of the discipline of psychology. They eventually gave way to modern approaches to psychology which continue to evolve to help us understand human and animal behavior and the human mind. Each of the approaches briefly described below will be covered in much more detail in later chapters.

Psychoanalytic Approach

Austrian neurologist **Sigmund Freud** (1856–1939) studied medicine but soon discovered that not all ailments were physical. Psychological ailments, he believed, could be treated by what one of his patients identified as "the talking cure." The **psychoanalytic approach** Freud developed emphasized the role of the **unconscious**, a depository of memories, feelings, and drives, many of them unwanted, that are beyond the reach of conscious awareness. He was also interested in the meaning of dreams. His book *The Interpretation of Dreams* emphasized the **latent** (or hidden) meaning of dreams.

Freud posited that we have three conflicting parts of our personality. The **id** holds our wants and desires and is primarily motivated by sex and aggression. The **superego**, in contrast, acts as our conscience and leads us to "do the right thing." Freud believed that the id and superego were often at odds with each other. To negotiate the conflicting forces, the **ego** allows people to get what they want and desire within the confines set by society. (Chapter 17 will examine this topic in depth.) Freud also believed that our personality was shaped by the time we were six or seven years old.

Freud was influenced by the theory of thermodynamics, which studies the flow and transfer of energy. Freud believed that the **libido,** instinctual desires such as those for sexual pleasure and self-preservation, was a source of psychological energy. The term **psychodynamics** is sometimes used to describe his approach.

Because the unconscious cannot be studied objectively, psychoanalytic theory was criticized for its lack of scientific objectivity. Many also believe that Freud's emphasis on sex and aggression was overstated and that he overemphasized the influence of the unconscious on behavior. Yet more than one hundred years after Freud's proposals, a significant subset of psychotherapists still practice some form of psychoanalysis.

Behavioral Approach

The **behaviorist approach** arose from criticisms of the psychoanalytic approach. Rather than focus on one's unconscious, behaviorists chose to focus on *observable* behavior. **John Watson** (1878–1958), like Wilhelm Wundt, believed behavior needed to be observable to be objectively and empirically measured. Watson built on the work of Edward Thorndike (1874–1949) who placed cats in **puzzle boxes** and found that once cats figured out how to escape from the puzzle box for a reward, they would repeat the behavior over and over again. He observed the *law of effect*—responses that produce a satisfying effect will likely be repeated; those that produce an undesirable effect will likely not be repeated. In a similar way, behaviorism rests on the tenet that behaviors that are rewarded will be repeated and those that are punished will eventually be extinguished. Behaviorism is often described as the study of **stimulus and response** learning.

Watson became infamous for asking the experimental question, "Can we condition fears in young children?" In a study of highly questionable ethics, Watson tested a young boy in his lab who became known as Little Albert. Little Albert had a particular affinity for a white rat. Watson presented Albert with the rat and at the same time made a loud noise, which scared Albert. After multiple pairings of the loud noise with the rat, Albert came to fear the white rat alone even when there was no frightening sound. This technique of paired associations is known as **classical conditioning**. Russian psychologist **Ivan Pavlov** (1849–1936) devised experiments in classical conditioning with salivating dogs.

Like Watson, **B.F. Skinner** (1904–1990) believed in **radical behaviorism,** the idea that behavior should be studied objectively using the scientific method and only what can be seen or observed is measurable. He created an **operant conditioning chamber** (also known as a *Skinner box*) in which an animal—often a rat or a pigeon—would be trained to complete a voluntary behavior, such as turning around or pecking the corner of the cage. Once the behavior was completed, the animal would receive a reward, which often increased the likelihood of the behavior occurring again. This process became known as **operant conditioning**. Like Thorndike, Skinner believed that behavior that was rewarded would be repeated, while behavior that was punished would not be repeated. Because Skinner emphasized the importance of learning through rewards and punishments, he believed that people have no free will and essentially operate like robots based solely on past learning.

The behaviorist approach is still popular today, but people have moved away from the radical approach taken by Skinner and Watson. While Skinner acknowledged that people had thoughts, he believed thoughts had little scientific value because they could not be studied objectively.

Cognitive Approach

The cognitive approach addresses the flaw Skinner identified in studying thoughts by examining thinking and perception. The cognitive revolution in psychology took place in the mid- to late 1950s. Psychologists such as Harry Harlow and others began to wonder why behaviorists were studying rats and pigeons to learn about human behavior rather than animals who were closer to humans, such as primates. They also believed that by failing to examine thought processes, the field of psychology was not studying the entire individual. The **cognitive approach** studies how thinking and perception influence behavior.

This field includes such topics as memory, problem-solving, decision-making, and perception. While cognitive psychologists do not necessarily discount observable behavior, they are more concerned with the internal functions driving behavior. Psychologists such as **Jean Piaget** studied how children's cognitive development unfolds. The cognitive approach remains a strong approach today, and new methods allow more objective study of how people think, interpret information, and make decisions in given situations.

Humanistic Approach

The **humanistic approach** also came to prominence in the 1950s. This approach addressed perceived flaws in both the psychoanalytic and behavioral approaches. Freud's belief that people were driven solely by sex and aggression was replaced in the humanistic approach with a more positive outlook on people related to their motivation to fulfill their potential. In addition, humanists focused on a person's future rather than the past. This approach also took issue with the behaviorists' idea that humans have no free will and are driven only by past rewards and punishments. The humanists believed that people do have free will and ultimately are responsible for the decisions they make regardless of what they may have learned in the past. Humanism focuses on the potential of people and their drive to be their best.

Carl Rogers (1902–1987) is one of the founders of the humanistic approach. Before Rogers went into the field of psychology, he was training to be a minister, a calling which perhaps helps to explain his optimistic view of the world. Rogers did acknowledge that environments may not always be ideal and can prevent individuals from reaching their potential. Abraham Maslow (1908–1970) built on these ideas and created a model of a **hierarchy of needs** in which people move from basic biological needs to their full potential, which he identified as self-actualization. Like Rogers, Maslow believed that people strive to reach their highest potential but can be limited by a poor environment.

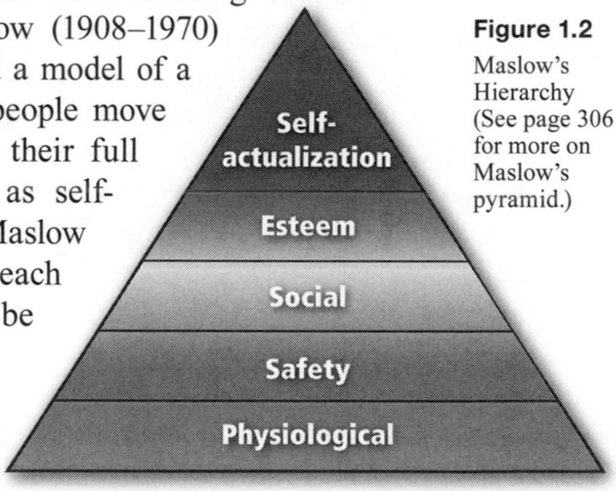

Figure 1.2

Maslow's Hierarchy (See page 306 for more on Maslow's pyramid.)

The humanistic approach today remains strong in the field of therapy but is criticized for what many describe as an overly optimistic view of human behavior. Also, many say it works well as a general approach to life but is not inclusive enough to be considered an explanation of all human thought and behavior.

Sociocultural Approach

The **sociocultural approach** emphasizes the impact of people's culture, religion, ethnicity, gender, income level, and overall environment on the individuals they become. To better understand the sociocultural approach, think about how your family, religion, high school environment, and peer group shape your beliefs and goals. Also consider how you might be different if you practiced a different religion, grew up in a different neighborhood, or had a different ethnic background.

Biological/Neurobiological/Physiological Approach

This approach focuses primarily on examining how genetics, the nervous system, hormones, and brain structures influence a person's thinking and behavior. Damage to certain areas in the left hemisphere of the brain can result in a lack of language functioning; an excess of a neurotransmitter called dopamine may lead to schizophrenic hallucinations. These types of findings are the focus of the **biological approach** to psychology. While examining biological factors that may cause a lack of functioning, this approach also focuses on how biological treatments may improve certain conditions. Treatments primarily involve medication to regulate levels of hormones or neurotransmitters in the brain and body. As brain scanning techniques continue to improve, biological psychologists are learning more than ever about how the brain operates.

Evolutionary Approach

This approach dates back to **Charles Darwin** and his thoughts on **natural selection** and the **survival of the fittest**, the process by which the genes that are most beneficial for survival are protected and strengthened, and the organisms that develop those genes survive and pass them on. However, **evolutionary psychologists** think beyond Darwin's famous study of the *physical* adaptations of finches to look for aspects of human thought and behavior that may give individuals or their genes a better chance for survival in the future. For example, evolutionary psychologists may examine why many people have an aversion to bitter tastes (they may have been an indication of poisonous foods that were dangerous to eat), or they may explain that we are attracted to those with certain physical traits because those traits tend to be associated with higher chances for successful reproduction.

Biopsychosocial Model

In the late 20th century, psychiatrist George L. Engel formulated a model of treating patients that looked for explanations of illness as well as potential treatments by examining the interactions of the patient's biology, personality, and social influences—the **biopsychosocial model**. While recognizing the biological and physiological elements of disease, Engel and others who followed believed that a patient's perception of an illness or condition as well as the social environment of the patient have an influence on treatment outcome. The interaction of these elements can also help explain the onset of disease: Someone who grows up in a family of smokers (social) might be more likely to become a smoker because of a desire to belong (psychological), and smoking is a known disease-causing behavior (biological). Some psychiatrists and medical doctors believe that Engel's ideas have helped medical doctors see patients as whole beings rather than just biological systems.

MODERN APPROACHES TO PSYCHOLOGY		
Perspective	**Image to Remember**	**Explanation**
Psychoanalytic	 Conscious Mind The Unconscious Mind	The iceberg represents Freud's levels of consciousness and shows the scope of the unconscious mind compared to that of the conscious mind.
Behavioral		Behavior that is observable and measurable is scientifically useful.
Cognitive		Thinking and perception influence behavior.
Humanistic		The flower is trying to reach its full potential and blossom. Even in a bad environment, it will try its best. People strive to be their best.

MODERN APPROACHES TO PSYCHOLOGY

Perspective	Image to Remember	Explanation
Sociocultural		The individual is influenced by the people and culture that surround them.
Biological	Hypothalamus Pituitary gland Amygdala Hippocampus	Brain structures and chemistry affect behavior.
Evolutionary	1. Geospiza magnirostris. 2. Geospiza fortis. 3. Geospiza parvula. 4. Certhidea olivasea.	Evolutionary adaptations help explain human thought and behavior.
Biopsychosocial	Hypothalamus Pituitary gland Amygdala Hippocampus	Interactions among a person's biology, personality, and culture help shape thoughts and behaviors.

The Strengths and Limitations of Theories

Theories in psychology, such as those you just read about, are like lenses or magnifying glasses. Lenses help us see things within the lens better, but things outside of the lens become less clear. Theories can make us blind to—or at least less aware of—other phenomena. For example, Freud's theory focused the lens on inner drives, taking little account of the kinds of influences the behaviorists examined. Humanism makes valuable contributions to understanding human potential but pays little attention to biological factors, beyond the requirement to meet basic needs. Thus, enduring theories help people see certain things well, but they explain other phenomena less well. Taken together, all applicable theories remain useful, at least to some subset of people—hence their endurance.

Subfields and Careers in Psychology

Psychologists are found in a vast array of careers, and for this reason and many others psychology is one of the most popular college majors. Most psychologists fall into one of two categories: applied psychologists and basic psychologists. **Applied psychologists** work face-to-face with clients, students, or patients. They use the knowledge of basic researchers to directly help individuals. **Basic psychologists** focus on completing research, often working in labs, to increase knowledge about human thinking and human and animal behavior. They may work to find a new antipsychotic medication, for example, but may never meet the people who use the drug. Some psychologists do work in both basic and applied psychology: A professor at a university may work in a lab studying how students learn (basic) and may also teach classes of students about the field (applied).

Applied Fields

Psychiatrists are medical doctors and can prescribe medication to patients who may benefit from them. In fact, psychiatric treatment today focuses on medication management—finding the right medications to successfully treat disorders and monitoring their effectiveness and side effects. Recently, some states have allowed psychologists who have the proper education to prescribe medications as well. Psychologists may be in a practice with psychiatrists, and their educational training as well as the approach (or approaches) to which they adhere will influence the type of treatment they provide.

Clinical psychologists are likely the professionals that most frequently come to mind when thinking about practitioners in psychology. Clinical psychologists work with individuals who may be suffering from psychological disorders. For example, they may help a person with an obsessive-compulsive disorder to cope with or potentially overcome the illness.

Counseling psychologists primarily work with individuals who are going through a difficult time in their lives but are unlikely to have a mental illness. Counseling psychologists generally try to help their clients work through such issues as divorce or transitioning into a new school. They work with their clients to develop strategies for coping with difficult situations so they can be positive and productive.

Human factors psychologists generally have a background in engineering. They study how the design of certain products can improve use. For example, human factors psychologists may design a comfortable chair that supports one's back properly or a coffee machine that is easy to use even by someone who has never seen it before. We have all had experiences with products that do not work as we might like; human factors psychologists seek to remedy these situations.

Industrial-organizational psychologists are often found in an office setting. They may work in human resources to find the best person for a particular job; they may work to increase worker morale; or they may be involved with training, such as sexual harassment training or other on-the-job seminars. They may also work as outside consultants to find a match between an employer and well qualified-employees.

School psychologists, not to be confused with educational psychologists who are often basic researchers, generally work in a face-to-face setting. They may evaluate students for special programs, such as special education or gifted programs. They are involved with proctoring IQ tests and creating plans, along with counselors, parents, students, and other school support staff, to meet each student's educational needs.

Basic Fields

Biological psychologists investigate how the structures in one's brain or nervous system influence behavior. Biological psychologists may also study how deficits in certain types of neurotransmitters may shape the behavior of their clients.

Cognitive psychologists investigate how people's thinking and perception of situations influence their behavior. They examine decision-making, problem-solving, memory, risk assessment, and metacognition (thinking about thinking).

Developmental psychologists study how people change and develop over their lifespan. The topics they examine may include cognitive development, linguistic (speech) development, moral development, motor development, and others. Developmental psychologists historically have studied children; however, as the population ages, gerontology (the study of old age) is attracting some practitioners as their focus.

Educational psychologists research how people learn and remember information. Their work may help teachers develop an effective curriculum for promoting student understanding.

Experimental psychologists generally work in laboratories and form the largest category of basic psychologists. What they study may run the spectrum from treating rats with a new type of drug to testing the interpersonal skills of college students.

Psychometric psychologists have a strong math background that they put to use by interpreting personality or intelligence tests or analyzing the data produced by basic psychologists to determine their findings. Psychometric psychologists often work as consultants to assist those collecting data to insure that they are analyzing the data correctly.

Personality psychologists often work closely with psychometric psychologists, providing personality inventories which are then analyzed and assessed. Personality psychologists may also work in a clinical setting to determine why certain personality characteristics seem to make getting along difficult for certain individuals or hold them back from reaching their potential.

Social psychologists are those who adhere to the sociocultural approach to psychology. They are primarily focused on examining the influence of family, culture, religion, and peer group on behavior. Social psychologists can work in teaching or research at universities, in the private sector in such positions as consultant and marketing director, or in the government or nonprofit spheres as researchers, conflict managers, or policy experts.

Regardless of the career one pursues in psychology, the key force underlying all careers is furthering an understanding of human behavior and helping to promote empathy and compassion for others. Even if you end up in the future on a path unrelated to psychology, your knowledge of psychology should help you better understand people's motives, behaviors, and thoughts.

THINK AS A PSYCHOLOGIST: APPLY GENERAL PRINCIPLES

The theoretical perspectives you have read about in this chapter are general frameworks that are applied to specific instances for purposes of therapy or understanding. For example, behaviorism rests on the conviction that behaviors are shaped by punishments and rewards. A psychologist applying behaviorism to a therapeutic situation would look for ways in which undesirable behavior in a client is being reinforced through rewards and seek opportunities to extinguish it. The ability to apply a general concept to a specific individual or situation is critical to a psychologist's success.

Practice: The American Psychological Association (APA) publishes the document "Ethical Principles of Psychologists and Code of Conduct" to enumerate the ways in which its members are to uphold high ethical principles. (See page 42 for more on ethics guidelines.) The first excerpt below is from the "General Principles" section of the document. The second is from the section devoted to "Human Relations." Read the excerpts carefully. Then review the experiments described in Chapter 1. Based on the information in this chapter, describe one experiment that seems to adhere to the ethical principles and one that does not, explaining why in each case.

Principle A: Beneficence and Nonmaleficence Psychologists strive to benefit those with whom they work and take care to do no harm. In their professional actions, psychologists seek to safeguard the welfare and rights of those with whom they interact professionally and other affected persons and the welfare of animal subjects of research. When conflicts occur among psychologists' obligations or concerns, they attempt to resolve these conflicts in a responsible fashion that avoids or minimizes harm. Because psychologists' scientific and professional judgments and actions may affect the lives of others, they are alert to and guard against personal, financial, social, organizational, or political factors that might lead to misuse of their influence.

Human Relations

3.04 Avoiding Harm
Psychologists take reasonable steps to avoid harming their clients/ patients, students, supervisees, research participants, organizational clients and others with whom they work, and to minimize harm where it is foreseeable and unavoidable.

REFLECT ON THE ESSENTIAL QUESTION

Essential Question: *How has the field of psychology been influenced by other disciplines and how has the field changed over time?* On separate paper, complete a chart like the one below to gather details to answer that question.

Influences from Other Disciplines	Changes Over Time

KEY TERMS			KEY PEOPLE
behaviorism	*PERSPECTIVES*	human factors	Mary Whiton
classical	behaviorist	psychologist	Calkins
conditioning	approach	industrial-	Charles Darwin
ego	biological approach	organizational	Dorothea Dix
empiricism	biopsychosocial	psychologist	Sigmund Freud
functionalism	model	personality	G. Stanley Hall
hierarchy of needs	cognitive approach	psychologist	William James
id	evolutionary	psychometrics	Jean Piaget
introspection	psychologists	social	Carl Rogers
latent	Gestalt psychology	psychologist	B.F. Skinner
natural selection	humanistic	*APPLIED*	Margaret Floy
nature vs. nurture	approach	*CAREERS*	Washburn
operant	psychoanalytic	applied	John Watson
conditioning	approach	psychologist	Wilhelm Wundt
operant condition-	psychodynamics	clinical	
ing chamber	sociocultural	psychologist	
psychology	approach	counseling	
puzzle box	*BASIC CAREERS*	psychologist	
radical behaviorism	basic psychologist	psychiatrist	
stimulus/response	biological	school	
stream of	psychology	psychologist	
consciousness	developmental		
structuralism	psychology		
superego	educational		
survival of the	psychology		
fittest	experimental		
theory of evolution	psychologist		
unconscious			

MULTIPLE-CHOICE QUESTIONS

1. Which of the following thinkers believed that people were born as blank slates and experiences formed their personality?

   (A) Plato

   (B) Aristotle

   (C) Freud

   (D) Descartes

   (E) Locke

2. Samantha believes all behavior originates from unconscious forces developed primarily in childhood and focused primarily on sex and aggression. With which approach to psychology is Samantha most likely to agree?

(A) Behaviorist

(B) Functionalist

(C) Humanistic

(D) Psychoanalytic

(E) Sociocultural

3. With which of the following statements would a behaviorist be most likely to agree?

(A) People are driven by subconscious forces.

(B) Religious and cultural beliefs determine values and morals.

(C) Psychology should study people's consciousness by asking them to report their conscious experiences.

(D) By studying how people think and solve problems, psychology can better understand how they behave.

(E) Psychology can only study what we can observe, because this is all that can be empirically tested.

4. Katelyn is struggling in school and fighting frequently with her parents. She is not sure about her future and what she wants to study in college. With which of the following statements about Katelyn would a humanistic psychologist most likely agree?

(A) Katelyn will work to the best of her ability to get her life back on track.

(B) Katelyn has been shaped by her parents' dysfunctional relationship and will have a difficult time forming deep relationships in the future.

(C) Katelyn is overthinking her problems, which are minor, and her misperception of the scope of the problems is inflating their importance.

(D) Katelyn has learned from her peers to treat her parents badly and to not put forth her best effort in school. Because this behavior is rewarded by her friends, it will continue in the future.

(E) Katelyn's problem is the result of changing hormones; once these level out, she will be able to concentrate on her goals and relationships.

5. How does the humanistic approach to psychology differ from the psychoanalytic approach?

(A) The humanistic approach studies thinking, and the psychoanalytic approach focuses on learning through rewards and punishments.

(B) The humanistic approach focuses on learning through rewards and punishments, while the psychoanalytic approach emphasizes the importance of the unconscious.

(C) The humanistic approach focuses on striving to be one's best, while the psychoanalytic approach examines unconscious forces and the importance of sex and aggression.

(D) The humanistic approach emphasizes one's religion and family, while the psychoanalytic approach emphasizes the unconscious and sex and aggression.

(E) The humanistic approach focuses on the good in all people, while the psychoanalytic approach emphasizes the impact of one's religion and peer group.

6. Edward Titchener followed the structuralist approach to examine human consciousness. With which of the following would he agree?

(A) We can only study people through direct observation and learning through rewards and punishments.

(B) We must examine the unconscious forces which influence an individual's behavior.

(C) We must examine how a person functions as a whole.

(D) We can use the process of introspection by asking people about their conscious experience to specific stimuli.

(E) We must examine problem solving and perception to better understand human consciousness.

7. Read the following quotation and answer the question that follows.

"Give me a dozen healthy infants, well-formed, and my own specified world to bring them up in and I'll guarantee to take any one at random and train him to become any type of specialist I might select . . . regardless of his talents, penchants, tendencies, abilities, vocations, and race of his ancestors" (1930).

To whom would the above statement most likely be attributed?

(A) Sigmund Freud

(B) John Watson

(C) Carl Rogers

(D) Wilhelm Wundt

(E) Descartes

8. Benjamin helps design cars that are easy to drive and intuitive to use. It is most likely that Benjamin is engaged in which of the following fields of psychology?

(A) Industrial-organizational

(B) Human factors

(C) Community

(D) Cognitive

(E) Psychometric

9. Denise just transferred from another school. She is having trouble adjusting to her new environment because she is very shy and is finding it difficult to make new friends. Which of the following types of psychologist might best help Denise work through this adjustment period?

(A) Clinical

(B) Personality

(C) Human factors

(D) Educational

(E) Counseling

10. Which of the following best describes how psychiatrists most often treat patients?

(A) Through intensive psychoanalysis

(B) Through behavioral therapy

(C) Through medication management

(D) Through dream analysis

(E) In partnership with psychologists

1. Eighteen-year-old Jennifer is afraid of heights. She has sought professional help to overcome this paralyzing fear but to little avail. When she is higher than two stories, she is reminded of a frightening trip to a high observation deck as a child. Each time Jennifer knows she will be in a high place, she plans out her approach days ahead but is anxious and agitated until the moment arrives. She realizes her fears are irrational but cannot seem to help her behavior.

   A) Explain how the following approaches to psychology would help Jennifer understand the causes of her fears.
      - Humanistic
      - Psychoanalytic
      - Cognitive
      - Behavioral
      - Sociocultural

   B) Explain how the following types of psychologists would attempt to examine Jennifer's behavior.
      - Counseling
      - Developmental

2. The field of psychology has evolved from the time philosophers first began asking questions about human behavior to today. Address the following questions about how the field has grown and changed.

   A) Philosophy has had a great impact on the field of psychology. Explain how the following theories were influenced by earlier philosophers.
      - Psychoanalytic
      - Behaviorism
      - Neurobiological

   B) Explain how the following modern day approaches addressed the flaws of earlier theories.
      - Behaviorism
      - Humanistic

   C) Explain how the following careers in the field of psychology ensure that the field continues to evolve and add to the body of knowledge regarding human behavior.
      - Clinical psychologists
      - Educational psychologists

Strong writing skills are essential to both psychologists and students of psychology. They are also necessary to provide clear answers on the AP®Exam. For example, when answering a free-response question, focus on the exact task each section of the prompt calls for by identifying the verb. In this chapter, both free-response questions ask you to *explain*. Explaining requires making connections among the parts of the prompt and the psychological concepts. You may also be asked to *identify, show, describe, discuss,* and *relate*. This book will provide practice in addressing each type of task. For more guidance on answering free-response questions, see pages xxii–xxiii.

UNIT 1: Review

In this unit, you sought answers to the following essential question about the history and scope of the field of psychology.

Chapter 1: How has the field of psychology been influenced by other disciplines, and how has the field changed over time?

Since the free-response questions on the AP® exam often ask you to draw on your knowledge and understanding of concepts across different topics and even different subject areas, the free-response questions at the end of each unit of the book will provide practice in answering questions that require that skill.

FREE-RESPONSE QUESTION

Psychology and philosophy as fields of study have attempted to explain human behavior. Each field has received both support and criticism of these attempted explanations.

A) Explain how the following thinkers attempted to make psychology a distinct field separate from philosophy.
- Wilhelm Wundt
- William James

B) Ana is having trouble adjusting after moving to a different country and changing schools. She is facing challenges with her mother at home. She also feels like she does not fit in with her peers at school and is struggling with the workload of her academic courses. Her classmates often ridicule her clothes and her accent. She feels embarrassed about this situation, but she is still attempting to make friends and is hopeful that she will eventually find a group who accepts her and allows her to be herself. Discuss how each of the following modern approaches to psychology would explain Ana's behavior.
- Behaviorism
- Humanism
- Neurobiological
- Sociocultural
- Cognitive

UNIT 2: Research Types and Designs

Chapter 2 *Research Methods*

Chapter 3 *Statistics*

Unit Overview

How did people learn about everything that fills this psychology book and so many others? How did people learn how babies see the world, how children imitate aggressive behavior, how teenagers are not "morning people," how adults respond to authority, how people strive for fulfillment? The answer is through systematic, well-designed research studies using the scientific method. The best of the researchers follow the advice of Ivan Pavlov, the physiologist known for his experiments with salivating dogs: "Don't become a mere recorder of facts, but try to penetrate the mystery of their origin."

This unit will explore various methods researchers use and what each can demonstrate. It will also explain how statistics can be used to create research results with significance and validity.

Key Topics

- Different types of research and their purpose, strengths, and weaknesses
- Research design and the reliability of reasonable conclusions
- Independent, dependent, confounding, and control variables in experimental designs
- Random assignment of experiment participants and random selection of participants in correlational studies and surveys
- Validity of behavioral explanations based on the quality of research design
- Purposes of descriptive statistics and inferential statistics
- Basic descriptive statistical concepts (graphs, calculations)
- Value of reliance on operational definitions and measurement in behavioral research
- Ethical and legal guidelines to protect research participants and promote sound ethical practice

Source: *AP® Psychology Course and Exam Description*

2

Research Methods

"For it all depends on how we look at things, and not on how they are themselves."

—Physicist Michio Kaku

Essential Question: How do psychologists use the scientific method to investigate questions about human thought and human and animal behavior?

Psychologists use different research methods to study questions about psychological phenomena. Which method a researcher chooses depends on the question, the characteristics of the participants, and the specifics of the study. By the end of this chapter, you will be able to identify which research method is appropriate for different research questions. Perhaps you will even consider a question you may wish to research in the future.

The Scientific Method in Psychology

To gather information about how humans think and humans and animals behave, psychology, like any other scientific field, uses the **scientific method**—a process of systematic observation, measurement, and experiment to formulate and test hypotheses. The process of science always begins with a question. Researchers conduct preliminary research to refine a question, make sure it is stated as clearly as possible, and connect it with related evidence or theories. Once they have refined the question, they restate it as a formal hypothesis and test it with an experiment or another type of measure, such as observation. The result of this systematic procedure is **empirical data**, which is evidence that comes from observation, experience, or experimentation. After gathering empirical data, researchers analyze the results, draw conclusions, and communicate with other researchers about what they learned. The steps in the scientific method are shown in Figure 2.1.

The scientific method allows researchers to achieve four general goals of psychological science. These goals include the following:

- *describe* psychological phenomena
- *predict* what will occur
- *control* factors that are believed to cause a phenomenon
- *explain* why the phenomenon occurs

The scientific method helps researchers think critically about the questions they are investigating and opens up the possibility for alternative explanations to a question.

Hypotheses

Researchers are curious by nature and may be tempted to begin a study as soon as they become interested in a psychological phenomenon. However, they must consider a number of factors and create a research plan before they begin. The first step is to restate the research question as a **hypothesis**, which is a specific and testable description of the expected outcome of a study. The hypothesis specifies the **variables**—anything that can change or be changed—and a

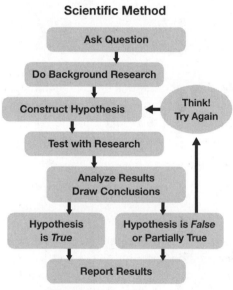

Scientific Method

Figure 2.1

relationship between them, and describes the circumstances or conditions that affect the relationship. For example, if prisoners are given the responsibility to train service animals, then social conditions in the prison improve.

Researchers often develop hypotheses from a **theory**, which is a coherent explanation or interpretation of facts and observations that have been identified in past studies. For example, there is virtually no empirical evidence of the positive impact on a prison population of dog training, yet anecdotal reports from inmates, prison employees, and those who are given a service dog trained by inmates are consistently very positive. Any number of hypotheses can be developed from these observations: "If service dogs are trained by inmates, the results of the training are more effective than if they are trained by

volunteers outside of prison," or, "Prisons in which inmates have the responsibility to train service dogs experience lower levels of violence than prisons without such programs." Hypotheses can support existing theories, lead to new theories, or reveal inaccuracies or errors in theories.

Researchers look for evidence that both supports a hypothesis and refutes it. If they look only for what they expect to occur, they may experience **confirmation bias**, which is the tendency to search for information that supports our preconceptions and to ignore or distort contradictory evidence. To effectively practice science and add to the body of knowledge, researchers need to be open to the conclusions to which the evidence points, even if the results are not expected or desired.

Methodology

The hypothesis specifies the phenomenon and variables you want to investigate. But what will you do in the study and how will you do it? The details of how you will measure the variables, how you will observe and measure the results, and how you will evaluate the hypothesis is the **methodology** of the study. Proper methodology follows directly from the hypothesis and is essential to good research. Clear and detailed statements about how you will measure the data collected about the variables are called **operational definitions**. For example, to measure the success of service-dog training by prisoners, you would need to develop an operational definition of success, such as, "Success is defined as a lower number of reported incidents of prison violence after the study was completed than before the study began."

When researchers carefully follow all the steps of the scientific method and communicate the details of what they did and how they did it, other researchers can attempt to **replicate** the study—repeat the original study as closely as possible. Researchers need clear operational definitions in order to successfully replicate a study. When a successful replication supports the results of the original study, the general scientific community has greater confidence that the results have not occurred by chance, and the study adds to the body of knowledge in a field.

The nature of the variables and the specified relationship between them often determine the type of study that needs to be done. Psychological researchers use three main research methods: experiments, correlational studies, and descriptive research.

The Experimental Method

The experimental method is the only research method for investigating *cause-and-effect relationships*. The experimental method can demonstrate **cause and effect** because it enables a researcher to manipulate one of the variables and observe the effect of that manipulation on one or more other measured variables. Research that uses the experimental method is sometimes known as laboratory experimentation and has been criticized for being too artificial to assess behaviors that most people usually exhibit.

Experimental Hypotheses, Independent Variables, and Dependent Variables

All research begins with a hypothesis, a prediction about the result of the study. Researchers generally write a hypothesis for an experiment in the form of an "if-then" statement. For example, "If participants drink a 12-oz cup of coffee before working on a puzzle, then they finish the puzzle faster than those who did not drink the coffee." An "if-then" statement makes it easy to identify the variables, the relationship between them, and the expected result of the experiment.

Suppose a team of sports psychologists who run noticed that they seem to run faster the day after eating a steak dinner. They decide to conduct an experiment to test their personal observations and write the following hypothesis for the experiment: "If people eat protein, then they run faster." This hypothesis specifies two variables, what people eat and running speed. It also specifies a cause-and-effect relationship between the two variables. Your running speed depends on what you eat.

To test this hypothesis, the sports psychologists will vary what people eat and then measure how fast they run. The *if* part of the sentence identifies the independent variable. The **independent variable** is the variable that the experimenter manipulates. This manipulation is what makes experiments distinct from other research methods. In other methods, such as correlational studies, naturalistic observation, surveys, and case studies, there is no direct manipulation of the independent variable. Researchers using these non-experimental methods cannot demonstrate cause-and-effect relationships.

In the running speed study, the amount of protein that participants eat is the independent variable. The researchers set up three groups. One group will eat a high-protein diet the day before the run. A second group will eat a low-protein diet the day before the run. A third group will eat what they usually eat, and the researchers will measure the amount of protein without controlling it. How much protein, what form the protein takes (chicken, beef, vegetable protein, a protein drink, and so on), and how and when the participants eat it are all part of the operational definition of the independent variable.

The second part of the hypothesis is: "… then they run faster." The *then* part of the sentence identifies the dependent variable. The **dependent variable** is the variable that researchers measure. The hypothesis makes a prediction that the dependent variable will vary or be influenced by the independent variable. Researchers must clearly define the dependent variable and clearly explain how they will measure it. This detailed statement of how the dependent variable will be measured is its operational definition. For example, the sports psychologists could measure running speed by having participants run on a treadmill that automatically records how fast they run. They could measure running speed with a stop watch while participants run on a track. Participants could wear electronic activity trackers while running on the track. There are a lot of options, and which one the researchers choose needs to be planned in advance and spelled out clearly.

Psychological researchers study many variables that are more difficult to define and measure than running speed. Self-esteem, intelligence, or personality type are some examples. Clear, well-defined operational definitions are critical for helping other researchers understand how dependent variables are being measured in a study. These details are necessary for any attempt to replicate a study.

Populations and Samples

Before conducting an experiment, researchers must also define the population to be tested, sometimes called the "population of interest." The **population** consists of all individuals who can potentially participate in the study. Psychologists would like to apply, or **generalize**, what they learn to all people. However, most of the time, it would take too much time or cost too much money to include all potential participants in a study. Even if the population of interest is narrower than *everyone*—for example, only people who like to run—the time and cost of a study would still make it impossible to include *everyone who likes to run*. Therefore, researchers use a smaller group of the population, or a sample.

Researchers use a variety of techniques to make sure the results from the sample will apply to the population of interest. At the most basic level, researchers use a **representative sample**, a sample that has characteristics that are similar to those in the population. When a study is conducted with a representative sample, researchers are able to generalize the results to the larger population.

Although people are unique, groups of people can share characteristics, such as sex, gender, age, socioeconomic status, and interests. If you asked for volunteers for your experiment on running or used a classified ad to recruit people, you might get a group of people sharing the characteristics of liking volunteer work; reading classified ads; running; and being mostly young, middle class adults. These samples would not be representative of the larger population, resulting in **sampling bias**, an error in the sampling process that allows some members of a population to be more or less likely than others to be included in a study. To ensure that a sample is representative and to avoid sampling bias, researchers use a **random sample**, one in which each member of the population has the same chance of getting into the sample as any other member. Any sampling process that has a pattern or that results in a sample with a pattern is not considered random. Non-random sampling techniques produce sampling bias, which limits the generalizability of an experiment.

Many inexperienced researchers define the population to be studied too broadly, making random sampling problematic and limiting the generalizability of experimental results. If the population is too broadly defined—for example, all people in the United States—drawing a random sample from the population becomes virtually impossible. In the same way, if researchers want to determine whether eating a diet high in protein has an impact on running speed, defining the population as everyone who runs will make selecting a random sample virtually impossible. If, in contrast, the researchers defined the population as "all students at City High School," they could reasonably expect to draw a random sample.

Researchers may also want to be sure that certain segments of the population are equally represented. For example, if you were to conduct an experiment on the students in your high school, you would want to be sure that you have an equal number of seniors, juniors, sophomores, and freshmen in your sample. In **stratified sampling**, subgroups within the population are equally represented, and members of those population subgroups have an equal chance of becoming members of the sample. Although a randomly selected stratified sample should come close to representing all subgroups equally, it may not be exact.

The population is everyone who *can* be in a study; the **sample** is those who actually participate in the study. Many factors may influence the number of people (or animals) to include in a sample, including the cost of or the funds available for the study, accessibility to potential participants, and the research question. Once researchers have defined the population (for example, all seniors in your high school), they can begin to select the sample.

When researchers use random sampling to select the participants in a study, they can generalize the results to the population they defined at the start of the study. This ability to generalize the results of a study to a larger population is called **external validity**. When researchers can establish external validity, they can apply the results of an experiment to other, similar populations. For example, if researchers used random sampling to select participants for a study of heartbeat recovery time of twelve-year-old children after running on a treadmill for 15 minutes, they would be able to generalize the results to other twelve-year-old children who were not in the study.

Experimental Groups, Control Groups, and Causality

Once researchers have randomly selected a sample of participants, they place them into the groups established by the independent variable and the methodology. To establish cause and effect in an experiment, researchers manipulate the independent variable in one or more **experimental groups**. They also measure the dependent variable in a **control group** or comparison group that doesn't receive the experimental treatment.

Researchers use **random assignment**, a process that ensures all members of the sample have an equal chance of being placed into either the control or experimental group(s), to determine who becomes a member of each group. Together, random sampling and random assignment allow researchers to assume that uncontrolled factors are spread randomly throughout the participants and will not have a systematic effect on the results. By comparing the results from the experimental and control groups, researchers are able to rule out other factors that might cause the results.

Researchers establish cause-and-effect relationships by creating an **experimental design** in which they randomly assign participants to groups, manipulate an independent variable, and observe the effect on a dependent variable. To isolate the impact of the independent variable on the dependent variable, researchers attempt to control or hold constant as many other differences as possible between the experimental and control groups. That is, conditions for the experimental and control groups, other than the independent variable, should be as similar as possible—the same time of day, for example, and the same environment. Both groups should be provided with the same instructions. If possible, both groups should be conducted by the same individual(s) who should have no desire to see one outcome over another in the study.

Suppose a researcher is studying whether drinking a glass of milk before bed provides more restful sleep than not drinking the milk. The experimental group would drink a glass of milk before bed. The control group would drink something that looks and tastes like milk but is not actually milk. If other differences between the groups are not held constant—darkness and noise in the room, temperature, comfort of the bed, for example—those other factors may influence participants' sleep.

At the conclusion of the study, the researcher may mistakenly attribute the effects of these other factors to the independent variable. The **internal validity** of the study, the likelihood that differences in the dependent variable are caused by the independent variable rather than some other factor, depends on how well the methodology controls factors other than the independent variable.

Even when both the experimental and control groups are treated similarly, extraneous factors, called **confounding variables**, may interfere with the independent variable and therefore have an impact on the outcome of the study. In the study about the effect of protein on running speed, confounding variables might be other foods in a participant's diet.

Controlling for Placebo Effects and Experimenter Bias

Sometimes when people simply *believe* that an action or a substance will have an effect, it actually *does*. The explanation for this phenomenon is the **placebo effect**—a real response, positive or negative, to an action or substance based solely on expectations, not on the actual properties of the action or substance.

To eliminate the placebo effect, researchers use the experimental methodology known as a single-blind study. A **single-blind study** is one in which the participants do not know whether they belong to the control group or the experimental group. For example, to test a new drug, researchers give the new drug to the experimental group and give a "dummy" pill—one that contains no active ingredient but looks like the new drug—to the control group. Neither group knows whether they have been given the actual drug or the placebo. The simple act of taking a pill, even one with no active ingredient, may cause improvements because of the placebo effect, so to prove the benefits of the new drug, the improvements in the experimental group must be substantially better than those of the control group.

When neither the experimenter nor the participants know to which group the participants belong, the experiment is called a **double-blind study**. Double-blind studies eliminate **experimenter bias**, an error resulting from the experimenter's unconscious expectations of results. If uncontrolled, experimenter bias can interfere with the objective outcome of a study because the researcher's expectations unintentionally interfere with how they treat participants in the study.

The benefit of the experimental method is its ability to demonstrate cause and effect through the manipulation of an independent variable. However, the controlled environment needed to demonstrate cause and effect leads some researchers to claim that the result of experimental research is too artificial to generalize to situations outside of a laboratory environment. Other research methods are available to use when the independent variable cannot be manipulated, if assignment to the groups cannot be randomized, or if the researcher does not want to directly interfere with the participants in a study.

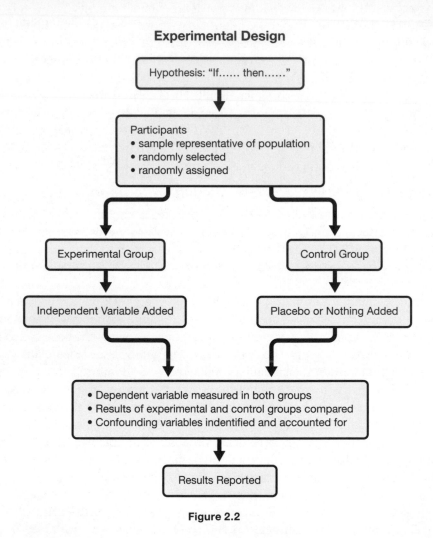

Figure 2.2

Correlational Studies

Occasionally, researchers want to study questions for which manipulating an independent variable would be unethical. Some examples include studying the long-term impact of methadone as a treatment for heroin addiction or the impact of smoking on teenagers' lung capacity. A researcher cannot ethically provide participants with heroin, withhold methadone from other participants, or ask teenagers to smoke. They can, however, investigate individuals who currently use heroin, currently participate in methadone treatment for heroin addiction, or are already smoking. In these cases, the researchers cannot manipulate the independent variable (heroin, methadone, or smoking). However, they can use correlational studies to investigate the relationships among these variables.

Correlational studies allow researchers to determine if there is a relationship between two variables. These studies do not involve manipulation of variables as in an experiment. Rather, they seek to examine how variables are related without interference on the part of the researcher.

The correlational method of research cannot demonstrate cause and effect because no independent variable is manipulated. However, correlational studies are often used as part of a larger research program before conducting an experiment. Combining the methods is one way that researchers can address concerns about the artificial nature of experimental results. When reading about the methodology or results of a study, look for words such as *link* or *relationship* to identify a correlational study.

Three types of relationships can be determined from correlational research. These include positive relationships, negative relationships, and illusory relationships.

In a **positive correlation**, the independent and dependent variables move together in the same direction. If one variable increases, the other also increases; if one variable decreases, the other also decreases. If you were to examine the relationship between time spent exercising and fitness level, you would likely find that as time spent exercising increases, fitness level also increases. Likewise, you would find that the less time people spend exercising, the more likely their fitness level will be low. Do not get confused when the variables are decreasing. As long as both variables are decreasing together, the relationship is still positive. Correlation coefficients indicate the strength of the relationship between two variables. A positive correlation will fall between 0 and +1.0. (See Chapter 3, page 63.)

In a **negative correlation**, the variables have an inverse relationship. For example, the more a person practices golf, the lower his or her game score will be. As the temperature decreases, the amount of clothing people wear generally increases. The key to identifying a negative correlation is that the variables move in opposite directions. The correlation coefficient for a negative correlation will be between 0 and -1.0. (See Chapter 3, page 63.)

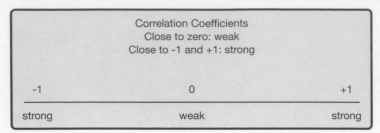

Figure 2.3 Correlation Coefficients

When analyzing relationships, draw arrows next to the variables. The directions of the arrows will indicate at a glance which type of relationship, positive or negative, you are considering. Avoid thinking of a positive correlation as indicating a "good" relationship and a negative correlation as indicating a "bad" relationship. The identifiers "positive" and "negative" simply indicate whether the variables move in the same or opposite directions.

Sometimes researchers expect a relationship to exist between two factors, but there is actually no link between the variables. An expected or suspected relationship that doesn't empirically exist is known as an **illusory correlation**. For example, a belief that height is related to grade in a psychology class is an illusory correlation because there should be no relationship between these two variables. However, a psychology instructor who recalls a few very tall students receiving As may be prone to believe

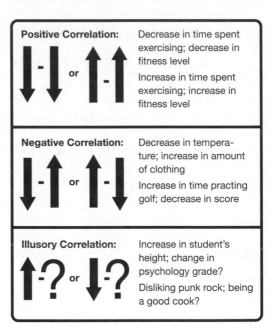

Figure 2.4 Types of Correlations

that these variables are related. Regardless of what the instructor believes, an analysis of data should demonstrate that no relationship exists. Illusory correlations should have correlation coefficients close to 0. (See Chapter 3, pages 63–64.)

Correlational studies are useful for making predictions—one of the goals of psychology—and decisions. For example, if parents learned there is a positive correlation between playing football and having a concussion, they may think twice about allowing their children to participate on a football team. Colleges value SAT scores because they correlate positively to, and therefore predict, the grades students get in their freshman year.

Correlational studies are also useful to avoid unethical experiments that would expose participants to harm. For example, suppose a researcher wanted to know if the death of a family member had an impact on levels of depression the following year. It is impossible to manipulate the independent variable (the death of a family member) in this study. But finding out if there is a link may allow proactive interventions to take place, which may benefit family members at risk for depression. A correlational study provides an ethical way to study how often depression occurs after the death of a family member.

Correlational studies may be misleading, however, because the relationship between the variables, especially which variable is affecting which, is sometimes hard to determine. For example, suppose there is a positive correlation between exercise and a good night's sleep. You cannot know if exercise causes better sleep or if getting better sleep provides more energy for exercise. It could be the case that both variables affect one another. Researchers also cannot rule out the possibility that a third variable causes both of the other variables to increase or decrease. This is known as a **third variable problem**.

Despite these challenges, correlational research is used often and produces valuable information. Correlational studies assist in making predictions about relationships and establishing links between variables. Figure 2.4 will help you review the types of correlation that result from this research method.

Descriptive Research

Descriptive research techniques are those that allow researchers to gather information that cannot be obtained using the experimental method while still using scientific questions, hypotheses, and careful data collection. Descriptive research methods include naturalistic observation, case studies, surveys, and interviews. Like correlational studies, descriptive research methods cannot provide a causal conclusion because of their lack of a control. But all of the following techniques are useful in their own right.

Naturalistic Observation

Naturalistic observation is the observation of human or animal behavior in its natural setting. In fact, participants often do not know that they are being observed, so they act naturally as a consequence. For this reason, naturalistic observation avoids the criticism leveled against experimental research as being artificial because of the intentional manipulation of variables, the necessity for control, and the location of testing in a laboratory.

An example of naturalistic observation is observing student behavior in the cafeteria at lunch. You might observe how students interact with one another, where they sit, with whom they sit, how many buy lunch vs. bring lunch from home, and other behaviors. Student behavior in this setting is likely to be different from behavior in a laboratory, and recreating the school lunch room in a lab may be too artificial to obtain results that are reflective of what actually happens in the lunch room.

Naturalistic observation has benefits when doing research with certain populations. This method may be helpful when conducting research with children who are too young to be interviewed or with animals who cannot be studied in a lab.

There is also potential for error with naturalistic observation. Although using naturalistic observation allows researchers to obtain information that is more reflective of the actual behavior of those being studied, it does not allow the researcher to interact with those being studied. In some cases, this lack of interaction with participants

Much coyote research uses naturalistic observation.

may lead to erroneous conclusions about why the behavior occurred.

Naturalistic observation is only descriptive; researchers cannot interfere as they may be able to in an experiment by adjusting variables. Careful and accurate observation is one goal of psychology.

Case Studies

Some descriptive researchers use case studies through which they conduct in-depth studies of either an individual or a group who share a common characteristic. Often individuals who are featured in case studies have some unique characteristic that researchers want to investigate.

A **case study** generally involves numerous testing methods to gather as much data about the participants as possible. In his book *Awakenings,* neurologist Oliver Sacks describes an instance in which he undertook an in-depth study of a group of individuals who had experienced years of paralysis. Many medical professionals had given up on these individuals, who were in a coma-like state, and believed that they could not interact with the outside world. Dr. Sacks evaluated their physical abilities and behavioral patterns and the individual differences within the group. He eventually treated them with L-Dopa, a synthetic form of the neurotransmitter dopamine, and many found at least temporary relief from their paralysis.

In an individual case study, a school psychologist might evaluate a child for a special education program. The psychologist would give the child a full battery of cognitive assessments to rule out some types of deficits, determine if there are environmental or physical causes, and identify precisely where a learning deficit lies. The psychologist would then create an Individualized Educational Plan based on the student's unique needs.

Case studies can be extremely beneficial for the individual involved but often cannot be generalized to the larger population because of the unique characteristics of the individual(s) studied. However, case studies may help researchers generate hypotheses for experimental testing.

The results of the case study method may also be influenced by the opinions of those conducting the research. For example, if researchers have preconceived notions about the individual or group under investigation, they may unconsciously find what they are looking for in the tests and miss other important factors. When researchers find only information that is consistent with their prior beliefs, they are demonstrating confirmation bias. (See pages 26 and 284.)

Surveys

Survey research is an inexpensive and quick method of gaining information about people's opinions, attitudes, and perceptions. In a **survey**, participants receive a list of questions to answer. Survey research may be helpful in obtaining information about individuals' political views, what features of a new car they like or dislike, or what aspect of a marketing campaign is appealing. Surveys can be conducted face to face, by phone, through the mail, or online. Surveys are often completed using an interview format.

If researchers want to know what students think about a potential new attendance policy at their high school, they could send an electronic survey to all students. The results of this survey could determine if the policy has the support of the student population, and that information could influence the administration's decision.

Other survey research occurs after an event, such as the review of a recently purchased product. Individuals who invested in a newly released smartphone may be asked what features they liked or did not like so that modifications can be made for future product releases.

As helpful as survey research is, it poses challenges. Participation in most survey research is not random. In many instances, people with extreme positions may respond to surveys. Often low response rates may cause survey results to not reflect the views of the population as a whole. Researchers conducting survey research can make efforts to use **random selection**, a technique for ensuring that all individuals in a population have an equal opportunity of being chosen to participate, to attempt to gather a variety of responses that reflect all views of a population. The Gallup Poll, for example, which conducts research about presidential elections, attempts to randomly call voters to predict who will win an upcoming election. This type of survey is, however, different from an experiment because even if random selection or sampling is used, there is no manipulation of an independent variable.

Another challenge with surveys is that the wording of the questions can have a strong effect on the way people respond, possibly skewing the results. For example, researchers have found that the words *forbid* and *allow* are especially potent in a question. In a now famous experiment from 1941, researcher Daniel Rugg posed a question two ways: 1) "Do you think that the United States should allow public speeches against democracy?" and 2) "Do you think that the United States should forbid public speeches against democracy?" When respondents were asked whether the United States should *allow* public speeches against democracy, 21 percent said yes and 62 percent said no, with the remaining percent undecided or without opinion. When other respondents were asked if the United States should *forbid* such speeches, 39 percent favored allowing the speeches and 46 percent favored forbidding them. The difference between the responses is significant: 21 percent vs. 39 percent in favor of allowing and 62 percent vs. 46 percent in favor of forbidding. Many later experiments built on this one, and many possible explanations have been offered, some suggesting that it is not the wording itself but rather the simple "either-or" nature of the question that tipped the outcomes. Specific wording, the context of the questions, the order of questions, the presence or absence of alternatives, the order of the alternatives if present, and whether problems were "framed" in terms of gains or losses all had an effect on survey results. (For more on framing and context and their effect on responses, see pages 288–289.)

Interviews

Interviews are often used for both formal and informal data collection. They can be conducted in a one-on-one setting or, less often, in groups. Like surveys, interviews can be useful for gathering much information quickly and relatively inexpensively. Interviews may be useful in developing an understanding of people's opinions and beliefs, and they make use of some of the same types of questions as surveys—with the same kinds of potential pitfalls in wording.

Interviews can be used for a variety of purposes. For example, they allow cognitive psychologists to understand someone's reasoning for choosing one answer over another on an exam. By interviewing the participants, researchers can know what participants experienced during a session, something naturalistic observation study does not allow. Participants can report their experiences, thoughts, and feelings during or after a study. Finally, interviews may help psychologists gain an understanding of a wide variety of topics, such as decision-making, interpersonal attraction, and emotions.

Interviews, like all research methods, have limitations. If you have ever seen a celebrity interviewed on a late-night talk show or participated in an interview yourself, you know that individuals may present a **subjective self-report**, portraying an overly positive view of themselves as they want to be viewed, not necessarily as they actually are. Also, **demand characteristics**—subtle cues interviewers may convey about their expectations—may cause interviewees to behave in ways they believe the interviewer wants them to behave. Interviewees also often exhibit a **social desirability bias** because they want to appear kind and empathetic to others.

In addition to limitations, the interview method poses at least two unique challenges. First, those conducting the interview must be careful to avoid leading questions—questions that encourage a certain answer. Second, the validity of interview data can be questioned because a participant could be lying. For example, most individuals would say that they would intervene if they saw someone else in trouble. Yet instances of the bystander effect (see page 641) tell a very different story.

In spite of challenges and limitations, the ease with which interviews can be conducted and the cost at which they can be completed makes them an attractive option for many researchers. You can use the table in Figure 2.5 to review the advantages and disadvantages of interviews along with all the other descriptive research methods.

a.bacall

"I'm an honest person but when I take an online survey, I'm a big liar."

Types of Descriptive Research	Advantages	Disadvantages	Example
All	Avoids artificiality of highly controlled experiments	Cannot demonstrate cause and effect	Observations, case studies, surveys
Naturalistic Observation	Participants act naturally—no artificial conditions	Lack of interaction between experimenter and participants may lead to erroneous results May be subject to experimenter bias	Researchers observe the hunting behaviors of coyotes living in a specified area
Case Studies (individual or group)	Collection of in-depth, detailed information Opportunity to investigate unique illnesses	May be distorted by the expectations of the researcher Cannot be generalized to the population	Researchers study how patient recovering from surgery to remove a brain tumor performs on cognitive, emotional, and physical tasks
Surveys	Quick, easy, and inexpensive collection of data Gathers information about people's opinions and beliefs	Possible low response rate Participants may be prone to demand characteristics and wording effects Respondents may lie	Researchers investigate student attitudes about gender stereotyping
Interviews	Quick, easy, and inexpensive collection of data Information directly from the participant to eliminate experimenter guessing	Possibility of subjective self-reports Participants may lie Participants may be prone to demand characteristics Possibility of researcher asking leading questions	Researchers evaluate responses after a community tragedy

Figure 2.5 Descriptive Research Methods Compared

The Science of Psychology: *Comparing Experimentation, Correlational Studies, and Case Studies*

As you read, there are three types of research methods psychologists use to collect and interpret scientific data: experimentation, correlational studies, and descriptive research, including case studies. To gain a deeper understanding of each method, consider the following question so you may determine which methods are most useful and appropriate given the researcher's goals, resources, and ethical limitations.

Research Objective: Suppose researchers in Oklahoma are attempting to examine the efficacy of a specific antidepressant as a treatment method for clinical depression in a local Native American tribe. They want to then expand the implications of their research to the national Native American community. List the pros and cons of using experimentation, case studies, and correlational studies in both local and national research. To help organize your answer, create a chart like the one below listing the pros and cons of each method if it were to be used both locally and nationally. Then determine which research method(s) would best suit the researcher's goals on both the local and national level, and write a paragraph explaining your answer.

Research Method	Level	Pros	Cons
Experimentation	Local		
	National		
Correlational Studies	Local		
	National		
Case Studies	Local		
	National		

Developmental Research Designs

In a method known as **longitudinal design**, researchers study individuals at several points during the life span. Some longitudinal studies last a few months or years, while others last many decades. This method would be useful for studying the impact of a degenerative illness over many years or to study language development in children. (For a description of a well-known and long-lasting longitutidinal study on attachment between babies and their mothers, see page 363.) Some case studies also employ this design because they investigate an individual in depth over a long period of time.

Although longitudinal research can generate in-depth and potentially interesting results, it has significant limitations. The longitudinal design can be very expensive to conduct. After many years, researchers may no longer be interested in their topic. Some unforeseen factors can affect the results of a longitudinal study. For example, over time participants could drop out of the study or die.

Instead of a longitudinal design, researchers often opt for a cross-sectional design. In a **cross-sectional design**, researchers compare several groups to one another based on variables such as age, socioeconomic class, and gender, resulting in a less expensive and quicker study than a longitudinal study. But because researchers compare different groups to one another, this design may find differences that do not actually exist.

For example, the results of one cross-sectional study about intelligence scores determined that intelligence declined over age. In fact, the differences were the result of **cohort effects**, the influences of being part of a group bonded on the basis of a time period or certain life experiences. Because young people today are tested far more frequently than in the past and have access to more information through technology than their predecessors, it appeared that young people were more intelligent, yet most research suggests that intelligence remains relatively steady throughout life. (See page 400.)

Ethics Guidelines for Conducting Psychological Research

Because the field of psychology is interested in human thought and human and animal behavior, humans and animals are the participants in most psychological research. Both humans and animals involved in studies must be treated according to the highest ethical standards. All institutions that conduct ongoing research have an **Institutional Review Board (IRB)** that must meet to review any study to determine if the proposal is ethical or if it poses risks to those involved. The IRB ensures the safety of those participating in research studies, and a study cannot begin until the IRB has given approval.

The American Psychological Association and other professional organizations which oversee and report on research set forth a number of specific criteria that must be followed in all research studies. Many institutional review boards have adopted the ethical guidelines set forth by the APA, but individual institutions may include additional guidelines or restrictions regarding what can and cannot be done with participants at their institutions.

Informed Consent

Humans participating in research studies must be participating by their own free choice. No **coercion**, or force, can be used to require individuals to comply. Even after a study begins, a participant may decide that the topic of the study makes him or her feel uncomfortable or unsafe, and the participant may leave the study without providing any reason or explanation.

Before the study begins, participants must be told all the details of the study and given a clear explanation of their role in the study. If the participants agree to take part in the study, they give their signed **informed consent** indicating that they understand the components and the potential risks of the study and agree to take part. Even if people have signed the informed consent form, they are not obligated to complete the study. For participants younger than eighteen, a parent must sign an informed consent form before the study begins.

Deception

Some studies require that the researchers mislead participants about the true nature of the study. In Stanley Milgram's famous research on obedience to authority, participants were told that they were involved in a test on learning and memory. They were told to administer what they thought were higher and higher levels of electric shock to another person, the "learner," who they believed was also a volunteer in the study but was actually a confederate (fellow researcher) of Milgram. (See page 606 for more on the Milgram experiment.)

Deception, which involves misleading participants about the nature of an experiment and its methodology, is acceptable when the researcher believes it is necessary for the efficacy of the study and the IRB agrees with the researcher's reasoning. The APA guidelines set limits on the types of deception researchers can use. Researchers may not deceive participants about the risk factors of the study. They also may not deceive participants after completion of the study by falsifying the results. If researchers use deception in a study, they must **debrief** the participants by explaining the deception at the conclusion of the study. The participants should be told the true intention of the study as soon as reasonably possible.

Milgram delayed debriefing participants in his studies because he was concerned they would share details of the study with their friends and neighbors in the small town of New Haven, Connecticut. Many of the participants in the study left without knowing that the individual posing as the learner was not harmed by the "electric shocks" they had administered (the person was never actually shocked). Some of the participants were deeply concerned because they believed that they had either harmed or possibly even killed the learner. Milgram sent a letter to all participants at the conclusion of the study. However, sending a letter is not sufficient to offset or diminish the risk faced by the participants. Some participants did not receive a debriefing letter until years after their involvement in the study.

The APA and IRB guidelines regarding debriefing participants were created to address ethical issues that became apparent in the wake of World War II and through Milgram's and others' research. Researchers and the IRB must consider both the physical and emotional risks of any study to be sure that neither will have a damaging impact on the well-being of participants.

Confidentiality and Anonymity

The identities of participants in a study must be kept confidential. **Confidentiality** protects their private information. Typically, participants are also not identified by name. Instead they are assigned a code or a number to protect their anonymity for the duration of the study. To prevent experimenter bias, even the researchers often do not know what data belongs with which participants. Once a study is complete, researchers must continue to protect the participants' anonymity and confidentiality; the information cannot be shared with anyone outside of the researchers without permission from the participants. For example, if researchers investigated the impact of teenagers' drug use on social relationships, they cannot release the names and drug use of individual participants during or after the study.

Animal Research

Historically, **animal experimentation** has played a large role in research. Researchers from different areas within psychology often use animals for gathering information that may help us better understand human behavior. Behavioral psychologists, such as B. F. Skinner, worked with rats and pigeons to demonstrate the impact of rewards and punishments on behavior. Although cognitive psychology did not become a formal approach until the late 1950s, psychologists were studying cognitive phenomena with nonhuman primates beginning in the early 1900s.

Today, animals are still used in many studies, and they must be treated ethically in all research. Harming an animal or placing one in unnecessarily risky conditions is unethical. Universities that use animals in research must have a committee that evaluates the proposed studies. That committee, which is for nonhumans what the IRB is for humans, is called the **Animal Care and Use Committee (ACUC)**. Review boards weigh the risks to the animal against the benefits of the research.

The American Psychological Association's **Committee on Animal Research and Ethics (CARE)** advocates for the ethical use of animals in research. The committee's main goals are to provide education on responsible research with nonhuman subjects and to establish clear guidelines about what ethical and responsible use of animals in psychological research means.

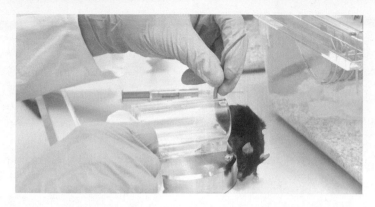

* * *

Occasionally, after research has been completed, individuals will experience **hindsight bias**—claiming to have known the result all along, like those who claim to have known the result of a presidential election or the Super Bowl before it occurred. Although we often have an educated guess about an outcome or turn out to be correct in a prediction, research must be conducted to know the results for certain and to know that they are reliable.

Strong research is essential to producing a growing body of knowledge in the field of psychology. Good methodology will ensure that researchers carefully consider all of the components of a research question and keep an open mind about information that might refute their expectations.

Each method of research has its merits and challenges, but all share the common goals of describing, predicting, controlling, and explaining human thought and human and animal behavior. All research must be conducted with careful consideration for the well-being of those participating.

REFLECT ON THE ESSENTIAL QUESTION

Essential Question: *How do psychologists use the scientific method to investigate questions about human thought and human and animal behavior?* On separate paper, make a chart like the one below and gather details to answer that question.

	Experimental Method	Correlational Studies	Descriptive Research
How Scientific Method Is Used			
Tools			
Advantages			
Disadvantages			

KEY TERMS			
Animal Care and Use Committee (ACUC) coercion Committee on Animal Research and Ethics (CARE) confidentiality confirmation bias deception experimental design experimenter bias hindsight bias hypothesis informed consent Institutional Review Board (IRB) methodology placebo effect random sample replication scientific method theory	*EXPERIMENTAL RESEARCH* cause and effect cohort effects confounding variable control group dependent variable double-blind study empirical data experimental group external validity generalizability independent variable internal validity operational definition population random assignment random sample representative sample sample sampling bias single-blind study stratified sampling third variable problem variables	*CORRELATIONAL RESEARCH* correlational studies demand characteristics illusory correlation negative correlation positive correlation	*DESCRIPTIVE RESEARCH* case study cross-sectional design debrief descriptive research interviews longitudinal design naturalistic observation random selection social desirability bias subjective self-report surveys

1. A researcher wants to determine if studying for a half hour each night for a week in preparation for an exam is better than studying for three-and-a-half hours on Sunday evening for an exam on Monday. Researchers will randomly select participants for the study and randomly place participants into either the massed (Sunday night) or distributed (half hour a night) study group. They will also measure the outcome of each unit exam (both groups will take the same exam). What is the dependent variable in this experiment?

(A) Massed practice

(B) Distributed practice

(C) Students in AP Psychology

(D) The content of the exam

(E) The score on each exam

2. An experimenter wants to determine the impact of caffeine on attention span. Which of the following best represents random assignment?

(A) Placing participants into either the caffeine or non-caffeine group without any set pattern

(B) Offering different levels of caffeine to the participants

(C) Observing the level of attention exhibited by participants given caffeine

(D) Selecting who will participate in the study without any specific pattern

(E) Selecting those who drink caffeine regularly and have built a tolerance to the effects

3. A researcher wants to investigate a unique brain tumor in a twelve-year-old child to see how the tumor affects the child's behavior. The researcher will conduct a battery of cognitive and physical tests with the child over the course of six months to account for potential changes in the tumor's size and impact. Which of the following would be the best research method to study this situation?

(A) Survey

(B) Naturalistic observation

(C) Individual case study

(D) Experimental design

(E) Group case study

4. A researcher determined that the less practice teenagers had driving, the more moving violations they received during the first year after receiving their drivers' license. This finding is an example of which of the following?

(A) Statistical significance

(B) A spurious correlation

(C) An illusory correlation

(D) A negative correlation

(E) A positive correlation

5. A graduate student wants to conduct a study to investigate people's opinions regarding the death penalty. Because he has not yet taken his research methods course, he does not know which technique would be best to gather data on this issue. Based on what you have read about research techniques, which of the following technique would work best for his proposed study?

(A) Individual case study

(B) Survey

(C) Experiment

(D) Group case study

(E) Naturalistic observation

6. A researcher who had a role in designing a new medication for headaches wants to promote it. She unconsciously suggests to those who took her medication that they are feeling better than those who had an alternative medication. This demonstrates which of the following phenomena?

(A) Spurious correlation

(B) Experimenter bias

(C) Hindsight bias

(D) Confirmation bias

(E) Placebo effect

7. What is the best way for a researcher to avoid unconsciously signaling any point of view to the participants in a study?

(A) Single-blind study

(B) Correlational design

(C) Case study design

(D) Double-blind study

(E) Survey research

8. Which of the following is the best example of random selection?

(A) Arbitrarily selecting names of everyone in the population to determine who will be in the study

(B) Selecting every tenth name from the census to determine who will be in the study

(C) Splitting the alphabet in half to determine who will be in the experimental or control group

(D) Determining all of the individuals who can potentially participate in the study

(E) Having all participants count off by twos and then placing all of the odd numbered participants into the control group and all even numbered participants into the experimental group

9. Mary is an undergraduate student who has volunteered for a study her professor is running. During the study, Mary picks up on cues from her professor about the expectations he has regarding the outcome of the study. The professor does not realize he is giving these cues, and she does not realize that she is picking up on them, yet she behaves as he expects. Which of the following phenomena has occurred?

(A) Mary's professor is demonstrating confirmation bias.

(B) Mary's professor had experienced sampling bias.

(C) Mary had displayed demand characteristics.

(D) Mary has participated in a double-blind study.

(E) Mary's professor has experienced hindsight bias.

10. A researcher has found that the more time athletes spend training in track and field, the lower their times in the 100-meter run. She determines that this result means that training causes drops in times. Which of the following is true about this study?

(A) The researcher has conducted a survey.

(B) The researcher has falsely determined that correlation proves causation.

(C) The researcher has conducted a correlational study that resulted in a positive correlation.

(D) The researcher has conducted a study that resulted in an illusory correlation.

(E) The researcher has conducted a longitudinal study.

1. Varad is a graduate student in psychology. He wants to study the impact of a high protein diet on muscle tone in students on his college campus. He plans on providing some students with high protein diets for six months while others will continue with their normal diets for the same time period. He will measure muscle tone at the start of the study and again at the end of the study.

   A) Identify how the following components would be applied to Varad's study.

   - Random selection
   - Random assignment
   - Double-blind study
   - Independent variable
   - Operational definition of the dependent variable
   - A potential confounding variable

   B) What is the benefit of the experimental design as it relates to the conclusion Varad can make about his study?

2. Elena wants to determine whether sun exposure influences the likelihood of developing skin cancer. The participants in the study will record their exposure to the sun on a scale of 1-5 using an electronic device each day, and Elena will record the amount of sun exposure each person has received over a five-year period. Also, the participants' skin will be inspected for sun spots and skin cancer both before, during, and after the study. Elena will not intervene to determine how much sun exposure each participant receives. If there are signs of skin cancer at any point during the study, the individual will be provided with treatment, and all participants will be given information about the dangers of sun exposure and rates of skin cancer at the conclusion of the study.

   A) Identify the following factors in Elena's study if she found that high levels of sun exposure led to higher levels of skin cancer.

   - What type of study is Elena conducting?
   - How could Elena report her findings in a graph?
   - What type of statement could Elena make at the conclusion of this study?

B) Explain how the following ethical issues apply to Elena's study.
- What are the ethical issues in this experiment?
- How has Elena accounted for an ethical issue that may have an impact on her participants?
- How could Elena have accounted for an ethical issue that was not clearly addressed by her study?

WRITE AS A PSYCHOLOGIST: BREAK DOWN THE QUESTION

In your responses to the free-response questions, clearly show where one answer ends and another begins. Skipping a line between your answers for each part of the question will help the readers clearly follow your response. It may also help you keep track of your progress in answering all the points raised in the prompts. Always write in complete sentences. For more guidance in answering free-response questions, see pages xxii–xxiii.

3

Statistics

"The greatest moments are those when you see the result pop up in a graph or in your statistics analysis—in that moment you realize you know something no one else does and you get the pleasure of thinking about how to tell them."

—Economist Emily Oster

Essential Question: How do researchers analyze data to determine if the results of a study are meaningful or significant?

In Chapter 2, you read about different research methods psychologists use to collect data for their studies. Before coming to conclusions about what those studies mean, researchers (and students) must analyze and interpret the collected data. The role of **statistics** is to summarize, analyze, and interpret that data.

Different research methods produce different types of data. You might find it useful to review Chapter 2 to keep research methods in mind while you learn how to use statistics to understand and report data and transform the data into information.

Thinking Critically About Statistics

Knowing how to use statistics has benefits beyond trying to understand research questions. Statistics have an official-sounding "factual" sense to them, but they are often misunderstood or intentionally misrepresented. People can select or cherry pick statistics to show a distorted picture of reality. For example, suppose a commercial says that three out of four dentists recommend a certain brand of toothpaste. Three out of four implies that 75 percent of dentists recommend the toothpaste. Thinking critically about the statistics, however, you might ask, "Were four dentists asked what toothpaste they recommend, or were 100 asked?" The number of dentists surveyed matters because the opinions of 75 dentists carry more weight than the opinions of three.

Consider another example. If you invested in a stock that was down 7 percent for the year, you might want to sell it to avoid more losses. However, you would make a better decision if you had more information. Perhaps the previous year the stock was up by 18 percent and the market is simply adjusting itself. In that case, you might be better off holding on to the stock and waiting to sell. Being aware of only part of a **data set**—or related groups of data—can lead to poor decision making or erroneous conclusions.

In addition to helping you become a savvy consumer or make better decisions, the ability to properly assess data is essential to understanding the results of research studies. Statistical analysis adds to the body of knowledge in psychology and other fields.

Descriptive Statistics

Descriptive statistics are techniques for organizing and describing data sets. The first step in working with a data set is to organize the data. Organizing the data set makes easier to manage and allows you to see patterns in the data.

Frequency Distributions

If your data set is small enough to do calculations by hand, start by making a **frequency distribution** table to show how often (how frequently) something occurs. For example, if you want to know how your study habits compare to those of your fellow students, you might poll your classmates to find out how many minutes a night they spend on homework. You might ask 20 students in your AP Psychology class and get these 20 answers:

45, 90, 60, 90, 120, 90, 150, 120, 90, 60, 150, 120, 120, 150, 90, 60, 175, 150, 120, 90

To make sense of these numbers, create a frequency distribution table by listing the responses in numerical order and tallying how many of each answer you received. Your table would look like this:

FREQUENCY DISTRIBUTION TABLE	
Number of Minutes Studied	**Frequency**
45	1
60	3
90	6
120	5
150	4
175	1

Figure 3.1 Frequency Distribution Table

In addition to helping you see patterns in data, a frequency distribution helps insure that you do not overlook any data points. With data organized into a frequency distribution, graphing, summarizing, and analyzing data become manageable.

Types of Data and Scales of Measurement

Before you can graph, summarize, or do other types of statistical tasks with data, you need to know the data's characteristics. Researchers study many kinds of variables in many different ways. The nature of a variable and how researchers measure it determine what type of data a study produces and whether you can perform mathematical calculations with that data.

Data are discrete or continuous. **Discrete data** have values that represent categories that cannot be further divided—things you can count, such as the number of students in your school or the number of channels a cable provider offers. **Continuous data**, in contrast, can take on any value—data you can measure rather than count. Examples include height, weight, and temperature. Whether data are discrete or continuous has an impact on the meaning and usefulness of the statistics you report. For example, you might read in the media that the size of the average American family in 2015 was 2.54 people. In reality, of course, there is no such thing as 0.54 of a person.

The categories of discrete and continuous data break down into subcategories depending on the scale of measurement researchers use. The subcategories of discrete data are *nominal* and *ordinal*; the subcategories of continuous data are *interval* and *ratio*.

Nominal Scale of Measurement The word *nominal* is derived from the Latin word *nomin*, which means "name." A **nominal scale** essentially labels or names categories of data. Nominal data do not lend themselves to mathematical computations. Rather, they count how many responses participants give in a study or how many people fall into a category. For example, for a study about political preferences, researchers would count the number of people who identified themselves as Democrats, Republicans, Independents, and others.

With a process called coding, you can assign a numerical value to each category of nominal data. For example, a researcher gathering data on political preferences might label all of the Democrats with a 1, Republicans with a 2, and Independents with a 3. The coding is for identification purposes only. You cannot arrange nominal data in rank order because the assigned numbers have no true numerical value. They represent only the different categories that exist in the nominal data.

Ordinal Scale of Measurement An **ordinal scale** produces data that can be rank ordered. With ordinal data, you can say that one value is more or less than another. For example, you can place the members of a baseball team in order from lowest to highest according to their batting averages; this is how a team manager determines the batting rotation for a game. An ordinal scale would work well to compare the GPA of high school students. Any variable you can place in order from highest to lowest or lowest to highest produces data on an ordinal scale.

Ordinal data do not have equal spacing between each number. For this reason, the types of calculations you can perform with ordinal data are limited.

For example, you can represent the first, second, and third runners to finish a 5K race with an ordinal scale, but there is not necessarily an equal amount of time between the first, second, and third runners in a race. The first-place runner could be far ahead in a race, while the second- and third-place runners might have running times relatively close to each other.

Interval Scale of Measurement How many times have you heard the phrase, "on a scale from one to ten"? Questions that begin with that phrase operate on the assumption that the difference between each degree of that scale is the same. An **interval scale**, then, represents data that can be placed in rank order *and* that have equal measurements between values on the scale. For example, the difference in time between 1:15 p.m. and 1:30 p.m. is the same as the difference between 9:00 p.m. and 9:15 p.m.—15 equal 60-second minutes. Because the spacing between measurements is equal for interval scale data, you can perform mathematical computations and compare scores to one another.

However, interval scale data do not have a true zero point. Standard temperature scales have an arbitrary zero point. Zero degrees Fahrenheit and zero degrees Celsius do not mean there is no temperature.

Ratio Scale of Measurement A **ratio scale** represents data that, like the interval scale, have equal values between measurements. In addition, a ratio scale has a true zero point. You can perform mathematical computations and compare scores with ratio scale data. Weight is a variable that has a true zero point. In addition, you can accurately state that 20 pounds is twice as heavy as ten pounds, whereas with the interval scale, you can't say that 20 degrees F is twice as warm as ten degrees F.

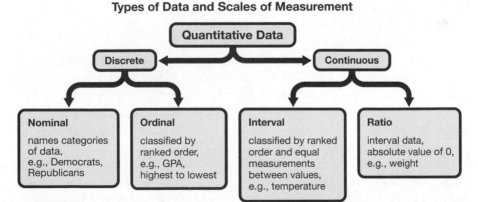

Types of Data and Scales of Measurement

Figure 3.2

Displaying Data

Once researchers have organized data, they should be able to display the findings and convey them concisely to others. Graphs and charts are useful in summarizing the results of experiments and surveys.

Following are several examples of graphs that researchers use to display data.

A **pie chart** is useful for displaying nominal or categorical data or any data that consist of percentages or proportions. Data on political preferences are simply and effectively displayed in a pie chart. Each slice of the pie would show the percentage of individuals who claimed affiliation to each of the political parties. A pie chart would enable you to see at a glance which party claimed more survey participants than the others. Another data set suitable for display in a pie chart is the percentage of students engaged in different fields of study at a college or university.

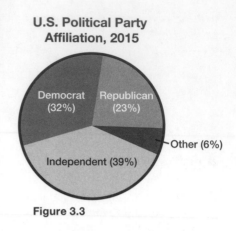

U.S. Political Party Affiliation, 2015

Figure 3.3

A **bar graph** is another useful way to display categorical or non-numerical data. For example, a bar graph can also display political party affiliation or other categorical data such

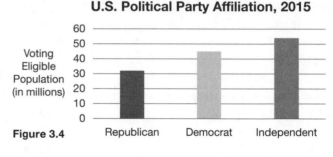

U.S. Political Party Affiliation, 2015

Figure 3.4

as the favorite color of students in a first-grade class. The graph would show frequency on the y-axis and a bar for each different color on the x-axis.

A bar graph is the most appropriate way to represent frequency for nominal or categorical data. For example, it is not meaningful to say that green is more than or less than yellow. However, it is meaningful to discuss how many students identified green or yellow as their favorite color.

When creating a bar graph for categorical data, leave space between the bars. This space between each of the bars signals that the data are categorical and measured on a nominal scale.

In a **histogram**, in contrast, bars touch one another to show data that are continuous rather than discrete. (See Figure 3.5.) Examples of data that can appear in histograms include time and age. For example, you could use a histogram to display the results of an experiment that measured the time it took rats to run through a maze. You would show equal segments of time on the x-axis and the number of rats running the maze within each time segment on the y-axis. Ages of students, lengths, weights, and heights—any data measured on an interval or ratio scale—can be grouped for display in a histogram. The histogram bars on the graph must touch one another to let viewers know that they are looking at continuous data.

A **frequency polygon** (Figure 3.6) is a line graph that is used to display continuous data generally measured on interval or ratio scales. It helps researchers and other viewers see themes and patterns in a data set. A frequency polygon line graph is useful for plotting multiple data sets, which can appear overwhelming on a histogram. For example, a graph of crime rates in Chicago over the past ten years would be easier to interpret if shown as a frequency polygon than as a histogram. The frequency polygon would allow viewers to identify peaks and valleys of crime at a glance.

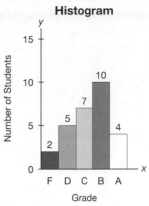

Histogram

Figure 3.5

Measures of Central Tendency

After organizing and graphing data, researchers summarize the data with a **measure of central tendency**, which indicates the point in a distribution of scores around which all the scores cluster.

The **mean** is the average number in a data set; it is the most

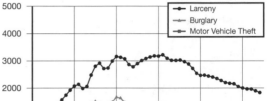

Frequency Polygon

Figure 3.6 Crime Rates in Chicago

commonly reported measure of central tendency. You can calculate the mean for data based on an interval scale or ratio scale; you cannot calculate the mean for nominal or ordinal data.

To calculate the mean, add all of the scores in the data set and divide by the number of scores (N). The number of scores or data points often represents the number of participants in a study.

How is the mean helpful to people? If your parents want to know how much lunch money to provide to you each week, the mean can help them decide. They could use the mean amount you spent on lunch each week last year to determine what you generally spend on lunch.

A disadvantage of the mean is that extreme values can pull it in one direction or another. For example, suppose you purchased lunch for all of your friends one week because they did not have money. The amount you spent that week will make the value of the mean higher than if you spent your usual weekly amount. In that case, the mean will not accurately reflect how much money you generally spend on lunch. The mean will also not accurately reflect what you generally spend if your parents include what you spent on lunch during school vacation week.

When a data set contains one or two extremely low or high data points, two other measures, the median and the mode, more accurately reflect the central tendency of the data set.

The **median** is the middle number in a set of scores. You calculate the median by determining the point in a distribution at which half of the scores fall above and half below.

Arranging the scores into a frequency distribution makes it easier to detect the middle number because the scores have already been arranged from lowest to highest or highest to lowest. For the data set 15, 17, 18, 21, 24, 26, and 28, the median or middle score is 21. Three numbers fall below 21 and three fall above. When the number of scores in the data set is even, you average the two middle scores to find the median.

When a data set has extreme scores, the median is a more useful measure to report than the mean because it is not as strongly affected by extreme scores. However, you always need to look at the particular data set to know whether there are extreme scores and what impact they may have on the median. The median is the measure of central tendency to report for ordinal data.

The **mode** is the most frequently occurring score in a data set. The mode is not how many times the score occurs. Rather, it is the score itself. For example, if you track how many points an athlete scores per game in a basketball season, the mode might be six. A mode of six means that the athlete most frequently scored six points per game. Some data sets are bimodal—they have two modes; some have none at all.

The mode is the most appropriate measure of central tendency to report for nominal data. For example, for data on political party affiliation, you would state the most commonly reported party.

Which measure of central tendency is best depends on your research question, the data set, your purpose, or your audience. If a psychology instructor wants to boost students' spirits about an exam on which a few students scored poorly but most scored well, she might report that the median score was an A. The median is useful in this case because it is not affected by extreme scores. However, if the instructor reported that there were two modes, 77 and 82, on the exam, students might end up confused because it does not give them a clear picture of how the class as a whole performed on the exam.

Measures of Variability

Measures of central tendency provide basic information about a data set —a snapshot—but do not reveal how spread out or dispersed the data in the distribution are. Measures of variability serve this purpose.

The simplest descriptive measure of variability is the **range**, which represents the span of the scores in a data set. You find the range by subtracting the lowest score in a data set from the highest score. In the data set 31, 44, 45, 48, 53, 57, the range is 26 (the highest score, 57, minus the lowest score, 31).

The range shows only the distance between the lowest and highest scores. It cannot reveal the average distance from the mean or other significant relationships between data points.

The **variance** of a data set indicates how widely spread scores are from one another and the mean. Typically, researchers report the measure of variability called the **standard deviation (SD)**, the average distance from the mean for a set of scores. The standard deviation becomes its own unit of measure, represented as a **z-score**—the number of standard deviations from the mean. A z-score of -1SD means a score is one standard deviation *below* the mean; a z-score of +1SD means a score is one standard deviation *above* the mean.

Since you cannot use a calculator on the AP Psychology exam, learn how to compute standard deviation. Work through the following steps with this simple data set: 1, 2, 3, 4, 5, 6.

1. Find the mean for the data set. Add all the scores and divide by the total number of scores. *(The six numbers in the data set add up to 21. Divide that by 6 and you get 3.5 as the mean.)*

2. Determine the difference between each score and the mean. *(With this data set, the differences between each score and the mean are -2.5, -1.5, -0.5, 0.5, 1.5, and 2.5.)*

3. Square each of the difference scores from step 2. *(The squares of the above numbers are 6.25, 2.25, 0.25, 0.25, 2.25, and 5.)*

4. Find the sum of squares by adding the squared difference scores from step 3. *(Add those squares for a total of 16.25.)*

5. Divide the sum of squares from step 4 by the total number of scores in the data set. This value is the variance, the mean of the squared difference scores. *(16.25÷6 = 2.7)*

6. Find the square root of the mean squared difference scores from step 5. This value is the standard deviation of the data set. *(The square root of 2.7 is 1.64, which is the standard deviation for this data set.)* The standard deviation is often not a whole number.

If the data set 1, 2, 3, 4, 5, and 6 were the scores on a six-point scale psychology exam, a score of 3 would have a z-score between +1SD (1.64) – +2SD (3.28).

Normal Distribution

Some variables, such as intelligence test scores and heights or shoe sizes of a large group of people, produce a symmetrical distribution. In a symmetrical distribution, the pattern of scores on one side of the mean is a mirror image of the pattern on the other side of the mean. Distributions of this sort are known as **normal distributions** and are sometimes referred to as a "bell curve" because of the shape of the distribution when graphed.

Normal distributions are useful because they are predictable. The data in a normal distribution fall around the mean in the same way each time. For example, Figure 3.7 shows that 68.26 percent of the scores in a normal distribution fall between −1 standard deviation (below the mean) and +1 standard deviation (above the mean). Fewer than one percent of the scores fall in the tails of the distribution. Because of this consistent pattern, you can use a normal distribution to understand some of the basic information a data set can communicate.

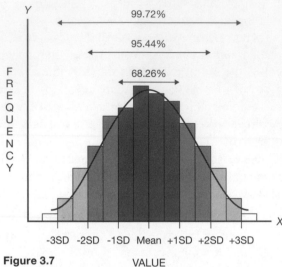

Figure 3.7

You can also use the normal distribution and the standard deviation to understand a score's **percentile rank**, the percentage of scores in a distribution that a particular score falls above. To determine the percentage of scores that fall between the mean and the standard deviation or to determine the percentile rank of a score, you need to know:

1. that the scores are normally distributed

2. the mean

3. the standard deviation

If you don't have access to a graph like the one in Figure 3.7, you also need to know the percentage of scores that fall between each pair (+ and −) of standard deviations around the mean, as shown in Figure 3.8.

PERCENTAGE OF SCORES FALLING BETWEEN PAIRS OF STANDARD DEVIATIONS AROUND THE MEAN	
Standard Deviations Around the Mean	**Percentage of Scores**
−1, +1	68.26%
−2, +2	95.44%
−3, +3	99.72%

Figure 3.8

The following mnemonic can help you remember the percentage of scores for a normal distribution:

1 sixty-eight year-old threw a huge birthday party for 2 ninety-five year olds. The 3 went all out for the event, hiring radio station 99.7 to DJ the party.

Working through a hypothetical example will help you learn how to use the normal distribution to find the percentile rank of a score in a data set. For example, scores on the ACT exam are normally distributed. Suppose that for a particular set of ACT scores, the mean is 21 and the standard deviation is 3. This is all the information you need to determine the percentile rank of any score on the test. To find the percentile rank of a score, start at the center of the distribution. An ACT score of 21 is in the center of the distribution. It has a percentile rank of 50, which means that half the scores are above 21 and half are below. Because the standard deviation is 3, a score of 24 (21 + 3) would have a percentile rank of 84. To see why, look at the figure below, which shows that 34 percent of the scores fall between the mean and 1 standard deviation above the mean. If a score of 21 has a percentile rank of 50, a score of 24 has a percentile rank of 50 + 34, which equals 84. Likewise, a score of 27 (21 + 2 standard deviations) has a percentile rank of 97 (50 + 34 + 13.6).

You can see that a data point of +3 SD (3 standard deviations above the mean) has a percentile rank of 99.7. A data point of –3 SD (3 standard deviations below the mean) has a percentile rank of 0.2. A data point of +3 or –3 is rare and is referred to as an outlier. **Outliers** are data points that fall beyond 3 standard deviations from the mean. In some cases, these data points are just very different from the data points in the rest of the distribution. In other cases, outliers may cause researchers to question the validity of their data collection. Before

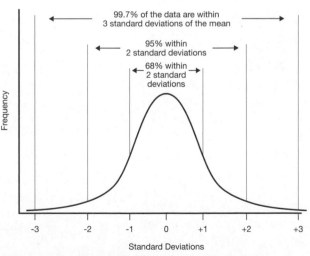

Figure 3.9 The percentages shown in the figure above apply to any data set that is normally distributed.

disregarding the outliers in a data set, researchers need to consider how the data were collected and if the measurement can be considered valid.

Normal distributions have one additional important feature. The measures of central tendency in a normal distribution are all the same and all fall directly in the center of the distribution. That is, in a normal distribution, the mean, median, and mode have the same value. Not all distributions are normally distributed, so you can use this fact to quickly assess whether a data set is normally distributed. When a data set is not normally distributed, the majority of the data points fall to one side or the other of the distribution.

Skewed Distributions

If your psychology instructor gave your class the Advanced Placement Psychology exam on the first day, you might expect that most students would perform poorly. Perhaps two students in your class took Introductory Psychology at the local community college over the summer, and their scores were high. If your psychology instructor gives your class a practice AP exam two days before the actual exam, most students would do well. There may be a few students who perform poorly because they were absent often during the year. In each case, the AP exam scores would pile up at one end of the distribution or the other. These types of distributions are referred to as **skewed**.

Measures of central tendency are more variable in skewed distributions than in a normal distribution. The mean is most affected by extreme scores, so it is pulled toward the side of the distribution where most of the scores fall. In a positively (right) skewed distribution, the mean falls to the right of the median and the mode. In a negatively (left) skewed distribution, the mean falls to the left of the median and the mode. (See Figure 3.10.)

A distribution in which there are many low scores and a few high scores is known as a positively (right) skewed distribution. The skew is defined by the slope of the graph, not the side to which most data points fall. Positive in this case does not mean "good"; rather, it indicates the side of the graph on which the slope falls. If you compare the values of the measures of central tendency, the mode will be less than the median, and the median will be less than the mean.

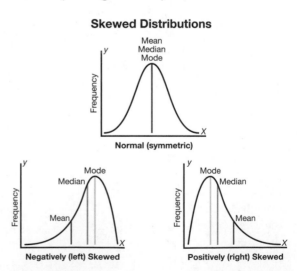

Figure 3.10 To determine the skew, look for the tail, the part of the graph where there are relatively few scores. The side on which the tail is located determines the skew.

A negatively skewed distribution occurs when a majority of data points are high and a few data points are low. In a negatively skewed distribution, the scores pile up on the right side of the graph and the slope falls on the left. The mean will be less than the median, and the median will be less than the mode.

A visual image can help you remember the difference between a positively skewed and a negatively skewed distribution. A positively skewed distribution looks like your right foot, with your big toe on the left side and a slope on the right. A negatively skewed distribution looks like your left foot, with your big toe on the right and the slope on the left.

Results of Correlational Studies

In Chapter 2 on research methods, you read about three different types of correlations: positive, negative, and illusory. Review the discussion in Chapter 2 to be sure you can distinguish among the different types of relationships. Recall also that correlational research does not reveal causality between variables, only whether they are related or linked.

The statistic used to describe the strength and direction of the relationship between two variables is called a **correlation coefficient (r)**. The value of a correlation coefficient falls between −1.0 and +1.0. A correlation coefficient with a value falling between 0 and +1 indicates a positive relationship between two variables. A negative relationship has a correlation coefficient between −1 and 0. The closer the value of a correlation coefficient is to +1.0 or −1.0, the stronger the relationship is between the variables. For example, a correlation coefficient of +0.34 indicates a moderately positive relationship between two variables, and a correlation coefficient of +0.78 indicates a stronger positive relationship. The strongest positive relationship between two variables is +1.0, although it is rare to find correlation coefficients above +0.80 in the field of psychology.

A **scatterplot** is a type of graph designed to display correlational data so that the relationship between the two variables is visible. The y-axis shows the values of one of the variables, while the x-axis shows the values of the second variable. Each dot on the scatterplot represents a pair of data points. Each point is plotted on the graph, and a line of regression is determined.

Once you have plotted all of the pairs of data points on the scatterplot, you can evaluate whether a relationship exists between the two variables. A cluster of points that tips up to the right, as in the left scatterplot in Figure 3.11 (on the next page), indicates a positive correlation. If you drew a line through the center of the cluster, it would begin at the bottom left of the graph and move toward the top right corner. The steeper the line, the stronger the correlation.

Negative correlations have a cluster of points that tips up to the left. A line running through the center of the cluster begins at the top left of the graph and moves toward the bottom right (see the center scatterplot in Figure 3.11). The steeper the line, the stronger the negative correlation.

Scatterplots and Correlation

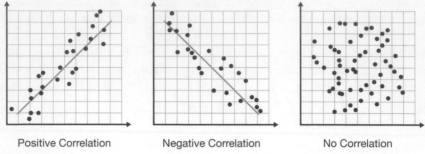

Positive Correlation   Negative Correlation   No Correlation

Figure 3.11

When the pairs of data points appear randomly scattered across the graph or do not form a cluster, as in the right scatterplot in Figure 3.11, there is no relationship between the two variables. The correlation coefficient will be zero or close to zero. An illusory correlation produces a random scatterplot.

Even when a correlation coefficient and scatterplot indicate a strong relationship between two variables, you cannot assume the relationship is causal. A third variable that is related to the original two variables may be responsible for the strong correlation, as occurs in a spurious relationship.

Inferential Statistics

While descriptive statistics provide basic information about a data set, such as measures of central tendency and variance, inferential statistics provide tools for determining causality and drawing conclusions from a data set. **Inferential statistics** are methods for determining the likelihood that the result of an experiment is due to the manipulation of the independent variable or variables or is due to chance.

Statistical significance is a measure of how likely the result of an experiment is due to the manipulation of the independent variable or due to chance. Significance is reported as a ***p*-value**, which is the probability of getting the experimental results. The closer the p-value is to zero, the less likely the result is due to chance. It is always possible that a variable outside the experimental manipulation is influencing the results. A p-value of zero, which would indicate 100 percent certainty that the result is due to the experimental manipulation, is therefore impossible.

In the field of psychology, a p-value of 0.05 or less is acceptable for results to be considered statistically significant. When $p \leq 0.05$, a researcher can conclude that the result is unlikely to have occurred by chance. A statistically significant finding does not rule out the possibility that a result is a fluke. With a p-value of ≤ 0.05, you can still expect to have a different result in one of every 20 trials.

When statistical analysis shows that the results of a study are significant, the researcher can reject the null hypothesis. Recall from Chapter 2 that the null hypothesis states that the independent variable has no impact on the dependent variable. When you reject the null hypothesis, you are saying that the independent variable had an impact on the dependent variable. A p-value that is less than or equal to 0.05 means that rejecting the null hypothesis will be the wrong decision 5 or fewer times out of 100.

Meta-Analysis

For some topics of interest, many researchers have published studies that use the same operational definitions of the independent variables. Each of these studies is useful in its own right, and together they provide even more insight into an area when someone examines the results as a whole. The process of analyzing the results of many studies that have measured the same variables is known as **meta-analysis**.

Meta-analyses allow researchers to see the "big picture" by combining like studies. For example, if many different high schools adopt a suicide prevention program that intervenes proactively to prevent student suicide attempts, each school could publish the results of its program. Then, a meta-analysis could examine the published results from all schools that had introduced the program and analyze the results as a whole.

Because this process examines multiple studies together, it provides a more comprehensive view than a single study. But meta-analysis may become complicated when studies have measured the same variable but used different operational definitions or measured the dependent variable in different ways. For example, if one school in the suicide meta-analysis exposed students to one session of an intervention program and others exposed students to four sessions, comparing the studies would be difficult. It would be equally difficult to compare studies if one school measured reported suicide attempts while others measured students' responses on a survey.

THINK AS A PSYCHOLOGIST: "REPLICATION CRISIS" . . . OR NOT?

In 2015, the Open Science Collaboration (OSC) published a report of their efforts to replicate 100 experimental and correlational studies published in three psychology journals. The results of their meta-analysis sent shock waves through the psychology field: only 39 of the studies were replicated successfully. The study became a landmark and created a "replication crisis" in the field of psychology.

Not so fast, said a team of professors and a graduate student from Harvard University (Daniel Gilbert, Gary King, and Stephen Pettigrew) and the University of Virginia (Timothy Wilson). Their study, published in 2016, revealed serious mistakes in the OSC study. For one, OSC failed to take into account that some replications would fail by chance alone, and in so doing they introduced statistical error into their findings. The team also found that some of the replications strayed too far from the original methods to be considered fair tests. Either of those alone would have been enough to call in question the OSC's findings. But the team also found that the OSC's study made a sampling error. In their choice of studies to replicate, they excluded many from subfields of psychology known for their rigorous methodology, thereby failing to select a random sample. Considering all these factors, the original studies failed only at the rate any group of studies would by chance.

The team critical of the OSC study stresses that they believe there was no intentional wrongdoing on the part of the OSC researchers—the scientists just made statistical and methodological mistakes, as scientists sometimes do. But they also note that the sensational headlines raising doubts about the reliability of psychological studies did harm to the field, creating a negative public perception.

Practice: With a partner, find out more about the study overturning the OSC's findings. The findings were published in *Science* in an article titled "Comment on 'Estimating the reproducibility of psychological science'" on March 4, 2016. In your research, focus on finding specific examples of statistical and methodological errors that the OSC researchers made. Share your findings with the class.

Researchers need to be equally skilled at gathering data and evaluating what that data may mean. Descriptive and inferential statistics allow researchers to organize, describe, and evaluate their data. As a student of psychology, if you have the ability to successfully organize sound research studies and evaluate their significance, any topic in psychology or any other scientific field is open to investigation.

The scientific method, which you read about in Chapter 2, relates to all other chapters because much of what we currently know about human thought and human and animal behavior has been gathered using these methods. Now that you know about good research design and statistical analysis, you also have the ability to identify and question flaws in the studies you learn about.

Ethical standards have changed over the years, and some studies that were performed years ago would not be approved by IRBs today. Furthermore, because the results of a study appear in your text or in this review guide does not mean that the study is without flaws. Use your knowledge to identify how the methodology and reporting of these studies could be improved.

REFLECT ON THE ESSENTIAL QUESTION

Essential Question: *How do researchers analyze data to determine if the results of a study are meaningful or significant?* On separate paper, make a chart like the one below and use it to gather information to help you answer the essential question.

	Descriptive Statistics	Inferential Statistics
Purpose		
Scenario showing how it is used and displayed		
Limitations		

KEY TERMS

continuous data	outliers
correlation coefficient	percentile rank
data set	positive skew
descriptive statistics	*p*-value
discrete data	range
frequency distribution	ratio scale
inferential statistics	standard deviation
interval scale	statistical significance
mean	statistics
measure of central tendency	variance
	z-score
median	
meta-analysis	*TYPES OF GRAPHS*
mode	bar graph
negative skew	frequency polygon
nominal scale	histogram
normal distribution	pie chart
ordinal scale	scatterplot

1. Paul has run a correlational study and found that as people age, their ability to hear high-pitched sounds decreases. While you do not have a written copy of Paul's study in front of you, which of the following scores likely describes the finding of Paul's study?

   (A) −1.02

   (B) +1.24

   (C) −0.48

   (D) −0.05

   (E) +0.66

2. Each semester, high schools across the country compute students' grade point averages. Which of the following is a measure of central tendency that best represents a student's cumulative grade point average?

   (A) Mode

   (B) Mean

   (C) Range

   (D) Standard deviation

   (E) Median

3. Tanya is helping the school's track and field coach recruit athletes for the upcoming season. She is timing her classmates as they run the 100-yard dash. She has tested 20 students so far and wants to show her coach the results. Which of the following would be the most appropriate way for Tanya to display her data for the coach?

   (A) A bar graph

   (B) A scatterplot

   (C) A normal distribution

   (D) A positively skewed distribution

   (E) A histogram

4. Which of the following is true about a negatively skewed distribution?

   (A) There will be a very small standard deviation.

   (B) The mode will be lower than the mean.

   (C) The mean will be lower than the median.

   (D) The mean, median, and mode will all be the same.

   (E) The mean will not be impacted by extreme scores.

5. Which of the following statements can be made about a normal distribution without knowing specific information about the data set?

(A) The mean will be pulled to the right by extreme scores.

(B) 84 percent of the population will score at or below a +1 standard deviation.

(C) 95 percent of the population will score within 1 standard deviation of the mean.

(D) The mean and median will be higher than the mode.

(E) The entire population will score within 3 standard deviations of the mean.

6. Alice has just found that the study she has been conducting over the last two years has yielded statistically significant results. She wants to tell her parents about her exciting news, but they do not know much about statistics. Which of the following statements can Alice share with her parents to summarize the meaning of statistical significance?

(A) The results are unlikely due to chance.

(B) The results will be an important contribution to the field of psychology.

(C) The independent variable is fully responsible for the result.

(D) The dependent variable is fully responsible for the result.

(E) The results will be easy to replicate.

7. Natasha is judging the science fair projects of the students in her class. The final round has narrowed the competition down to the top ten students who all must be placed in rank order and compared to one another in regard to their scientific abilities and the quality of their projects. Which type of data is Natasha working with?

(A) Ratio

(B) Interval

(C) Nominal

(D) Ordinal

(E) Statistically significant

8. Which number best represents the median for the following data set?
4, 4, 5, 7, 7, 9, 11, 12, 15, 18, 18, 22

(A) 8

(B) 9

(C) 10

(D) 11

(E) 12

9. Jessica's chemistry instructor told the class that the results of the final exam were normally distributed. Because Jessica had been paying attention in her psychology class, she knows what this means. The instructor hands back the exams, telling the students that the mean was 80 and the standard deviation was 4. Jessica's score on the exam was 88. She wants to compute her percentile rank to see how she did in comparison to her classmates. Which of the following is correct about Jessica's exam score?

(A) Jessica's percentile rank is 2.5.

(B) Jessica's percentile rank is 99.85.

(C) Jessica's percentile rank is 84.

(D) Jessica's percentile rank is 0.015.

(E) Jessica's percentile rank is 97.5.

10. Varun is graduating from college. He is excited to have received a job offer from a small accounting firm near his home. During his research on the company, he found that most of the firm's 50 employees are recent college graduates like himself who make $43,000 per year. There are five managers who make $80,000 per year, a vice president who makes $120,000 per year, and a CEO who makes $300,000 per year. Which of the following best represents Varun's findings on the salaries of the employees at the accounting firm?

(A) A positively skewed distribution

(B) A normal distribution

(C) A correlation coefficient of -0.67

(D) A negatively skewed distribution

(E) A p-value of ≤ 0.05

1. Mr. Jones has just given a review test in preparation for the AP Psychology exam in May. He wants to be certain that he can provide those who need extra assistance the opportunity to attend a study session if they don't do well on the practice test. During the study session, he will review the topics covered by the exam. Mr. Jones is going to ask any student whose score is more than 1 standard deviation below the mean on the review test to attend the study session. As an expert statistician, you will be asked to examine the data provided below, which represent the students' scores, and make a recommendation to Mr. Jones regarding who should attend the study session.

Student #1	Student #2	Student #3	Student #4	Student #5	Student #6	Student #7	Student #8	Student #9	Student #10
97	78	92	88	67	65	81	83	86	73

(You may need a calculator to solve this problem, but remember you may not use calculators on the AP exam.)

A) For the population above, determine the following and indicate which each of the scores represents.
- The mean
- The median
- The range
- The standard deviation

B) Make your recommendation to Mr. Jones regarding which students should attend the study session.
- Determine and explain which type of graph would be best to summarize the information from this data set.
- Graph the data. Also label the axes and title the graph.

2. Ashley is working for the Olympic committee that is trying to determine which athletes to train by providing coaching and funding to those who may be future Olympians. Unfortunately, Ashley does not have funding to train all of the interested athletes, so she must first perform a battery of tests to determine which athletes are the highest ranking—these are the athletes (top 2.5 percent) who will receive funding and coaching. The results from her tests indicate that the mean on the battery of tests was 80 and the standard deviation was 5. Based on this information, answer the questions below.

A) Create a normal distribution that represents the athletes' scores (go out 3 standard deviations on either side of the mean).

B) Ethan, one of the athletes, received a score of 90.
   • What is his percentile rank, and what does this mean?
   • What is Ethan's z-score on the battery of tests, and what does this mean?
   • Will Ethan receive funding from Ashley's committee? Explain why or why not.

C) Interpret the results of Ashley's test.
   • Where will the measures of central tendency fall on this graph?
   • If Ashley were dealing with only the "best of the best" and most of these athletes performed extremely well with only a few performing poorly, what type of distribution could Ashley expect?

UNIT 2: Review

In this unit, you sought answers to the following essential questions about research methods and statistics.

Chapter 2: How do psychologists use the scientific method to investigate questions about human thought and human and animal behavior?

Chapter 3: How do researchers analyze data to determine if the results of a study are meaningful or significant?

Apply what you have learned about research methods and statistics by answering the free-response question below.

FREE-RESPONSE QUESTION

Nicole, an athletic trainer, believes if she has evidence that her program of exercise works, she can recruit more clients. She is planning to conduct a study to determine if working out for one hour per day with her fitness program causes a person to lose weight. She will track the participants' progress over a twelve-week period. Nicole mandates that her clients at the gym participate in her study, and she asks them to each find one friend who is not a member of the gym to also participate. Each of the participants weighs in at the start and again after the twelve-week period has ended. At the conclusion of the study, she will compare the results of both groups. Unfortunately, because she has not had any formal training in research methodology, she is not certain how to label the different components in her study or identify any potential flaws. Help Nicole to identify the following components of this study.

A) Identify the following factors:
- Independent variable
- Operational definition of the dependent variable
- Control group
- Experimental group

B) Identify the following issues with the study described:
- Ethical concerns
- Sampling bias

C) What type of research methodology should Nicole use if she wants to determine if exercising for one hour per day causes a person to lose weight? Explain why this method would be preferred to others.

UNIT 3: Biological Bases of Behavior

Chapter 4 *Understanding the Brain: Its Structure and Functions*

Chapter 5 *Neurons, Neural Communication, and Behavioral Genetics*

Unit Overview

In an article called "My Genome, My Self," psychologist Stephen Pinker explores the field of behavioral genetics—the study of ways in which human behavior is determined by biology. "Of course genes can't pull the levers of our behavior directly," he writes. "But they affect the wiring and workings of the brain, and the brain is the seat of our drives, temperaments and patterns of thought." In this unit, you will explore the "wiring and workings of the brain" as well as a persistent question of psychological studies: How much of our behavior is "nature"—determined by biology—and how much is "nurture"—the result of our environment.

Key Topics

- Basic processes and systems in the biological bases of behavior, including parts of the neuron and the process of transmission of signals between neurons
- The influence of drugs on neurotransmitters (e.g., reuptake mechanisms, agonists, antagonists)
- The effect of the endocrine system on behavior
- The nervous system and its subdivisions and functions:
- central and peripheral nervous systems
- major brain regions, lobes, and cortical areas
- brain lateralization and hemispheric specialization

- The role of neuroplasticity in traumatic brain injury
- Historic and contemporary research strategies and technologies that support research (case studies, split-brain research, imaging techniques)
- How heredity, environment, and evolution work together to shape behavior
- Traits and behavior selected for their adaptive value
- Key contributors (Paul Broca, Charles Darwin, Michael Gazzaniga, Roger Sperry, Carl Wernicke)

Source*: AP® Psychology Course and Exam Description*

4

Understanding the Brain: Its Structures and Functions

"The brain is more than an assemblage of autonomous modules, each crucial for a specific mental function. Every one of these functionally specialized areas must interact with dozens or hundreds of others, their total integration creating something like a vastly complicated orchestra with thousands of instruments, an orchestra that conducts itself, with an ever-changing score and repertoire."

—Neurologist Oliver Sacks

Essential Question: How do the parts of the brain and nervous systems work together to process information and control behaviors?

"**E**verything psychological is simultaneously biological." This commonly cited quote suggests everything people think, feel, and do has biological roots—everything. From daydreaming to sleeping, from practicing jump shots to rehearsing lines in the school play, the brains of humans and other animals are constantly at work, operating behind the scenes and making decisions. In fact, a person's brain has made some decisions even before that person becomes aware that he or she is thinking or feeling something. How does the brain do this? A tour through the nervous system illustrates how the brain and the rest of the nervous system work to direct behavior and play important roles in a person's daily life.

Neuroanatomy and Organization of the Nervous Systems

Neuroanatomy is the study of the structures of the nervous systems, which include the brain and the nerves that run throughout the body. Figure 4.1 shows the basic organization of the nervous system and its subsystems.

The **central nervous system (CNS)** is literally "the brains of the operation"—it coordinates the actions and interactions of the other systems in the body. The **brain** is the dominant part of the CNS. The **spinal cord** is the avenue through which the brain communicates with the rest of the body.

The Brain

Inside a person's skull is arguably the most fascinating and complex structure in the universe, the human brain. The brain has a role in nearly every thought, emotion, and action that a person expresses. It processes information and experiences before we are even aware that we experienced something. The brain doesn't "read" a person's mind; it creates the mind.

Researchers are still discovering the complexities of this wondrous organ. The 1990s and the 2010s have each earned the title "Decade of the Brain." Researchers have learned more about the brain in the last 50 years than had been learned in the entirety of human history before that point.

The brain makes up about 2-3 percent of a person's total body weight, uses about 20 percent of a person's total

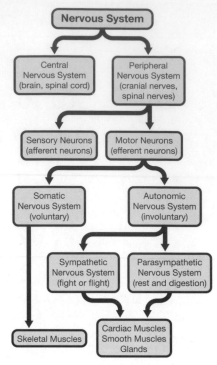

Figure 4.1

oxygen consumption, and consumes about 17 percent of the glucose (energy) the body uses. It is composed of many billions of cells and connections among cells, the details of which are discussed in Chapter 5, and surrounded by the **meninges**, three layers of covering that protect the brain:

- the **dura mater** (meaning "tough mother" in Latin), which is the outermost layer
- the **arachnoid mater**, a spider web-like layer in the middle
- the **pia mater** (meaning "soft mother")

The brain also sits in the skull and is surrounded by **cerebrospinal fluid**, which cushions and protects the brain.

The spinal cord extends down from the and descend through the center of the vertebral column (backbone). Pathways within it carry sensory messages to and motor messages from the brain. The spinal cord is also enclosed in protective meninges and surrounded by cerebrospinal fluid.

The **peripheral nervous system (PNS)** includes the nerves outside the brain and spinal cord that connect the the central nervous system to the rest of the body. It has two major divisions: the motor pathway and the sensory pathway. Signals from the brain travel via the motor pathway and then to muscles or glands to influence behavior, and signals from sensory receptors travel via sensory nerves from the body to the brain via the sensory pathway.

The motor pathway of PNS contains two subsystems, or divisions:

- The **somatic nervous system** includes the nerves that transmit signals from your brain to the skeletal muscles to allow voluntary movement. For example, when you raise your hand, walk, jump, wave to a friend, or end a text, the brain sends signals through the somatic nervous system to initiate these movements. If you get up and get a snack before finishing this chapter, your somatic nervous system is hard at work.

- The **autonomic nervous system (ANS)** controls functions that we do not have to think about. These functions are automatic and involuntary: breathing, blood pumping through the veins and arteries, digestion, gland functioning, the work of other internal organs. People can choose to influence and sometimes override these basic signals, such as by slowing down breathing or increasing heart rate through exercise, but for the most part, this system operates without intervention.

The autonomic nervous system is further subdivided into two divisions:

- The **sympathetic nervous system** is the emergency response system. When a person is frightened by a loud sound or startled when someone sneaks up from behind, the sympathetic system goes to work (i.e., is activated). The person's heart rate increases, attention becomes more focused, digestion slows, muscle tension increases, and adrenaline flows into the bloodstream. The system enters "fight, flight, or freeze" status.

- The **parasympathetic nervous system** is the default condition of the ANS. It functions to calm the person, reduces energy expenditure, decreases blood sugar, increases blood flow to the digestive organs, and decreases heart rate, among other things. It allows us to rest and digest, relax and recuperate.

The two systems work together to balance energy use and energy conservation. Figure 4.2 on the next page shows the detailed connections between the brain and spinal cord (i.e., the CNS) and the organs in the body, by way of the two divisions of the autonomic nervous system.

Typically, the brain and the spinal cord are both involved in any action, but the body does have one trick up its sleeve—the **reflex arc**. A reflex arc occurs when a signal is sent from a sensory organ to the spinal cord, which processes the information instead of passing it on to the brain. For example, when a person touches a hot surface with a finger, sensory cells in the skin pass the information ("Hey, that's really hot!") to the spinal cord, which responds immediately with a message to initiate action ("Get your hand off that thing right now!"). This system is faster than if the signal had to travel to the brain to make a decision about how to respond to the sensation.

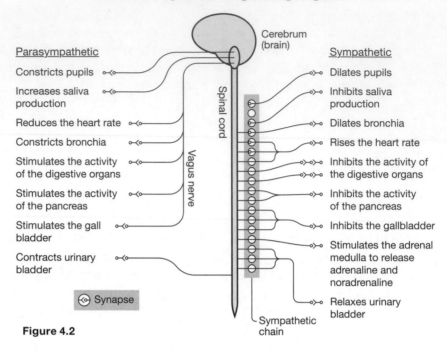

**Parasympathetic and Sympathetic
Nervous Systems Regulating Organs**

Cerebrum (brain)

Spinal cord

Vagus nerve

Sympathetic chain

Parasympathetic

Constricts pupils

Increases saliva production

Reduces the heart rate

Constricts bronchia

Stimulates the activity of the digestive organs

Stimulates the activity of the pancreas

Stimulates the gall bladder

Contracts urinary bladder

Synapse

Sympathetic

Dilates pupils

Inhibits saliva production

Dilates bronchia

Rises the heart rate

Inhibits the activity of the digestive organs

Inhibits the activity of the pancreas

Inhibits the gallbladder

Stimulates the adrenal medulla to release adrenaline and noradrenaline

Relaxes urinary bladder

Figure 4.2

Methods for Understanding the Brain

People have tried many ways to understand their own and others' behavior. As researchers began to recognize an important link between behavior and the brain, they wanted to find ways to see what happens inside the skull. Today, scientists use a variety of techniques to examine and learn about the brain. Following is a brief look at the techniques most commonly used.

Case Studies

Before modern brain scanning techniques, studies of individual cases were the primary means to understand brain functions. Detailed descriptions of case studies allow professionals and students alike to wonder at the complexity of the brain. One early case study was that of Phineas Gage. In 1848, Gage was working as the foreman of a crew cutting a railroad line in Cavendish, Vermont. He was packing blasting powder into a hole in the rock with a tamping iron when, unexpectedly, the powder exploded. The tamping iron shot upward, traveling through his left cheek, passing behind his eye, and protruding out of his skull. The force of the explosion

Figure 4.3

and the speed of the rod seem to have generated enough heat to cauterize (seal off) many of the blood vessels, preventing him from dying instantly. In fact, he remained conscious—he walked over to a cart so he could be taken to a doctor.

For many years, popular press articles and most introductory psychology textbooks reported that Gage had a severe change in his personality following the accident, in particular that he became loud and socially uninhibited, acting in ways that were seen as inappropriate at the time. Although recent reports suggest that this belief may not be accurate, it is certain that Gage was not able to go back to his job as a foreman and had difficulty holding new jobs. Recent research using new technology suggests that Gage probably lost about 4 percent of his cerebral cortex, including about 11 percent of the frontal lobe. The changes in his behavior and the location of the damaged parts of Gage's brain have helped scientists understand where certain functions are located in the brain. (You will read more about the functions of these parts of the brain later in this chapter.)

Other case studies also revealed knowledge of the brain. **Paul Broca** studied patients who had lost the ability to speak; **Carl Wernicke** studied patients who had lost the ability to understand language. Because of these case studies, parts of the brain are now known as **Broca's area** (which moves the muscles to create speech) and **Wernicke's area** (which processes both spoken and written language). More recently, Oliver Sacks published a number of books telling the stories of individuals with unique neurological disorders. His books appeal to a wide audience, and the cases have educated the public about color blindness, autism, memory, deafness, facial recognition, and many other behaviors.

Damaging or Stimulating Parts of the Brain

Usually to control or eliminate some unwanted behavior, brain surgery (psychosurgery) typically involves destroying parts of the brain. **Ablation** is the process of removing or destroying some brain tissue, leaving **lesions**, or tissue damaged from the surgery, behind.

An operation called a **prefrontal lobotomy** uses ablation to control behavior. Developed in the 1930s, this process involved disconnecting

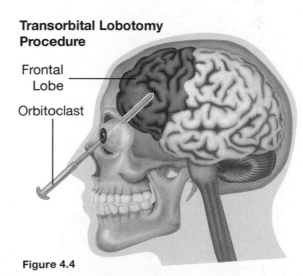

Transorbital Lobotomy Procedure

Frontal Lobe

Orbitoclast

Figure 4.4

the prefrontal cortex, a part of the brain directly behind the forehead, from the rest of the brain. Early lobotomies involved drilling holes on each side of the forehead just behind the hairline and injecting alcohol, which destroyed the brain tissue in that area. Other methods involved inserting sharp tools into the brain and removing some brain tissue. A later method was to insert an icepick-like instrument through the orbital bones (i.e., the eye socket) into the frontal lobe. Dr. Walter Freeman was the first to perform the transorbital lobotomy in 1946. He traveled the country performing the surgery on hundreds of patients.

As you might expect, after this type of surgery, patients did show behavior changes: Many stopped acting out, but many also had personality changes, loss of long-term memories, and loss of emotional expressiveness. Although this procedure is controversial today, it helped two doctors win the Nobel Prize in medicine in 1949 for its treatment of schizophrenia.

A **hemispherectomy** is another type of brain surgery used to treat behavioral disorders or illnesses; it involves the removal of one of the halves (i.e., **cerebral hemispheres**) of the brain. Hemispherectomies have been successfully used to control seizures in people who have epilepsy. For example, Jodi Miller was diagnosed with Rasmussen's Syndrome (a type of epilepsy with severe seizures) at age 3; her doctors and family chose to remove her right hemisphere in an effort to control it. Jodi grew up with some motor coordination challenges, but she later become a successful college student.

Deep brain stimulation is a newer, less invasive method of altering the brain to eliminate behavioral symptoms. A surgeon first creates an opening in the skull and then carefully inserts an **electrode** through the opening and deep into the brain, all the way down into the brain stem. The electrode doesn't damage the brain, but rather it stimulates a specific area. This stimulation interrupts communication in that area of the brain, reducing or eliminating behavioral symptoms that are associated with that area. Deep brain stimulation has been used to treat epilepsy, Parkinson's disease, tremors, acute depression, and Tourette Syndrome.

Transcranial Magnetic Stimulation (TMS) is a noninvasive technique that alters brain activity. TMS involves the use of an electromagnetic wand that alters the magnetic fields that affect how the brain processes emotions and moods. TMS is sometimes used to treat depression.

Brain Scanning

Scans of the brain are not used to treat disorders directly; rather, they provide information about the structure of the brain or about the activity of the brain. This section presents the most common methods for each purpose.

X-rays primarily show bones and other solid structures. They are especially useful when a person has broken bones. When a head injury occurs, an x-ray can show skull fractures. However, an x-ray will not show details of the soft tissue in the body, so it can't be used for a complete evaluation of ligaments, tendons, or brain tissue.

Scientists use the process of **electroencephalography** to measure electrical activity in the brain. The brain communicates with the body via electrical and chemical signals (see Chapter 5). The electricity in the brain at any one time is enough to light a bulb from 10–25 watts! To create an **electroencephalogram (EEG)**, technicians attach electrodes to a person's scalp to record the waves of electrical activity that travel across the brain's surface during various states of consciousness (discussed in more detail in Chapter 8). Brain waves should be occurring at predictable patterns, so if neurologists see abnormal patterns, they can make inferences about the patterns of behavior that may be caused by the unusual electrical activity.

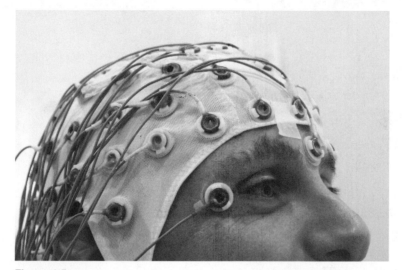

Figure 4.5

A common use of EEG is to measure a person's brain waves while the person is asleep. Different sleep stages have different brain waves (see Chapter 8), which can be seen in the EEG recording. An EEG can help to identify the occurrence of disorders, such as sleep apnea.

Magnetic Resonance Imaging (MRI) is an imaging technique that uses a magnetic field and pulses of radio waves to generate detailed images of parts of the body made up of soft tissue, so they are especially useful when it's necessary to see the structure of the brain or other internal organs (Figure 4.6). You may be familiar with MRIs because they are often used to show damage to ligaments and cartilage after a sports injury, such as a severely twisted knee or ankle. MRIs can be used to help diagnose strokes, tumors, inner ear and eye disorders, aneurysms, and spinal cord injuries.

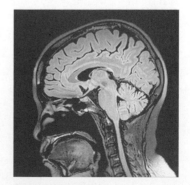

Figure 4.6 MRI

Functional Magnetic Resonance Imaging (fMRI) is a variation on the MRI process; it involves using magnetic resonance imaging to visualize blood flow and oxygen metabolism to infer brain activity (Figure 4.7). No matter what activities a person is engaged in, blood is carrying oxygen to the brain. fMRI will show where the oxygen is taken up from the blood during any particular activity, and scientists can then identify the parts of the brain that are involved in that activity. The development of fMRI technology has allowed scientists to create 3-D activation maps of the brain in real time.

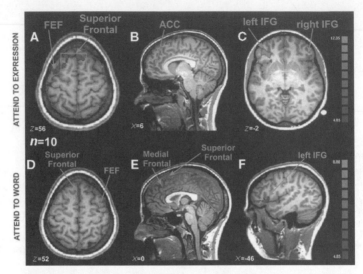

Figure 4.7 Functional Magnetic Resonance Imaging

Computerized Axial Tomography (CT or CAT scans) involves taking two-dimensional x-ray photographs from different angles and using them to create a three-dimensional representation of an organ or other body part. CT scans can detect brain damage and measure blood flow in the brain, but the most common and probably most effective use is to identify a muscle or bone disorder, a tumor, or a blood clot. CT scanning is often used in emergency rooms because the technique helps doctors to identify critical problems in the lungs and abdomen very quickly. A major advantage is that the CT scan can examine bones, soft tissue, and blood vessels all at the same time.

Positron Emission Tomography (PET Scan) images allow researchers to visualize slices of the brain to examine deep brain structures that had previously been reachable only via invasive procedures such as surgery. During a PET scan, scientists inject a radioactive "tracer" molecule into a person's bloodstream. This molecule is taken up by the body's cells in the same way that glucose is. The brain uses glucose as a form of energy, so blood carrying the tracer flows to parts of the brain that need energy to support its activity. The radioactive "glucose" will be carried to the active parts of the brain via the bloodstream and its path can be "traced" via the positrons (charged particles) that show up on the scan (Figure 4.8).

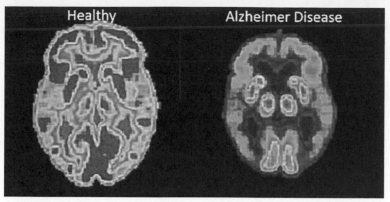

Figure 4.8 PET Scan

Researchers use PET scans to measure the total amount of energy that the brain uses during a particular activity and also to identify the portions of the brain that are active during different tasks, such as reading, recognizing photos, listening to music, and more. Doctors may also use PET scans to help figure out why a person is experiencing health problems.

Scientists and doctors sometimes use other techniques to monitor and record the flow of blood or cerebrospinal fluid, measure tumors or blood pressure, and visualize and evaluate other parts of the body. Some methods create static (non-moving) images, and others create a dynamic series of images that can be used to show organ function. New techniques are continually being developed.

The Endocrine System and Behavior

Whereas the central and peripheral nervous systems communicate using nerve impulses transmitted in the brain, spinal cord, and nerves, the slower-acting **endocrine system** sends its signals by passing **hormones** through the bloodstream. These hormones are secreted (produced and passed on) from a number of different parts of the body and select parts of the brain. The endocrine system plays a critical role in raising and lowering a person's blood sugar (glucose) levels, making a person feel hungry or full, regulating metabolism and sleep, and determining sex drive. While the endocrine system is slower to operate than the CNS, its effects last longer.

Figure 4.9 on the next page shows some of the parts that make up the endocrine system, along with the hormones that each part secretes. The parts of the system work with the nervous system as an interconnected team.

The **hypothalamus** signals the **pituitary gland**, which is sometimes called "the Master Gland." The pituitary gland regulates stress, growth, and reproduction, including some parts of pregnancy and childbirth. For example, the pituitary gland plays an important role in the production and secretion of milk from the mammary glands (lactation). The pituitary gland sends signals to other glands, including the testes, ovaries, and thyroid gland, which then release their own hormones.

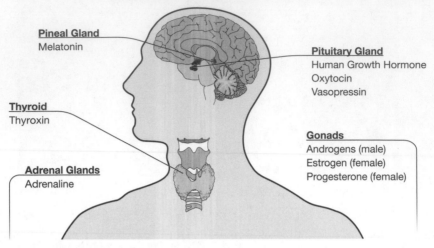

Major Glands and Hormones

Pineal Gland
Melatonin

Pituitary Gland
Human Growth Hormone
Oxytocin
Vasopressin

Thyroid
Thyroxin

Gonads
Androgens (male)
Estrogen (female)
Progesterone (female)

Adrenal Glands
Adrenaline

Figure 4.9 The Endocrine System

If the pituitary gland malfunctions and releases excess growth hormone, a person may experience **gigantism** (excessive growth and height) or **acromegaly**, a potentially disfiguring and deadly condition that includes visible swelling of the soft tissue, resulting in large hands, feet, nose, lips, and ears. Some well-known individuals with acromegaly include actor Richard Kiel (played "Jaws" in the James Bond films), Tony Robbins (motivational speaker), pro wrestlers "The Big Show" and "The Great Khali," and the late pro wrestler, Andre the Giant. If the pituitary gland does not secrete enough human growth hormone early in development, a person may experience **pituitary dwarfism**, a condition in which a person grows very slowly and as an adult is typically proportioned but notably shorter than average.

The **thyroid gland** secretes thyroxin, which affects body metabolism. The thyroid hormones increase oxygen use by the cells, tissues, and organs of the body. Without that oxygen, those organs atrophy (waste away). People with damage to the thyroid gland often have poor sleep and concentration, fatigue, depression, dry skin and hair, sensitivity to cold, and joint and muscle pain. If a person's thyroid isn't working properly, or if it has to be removed, the person will have to take medication daily to replace its important function.

Other important glands are the **pineal gland**, the **adrenal glands**, and the **gonads**. The pineal gland releases melatonin, which is a hormone that helps to regulate sleep and body rhythms. The adrenal glands sit atop the kidneys and release adrenaline, which helps to regulate arousal, and corticosteroids, which are involved in long-term stress response and glucose metabolism. The gonads secrete hormones that regulate development of sex characteristics and possibly sex-typical behaviors; these hormones include androgens, estrogen, and progesterone. (See Chapter 13 for more on these glands.)

Structure of the Brain

Although the brain has discernible parts, it is best thought of as a single organ because its parts are so tightly interconnected. In addition, although it's common to say that a brain part is responsible for a specific function, brain–behavior connections are far more complex than that would suggest. The brain's circuits are constantly communicating with one another, and no part works in isolation. This complexity means that an introduction to the structure of the brain will necessarily be simplified, and not every part or function can be included. The following discussion reflects how the organization of the brain is usually discussed and what researchers currently believe about the function of some key areas of the brain.

No two brains are exactly the same, but every intact brain has some distinguishing features. First, the brain (cerebrum) has two **hemispheres**, which are sometimes referred to as the "left brain" and the "right brain." The two hemispheres are similar but not mirror images; for example, some areas in one hemisphere are bigger than in the other hemisphere.

In general, the left hemisphere controls the right side of the body, and the right hemisphere controls the left side of the body. For example, when a right-handed person is writing, the left hemisphere is more involved than the right hemisphere in coordinating the hand movements. However, the right hemisphere isn't uninvolved in the writing process, and it communicates with its partner on the left by passing information through the **corpus callosum** (Latin for "tough body"), a bundle of nerve fibers that connects the two hemispheres. Messages also move from one side of the brain to the other in the brainstem, where the motor and sensory "crossover" occurs. Visual signals cross in the optic chiasm.

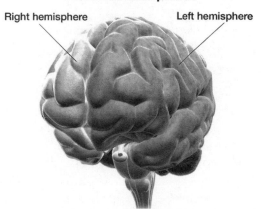

Cerebral Hemispheres

Right hemisphere   Left hemisphere

Figure 4.10

The Cerebral Cortex

The outer layer of the brain is the **cerebral cortex**, also known as the **cerebrum**. The tissue of the cerebral cortex is folded in on itself, forming **sulci** (peaks; *sulcus* is the singular) and **gyri** (valleys; *gyrus* is the singular). Squeezing the skin on the back of your hand can provide an analogy: you'll see ridges and grooves similar to those in the brain. This folding and wrinkling allows for more surface area of cortex to fit into the skull. The more wrinkles, the more tissue surface the brain has to work with, and the more computational power the organism has. A rat brain is almost smooth on its cortex. Compared to dogs, cats, and even dolphins and primates, the human brain has a more wrinkly cortex. If a scientist unfolded a monkey's brain so that the sulci and gyri became flat, the unfolded brain would have roughly the surface area of an 8.5 x 11 piece of paper. The human brain has even deeper sulci and gyri, and when spread out flat, a typical human brain has a surface area similar to four sheets of paper. That translates into a lot of computational power.

Though the cerebral cortex is divided, researchers generally talk about four distinct **lobes**, or areas of the cerebral cortex, distinguished by their locations and primary functions. In graphics, the lobes are often color coded, but in reality the edges aren't always clear because the cortex looks mainly uniform throughout. Even brain surgeons cannot always tell just by sight—patients undergoing brain surgery are often conscious so that the neurosurgeon can temporarily stop activity in a section of the brain and see how behavior is affected. For example, one patient had a tumor near Broca's area, which is important for speech production. During surgery, the patient looked at a set of cards showing simple images like a red triangle or a blue hammer and had to tell the nurse what she saw. Depending on how she answered, the surgeon could tell whether he was probing the damaged area and was able to avoid affecting a healthy part of the brain. After doing dozens of these little procedures and mapping out the language areas, the surgeon could confidently move around the brain and remove the offending tissue.

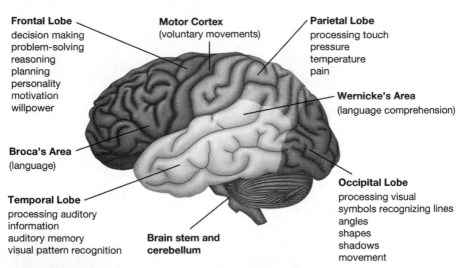

Figure 4.11 Lobes and Functions

The Frontal Lobes The **frontal lobe**, which is the part of the brain directly behind the forehead and above the eyes (in each hemisphere), is "command central" for decision making, problem solving, reasoning, planning, personality, and language. These cognitive processes are often called executive functions. The frontal lobe is also important for motivation and the exercise of willpower, guiding the ability to say no to unhealthy foods or yes to challenging activities such as studying or exercising when it would be easier to sit on the couch and relax. The memory and problem-solving skills required to answer the questions at the end of each chapter engage the frontal lobe; so does the experience of figuring out whether you can afford to buy groceries, the newest music release, or a car with the money in your wallet or bank account.

Many scientists believe that the sophistication of the frontal lobe is what makes humans different from animals with simpler brains. Our hopes and dreams for the future, our awareness of eventual death, and our ability to reflect on our past are complex thought patterns that other animals do not seem to have.

The frontal lobe is also where the **motor cortex** is located. The motor cortex plays a large role in voluntary movements, receiving information from and working with other parts of the brain.

The Parietal Lobes Behind each frontal lobe—roughly on the top of the head—is the **parietal lobe.** This area of the brain is important for processing certain sensory signals from the body: touch, pressure, temperature, and pain. A specific area of the parietal lobe, the **somatosensory cortex**, has been carefully mapped to show where signals from each body part are received.

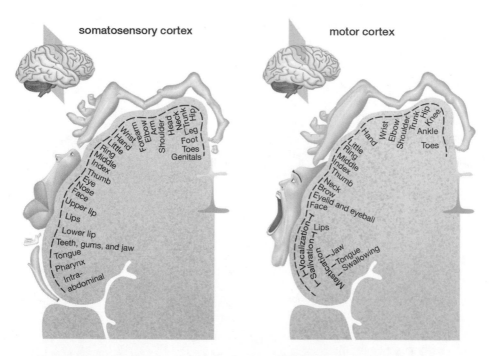

Figure 4.12 The image of a homunculus, or "little person," is distorted so that its body parts map to the region of the sensory or motor cortex that receives that part's signals. The figure is an aid for remembering what regions of the brain process which sensory and motor signals.

The Occipital Lobes At the back of each hemisphere lies the **occipital lobe**. This lobe processes visual signals and coordinates various aspects of vision. The part of the occipital lobe at the very back, directly behind the eyes, is the primary visual cortex, which has an important role in taking information from the eyes and interpreting it so that a person knows what he or she is seeing. Another part of the occipital lobe, the **visual association cortex**, helps us recognize lines, angles, shapes, shadows, and movement. (See Chapter 6 for more on the visual system.)

The Temporal Lobes The **temporal lobes** are near the ears; they are important for processing auditory information and auditory memory. One major role of the right temporal lobe is processing the melody and tonal changes in music. Part of the left posterior temporal lobe is known as Wernicke's area, which is important for language comprehension. See Figure 4.16 on page 92 for more brain functions.

The lower part of each temporal lobe is responsible for some visual processing, in particular the processing of patterns. People with damage to this part of the temporal lobe may experience **agnosia**, a condition in which familiar objects become unrecognizable. One particularly dramatic form of agnosia is prosopagnosia, also known as face-blindness. People with prosopagnosia can see faces—they can point out ears, eyes, mouth, and other facial parts—but they cannot identify the person whose face it is. In fact, when shown photos, they can't even recognize people they know very well. Brain scientist and author Oliver Sacks, mentioned earlier, suffered from prosopagnosia.

The Brain Stem

The oldest part of the brain is the **brain stem**, which is shown below. One critical part of the brain stem, the **medulla oblongata** (sometimes just called the medulla), is respon-sible for maintaining and regulating heart rate, breathing (respiration), digestion, swallowing, and even sneezing. Dam-age to the medulla often results in death.

Above the medulla is the **pons**, a mass of nerve fibers that serve as relay stations, sending infor-mation from the brain stem to the cerebellum (see below) and cortex.

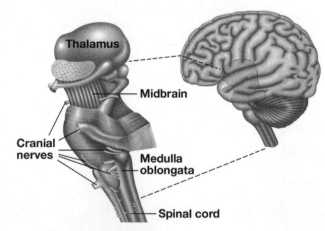

Figure 4.13 The Brain Stem

Four cranial nerves in the pons are involved in movements in the facial region to the teeth, tongue, jaw, eyes, and lower face.

The **midbrain**, located just above the pons, is involved in vision, movement, hearing, and muscle coordination, although it is not the central processing unit. Rather, the midbrain is an assistant, just one part of the circuitry that makes up brain function. Think of the midbrain as a point guard that gives lots of assistance to teammates but does little of the scoring itself.

The **cerebellum**, or "little brain," is a collection of brain cells with some major responsibilities, including fine motor control, coordination, posture, and balance. If the cerebellum is damaged, a person might experience problems with balance and coordination, judging distances, and knowing when and where to stop moving forward. Some people with cerebellar damage have trouble walking in a straight line, and many also develop tremors. Researchers are continually learning more about how the cerebellum influences motor and cognitive skills, and recent research suggests it plays a role in both speech and reading.

The **reticular formation** is a network of nerves that carry messages between parts of the brain stem. It helps regulate the intensity of pain and controls some parts of the body. The reticular formation also helps people focus on useful sensory input while filtering out unnecessary stimuli. For example, activity in the reticular formation allows people in a train station to hear a baby crying but at the same time ignore the sound of the train on the tracks.

The **reticular activating system (RAS)** is a part of the reticular formation. It is responsible for regulating the sleep–wake cycle—it turns the processing of sensory stimuli on (when we need the sensory information) and off (when we need to sleep). Should you start dozing off during class, the RAS is likely to blame. If a person's RAS is damaged, that person typically falls into an irreversible coma.

The Limbic System

The **limbic system** sits at the top of the brainstem. The limbic system is sometimes called the "mammalian brain," because other mammals (but not reptiles, for example) have a similar structure in their brains.

The limbic system includes the thalamus, the hippocampus, the amygdala, the fornix, and the hypothalamus. Together they help us to process pleasant emotions like joy, happiness, excitement, or pleasure and unpleasant emotions like fear, anger, desperation, or nervousness.

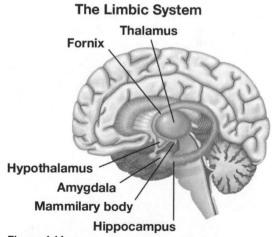

The Limbic System

Thalamus
Fornix
Hypothalamus
Amygdala
Mammilary body
Hippocampus

Figure 4.14

The **thalamus** serves as a relay station between the brain stem and the cortex. For example, sensory signals are sent from the sense organs to the thalamus. The thalamus then sends signals from the eyes to the occipital lobes, signals from the ears to the temporal lobes, and signals from the skin and mouth to the parietal lobes. The information is ultimately processed in these lobes of the cerebral cortex.

The **hippocampus** (Latin for *seahorse* because of its shape) is a rounded part of the limbic system near the center of the brain. The hippocampus plays an important role in turning information into long-term memories and in recalling facts and events. Movies such as *50 First Dates* and *Memento* tell fun or dramatic stories about people who cannot store new memories, but they do not truly reflect the challenges of someone who cannot lay down new long-term memories. Damage to the hippocampus can result in serious cognitive problems. For example, British musicologist, conductor, and pianist Clive Wearing contracted a virus that damaged his hippocampus, and he is now unable to convert any new information into lasting memories. Although he has memories of people and friends he knew before his illness, he has difficulty conversing because he can't remember what another person said only a moment ago. To help make sense of his life, he keeps a journal, but almost all the events are repetitions of "2:15 I am awake now," which would later be crossed out and followed with "3:30 I am fully awake now." He can, however, still read music, and sometimes when he sits down at the piano he can play a familiar piece, sometimes even with comic flourishes at the end. Although he cannot make new memories and has no store of episodic memories, he retains procedural memory. Wearing's story has been the subject of a number of documentaries and articles, and his wife Deborah, whom Wearing greets with excitement and love after even brief partings, wrote a book about it called *Forever Today: A True Story of Lost Memory and Never-Ending Love.*

The hippocampus is also involved in spatial perception, in being aware of the location of objects (or oneself) in the environment. Gymnasts, dancers, and other athletes need the hippocampus to help them land on their feet, catch the pass, or hit the ball with the bat.

Whereas the hippocampus is primarily involved in cognitive processes, the **amygdala** is primarily involved in processing emotion and survival responses (*amygdala* comes from the Latin word for "almond," which this cluster of cells resembles). The amygdala becomes active during potentially threatening situations, such as when a person is focused intently on something and is unexpectedly startled or even when a person is watching a scary movie. A moment of silence on screen builds anticipation, and if a quick movement is paired with a loud sound or music, the movie watcher jumps high and spills popcorn everywhere, thanks to the activation of the amygdala.

When scientists create lesions in parts of an animal's amygdala, the animal becomes excessively tame. It seems as if all aggressiveness is gone. Humans with lesions or tumors in the amygdala show similar behavior: flat affect, very little emotion, either positive or negative. (See Chapter 14 for the role of the amygdala for survival.)

Another part of the limbic system that plays a major role in survival drives is the hypothalamus. The hypothalamus is one of the most important parts of the brain, working in conjunction with many other brain parts to regulate the autonomic nervous system. It releases hormones that are important for feeling sexually attracted to others (oxytocin) and bonding emotionally with others (oxytocin and vasopressin). For example, the hypothalamus is part of a circular loop system that involves the pituitary gland and the gonads. The hypothalamus sends signals of arousal to the pituitary gland, which then releases chemicals (gonadotropins) into the bloodstream. The gonadotropins target the gonads, which then release hormones into the bloodstream. The rising levels of hormones (such as testosterone) in the bloodstream provide feedback to the hypothalamus, leading to a sexual response. The hypothalamus also helps to regulate body temperature and plays a role in sleep and fatigue.

Two nuclei in the hypothalamus, the **lateral hypothalamus (LH)** and the **ventromedial hypothalamus (VMH)**, play a key role in eating (a **nucleus** is a bundle of cells that work together). The lateral hypothalamus regulates hunger: Signals from the stomach are carried to the brain by the vagus nerve, where they are received by the LH. If this nucleus is removed or damaged, the person or animal will not experience hunger. The ventromedial hypothalamus, in contrast, regulates feelings of fullness (satiety). Individuals with damage to the VMH never feel full. They continue eating well beyond when most people would stop, consuming much more food than they need to survive and typically gaining massive amounts of weight. This disorder is known as hyperphagia. The LH and/or the VMH may potentially play a role in eating disorders such as bulimia nervosa and anorexia nervosa. (See Chapter 14 for more about the role of the hypothalamus for survival behaviors.)

The **nucleus accumbens** is located near the hypothalamus but is a part of the frontal lobe (and is a part of the basal ganglia which is connected to learning habits and motor skills). It has a primary role of cognitive processing of pleasure, aversion, motivation, learning, and reward. It is where dopamine is released when we experience pleasure. Therefore, it plays a role in addiction.

The Divided Brain

As you read, each of your cerebral hemispheres is performing its own primary set of functions. For many tasks, one hemisphere is more active than the other. This division of labor is called **brain lateralization** or **hemispheric specialization**. Remember, however, that the two hemispheres are connected via the corpus callosum, and information passes from one side to the other. All people with intact (i.e., not damaged) brains use both hemispheres and have access to the abilities that are dominantly controlled by each.

For most people, the left hemisphere of the brain controls most actions for the right side of the body; the information crosses over in the brain stem. In addition, for most people, the left hemisphere is more active than the right when people engage in language and cognitive skills.

Because of this dominance, many people refer to the left hemisphere as the "language side" of the brain. Similarly, the right hemisphere of the brain controls most actions for the left side of the body. It is more active than the left for some kinds of cognitive tasks, as shown below.

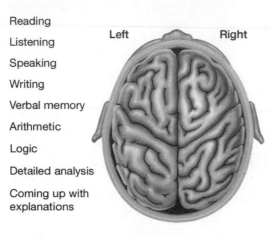

Reading

Listening

Speaking

Writing

Verbal memory

Arithmetic

Logic

Detailed analysis

Coming up with explanations

Recognizing faces

Interpreting emotions (emotional cognition)

See and comprehending patterns

Making inferences

Processing spatial relationships (such as determining the location and relationships of objects in space)

Mentally rotating objects

Processing nonlinguistic sounds, including music

Recognizing and interpreting rhythms

Creating a sense of self

Figure 4.15 Hemisphere Functions

In general, the right side is more influential for global, intuitive, spatial, and creative tasks, while the left side is more active for tasks that are logical, verbal, and linear. Ultimately, an intact brain processes information in both hemispheres—but what about a brain that's not intact?

Split-Brain Research

During most cognitive tasks, the two hemispheres of the brain communicate extensively, with information passing back and forth via the corpus callosum. When the two hemispheres can't communicate, each side of the brain seems to act independently, seemingly without awareness or knowledge of the other. This intriguing phenomenon, known as the "**split brain**," has been demonstrated in a series of well-known studies.

Epilepsy is a medical condition that involves a disruption of communication pathways in the brain, resulting in abnormal, "out of control" electrical activity which leads to seizures. This condition provided an opportunity for researchers to study a split brain. Research with nonhuman animals suggested that seizures might be eliminated if the defective pathway were destroyed entirely; in other words, if the scientists cut the corpus callosum so that the two hemispheres were isolated, or "split." Because epileptic seizures can be severe and debilitating, neurosurgeons made the decision to try this unconventional approach with humans who had not responded to more conventional treatments for epilepsy.

As the scientists had predicted, the surgery reduced or eliminated the epileptic seizures, and for the most part the split-brain patients appeared able to function effectively in their daily lives. They could talk and walk, they remembered events from the past, and they could make new memories. In most ways, life seemed normal—except, in certain ways, it wasn't.

In a series of clever experiments with split-brain patients, neuroscientists **Roger Sperry** and **Michael Gazzaniga** showed that some information, in particular visual information, seemed to get "stuck" in one hemisphere. This phenomenon is partly due to the anatomy of the visual system. Although each hemisphere generally controls the opposite side of the body, the visual system works a bit differently. Each eye takes in information from an entire scene, known as the visual field. All information about the right side of the visual field is sent from each eye to the left hemisphere, and all information about the left visual field is sent to the right hemisphere. The information is then combined in an intact brain because the signals from each hemisphere can cross via the corpus callosum.

The researchers asked patients with a severed corpus callosum to focus on a single spot in the center visual field, and then they presented a stimulus—a pencil or an apple, for example—in the far right (apple) or the far left (pencil) of the visual field, or sometimes both at once. Then, when the researchers asked the people to report what they saw, the patients said they saw the apple but they didn't mention the pencil. However, when asked to draw what they saw and were instructed to draw with their *left* hands, they drew a pencil. When asked to pick up what they saw, both hands reached out—the right hand picked up the apple, and the left hand picked up the pencil. Many of the participants were surprised by the actions of their hands.

The apple in the *right visual field* is seen by both eyes, but a representation of the apple is sent only to the *left hemisphere,* which controls speech processing. Thus the person can say, "it's an apple." At the same time, a representation of the pencil in the *left visual field* is sent only to the *right hemisphere,* which controls motion of the *left hand*. Thus the left hand will draw the pencil.

In a related study, Gazzaniga and his colleague Joseph LeDoux briefly showed split-brain patients two pictures simultaneously, a picture of a chicken claw in the right visual field and a picture of a winter scene in the left visual field. As expected, when asked to point to cards representing each scene, each patient's right hand pointed to a card with a chicken and the left hand pointed to a card with a shovel. The researchers then asked the patients why they were pointing to a shovel, and they responded by making up an explanation that incorporated both items, for example saying that the chicken claw goes with a chicken, and a shovel is needed to clean out a chicken shed. Because the left hemisphere did *not* have the information that "my eyes saw a shovel" but *did* have the information that "I am now pointing to a shovel," the brain processed both stimuli and spontaneously created some explanation for this odd behavior. Gazzaniga and LeDoux called this phenomenon the "left brain interpreter," which creates a story about events that goes beyond information available to the person. Gazzaniga concluded, "These findings all suggest that the interpretive mechanism of the left hemisphere is always hard at work, seeking the meaning of events. It is constantly looking for order and reason, even when there is none—which leads it continually to make mistakes."

Hemispherectomy and Brain Plasticity

As you read, a hemispherectomy is the removal of one of the halves (i.e., hemispheres) of the brain. Hemispherectomies have been successfully used to control seizures in people who have epilepsy, with fewer side effects than those resulting from severing the corpus callosum. In fact, when a hemisphere is removed from a young child, that child develops what would otherwise be lateralized skills in the remaining hemisphere. This incredible ability to recover from having only "half a brain" is an example of **neuroplasticity**— the reorganization of neural pathways as a result of experience. Plasticity is stronger when we are young and reduces as we age, so many older adults experiencing a stroke never recover full functioning. Nevertheless, even adult brains are plastic to some degree. (See pages 113 and 138 for more on neuroplasticity.)

The idea of plasticity is sometimes confused with a longtime but very inaccurate belief about the brain, that people use only 10 percent of their brains. People use their entire brains, whether that's both hemispheres or only one. The origin of this "10 percent myth" is unclear, but it likely came about because people misunderstood early research and commentary about not living up to one's potential. Marketers and advertisers have continued to perpetuate it, often to encourage consumers to purchase products that allow us to use "more" of our brains. It is a comforting fantasy that people somehow all have more potential and would be smarter, stronger, or faster if there were only a magic pill or a quick fix that allowed people to use "more" of the brain. But it's just that—a fantasy. The best way to "grow" a brain is to engage in the world, building connections among brain cells by learning new things. This process is described in detail in Chapter 5.

Going for a Drive: An Example of Brain Processing

Now that you know the basic functions of the brain structures, you can take a look at how each part of the nervous system plays a role in your behavior. Consider the example of going for a drive with your best friend. What is your brain doing during this driving experience? Initially, as you're making the decision to go on this drive, your frontal lobe is active, helping you plan out your trip. As you get into the car, your legs and back feel the pressure from the seat. The seat belt comes across your chest. These sensations are passed, via sensory nerves in the peripheral nervous system, to the spinal cord and then the brain (the central nervous system). The thalamus processes the information and then sends it to the somatosensory cortex, the part of the brain that ultimately processes the meaning in the message. The cerebellum helps keep you vertical, assisting your balance and helping you to coordinate all your movements. You are not feeling dizzy, so you can maintain your balance.

Because you have driven many times, you hardly have to think about putting the key into the ignition and turning the key (or maybe you have to push a button). Turning on the radio requires the motor cortex and the cerebellum, and you realize that you don't even remember starting the car. Your basal ganglia took care of that basic repetitive motor function for you.

As the music plays, you recognize the song because your thalamus sent the signals to the temporal lobes, which worked hard to help you identify the melody. The left hemisphere is especially active in processing the lyrics; with help from the hippocampus, it pulls information from the cerebral cortex so you can sing along. When your friend asks, "Who sings this song?," Wernicke's area helps you to recognize the words, and your frontal cortex is active as you formulate a response. Broca's area helps you say the name of the artist, and as soon as it's out of your mouth you realize that your frontal lobe let you down, allowing you to miss the forthcoming comeback: Your friend says, "Then shut up and let them sing it!" As you realize that you just walked into that joke, your frontal lobe begins to feel a bit of shame for having fallen for such a transparent and predictable put down of your singing skills.

Now you are ready to pull out of the driveway. Your parietal lobe helps you to judge the distance and speed as you move backwards into the street, but first your eyes must process the signals of light bouncing off all the surfaces. As you look at the car, the rearview mirror, and out the back window, your eyes are bringing all that data into the thalamus and then the occipital lobe, where all that visual data is processed.

Your arms are controlling the steering wheel and gear shift, thanks to your motor cortex working as you switch from reverse to drive. The pressure you feel on the bottom of your foot as you move from the brake to the accelerator pad is processed by the somatosensory cortex, and the hippocampus is busy searching your memory for information about which roads to take to get to your destination.

As you are driving and talking, the lateral hypothalamus processes a signal from your body and messages your frontal lobe, which lets you know that you feel hungry. You ask your friend, "Hey, wanna get something to eat?" When your friend says, "I could go for some tacos," your frontal cortex helps you evaluate the possibilities of restaurants. The hippocampus is at work again, searching for the two best choices. You recall that the taqueria where you most recently ate had the best salsa you've ever had. Your frontal lobe goes into action and you respond, "Let's go to the taqueria on Main Street."

On your way, another favorite song comes on the radio. You both are singing and laughing. As your attention is diverted from the road, you do not notice the cars stopped in front of you. Out of the corner of your eye, you see lights and movement (eyes, thalamus, occipital lobe). The thalamus and the RAS help focus your attention. Your amygdala activates the sympathetic nervous system via the hypothalamus. Adrenaline pours into your bloodstream. Your body knows what to do; you hit the brakes. You begin to sweat as your muscles tense and your body temperature rises. You somehow swerve to the right and avoid hitting the cars in front of you. The frontal lobe is working overtime to get you to stop on the side of the road. You pull over and turn on the hazard lights, but you are still breathing heavily and stunned about what just happened. Your frontal lobe sends the signal, and you realize everyone is safe. Your friend, and your parasympathetic nervous system, help to calm you down—your breathing slows, the chemicals move out of your bloodstream, and your body resets itself. The sympathetic nervous system sends a signal telling you that digestion isn't a priority right now, and you realize you're no longer hungry.

You reflect about the near accident, with your frontal lobe humming as you process all the activities that were going on during the drive. Your hippocampus helps you to remember and second-guess every decision you made—from the music to the singing, even to having your friend in the car. As you review everything, your cerebral cortex is working to make those memories into long-term ones: the melody of the song, the smell of the burning rubber, the squealing of the tires, the feeling of your body in the danger zone, and the sense of relief as you realize it was not an actual crash, only a near one.

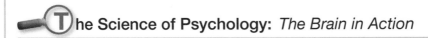

The Science of Psychology: *The Brain in Action*

With a partner, develop your own explanation of what your brain is doing when you perform a routine task, such as jogging outdoors while listening to music or responding to a funny meme someone posted on social media.

REFLECT ON THE ESSENTIAL QUESTION

Essential Question: *How do the parts of the brain and nervous systems work together to process information and control behaviors?* On separate paper, make a graphic organizer using the KEY TERMS to gather details to answer that question.

KEY TERMS			KEY PEOPLE
FRAMEWORK OF THE NERVOUS SYSTEM brain central nervous system spinal cord autonomic nervous system parasympathetic nervous system peripheral nervous system somatic nervous system sympathetic nervous system *BRAIN ANATOMY* amygdala arachnoid mater brain stem Broca's area cerebellum cerebral cortex cerebral hemispheres cerebrospinal fluid cerebrum corpus callosum dura mater hemispheres hippocampus frontal lobe gyrus/gyri hemisphere specialization hypothalamus lateral hypothalamus (LH) limbic system lobes	medulla (medulla oblongata) meninges midbrain motor cortex nucleus accumbens occipital lobe parietal lobe pia mater pituitary gland pineal gland pons reticular activating system (RAS) reticular formation somatosensory cortex sulcus/sulci temporal lobes thalamus thyroid gland ventromedial hypothalamus (VMH) visual association cortex Wernicke's area *RELATED TERMS* acromegaly adrenal glands agnosia brain lateralization (hemispheric specialization) electrode endocrine system gigantism gonads hormone neuroanatomy neuroplasticity	nucleus pituitary dwarfism reflex arc "split brain" *TECHNIQUES FOR STUDYING AND TREATING THE BRAIN* ablation computerized axial tomography (CT or CAT scan) deep brain stimulation electroencepha-lography/ electroencepha-logram (EEG) functional magnetic resonance imaging (fMRI) hemispherectomy lesions/lesioning magnetic resonance imaging (MRI) positron emission tomography (PET scan) prefrontal lobotomy transcranial magnetic stimulation (TMS) x-ray	Paul Broca Michael Gazzaniga Roger Sperry Carl Wernicke

1. Liz is a high school tennis player. She started to lose weight rapidly during the season. She couldn't control her emotions and acted out on them, never holding back. It appears that Liz could have a classic case of anorexia. Which part of the brain are new studies focusing on in understanding the role of the brain in this eating disorder?

   (A) Hippocampus

   (B) Hypothalamus

   (C) Thalamus

   (D) Brain stem

   (E) Nucleus accumbens

2. Mrs. Johnson took her husband to see a doctor after being in the car with him for one day. He repeatedly ran red lights and drove right past the building where he was supposed to drop her off, even though he had been there several times. After many tests, the doctor told Mrs. Johnson that her husband had a brain tumor and it had already started to spread. Where did the tumor likely begin?

   (A) Hippocampus

   (B) Cerebellum

   (C) Thalamus

   (D) Brain stem

   (E) Nucleus accumbens

3. Sasha has tried every diet in the book. Cutting portions has not worked because she finds herself constantly hungry. Her weight gain has been depressing her, and her mom has gotten very worried. She also consumes large quantities of water. What part of the brain might be damaged and responsible for Sasha's behavior?

   (A) Amygdala

   (B) Hippocampus

   (C) Lateral hypothalamus

   (D) Pons

   (E) Ventromedial hypothalamus

4. Susie works in an ice cream shop and suffered brain damage from an accident. Now when something goes wrong in the store, she has no idea how to fix it. Her favorite type of ice cream has always been chocolate chip, yet now she can never decide what flavor she wants to eat on her break. Susie's coworkers have also noticed that she just doesn't seem like her herself. Where did Susie suffer the brain damage?

(A) Occipital lobes

(B) Temporal lobes

(C) Reticular formation

(D) Parietal lobes

(E) Frontal lobes

5. As a result of a surgical procedure, Hakim's career as a violinist is over. He finds that he can no longer compose music. When he tries to play, he gets confused because he can't retain what he hears. What part of the brain is likely implicated?

(A) Occipital lobes

(B) Temporal lobes

(C) Reticular formation

(D) Parietal lobes

(E) Frontal lobes

6. Lately, Maria has not been sleeping well. It seems like she hears everything at night. Even the faintest noises, such as the refrigerator humming and the toilet down the hall flushing, wake her up. If she does fall asleep, she has a very hard time getting up. Maria is desperate for some rest. What part of her brain is not functioning properly?

(A) Occipital lobes

(B) Temporal lobes

(C) Reticular activating system

(D) Parietal lobes

(E) Frontal lobes

7. Valeria is a dancer. She has been dancing for years, but one day at a late-night rehearsal, her tired partner accidentally dropped her on her head. Now, Valeria has problems dancing. She knows the correct steps she must make, but she feels as if her legs and arms are moving as if directed by someone else. What area of her brain was damaged by her fall?

   (A) Amygdala

   (B) Hippocampus

   (C) Lateral hypothalamus

   (D) Pons

   (E) Cerebellum

8. Jon has a very strong fear of spiders. One day while he was lying in bed, a spider fell on his head. Jon quickly jumped out of bed as a result of his fear. However, the spider still managed to bite him. Jon darted toward the door, and within seconds he collapsed to the ground. When his mother rushed into the room to ask what was wrong, he was unable to understand her question. He saw her mouth move, but was unable to make sense of the words. What area of the brain did the poison affect?

   (A) Amygdala

   (B) Hippocampus

   (C) Lateral hypothalamus

   (D) Pons

   (E) Cerebellum

9. Dr. Ramachandran needs to examine a patient's brain to find out if there is a tumor and, if so, where it is. Which method should he use?

   (A) PET Scan

   (B) EEG

   (C) CT Scan

   (D) Deep Brain Stimulation

   (E) fMRI

10. Mr. Murphy has suffered a stroke and is no longer able to communicate the ideas he has in his head. He knows what he wants to say but is unable to speak. What part of Mr. Murphy's brain has been damaged by the stroke?

    (A) Wernicke's area

    (B) Broca's area

    (C) The amygdala

    (D) The hypothalamus

    (E) The reticular formation

1. "Everything psychological is simultaneously biological." Support this statement by connecting biology and behavior. Define and use the following terms in your explanation:
   - Cognition
   - Emotions
   - Language
   - Perceptions
   - Attitudes

2. Describe the process of how the brain influences the daily lives of humans. For each term below, describe its basic function, and give an example of how each would work in a day at school.

   Please go in this order:
   - Medulla
   - Reticular formation
   - Amygdala
   - Hypothalamus
   - Wernicke's area
   - Broca's area
   - Frontal cortex

5

Neurons, Neural Communication, and Behavioral Genetics

"A typical neuron makes about ten thousand connections to neighboring neurons. Given the billions of neurons, this means there are as many connections in a single cubic centimeter of brain tissue as there are stars in the Milky Way galaxy."

—David Eagleman

Essential Question: How do the biological fields of neuroanatomy and genetics help to explain the behaviors of an individual?

In Chapter 4, you read about the structures and organization of the nervous system, which includes the brain and the nerves that run throughout the body. This chapter will explore neuroanatomy on a cellular level—what types of cells make up the nervous system, how they are organized, and how they communicate.

Neuroanatomy: The Structure and Organization of Nerve Cells

The brain is composed of hundreds of billions of cells that connect to and communicate with one another in intricate networks. Arguably, the most important of those cells are the **neurons**—the basic units on which the entire brain and nervous system are built: no neurons, no brain.

Nerves are bundles of neuron **axons**—slender protrusions from the cell body, often called *fibers*—outside of the brain and spinal column. **Cranial nerves** are nerves that come out of the brain and generally send messages to the head and neck (*cranium* is another name for the skull). Some bundles of neuron axons (called *tracts* in the brain and spinal cord) join together in the brain stem; as those tracts exit the brain, they become a major part of the **spinal cord**. Figure 5.1 shows how other nerves then extend through the body.

But neurons aren't the most abundant cells in the brain. They are outnumbered by as many as 50 to 1 by **glial cells**, which provide nutrition and protection for the neurons. The glial cells function like glue to hold the neurons together (in fact, *glia* comes from the Greek word meaning "glue").

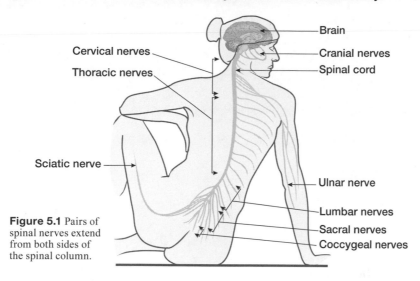

The Nervous System of the Human Body

Brain

Cervical nerves

Cranial nerves

Thoracic nerves

Spinal cord

Sciatic nerve

Ulnar nerve

Lumbar nerves

Figure 5.1 Pairs of spinal nerves extend from both sides of the spinal column.

Sacral nerves

Coccygeal nerves

Neural Diversity

Neurons come in many shapes and sizes; they can be as small as four microns (4/100 of a millimeter) or as large as 100 microns (1/10 of a millimeter). They also have varying functions.

- **Sensory neurons** take input received through sensory receptors throughout the body, such as in the skin, eyes, nose, ears, and tongue, and pass it on toward the brain and spinal cord to initiate a response. These neurons are also known as **afferent neurons**.

- **Motor neurons** transmit signals from the brain to our muscles and other organs. Motor neurons are also known as **efferent neurons**.

- **Interneurons** are relay neurons, or connectors, allowing for information to pass between neurons.

Neural Structure

In general, every neuron has the same basic structure. If you have taken biology or anatomy/physiology, you may recognize that neurons are similar in many ways to other cells in the human body. They are surrounded by membranes, have a nucleus with genes inside, and contain mitochondria, cytoplasm, and other organelles. However, they also have distinct parts that play key roles in the communication process.

The body of a nerve cell is known as the **soma** (as you might now expect, the name *soma* comes from the Greek word for "body"). The soma contains the nucleus and other parts that are important for the creation of proteins and membranes needed for a neuron to function. Cell bodies can vary in size and shape, as you can see in Figure 5.2 on the next page.

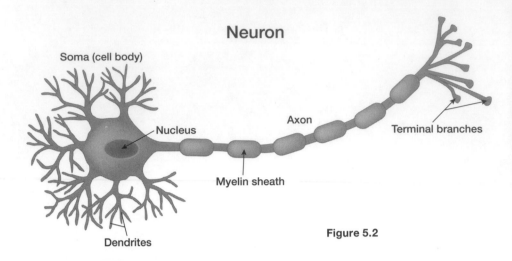

Neuron

Soma (cell body)

Nucleus

Axon

Terminal branches

Myelin sheath

Dendrites

Figure 5.2

Tree-like protrusions extending from the cell body are known as **dendrites**. The dendrites receive signals from other cells. Each neuron can have hundreds or thousands of dendritic spines, each of which may make multiple connections with other neurons.

Messages from the soma travel down the length of the axon, where it branches out. The **terminal branches** end in little bulbs called **terminal buttons**. The terminal buttons contain small sacs, known as **vesicles**, that contain chemicals (called **neurotransmitters**) that are necessary to pass on the signals.

Because the axons carry electrical charges, they need to be insulated. Glial cells help to perform this function in the **central nervous system (CNS)**, developing into a covering known as **myelin**. This myelin sheath is critically important in the nervous system, and when it degenerates, it disrupts communication in the central nervous system. Multiple sclerosis (MS) is an example of a disease caused by demyelination (i.e., the degradation or loss of the myelin sheaths) in the CNS. People with MS often have severe fatigue, problems with sensation, and difficulty with motor skills. Many lose the ability to walk. In the **peripheral nervous system**, glial cells form a myelin sheath around the axons. This membrane is known as the **neurilemma**. This outer covering of the myelin protects the cell and creates a tunnel for regenerating the nerve fiber after damage. The newly regrown fibers help patients regain some control when their limbs are injured.

Neurons do not typically touch one another. They communicate chemically across very small gaps called **synapses** (Figure 5.3). Neurotransmitters from the terminal buttons of one cell are released into the synapses between that cell and other cells. This transfer of information is known as **electrochemical communication**.

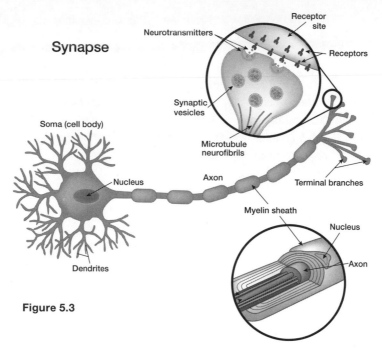

Synapse

Neurotransmitters

Receptor site

Receptors

Synaptic vesicles

Soma (cell body)

Microtubule neurofibrils

Nucleus

Axon

Terminal branches

Myelin sheath

Nucleus

Axon

Dendrites

Figure 5.3

Communication Among Neurons

Neural conduction is the process by which information travels through a neuron. This process is commonly known as **neural firing**. Neural firing is both electrical (within the neurons) and chemical (between neurons).

The Electrical Component: Resting and Action Potentials

Input from the environment is received by sensory receptors, passed on to the dendrites, and then sent to the cell body in the form of electrical impulses. As you may recall from other science classes, cell bodies contain various charged particles called ions. Some ions have positive charges, and others have negative charges. Neurons are no different. When a neuron is in a resting state, it has an overall negative charge, at negative seventy millivolts (–70 mv). The inside of the neuron contains more potassium and chloride ions than the outside, and the outside contains more sodium ions than the inside. Because this imbalance creates a *possibility* of voltage change, the resting state is called **resting potential**.

An easy way to remember resting potential is "salty bananas." Bananas contain lots of potassium. If you dip the banana into a tub of salt water (sodium), the banana is in its resting state—the inside has lots of potassium, and the outside has lots of salt. If you then peel the banana and take a bite, it might taste a little salty, because a banana peel is semi-permeable, which means that some ions can pass through it. The "peel" or membrane of a neuron is also semi-permeable, so that sodium and potassium can move in and out. This movement is altered when gated sodium and/or potassium channels are opened. Continuous, tiny pumps in the cell membrane move sodium ions out of the cell and potassium ions into the cell. These pumps rely on the energy-releasing molecule adenosine triphosphate (ATP).

When an electrical impulse reaches the cell body, gated channels open up and allow sodium ions to rush into the cell. This increase in sodium alters the balance of charge, making the cell more positive than it was when it was resting (-70mv). This change in charge is known as **depolarization**. The brief positive charge creates an electrical impulse known as an **action potential**. The charge in the cell briefly rises to around +30 mv. In simpler terms, the cell has reached an electrical **threshold**—the point at which it fires, usually about –55mv. The action potential travels down the axon as a voltage spike, like a chain reaction of dominoes falling, as the energy moves down the neuron.

Action potentials follow the **all-or-none principle**: Cells either fire (if the electrical charge inside the cell reaches a threshold) or they don't fire, and when an action potential does occur in a cell, it always occurs with the same charge. Some people describe the process as similar to turning on a television. Either the TV is on or it is off. A TV can't be partially on.

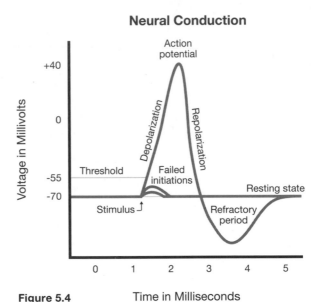

Neural Conduction

Figure 5.4 Time in Milliseconds

For a brief moment after firing, the neuron is in its refractory period during which it is not able to fire again. The sodium gated channels then close, and voltage-gated potassium channels open, allowing the cell to return to its normal resting state of –70mv.

A neural impulse might speed through your nervous system in an autonomic response to a sudden pain stimulus—when you touch something hot, for example. Less urgent messages that require processing and thought, such as those from your eyes to your brain about the words on this page, take longer. The speed of a neural impulse can range from 2 to 200 miles per hour, depending on a number of factors, including the size of the nerve fiber and the type of signal. Researchers usually record the speed in milliseconds, or thousandths of a second.

By age four, children's nerve speed is the same as adults'. Conduction speed in some nerves, such as the ulnar nerve that runs through the elbow, slows as people age.

The Chemical Component: Neurotransmitters

When a neuron fires, the electrical charge from its action potential travels all the way down the axon. When this charge gets to the vesicles in the terminal buttons, the neuron releases its neurotransmitters—the chemical component—into the synapse. Neurotransmitters that enter the synapse are picked up by **receptors** in the dendrites of adjoining neurons. If enough neurotransmitters are received by the dendrites to change the ionic balance of these new neurons, they create electrical charges that move the neurons from their resting potential of –70mv, and the cycle begins again.

After they complete their work at the receptor cells on the dendrites, the neurotransmitters are released back into the synapse. In some cases, the originating neuron reabsorbs the chemicals in a process called **reuptake**. In other cases, an enzyme destroys the neurotransmitter, breaking it down into parts that can be used elsewhere in the brain in a biological recycling service.

Consider what happens when cells in the eye respond to light. The light is taken in by sensory receptors, passed on to the dendrites, and then sent to the cell body in the form of electrical impulses, which ripple down the axon through the terminal branches, buttons, and vesicles. They are then sent on their way by neurotransmitters, which are released into the synapses. An overview of the process is described below.

{sensory receptor}→ {dendrites of cell #1}→ {soma}→ {axon}→ {terminal branches}→ {terminal buttons}→ {vesicles}→ {neurotransmitters released into the synapse}→ {dendrites of cell #2}→ {soma}

Functions of Neurotransmitters Some neurotransmitters are classified as **excitatory neurotransmitters**. When these chemicals are released from the terminal buttons, they excite connecting neurons and cause them to fire. Others are classified as **inhibitory neurotransmitters**. These inhibit (prevent) the next neurons from firing. Inhibitory and excitatory neurotransmitters balance each other out, attempting to create a homeostasis within the brain and body.

Approximately 30 neurotransmitters are known. Of those, only about 10 do 99 percent of the work. Often, neurotransmitters work in concert with other neurotransmitters, but the focus here is on the primary responsibilities and functions of some of the most important neurotransmitters.

Acetylcholine (ACh) Acetylcholine was the first neurotransmitter discovered. It is active in both the peripheral and central nervous systems. ACh is connected to movement; its primary function in the somatic nervous system is to activate muscles and carry out voluntary movements. It is involved in decreasing heart rate, increasing sweat and saliva, and increasing muscle contractions. Acetylcholine also plays a role in memory: Levels of ACh can drop up to 90 percent in people with Alzheimer's disease.

Figure 5.5 shows ACh being released into the synapse and activating the skeletal muscle cell in the neural communication process. If key receptors for ACh are blocked, paralysis may result. Because the ACh cannot bind to the receptors, the motor neurons don't get the message to fire, and the somatic nervous system is paralyzed. Various tribal groups in Central and South America have paralyzed their prey for hundreds or even thousands of years with curare, a poison that blocks the acetylcholine receptors in motor neurons.

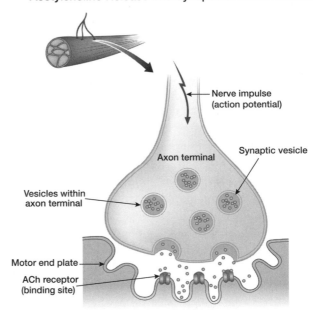

Acetylcholine Release into Synapse of Motor Neuron

Nerve impulse (action potential)

Synaptic vesicle

Axon terminal

Vesicles within axon terminal

Motor end plate

ACh receptor (binding site)

Figure 5.5

Serotonin One of the most important neurotransmitters is serotonin, which is connected to mood, emotion, appetite, sleep, and sexual desire. Only about 10 percent of the serotonin in our bodies is produced within the brain; the remaining serotonin is located in the gastrointestinal tract. High levels of serotonin in the brain increase happiness, and low levels are associated with depression, anger control, obsessive-compulsive disorder, and suicide.

Depression is often treated using drugs called SSRIs (selective serotonin reuptake inhibitors). These drugs increase the levels of serotonin in the brain, reducing feelings of depression and decreasing compulsions. SSRIs work by blocking the reabsorption or reuptake of the serotonin into the sending neuron, leaving it in the synapse longer and thus allowing the neural signal to continue repeatedly, increasing its effect.

Dopamine Sometimes called the pleasure chemical of the brain, dopamine is released into the pleasure centers of the brain, specifically the nucleus accumbens, which is a part of the mesolimbic or "reward" pathway.

Dopamine plays a role in a number of behaviors related to reward and motivation. For example, dopamine is released when we anticipate something pleasurable, such as making a long-desired purchase, winning a game, or—for addicts—getting the next hit of heroin. This anticipation releases dopamine which makes us feel better temporarily.

Low dopamine levels have been connected to addictive behaviors, including drugs, gambling, and sex. Dopamine also affects alertness and happiness, reduces hunger, aids in perseverance, and helps with fine motor coordination.

Dopamine is also connected to muscle control, or specifically the lack of it. People with Parkinson's disease (for example, actor Michael J. Fox or the famous boxer Muhammad Ali) exhibit tremors and loss of key motor skills, because their brains have stopped producing adequate supplies of dopamine. A common treatment for Parkinson's disease is a drug that stimulates creation of dopamine. On the other hand, excessive levels of dopamine production in the limbic system have been linked to schizophrenia.

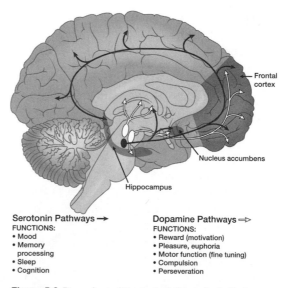

Serotonin Pathways →
FUNCTIONS:
• Mood
• Memory processing
• Sleep
• Cognition

Dopamine Pathways ⇒
FUNCTIONS:
• Reward (motivation)
• Pleasure, euphoria
• Motor function (fine tuning)
• Compulsion
• Perseveration

Figure 5.6 Dopamine and Serotonin Pathways in the Brain

Epinephrine Epinephrine in the endocrine system is associated with energy; in the sympathetic nervous system, it is associated with response to high-emotion situations, such as emergencies. High levels lead to muscle tension, increased heart rate, increased blood pressure, and more blood being released to the skeletal muscles. Epinephrine is also connected to forming memories, especially those related to traumatic events or emotionally charged incidents. Epinephrine is the same chemical as **adrenaline**.

People with serious allergies are often prescribed a device to inject epinephrine. Epinephrine reduces life-threatening responses, such as swelling, difficulty breathing, and a drop in blood pressure. It opens the airways and increases blood pressure by reducing the size of the blood vessels.

Norepinephrine Norepinephrine is active in the sympathetic nervous system response to danger. Higher levels of norepinephrine increase alertness, blood pressure, and heart rate. Norepinephrine also releases glucose stores (energy) so that a person can respond quickly, as in the **fight-or-flight response**, which occurs when people encounter something dangerous or even life-threatening and respond physiologically in a way that prepares them to fight or flee. Norepinephrine is involved in developing fears, and low levels of norepinephrine are connected to depression. One treatment for depression is a selective norepinephrine reuptake inhibitor (SNRI). Like SSRIs, SNRIs are drugs that reduce the reuptake of the neurotransmitter, leaving it in the synapse longer and allowing the neural signal to continue repeatedly.

GABA GABA is the acronym for **gamma-aminobutyric acid**, the primary inhibitory neurotransmitter that slows things down, calming the central nervous system. It is sometimes considered a natural tranquilizer. GABA increases sleepiness and decreases anxiety, alertness, memory, and muscle tension. Too little GABA is associated with anxiety disorders. Without GABA, neurons fire too easily and too often, destabilizing the brain systems.

Glutamate Glutamate, the major excitatory neurotransmitter, is the opposite of GABA. It is involved with most normal operations of the brain, including thinking, memory, and learning. It plays a key role in **long-term potentiation (LTP)**, a pattern of neural firing that strengthens synaptic connections over time. As we repeat a behavior or a cognitive task, we make the connections in our brains stronger. Glutamate facilitates this process.

Other chemicals are also involved in the electrochemical process. Neuropeptides regulate the activity of other neurons. Enkephalins and **endorphins** relieve pain and stress. Endorphins, which are released by the pituitary gland, are often called the brain's natural aspirin. You may have heard about people getting an "endorphin rush" while participating in physical activities such as running.

Agonists and Antagonists Some chemicals function as neurotransmitters but aren't actually neurotransmitters. **Agonists** activate the receptors for certain neurotransmitters and ultimately make the effects of the neurotransmitter stronger. Well-known agonists include heroin, oxycodone, methadone, hydrocodone, opium, and morphine, which mimic the actions of endorphins throughout the entire nervous system. **Antagonists** are chemicals that inhibit or oppose the actions of neurotransmitters. Often, they sit in receptor sites and block the neurotransmitter from binding with the receptors on the dendrites. An example of an antagonist is haloperidol, a drug that blocks dopamine and is used to treat schizophrenic symptoms.

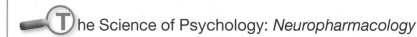

The Science of Psychology: *Neuropharmacology*

By the early 20th century, Sigmund Freud had proclaimed that the cause of depression lay in repressed oral stage childhood trauma, and the cure was to release those traumatic experiences and emotions from the unconscious through psychoanalysis. (See pages 552–553 for more on Freud's approach.) At the same time, however, scientists were discovering the chemical communication of neurotransmitters. By the 1950s, prescription drugs were being developed to influence the actions of neurotransmitters, and in the decades that followed, more and more drugs were developed to manipulate neurotransmitter communication. By the 1990s, pharmaceutical companies had flooded the market with new and better antidepressants.

In this contest between Freud and pharmaceuticals, who won? Would you be surprised to hear Freud did? Empirical evidence indicates the best way to treat at least one disorder, post-traumatic stress disorder (PTSD), is through a form of psychotherapy called cognitive-behavioral therapy (CBT), specifically prolonged exposure therapy. (See Chapters 22 and 23 for more on disorders and the therapies to treat them.)

Yet what is the most widely used form of treatment for PTSD? Psychopharmaceutical drugs. Freud's oral stage trauma theory may have been the product of bad science and speculation, but he was right about one thing: The symptoms of PTSD are the result of a traumatic event, and the best way to treat it is to bring the trauma to the surface and confront it, and by so doing, you reduce its painful effects. Neuropharmacology offers a solution as well, but it is one that reduces the symptoms rather than addresses the cause.

Practice: With a group of students, collaborate to find out why drugs that reduce the symptoms but don't address the underlying disorder are more widely used than a psychotherapeutic treatment that evidence shows to be much more effective and permanent. Divide the following tasks among your group. When everyone has finished the tasks, come together to discuss, prepare, and present your findings.

- Research meta-analyses of studies into the effects of CBT and prolonged exposure treatment for PTSD.

- Research empirical studies into the effects of the top three types of drugs used for PTSD: antidepressants, mood stabilizers, and antipsychotics.

- Investigate the ways that pharmaceutical companies market their products.

- Investigate evidence of pharmaceutical marketing on mental health or medical informational websites.

Life and Death of a Neuron

Until very recently, scientists believed that we were born with all the neurons we were ever going to have, about 100 billion cells that developed prenatally, but research in the last two decades suggests that under certain circumstances, new neurons develop even in adults. However, researchers still believe that babies are born with many, many more neurons than they'll ever use, many of which will die off before the second year of life.

What causes some neurons to survive and thrive, whereas others simply die? The answer lies in how they're used. When infants (or adults) interact with the environment in some way, the neurons that are active during the interaction form new connections or strengthen the connections they already have with other neurons. On the other hand, neurons that are not active in any interactions will stop functioning and eventually be reabsorbed by the body. This process of neural connection and neural death describes learning at a microscopic level—when we learn something new, we build connections among brain cells, and when we forget something, we've weakened or lost some already-established connections among brain cells. The primary reason, then, that infants are born with so many "extra" neurons is that they need to be prepared to learn almost anything.

Also, neurons can be injured or damaged. Traumatic brain injury that results in a concussion can damage neurons. The word *concussion* comes from the Latin word meaning "to shake violently." Imagine an egg yolk in a shell— the brain in a skull is a lot like that. A concussion occurs when a strong force to the head results in the brain slamming into the side of the skull. For example, a concussion often occurs when a football player is running at full speed to catch a ball and a defensive player running in the opposite direction stops the player in mid-catch, hitting helmet on helmet. Or a distracted driver slams into the car stopped in front of her and hits her head on the steering wheel.

When these violent events take place, a process called neural metabolic crisis occurs. During this time, neurons can become depolarized, and excitatory neurotransmitters may be released, resulting in altered blood flow in the brain. When this type of injury occurs, calcium ions may be released and make their way into the neurons, leading to cell death. The person may experience dizziness, disorientation, confusion, headaches, loss of consciousness, memory issues, problems with vision, and more.

Researchers have examined the brains of former NFL players who committed suicide and found neurofibrillary tangles. Normally, the damage is found only in people of advanced age, but these athletes were in their thirties and forties when they died. Their brains appeared to have aged prematurely. This process of repeated damage to the brain cells is called chronic traumatic encephalopathy (CTE). Research has shown that repeated exposure to concussions, without the proper time to heal, creates this metabolic damage. CTE can result in memory loss, aggression, depression, and other cognitive, motor, and behavioral problems. Concussion protocols are now in place for professional athletes, college athletes, and even children.

Neuroplasticity provides hope for many people with traumatic brain injury. **Neuroplasticity** is the ability of the brain to create new neurons, form new neural connections, and recruit neurons from other parts of the brain to perform functions once performed by the damaged neurons. Rehabilitation that focuses on relearning and repeating behaviors strengthens the new neural wiring.

Behavioral Genetics

Throughout the history of the field, psychologists have studied the genetic basis of behavior. Some researchers claim that behavior is determined by biology; not surprisingly, they are known as biological determinists. Others claim that behavior occurs as a response to an organism's environment and surroundings; they are known as environmental determinists. Over time, researchers have come to believe that both are correct—nature (i.e., heredity, a person's biological makeup) and nurture (i.e., the environment, life experiences, family, and education) both play roles in influencing behavior. Researchers have identified predictable patterns of behavior that develop as a result of interactions between what people inherit and the surroundings in which they grow up. The field called **behavioral genetics** focuses on discovering how genes and experiences interact and lead to specific behaviors and mental abilities.

Every individual has a unique **genome**; a genome is the entirety of that individual's hereditary information. A person's **genotype** refers to the person's specific genetic blueprint, which is determined by the total pattern of chromosomes inherited from each parent. The actual characteristics a person develops, taken together, are known as the person's **phenotype**. For example, we may have genes that predispose us to a particular height, but the environment might moderate that, leading to a slightly taller or slightly shorter phenotype. People growing up in impoverished environments might be shorter than they would have been had they lived in an environment with more resources, despite a genetic predisposition to a certain height.

DNA and Genetic Expression

The human body contains 100 trillion cells with a nucleus inside each one, except for red blood cells. Each nucleus contains 46 chromosomes, 23 inherited from each biological parent and arranged in 23 pairs. The chromosomes are filled with tightly coiled strands of **DNA—deoxyribonucleic acid**—which contain the basic building blocks of all life (Figure 5.7). DNA is the means by which specific characteristics of an individual or species pass from one generation to the next. The nucleus of each cell in the body contains chromosomes made up of tightly wound coils of DNA.

An entire strand of DNA is composed of billions of smaller molecules, and any drawing of DNA shows only a small section. The molecular structure of DNA is a double helix. This structure is shaped like twisting parallel lines around a central axis. Specific areas on the helix carry information about hereditary traits and processes of the body. Linked molecules make up the rungs on DNA's twisted molecular ladder. The order of these molecules serves as a code for genetic information. This code provides the unique genetic blueprint for the individual.

Genes are segments of DNA that contain instructions to make proteins—the building blocks of life. Humans have 20,000–25,000 genes that produce the proteins needed to express a phenotype. When genes are active, they are called expressed genes. When genes are inactive, they do not make proteins that influence our characteristics and behaviors.

Figure 5.7   The structure of a DNA molecule is a double helix, shown above.

Genes may be dominant or recessive. When a gene is dominant, the features associated with it will appear if the gene is present. If a gene is recessive, the features associated with it will appear only if it is paired with another recessive gene. A classic (though theoretical) example of how dominant and recessive genes work is eye color. Figure 5.8 shows possible gene patterns for children with brown-eyed parents who each have one brown-eye gene and one blue-eye gene. Note that it is possible for two brown-eyed parents to have a blue-eyed child.

Punnett Square Diagram: Eye Color

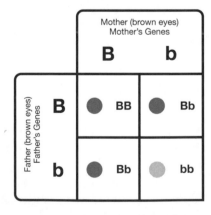

B – Dominant Genetic Trait
(Brown eye color)
b – Recessive Genetis Trait
(Blue eye color)
● – Brown Eyes
Figure 5.8   ● – Blue Eyes

Because the brown-eye gene is dominant, the likelihood of a child having blue eyes is one out of four.

Sometimes, an individual inherits genes from parents that lead to the development of disorders or diseases, and sometimes genes are damaged during prenatal development. Some examples of genetic disorders include cystic fibrosis, neurofibromatosis, and Down syndrome (in which an individual has an extra chromosome). Some congenital disorders (i.e., defects or disorders that are due to a genetic disorder or that occur during prenatal development and are present at birth) may have a genetic and/or an environmental link, including spina bifida, hydrocephalus (often known as "water on the brain" but actually an accumulation of cerebrospinal fluid), and microcephaly (underdevelopment of the brain).

Gene-Environment Interactions

Genes set a blueprint for development, but the environment also plays a key role. For some behaviors or physical characteristics, a particular environment is important at a particular time in life for the genetic information to be expressed. This time in life is known as a **sensitive period** (sometimes called a critical period) because the organism has a period of increased sensitivity to environmental influences. For example, children have sensitive periods for the development of binocular vision (i.e., focusing both eyes to see depth), hearing, and learning the sounds of their first language. Another well-known example of this type of sensitive period is **Konrad Lorenz**'s study of imprinting in ducks and geese. Hatchling chicks are genetically driven to bond to and follow a "parent"—that is, the first large moving object they see. In Lorenz's study, goslings without an adult goose imprinted to Lorenz himself. If you search the Internet, you can see video clips that show the baby geese walking behind Lorenz and even swimming behind him. You may also have seen the movie *Fly Away Home,* in which orphaned geese imprint to a young girl who then uses an ultralight glider built by her father to help the geese fly south. During a sensitive period, some connections between neurons in the brain become stronger, and some unnecessary or unconnected cells die.

Another example of gene-environment interaction is the development of personality. Every individual has a genetically influenced temperament. In other words, we each have our own patterns and characteristic ways of responding to the environment. Temperamental characteristics appear right at birth and include how sensitive, irritable, distracted, approachable, or moody we are. Some children (about 40 percent) show an overall pattern known as an easy temperament. They are relaxed and agreeable. Others (about 10 percent) are described as difficult; they tend to be moody, intense, and easily angered. Another group of children are considered "slow to warm up." These children tend to be restrained, unexpressive, and shy.

Our temperaments influence how we react to, and therefore how we affect, our environments. For example, consider how a parent might respond to his two children, one of whom is easily distracted and irritable and one of whom is slow to warm up. That parent might act differently during play sessions with each child—the irritable one might need more direction or intervention, whereas the slow-to-warm-up child might need quiet time to get used to an activity. The temperamental characteristics of the children influence the parent's behavior, and the parent's behavior simultaneously influences the development of the child's personality. This dual influence is called **reciprocal determinism**. In other words, by interacting with the world around us, we have a role in changing the environment in which we live.

Twin Studies

Researchers who are interested in the interaction of genes and environment often study twins. To understand why, consider the difference between identical and fraternal twins. Identical twins are also known as monozygotic (MZ) twins because one fertilized egg (known as a zygote) splits in half and develops into two people. Monozygotic twins have identical genotypes—the same genes, although not necessarily the same number of copies of those genes. Fraternal twins, in contrast, develop from two separate fertilized eggs and so are known as dizygotic (DZ) twins—two zygotes. On average, any pair of dizygotic twins have 50 percent of their genes in common, the same as other non-twin pairs of siblings.

Because monozygotic twins share the same genetics, any differences between them are most likely—though not certainly—caused by interaction with the environment. Because shared genes can also mean a shared experience, most, not all, monozygotic twins share placentas and are treated similarly by people in their worlds.

This close interaction between genetics and environment creates a prime research opportunity for psychologists. In recent years, researchers have learned a number of things from twin studies, including:

- A person whose identical twin has schizophrenia has a 30–50 percent chance of developing it too.

- If one twin is on the autism spectrum, an identical twin is on the spectrum 70 percent of the time.

- A person whose identical twin has Alzheimer's disease has a 60 percent chance of developing it, but a person whose fraternal twin has Alzheimer's disease has only a 30 percent chance.

- Identical twins are more alike on measures of extraversion and emotional stability than fraternal twins.

As always, any conclusions need to be evaluated based on the methodology of obtaining them. Systematic research, for example, carries a different weight from that of anecdotes (i.e., stories or reports that aren't scientifically evaluated). Consider the case of the famous set of twins, "The Jim Twins," who were separated at birth and reconnected after thirty-eight years. They weren't systematically studied, but reports show they were very much alike. Both were named Jim (Lewis and Springer). Both liked woodworking, driving their Chevys, watching stock car races, and drinking the same brand of beer. Their voices were nearly identical, and they had similar personalities, intelligence, heart rates, and brain waves. Does this story suggest that shared genes are much more influential than different environments?

Geneticists and other systematic researchers are working to answer this question. Any answer, however, is bound to be incomplete. We know that families, peer groups, and other aspects of our lives influence our attitudes, values, manners, religious beliefs, and political viewpoints. Ask yourself: Would you be the same person if you had been raised in a different family? a different culture? a different continent?

Twin studies offer insights into the nature vs. nurture debate.

Heritability

Research on heritability can help answer questions like those above. The word *heritability* is often confused with the word *inherited,* but the two words have very different meanings. Heritability is a statistic used to determine how much of the variation among members of a group is attributable to genes. In other words, **heritability** is a measure of the degree to which our traits are inherited. The heritability of a trait may vary, depending on the range of populations and the environments studied. Heritability involves comparisons of specific traits among populations, genotypes (genetic makeups), and phenotypes (outward, physical manifestations of characteristics). Fully understanding heritability involves mathematics and analysis that is far beyond this course; you may learn more about this concept in advanced biology or genetics courses.

A simple way to think about this concept is to remember that behaviors themselves are not inherited, but genetic predispositions that may lead to the behavior may be. For example, a person with a predisposition to anger may be more likely to divorce than a person who is not predisposed to become angry during conflicts and can work through problems. Heritability is a way to discuss how these differences play out in a population. As another example, consider that some humans in a population are taller than others. Heritability attempts to identify the extent to which genetics causes a part of the population to be extra tall and the extent to which extra height is a result of the environment.

Genes, then, are part of the story of why we are the way we are but not the whole story. Genes and environments work together like two hands clapping; the genes in any organism must interact with the environment. Interaction is the interplay when the effect of one factor (such as the environment) depends on another factor (such as heredity). Genes point a person in one direction, drawing in particular responses that reinforce the genetic direction. For example, a happy baby draws in adults who respond to the happiness with warmth of their own. This interaction can become a cycle, with the happy baby becoming more outgoing and socially confident and then interacting more with the environment. Environment-gene interaction plays a role in the development of almost any trait or behavior.

Evolutionary Psychology

Evolution is the study of inherited traits over successive generations of a species, and natural selection is the process that governs evolution. As **Charles Darwin** demonstrated, the basic principle of natural selection is that, given a range of possible inherited trait variations, those traits that lead to increased reproduction and survival of the species are most likely to be passed down to generations that follow. The process by which an organism or species becomes better suited for life in its environment is known as **adaptation**, and the specific traits that make the organism or species better suited are known as adaptive traits.

Evolutionary psychology is the study of the evolution of mind and behavior based on principles of natural selection. Evolutionary psychologists ask, How have the principles of adaptation served to create the current range of behaviors and responses that humans have? How are those behaviors helpful for the organism to live within the environment? In general, these scientists agree that "only the strong survive" is a myth—it's the organisms with the most adaptive traits for their environments that survive and reproduce.

The Process of Natural Selection

With every generation, random errors in gene replication lead to changes in a species. These errors are known as **genetic mutations**. Sometimes these mutations lead to the development of a trait that is adaptive for the organism; the organism lives effectively in the environment and passes that trait down to the next generation. If mutations lead to traits or behaviors that are not adaptive, the organisms with those genes may live to pass them on, or—if the adaptations make life difficult—they may die without reproducing.

The evolutionary success of the traits that most humans possess helps explain the similarities of people around the world. Because emotions, drives, and reasoning are similar across many cultures, evolutionary psychologists conclude that they have been adaptive in the past and perhaps are still adaptive now. For example, the nausea of pregnant women, especially after eating bitter or strongly flavored food, provides one example of a universally adaptive response. Bitter tastes often accompany poisonous foods, so developing nausea will increase the likelihood that the woman will spit the poison out. Historically, then, when people lived as hunter-gatherers, women with strong responses to bitter tastes were more likely to survive, but women without strong responses often died, reducing the likelihood that future generations would have a weak response to these flavors.

Human mate preferences provide another example of the impact of natural selection through the lens of evolutionary psychology. Both men and women look for physical signs of a strong and healthy mate, including symmetry in face and body, healthy skin, certain ratios of shoulders to hips, and muscle strength. Some evolutionary psychologists argue that a male's evolutionary goal is to procreate as much as possible; therefore men would seek out many partners. Females have different evolutionary goals, including finding one suitable mate with good genes who can be a good protector. Women, then, are more likely to have fewer partners than men and likely only one at a time.

Some previously adaptive behaviors no longer serve us. For example, eating sweets was once an adaptive behavior. In hunter-gatherer societies, fruits were relatively rare. People ate fruits when they were available and over time developed a taste for sweets. This adaptive behavior was useful especially in periods with little or no food because fruits and other sweets are typically high in calories. These natural sweets were never in such abundance that they could lead to such health problems as diabetes or obesity. However, they are very abundant now, and this taste for sweets has led to the production of processed foods which are associated with health problems today, especially in the United States.

Another simple example of an outdated behavior is the fight-or-flight response. Neanderthals and early humans were wary of the dark and of potentially dangerous noises. Those who responded strongly to these potential dangers were more likely to survive and reproduce, so the trait was passed along to future generations. Those without the trait were more likely to die or not reproduce. In our modern world, people generally do not need that intense level of response, so most of us do not show it. People who do show that intense response to potential dangers are often diagnosed with anxiety disorders.

In early genetics studies, some researchers believed that an individual's genes could change as a result of behavior. For decades, this idea was rejected by the scientific community. Research over the past few decades, however, has shown that how we live our lives can indeed influence whether genes become active or stay inactive—that is, whether they are expressed or not. An individual could change gene expression to adapt to the environment without having to wait generations for a trait to become active through the DNA. The emerging field of study is known as **epigenetics**.

Evolutionary psychologists examine psychological traits, such as memory, perception, and language, always asking what their evolutionary advantage might have been. Consider our ability to infer or interpret emotions of others, discern kin (family) from non kin, identify and prefer healthy mates, and cooperate with others. Which human psychological traits, tendencies, and behaviors are evolved adaptations—that is, the products of natural selection? Our cognitive processes may have been adaptive at one time in our history, but how are they affecting us now? Does our attempt to simplify a complex world contribute to prejudice and war? Evolutionary psychologists hope to help answer these questions.

Criticisms of Evolutionary Psychology

Evolutionary psychology identifies modern traits and looks backward to propose an explanation for why we have them. This type of explanation is sometimes called a hindsight explanation. Hindsight explanations are not testable scientifically, no matter how much intuitive sense they may make.

Critics of the field ask important questions. To what extent does this hindsight view confuse or conflate the impact of genetics and environment on particular behaviors? Not knowing the environments of the past, what details could we be overlooking when reaching tentative conclusions?

Critics also ask about the social and moral implications of the evolutionary psychology perspective. Could evolutionary psychology be used to justify such practices as high-status men mating with a series of young, fertile women? What about cultural differences that seem to work against evolutionary explanations? Evolutionary psychologists recognize these criticisms and continue to develop techniques and research programs to respond to them.

REFLECT ON THE ESSENTIAL QUESTION

Essential Question: *How do the biological fields of neuroanatomy and genetics help to explain the behaviors of an individual?* On separate paper, make a chart like the one below. Use the Key Terms to complete the chart to help answer that question.

Neural Structure	Neural Communication	Behavioral Genetics	Evolutionary Psychology

KEY TERMS

NEURAL STRUCTURE

axon
central nervous system
cranial nerves
dendrites
glial cells
myelin
neurilemma
neurons
peripheral nervous system
soma
spinal cord
synapses
terminal branches
terminal buttons
vesicles

NEURAL COMMUNICATION

acetylcholine (ACh)
action potential
adrenaline
afferent neurons
agonists
all-or-none principle
antagonists
depolarization
dopamine
efferent neurons
electrochemical communication

endorphins
epinephrine
excitatory neurotransmitters
fight-or-flight response
gamma-aminobutyric acid (GABA)
glutamate
inhibitory neurotransmitters
interneurons
long-term potentiation (LTP)
motor neurons
neural firing
neurotransmitters
norepinephrine
receptors
resting potential
reuptake
sensory neurons
serotonin
threshold

BEHAVIORAL GENETICS

behavioral genetics
deoxyribonucleic acid (DNA)
genes
genome
genotype
heritability
phenotype
reciprocal determinism
sensitive period

EVOLUTIONARY PSYCHOLOGY

adaptation
epigenetics
evolutionary psychology
genetic mutations

KEY PEOPLE

Charles Darwin
Konrad Lorenz

1. Which of the following is the correct sequence of parts of a neuron firing?

   (A) Dendrites, soma, axon, vesicles, neurotransmitters

   (B) Synapse, soma, axon, dendrites, neurotransmitters

   (C) Ions, axons, soma, dendrites, synapse

   (D) Nucleus, axon, soma, synapse, dendrites

   (E) Dendrites, soma, axon, synapse, ions

2. The branching fibers of the _____ end in _____ and link with parts of other neurons.

   (A) soma; somatic membranes

   (B) nucleus; nucleic dampers

   (C) dendrite; dendritic arcs

   (D) axon; axon terminals

   (E) synapse; dendritic spines

3. Which of the following is the closest voltage to the threshold for firing inside a nerve cell?

   (A) The electrical charge reaches –10 millivolts

   (B) The electrical charge reaches –50 millivolts

   (C) The electrical charge reaches +100 millivolts

   (D) The electrical charge reaches +10 millivolts

   (E) The electrical charge reaches +110 millivolts

4. If the electrical charge of the neuron changes to about –55 millivolts, the neuron will reach its _____ for firing.

   (A) synaptic potential

   (B) soma

   (C) negative after-potential

   (D) threshold

   (E) fusion level

5. Communication within a neuron is _____, while communication between neurons is _____.
   (A) chemical; electrical
   (B) electrical; mechanical
   (C) electrical; chemical
   (D) mechanical; electrical
   (E) electrical; mechanical

6. The paralyzing effect of poison is caused by its ability to
   (A) block the action of acetylcholine at neuron-muscle synapses
   (B) create an imbalance in the sodium content in the dendrite
   (C) produce an overproduction of acetylcholine in the neural soma
   (D) produce a disintegration at the synapse
   (E) slow cell growth

7. Madison is suffering from an inability to move. She likely has unusually low _____ levels.
   (A) neuropeptide
   (B) endorphin
   (C) epinephrine
   (D) dopamine
   (E) GABA

8. Some peripheral nerves can regenerate after being damaged because of the presence of
   (A) neurilemma
   (B) myelin
   (C) acetylcholine
   (D) none of these, since peripheral nerves cannot regenerate
   (E) dopamine

9. Carlos is under a great deal of stress at work. The brain produces opiate-like neural regulators called _____ to help relieve his stress and pain.
   (A) acetylcholine
   (B) catecholamine
   (C) enkephalins
   (D) dopamine
   (E) glutamate

10. The release of ____ seems to underlie the "runner's high," the effects of placebos, and the occasional euphoria associated with childbirth.

(A) acetylcholine

(B) endorphins

(C) neurilemma

(D) epinephrine

(E) GABA

FREE-RESPONSE QUESTIONS

1. You have just stepped on a nail. Explain how the electrochemical process of neural communication works, both within and between neurons, to respond to that experience. In your response, describe the importance of the following.
   - Resting potential
   - Action potential
   - All-or-none response
   - Threshold
   - Synapse
   - Dendrites
   - Neurotransmitters

2. How might evolutionary psychology explain how genetics and environment interact to create alcoholism? In your explanation, include the role and importance of each of the following factors.
   - DNA
   - Active genes
   - Family environment
   - The mind-altering impact of alcohol
   - Epigenetics

WRITE AS A PSYCHOLOGIST: SUPPORT YOUR ANSWER WITH EXAMPLES

Vivid examples will strengthen your answer, even if they are not necessarily required. For example, in the second free-response question, when you are discussing the family environment, a specific example or two of what such an environment might be like would help clarify your general ideas. For more guidance on answering free-response questions, see pages xxii–xxiii.

UNIT 3: Review

In this unit, you sought answers to the following essential questions about the anatomy of the brain and nervous systems and the role of neurons and genes in influencing behavior.

Chapter 4: How do the parts of the brain and nervous systems work together to process information and control behaviors?

Chapter 5: How do the biological fields of neuroanatomy and genetics help to explain the behaviors of an individual?

Apply what you have learned about the brain and neuroanatomy by answering the free-response question below.

FREE-RESPONSE QUESTION

Dr. Mboda just completed medical school. She took many courses on anatomy and biology and studied hard to serve her future patients to the best of her abilities. One of the first patients Dr. Mboda sees has symptoms of uncontrollable movement in the form of small tremors, trouble remembering new information, and difficulty understanding complex problems.

A) Explain how the following brain structures might play a role in the symptoms the patient is displaying.
   - Cerebellum
   - Frontal lobe
   - Hippocampus
   - Motor cortex

B) Dr. Mboda wants to examine her patient's brain in more detail and has decided to do a brain scan to determine if there is any structural damage. Identify two brain scanning techniques that would be appropriate to determine this patient's problems, and explain why these techniques would be beneficial.

C) Upon further examination, Dr. Mboda determines that the patient may have an imbalance of neurotransmitters. Explain which neurotransmitters may be at the root of the patient's challenges and whether an agonist or an antagonist would most benefit the patient and why. Be sure to explain your reasoning for both of the following.
   - Type of neurotransmitter affected
   - Agonist or antagonist

UNIT 4: Sensation and Perception

Chapter 6 Sensation

Chapter 7 Perception

Unit Overview

The sight of flickering candles, their smoky smell after they've been blown out, the taste of frosting and the sticky feeling after your hand accidentally brushes the cake, the sound of ripping paper as presents are being opened: These are all *sensations*—stimuli that your senses take in. But without a way to make order out of all the stimuli we experience, our worlds would seem chaotic. Fortunately, we do have a way, through perception. *Perception* is what ties the flicker and the smoke and the sweet stickiness and the ripping paper together: birthday party. This unit will explore sensory processes and how our brains integrate sensory input through perception.

Key Topics

- Basic principles of sensory transduction, including absolute threshold, difference threshold, signal detection, and sensory adaptation

- Sensory processes (e.g., hearing, vision, touch, taste, smell, vestibular, kinesthesis, pain), including the specific nature of energy transduction, relevant anatomical structures, and specialized pathways in the brain for each of the senses

- Common sensory disorders (e.g.,visual and hearing impairments)

- General principles of organizing and integrating sensation to promote stable awareness of the external world (e.g., Gestalt principles, depth perception)

- How experience and culture can influence perceptual processes (e.g., perceptual set, context effects)

- The role of top-down processing in producing vulnerability to illusion

- The role of attention in behavior

- Challenges to common beliefs in parapsychological phenomena

- The major historical figures in sensation and perception (e.g., Gustav Fechner, David Hubel, Ernst Weber, Torsten Wiesel)

Source: *AP® Psychology Course and Exam Description*

6

Sensation

"All our knowledge begins with the senses, proceeds then to the understanding, and ends with reason."

—Immanuel Kant

Essential Question: How are stimuli in our environment detected by our five senses and communicated to and processed by our brains?

Daniel Kish was barely a year old when he lost both of his eyes to retinal cancer. Yet, by developing a system of echolocation—the process bats use to "see" in the dark—now as a grown man he is able to detect the presence of a building 1,000 feet away, go mountain biking, and do many other things sighted people can do. He sends out sounds by clicking his tongue and then listens for echoes. Scientists who have studied his brain scans have found that even though he uses the sense of hearing to receive and draw information from the echoes, the part of the brain that is responsible for vision shows activity when he is using echolocation. Other studies confirm that the brain remodels itself after the loss of one sense. This chapter will examine **sensation**, the process by which our brain and nervous system receive input from the environment through our five senses.

Vision

Many animals primarily use smell, sound, or touch to understand their environments. Humans use these senses too, but none as much as vision. For this reason, a very large part of our brain is devoted to processing visual input. We do this through a process called **transduction**, which transforms one form of energy into another. In the case of vision, transduction transforms electromagnetic light waves received by our sense of vision into electrochemical energy our brains can understand.

What Can We See?

Energy moves in waves in an *electromagnetic spectrum*, each type of energy having a different **wavelength**, the distance from one wave peak to the next. The **intensity** of a wave is the amount of its energy measured by amplitude or height. The visible region of the electromagnetic spectrum of energy is known as visible light. White light has a range of different wavelengths. When white light travels through a medium—air, water, or glass, for example—it is refracted (bent). The refraction separates the colors of light into their specific wavelengths. This is why, as a beam of white light passes through a glass prism (which refracts the light), the result is a rainbow of colors. The human eye has millions of **photoreceptor** (light receptor) cells that transduce light energy into electrochemical energy (nerve impulses). **Hue**, the color we experience, comes in the basic colors of red, green, or blue.

Compared to other animals, humans may be seen as having fairly limited vision. Figure 6.1 shows that the band of wavelengths we can see, called the **visible spectrum**, is small, whereas some other animals can see further up or down the spectrum as well. For example, some fish can see *infrared* (IR) light, which can help them navigate murky waters (infrared light waves travel well through mud and dirt). And cats, dogs, cattle, and many other animals can see *ultraviolet* (UV) light, an ability known as having *night vision*.

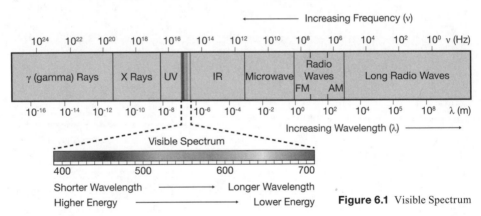

Figure 6.1 Visible Spectrum

Structure of the Eye

Figure 6.2 shows the parts of the eye. Each has a different function in relation to processing light waves. The outer layer is the **cornea**, a transparent, convex structure that covers the front part of the eye. The shape of the cornea bends light toward the center of the eyeball. The **iris**, or colored part of the eye, is a muscle that adjusts by opening and closing (dilating and constricting) in response to the brightness in the environment to let in more or less light. The opening the iris creates is the **pupil**, the black part at the center of eye. Light then passes through the **lens**, a transparent structure behind the pupil that is curved and flexible and changes its curvature to help focus images. Behind the pupil and the iris is a chamber called the **aqueous humor** that is filled with a watery fluid. Light waves then pass through a jelly-like fluid called the **vitreous humor** before hitting a light-sensitive layer at the back of the eye called the **retina**. Before passing through to the retina, the lens flips an image and focuses the inverted image. This focusing process is called **visual accommodation** (not to be confused with accommodation in the theory by Piaget).

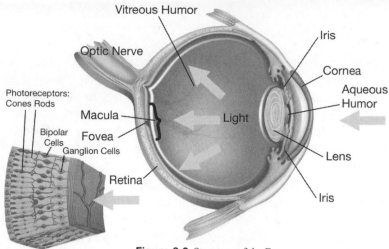

Figure 6.2 Structure of the Eye

The retina contains *photoreceptor cells* which are called rods and cones. The **rods** are photoreceptors that detect black/white/grey and work in very dim light for night vision, and the **cones** are photoreceptors that function only in bright light. Rods and cones are responsible for transforming (or *transducing*) electromagnetic energy into electrochemical energy that the brain can translate. There are more than 120 million rods and 5 million cones in each eye; they can be damaged easily from excessive exposure to light (e.g., staring at a solar eclipse or into the sun directly).

Cones are located in and around the **fovea**, the central point of the retina and a part of the *macula*, which has multiple structures to ensure focused vision. Three types of cones—red, green, and blue—allow us to perceive color. The brain is able to determine the wavelength by how active each of the color cones is. The more active, the more of that color is perceived. If a large enough number of rods and cones fire, then *bipolar cells* are activated. If enough bipolar cells are activated, ganglion cells, which meet at the back of the eye at an *optic disc*, fire. Axons of the ganglion cells comprise the **optic nerves** (the nerves that send signals from the eyes to the brain). Some of the fibers from each optic nerve cross into the opposite side of the brain (the thalamus) at the **optic chiasm**.

Steps in Vision

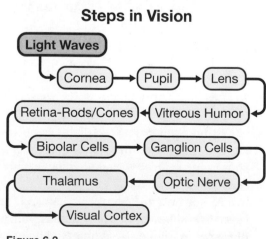

Figure 6.3

From there, the signals travel to the occipital lobe, the primary visual cortex, and the visual association cortex.

Focusing

Each eye has six muscles, one on each side, one on the bottom, one on the top that extends straight back from the eye, and two that extend diagonally. Through the coordination of these muscles, the eyes can look in a variety of directions. There are subtle fluctuations as you try to focus on things closer to your face. To show you how this focusing works, choose a word on this page and stare at it. Do the words to the side, above, and below seem blurred? The reason for the differences is because the word you focus on hits the cones, which are detail oriented, and the words around it hit the rods, which are less oriented to detail and are located on the outer portions of the retina.

Or, if you place your finger at arm's length, then slowly bring it to your nose, your eyes will cross. Some people are born with some of these muscles tighter than they should be, and that condition results in crossed or differently facing eyes in a condition called *strabismus* (misaligned eyes). Other processes and phenomena concerned with how we focus our vision include peripheral vision, blind spots, saccade, and dark adaptation.

Peripheral Vision The eye's ability to see things on the side of our field of vision when looking straight ahead is called **peripheral vision.** Our ability to see things in the periphery is not as good as our ability to see things looking straight-on—objects often seem blurred and their colors hard to discern. Still, many superstar athletes have excellent peripheral vision. For instance, a quarterback can look straight ahead to where he wants to throw a ball but can see in his peripheral vision a player from the opposing team who is approaching to tackle him. So, it appears that we may be able to train our peripheral vision to be stronger. On the other end of the spectrum is *tunnel vision*, the absence of peripheral vision. Imagine looking at the world through a paper towel tube and you'll get an idea of what tunnel vision is like.

Figure 6.4

Blind Spot Since the disc where the ganglion cells meet at the back of the eye is a hole in the retina, there are no photoreceptors there and a **blind spot** is created in your field of vision. This "spot" is literally a place where you cannot see.

To see how the blind spot works, close your left eye and hold the page about 10 inches from your face as you focus your right eye directly on the plus sign in Figure 6.4 above. Slowly adjust the distance from your face until the emoji disappears. You can do the same experiment all around the circle of your blind spot.

Saccade Eyes have a reflexive, rapid movement from side to side called a *saccade*. This small movement keeps different neurons firing and helps fill in the missing information created by the blind spot. Saccades occur during reading, while taking in a scene, and even during certain stages of sleep.

Dark Adaptation One feature our eyes possess is the ability to adapt to quickly darkening conditions such as when we go from daylight into a dark movie theatre. This ability is called **dark adaptation.** In addition to the pupil opening quickly to allow for more light waves to enter the eye, this shift in available light creates increased retinal sensitivity in the rods. *Rhodopsin* is a light-sensitive pigment in the rods that helps the rods deal with low-light conditions. A bleaching of the rods, or overexposure to sunlight, reduces this chemical and results in night blindness, or blindness in low-light conditions. The eyes adapt similarly when going from a dark condition to one with more light. The chemical changes in the retina allow for us to adapt quickly to changes in light as the pupil constricts.

Visual Information Processing

Figure 6.5 summarizes the pathway of visual sensory stimuli to the visual cortex. That is where visual sensory stimuli is interpreted.

Feature Detectors In the visual cortex, thousands of specialized neurons called **feature detectors** react to the strength of visual stimuli, responding to shapes, angles, edges, lines, and movement in our field of vision. Feature detectors in other locations in the brain have specialized functions (color, form, and depth for example). Recent research has found there are even some

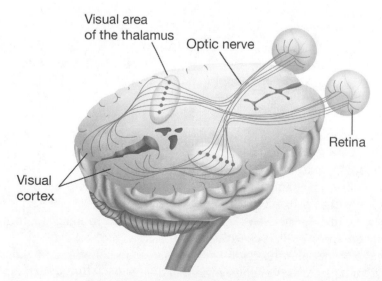

Figure 6.5 Pathway to the Visual Cortex

feature detectors that process faces, smiles, and parts of the body. The brain, both in the visual cortex and other parts, takes all the information it receives from the feature detectors and makes a series of interpretations that allow us to see what we see.

Parallel Processing Different feature detectors can react to visual stimuli simultaneously through **parallel processing**—the ability of the brain to do many things at once. For visual processing, color, motion, shape, and depth are processed simultaneously.

Theories of Color Vision

We can perceive color only within the visible wavelengths of light, ranging from violet to red. There are two different though complementary theories explaining why this is so.

Trichromatic Theory The earliest theory about why we can see color only within the visible spectrum is called the **trichromatic**, or **Young-Helmholtz**, **theory**. The trichromatic theory explains a process that takes place within the eye. It hypothesizes that the three cone types in the retina, each producing only red, green, or blue, work together to let us perceive a range of colors. Blue and red make purple, for example, and red and green make yellow. Black and white are produced by rods.

According to this theory, we see a specific color by comparing responses from the three kinds of cones, each of which is most sensitive to a short, medium, or long wavelength of light. Therefore, the color we see depends upon the mix of strengths of cone types that are firing. Since there are fewer short-wavelength cones (blue), we see red, yellow, and green colors better than blues. When all three cones are equally active, we see white or gray.

Opponent-Process Theory Have you ever wondered why we can't see reddish green or bluish yellow? The second theory, **opponent-process theory**, answers this question by focusing on what happens in the brain rather than in the eye. It postulates three "systems" or opponent channels (red-or-green, blue-or-yellow, black-or-white). The theory states that light waves will excite one color in a pair (red, for example), which will then inhibit (prevent) the excitation in its opposing color (green). The black-white set are achromatic (or without color) and detect luminance (light-dark changes).

A phenomenon known as **afterimage** (a visual sensation that remains after stimulus is removed) helped point in the direction of the opponent-process theory. Staring at one color will fatigue the sensors for that color. If you were to stare long enough at an American-style flag with black and green stripes, a yellow upper left square and black stars then look at a white page background, you will see a fuzzy American flag. This fuzzy perceived image is known as an afterimage, specifically, a negative afterimage.

With the proper photo software, you can take any photograph and create a negative of it. Stare at the center of that and then at a white screen or paper and you will see a version of the original. Another common example of afterimage is when you look into the yellow/white flash of a camera and then see a purple/black spot that follows your eyes around, even when they are shut.

Both the trichromatic and opponent-process theory are correct—they just explain color vision on different levels.

Problems in Vision

Young and old alike may experience problems with *visual acuity* (the sharpness of visual perception). One such problem is *myopia* or nearsightedness, having good near vision but difficulty focusing on things in the distance. Another is *presbyopia*, or farsightedness, being able to see things in the distance well but having difficulty focusing on things that are close by. Glasses or contact lenses can often help correct these impairments. The standard test for visual acuity is called a Snellen Test. When administering the Snellen test, a doctor will ask a patient to read a chart of letters to see what size font the patient can read from a certain distance.

People can develop numerous other problems with their vision. A cornea that is irregularly shaped creates *astigmatism*, which causes blurriness at any distance. Cataracts occur when some of the proteins in the lens break down and create increasing cloudiness in the eye. Surgery can replace the lens and restore vision. *Conjunctivitis* (pink eye) is inflammation of the conjunctiva, the transparent layer that lines the inside of the eyelid and covers the sclera (the white part of the eye). *Glaucoma* damages the optic nerve and destroys vision.

Eyes are made of soft tissue; they can be easily damaged or infected. There are many ways eyes can become irritated, including a scratch on the cornea, an infection from a contact lens, and excessive exposure to UV light. Be sure to use sunglasses that block ultraviolet radiation.

A less common vision deficiency is **color blindness**, the inability to perceive color differences. Color blindness is caused by a lack of short-, medium-, or long-wavelength cones in the fovea. Some people lack two types of cones while others have a low number of all three. Color blindness is a genetic condition caused by a recessive trait on a chromosome and can be diagnosed using the Ishihara Test. You have probably seen examples of the Ishihara Test: a circle filled with dots of various sizes and colors with a number "hidden" within it that people without color blindness can see. The inability to distinguish red from green is the most common deficiency, caused by a sex-linked, recessive trait on the X chromosome. This color vision deficiency occurs in 8 percent of men and 1 percent of women. Total color blindness is rare. Most people will experience only *color weakness*, the inability to distinguish some colors.

Hearing

Audition is the biological process by which our ears process sound waves. If a tree falls in the forest and there is no one around to hear it, does it make a sound? Take a moment and ponder that. Certainly sound waves are created. But the answer depends on how we define the concept of sound. In psychology, in order for something to be a sound, it has to be perceived. So, if no one (or no animal) is around to hear it, a falling tree makes only waves, not sound.

Using specialized brain and body parts, not only are we able to understand sound waves that move through the air, but we also can determine their original source and the source's direction, and we can understand and appreciate sophisticated combinations of sound such as language and music.

Sound Waves

Sound waves are vibrations of molecules that travel through the air. They move much more slowly than light, which explains why you can see lightning but not hear the accompanying thunder until several seconds later. Sound waves are created by vibrating objects such as a plucked guitar string, vocal cords when air passes over them, or one object (e.g., a drum) that has been struck by another (e.g., a drum stick). Sound waves can also be created by forcing air through a chamber, such as a flute, or by releasing a burst of air, such as when air whooshes out of a popped balloon. These waves are characterized by their amplitude, wavelength, and purity.

Amplitude affects the psychological quality of *loudness* (sound pressure or intensity)—how much pressure is being forced through the air. The intensity or power of sound is measured using a scale of *decibels* (dB). Decibels at 120 or higher can cause immediate damage to one's hearing, and one's eardrum will rupture at 150 dB. For each ten-decibel increase, the loudness increases by ten times; that is, 110 dB is ten times louder than 100 dB, and 100 dB is ten times louder than 90 dB.

The wavelength of sound waves affects the **pitch** (or note, *A* through *G* in various octaves). A sound's **frequency** is the number of wavelength cycles in a unit of time (i.e., the number of wavelengths per second). These are measured using

Typical Sound Levels (dBA)

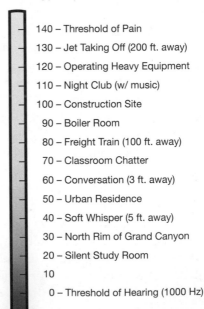

- 140 – Threshold of Pain
- 130 – Jet Taking Off (200 ft. away)
- 120 – Operating Heavy Equipment
- 110 – Night Club (w/ music)
- 100 – Construction Site
- 90 – Boiler Room
- 80 – Freight Train (100 ft. away)
- 70 – Classroom Chatter
- 60 – Conversation (3 ft. away)
- 50 – Urban Residence
- 40 – Soft Whisper (5 ft. away)
- 30 – North Rim of Grand Canyon
- 20 – Silent Study Room
- 10
- 0 – Threshold of Hearing (1000 Hz)

Noise

Figure 6.6 Sound Levels

hertz. Sound is perceivable by humans only in a range from 20 hertz (Hz) to 20,000 Hz. One hertz is one vibration per second; 20 Hz is 20 vibrations per second. Toward each end of the spectrum, sound is more difficult for humans to detect, but some animals are able to hear in these ranges. For example, elephants are able to create *infrasound*, a low, rumbling sound humans cannot perceive. Some researchers assert that infrasound is associated with earthquakes, because the strange way some animals act before an earthquake would suggest they are detecting something that humans are not.

On the other end of the sound spectrum, some animals can hear high-frequency sounds that humans cannot. For example, dogs can hear a dog whistle, but humans cannot, and bats can use high-frequency sounds to navigate in the dark (this is called *echolocation*).

Beyond 20,000 Hz is the *ultrasound* range. Ultrasound machines use sound waves to determine tissue density and blood flow, and navies around the world determine the location of objects under the water using sonar (originally SOund Navigation And Ranging).

The Anatomy of the Ear

As with visual waves, sound waves go through a series of "steps" before they become neural impulses. The funky-shaped outer ear is called the **pinna**. It has a design that allows it to catch sound waves and direct them into the ear canal, also called the **auditory canal**. Next, the waves make the **tympanic membrane** (often called the eardrum) vibrate. This series of vibrations is called *conduction*. You may have noticed your older relatives and friends cupping their ear and turning it toward you in order to hear you better (to "catch" sound better). Many other animals have the ability to move their pinna in the direction of a sound.

Sound waves then travel to the **middle ear** where they vibrate the bones (*auditory ossicles*) of the ear. These typically unbreakable bones are called the **malleus** (hammer), the **incus** (anvil), and **stapes** (stirrup). (You can see in Figure 6.7 how these bones got their nicknames.) These bones concentrate the vibrations of the eardrum on the cochlea's **oval window**.

The **inner ear** begins where the stapes meets the oval window as part of the snail-shaped organ called the **cochlea** (pronounced "coke-lee-uh"). The inner surface of the cochlea (*basilar membrane*) resonates to different sounds in different locations. On the top of this membrane, along with dendrites of auditory nerve fibers, is the organ of Corti which contains *hair cells* (receptor cells). Transduction occurs when these hair cells convert vibrations into nerve impulses and send them to the **auditory nerve**.

From the auditory nerve, the new neural signals travel to the *thalamus* (sensory relay station) via the brain stem and then on to the temporal lobe's *auditory cortex* where your brain perceives and makes sense of what you just heard.

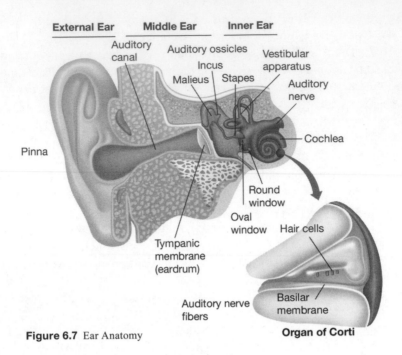

External Ear   Middle Ear   Inner Ear

Figure 6.7 Ear Anatomy

Organ of Corti

Theories of Sound and Hearing

How do we hear certain pitches or tones? The first theory to describe this process was **place theory**, proposed by Hermann von Helmholtz. It says that higher and lower tones excite specific areas of the cochlea along the basilar membrane, each location (place) responding differently to different pitches. As sound waves enter the cochlea, higher-pitched sounds displace the fluid in the inner ear, making the stiffer *cilia*—the microscopic hairs on sensory cells—vibrate in the narrow beginning, whereas the lower frequency sound waves travel down the length of the cochlea and stimulate the softer cilia in the wider rear, or apex, of the cochlea.

A second theory, **frequency theory** suggests that, as a pitch rises, the entire basilar membrane vibrates at that frequency, with nerve impulses that correspond with the frequency of the pitch traveling up the auditory nerve enabling us to perceive pitch in a kind of frequency coding.

Researchers have determined that these two theories are similar to the trichromatic and opponent-processes of vision in that together they can be used to describe how pitch is perceived. Current conclusions show that pitch perception depends on both place *and* frequency coding. Frequency coding is used for sounds under 1000 Hz. For sounds between 1000 and 5000 Hz, a combination of frequency and place along the basilar membrane seems to work. And sounds over 5000 Hz appear to respond to the place along the basilar membrane.

Locating Sound

You are walking across campus and you hear someone call your name. It gets louder, but where is it coming from? Is the voice in front of you? Behind you? Off to one side? To determine the location from which a sound is coming, your ears attend to two things. The first is loudness—the louder the sound, the more likely it is to be closer. The second concerns the timing of when each ear receives the sound. There will be a greater intensity of the sound in the ear closer to the origin because it hears it first and therefore hears a slightly stronger signal. The brain puts all this together to determine the approximate or even exact source of the sound. We are pretty accurate in locating sounds except when they come from directly in front of us, directly behind us, or directly above us. In these cases, the timing and intensity are experienced as the same in each ear, leaving the brain without the detailed information needed to make the judgment.

Problems in Hearing

Conductive hearing loss is a condition in which there is a poor transfer of sounds from the tympanic membrane to the inner ear. Conductive hearing loss is common as people get older, but hearing aids can compensate for the loss.

Nerve deafness is caused by damage to hair cells or the auditory nerve. Hearing aids are ineffective in these cases since no auditory messages can reach the brain. However, people with nerve deafness can receive a **cochlear implant**. An "electrode array" is surgically placed within the cochlea of the affected ear, and an external device is placed behind the pinna to collect and process sounds and transmit the signals to the cochlear implant, which stimulates the auditory nerve. Small children whose hearing problems cannot be solved otherwise often receive cochlear implants.

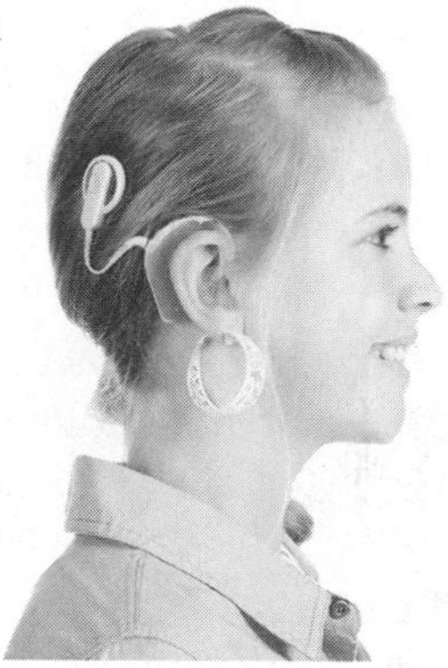

Figure 6.8 Cochlear Implant

Sensorineural hearing loss is caused by damage to the inner ear (the cochlea or the hair cells), the auditory nerve, or auditory processing areas of the brain. The hair cells can be abnormal at birth, or infection or trauma can damage them, but once damaged, they are dead and can no longer function or be replaced.

Roughly 90 percent of sensorineural hearing loss is preventable. This kind of damage was once caused primarily by frequent exposure to excessively loud sounds—from rock concerts, airplane engines, and explosions, for example. However, hearing damage has increased significantly in the past few decades with the invention of earbuds-style headphones that channel intense sound directly down the auditory canal. Normal aging reduces the number of hair cells too. By age sixty-five, 40 percent of hair cells are gone. Their loss leads to a reduction in the ability to perceive higher pitched sounds.

The Science of Psychology: *Neuroplasticity*

You read earlier about Daniel Kish, who lost his vision as an infant and developed echolocation to "see" with his ears. Like Kish, Ben Underwood lost his eyes to cancer early in life, but by age five he began "seeing" with echolocation as well. By the time his friends were riding their bikes and shooting baskets, so was he.

The brains of people without vision, such as Underwood and Kish, who have mastered echolocation hold a key to solving some of the mysteries of sensation and perception, because they demonstrate the ability of the brain to rewire itself and the ability of neurons to perform different functions. Neuroscientists call this ability *neuroplasticity.*

Many experiments have confirmed the hypothesis of *cross-modal recruitment*—the brain's recruitment of neurons associated with another sense after the loss of one sense. For example, temporary disruption of the visual cortex of blind, Braille-proficient subjects with transcranial magnetic stimulation (TMS) led to impaired Braille reading. In other words, when there was disruption to their *visual* cortex, these subjects felt the effects in their *tactile* sensation. Other studies showed that people who lost vision at an early age and had it restored much later demonstrated many difficulties in visual processing, suggesting that their visual processing neurons may have deteriorated after having been recruited to support another sense. PET (positron emission tomography) studies with profoundly deaf people who received a cochlear implant show that those whose auditory cortical areas showed a near-normal metabolism, suggesting they were actively recruited for another sense, had poorer speech performance outcomes because their brains were so well rewired in support of another sense.

Practice: In a small group, consider this scenario: At age two, Ahmal lost his hearing after being too near a blast. With your group, discuss what is likely going on in Ahmal's brain to compensate for that loss. Would the neuroplastic adjustments be an overall gain or loss for Ahmal? How well might he respond to a cochlear implant or other rehabilitative efforts? How might you test your hypotheses? Do research to help you answer these questions. Then develop a presentation answering these questions. Find and use videos and other visuals in your presentation to help explain your points.

The Other Senses

Each of our other senses has its own specialized name. Smell is **olfaction** or the olfactory sense. Taste is **gustation** or the gustatory sense. The skin senses of touch, pain, hot, and cold are the **somesthetic senses**. Balance is the **vestibular sense**, and movement is the **kinesthetic sense**. Smell and taste work together and are known as the **chemical senses** (or chemoreception).

Smell

Smell is the most evocative of the senses. Smells can bring back long-forgotten memories of childhood or people—the smell of your grandmother's house when she was cooking holiday dinner, or the smell of the cologne your father or grandfather wore. You can smell those again and be immediately transported back in time. So how does smell work?

Evocative aromas from a cookout can bring back memories of family times together.

Olfaction begins with receptors in the mucous membrane in the upper nasal cavity. Hundreds of different kinds of receptors may exist. Olfactory nerve fibers respond to gaseous molecules in a "lock and key" system. Each receptor can be triggered when a chemical "key" fits the "lock" of the receptor. Odors are related to the shape of the molecules that create the smells. Each nasal cavity has roughly five million receptors which then send nerve signals through the nerve fibers to the amygdala and then to the hippocampus (where emotions and memory are processed).

Pheromones are airborne chemical signals that animals can perceive. You may have heard the word used in relation to animal mating. When dogs meet, they sniff each other, their hind quarters in particular. Male dogs typically know when a female dog is in heat (ready to mate) because of the pheromones her body gives off. The *vomeronasal organ* in the nose senses pheromones. Since humans have this as well, we are susceptible to the smell of pheromones.

Diane Ackerman in *A Natural History of the Senses* describes the tendency of ancient males to heavily scent themselves: "In a way, strong scents widened their presence, extended their territory . . . mint for the arms, thyme for the knees, cinnamon, rose or palm oil for the jaws and chest, almond oil for the hands and feet, and marjoram for the hair and eyebrows." That book contains hundreds of fascinating examples of people modifying their scents. Manufacturing the right scent is big business. Research departments at perfume and food companies work hard to determine what particular smells, and in what quantity and combination, will produce the best-selling products. And restaurants will often pump out smells in order to draw you in.

Our ability to smell peaks between ages thirty and fifty, and women tend to be able to smell more accurately than men at all ages. After fifty, our sense of smell declines, and we adjust how much perfume or cologne we wear as well as how much spice we put on our food, since our sense of taste decreases with age as well. Without smell, everything becomes bland, because much of what we experience as taste is actually the result of smell.

Taste

If you look closely at your tongue, you will see small bumps on the surface. These are called *papillae*, the taste receptors on the tongue. These receptors absorb the chemical molecules of what we eat and drink. The signals are then routed to the thalamus and then to the cortex. The more papillae we have, the more packed together they are, and the more chemicals that are absorbed, the more intense the taste. Our perception of taste quality appears to be connected to complex patterns of neurons firing.

Gustation, the sense of taste, has five sensations—sweet, salty, sour, bitter, and umami (this is a brothy, meaty, savory flavor, a combination of L-glutamate and sodium). Humans are most sensitive to bitter and least sensitive to sweet. Tastes serve specific survival functions. Sweet foods such as fruit provide a source of energy (glucose). Salty foods help us maintain the sodium that we need for our basic physiology (recall proper brain function requires Na+). Sour helps us perceive a potentially toxic acid, while bitter alerts us to a potential poison. And umami (often found in foods with monosodium glutamate, or MSG), helps us identify food with proteins for growth and tissue repair.

Dr. Linda Bartoshuk has performed extensive research on *supertasters*, people with particularly dense papillae-filled tongues (which appear to be genetic). While non-supertasters may try a food and not have any idea of the levels of sweetness or bitterness in it, supertasters will be able to detect those levels. Supertasters are very picky about the amount of specific spices in their foods because they are much more sensitive to chemicals, like capsaicin in hot peppers. They can taste the smallest changes in flavor and may insist on modifying recipes because of them. At the other end of the spectrum, non-tasters, who make up about the same percentage as supertasters, like spicy foods and tend to crave sweets.

Touch and the Body Senses

The senses of the skin, called the somesthetic senses, allow us to feel light touch, pressure, pain, cold, and warmth. Inside the layers of the skin (the epidermis and dermis), there are several different kinds of cells that sense pressure. They are spread out and perceive constant pressure as force. Multiple receptors respond to fluctuations in temperatures. Signals received by the receptors are sent to the thalamus and then to the corresponding part of the somatosensory cortex at the front of the parietal lobe. The more receptors there are in a given body area, the more brain area there is devoted to it.

Balance, Movement, and Our Bodies in Space

The vestibular system helps us sense our balance, gravity, and the acceleration of our heads. The *otolith organs* are located in the inner ear and are sensitive to movement and acceleration. The *semicircular canals* are three fluid-filled tubes located adjacent to the cochlea and arranged at right angles to one another. Movement of the fluid within each gives the brain a sense of where we are in space and helps us keep our balance.

Kinesthesis is our sense of movement, while **proprioception** is the sense of our body in space. If the receptors (found in our muscles, tendons, and ligaments) have sustained responses, our body perceives muscle force and joint position. If the receptors have short-term (transient) responses, we sense movement, or kinesthesis. The transient receptors allow us to reach out quickly to catch a ball or swat something away from our face. Gymnasts, divers, and dancers have finely developed kinesthetic and proprioceptive senses.

One condition directly related to the vestibular system is *motion sickness,* the feeling of nausea resulting from motion. *Sensory conflict theory* posits that it results from a mismatch between information from vision, the vestibular system, and kinesthesis. When you spin and then stop your body, the fluid in the semicircular canals is still spinning, but your head is not. This mismatch leads to sickness. If you've ever watched dancers or skaters carefully as they do pirouettes, you will notice they quickly move their heads to the same direction while their bodies play catch up. Their heads do not move at the same pace as their bodies in order to reduce the potential for motion sickness or dizziness. Medications, relaxation, and lying down also can help with motion sickness.

Adaptation

Do you have a dog or cat, but your friend does not? Why can your friend smell your pet but you cannot? **Sensory adaptation** occurs when sensory receptors respond less to unchanging stimuli. For example, the longer you are in your house, the more likely you will become "noseblind" (as a popular air freshener commercial says). In other words, you will stop being able to smell the odor of your pet because your receptors are responding less. Another example of sensory adaptation would be feeling cold when you first jump in water but after a time no longer feeling cold because your body has adapted to the temperature.

Sensory habituation (a type of adaptation) is slightly different and occurs in the brain rather than in the body's receptors. Our perceptions of our senses depend on how focused we are on them. For example, you may no longer hear nearby traffic after living in an area for a time. Or you may stop noticing the train going by since it no longer grabs your attention. You are shifting your attention away from the stimulus and onto something else. The stimuli haven't gone away, but you are no longer paying attention to them. However, the feeling you get from a stimulus can come back once you attend to it again.

If you live near an airport, you might become habituated to the sound of the airplanes and stop noticing the takeoffs and landings..

Pain

Pain is experienced through receptors called *nociceptors* and comes in many varieties and intensities that differ in how they are sensed and processed in the brain, body, and spinal cord. *Visceral pain* originates in the internal organs. *Referred pain* is felt on the surface of the body, away from the origin point. And *somatic pain* is sharp, bright, and fast and comes from the skin, joints, muscles, or tendons.

Despite being unpleasant to feel, pain can serve important functions. It can be a good warning system—it demands your attention, makes you focus, and communicates that damage may be occurring to your body. It can also be a good reminder that you have an injury, prompting you to treat an affected area of the body carefully or give it rest. The firing of smaller nerve fibers creates a slower, nagging, aching, widespread pain that serves this purpose.

The **gate-control theory of pain** posits that the more neurons fire in response to a pain stimulus, the more intense the pain. The theory also says that pain messages from different nerve fibers pass through the same neural "gate" in the spinal cord. If the gate is closed by one pain message, other messages may not be able to pass through. For instance, when scratching an itch, messages are stronger for the scratch than the itch, so the scratch messages get through, reducing the message of the itch.

Other factors also influence the degree to which we feel pain. Fear, high levels of anxiety, and memories of pain nearly always increase pain perception. If we expect high levels of pain with our upcoming root canal or wisdom teeth removal, we will likely experience more pain, both immediate and residual. Also, if people around us tend to be in pain, we might experience pain ourselves as we sympathize with others, a phenomenon that demonstrates a psychosocial influence on pain.

If you can learn to regulate a painful stimulus, you have control over it. One way to regulate pain is through distraction. Athletes often play on in a game even though they experience pain. Women in childbirth sometimes meditate or use deep breathing to distract themselves from labor pains.

How we interpret pain stimuli can also affect pain levels. For example, after a strenuous workout, your muscles may feel tired and sore. At the same time, however, beta-endorphins (endogenous opioid peptides) may give you the upbeat feeling known as the runner's high. To which stimulus do you give the most importance? If you interpret your muscular pain as the result of life-affirming activity and focus on the feeling of well-being you experience, your pain levels are likely to go down.

Interactions Among the Senses

As part of a holistic system, your senses almost always experience stimuli together. The sense of taste is heavily influenced by the sense of smell. Try closing your eyes and having someone you trust feed you various foods. You will have a hard time telling apples from raw potato. Steak is similar to a piece of cardboard. Cold coffee will seem the same as a sports drink. Many students over the years have bit into onions thinking they were apples—until they could smell them. Sensory interactions reflect the way your brain assembles stimuli from different sensory systems to make sense of experience.

The **McGurk effect** is an interaction with vision and hearing—an illusion when the auditory component of one sound is paired with the visual component of another sound leading to a third sound. You can find a number of videos on YouTube demonstrating this effect. In one, an actor repeats a sound. When you watch it, you see and think the actor is saying "ba, ba, ba." Then, with your eyes closed, it will sound like "da, da, da." However, with no sound, it will appear that the actor is saying "ga, ga, ga." In reality, the actor is saying, "ga, ga, ga." Our eyes are seeing "ba, ba, ba" but our brains are hearing, "da, da, da." This demonstration vividly shows that the accurate perception of information can involve more than one sensory system—in this case, vision and hearing. This process is called **multimodal perception**. Multimodal perception supports the idea that our senses did not evolve separately but rather in tandem to help create a complex web of perceptions of our world.

REFLECT ON THE ESSENTIAL QUESTION

Essential Question: *How are stimuli in our environment detected by our five senses and communicated to and processed by our brains?* On separate paper, complete a chart like the one below and use it to gather information to help you answer that question. Leave enough room in your chart to sketch pathways in the transduction process.

Senses	How stimuli are detected	How stimuli reach brain	How brain interprets stimuli
Vision			
Audition			
Olfaction			
Gustation			
Somesthetic Senses			
Vestibular Senses			
Kinesthesis			
Proprioception			

KEY TERMS

GENERAL	EYE ANATOMY	nerve deafness	OTHER SENSES
sensation	aqueous humor	pitch	chemical senses
transduction	cones	place theory	gate-control
	cornea	sensorineural	theory of pain
VISION	fovea	hearing loss	gustation
afterimage	iris		kinesthesis
blind spot	lens	EAR ANATOMY	kinesthetic sense
color blindness	optic chiasm	auditory canal	McGurk effect
dark adaptation	optic nerves	auditory nerve	multimodal
feature detectors	pupil	cochlea	perception
hue	retina	cochlear implant	olfaction
intensity	rods	incus	proprioception
opponent-pro-	vitreous humor	inner ear	sensory
cess theory		malleus	adaptation
parallel	HEARING	middle ear	sensory
processing	amplitude	oval window	habituation
peripheral vision	audition	pinna	somesthetic
photoreceptor	conductive	stapes	senses
trichomatic/	hearing loss	tympanic	vestibular sense
Young-	frequency	membrane	
Helmholtz	frequency theory	(eardrum)	
theory			
visible spectrum			
visual accommo-			
dation			
wavelength			

MULTIPLE-CHOICE QUESTIONS

1. Negative afterimages can be explained by which of the following?
   (A) Dichromatic color perception
   (B) Color detection by rods
   (C) The opponent process theory
   (D) The trichromatic theory
   (E) A lack of dark adaptation

2. What is true about the blind spot in each eye?

    (A) It is caused by an excess of iodopsin in the cones.

    (B) It is stimulated by low levels of illumination.

    (C) It exists only in high levels of illumination.

    (D) It occurs where the optic nerve leaves the eye.

    (E) It is caused by an excess of ganglion cells in the retina.

3. The perceived pitch of a tone is mostly determined by its

    (A) complexity

    (B) amplitude

    (C) frequency

    (D) loudness

    (E) timbre

4. In audition, transduction occurs within the

    (A) tympanic membrane

    (B) incus

    (C) stapes

    (D) malleus

    (E) basilar membrane

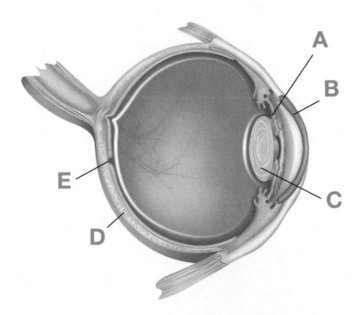

5. In the diagram on page 146, which letter indicates the part of the eye that inverts and bends the light waves?

(A) A

(B) B

(C) C

(D) D

(E) E

6. In the diagram on page 146, which letter indicates the part of the eye that contains the cones and makes color vision possible?

(A) A

(B) B

(C) C

(D) D

(E) E

7. Visual acuity is best in the

(A) lens

(B) iris

(C) cornea

(D) fovea

(E) pupil

8. Photoreceptors relay visual information to the brain through which of the following cells?

(A) Vestibular and dendritic

(B) Bipolar and ganglion

(C) Bipolar and vagus

(D) Ganglion and vestibular

(E) Vestibular and terminal nerves

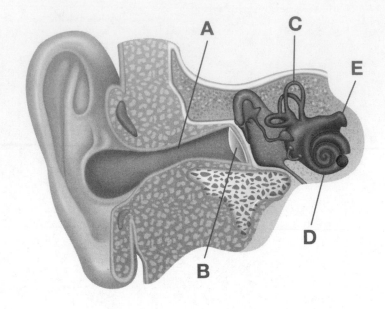

9. In the diagram above, which part of the ear can be ruptured when exposed to explosives?

(A) A

(B) B

(C) C

(D) D

(E) E

10. In the diagram above, which part of the ear is involved with balance rather than hearing?

(A) A

(B) B

(C) C

(D) D

(E) E

1. A number of factors determine how one experiences pain. Explain the variations in how an individual might experience pain. Include the following.
   - The gate-control theory
   - Memories of pain
   - The biology of the brain/body
   - Sociocultural influences
   - Pain control techniques

2. Transduction plays a role in both vision and hearing. Explain the process of transduction in both the ears and the eyes. In doing so, discuss the role of the following.
   - Light waves
   - Retina
   - Optic nerve
   - Sound waves
   - Middle ear
   - Cochlea
   - Basilar membrane
   - Cilia

WRITE AS A PSYCHOLOGIST: USE ACTIVE VOICE

Free-response questions may ask you to explain how some facet of the body or brain produces a certain outcome. You'll find that anatomical parts as well as various theories become the subjects of your answers. Make them the subjects of your sentences as well by using the active voice. When explaining some sensory process, write "The papillae absorb the chemical molecules of what we eat and drink" rather than "Chemical molecules of what we eat and drink are absorbed." The second sentence, which hides the subject in the passive voice, leaves the reader wondering what absorbs the chemical molecules. This approach allows you to add one more bit of information, to show your expertise, and to present a clear response. For more guidance on answering free-response questions, see pages xxii–xxiii.

7

Perception

"There are things known and there are things unknown, and in between are the doors of perception."

—Aldous Huxley

Essential Question: How can two people see or hear the same thing and each have an entirely different interpretation of what was sensed?

In Chapter 6, you read about how the body brings stimuli from the outside world into the brain through the senses. This chapter explores how the brain interprets or makes sense of those stimuli. A key aspect of our human experience, **perception** is the mental process of organizing sensory input into meaningful patterns.

General Properties of Perceptual Systems

Estimates suggest that we process between one and ten million bits of information through our senses every *second*. As you read in Chapter 6, one set of systems takes that external stimuli and converts the energy into neural messages the brain can understand. But our brains still need a way to reduce that huge amount of input into manageable bits. To help with that process, another set of systems selects, analyzes, and condenses information to form patterns or perceptions. These processes are not as straightforward as they may seem though, for what we *sense* is not always what we *perceive*.

Psychophysics

Ernst Weber (1795–1878) was a German physician whose study of sensation using strict experimental techniques brought scientific credibility to psychology. It also cemented his place as a founder in the field of **psychophysics**, the study of the relationship between stimuli and our responses to them. In examining weights, he found that while we can detect differences between the weights of two items, we can not determine the degree of difference. However, the greater the difference in the weights of the items, the easier it was to discriminate between them. He looked for the smallest amount two stimuli had to differ for us to be able to tell them apart—the **difference threshold**, or the **just noticeable difference (JND)**. He found that to be perceived as different, two stimuli must differ by a constant percentage (rather than a constant amount). The amount of change needed to produce a constant JND is a constant **proportion** of the original stimulus intensity. **Gustav Fechner** (1881–1887), who was also studying the relationship between stimuli and sensation, called this finding **Weber's Law** (it is also called Weber-Fechner's law).

For example, if you were to hold a 100 gram weight in one hand, you could not notice the difference between that one and another weight of 101 grams or 102 grams in your other hand. However, with a 103 gram weight, you could detect a difference. This proportion for weight difference detection is three percent. If you were given two different weights, their weights also would need to be three percent different before you could detect the difference no matter what their actual weights are.

Other senses have different proportions. The proportion for determining a difference in line length is 0.01. For musical pitch, there must be at least 0.006 vibrations per second difference before a difference can be detected.

Absolute thresholds are our lowest levels of awareness of faint stimuli with no competing stimuli present. In order to meet the threshold, the stimulus has to be detected at least 50 percent of the time. In vision, the absolute threshold is the equivalent of seeing a candle thirty miles away in a perfectly dark night—any farther than that and we see nothing. In hearing it is the equivalent of registering a watch ticking 20 feet away (but not 20.5 feet). The absolute threshold for smell is the equivalent of a drop of perfume diffused in a three-room apartment; for taste, it is a teaspoon of sugar in a gallon of water. The level for touch is the equivalent of a wing of a fly dropped on your cheek from one centimeter.

Subliminal Perception   Perception of a stimulus below the threshold for conscious recognition is called **subliminal perception**. Various claims have been made that somehow our brains are capable of being influenced by stimuli below the threshold that will make us change our behavior. However, there is currently no research to support claims that subliminal advertising or subliminal therapy can elicit behavior change.

Signal (or Stimulus) Detection Theory The **signal detection theory** is a way to measure how we discern a faint stimulus (signal) that conveys information and separate it from random background stimulation (noise). A key component of this process is separating the important information from the irrelevant information we are sensing all around us. This theory assumes that detection depends partly on a person's experience, expectations, motivation, and alertness. For example, a new parent will be much more sensitive than the average person to the stimulus of a baby's cry.

Processing Incoming Information

If you looked at an unfamiliar object, what would you do first? Would you mentally search for a match with broad patterns or schemas from your experience before you discern the specifics of the object? Or would you start by looking at specific details and then piece them together to form an overall understanding of what you are seeing? Both are methods of filtering the sea of information in which our senses are always swimming.

Top-Down Processing

Top-down processing is an approach to processing information that is guided by our thoughts or higher-level mental processes—we move from the general concept to the specific example. We use top-down processing when we create perceptions from our senses, drawing on our experience and expectations. When we use top-down processing, we look at the whole big picture, try to find patterns in it to make meaning, and then examine the details. We use background knowledge to fill gaps. **Deductive reasoning**—an approach to logical thinking that begins with a general idea, such as an hypothesis, and then develops specific evidence to support or refute it—is an example of top-down processing.

You may have seen examples that demonstrate top-down processing on the Internet. Here is one that shows how our brains rely on experience and context for perceiving meaning in words:

> Aoccdrnig to rscheearch, it deosn't mttaer in waht oredr the ltteers in a wrod are, the olny iprmoatnt tihng is taht the frist and lsat ltteers be at the rghit pclae. The rset can be a toatl mses and you can sitll raed it wouthit porbelm. Tihs is bcuseae the huamn mnid deos not raed ervey lteter by istlef, but the wrod as a wlohe.

Our top-down processing lets us bring past experience to bear on making meaning out of these words with mixed up letters. However, reading this way is clearly a little more difficult than reading a regular passage.

Bottom-Up Processing

Bottom-up processing (or feature analysis) is an information processing approach that starts by noticing individual elements and then zooms out to appreciate the whole picture. **Inductive reasoning**—an approach to logical thinking that begins with specific details or observations and forms broad perceptions or generalizations based on them—is an example of bottom-up processing. In contrast to top-down processing which begins in the mind with previous knowledge, bottom-up processing begins with sensory inputs and works up to mentally organizing them into a whole.

A good example of bottom-up processing is the way people with only rudimentary knowledge of a different language try to understand the meaning of a message. They will try to pick out words they understand and piece the overall message together to get a sense of what is being communicated.

Top-down and bottom-up processing work together. An example of what can happen when they don't work together is the case of a man named John who suffered a stroke and is unable to recognize faces (a condition called *prosopagnosia*). When he looks at himself in the mirror, he can see eyes, glasses, ears, nose, mouth, and jaw, but he has absolutely no idea who he is looking at. John's bottom-up processing allows him to see features, but because of the stroke, his brain can no longer provide the higher-level mental processing needed to achieve the perception of faces.

Feature Detectors

David Hubel (1926–2013) and **Torsten Weisel** (b. 1924) discovered neurons in the visual association cortex that focus specifically on edges, lines, angles, curves, and movements. These are known as **feature detectors.** In experiments with cats, the researchers discovered that some neurons in the cats' brain would fire or respond to certain lines—the researchers called these "simple cells." Other neurons responded to motion and were called "complex cells." The researchers showed how the cat's visual system built an image from simple stimuli by combining them into more complex formats. In humans, feature detectors work much the same way. They help sort the rush of impulses from the optic nerve to the thalamus to the visual cortex, recognizing discrete features and putting them together to gradually create an image in the mind.

Attention

We cannot perceive all sensory stimuli at once, nor would we want to. We would drown in a sea of sensory stimuli, and nothing would make sense. The basic function of perception is to help make sense out of our world. Toward this goal, our brains automatically pay attention to just one thing at a time. When we pay attention to one thing, our brains must ignore all the other stimuli that are occurring at the same time. While we can perform some simple motor skills simultaneously (like the famous walking and chewing gum), for more cognitively complex tasks, we can focus on only one thing at a time. When people try to multitask they use **divided attention**—focusing on two or more tasks or stimuli. Some tasks, such as singing along with music while driving, are possible to perform with divided attention, because one of them—in this case singing—does not require much thought. However, our brains can really only focus well on one thing at a time.

So what do we pay attention to? How does attention work? How much can we pay attention to at once? While our brains are processing upwards of one million to ten million bits of information, we can consciously process only a few dozen at most.

Focused Attention With **focused** or **selective attention**, we home in on one particular stimulus in our environment, such as a cat meowing, birds chirping, muscles tensing in our left leg, the pressure of our watch, or the sound of our own breathing. We can flit from stimulus to stimulus consciously while the brain processes everything else (filtering in relevant information and filtering out irrelevant information).

A classic example of selective attention is called the *cocktail party effect*. When talking at a party, our attention can be drawn away from our own conversation if we hear our own name said by someone across the room. The stimulus of our name immediately demands our attention and produces the effect.

Another demonstration of factors that affect our ability to directly attend to (pay attention to) information is called the *Stroop effect*. When asked to read the words for colors printed in black ink, you can read them more quickly and with fewer errors than if they are presented in incongruent colors—that is, if the word *red*, *blue*, or *green* were presented in non-matching colors. Our brains recognize the color of the word first, which interferes with our ability to decode the word itself, and this interference pattern slows down our ability to read the word aloud. To correctly respond to each incongruent word, the brain has to compete between two processes. It must suppress the easier perceptual process, which is identifying the word, in order to correctly identify the color of the word, which takes longer. This inhibition of the easier perceptual process requires selective attention.

Selective Inattention The expression, "you hear what you want to hear" describes **selective inattention**—the screening out of unwanted stimuli because it causes anxiety or feels threatening or because it is thought to be of no importance. For example, during an all-school assembly, you might tune out the instructions given to the freshmen and sophomores because you are a junior, and the other instructions are not important to you. Or perhaps you are having a wisdom tooth extracted and the dentist tells you the possible side effects of the anaesthesia. You may tune those out because of the anxiety they cause about the procedure.

Inattentional Blindness When our focus is directed at one stimulus, leaving us blind to other stimuli, we are experiencing **inattentional blindness**. Classic research that demonstrates inattentional blindness involved showing subjects a film clip of a group of people tossing around a basketball. Subjects viewing the film were asked to count how many passes were made. The subjects' responses for this task were pretty accurate. But the film clip included other images as well—a woman with an umbrella and even someone in a gorilla suit. Few subjects noticed these. Their attention was fixed on counting the passes and they were blind to other stimuli. Magicians take advantage of inattentional blindness to successfully perform their magic tricks. For instance, because an arc movement of one's hand will distract a person's attention, magicians often use this maneuver to distract you from what the other hand is doing (e.g., picking your pocket or making something "disappear").

Change Blindness One type of inattentional blindness, **change blindness**, is the inability to see changes in our environment when our attention is directed elsewhere. The National Geographic series "Brain Games" has demonstrated this phenomenon multiple times. In one scenario, people were signing up to be on television. While one person went below the desk level to get a pen, a different person appeared back up with the pen. Few people noticed that it was a different person.

Perceptual Adaptation

When you are accustomed to your surroundings, you can easily filter out certain information. The term for this is **perceptual adaptation** —the ability of the body (and brain) to adapt to an environment and filter out distractions.

One kind of adaptation is called **sensory adaptation** (also known as neural adaptation). This occurs when neural or sensory receptors alter or reduce their sensitivity to a continuous or unchanging stimulus. (Recall the example from Chapter 6 of jumping into cold water and adjusting to the temperature.) A second kind of adaptation is called **habituation**, which occurs when we stop having an interest in a stimulus or lack attention to it. For example, people with chronic ringing in the ears (tinnitus) may get so used to it that they stop paying attention to it.

Perceptual Organization

Gestalt is a German word meaning "pattern" or "whole." Gestalt psychologists, such as Kurt Koffka, have emphasized the brain's tendency to integrate pieces of information into meaningful wholes. This perception, or interpretation, of the external world is done in predictable ways, and Gestalt psychologists describe several patterns through which we see the world.

Figure 7.1 The figure and ground are obvious in this photograph.

Figure and Ground

In a **figure-ground** pattern, the figure is what is focused on and the ground is the blurry background which is likely ignored. As a demonstration, hold your finger out in front of you at eye level. Focus on it. Your finger is the figure. But now take your focus and look past the thumb and focus on the other side of the room. That wall/ bookcase/window becomes the figure as your thumb becomes the ground.

Figure 7.2 Faces or Vase?

When you look at the image in Figure 7.2, however, the figure and ground are ambiguous. You might see the white vase as the figure and the black as the ground. Or maybe you see two facing profiles as the figure and the white as the ground. Viewers can see both images, but not at the same time. They need an attentional shift to go back and forth. This classic example of *ambiguous figures* is yet another way our brains can be fooled when examining our external reality.

Grouping

Gestalt psychologists posited that our brains have a tendency to organize stimuli into groups, called **grouping**, in order to process the complexity of the world. The five types of grouping patterns demonstrated in Figure 7.3 are common to everyone. In this figure, we see:

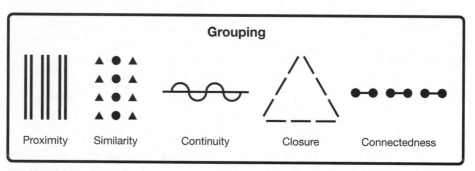

Figure 7.3

- *Proximity*—We see three sets of parallel lines rather than six unrelated lines because of the nearness, or proximity, of the pairs of lines.

- *Similarity*—We note two columns of triangles and a column of circles rather than three columns of shapes because we group similar items.

- *Continuity*—We perceive a horizontal line and a curved line running over and under the line rather than a series of half circles along a common edge because our eyes want to move through one object and continue to another.

- *Closure*—We see a triangle rather than a series of broken lines in the form of what could be an unfinished triangle because we fill in the missing pieces to form a whole.

- *Connectedness*—We see three dumb-bells rather than six circles with sets of connecting lines because we see items connected by a visual element, in this case a line, as more related than similar items that are not related.

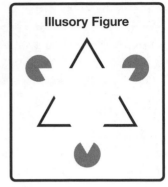

Illusory Figure

Figure 7.4

Using closure, our brains will envision things that are not even there. For example, what do you see in Figure 7.4? Do you see two triangles surrounded by three black dots? Take away the dots and the top triangle disappears. Your brain made that triangle. It does not exist outside of your brain. This is called an *illusory figure*.

Depth Perception

Depth perception is the ability to see the world in three dimensions and know how far away an object is. Depth perception gives us two ways of judging distance. How and at what point in life do we have depth perception?

Researchers Eleanor Gibson and R.D. Walk conducted an experiment to find out if depth perception is inborn. In their experiment, they created a *visual cliff*, a table with one half of the top appearing solid and the other half made of clear Plexiglas. The meeting of the solid side with the clear side created the appearance of the drop-off of a cliff. Babies from six to fourteen months of age were placed on the opaque side of the table and their mothers stood at the other end of the table beyond the "drop-off," encouraging their babies to crawl toward them. The babies experienced increased heart rate moving over the perceived drop-off, indicating they perceived a difference in depth and potential danger.

Figure 7.5 The baby in this photo has to make a decision: Is there a drop-off or is it safe to crawl forward?

Binocular Cues With **binocular cues**, we use both of our eyes in concert to judge depth. One cue is *retinal disparity*—the difference between the images the eyes perceive because of their slightly different perspectives, or angles. We use that to perceive distance based on differences detected between the two. A second cue, called *convergence*, is based on how far inward the eyes need to move when focusing on an object. To demonstrate, take an index finger and hold it as far away from your face as you can. Then slowly bring it closer to your nose. As it gets closer, your eyes begin to cross, or converge onto the same location. The more convergence the eyes must use, the closer the object is to the middle of the face.

Monocular Cues If you were to lose the use of an eye, you would not lose all your depth perception because you would still have **monocular cues**, or depth perception cues that require only one eye. There are several types of monocular cues (six of these are demonstrated in Figure 7.6):

- **Linear perspective** is a depth cue that makes parallel lines appear to converge at a vanishing point on the horizon. The closer the lines are, the greater the distance. As we are standing on railroad tracks while looking down the tracks into the distance, we can see this easily. The further the distance, the closer the sides of the tracks appear to be. Because of Gestalt principles and linear perspective, we perceive that the point at which the black line leading to the mountains in Figure 7.6 is most narrow is the farthest away.

- **Interposition** (sometimes called occlusion) is the partial blocking of one object by another object, leaving the viewer with the perspective that the blocking object is closer. If you see a chair blocking a complete view of a table, you know the chair is closer to you than the table. Interposition in Figure 7.6 leads us to believe that the female on the far left is in front of the man with the dog—closer to us—because her hand blocks his.

- **Relative size** is a depth cue that causes us to perceive something as farther away because it looks smaller than an object in the foreground that we assume is similar in size. In Figure 7.6, we perceive the people in the background as more distant, not smaller, than the man and the woman with the dog because of the relative size cue.

- **Relative height** is a cue that makes objects higher in your field of vision appear farther. If we draw a horizontal line across a picture half way up, our brains assume the top half is more distant and the lower half closer. In Figure 7.6, the mountains above the horizontal line appear to be more distant in part because they are higher in our field of vision.

- **Relative clarity** is a cue that makes clear objects appear closer than blurry or fuzzy objects. The farther something is from us, the less detail it conveys. In Figure 7.6, the blurry female in the center left appears farther away and taller than the female next to her because of relative clarity cues.

- **Light and shadow** play a role in depth perception because nearby objects reflect more light to our eyes than distant objects, so if there are two identical objects, the dimmer one seems farther away. The dimmer male in the center of Figure 7.6 appears farther away and taller than the females to the left. Shadows are also cues, because our brains assume that light comes from above an object, casting a shadow. Shadows help our brains position an object in space and create a 3-D effect. (See Figure 7.7 on the next page.)

- **Texture gradient** combines several monocular cues. Take a look at the floor nearest you. It will likely have some kind of texture—carpet fibers, wood patterns, or tile designs. The closer the object is, the clearer the gradient, or degree of detail. The farther away it is, the smoother and less detailed the texture becomes.

- **Motion parallax** is a monocular cue that makes objects closer to us appear to move faster than those farther away. Imagine sitting in the passenger seat of a car and looking out the window at the pavement. It appears to be moving quite fast. Look up to the side of the road, however, and the objects there appear to be moving slower. Then look out into the distance, and objects will appear to move even more slowly.

Figure 7.6 Monocular Cues and Gestalt Principles

Figure 7.7 is another example of the monocular cue of light and shadow. All the circles are on a flat page, but because our brain is accustomed to a three-dimensional world where light and shadow operate in predictable ways, we see these circles as either divots (concave) or mounds (convex). The circles on the outside have the lightest parts at the bottom of the circle. That is consistent with the light source being at the top. Therefore, our brain perceives the outer circles as being divots. The ten inside circles appear different because the shading is the opposite—the light appears to hit the far/top side

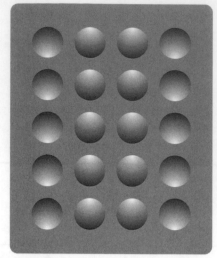

Figure 7.7

and create a shadow on the distant side. We interpret these as mounds.

Motion Perception

The human visual system can process up to 10 to 12 images per second and still perceive the images as individual pictures. The movement of a series of pictures at a rate that suggests motion is called *stroboscopic movement,* also known as the **phi phenomenon**. Motion pictures are a familiar example— old-fashioned film projectors displayed a series of still images at a rate of 24 frames per second. Digital "film" works at 29.95 frames per second, and Blu-ray machines project images at 60 frames per second. Our brains do not perceive these as still images but rather as movement on the screen.

We can also perceive movement in stationary lights because of the pattern of their illumination. Picture a circle made up of eight lights. Only one light is lit at a time. Every time a light in the circle turns off, the light to the right of it turns on, all around the circle. That pattern of briefly lit lights will make it appear that the lights are moving in a circle. You may have seen lights on signs spelling out words that appear to move across the sign. There is no actual movement—the lights are just blinking on and off according to a prearranged pattern.

Relative motion occurs when we ourselves are the moving objects. Objects that are fixed in one place appear to move along with us. When riding in a car (or train, or bus), if you focus on some distant object, the objects beyond that point will appear to move along with you, and objects nearer will appear to move backward. The further away you are from the fixation point, the faster the nearby objects appear to move.

The Science of Psychology: *Virtual Reality in Perception Research*

What if, instead of looking at examples of visual cues in a textbook, you were wearing virtual reality (VR) goggles, called head-mounted displays or HMDs, and could experience the cues in a more naturalistic but highly controlled environment? What might be different in what you could learn about perception?

Since the cost of such devices has been steadily declining, more research facilities are able to afford them, and VR has been applied to many different areas of psychology. (See page 564 for an examination of its use in treating phobias.) In the field of perception, a number of different studies have looked at how perception is affected in a virtual reality environment. For example:

- Participants in VR consistently misjudge distance and location when they try to "reach" for an object. Explanations of this disconnect include the idea that when judging the distance of an object in reality, there are two factors involved: our eyes, which use retinal disparity and convergence as cues, and the object. In VR, however, a third factor is introduced—images on a display. The user is not actually looking at the object but rather at a series of images that are representing the virtual object, so the usual cues are not reliable.

- Researchers have also looked at the phenomenon of change blindness in a virtual environment. Would you expect that participants in a virtual reality environment would be more likely to notice large changes (such as the woman with an umbrella)? They are not. This research on change blindness in a virtual environment has been applied to eyewitness testimony and driving behavior, among other areas.

- One important practical application of VR research focuses on texting and driving. HMDs offer a fully-immersive yet completely safe environment in which researchers can observe selective attention, inattentional blindness, and change blindness as it applies to texting and driving and objectively measure variables such as the effects of texting and response time to changes in the visual environment.

Practice: In small groups, investigate VR research on texting and driving. Create a presentation that shows the empirical data supporting the claim that texting and driving is truly dangerous. If possible, use in your presentation a VR device that includes a texting-while-driving simulation. VR goggles are inexpensive and readily available. ATT® offers a free texting-while-driving VR app called *It Can Wait Driving Simulation*. Other iPhone® and Android® driving simulator apps are also available.

Perceptual Constancy

Perceptual constancy is our ability and need to perceive objects as unchanging even as changes may occur in distance, point of view, and illumination. Our brain makes adjustments and interpretations without our awareness to perceive the objects as the same, because otherwise our world would not make sense.

Color constancy is the perception that the color of an object remains the same even if lighting conditions change. For example, a person can walk in and out of the shade, but our brain does not conclude that the color of the person or the person's clothes has changed.

Size constancy is the tendency for the brain to perceive objects as the same apparent size regardless of their distance from us. When someone walks away from us, the retinal image is shrinking, but we do not think the person is also shrinking. Our brains make this determination automatically in what is called "unconscious inference." Our visual system infers the size of an object using cues from the image.

Shape constancy occurs when our viewing angle changes or an object rotates and we still perceive the object as staying the same shape. For instance, if you look at a computer monitor straight on, it appears to be a rectangle that is wider than it is high. If look at from the side, however, it appears to be a very thin rectangle much taller than it is wide.

Size and shape constancy are dramatically illustrated in the illusion of the *Ames Room* (Figure 7.8). When this specially designed room is viewed through a peephole, it appears that a person in one back corner is tiny and a person in another corner is very large. When they switch positions, the effect reverses itself.

Figure 7.8 The Ames Room, when viewed through a peephole with one eye, appears to be a rectangle with the back corners equally distant from the front, the walls perpendicular to the floor, and the floor flat. Why, then, does the adult woman standing in the back left corner appear shorter than the children in the back right corner? And when they change places, why do their sizes appear to change as they move and their relative heights reverse when they reach the corners?

Ames Room

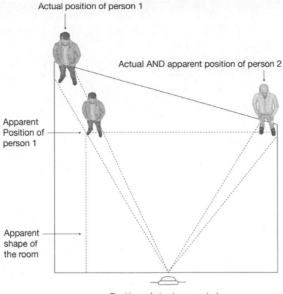

Actual position of person 1

Actual AND apparent position of person 2

Apparent Position of person 1

Apparent shape of the room

Position of viewing peephole

Figure 7.9 In reality, the Ames room is trapezoidal, not rectangular, as this view from above shows. The walls are slanted, the floor inclines toward the front, and the right corner is much closer to the viewer than the left corner. In this illusion, our shape constancy overrides our size constancy—it's easier for us to see the room as the expected rectangle than to see relative heights.

Lightness constancy occurs when our perception of the whiteness, blackness, or grayness of objects remains constant no matter how much the illumination has changed. We perceive lightness based upon the intensity of light reflecting off an object. In other words, we see a constant *proportion* of lightness reflected rather than a total amount. Objects that look black reflect little light, and we will see them reflecting that same proportion of light whether they are outside in bright sunlight or inside in a dim room. White objects reflect the most light, and again we see the same proportion of light reflecting off of white despite varying lighting. A white rose appears white under both sunny skies and cloudy skies.

Optical Illusions

There are many optical illusions, some of which occur in the eyes, some of which occur in the brain. For the purposes of AP Psychology, there are a three with which you should become familiar:

- **Müller-Lyer illusion** In the pair of lines at the top of Figure 7.10, which line is longer? Most people in the Western hemisphere view the lower line as longer because of its extended protrusions. As the bottom part of the figure shows, they are actually the same length. Those who live in homes and buildings with lots of rectangles and lines are more susceptible to this illusion. Research with many non-Western cultures show a lower rate of falling for this illusion.

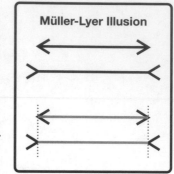

Figure 7.10

- **Ponzo illusion** Most people will judge the top grey line in Figure 7.11 as being wider than the grey line near the bottom of the image. The parallel lines of the "railroad tracks" lead our brains to believe that the top line, in crossing the tracks, is wider than the lower one that does not extend across the tracks.

Figure 7.11

- The **moon illusion** occurs when the moon is near the horizon and appears to be larger than when it is rising or setting in the middle of the sky, away from the horizon. The most easily observed explanation for this illusion is the relative-size cue. When the moon is just above the horizon, everyday objects—trees, mountains, and buildings—give you context for comparison. When at the moon is at its zenith, the sky is wide open and empty, making it look very small. When you look at the moon through a rolled up piece of paper, however, taking away contextual cues, it looks the same size whether it is on the horizon or straight up in the sky.

Perceptual Set

Perceptual set, a top-down mental processing skill, refers to our disposition to perceive one aspect of a thing and not another, and it influences nearly everything we perceive. Look at Figure 7.12. Read it from the top (at the A) and read down. Then read left to right (starting at 12). What is different? The figure in the middle can be perceived as either the letter "B" or the number "13" depending on the context.

Figure 7.12 Perceptual Set

Schemas Mental filters or maps that organize our information about the world are called **schemas**. Schemas have a significant influence on our perceptual sets, and they vary from person to person. For example, in a story that may or may not be true, it is said that the famous television correspondent Walter Cronkite, called "the most trusted man in America" during the 1960s and 1970s when he anchored the evening news, was sailing into port one day and thought the crowd on shore was saying, "Hello, Walter!" repeatedly. They were really saying "Low water!" In his personal schema, he identified himself as a celebrity and therefore imagined the crowd obviously would be saying hello to him. He filtered out the idea that the crowd might be warning him.

Context and Culture Effects Our tendency or bias to perceive some aspects of stimuli and ignore others can be influenced by our expectations, emotions, motivation, and culture, and our moods and circumstances can create some top-down processing errors. For instance, have you ever been in a bad mood and thought someone disrespected you, when objectively the person actually just said something neutral or even positive? Or, if you feel unsafe or out of place in a neighborhood, you may see other people looking at you strangely or threateningly. How much is real and how much is your emotional context affecting your perceptions?

Cultures affect perceptions as well. Not all cultures perceive the same stimuli in the same way. For example, a team of researchers from the Netherlands under the leadership of Asifa Majid and Stephen C. Levinson found that speakers of Persian, Turkish, and Zapotec (indigenous people of Mexico) do not perceive musical pitch as high or low as English and Dutch speakers do—they hear the different sounds as thin or thick.

Culture directs our attention, tells us what is important to notice and what is funny or offensive, and can even shape stereotypes. We change our perceptions to make the stimulus fit what we think it should be. Reality is not reality. Reality is what we think it is, regardless of the objective facts in front of us.

Parapsychology

Because the word *psychology* appears in the words **parapsychology** and *pseudopsychology*, some people mistakenly conclude that these topics are legitimate subfields of psychology. Nothing could be further from the truth. *Pseudo* means "false" or "fake." The fraudulent field of parapsychology claims that people have perceptual powers or abilities outside the realm of existing scientific laws. In popular culture, there are many beliefs about phenomena that have no scientific evidence to support them, such as mind-reading, astrology, and palm reading.

Parapsychology falsely claims the legitimacy of **extrasensory perception**, or **ESP**, perception without specific sensory input. ESP includes *telepathy,* or mind reading; *clairvoyance*, which includes the ability to speak with the dead; and *precognition*, an ability to foretell the future. A related power, *psychokinesis* (from *psyche* meaning "mind" and *kinesis* meaning "movement") is the ability to move objects with one's mind.

All the research indicates that ESP is not possible. As you read in Chapter 2, one characteristic of good science is skepticism, a "show me the evidence" attitude. What scientific evidence is there to support the claim that telepathy or any of the other paranormal claims are real? To date, there is *none*.

REFLECT ON THE ESSENTIAL QUESTION

Essential Question: *How can two people view or hear the same thing and each have an entirely different interpretation of what was sensed?* On separate paper, complete a chart like the one below to gather details to help answer the question. Then write a paragraph or two answering the essential question.

General Properties of Perceptual Systems	Processing Incoming Information	Perceptual Organization

---

KEY TERMS

absolute threshold	habituation	relative motion
binocular cues	inductive reasoning	relative size
bottom-up processing/ feature analysis	interposition	schemas
	light and shadow	selective (focused) attention
change blindness	lightness constancy	
color constancy	linear perspective	selective inattention/ inattentional blindness
deductive reasoning	monocular cues	
depth perception	moon illusion	sensory adaptation
difference threshold/ Weber's Law/just noticeable difference (JND)	motion parallax	shape constancy
	Müller-Lyer illusion	signal detection theory
	parapsychology	size constancy
divided attention	perception	subliminal perception
	perceptual adaptation	texture gradient
extrasensory perception (ESP)	perceptual constancy	top-down processing
feature detectors	perceptual set	
figure-ground	phi phenomenon	*KEY PEOPLE*
focused (selective) attention	Ponzo illusion	David Hubel
	psychophysics	Ernst Weber
Gestalt	relative clarity	Gustav Fechner
grouping	relative height	Torsten Weisel

MULTIPLE-CHOICE QUESTIONS

1. In a photograph, the detail in the bottom part of the picture is much greater than the detail in the top part. This illustrates which monocular cue?

(A) Interposition

(B) Relative brightness

(C) Relative clarity

(D) Texture gradient

(E) Motion parallax

2. The outfielder focuses her eyes on the approaching ball and as it gets closer they move inward. This phenomenon is the binocular cue of

(A) linear perspective

(B) texture gradient

(C) retinal disparity

(D) interposition

(E) convergence

3. The faces or vase figure illustrates the Gestalt organizing principle of

(A) figure-ground

(B) closure

(C) common fate

(D) continuity

(E) proximity

4. You see a friend approaching from the far end of the school courtyard. He looks small, but you assume he is his usual height because of

(A) Weber's law

(B) the phi phenomenon

(C) shape constancy

(D) size constancy

(E) top-down processing

5. An artist paints distant trees closer to the top of the canvas than the flowers near by. The artist is using the distance cue called

(A) linear perspective

(B) light and shadow

(C) continuity

(D) relative size

(E) relative height

6. When you restart your computer, you may see what appears to be a circle with spokes spinning until start-up is complete. This is an example of

(A) retinal disparity

(B) stroboscopic movement

(C) the phi phenomenon

(D) the Ponzo illusion

(E) frequency theory

7. When looking at the book in front of you, you probably perceive it as rectangular rather than trapezoidal as it appears on your retina. This shows the importance of

(A) shape constancy

(B) perceptual adaptation

(C) figure-ground

(D) retinal disparity

(E) the principle of continuity

8. Trisha was watching a scary movie while home alone. She heard a storm rattling the windows and interpreted that as the sound of an intruder trying to break in. Her error was due to the influence of

(A) phi phenomenon

(B) clairvoyance

(C) perceptual adaptation

(D) bottom-up processing

(E) perceptual set

9. A painter who wants to show that one figure is closer to the viewer than another, partially blocked figure standing slightly behind it is using the principle of

(A) relative height

(B) light and shadow

(C) interposition

(D) relative clarity

(E) relative size

10. What conclusion can you draw from the visual cliff experiment about depth perception?

(A) It is inborn.

(B) Children begin to experience it when they are older than fourteen months old.

(C) Children with a strong attachment to their mothers do not seem to display it.

(D) Increased heart rate among babies showed anxiety as they approached the cliff, so they likely perceived the "cliff" and therefore have depth perception.

(E) If babies had depth perception, they would have known there was no real cliff.

1. Perceptions are the interpretations our brains make of sensory stimuli.
   A) Define the following terms.
      • Perceptual set
      • Top-down processing
   B) Explain how perceptual set relates to top-down processing. Cite one example.
   C) Further explain how a) context effects and b) schemas can influence our perceptions. Cite one example using either concept.

2. In a variety of movies, characters such as pirates wear eye patches. Explain how they could still navigate the world despite having vision in only one eye. Do so using the following concepts:
   • Depth perception
   • Retinal disparity
   • Relative height
   • Relative motion
   • Relative size
   • Interposition

UNIT 4: Review

In this unit, you sought answers to the following essential questions about sensation and perception.

Chapter 6: How are stimuli in our environment detected by our five senses and communicated to and processed by our brains?

Chapter 7: How can two people view or hear the same thing and each have an entirely different interpretation of what was sensed?

Apply what you have learned about sensation and perception by answering the free-response question below.

FREE-RESPONSE QUESTION

Tayma is excited to finally see her favorite band in person. She is planning on meeting up with a few friends, but she cannot find them before the concert begins. She enters the crowded facility so that she will not miss any of her favorite songs. Even though she is far away from the stage, she can still see the members of the band and she enjoys the energy from the others at the concert.

A) Explain how the following factors may affect Tayma's experience of the concert using the musicians on the stage and the audience members to frame your responses.

- Relative size
- Just noticeable difference
- Interposition
- Sensory adaptation

B) After Tayma's friends arrive, they see her ahead of them in the crowd and begin calling her name but she does not hear them. Explain how the following areas/factors may hinder Tayma's ability to hear her friends calling her name.

- Lobe of the brain
- Signal detection theory
- Selective attention

UNIT 5: States of Consciousness

Chapter 8 *Sleep, Dreams, Hypnosis, and Drugs*

Unit Overview

How do you know you exist? How are you aware of your surroundings? Do you think your perceptions are shared by everyone else? Are you living in someone else's dream or some sort of Matrix? Philosophers have asked questions like these for thousands of years in their attempts to explain human consciousness.

Key Topics

- Various states of consciousness and their impact on behavior
- Aspects of sleep and dreaming:
  - stages and characteristics of the sleep cycle
  - theories of sleep and dreaming
  - symptoms and treatments of sleep disorders
- Historic and contemporary uses of hypnosis (e.g., pain control, psychotherapy)

- Hypnotic phenomena (e.g., suggestibility, dissociation)
- Major psychoactive drug categories (e.g., depressants, stimulants) and specific drugs, including their psychological and physiological effects
- Drug dependence, addiction, tolerance, and withdrawal
- The major figures in consciousness research (e.g., William James, Sigmund Freud, Ernest Hilgard)

Source: *AP® Psychology Course and Exam Description*

Sleep, Dreams, Hypnosis, and Drugs

*"Now I do not know whether it was then I dreamt I was a butterfly,
or whether I am now a butterfly dreaming I am a man."*

~Chuang Chou

Essential question: How do levels of human consciousness change through our wake/sleep cycle, biological rhythms, hypnosis, and the use of certain drugs?

As you read in Chapter 1, American philosopher and physician **William James** (1842–1910) saw consciousness as a continuous flow, a "stream of consciousness." Influenced by the work of Charles Darwin (1809–1882) and his theory of evolution, James saw the function of consciousness as an evolutionary adaptation to environment that made it possible for humans to thrive and to continue to adapt. James began to explore the nature of consciousness, but his efforts were cut short because he lacked appropriate tools to adequately examine these ideas. Only since brain scanning was introduced in the 1990s have scientists been able to answer questions about human consciousness as it occurs. However, even with this capability, the study of consciousness is still in relative infancy.

Consciousness

Consciousness is our state of awareness of our existence, sensations, thoughts, and environment. We are conscious to the degree that we are aware of what is going on both inside and outside our bodies. Psychologists examine our waking consciousness and compare it to other levels of consciousness, including sleep, hypnosis, and altered states of consciousness achieved through meditation and drug use. Philosophers have continued to examine the nature of consciousness, asking such questions as: "What is the mind? Does the brain create the mind? Does the mind exist independently of the brain? Does the mind—or consciousness— exist beyond death? Does the mind influence the body, the body influence the mind, or are they interdependent?" In philosophy, **dualism** holds the point of view that mind and brain are distinct entities; the mind (nonphysical) is one thing and the brain/body (physical) is another. Neither mind nor brain can be inferred from the existence of the other. **Materialism** proposes that either matter or energy or matter *and* energy are all that can exist. In other words, all phenomena are matter, energy, or the interaction of the two. Materialism asserts that the mind exists as a function of the brain.

As you read this passage, you are conscious of the words on the page and what they mean. You may be less aware of movements like adjusting your glasses, tapping your foot, or wiggling in your seat. If you check the time or begin to focus on how warm the room has become, your awareness may shift and you may suddenly lose track of what you are reading. Although several biological activities—cognitive and physical—may be happening simultaneously in a given moment, your awareness is directed toward only one at a time.

Consciousness has a single focus. We give our attention to one thing at a time, focusing our entire awareness on something within ourselves or in the environment outside ourselves. New things and novel ideas tend to capture our attention. Have you ever noticed a new building or business on your way to school? Is it really new, or has it been there for months and you just never focused on it before? Suppose your family has just purchased a new blue Chevy minivan and now, all of a sudden, you see blue Chevy minivans on every street. Although these vehicles have been popular for a while, having one in your family has clearly shifted your conscious awareness. You can be sure, however, your focus will shift again. Once we are exposed to a stimulus repeatedly, we often begin to ignore it or to become habituated, as you read in Unit 4.

The different levels of consciousness that have been identified and named are described below.

- **Conscious awareness** includes all the sensations, perceptions, memories, and feelings you are aware of at any given moment. Waking consciousness is your normal, alert awareness that includes your working memory.

- The **nonconscious** level includes all the various biological processes that are taking place internally and constantly without your noticing, including heart rate regulation, breathing, digestion, biochemical pathways that control organ functions, and other autonomic responses.

- The **preconscious** level includes stored information about yourself or your environment that you are not currently aware or thinking of but can easily call to mind when asked. At the preconscious level you can easily recall your favorite childhood spot to play or your embarrassment at being locked out of your school when you arrived after the late bell.

- The **subconscious** level includes information you have been exposed to but cannot recall. However, this hidden information or experience can and does influence your behavior. If you have a memory such as the time a dog barked loudly and charged at you at age three, you may not recall your terror overtly, but you are still not likely to buy a product advertised with a barking dog. The influence of this kind of experience is known as the "mere exposure effect" or familiarity principle, which can happen at the conscious level as well. Some psychologists and psychotherapists use subconscious and preconscious interchangeably. The clear distinction between the two is made only at the college level and higher.

- The **unconscious** level is Sigmund Freud territory. He and other psychoanalysts theorized that the unconscious level is an invisible force deep within our minds, a series of unconscious conflicts between competing parts of our personalities that influence our attitudes and actions. Included in the unconscious are the id (life and death instincts, immediate gratification, pleasure-seeking), superego (societal or parental standards that we try to live up to), and ego (self-image and reality-based part of the mind that tries to balance the id and superego).

LEVELS OF HUMAN CONSCIOUSNESS	
Conscious Awareness	All the ideas in your immediate awareness, such as your thoughts, feelings, senses
Nonconscious	Biological functions occurring without your awareness, such as respiration and digestion
Preconscious	Items we can access from long-term memory
Subconscious	Hidden memories that influence behavior despite no clear memory of them: e.g., the mere exposure effect (familiarity principle) (See page 637.)
Unconscious	From the psychoanalytic perspective, hidden memories that influence behavior but can never be known to the conscious mind

Biological Rhythms and Sleep

The human body experiences various **biological rhythms** (see Figure 8.1 on the next page) that are not detected by our conscious awareness. For example, we are not usually aware of normal changes in body temperature, hormone levels, or energy levels during the day. Night owls and early risers do exist, but how do most humans operate in their daily wake/sleep cycle?

Waking and sleep fall into a biological rhythm known as the **circadian rhythm**. Defining the wake/sleep cycle, the circadian rhythm ebbs and flows for roughly twenty-four hours without external cues. **Ultradian rhythm** is another cycle in which changes occur in a shorter time than a day but longer than an hour. Blood circulation, hormonal changes, blinking of the eyes, heart rate, and bowel regulation are all ultradian rhythms. Rhythms that last longer

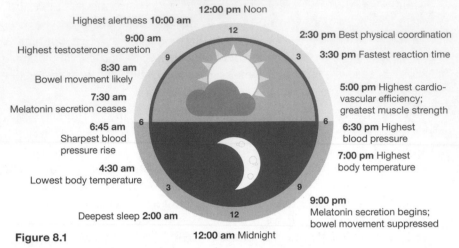

Biological Rhythms

12:00 pm Noon

Highest alertness **10:00 am**

9:00 am
Highest testosterone secretion

8:30 am
Bowel movement likely

7:30 am
Melatonin secretion ceases

6:45 am
Sharpest blood
pressure rise

4:30 am
Lowest body temperature

Deepest sleep **2:00 am**

Figure 8.1

2:30 pm Best physical coordination

3:30 pm Fastest reaction time

5:00 pm Highest cardiovascular efficiency;
greatest muscle strength

6:30 pm Highest
blood pressure

7:00 pm Highest
body temperature

9:00 pm
Melatonin secretion begins;
bowel movement suppressed

12:00 am Midnight

than a day, including the menstruation cycle, seasonal migration of animals, breeding cycles, and the four seasons, are called **infradian rhythms**

Human circadian rhythms are day-long biological patterns. Our cycles are roughly twenty-four hours, with sixteen hours awake and eight hours asleep. Humans are also considered **diurnal** creatures, because we are typically awake during the day. Many other animals are **nocturnal**, meaning that they do most of their foraging and hunting at night and sleep during the day. Bats, lions, tigers, and many rodent species are nocturnal animals (along with fictional vampires). If you've ever had hamsters, gerbils, or rats as pets, you've probably been awakened by the various noises they make at night. The study of these various temporal biological rhythms is called **chronobiology**.

Brain Waves—The Key to Sleep Studies

Learning about the different wave patterns present in each known level of consciousness helps us understand the mind, the brain, and their interactions. **Electroencephalography (EEG)** was introduced in the 1950s to measure electrical currents in the brain, recording them as a visual tracing called an encephalogram. Researchers first began to use this measurement technique to examine the brains of people with epilepsy and, in time, began to focus on evaluating sleep. During a sleep study, electrodes are attached to the scalp to measure the brain's electrical currents during sleep and compare the results to those recorded in waking hours. Since the brain is electrochemical, EEG measures electrical currents produced as brain cells communicate with one another. EEG measures wave patterns in hertz (Hz). Brain waves are categorized by their speed: **delta waves** up to 4 Hz; **theta waves** from 4 Hz to 7 Hz; **alpha waves** from 7 Hz to 12 Hz; and **beta waves** from 15 Hz to 30 Hz.

MEASUREMENT OF ELECTRICAL ACTIVITY IN THE BRAIN			
Types of Waves	Speed (vibrations per second)	What they show	EEG tracings
Delta waves	Up to 4 Hz, slow waves	Deep sleep; stage 3 of NREM	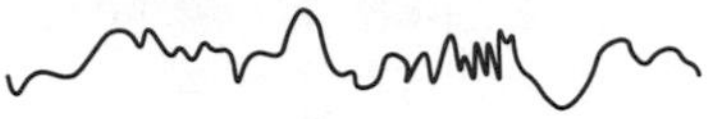
Theta waves	Between 4 and 7 Hz	Stages 1 and 2 of NREM sleep	
Alpha waves	Between 7 and 12 Hz	Relaxed, ready for sleep	
Beta waves	Between 15 and 30 Hz	Awake, alert, anxious	

Figure 8.2

If we are awake, alert, or anxious, we will display beta waves—quick, rapid brain waves. If we are relaxed and possibly ready to fall asleep, we display alpha waves. Our minds wander and are more open to reflection, while our body's internal states begin to slow down. We may even experience hallucinations just before falling asleep. At some point, we shift from being awake to being asleep, but we do not perceive that moment of changeover. An EEG, however, can detect the wave changes in this period of sleep onset.

The Wake/Sleep Cycle

In studies with subjects prevented from exposure to outside light so they had no way to tell the time of day or what day it was, subjects still exhibited twenty-one- to twenty-eight-hour internal clocks, averaging close to the actual twenty-four-hour day. However, for the rest of us, environmental cues signal our brains that it's time to sleep. The first cue is our ability to perceive nighttime. As daylight lessens, the eyes (rods/cones in the cornea) detect lower light levels, and cells in the retina (ganglion cells) communicate directly with the **suprachiasmatic nucleus (SCN)** or "master clock." The SCN resides in the hypothalamus, a gland that also regulates hunger, thirst, body temperature, sex drive, and more. It interprets information taken from the eye and signals the pineal gland to secrete **melatonin**—the sleep hormone—into the bloodstream. Melatonin production increases naturally at night as darkness falls and then decreases during the day when the light returns.

Stages of Sleep Once we are asleep, we enter Stage 1, a non-dreaming stage or **non-REM (NREM) sleep**. (REM stands for Rapid Eye Movement and represents what is known as "dream sleep.") In Stages 1 and 2 of NREM sleep, our brains produce high frequency/low amplitude theta waves. As these waves begin to slow down, progressing into **slow-wave sleep**, the sleep spindles and k-complexes of Stage 2 begin to appear. **Sleep spindles** are slower-paced waves with spikes comparable to the low amplitude theta waves of Stage 1. **Sleep talking** is associated with sleep spindles. **K-complexes** are large, high-voltage waves that often appear in response to such outside stimuli as sounds.

As we move into Stage 3, slow-wave sleep (delta waves) begin to appear more often, hormones are released into the bloodstream for growth in children, our immune system refreshes itself, and sleep is so deep that we cannot be easily awakened and are completely unaware of our environment. This deep stage of sleep is essential for good health. Without such deep sleep, we are at greater risk for illness and may have difficulties with concentration and coordination throughout the day.

REM Sleep During the initial period of slow-wave sleep in Stage 3, our brain waves increase in frequency, taking us back into Stage 2 and then into **Rapid Eye Movement (REM) sleep**. This sleep stage is often called the **paradoxical stage** because brain waves move as if we are awake. Though the brain is active, the brainstem acts to block communication between the cerebral cortex and the motor neurons to produce **REM paralysis** so our bodies remain still during dreams. We do, however, experience muscle twitches. Sleeping dogs moving their legs in running motions are in REM sleep. We also dream while in REM sleep, sometimes vividly, and our heart rate, blood pressure, and breathing rate may become irregular. Males will experience erections and sometimes nocturnal emissions, and females will experience vaginal lubrication. However, dreams with those physical effects are not actually sexual in nature; they are merely a by-product of the sleep process. If we do not experience REM sleep one night, we may make up for it the next with REM rebound—more REM sleep—to help the body recover.

The process of sleeping follows this pattern: sleep onset, Stage 1, Stage 2, Stage 3, Stage 2, REM, and repeat. The pattern occurs three to five times per night of sleep in roughly 90-minute segments (see Figure 8.3). Notice that the amount of Stage 3 sleep declines during the night and REM and Stage 2 increase.

Although researchers do not fully understand all the functions of REM sleep and consider REM to be somewhat mysterious, evidence shows that REM sleep plays a role in memory formation and consolidation, specifically for procedural and emotional memories. This evidence may explain why infants, who are so busy processing new information, sleep sixteen hours a day, half of it REM sleep. The percentage of REM sleep reduces considerably as we age. Research on the precise function of REM sleep continues.

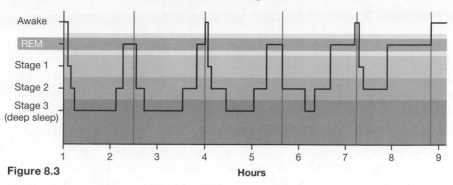

REM Sleep over Eight Hours

Figure 8.3

Hours

Why We Sleep

Many different theories attempt to explain why we sleep, but no single theory holds all the answers. These are just a few of the theories briefly described.

- From an evolutionary perspective, sleep kept us safely "tucked away" during the hours when our vision was limited and predators were active.

- Sleep helps restore health and efficiency. NREM sleep helps restore physiological functions; REM sleep helps restore mental processes. Recent evidence suggests that during sleep, the brain removes neurotoxic waste.

- Sleep helps us consolidate the information of the day and support long-term memory.

- Sleep helps us replay and process stressors from the day through dreaming. (See page 183 for more on dreaming.)

Some of what researchers theorize about why we sleep comes from research into what happens when we are deprived of sleep. Research has shown that **sleep deprivation** contributes to many negative outcomes, including memory impairment and moodiness. Lack of sleep is also associated with overeating and eating unhealthy foods. If lack of sleep becomes habitual over time, we experience what is called a "sleep debt." Chronic sleep deprivation can lead to chronic irritability, lack of motivation, anxiety, an inability to concentrate, reduced vigilance, longer reaction times, distractibility, reduced energy, restlessness, lack of coordination, poor decision-making, increased errors, forgetfulness, and physical symptoms such as high blood pressure, high blood sugar, and obesity. Someone lacking REM sleep may have waking hallucinations as adenosine, a central nervous system neuromodulator, slows down brain activity and causes sleepiness. Staying awake increases adenosine production, which can lead to visual and auditory false sensory signals in people who are genetically susceptible. Some people may find such experiences pleasurable, but perceptions vary from person to person. Some individuals may instead suffer breaks from reality referred to as **sleep-deprivation psychosis**.

Microsleep When our need for sleep is so great that we are exhausted, **microsleep**, a brief shift in brain activity from waking to sleeping brain waves, may occur. During this half-second to thirty seconds, we lose consciousness and are unaware of our surroundings. Symptoms may include nodding of the head, drooping eyelids, constant blinking, having a blank stare, and difficulty concentrating. We are often unaware that microsleep has occurred. We assume we just zoned out for a moment. Microsleeps while driving can be deadly.

Circadian Rhythm Disruption An out-of-sync sleep/wake cycle is called **circadian rhythm disruption. Jet lag**, for example, occurs when you travel across several time zones. Imagine you are traveling from Chicago to London. You leave from Chicago during the day and arrive in London the next morning. You were not able to fall asleep on the plane, remaining awake during your normal "night's sleep," and yet you arrive in London on the same day you left, with a five-hour shift in time zones. Your new 7 a.m. is actually 2 a.m. Chicago time! Adjusting to the time change mentally and physically may take you more than a week. This type of circadian disruption also happens every spring in geographic areas that shift from standard time to "daylight saving time." As time shifts "forward," people need to wake up an hour earlier—a challenge as people adjust their circadian clocks. The somewhat minor disruption in circadian rhythm is even associated with an increase in automobile accidents in the few days after the time change.

Cultural Influences on Sleep Patterns

How many people have been taught the importance of getting a solid eight hours of sleep? With this as a mandate, waking up in the middle of the night and not falling back to sleep right away could cause stress. Historically, the American pioneers did not get an eight-hour block of sleep. They would go to bed, sleep three or four hours, wake up for a couple of hours, then go back to sleep. Albert Einstein, one of the world's greatest thinkers, was known to work around the clock, taking only cat naps for a few hours when he needed it. Eight hours is a culturally developed norm, and people in all parts of the world have their own sleep patterns without necessarily experiencing sleep deprivation.

In our culture today, sleep deprivation may be the result of keeping lights on all night, including lights associated with television, computers, tablets, and cell phones. Although we may want to sleep, we maintain a certain level of alertness for that text signal or that social media message from our friends. We do not unplug and therefore may not sleep—or may not sleep as deeply as the body requires. Be honest. Do you sleep with your phone close? Is the volume up? Is the vibrate on? Do you wake up to respond to messages? If so, you may be making challenging sleep issues even worse.

In our 24/7 world, people work in the evenings and even overnight. Firefighters, police, nurses, doctors, and assembly workers often do shift work, sometimes working three twelve-hour shifts instead of a standard work day of eight hours. Nurses and other hospital personnel who work shifts suffer high rates of sleep deprivation and poor concentration; their lack of attention is even known to reduce the quality of patient care.

Studies show that shift work and sleep deprivation are almost synonymous and are challenging for mind and body. Shift workers are prone to sleeping on the job, making mistakes, and taking frequent sick days. People driving home after evening and night shift work are more likely to fall asleep at the wheel and have auto accidents.

Most people find that changing from working days to working early evenings is easier than changing from working days to working the night shift. Shifting employees back and forth between shifts is disorienting to the employees—and a sure way to encourage them to leave their jobs.

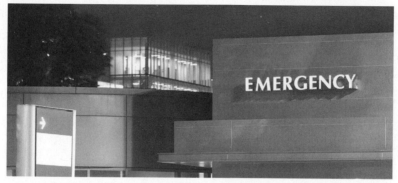

Many medical workers have to work the night shift. Researchers have found that workers who are exposed to intermittent bright lights during their shift, wear sunglasses while driving home, and sleep in a dark room at home can counteract the disruption to their circadian rhythms.

Good Sleep Habits

Good sleep habits emphasize behaviors that promote good health. Guidelines for good sleep habits include the following:

- Stick to a regular sleep schedule, even on weekends. Go to bed and wake up at the same time every day.

- Avoid ingesting stimulants (e.g., caffeine, alcohol, nicotine) for at least six hours before bedtime.

- Avoid taking extended naps during the day. No naps after 3 p.m.

- Reserve your bedroom for only sleeping. Keep your cell phone and other electronics away from your bed—they can interfere with sleep.

- Make sure your sheets are clean, and shower before bed to relax the body.

- Avoid eating large meals before bedtime, and make evening snacks easy to digest (no cheese, meat, or nuts, for example).

- Make sure your room is dark and at a cool temperature (low to upper 60s).

- Develop and follow a relaxation ritual before you attempt to go to sleep.

Sleep Disorders

Have you ever been so excited about an upcoming event that you slept very little the night before? Have you ever been so stressed that you took more than an hour to fall asleep? If so, you are normal. These sleep issues happen to nearly everyone at some time. However, while most of us are inconvenienced by occasional sleep irregularities, we do not experience the degrees of distress that sleep disorders such as the following create.

- **Insomnia**, the inability to fall asleep or stay asleep, can be temporary or chronic. Roughly 10 to 20 percent of the population suffer from insomnia from time to time or chronically. Insomnia can be caused by many factors, including underlying medical or psychiatric conditions, stress, emotional or physical discomfort or pain, use of medications or stimulants, or disruptions to the normal sleep cycle such as shift work.

- **Narcolepsy** is a disorder in which a person suddenly falls into REM sleep during waking hours. These sudden sleep episodes can occur either during periods of excitement or periods of low activity—from laughing or cheering at a ball game, to sitting quietly during a lecture or concert. Some people with narcolepsy also experience cataplexy, the sudden loss of muscle tone. Lack of activity and staying still for long periods can make narcolepsy symptoms worse. The condition occurs because the brain does not produce enough orexin, a neuromodulator that influences wakefulness, arousal, and appetite.

- **Sleep apnea** is a condition in which breathing stops and starts repeatedly during sleep. A person may fall asleep normally but awaken suddenly when breathing stops in order to gasp for breath and resume breathing.

In the most common type of sleep apnea, obstructive sleep apnea, the throat muscles relax and decrease the opening of the esophagus, disrupting normal breathing. People who are overweight and obese are especially susceptible to obstructive sleep apnea because excess fat presses on the airway and cuts off oxygen (a condition called anoxia). Sleep apnea can also be caused by a lack of signals from the brain to the muscles that control breathing, a condition called *complex sleep apnea syndrome*. Diagnosis of sleep apnea is done in a sleep lab using EEG and EMG to measure brain waves and muscle movement. Apnea can be treated with a breathing device that helps force air into the lungs through a mask. While the mask may be uncomfortable at first, most people with sleep apnea readily adjust to the mask because they are eager to get a good night's sleep and avoid exhaustion.

- **Sleepwalking** (somnambulism) occurs in NREM sleep during Stage 3, deep sleep. Contrary to myth, no harm will come to sleepwalkers if you wake them while walking. Simply wake the person if needed and direct him or her gently back to bed. Sleep talking is speaking while asleep and also occurs in NREM sleep.

- **Nightmares** are dreams occurring during REM sleep that have disturbing content. We often recall these dreams well when we wake up. **Night terrors** are extreme episodes that occur in NREM, Stage 3 sleep. They are accompanied by arousal, sweating, agitation, and dilated pupils. Children will often scream and continue being terrified for several minutes until finally relaxing and falling back to sleep. Night terrors usually occur early in the night and can be combined with sleepwalking. Details of the experience are often vague or not remembered at all.

- **REM sleep behavior disorder** is a disorder in which the body is not motionless or "paralyzed" during REM sleep and the person can physically act out dream behavior. Movements can include punching, kicking, jumping from bed, acting out the actions of a violent dream, making noises, talking, laughing, and shouting. People have harmed their partners during episodes, though they are actually asleep.

Theories of Dreaming

Dreams include all images, events, sounds, and other sensations experienced during sleep. We all dream, even if we cannot recall our dreams. For as long as there have been dreamers, there have been people trying to make sense of dreams. Peruse any book store and you'll find books telling you how to interpret your dreams. Some cultures believe that dreams foretell the future or are oracles of prophecy; other cultures view dreams as pathways to other dimensions; and still others see dreams as a path to an inner world.

Dreamcatchers originated with the Ojibwe people. According to legend, "dreamcatchers" represent the Spider Woman, who protected children. The web in the dreamcatcher is thought to filter out bad dreams.

Freud's Theory of Dream Interpretation

Psychologist and physician **Sigmund Freud** (1856–1939) created a fascinating theory of dream interpretation, although it lacks empirical evidence to support it. Freud saw dreams as a method for reaching into the unconscious mind, a part of the mind that influences behavior but that could not be accessed directly. He theorized further that dreams might represent a form of wish-fulfillment by the unconscious mind that people could not deal with while awake. The ego, Freud thought, was busy trying to protect us from open conflict and so could redirect our impulses into a safe place in our dreams. When Freud examined dreams, he saw them as either manifest (obvious and open) or latent (hidden). **Manifest content** is what we recall from the "story line" of our dreams—being chased, flying, riding horses, moving through windows, interacting with people we know or have met only in a dream. To Freud, the manifest content was only symbolic of something deeper within the unconscious and was, perhaps, symbolic of repressed desires (the ego protects the conscious mind with symbols). **Latent content** is what the dream content actually represented. Freud often viewed these symbols as being sexual. (For more on Freud's theories, see pages 414–421 and

Sigmund Freud

552–554.) To Freud, dreams provided a window to the unconscious and were worthy of interpretation by a trained psychoanalyst.

The Activation-Synthesis Theory

The **activation-synthesis theory** of dreams comes from a purely physiological/biological point of view. During sleep, the pons sends signals to the cerebral cortex, creating what we perceive as dreams. Neural activity during REM sleep periodically stimulates the brain. The activation-synthesis theory views dreams as the mind's attempt to make sense of random neural firings in the brain as we sleep. However, the activation-synthesis theory says there is nothing to interpret. Dreams are meaningless.

The Information-Processing Theory

Combining ideas from both Freudian and activation-synthesis theories, the **information-processing theory** explains dreams as the brain's attempts to make sense of what we encounter during the day. Proponents see the main functions of REM dream-filled sleep as problem-solving and information-processing based on what has occurred during the day. Our brains are very active while we sleep, and as we shut down our sensory experiences during sleep, the brain has time to process new data acquired during the day, consolidate memories, and rewire connections between brain cells, a process called "pruning neurons." The information-processing theory adds even more importance to getting sufficient REM sleep. According to this theory, dreams are one way we actively process and analyze information rather than just respond to stimuli.

Hypnosis

You may have seen an old movie in which a hypnotist or performer holds up a pocket watch, lets it swing slowly, and asks another person to concentrate on the watch. The victim surrenders her will to the hypnotist and is then told to do something illegal like rob a bank. Or perhaps you have been to a county fair or a stage show in which a hypnotist makes volunteers from the audience squawk like chickens, flap their arms, run around, or do some other strange behavior. Practitioners of hypnosis have been fighting such mythical depictions of hypnosis for years. Stage hypnotists are known to screen possible collaborators among their audiences to find people who can focus well and who are exhibitionists who like to perform in front of crowds. True hypnotism is a science—the induction of a state of altered consciousness that uses the power of suggestion to change specific mindsets but does not make individuals behave contrary to their core principles.

Modern hypnosis was devised and introduced by Franz Mesmer (1734–1815), from whose name the terms *mesmerism* and *mesmerize* derive. Although trance states and forms of hypnosis have been around for as long as humans, Mesmer brought hypnosis from the realm of magic into the realm of science. While he did not bring it very far, researchers in the fields of medicine and psychiatry began to study hypnosis. In current views, **hypnosis** is an induced **altered state of consciousness** that heightens a person's **suggestibility**—openness to responding to suggestion—without losing his or her sense of self or control. People do under hypnosis only what they would be willing to do in their usual, fully conscious state of mind, nothing more.

In the past, hypnosis was thought to be able to help someone recover repressed memories—overwhelming emotional experiences that are consciously or unconsciously forgotten. However, research has shown that hypnosis is ineffective in memory recovery. Most recovered memories are nothing more than falsely created memories made at the suggestion of an overeager hypnotherapist. Similarly, research shows that age regression therapy—inducing through hypnosis the state of mind of a younger version of the client—is also not a viable technique, lacking empirical support.

In therapeutic hypnosis, a **state of suggestibility** makes someone more able to respond positively to recommendations, such as those for reducing a smoking habit or feeling no pain during a visit to the dentist. Hypnosis is especially effective at reducing pain. Some people have used hypnosis successfully to treat anxiety, depression, gastrointestinal disorders, skin conditions, and many other troublesome conditions, though the positive results may be nothing more than the placebo effect. Therapists can use **post-hypnotic suggestion** to encourage a client to respond to desired outcomes. Hypnosis is a useful tool that trained therapists can use effectively, but it is not appropriate for everyone.

The ability to be hypnotized varies from person to person. The more a person can concentrate or focus, the more likely he or she is to be hypnotizable. Three main theories attempt to explain why.

1. **The social influence theory** emphasizes the human desire to be viewed favorably. The research of psychologist Joseph Spanos (1942–1994) concluded that hypnosis was not an altered state of consciousness at all. People pretending to be hypnotized are indistinguishable from people who are "really" hypnotized. The social influence theory postulates that no special physiological state is acquired during hypnosis, but that individuals with rich fantasy lives, who follow directions well and can focus intensely on one task for a period of time, are those who respond more readily to suggestion. During hypnosis, individuals act out the role expected of them.

2. **Hilgard's divided consciousness**, introduced in the 1950s by **Ernest Hilgard** (1904–2001), proposes that hypnosis creates a *dissociative state*—an altered state of divided consciousness. This **dissociation theory** posits that the hypnotic state divides the higher executive functions of the brain, including a "hidden observer," or second part of the mind, that keeps the mind aware during hypnosis and lets the individual remain open to suggestion. Divided consciousness allows a person to feel no pain (hypnotic analgesia) and to put suggestions into effect.

3. **Hypnotic susceptibility scales** were introduced in the 20th century to measure how easily a person can be hypnotized. The Stanford Hypnotic Susceptibility Scales were developed by Andre Muller Weitzenhoffer (1921–2004) and Ernest Hilgard in 1959 and are still used widely. Used only with individuals, not large groups, the Stanford research instrument assesses a series of twelve motor and cognitive tasks of progressive difficulty, up to and including submerging an arm in an ice bath, to determine how deeply hypnotizable an individual can be. The entire process can be accomplished in less than an hour. Research indicates that while a majority of people can be at least mildly hypnotized, only a minority (around 20–30 percent) can be hypnotized at a deep level.

Psychoactive Drugs

Psychopharmacology is the field of study that examines changes induced by drugs in mood, thinking, and behavior. Synthetic drugs and those derived from natural sources have various effects on the body; they can slow it down or speed it up. Humans have been using consciousness-altering substances for all of human history. Humans are not the only ones to seek alternatives, it seems. Elephants are known to raid fermented alcohol reserves, most cats are attracted to catnip, and reindeer ingest a mind-altering mushroom.

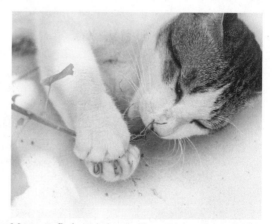

Most cats find catnip irresitable.

 Psychoactive drugs are chemical substances that alter perceptions, mood, or behavior. These chemicals can change consciousness by changing brain chemistry through their specific effects on neurotransmitters. Psychoactive drugs affect nerve synapses and neurotransmitters in three ways: they bind with receptors (**agonists**) on cell surfaces to support an action, block receptor sites (**antagonists**) to suppress an action, or block the reuptake of neurotransmitters by certain neurons. All mind-altering chemicals are able to pass through the **blood-brain barrier**, a semi-permeable membrane that protects the brain from substances that may cause brain injury.

If a chemical is being supplied synthetically by a psychoactive drug, after long-term use the brain then produces less of that specific neurotransmitter, developing a **tolerance** to the drug. The tolerance creates a need for increasing amounts of the drug to experience the same effects the brain would normally produce on its own. The impact of the drug also weakens over time, and increasing doses are required to achieve the same effect a lower dose once provided. These changes are a form of **neuroadaptation**—a process whereby neurons increase or decrease the production of neurotransmitters in response to the chemicals ingested.

Withdrawal—a set of symptoms associated with discontinuing a drug—reverses neuroadaptation. Symptoms may include cravings, tremors, anxiety, depression, seizures, and even death. Withdrawal symptoms vary by drug but can be psychological, physical, or both.

Drugs and the DSM–5

The *Diagnostic and Statistical Manual of Mental Disorders*, 5th edition (DSM-5), the official guide to diagnosis published by the American Psychiatric Association, lists addictions in the substance-abuse and addictions category of disorders, describing substance abuse and addiction as follows:

> "All drugs that are taken in excess have in common direct activation of the brain reward system, which is involved in the reinforcement of behaviors and the production of memories. They produce such an intense activation of the reward system that normal activities may be neglected. Instead of achieving reward system activation through adaptive behaviors, drugs of abuse directly activate the reward pathways. The pharmacological mechanisms by which each class of drugs produces reward are different, but the drugs typically activate the system and produce feelings of pleasure, often referred to as a 'high.' Furthermore, individuals with lower levels of self-control, which may reflect impairments of brain inhibitory mechanisms, may be particularly predisposed to develop substance use disorders, suggesting that the roots of substance use disorders for some persons can be seen in behaviors long before the onset of actual substance use itself."

The brain reward, memory, and motivation structures include the nucleus accumbens, the anterior cingulate cortex, the basal forebrain, and the amygdala. (See page 109 for the dopamine pathways in the brain.) Addictive behaviors replace healthy behaviors and self-care actions. People who are addicted will have altered motivations, making the substance the primary reward rather than other motivations such as relationships, career, and family. Addicts ignore negative memories resulting from addiction as well as positive memories before addiction began. Addicts also lack **impulse control**, the frontal lobe inhibitor to make proper judgments about what to do and not do. The DSM has also applied the idea of addiction to behaviors such as exercise, gambling, or shopping, though this application is still controversial.

Drug Categories

In the substance-abuse category, the DSM includes alcohol, caffeine, cannabis, hallucinogens, inhalants, opioids, sedative-hypnotics, stimulants, and tobacco. The DSM specifies the symptoms, diagnoses, intoxication levels, withdrawal symptoms, and indications for each listed drug.

Depressants and Sedatives These drugs lower neural activity and slow body functioning. All depressants can cause dependence, tolerance, withdrawal, and psychological addiction. Examples include alcohol and barbiturates.

- **Alcohol** slows neural processing and thinking and impairs physical activity. It does so by reducing activity in the prefrontal cortex, the part of the brain responsible for controlling inhibitions and making judgments. Alcohol reduces self-awareness and impairs memory by suppressing the processing of events into long-term memory. Alcohol also impairs REM sleep, further interfering with memory storage. Alcohol also disrupts neurotransmitters. It intensifies the effects of gamma-aminobutyric acid (GABA), an inhibitory neurotransmitter in the brain—hence the characteristic sluggish movements and slurred speech of someone who has had too much to drink. Alcohol also reduces glutamate, an excitatory neurotransmitter, slowing down reactions and impairing judgment. Alcohol affects balance and fine motor coordination, which is why drinking and driving are so dangerous. Alcohol also causes the release of dopamine in the reward system of the nucleus accumbens.

- **Sedatives**, sometimes called **tranquilizers** or hypnotics, are drugs that reduce anxiety or induce sleep, These include barbiturates, drugs that depress the activity of the central nervous system, reducing anxiety while also impairing memory and judgment (e.g. phenobarbital and Seconal®). Sedatives work by making receptor sites more efficient, thereby increasing the efficiency of GABA, inhibiting brain functions, and exerting a calming effect.

- **Benzodiazepines** are anti-anxiety drugs (e.g., Valium® and Xanax®). They work by slowing the central nervous system, leading to muscle relaxation and sedation. They also depress heartbeat and breathing. These depressants can be lethal in overdose, and they interact with other drugs, especially alcohol, impairing memory and judgment.

Opiates **Opiates** are drugs that reduce neurotransmission and temporarily lessen pain and anxiety. They work by reducing GABA, the inhibitory neurotransmitter that normally slows the release of dopamine in the nucleus accumbens. Without that controlled release, the brain releases more dopamine, creating a euphoric feeling.

The body produces natural opiates called endogenous opioid peptides, better known as endorphins. Endorphins regulate reaction to pain and also influence hunger, thirst, mood control, and other processes. Opiates from outside the body, such as opium, morphine, codeine, heroin, and the prescription drug oxycontin, bind to the same receptors as endorphins, essentially as endorphin agonists. With continued use of opiates over time, the brain eventually stops producing dopamine and natural endorphins. When dopamine production stops, people may experience a condition called **anhedonia**, the inability to feel pleasure physically.

All opiates can result in dependence, tolerance, withdrawal, physiological and psychological addiction. The rise of heroin addiction in suburbia is associated with the rise of prescription drug abuse. When people can no longer get prescriptions from their doctors, they often turn to street opioids and can become addicted to heroin.

Stimulants Caffeine, nicotine, cocaine, and amphetamines are all **stimulants**—drugs that speed up the body's functions. Stimulants provide users with a sense of increased energy, mental alertness, and forced wakefulness. All stimulants can cause dependence, tolerance, withdrawal, and psychological addiction as well as irreversible changes in mood.

- **Caffeine** is the most used drug in the world. It affects *adenosine,* a central nervous system neuromodulator that has receptors to slow a person down and induce sleepiness. Caffeine acts as an adenosine-receptor antagonist. That is, caffeine slows down the impact of adenosine.

- **Nicotine** imitates acetylcholine by attaching to a type of acetylcholine receptor (AChR) called a nicotinic receptor. These receptors connect to the nucleus accumbens, the reward center in the brain, and increase dopamine, making a smoker feel good. Though nicotine is the addictive substance, tar in tobacco is cancer-causing (carcinogenic), compounding the health risks of smoking.

- **Cocaine** is an illegal substance that blocks the reuptake of neurotransmitters such as dopamine, serotonin, and norepinephrine. Rather than being reabsorbed by the sending neuron, the chemicals stay in the synapse, acting as an agonist and increasing their effects on the next neuron. This interaction creates dopamine dependency, boosting feelings of confidence with serotonin and generating more energy with epinephrine. The result is an immediate rush—and an eventual crash.

- **Amphetamines** are drugs used to increase wakefulness and enhance cognitive performance. Prescribed as racemic amphetamine (trade name, Adderal®), amphetamine is used to treat ADHD, narcolepsy, and weight gain. Amphetamine works by increasing the concentration of dopamine in brain synapses, which increases metabolism and mental clarity and creates wakefulness. Amphetamine has a high potential for abuse and dependence. With its euphoria-inducing properties, racemic amphetamine (Adderal) has become a relatively cheap addictive substance. When used properly, it reduces symptoms of the disorders for which it is prescribed. However, it is often abused by college students and other individuals who need to stay awake for hours beyond normal sleep time. High doses can cause an irregular heartbeat, anxiety, and even psychosis with delusions and paranoia.

- **Methamphetamine** is an illegal substance, a "super" stimulant used mainly as a recreational drug and not prescribed medically. While it is chemically similar to amphetamine, its differences are significant. Unlike amphetamine, methamphetamine is methylated twice, making it faster acting, more potent, and more dangerous. Although the street drugs "meth" and "crystal meth" are chemically similar to prescribed amphetamine, their effects can be more extreme. One specific methamphetamine (MDMA), nicknamed "Ecstasy," was used originally in therapy sessions in the 1960s but became a street drug in the 1980s at raves, music festivals, and concerts. Feelings of euphoria, an increased sensitivity to light and touch, and reduced inhibitions are produced as MDMA increases serotonin levels released into synapses of the brain and blocks reabsorption. Increased norepinephrine increases energy while increased dopamine creates euphoria. The dehydrating effect of this drug is exacerbated by an increase in body heat, made worse during dancing. This, in turn, increases blood pressure and may result in death. MDMA also suppresses the immune system, impairs memory, and disrupts sleep. Long-term use reduces serotonin production and may lead to depression.

Drugs that cause hallucinations and distort perceptions of reality are known as **hallucinogens (psychedelics)**. Primary examples are **LSD** (lysergic acid diethylamide) and marijuana. MDMA/Ecstasy is sometimes considered a hallucinogenic drug as well as a stimulant.

- LSD effects vary from person to person, influenced by context and environmental factors, but common experiences include hallucinations (visual, auditory, and tactile). Many users have had a "near death" type of experience related to oxygen deprivation. LSD can cause physiological dependence/tolerance and psychological dependence.

- **Marijuana**, or cannabis, refers to the leaves, stems, resin, and flowers from the hemp plant that, when smoked, lower inhibitions and produce feelings of relaxation and mild euphoria. THC (delta-9-tetrahydrocannabinol) is the active ingredient. The sensations of mild euphoria, relaxation, and increased auditory and visual perceptions are products of cannabinoid receptors in the brain. The neurotransmitter anandamide, called the "bliss molecule," binds to the THC receptors. Anandamide also appears to be involved in regulating mood, memory, appetite, pain, cognition, and emotions. When cannabis is ingested, THC can interfere with all of these functions. Chronic cannabinoid use also disrupts memory function, lowers attention, and impairs learning ability. In addition, lung damage can result from inhalation of the smoke. Marijuana can cause physiological dependence/tolerance and psychological dependence.

The Roots of Substance Abuse

Psychological dependence occurs when drugs that reduce stress become an increasingly important part of a user's life, often as "self-medication" to relieve negative emotions. Drug addiction or abuse of any substance is a brain disorder, and medical and/or psychiatric treatment is needed for those who abuse drugs.

Why do people abuse drugs? While there may be as many reasons for taking drugs as there are drug users, several sociocultural, psychological, and biological factors play a role in drug use and abuse.

Sociocultural factors, especially for teens, include the effect of drugs on friendships and other relationships. Drugs and alcohol lower inhibitions, so they might help people overcome shyness and make friends more easily. If their friends are taking drugs and drugs are readily available in their neighborhood, young people might become drug users to feel a sense of belonging and fitting in. Rebelling against parental and societal norms may be another sociocultural factor in taking drugs. Also, teens encounter so many of life's challenging situations for the first time—relationships, deaths of friends and family members, dysfunctional families, bullying—that they may experience significant stress and adopt avoidance behaviors, including drug use, to cope.

Psychological influences abound. Feeling a lacking of purpose in life, a relatively common experience in teens as they figure out who they are, can lead to experimentation. The prefrontal cortex, which controls impulsivity and evaluates consequences, is not fully developed in teenagers, perhaps explaining why teens tend to take more risks than older people, especially with drugs. Those with a sensation-seeking personality may take risks even beyond those of the average teen. Adrenaline junkies often like to do exciting things—driving at high speeds, skydiving, spending time in dangerous situations, or taking drugs—to feel more alive. Some people with untreated mental illnesses may self-medicate, using illicit drugs to treat the pain from their psychological disorder, especially anxiety and depression.

Finally, brain biology may be involved in addiction, since genes influence neurotransmitter production in our brains and endocrine system. Some people are born with genetics that, in certain environmental conditions, make initial experiences with drugs especially pleasant. People with those same gene combinations, however, may never become users, let alone addicts, because they never have the "right circumstances" in which to begin drug use. Some people can be mild to moderate users of a drug while others become addicted after the first use. Our brain biology can make us more susceptible to addiction, but genetics alone cannot explain it.

The Science of Psychology: *Rat Park—A Study of Addiction*

Imagine for a moment that you are a laboratory rat. What kind of life do you imagine? Are you bored, scared, lonely? What would it take to have a happy life as a rat? Researcher Bruce Alexander conducted an experiment in the late 1970s using laboratory rats to explore the nature of addiction and how it might worsen in isolation, or, in contrast, how it might wane with social connectedness in what he imagined would be an ideal environment for rats. In the experiment, one group of rats was caged in isolation. Another group was allowed free access to a large area—"Rat Park"—with other rats, stimulating toys, and the freedom to interact sexually with other rats. Both groups were given two sources of water: one filled with plain water, and one laced with morphine. The experiment's results showed that most of the rats in isolation became addicted to the drugged water and chose it over plain water, relentlessly drinking the drugged water until they died. The rats in Rat Park, with a positive, low-stress environment with social connections, drank less than a quarter of the drugged water the isolated rats drank. None of the socially connected rats died.

As promising as the results seemed to be for an understanding of addiction, the study lost funding after a few years because of difficulty in replicating the results. In addition to the problems with replication, this experiment, like all animal experiments, raises questions about the extent to which animal studies apply to the science of human behavior.

Practice: Working in teams of three or four students, research studies in human addiction and determine what methodologies are used. Choose a specific drug that your team would like to study and, based on what you

learned in your research, develop a proposal for an experiment in which the effects of that drug and the factors that contribute to addiction can be studied. In your proposal, consider methodology, experimental ethics, and what type of study might yield the best results.

REFLECT ON THE ESSENTIAL QUESTION

Essential Question: *How do levels of human consciousness change through our wake/sleep cycle, biological rhythms, hypnosis, and the use of certain drugs?* On separate paper, complete a chart like the one below to gather details to help answer that question.

Biological Rhythms	Dreaming	Hypnosis	Psychoactive Drugs

KEY TERMS			KEY PEOPLE
CONSCIOUSNESS AND SLEEP	microsleep	*DRUG CATEGORIES AND EFFECTS*	Sigmund Freud
activation-synthesis dream theory	narcolepsy		William James
	night terrors		Ernest Hilgard
altered state of consciousness	nightmare	alcohol	
	nocturnal	agonists	
alpha waves	nonconscious	amphetamines	
beta waves	NREM sleep	antagonists	
anhedonia	paradoxical stage	benzodiazepines	
biological rhythm	post-hypnotic suggestion	caffeine	
chronobiology		cocaine	
circadian rhythm disruption	preconscious	depressants	
	psychopharmacology	drug tolerance	
conscious awareness	rapid eye movement (REM)	hallucinogens/ psychedelics	
consciousness		impulse control	
delta waves	REM paralysis	LSD (lysergic acid diethylamide)	
disinhibitor	REM sleep		
dissociation theory	REM sleep behavior disorder	marijuana	
electroencephalography (EEG)		methamphetamine	
	sleep apnea	nicotine	
diurnal	sleep deprivation	neuroadaptation	
dissociative state	sleep spindles	opiates	
dreams	sleep stages	psychoactive drugs	
dualism	sleep talking		
hypnosis	sleepwalking	psychological dependence	
hypnotic susceptibility	sleep-deprivation psychosis	sedatives	
information-processing dream theory	slow wave sleep	stimulants	
	social influence theory of hypnosis	tolerance	
		tranquilizers	
infradian rhythms	state of suggestibility	withdrawal symptoms	
jet lag			
k-complex	subconscious		
insomnia	suggestibility		
latent content	suprachiasmatic nucleus (SCN)		
manifest content	theta waves		
materialism	ultradian rhythm		
melatonin	waking consciousness		

1. Which of the following is true regarding REM sleep in healthy adults?

    (A) It involves a decrease in blood pressure and heart rate.

    (B) It occurs only in the first half of a person's sleep cycle.

    (C) It alternates with NREM sleep in thirty-minute cycles.

    (D) It correlates with an increase in muscle tone.

    (E) It correlates with dreaming.

2. An office worker is concerned about constant sleepiness. Her doctor refers her to a sleep clinic, where they discover her sleep is interrupted by gasping for breath, waking up, and falling back to sleep dozens of times each night. Her doctor would likely diagnose her with

    (A) sleep paralysis

    (B) REM behavior disorder

    (C) narcolepsy

    (D) night terrors

    (E) sleep apnea

3. Maritza is able to be hypnotized easily. She is able to place her arm in a bucket of ice water without showing any signs of pain or discomfort. When asked to give a signal if some part of her is aware of the pain, she raises her hand. Which of the following is a theory that best explains Maritza's behavior?

    (A) Dissociation

    (B) Age regression

    (C) Social influence

    (D) Role

    (E) State

4. Which of the following most accurately characterizes the role of the suprachiasmatic nucleus in the regulation of sleep?

    (A) It responds to visual cues related to sleeping and waking.

    (B) It monitors levels of adenosine in the brain.

    (C) It acts with the endocrine system to control hunger and satiety.

    (D) It acts with the eyes and the pineal gland to regulate circadian rhythms.

    (E) It inhibits the release of melatonin.

5. A person who drinks alcohol daily finds he needs to keep increasing his alcohol intake to get the same pleasure. He is experiencing
   (A) symptoms of withdrawal
   (B) state-dependent learning
   (C) delirium tremens
   (D) alcohol tolerance
   (E) fetal alcohol syndrome

6. Whether a person can be hypnotized or not depends mainly on
   (A) the skill of the hypnotist
   (B) the willingness of the person to be hypnotized
   (C) the intelligence and logical reasoning abilities of the person to be hypnotized
   (D) how well the person and hypnotist can fake the "hypnosis"
   (E) the presence of a psychological disorder

7. Mona has been abusing cocaine and now suffers from an inability to feel pleasure. This condition is called
   (A) hypomania
   (B) anhedonia
   (C) affective neurosis
   (D) cyclothymia
   (E) orexin

8. Paradoxical sleep is to slow-wave sleep as _____ sleep is to _____ sleep.
   (A) REM; Stage 3
   (B) REM; Stage 1
   (C) Stage 1; REM
   (D) REM; Stage 2
   (E) Stage 2; REM

9. Obesity is a risk factor for developing which of the following sleep disorders?
   (A) Sleep talking
   (B) Sleepwalking
   (C) Night terrors
   (D) Insomnia
   (E) Sleep apnea

10. While Emily was hypnotized, her therapist recommended that she eat a specific and healthy diet over the next week. The therapist was making use of

(A) age regression

(B) post-hypnotic suggestion

(C) paradoxical sleep

(D) post-hypnotic amnesia

(E) psychoanalytic approach

FREE-RESPONSE QUESTIONS

1. David is a 6'3", 320-pound middle-aged man who feels tired all the time and suffers from a variety of issues, including sleep difficulties, irritability, memory issues, and depression. Use each term below to explain why David might be having those issues.
   - Sleep deprivation (sleep debt)
   - Stage 3 sleep
   - REM sleep
   - Sleep apnea
   - Suprachiasmatic nucleus
   - Alcohol

2. Explain why drug abuse is such a common problem. Why are adolescents more susceptible to drug use? In your explanation, include the following concepts.
   - Genetics
   - Neurotransmitters
   - Major stressors
   - Brain development
   - Sociocultural factors

WRITE AS A PSYCHOLOGIST: ESSAY VS. FREE-RESPONSE

Free-response questions do not call for an essay answer. An essay has an introduction, thesis statement, supporting paragraphs, transitions for coherence and flow, and a conclusion. The answer to a free-response question, in contrast, should not restate the question or try to work it into an introduction, and it should not have the structure of a full essay. For more guidance in answering free-response questions, see pages xxii–xxiii..

UNIT 5: Review

In this unit, you sought answers to this essential question about states of consciousness.

Chapter 8: How do levels of human consciousness change through our wake/sleep cycle, biological rhythms, hypnosis, and the use of certain drugs?

Apply what you have learned about consciousness by answering the free-response question below.

FREE-RESPONSE QUESTION

Patricia is forty-three years old. Her husband complains that she tosses and turns all night long. She is irritable during the day because she never feels like she has had enough sleep, and she has little patience for her children or coworkers.

A) Explain how the following might relate to Patricia's situation.
- What sleep disorder is Patricia likely experiencing?
- What are the symptoms of this disorder?
- What type of brain waves is Patricia likely missing out on because of the disorder?
- How can this disorder be treated?

B) Because of Patricia's experiences with this sleep disorder, she is interested in reading about and studying sleep and dreams. In order to help Patricia understand these issues better, address the following.
- Assuming an eight-hour sleep cycle (without any disruptions), describe how the time spent in different stages changes as the sleep cycle continues.
- Explain to Patricia how the activation-synthesis theory explains why we dream.

C) What area of the brain is responsible for sleep and dreaming?

D) If a researcher was interested in conducting a case study on Patricia because of her illness, what is at least one ethical consideration the researcher would have to consider?

UNIT 6: Learning

Unit Overview

For psychologists, learning is not just studying for exams or finding out how to mix recorded music to create mash-ups. Psychologists view learning as producing a permanent change in behavior. For example, if you touch a hot stove in childhood, you will likely remember the experience, and the memory will persist into adulthood, affecting behavior—you won't do it again!

Some evidence of learning is also required to indicate a permanent change. Teachers typically use quizzes, tests, papers, projects, and more to determine how well you have mastered, or learned, specific content. Learning a skill set requires that you practice—perform certain tasks over and over again until the skills are acquired. Learning, then, is inferred from a change in behavior or performance.

The two chapters in this unit will examine learning by association, by consequence, and by observation and will review the biological and cognitive factors involved in learning.

Key Topics

- General differences between principles of classical conditioning, operant conditioning, and observational learning (e.g., contingencies)
- Basic classical conditioning phenomena, such as acquisition, extinction, spontaneous recovery, generalization, discrimination, and higher-order learning
- The effects of operant conditioning (e.g., positive reinforcement, negative reinforcement, punishment)
- How practice, schedules of reinforcement, and motivation influence quality of learning
- Graphs that exhibit the results of learning experiments

- How biological constraints create learning predispositions
- The essential characteristics of insight learning, latent learning, and social learning
- Application of learning principles to explain emotional learning, taste aversion, superstitious behavior, and learned helplessness
- The use of behavior modification, biofeedback, coping strategies, and self-control to address behavioral problems
- Key contributors in the psychology of learning (e.g., Albert Bandura, John Garcia, Ivan Pavlov, Robert Rescorla, B. F. Skinner, Edward Thorndike, Edward Tolman, John B. Watson)

Source: *AP® Psychology Course and Exam Description*

9

Classical and Operant Conditioning

"I never teach my pupils, I only attempt to provide the conditions in which they can learn."

—Albert Einstein

Essential Question: How do humans learn, and how do experience and association contribute to the learning process?

Psychologists define **learning** as a relatively permanent change in behavior resulting from experience or practice. Some behavior changes are not learned but instead are either the effect of a temporary biological change (e.g., using substances that alter behavior) or behavior that occurs naturally as a part of development and reflexive actions. For example, you do not learn to flinch when an object approaches your face or to blink when something blows into your eyes. These responses tell us that learning does not include instincts, reflexes, and maturation.

The learning theorists, known as the **behaviorists** (adherents to the **behavioral perspective**), theorized that thoughts, or cognition, played no role in the study of behavior. Behaviorists did not accept Freud's view of an unconscious mind; only observable behavior had meaning to them. The behaviorists' thoughts were strongly influenced by those of political philosopher John Locke (1632–1704)—the Father of Liberalism noted for his social contract theory. According to Locke, to be born human was to be born with a *tabula rasa*, Latin for "blank slate." In this view, everything an individual becomes is the result of experience. In other words, our environment shapes every aspect of who we were, are, and will become. This view is known as **environmental determinism**. It allows us to understand the world in a way that makes the world controllable and suggests that we can change who people become by manipulating the circumstances in which they develop. **John Watson** (1878–1958), who founded the psychological field of **behaviorism**, claimed: "Give me a dozen healthy infants, well-formed, and my own specified world to bring them up in and I'll guarantee to take any one at random and train him to become any type of specialist I might select—doctor, lawyer, artist, merchant-chief and, yes, even beggarman and thief, regardless of his talents, penchants, tendencies, abilities, vocations, and race of his ancestors." Such confidence was characteristic of early behaviorism.

Classical Conditioning

Russian physiologist **Ivan Pavlov** (1849–1936) provided experimental support for the views of behaviorists—but with dogs, not people. Pavlov studied digestion and salivary reflex in dogs. While conducting this research, Pavlov discovered the process now known as **classical conditioning**, a type of learning that links a **neutral stimulus**—one that evokes no special response except to call attention to it—to another stimulus that elicits a natural or involuntary response in a given organism. The association between the two stimuli is one form of **associative learning**—a learning mode in which ideas and experiences are mentally linked and thereby reinforce each other.

Stimulus-Response Learning

The conditioning concept is based on the premise that behavior can be learned or modified through a stimulus and a response. For example, dogs salivate when they are presented with food—an unconditioned (unlearned) stimulus-response mechanism. However, while observing this process, Pavlov noticed that the dogs in his experiments began to salivate *before* being presented with food; they salivated as soon as they saw a person in a white lab coat, because it was a person in a white lab coat who brought them food. Obviously, this was a learned response. The dogs experienced an association between the lab coat and the food, which, in turn, induced salivation. The steps in the **stimulus-response learning** process were:

1. White coat → food → salivation

2. Repeat many times

3. White coat → salivation

The dogs learned that seeing the white coat signaled that they were about to receive food—a learned stimulus-response. The formation of a learned association is called **acquisition**. This process is illustrated in Figure 9.1. The labels identify the stimuli and the responses in this type of associative learning.

- **Unconditioned Stimulus** (US or UCS): any stimulus that elicits (produces or causes) an autonomic/automatic/reflexive response in an organism

- **Unconditioned Response** (UR or UCR): behavior that is a reflex or autonomic response (e.g., blinking of the eyes, nausea, muscle tension, salivation, blood pressure or heart rate increase, or other physical response)

- **Conditioned Stimulus** (CS): neutral stimulus paired with the US that becomes part of a new stimulus-response association (e.g., anything we can perceive, hear, smell, feel, see, or taste)

- **Conditioned Response (CR)**: behavior that is considered a reflex or autonomic response, now paired with a CS (similar to UR)—anything that can be considered a UR/UCR can become a CR after being paired with a CS. For the purpose of this class, the UR is *always* the same as the CR.

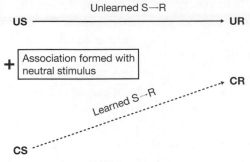

Figure 9.1 Process of Acquisition

The top line shows a natural response between the unconditioned stimulus (US) and the unconditioned response (UR). If you pair the US with a neutral stimulus, it becomes a conditioned stimulus (CS), which leads to a conditioned response (CR).

Figure 9.2 applies these labels to Pavlov's experiments. Salivation in the dogs at the presentation of food was reflexive (autonomic); the dogs did not need to *learn* how to salivate. The food is the unconditioned (unlearned) stimulus (US). Salivating at the presentation of food is the unconditioned (unlearned) response (UR). In the process, a neutral stimulus, the white lab coat, was paired with an unconditioned stimulus, producing a learned or conditioned response.

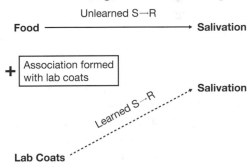

Figure 9.2 Acquisition Applied to Pavlov's Experiments

The specific stimuli and responses of the acquisition process are labeled in this version of the diagram.

Once Pavlov noticed the *lab coat → food → salivate* pattern, he tried ringing a bell as the conditioned stimulus. The pattern switched to *bell → food → salivate, bell → food → salivate, bell → food → salivate*, and so on, and, after a number of repeated trials, the learned pattern became *bell → salivate,* with the food portion of the pattern eliminated. The bell was the conditioned stimulus (CS), the food was the unconditioned stimulus (US), and salivation was both the unconditioned (UR) and conditioned response (CR). Pavlov noticed that the shorter the time between the conditioned stimulus and the unconditioned stimulus, the quicker and stronger the learned association. The closeness in time between the CS and US is called **contiguity**.

Learned Responses in Everyday Life Advertisers routinely take advantage of learned responses. They link an attractive US with a CS (the product being sold) so consumers feel as good about the product as they do about the US. Psychologist Robert Cialdini reports that in a study about car commercials, men who were shown a commercial featuring an attractive woman rated the advertised car as faster, more appealing, and better designed than did the men who were shown a commercial for the car without the woman. A similar process unfolds when companies license music to be associated with their brands. If a beloved song is associated with a product, advertisers hope that the positive feelings stirred by the song become associated with the product.

Taste Aversion If you have ever lost your taste for a food after having a bad experience with it—food poisoning, or even the onset of a stomach bug—then you have experienced **taste aversion**—a unique conditioned aversion that is accomplished rapidly by a single pairing of an illness or symptoms such as nausea with eating a specific food, even though the specific food is not the actual cause. While studying radiation effects in rats, psychologist **John Garcia** (1917–2012) discovered that initial exposure to flavored water followed by a toxic reaction to radiation (even if several hours later) made rats averse to the water. Radiation made the rats feel sick (US → UR), and the sickness was paired with the taste of the flavored water (CS). The animals were then conditioned to avoid foods paired with a previously aversive taste. Taste aversion is also known as the **Garcia effect.**

The Garcia effect was put into practical application to protect sheep from coyotes. Sheep carcasses were laced with a poison that would sicken but not kill coyotes who ate it. The Garcia effect was so strong that not only did the coyotes stop preying on sheep, but they also ran away from them in fear.

As research has shown, this type of conditioning applies to tastes but not to sights and sounds. The conditioning process is not the standard CS → US → CR/UR process, since CS occurs long after the taste, not immediately. The taste aversion is learned. It is especially common in chemotherapy patients who associate post-chemotherapy nausea with the taste of a specific food consumed after treatment rather than with the chemotherapy.

Stimulus Discrimination and Stimulus Generalization

Stimulus discrimination is a response to only the specific stimulus that has been conditioned. **Stimulus generalization**, in contrast, is a response to another stimulus that is similar to the original conditioned stimulus. For example, if a dog is conditioned to respond to a plastic bowl as a conditioned stimulus but not to a metal bowl, the dog exhibits stimulus discrimination if it does not salivate when a metal bowl appears. If a dog responds with salivation regardless of the material of the bowl, then the dog has generalized its response, exhibiting stimulus generalization.

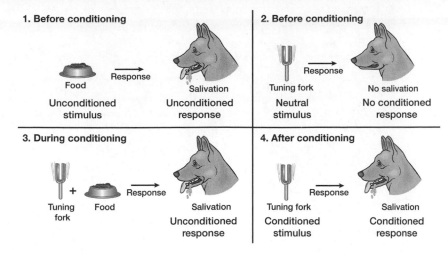

Figure 9.3

In one version of his research, Pavlov used a tuning fork (see Figure 9.3) as a strong CS paired with food to encourage dogs to salivate (CR). After losing his original tuning fork, Pavlov found that other tuning forks worked as a CS for salivation. When the pitch was closest to that of the original tuning fork, the dogs' response to it was stronger.

Following are other examples of stimulus discrimination and generalization. Try to identify the US, UR, CS, and CR in each example.

- A young woman listening to a popular song while driving is suddenly hit by another car, pushing her headlong into oncoming traffic. Although she survives the crash, the song later elicits an emergency response of the sympathetic nervous system, mimicking her experience in the accident.

- A college professor was robbed at gunpoint by a young man who gave him the choice, "Your money or your life." The unexpected and frightening experience occurred at just about dusk, and for a long time thereafter the professor experienced moments of dread in the late afternoons as he walked around campus. Even though he was quite safe, the lengthening shadows of the day were so strongly associated with the fear experienced in the robbery that he felt the emotion over and over again.

- Alcoholism is sometimes treated medically by administering a drug called disulfiram (trade name, Antabuse®). If the individual being treated ingests any alcohol at all, serious vomiting will develop. The objective of treatment is to pair, or associate, the vomiting with drinking alcohol, and thus prevent or eliminate alcohol abuse.

Military veterans who had been exposed to bombs and their associated injuries and destruction in war zones have often experienced classical

Many vets returning from war experience post-traumatic stress disorder (PTSD), a condition in which a sound once paired with danger triggers intense fear even when the vet is safe at home.

conditioning. After they return home, sudden sounds from a branch snapping or a loud explosion may elicit intense fear or emotional responses in these veterans, despite their being in relatively safe situations. The initial fear response to land mines had been generalized to cars backfiring or sudden loud sounds, even the sharp crunch of celery.

Watson and Little Albert

Can you name one thing humans are naturally afraid of? You've got it—loud noises. They startle us and make us focus our attention on the source of the sound. However, people are less afraid of the noise itself than of the circumstances associated with the loud sounds.

Imagine the sound of a hammer hitting a heavy metal bar. While it would definitely be startling for an adult, imagine the impact on a nine-month-old infant. Psychologist John B. Watson and his assistant, Rosalie Rayner, tested that impact on a nine-month old baby nicknamed "Little Albert." The research goal was to determine whether people—like Pavlov's dogs—could be classically conditioned. Watson also wanted to show that many fears are learned, not genetic, as many scientists in the early 1900s proposed.

Before beginning the classical conditioning process on Little Albert, Watson performed baseline readings to see if Albert responded to any of the stimuli he would use after conditioning occurred. Watson tested a white rat, a rabbit, a dog, a monkey, masks (with and without hair), cotton, wool, burning newspapers, and other stimuli, and Albert showed no fear of any item but special interest in the white rat. However, after exposure to several pairings with the loud sound of a hammer on steel while he played with the rat, Albert began to respond to the rat with fear, crying and pulling away. Albert had begun to anticipate the loud sound (US) and the feeling of fear that accompanied it (UR). The rat was paired with the loud sound and became the conditioned stimulus (CS). After the initial fear exhibited toward the rat, Albert began to respond to all furry objects (a rabbit, a mask with a cotton-ball beard, a dog, and a monkey) in a fearful way, exhibiting stimulus generalization. This series of experiments with Little Albert clearly showed the ease with which people can learn fears and phobias.

Little Albert's fate and actual identity remain somewhat uncertain. One team of researchers believe Little Albert's real name was Douglas Merritte, his mother was paid $1.00 for her baby's participation in the experiment, and he died at the age of six from hydrocephalus. Other researchers, including a Watson scholar, believe he was William Barger, whose nickname was Albert and who lived to the age of eighty-seven. Barger exhibited no special fears of white fluffy things, though he was afraid of dogs.

Now he fears even Santa Claus

This is a still from a movie taken of the Little Albert experiment. You can see the entire film on YouTube.

Many criticisms have been leveled against this research because of the stress it caused Little Albert. Researchers must now follow set procedures protecting subjects of psychological research.

Higher Order Conditioning

Higher order conditioning, also called **second order conditioning**, is classical conditioning with an extra conditioned stimulus. Think about the model of Pavlov's dogs: first the bell (CS), then the presentation of food (US), and finally the dogs salivating (UR). Second order conditioning adds another layer to this model. For example, a light might be added to the mix, changing the sequence from bell→ food→ salivation to bell→ light→ food→ salivation. After the sequence is repeated sufficiently, the dog will salivate at the light. With higher order conditioning, a new neutral stimulus becomes associated with the conditioned stimulus.

For a personal example, let's say you have a favorite aunt or grandmother who always makes you feel warm, wanted, and loved. Her loving behavior elicits warm feelings. Although everyone's experience is different, many grandmothers' homes have a particular grandma smell—maybe from the food cooking on the stove, or the furniture polish, or grandma's lavender soap. So you associate the aroma with your loved one: Grandmother (CS)→ smell (CS)→ loving behavior (US)→ feeling loved (UR). The image of the house may trigger feeling loved. Or perhaps driving onto her street creates those feelings of being loved.

Higher order conditioning extends the conditioning concept to more complicated reflexive human responses and to seemingly unrelated stimuli.

We are not typically aware of when we are being classically conditioned or when we experience higher order conditioning. However, these psychological concepts likely explain many experiences we have had, especially those involving fears. We may not recall an experience from our early childhood, but we may have been conditioned to respond in a fearful way that was extended into a higher order conditioning response.

Extinction and Spontaneous Recovery

Extinction is a process that leads to the gradual weakening and eventual disappearance of the conditioned response to the conditioned stimulus by presenting the CS repeatedly without pairing it with the UCS. Over time, pairing without reinforcement of the US will break the association. The association becomes extinct, or extinguished, and the neutral and unconditioned stimuli are no longer paired. That is, the conditioned stimulus no longer produces the conditioned response.

Occasionally, after a stimulus–response has been extinguished, it recurs without any obvious reason. Reappearance of the stimulus-response is known as **spontaneous recovery**. During spontaneous recovery, suddenly, and seemingly without cause, the learning reappears after a period of time during which the organism did not respond to a previously learned stimulus. The reappearance indicates that the learning has not disappeared at all but has been inhibited in some manner.

You can find examples of spontaneous recovery in almost everyone's life. As a child, you may have paired the sound of calliope music coming from an ice cream truck with your hunger or thirst for a treat. After not hearing those sounds for a while, you may no longer salivate when the truck and its music appear. However, even after years have passed, you may suddenly hear the calliope again and salivate. Similarly, in Pavlov's experiments with his dogs, after salivating was extinguished, the dogs recovered the salivating spontaneously when they heard a certain tone.

Operant Conditioning

After Watson left psychology to work in advertising, psychologist **B. F. Skinner** (1904–1990) assumed the behavioral mantle and rose to such prominence that he is considered the founder of the modern behavioral perspective. While Skinner understood the existence of mind, he viewed it as unworthy of study, since observable behaviors were far more intriguing. Skinner thought Watson's view of classical conditioning was too simplistic to fully explain human behavior. Skinner hypothesized that an organism "operates" in its environment, exhibiting some behaviors that are inborn and some behaviors that are learned. Skinner saw that every behavior has a consequence, pleasant or unpleasant. Behaviors that elicit a pleasant response are more likely to be repeated than those that are neutral or unpleasant. These observations led Skinner to develop **operant**

conditioning, a type of learning in which voluntary behavior is modified by subsequent **consequences**. Behavior is strengthened when followed by reinforcement—a reinforcing stimulus or reward—or diminished when followed by punishment, or a punishing stimulus. Operant conditioning is also referred to as **instrumental conditioning** and Skinnerian conditioning.

Thorndike and the Law of Effect

Skinner built upon the learning theory of **Edward Thorndike** (1874–1949). One of Thorndike's major contributions to psychology is the **law of effect**, which states that any behavior followed by pleasant consequences is likely to be repeated, while any behavior followed by unpleasant consequences is likely to be reduced or stopped.

Thorndike devised an experiment to empirically test the idea that there are laws of learning related to consequences of behavior. Using cats as his subjects, Thorndike designed a "puzzle box," a cage with a lever inside that would open a door for the cat to get out. He placed a cat in the puzzle box and placed a piece of fish outside of the box. The cat would attempt to escape and reach the fish.

The cats used **trial and error,** attempting various ways to escape the box to reach the fish until they found a way that worked. The cats would scratch at the bars, push at the ceiling, and dig at the door as the most common behaviors, but the only way out was to press the lever that opened the cage. Thorndike measured both the behaviors the cats used and the time it took for the cat to escape the box. After escape, a cat would be rewarded with the fish and returned to the box, and the process was repeated. Over successive trials, the cat would learn that pressing the lever had more positive consequences than the other behaviors. In time those other behaviors reduced as the cat learned to press the lever (see Figure 9.4).

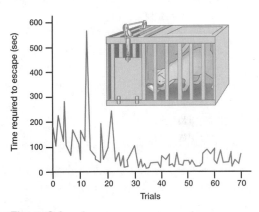

Figure 9.4

Thorndike demonstrated successfully that responses that produce a satisfying effect in a certain situation are likely to occur again in that situation, and responses that produce a discomforting effect are less likely to occur again in that situation. In other words, when good things happen after we do something, we are more likely to do it again. This pattern can sometimes lead to **superstitious behaviors**—actions that are only incidentally tied to good results. For example, if you use a certain pen on a test and get a good grade, you might start using that pen for every test, even though it was your studying that earned you the good grade.

Reinforcement and punishment can be interpreted differently by different organisms. What seems pleasant to one organism may not be pleasant to another. Organisms are individual, so sometimes certain kinds of reinforcer stimuli work better than others. Some people cannot stand hugs while other people love them. The allure of cash may outweigh all other consequences for some individuals, even dangerous and deadly consequences.

While classical conditioning or conditioned learning requires making associations between events, operant conditioning is learning from the consequences of our behavior. In classical conditioning, a response/behavior is *elicited* from an organism when an association is made. In operant conditioning, an organism *emits* a behavior that is linked to a consequence, and the consequence influences the likelihood of repeating the behavior.

Skinner's Experiments

The results of Thorndike's studies—the cats' behavior responding to positive reinforcement—led directly to B. F. Skinner's development of operant conditioning, a key component of behaviorism. In his experiments, Skinner conditioned rats, birds, people, and others. Videos have captured Skinner training pigeons to play ping pong, pull toys, and play the piano. Skinner once said, "I don't deny the importance of genetics. However, the fact that I might be altruistic isn't because I have a gene for altruism; the fact that I do something for my children at some cost to myself comes from a history that has operated on me." The attitude expressed by Skinner derives from environmental determinism, a point of view holding that all behavior is the result of our interactions with our environment. It acknowledges the existence of genetics and the mind but sees them as incidental to or nonfactors in behavior. In modern psychology, this extreme mindset is held by only a few, though the influence of behaviorism is still in evidence.

Reinforcement and Punishment

The terms used to describe the elements of operant conditioning usually refer to behavior that has already been exhibited.

- A **reinforcing stimulus** (**reinforcement**) is a consequence that increases the likelihood of a behavior occurring again. Examples may include food, water, a hug, payment, and praise, such as "great job, nice improvement" from a teacher or coach.

- A **punishing stimulus** (**punishment**) is a consequence that decreases the likelihood of a behavior occurring again. Examples may include a slap or punch, a traffic ticket, exclusion from a group, or having your phone confiscated.

A **primary reinforcement** is an innately valued reinforcing stimulus, such as one that satisfies a biological need (e.g., food, drink, or pleasure). **Secondary reinforcers**, or **conditioned reinforcement** learned through association (e.g., money and good grades), are very common. Money is not innately valuable, but it can be exchanged for other items that are closer to primary reinforcers.

The timing of a consequence, as in the contiguity concept of classical conditioning, must be close to the behavior to make it effective. For example, working people sometimes come home to a dog who has been inside all day and has relieved himself on the floor. A dog owner may grab the dog, take it to the scene, push the dog's nose near the waste, and yell "Bad dog!" Since so much time has passed since the accident, however, the dog does not connect the scolding with relieving himself. A time-based (temporal) connection is missing between the dog's accident and being punished. What the dog learns is to avoid people when they come home.

Both punishment and reinforcement can be either positive or negative. How can a punishment be positive? How can reinforcement be negative? To answer these questions, view positive and negative as they are used in mathematics. *Positive* means the *addition* of a stimulus while *negative* means the *removal or subtraction* of a stimulus. All punishment, positive or negative, is a consequence that reduces a specific behavior.

Figure 9.5 shows how positive and negative apply to punishment and reinforcement. The stimuli described here are all consequences of behaviors emitted by an organism.

OPERANT CONDITIONING: REINFORCEMENT AND PUNISHMENT		
	Reinforcement (Increase behavior)	**Punishment** (Decrease behavior)
Positive (add stimulus)	*Positive Reinforcement* ADD pleasant stimulus/ consequence to increase behavior	*Positive Punishment* ADD aversive stimulus/ consequence to reduce behavior
Negative (remove stimulus)	*Negative Reinforcement* *REMOVE* aversive stimulus to increase behavior	*Negative Punishment* *REMOVE* pleasant stimulus to decrease behavior

Figure 9.5

Positive Reinforcement A pleasant consequence (reinforcing stimulus) that increases the likelihood of repeating a behavior, whether intentional or not, is a **positive reinforcement**. The reward occurs after a desired behavior. Spend time in a public park and you'll see many birds hovering near people, repeating behavior that was rewarded previously with handouts of food. An old saying advises, "If you feed a stray cat, you've made a friend for life." Cats are creatures of habit, and if someone offers a cat a primary reinforcing stimulus of food, the cat will surely return to get more of that reinforcement. The behavior that has been reinforced is showing up on the person's doorstep. Similarly, when a young boy receives five dollars for every A he receives on his report card (desired behavior), the good grades will likely continue. A child who receives dessert after finishing the food on her plate (desired behavior) will continue to eat what she's served. A dolphin may be thrown a fish after performing a trick. Every time you give your pet food from your plate under the table, you are reinforcing begging for food at the table.

Negative Reinforcement The removal of an unpleasant/aversive stimulus to increase a behavior is called **negative reinforcement**. Since the goal is still to increase the occurrence of a specific behavior, the removal is still a reinforcement, but it is accomplished by eliminating something painful or annoying. Car technology applies this principle fairly often. If you start the car and do not fasten your seat belt, that annoying buzzer continues to sound until the seat belt is buckled. The desired behavior is achieved not by a pleasant consequence, but by removing an aversive one. When siblings wrestle each other, the dominant sibling may hold the other sibling in a painful position. Once the desired behavior of having the pinned sibling say "uncle" or "you're the best brother ever" occurs, the painful stimulus is removed. Also, an itch is often considered an aversive stimulus. Scratching it removes the unpleasantness and simultaneously reinforces the behavior of scratching.

Negative reinforcement, however, can sometimes be an **avoidance behavior**—a behavior that prevents an aversive event by emitting target behaviors early. For example, if we see that it is raining, we open an umbrella to avoid getting wet. Similarly, we take out the trash or do the dishes to avoid being nagged by our parents or partner. We may obey the speed limit in order to avoid tickets and fines.

Positive Punishment If you *add* an unpleasant or aversive stimulus to reduce a behavior, you are using **positive punishment**. An officer giving the driver of a speeding vehicle the consequence of a ticket reduces the speeding behavior by adding an unpleasant stimulus. If a student dresses inappropriately for school, he may receive a verbal reprimand and dress appropriately the next time. Parents whose young child dashes into the street without looking use positive punishment when they grab the child and raise their voices in a harsh tone (unpleasant consequence) to emphasize that running into the street is not a desired behavior. One of the clearest examples of positive punishment is the use of shock collars on dogs. Dogs can be fitted with collars designed to produce an electrical shock if they go beyond a specific area of a property bordered by an underground, electrified "invisible fence." The undesirable behavior is leaving the specified area. When the dog moves beyond the invisibly fenced border, the shock is administered. The dog responds to the positive punishment by learning not to leave the area.

Negative Punishment The removal of a pleasant stimulus to decrease or eliminate a specific behavior is called **negative punishment**. Fighting between siblings over a new toy may be stopped when the mom takes the toy away from one child, which effectively removes it from both children. Removal of the toy is the consequence for the behavior of fighting. If the fighting behavior decreases, punishment has worked. If a teenage girl stays out past her curfew and her parents ground her for a week during the summer, the pleasant stimulus of being with friends has been removed, most likely reducing the behavior of exceeding the curfew. If a soccer player receives two

Flow Chart of Operant Conditioning

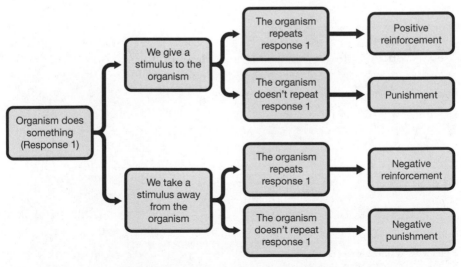

Figure 9.6

warnings for violations, he or she receives a red card and must leave the game permanently, and the team must play with one fewer member. The pleasant stimulus of playing the game was removed to reduce a behavior, making the removal a negative punishment.

Both punishment and reinforcement are most effective when the consequence follows the response *immediately* and is applied *consistently*.

Humans may respond uniquely to punishment. For example, Ryan was getting in trouble in school almost daily, talking in class and bullying other kids. Teachers and administrators spoke with him and scolded him, sometimes loudly, for misbehaving. Strangely, such consequences, even though intended as punishment, turned into rewards or reinforcing stimuli. Ryan appeared to need human interaction, no matter what form it took. For him, interaction of the teachers was reinforcement, even if it was in the form of punishment. Schools may also use suspension as a "punishment" for students. Quite often, however, it is the response the student is seeking. Being away from school reinforces the undesirable behavior.

Escape and Avoidance Conditioning

Escape conditioning is operant conditioning that occurs when an organism learns to perform an operation to terminate an ongoing, aversive stimulus. It is a "get-me-out-of-here" or "shut-this-off" reaction aimed at escaping pain or annoyance. The behavior that produces escape is negatively reinforced by eliminating an unpleasant stimulus. For example, picture a rat in a box with two compartments that are separated by a low-enough barrier for a rat to jump over. If the rat is administered a harmless electric shock, it will jump to

If a parent gives in to a whining child in a public place, the parent is being conditioned to remove an unpleasant stimulus (the child's whining) with a pleasant consequence for the child, establishing a pattern that could possibly last a lifetime.

Effective parents take a different approach. This father discussed with his son how he expected him to behave at the store and told him he would get a treat if he behaved well. The son complied and was rewarded with bubbles after the shopping was done.

the other compartment to escape it. The jump is an *escape behavior*. Escape conditioning happens only after a stimulus has already occurred.

Avoidance conditioning is similar to escape conditioning but includes a CS and is preventive in nature. If a tone is sounded (CS) before the rat feels an electric shock, the rat will soon not wait around for the shock but will learn to avoid it by jumping over the barrier as soon as the tone is sounded. This conditioning occurs quickly and is maintained well. Avoidance behaviors are very persistent and are often still in place when there is no longer anything to avoid. For example, if the tone sounded but no electric shock follows it, the rat would still jump over the barrier.

The Operant Conditioning Chamber

Psychologist B. F. Skinner invented the **operant conditioning chamber**, a conditioning chamber often called a **Skinner box** (Figure 9.7). The box was designed to train research animals such as rats and birds. With the box and associated methods, Skinner created a revolution in conditioning research. His approach is still used by many investigators and is one of the most scientifically validated theories applied to understanding human behavior.

Skinner placed hungry or thirsty research animals in the operant conditioning chamber, using their existing behaviors as a basis for training them to do specific and sometimes amazing tasks. A hungry rat is obviously receptive to having food as a reinforcer. Hungry rats were placed in the chamber where they did what rats do—sniff around, explore every corner, put their paws on everything, including a lever constructed in the box, and generally operate within their new environment.

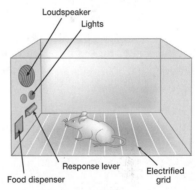

Figure 9.7

As soon as Skinner noticed the lever being pressed, he would release a pellet of food—a positive reinforcement. After several repeat trials, rats that pushed the lever made a clear connection between the bar press and the food. Skinner could then manipulate any natural rat behavior and have the rat running circles, doing multiple bar presses, and even more before obtaining food.

Schedules of Reinforcement

Over time, Skinner developed a set of principles that are now called the **schedules of reinforcement**. These systematic consequences reinforced behavior that was increasingly close to the desired behavior. Using this method, Skinner modified his lab rats' behaviors successfully.

Continuous reinforcement occurs when every instance of a desired behavior that occurs is reinforced. Examples of continuous reinforcement include rats getting food every time they press a bar or monkeys getting food every time they insert a token into a slot. Each time they do the behavior, they get the reinforcement.

Partial (intermittent) reinforcement, or not reinforcing a response every time, is a more common type of reinforcement. The intermittent format results in slower acquisition of a response but much greater resistance to extinction than continuous reinforcement. Intermittent response schedules can be carried out in four ways:

1. **Ratio schedules** are reinforcements based on the number of behaviors required.

2. **Interval schedules** are reinforcements based on the passage of time.

3. **Variable reinforcement** is reinforcement for a) variable number of times/behaviors (ratio schedule) or b) variable time intervals (interval schedule).

4. **Fixed reinforcement** is reinforcement for a definite or certain a) number of times/behaviors (ratio) or b) intervals of time (interval schedule).

Some reinforcing stimuli are immediate and others are delayed. As with Pavlov and contiguity, longer delays are associated with a weaker connection between the stimulus and response, indicating that immediate reinforcers are more effective.

Interval Schedules Interval schedules can be fixed or variable. A **fixed interval schedule** of reinforcement provides reinforcement for the first behavior after a fixed period of time. If the desired behavior is that the rat press the bar every 30 seconds, then the rat will be rewarded the first time it presses the bar after 30 seconds. The reinforcer is dependent upon the organism performing the behavior but is reinforced based upon a definite, unchanging time interval. The organism will learn to time its activity to correspond to the reward. For example, the rat will relax after a reinforcement but start pressing the lever again at 28 or 29 seconds.

Think about fixed interval schedules of reinforcement in your own life. If you have weekly music lessons, you might find yourself relaxing a bit right after a lesson but picking up your practicing as the next lesson approaches so you can get the reinforcement of praise from your teacher. Or if you finish your weekly chores by Thursday night you will get your allowance for the week.

Variable interval reinforcement is unpredictable reinforcement—that is, the first behavior after variable amounts of time is rewarded. You do not know when a behavior will be reinforced. For example, when you check your phone for text messages, you do not know if or when you will be rewarded with a message, but you will likely continue to check until you are. If a teacher tends to give pop quizzes, a steady rate of studying may develop, at least theoretically, because students cannot know when the quiz, which reinforces preparation, may occur. If you call a friend repeatedly and you keep getting the voicemail option (or a busy signal), you'll have to keep calling to finally speak to the person. You will likely call at variable times because you cannot know when the line will be free.

Ratio Schedules Ratio schedules can also be fixed or variable. With a **fixed ratio reinforcement schedule**, a behavior is reinforced after a specific *number* of behaviors. The classic example is a factory worker who receives a certain amount of money for each item she or he produces. A car salesperson on commission receives a payment after each car sold. A child receives her favorite candy every time she picks up all of her toys. In some schools, students may be given a prize for reading ten books. Some restaurants offer a "buy ten, get the eleventh sandwich free." Sometimes when a college student completes an exam (e.g., 50 multiple-choice questions), he or she can leave the exam room (negative reinforcement).

With the **variable ratio reinforcement schedule,** behavior is reinforced after a variable number of behaviors. The variable ratio is the most powerful reinforcement schedule, the one that most reliably produces desired behaviors. The organism does not know when reinforcement will occur. Since the variable ratio form is based on a behavior that *has been* or *could be* reinforced, the organism must continue to exhibit the behavior in order to get any possible reinforcement. This is the power source behind variable ratio reinforcement, a process that occurs around us every day. A salesperson doing cold calls must continue making the sales pitch to get the sale (reinforcement). The desired outcome is the sale, but the salesperson does not know which calls will lead to the sale.

Gambling is another classic example of the power of the variable ratio schedule of reinforcement. An entire city—Las Vegas, Nevada—is founded on the variable ratio schedule of reinforcement. A gambler will sit and feed nickels, quarters, dollars, or even more into a slot machine, facing a possible payoff each time. If the guest does not play (playing is the casino's desired behavior), the person cannot win (get reinforcement). The same can be said of those who play poker or blackjack. In order to win (reinforcement), one must play (the desired behavior). The timing or number of hands a person must play to win is not established, so the possibility of winning is variable.

Dating may be an example closer to your experience. Asking someone out can be anxiety-producing, and it may or may not yield positive responses, but you must ask—i.e., do the behavior, asking—in order to receive the reinforcement of acceptance and a date.

Figures 9.8 and 9.9 provide an overview of the schedules of reinforcement.

THE FOUR SCHEDULES OF REINFORCEMENT		
Type	**Ratio** (based upon behavior)	**Interval** (based upon time)
Fixed (number of behaviors or length of time intervals is constant)	*Fixed Ratio* (e.g., reinforces every third bar press)	*Fixed Interval* (e.g., reinforces first bar press after 30-second intervals)
Variable (number of behaviors or length of time intervals is variable)	*Variable Ratio* (e.g., reinforce bar press after 3, 8, 2, 5, 3, 6, presses of the bar)	*Variable Interval* (e.g., reinforce bar press after 30 seconds, 12 seconds, 8 seconds, 33 seconds, 15 seconds)

Figure 9.8

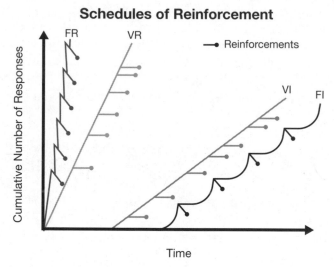

Schedules of Reinforcement

Figure 9.9 The fixed and variable ratios (FR and VR) reflect reinforcements in relation to the number of times a behavior is performed (the *y*-axis). The fixed and variable interval (FI and VI) reinforcements are based on time span (the *x*-axis).

Shaping

Shaping is a technique using a series of positive reinforcements to create more complex behavior. By rewarding **successive approximations**, steps toward a target goal, reinforcement can make a rat turn in a full circle to obtain food. First, when the rat makes a quarter turn, that behavior is reinforced. If the rat then turns a bit more, perhaps a half turn, that behavior is once again reinforced. That process continues until finally the rat is turning a complete circle. By doing this serially and properly, humans and nonhuman animals can be taught to do just about anything within their physical capability.

A familiar example in the classroom is a variation on the game of Hot & Cold. One student is asked to leave the room while the class decides on a desired behavior they want the student outside to perform. When the student returns, clapping is the reinforcer. The subject student must move about the room being sensitive to which behaviors are being reinforced by the clapping and which are being ignored. As the student gets closer to the desired behavior (using successive approximations by the class), she changes her behavior accordingly. Whether the task is to open a window, sit in the teacher's chair, or pick up a book, it is learned relatively quickly. When changed to punishment, in which the class says "No!" to any behavior that is not the desired behavior, the subject may be left in a corner of the room, afraid to move, feeling helpless and foolish. The power of reinforcement over punishment is clearly demonstrated.

Nebraska Wesleyan University holds an annual Xtreme Rat Challenge in which students train their rats to jump hurdles, climb ropes, navigate an obstacle course, and more. Students use shaping to teach their lab rats to perform specific behaviors. But that's not all. After specific simple behaviors have been taught, a process known as **chaining** can be used to combine learned behaviors. Mastery of the process of chaining can make a rat run hurdles, then climb a rope, jump from one platform to another, and then navigate a maze. Each behavior was taught separately, but behaviors were combined later to create the more complex course.

PAVLOV'S DREAM

Classical and Operant Conditioning Together

While we study classical and operant conditioning separately to understand the details behind learning, the reality is that they often occur within the same sets of behaviors. Humans and other animals are more complex than those represented by research animals in a laboratory environment.

An episode from the discontinued TV hit, *The Office*, provides a good example of how classical and operant conditioning can work together. In one scene, Jim is pranking his office mate Dwight as usual. Jim begins by restarting his computer, which makes its familiar start-up chime. Seconds later, Jim offers Dwight a mint. The sequence is repeated several times. Finally, when Jim restarts his computer and the chime is heard, Dwight reaches out his hand for a mint. Jim asks him, "What are you doing?" Dwight replies, "I don't know . . . I have a bad taste in my mouth."

You can probably see that both classical and operant conditioning were in play in this scene. The taste in Dwight's mouth is the UR part of the classical conditioning process (the computer tone is the CS and the mint is the US). Dwight puts out his hand, an operant behavior; clearly he has been conditioned to put his hand out after the tone, and the mint reinforced the behavior.

Figure 9.10 summarizes the characteristics of classical and operant conditioning.

CHARACTERISTICS OF CLASSICAL VS. OPERANT CONDITIONING		
	Classical Conditioning	**Operant Conditioning**
Terminology	CS, US, CR, UR	Response, reinforcement, consequence
How behavior occurs	Elicited involuntarily from organism	Emitted voluntarily by organism
Subject's behavior	Does not control US	Controls reinforcement
Paired during acquisition	Two stimuli (CS and US)	Response and reinforcement in the presence of certain stimuli
Responses studied	Mostly involuntary reflexive and visceral (internal organs)	Mostly voluntary skeletal (movements)

Figure 9.10

One-minute math tests—do you remember those from your elementary school days? If you are like many students, being tested on math facts under time pressure produced anxiety for you, and possibly you were conditioned from those early experiences to feel anxiety even today in the form of a more generalized test anxiety. In timed testing situations, you may feel your heart race and experience shortness of breath. Your mind may be filled with negative thoughts: "I can't do this. I don't know what I'm doing. I'll never amount to anything." How can you relieve yourself of that anxiety?

As you will learn in the next unit, preparing well for a test with sound study methods is the best way to reduce test anxiety. But you can also use *counterconditioning*—replacing unpleasant responses to stimuli with more positive ones. Using a three-step process called systematic desensitization developed by South African psychiatrist Joseph Wolpe in the 1950s, you can gradually replace anxious responses to stimuli with relaxed responses. (You will read more about this process in Chapter 10.)

Step 1 is to identify the stimuli that trigger your anxious responses, arranging them from weakest to strongest. These stimuli can be material— the exam booklet and pen, the ticking clock that indicates the time remaining on the exam, or even the room in which the exam is taken, and they can also be internal—expectations of the difficulty of the exam, for example, or estimations of your likelihood to pass the test. Step 2 is to develop relaxation techniques—deep breathing, meditation, whatever opposes the physiological effects of anxiety. Step 3 is to replace the negative responses to each of your identified stimuli with a relaxed response, starting with the weakest stimulus and gradually working your way up to the strongest. You may begin, for example, by sitting near an exam booklet while you are in a deeply relaxed state. You must practice the new responses many times for them to "hold," and when you can be completely relaxed in the presence of the weakest stimulus, you would move on to the next strongest stimulus. You might end the process by actually going to the examination room and practicing your relaxation techniques there.

Practice: Recognizing that counterconditioning is just one way of many to reduce test anxiety, follow the steps outlined on the previous page to develop a personalized plan for overcoming test anxiety. If you are lucky enough not to experience test anxiety, ask to partner with someone who does experience it. Write up the plan, listing the hierarchy of anxiety-producing stimuli and the relaxation methods you will use to replace the unwanted anxious response with a relaxed response. Share your work with your classmates.

REFLECT ON THE ESSENTIAL QUESTION

Essential Question: *How do humans learn, and how do experience and association contribute to the learning process?* On separate paper, complete a chart like the one below to gather details to help answer that question.

Topics	Classical Conditioning	Operant Conditioning
Key Experiments and Their Findings		
Terminology		
Relationship Between Stimuli and Behavior		

KEY TERMS			KEY PEOPLE
associative learning	*CLASSICAL CONDITIONING*	fixed ratio reinforcement schedule	John Garcia
behavioral perspective	acquisition	fixed reinforcement	Ivan Pavlov
behaviorism	conditioned response (CR)	higher order (second order) conditioning	B. F. Skinner
behaviorists	conditioned stimulus (CS)	interval schedules	Edward Thorndike
classical conditioning	consequences	negative punishment	John Watson
environmental determinism	contiguity	negative reinforcement	
instrumental conditioning	extinction	operant conditioning chamber	
law of effect	Garcia effect	partial (intermittent) reinforcement	
learning	neutral stimulus	positive punishment	
operant conditioning	spontaneous recovery	positive reinforcement	
	stimulus discrimination	primary reinforcement	
	stimulus generalization	punishing stimulus/ punishment	
	stimulus-response learning	ratio schedules	
	taste aversion	reinforcing stimulus/ reinforcement	
	unconditioned response (UR)	schedules of reinforce- ment (FI, FR, VI, VR)	
	unconditioned stimulus (US)	secondary reinforcer/ conditioned reinforcement	
		shaping	
	OPERANT CONDITIONING	Skinner box	
		successive approximations	
	avoidance behavior	superstitious behaviors	
	avoidance conditioning	trial and error	
	chaining	variable interval reinforcement schedule	
	continuous reinforcement	variable ratio reinforcement schedule	
	escape conditioning		
	fixed interval schedule	variable reinforcement	

1. An untrained dog's salivation at the sight of a food dish is (a, an)
   (A) neutral stimulus
   (B) unconditioned stimulus
   (C) conditioned stimulus
   (D) conditioned response
   (E) unconditioned response

2. Bailey had to get allergy shots weekly. Before administering them, the doctor would put rubbing alcohol on her skin. Now Bailey becomes fearful every time she smells rubbing alcohol. Which concept best explains Bailey's fear?
   (A) Negative reinforcement
   (B) Positive reinforcement
   (C) Classical conditioning
   (D) Operant conditioning
   (E) Variable interval reinforcement

3. Pavlov is to _____ as Skinner is to _____
   (A) positive reinforcement; negative reinforcement
   (A) classical conditioning; operant conditioning
   (B) observational learning; operant conditioning
   (C) primary reinforcers; secondary reinforcers
   (D) operant conditioning; classical conditioning

4. Which of the following could be considered an unconditioned response?
   (A) Getting money as a reward
   (B) Navigating a maze
   (C) Playing jacks
   (D) Sweating in hot weather
   (E) Cheering when the artist plays your favorite song at a concert

5. In Watson's Little Albert experiment, Albert became fearful of furry masks, rabbits, and dogs in addition to the original rat. Which concept did this best illustrate?

(A) Unconditioned stimulus

(B) Unconditioned response

(C) Stimulus generalization

(D) Stimulus discrimination

(E) Neutral stimulus

6. Service dogs are often trained to assist in such tasks as letting their person know someone is at the door, safely crossing the street, or pushing buttons on the elevator. Which concept best describes how dogs were trained for these behaviors?

(A) Shaping

(B) Unconditioned response

(C) Latent learning

(D) Operant discrimination

(E) Variable interval schedule of reinforcement

7. Reyna's therapist reminds her of her father in a variety of ways. As a result, she has many of the same reactions to the therapist as she has to her father. Her reactions to her therapist best illustrate the concept of

(A) habituation

(B) shaping

(C) delayed reinforcement

(D) generalization

(E) spontaneous recovery

8. Adriana is addicted to heroin. The room in which she usually takes heroin will likely become what for her drug cravings?

(A) Primary reinforcer

(B) Autonomic response

(C) US

(D) CS

(E) CR

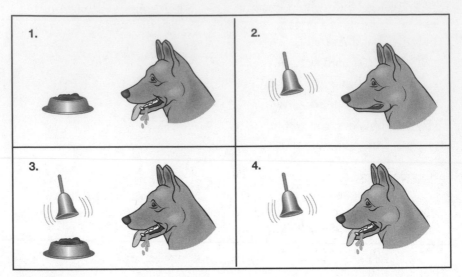

Figure 9.11

9. If Figure 9.11 represents the sequence in classical conditioning, what does the bell represent in slide 2?

   (A) Unconditioned stimulus

   (B) Unconditioned response

   (C) Conditioned stimulus

   (D) Conditioned response

   (E) Neutral stimulus

10. If Figure 9.11 represents the sequence in classical conditioning, what does the bell represent in slide 4?

    (A) Unconditioned stimulus

    (B) Unconditioned response

    (C) Conditioned stimulus

    (D) Conditioned response

    (E) Neutral stimulus

1. Classical (Pavlovian) conditioning contains several different elements.

A) Explain and give examples of each of the following:
- Unconditioned stimulus
- Unconditioned response
- Neutral stimulus
- Conditioned stimulus
- Conditioned response
- Stimulus discrimination
- Stimulus generalization

B) Explain how classical conditioning elicits behavior from an organism.

2. Punishment and reinforcement are often confused, especially when the terms positive and negative are involved.

A) Explain as simply as you can the purposes of reinforcement and punishment.

B) Explain how one might accomplish those purposes with the following. Include examples where appropriate.
- Positive reinforcement
- Negative reinforcement
- Positive punishment
- Negative punishment

WRITE AS A PSYCHOLOGIST: COUNT POINTS TO DETERMINE RUBRIC

For each lettered or bulleted items, notice how many topics you need to explain and how many examples you must provide. The total will be the number of points that question is worth. Be sure to cover all of the bulleted items to gain full credit for the questions. Based on the construction and components of the question, try to imagine the rubric the readers will be using to evaluate your response. For more guidance on answering free-response questions, see pages xxii–xxiii.

10

Social Learning and Biological Factors

"People not only gain understanding through reflection,
they evaluate and alter their own thinking."

—Albert Bandura

Essential Question: How do the principles of conditioning work with biological principles to modify human responses, and how does observing others influence behavior?

As you read in Chapter 9, classical conditioning occurs when a neutral stimulus pairs with a naturally occurring stimulus to create a conditioned response in an organism. The biological influence is clear—biology limits what an organism can be classically conditioned to learn. Psychologists and behavioral scientists have discovered that certain biological principles that help control body functions can also be applied to modify behavior. This chapter will revisit classical and operant conditioning, exploring the way conditioning principles and biological factors work together to treat **phobias**—irrational fears—and anxiety. It will also explore how learning takes place in a social context as humans observe the behavior of others.

Biology and Cognition in Classical Conditioning

As you recall from the Little Albert study conducting by John Watson and Rosalie Rayner (page 206), Little Albert was conditioned to fear the rat at first, and he then generalized the fear to other objects that were white and/or furry (dog, monkey, Santa Claus mask, among others). After hearing a lecture by John Watson on classical conditioning and generalization of responses, psychologist **Mary Cover Jones** (1897–1987) wondered if the process could work in reverse—if classical conditioning could reduce a fearful or phobic response rather than bring it on. After conducting studies of her own on various phobias and developing a form of therapy to treat them, Jones became known as "the mother of **behavior therapy**."

The **desensitization** therapy she developed and tested—therapy designed to reduce sensitivity to a feared stimulus—involved introducing a series of stimuli that approximated a person's phobia. Her most famous subject was Peter, a three-year-old with a fear of rabbits. During her treatment of Peter, she exposed the child to a rabbit, gradually moving Peter and the rabbit closer together while she simultaneously presented Peter with his favorite sweet, candy. Eventually, as the visits with dual stimuli progressed, Peter was able to touch the rabbit without manifesting a fear response.

Although the work of Mary Cover Jones was initially ignored, her friend and colleague, psychiatrist **Joseph Wolpe** (1915–1997) built on her original work in behavioral therapy. Wolpe took the idea of relearning a response and expanded it to include the biological principle of *reciprocal inhibition*, a process in which two sets of opposing muscles—flexors and extensors—work in synchrony. Muscles on one side of a joint relax to allow muscles on the other side of the joint to contract—a reciprocal agreement of sorts that allows a joint to function. In psychology, **reciprocal inhibition** is a process of extinguishing an undesired response to stimuli by evoking a desired response in its place. Wolpe applied this principle to anxiety, hypothesizing that if a desired emotion is invoked at the presentation of an anxiety-producing stimulus over many repetitions, the undesirable anxiety response can be extinguished because the favorable and nonfavorable responses cannot be evoked at the

Dogs trained for use in the military are gradually desensitized to loud noises.

same time. Wolpe first worked with cats who had received electric shocks in boxes and therefore had a strong fear response to the boxes. He found that by feeding the cats—providing a pleasurable activity for them—and gradually moving the food dishes closer and closer to the boxes, he could successfully weaken or extinguish the cats' fear response to the boxes, replacing it with a contrasting and incompatible favorable response associated with eating. In humans, the emotional state of relaxation is not compatible with anxiety, so Wolpe reasoned that developing techniques to produce a relaxed response to an anxiety-producing stimulus should, in theory, extinguish the undesirable anxiety response.

Wolpe had a further insight that led to a phobia treatment still in common use. **Systematic desensitization** is a process that first trains individuals with phobias in relaxation techniques and then exposes them to progressively more anxiety-provoking stimuli while they are relaxed.

Before beginning the process, a therapist and patient must compile an **anxiety hierarchy**, or exposure hierarchy, a list of feared objects and situations ranked from the least anxiety-provoking to the most anxiety-provoking. Then the patient learns to identify the relaxed state by how it feels and, in some cases, by how it is displayed on a **biofeedback** device that monitors such functions as heart rate, blood pressure, and respiration.

Once relaxation is learned, the step-by-step desensitization process begins. For example, the first item on the hierarchy of a person terrified of dogs might be seeing a picture of a dog. The therapist and client work on that level until the patient can view a picture of a dog while remaining completely relaxed. After mastering that, the therapist and patient move on to the next item, such as hearing a dog behind a closed door, again remaining at that level until the situation can be experienced with relaxation. The therapist may remind the person to focus on breathing and other relaxation techniques as they progress through the hierarchy. Only when one item on the hierarchy is mastered do the therapist and patient move on to the next. By the end of the process, the relaxation response will have gradually replaced the incompatible anxiety response, and the patient should be able to play with and pet a dog or master whatever was identified as the most anxiety-producing situation.

Biology and Classical Conditioning

An organism's autonomic responses—changes in heart rate, blood pressure, digestion, and respiration, for example—are part of the nervous system's regulation of body functions. In humans, autonomic responses and body functions typically happen without our awareness. At the same time, the autonomic nervous system is influenced by our external environment and by how we think and feel about things that occur or exist in the environment. Our responses to any given situation, event, or object can be wanted or unwanted, desired or undesirable. **Taste aversion** is a perfect example. If you ingest a certain food or drink and your biological response is nausea, you are likely to learn an avoidance response (permanent distaste for that food) even after only one pairing of the responses.

Psychologist **John Garcia** and colleagues, as you read in the previous chapter, found that taste aversion experiments modified previous assumptions about classical conditioning. First, they showed that the time gap between the conditioned stimulus and the biological response (the unconditioned stimulus) can be much longer than originally thought. Garcia's experiments demonstrated that aversion can be learned even if nausea occurred hours after exposure to radiation or drugs and that the aversion response can occur after only one trial rather than multiple trials. They also challenged the idea that anything perceivable could be a conditioned stimulus. Garcia found that taste was the perception with the powerful connection and that the rats did not connect perceivable sounds and sights to the nausea. Taste aversion appeared to be a survival mechanism because it allowed the rats to learn quickly how to avoid poisonous food and to retain the aversion, and thus avoidance of the potentially poisonous food, over time.

Aversions may differ from one species to another and are learned differently. Humans cannot always visually notice that food has been contaminated and may learn the taste aversion later after becoming sick. Birds hunt by vision alone and appear biologically primed to establish aversions at the sight of tainted food. Other animals may learn to identify potentially poisonous food through its smell. Cancer patients have been shown to learn an "anticipatory nausea" associated with chemotherapy treatments. Depending upon the drugs used, nausea and vomiting can occur during chemotherapy and for several days after. Before the treatment is started, patients are typically given medications to reduce nausea and vomiting. Studies have shown, however, that a large percentage of patients still become nauseated, because the anti-nausea treatment given just before the start of chemotherapy acts as a stimulus associated with the chemo-induced nausea.

Cognition and Classical Conditioning

Classical and operant conditioning influence behavior that reflects learning. Sometimes, however, learning is not exhibited when it is first acquired. In other words, one can learn something but not show the behavior right away. This kind of learning is called **latent learning**. Animal studies conducted by psychologist **Edward Tolman** (1886–1959) attempted to teach rats to run a maze during a series of one-day trials. The rats were divided into different groups, each group with a different reinforcement schedule. During the trials, Tolman noticed that one group did not exhibit the learned behavior until after it was reinforced. Although the rats had learned the maze, they were not compelled—or had no reason—to run it correctly until the behavior was reinforced with food. The rats had learned the behavior but lacked the motivation to demonstrate the learned behavior. The results of Tolman's research suggest two important aspects of learning.

1. Learning can take place in an organism without the presence of a reinforcer.

2. Organisms that display latent learning have formed a **cognitive map**, a mental representation that allows an organism to acquire, store, and recall information both in a real, spatial world, or in a metaphorical spatial environment. (The term *cognitive map* will be described in more detail in the upcoming unit on cognition.)

The mental representation, or cognitive map, of the rats in Tolman's experiment was of the spatial layout of the maze. An example of stored spatial information for humans might be images viewed on a video game. You need to create a cognitive map of the world of the video game to remember where certain features are and be able to proceed to the next level.

Psychologist **Robert Rescorla** (b. 1940) also demonstrated that cognition is at work within classical conditioning. **Contingency theory** posits that for learning to take place, a stimulus must provide the organism with a reliable signal (**signal relations**) that certain events will take place. The predictive nature of a stimulus is key to establishing an effective association between a stimulus and response. For example, if the tuning fork in Pavlov's experiment had not been a predictable precursor to food, the dogs would likely not have learned to salivate so quickly or strongly in response to that stimulus.

In the same way, if a teacher pulls out an air horn in class and activates it, students will likely cringe at the harsh sound. When students cringe at the *sight* of the air horn, conditioning may have occurred. Students may not respond, however, if the teacher pulls out a picture of the air horn or plays a loud recording of an air horn (easily found online) without actually presenting the air horn. In these cases, the predictive value of the stimulus may be lost or less significant. The air horn sound without the presence of the air horn is less likely to produce as great a response as the simultaneous sound and sight of the horn.

Biology and Cognition in Operant Conditioning

Animals can be trained to adopt only those behaviors that are consistent with their biological predispositions. This fact indicates that biology limits what can be learned. For example, rats do not walk backwards and cannot be trained to do so because it's contrary to their natural inclinations.

Using food as reinforcement, psychologists Marian and Keller Breland trained raccoons to perform humanlike activities, such as putting a coin into a metal container. However, they could not train the raccoons to place *two* coins into the container. Rather than dropping the coins in, the raccoons held the coins, rubbed them together, and dipped them into the container. They essentially mimicked the natural raccoon behavior of washing food in a stream. This reversion to a natural behavior is called **instinctive drift**. The Brelands also trained the raccoons to put a large ball, too large for raccoons to wash, into a basketball hoop. Results of the experiment and others suggested that behaviorists must take species-specific behaviors into account when attempting to condition their behavior. The Brelands' focus on modifying animal behavior brought conditioning and biology together, changing the experimental methods applied in the field from primarily punishment of animals to reinforcement of naturally occurring animal behaviors.

Cognition in Operant Conditioning

Strict adherents of behaviorism, including Skinner, largely ignored the thought process as a factor in their work with animals. Nevertheless, many studies have demonstrated the role of cognition in operant conditioning. Results of these studies introduced ideas such as abstract learning, insight learning, the Premack Principle, learned helplessness, and locus of control. Each learning

The Brelands worked with animals' natural behaviors when conditioning them. They ran into instinctive drift when the raccoons they worked with reverted to their natural inclination to wash their food.

concept recognizes elements of cognition that influence behavior, carrying behavior modification beyond consequences and basic biology.

Abstract Learning Understanding complex cognitive concepts or qualities such as *same* or *different*, *love* or *hate*, *honesty* or *dishonesty*—concepts that involve rules about relationships—rather than concrete stimuli such as specific objects, actions, or situations is called **abstract learning.** Pigeons in operant conditioning boxes have been able to learn abstractions such as shapes in order to receive reinforcement. Rats can exhibit abstract learning if they press a lever when they see a picture of a dog because they know they will receive reinforcement for that behavior, but they do not press the lever when they see a cat picture because doing so will not produce reinforcement. Animals, then, can learn to respond not only to concrete stimuli connected to a stimulus-response mechanism but also to less tangible (more abstract) concepts. One study trained eight pigeons to distinguish "same" from "different" and tested them in a simultaneous *same/different* task. After the pigeons pecked at an upper picture, they pecked a lower picture if it was the *same* or a white rectangle to indicate it was *different*. This cognitive complexity shows that some animals can think beyond the simple stimulus-response premise that Thorndike and Skinner considered a central premise of behaviorism.

Insight Learning In 1912, German psychologist Wolfgang Köhler (1887–1967) co-founded the school of psychology known as **Gestalt psychology**, which is based on the view that perceptions are organized wholes (*gestalts*) rather than a summary of their constituent parts. The age-old phrase from Aristotle, "the whole is more than the sum of its parts," explains gestalt perfectly.

Köhler's work with monkeys helped demonstrate **insight learning**—the term for a sudden realization that "just came to you" of how to solve a problem the first time you are exposed to it. In one study, Sultan, a chimpanzee, was given two sticks in his cage with bananas placed outside the cage just beyond the reach of each stick. After trying each stick unsuccessfully, Sultan fashioned the two sticks together to pull the bananas into his cage successfully. The experiment demonstrated once again that stimulus-response conditioning alone is not responsible for behavior—that some level of unobservable cognitive processes are at work. This finding supports the Gestalt psychology perspective which looks for an understanding of the whole—in this case, conditioning as well as cognition.

The Premack Principle In his original studies conducted with monkeys, psychologist **David Premack** (1925–2015) discovered a principle that worked extremely well with humans, named the **Premack principle**. The Premack principle states that a person will perform a less desirable activity in order to perform the more desirable activity as a consequence. To arrive at this conclusion, Premack had presented monkeys with two kinds of toys they had liked during his earlier research. The monkeys had to play initially with the "second-rate" toys for a period of time before being allowed to play with the "top-tier" toys they preferred, and they eventually understood the sequence.

Since each organism, including each human, is unique, a psychologist or teacher or parent may benefit from knowing what is desirable and not desirable for each person. Parents typically receive clues from observing their own children. Sometimes parents will name a desired behavior "Grandma's rule"—"no dessert until you finish dinner."

Parents may often use a variation of this when they want their children to eat vegetables. Vegetables first; ice cream second. When therapists practice applied behavior analysis using the Premack Principle, they notice especially how the activities themselves become reinforcers. Individuals are motivated to perform an activity if they know that a more desirable activity will follow as a consequence.

Sultan demonstrated that unobservable cognitive processes are at work in stimulus-response conditioning.

Learned Helplessness and Control

In his book, *Learned Optimism: How to Change Your Mind and Your Life,* psychologist Martin Seligman (b. 1942) recounts that as a student he conducted experiments involving dogs and a mild shock. Seligman observed that dogs who tried to stop the shock by pressing a lever that was designed *not* to work finally stopped trying and lay down whimpering. That led him to the realization that the dogs must have *learned* how to be helpless. After struggling with the ethical and practical issues, Seligman began to investigate further using dogs in a cage with a partially electrified floor. Dogs who in previous experiments had been able to control the shock by pressing a working lever learned fairly quickly that jumping over a short barrier allowed them to escape the shock, while the dogs who in previous experiments had no control over the shock lay down on the electrified floor and did nothing. Seligman and his research partner hypothesized that dogs in the second group had learned that nothing they did mattered, so they would just become helpless, lying down in the shock and doing nothing. After running variations and replications of the research, Seligman concluded, "Clearly, animals can learn their actions are futile, and when they do, they no longer initiate action; they become passive."

Seligman's research results, when published, were challenged by traditional behaviorists who argued that animals could not learn in this way, using cognition. However, some learning theorists supported these findings, recognizing that the most basic premise of behaviorism, that thought is irrelevant, was clearly incorrect. Until that point, the learning theorists firmly believed that animals and humans could learn only actions, not thoughts or expectations, or **expectancies**.

Although they encountered resistance for years, Seligman and others continued to research **learned helplessness**, a mental state in which an organism continues to experience a painful, unpleasant, or aversive stimulus. Their assumption was that organisms become helpless because they have learned that, regardless of their actions, they have no ability to change the outcome.

Psychologist Donald Hiroto attempted a variation of these studies, observing humans escaping a loud noise by learning how to turn it off. He concluded that placing humans in a situation they are unable to control demonstrates in the lab the process of learning to be helpless.

What about in real life? Can people learn to become helpless and then stop trying to accomplish something? Consider national politics. When people feel that they are unable to affect the development of public policy or to change unfair practices, they may stop voting. Similarly, some students who have experienced failure in school may come to think they will never succeed and will stop trying—and as a result they experience more school failure, reinforcing their belief. Unemployed people may search for jobs for a period of time, eventually giving up if they lack skills and connections or if they perceive some bias against them associated with age, gender, sexual orientation, or race. Humans and other animals who experience a sense of powerlessness after repeated failure to avoid aversive stimuli have essentially lost control. Many will give up after acquiring learned helplessness.

The Brain and Personal Control

Psychologist Steven Maier, one of Seligman's original research partners, searched for a neural understanding of the learned helplessness phenomenon. In the original experiments, the dogs had lost control of their situation, and that loss of control triggered stressors. Fear and anxiety derived from stressors provoke the well-known fight-or-flight response in which the amygdala in the brain plays a part. A nearby brain region releases serotonin into the forebrain and limbic systems to mediate the stressed responses. In a series of studies, Maier and his colleagues found that when an individual is stressed, the body's stress responses are activated, but if the stressor is controllable, serotonin steps in and calms brain activity. If an individual does not feel in control, the serotonin cannot mediate the stress.

Coping Mechanisms and Mindset

Since life does contain many stressors, multiple approaches have been developed to deal with the challenges. One way is **problem-focused coping**, in which we attempt to take control of a situation either by changing our behavior or changing the situation. If someone has a fight with a friend, for example, he goes directly to the friend to work it out. If we believe we *do not* have control over a situation, or lack control over anything, we may engage instead in **emotion-focused coping**, seeking out the support of others, trying to find a positive side to the stressor, or taking our minds off the problem. Distractions like playing games or altering mood by using alcohol, drugs, food, or sex, do not help us solve the problem at hand and are maladaptive.

In education, the idea of *fixed vs. growth mindsets* examines influences on our sense of control. Individuals with a fixed mindset perceive no level of self-efficacy and do not believe that anything they do will change a situation. In the world of learning, sentiments expressing a fixed mindset may include, "I'm terrible at math," "I just can't understand physics," or "no matter what I do, I cannot learn a second language." The fixed mindset is essentially a form of learned helplessness. Individuals with a growth mindset, in contrast, understand that perfection of a skill will not occur immediately or even soon, but the right practice will lead to it.

Locus of Control

Psychologist Julian Rotter (1916–2014) began as a social learning theorist by moving away from both psychoanalytic thought and behaviorism. He proposed that people actively seek pleasant outcomes and avoid aversive outcomes by engaging in specific behaviors. If people anticipate a pleasant outcome from a certain behavior, or think that the odds favor a pleasant outcome, they are likely to do the behavior.

Rotter's early research indicated that social context and related factors influenced behavior, not just psychological factors. Later, as his career moved in the direction of personality, he studied the **locus of control**, the perception of where control over life events resides. An *internal locus of control* is the belief that people have the ability to control their lives, choices, and the world. They direct their life—life does not just happen—and they can influence people and situations. Such inner-driven individuals tend to have a high motivation level and an orientation to success. Those with a high internal locus of control will be equipped with proactive ways to handle life's stressors, including

- Engaging in activities that will improve their situation

- Striving for achievement—working hard to develop their own abilities, skills, and knowledge base

- Being curious and wanting to find out why things happen the way they do

- Using current information to create positive outcomes

However, people with an internal locus of control are also more likely to blame themselves for circumstances beyond their control, a tendency that can be damaging.

Self-control—the ability to delay the satisfaction of immediate desires for a long-term benefit—is effective in addressing behaviorial problems and correlates significantly with happiness.

In contrast, people with a high *external locus of control* believe that they have little or no control over their lives or over what people do. They often believe that life is a "function of chance, luck, or fate, is under the control of powerful others, or is simply unpredictable" (J. Rotter). These people tend to be fatalistic, passive, and accepting.

Behavioral Psychology and Observational Learning

Psychologist **Albert Bandura** (b. 1925) has influenced both behavioral psychology and social cognitive theory with his **social learning theory**. The social learning theory postulates that people learn behaviors through **observational learning**—watching and mimicking others. A child imitating her parents or older siblings plays out the old adage "monkey see—monkey do." The idea of **modeling** behavior—showing how something is done—has profound implications in our media-driven world. YouTube presents thousands of tutorials on subjects ranging from using computer programs to applying makeup and painting with watercolors. If something can be learned, a how-to can probably be found online. The visual demonstrations are easy to access, ideal for imitation, and a way to learn something new.

As Bandura examined learning, he looked beyond Skinner's view that behaviors were learned only via stimulus and response. He posited that learning takes place in a social context and has a cognitive basis. He suggested that learning can take place solely through observation or by direct instruction, and he discovered several social learning factors at work.

A key element of social learning is a model—a member of the same species exhibiting a behavior. A second element is an observer, an organism viewing the model. For example, a toddler can watch her older sibling pet the family dog gently and see how it is done. Learning something by watching someone model a behavior is called **vicarious learning**. *Vicarious* means "experienced in the imagination through someone else's actions." The model exhibits the behavior, and it is observed and interpreted by a viewer who can imitate it.

The viewer can also see the consequences of a behavior, an element of social learning called **vicarious reinforcement**. The toddler observing her mother praise the child for being so gentle with the dog is an example of vicarious reinforcement. Although reinforcements are often observed, Bandura felt that they are not needed for learning.

Reciprocal Determinism

Bandura does not regard an organism operating within its environment as a passive entity but rather as an active creator of the environment. Therefore, the environment influences the organism and its cognition which in turn influence the environment. Bandura called this mutual influence **reciprocal determinism**.

The social learning theory describes three possible models for imitation: live modeling, verbal instruction, and symbolic modeling. You imitate a live model when you learn how to use silverware by watching your parents. You experience verbal instruction anytime someone explains something—at home, in a classroom, or anywhere else. You experience symbolic modeling through various media (e.g., television, movies, the Internet, and literature). You probably know firsthand how pop culture experience on social media has influenced the behavior of many of your friends.

The Bobo Doll Experiments

Bandura reached many of his conclusions about vicarious learning by studying the behavior of children using a Bobo doll, an inflated plastic clown weighted at the bottom. When the doll was pushed over, it popped right back up.

The original experiment included four groups of children, two adults—one male and one female—and the experimenter. A child was brought into a playroom with an adult serving as a model. The experimenter instructed the child to play in one corner of the room with appealing toys while the adult was in another corner with other toys, including the Bobo doll, which the child was told were reserved only for the adult. In one scenario, the adult played with the toys for one minute and then played with the Bobo doll in an increasingly aggressive manner, including hitting, punching, and verbally assaulting. In a second scenario, a nonaggressive adult played with the other toys in his or her corner for ten minutes (and didn't play with the Bobo doll at all). After ten minutes, the experimenter returned and took the subject child to a different playroom. The experimenter told the children they could play with the toys in that room, but after two minutes, the experimenter took away that permission to increase the child's frustration. The experimenter told the child that he or she could instead play with all the toys in the original room.

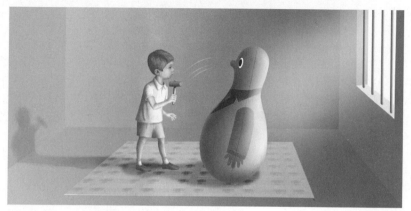

Figure 10.1 The Bobo doll experiments demonstrated vicarious learning. A video of segments of the experiment is available on YouTube.

Investigators observed the children from both groups (i.e., those exposed to the aggressive or nonaggressive models) and recorded acts of physical aggression, including kicking, punching, sitting on the Bobo doll, hitting it with a mallet, and tossing it around. They also recorded verbal aggression, including how many times the children imitated the adult model and/or used the phrases the model had used against Bobo, and they recorded any forms of aggression exhibited by the children but not modeled during the study.

Bandura found that children exposed to the aggressive model were more likely to act in a physically aggressive manner than those who were exposed to the nonaggressive model. Gender differences were also noted, with boys acting more aggressively than girls overall. Bandura predicted accurately that the children were more influenced by same-sex models than opposite-sex models.

Later variations of the experiment included children viewing video recordings of models acting aggressively toward the Bobo doll. Some models received a reward, some models received punishment, and some received no consequences at all for acting aggressively. After viewing the videos, the children stayed in the same room and were permitted to play with many toys, including Bobo. Children who viewed the model receiving punishment tended to play less aggressively with Bobo than children who viewed the model receiving rewards. Children who witnessed both neutral and rewarded models played as aggressively with Bobo as had the models.

The Science of Psychology: *The Doll Test and* Brown v. Board of Education

The Bobo doll test is a famous and influential experiment in the field of psychology. However, another doll test, one devised by psychologists Kenneth Clark and his wife Mamie Clark in 1939, became the basis for a landmark study exerting influence far beyond the field of psychology. In fact, it became the first psychological study to be used as evidence in a Supreme Court case.

The Clarks designed the experiment to test the effects of segregation on African American children—in other words, to measure the influence of a child's environment on self-image. The test was simple. An African American child was shown two dolls that were identical except for the color of their skin. They were then asked to pick a doll in response to such directions as

- Show me the doll you like best or that you'd like to play with.
- Show me the doll that is the "nice" doll.
- Show me the doll that looks "bad."
- Give me the doll that looks like you.

Most of the children chose the white doll as the "nice" one and the black doll as the "bad" one.

The Clarks repeated the experiment over a number of years in different settings, including the segregated schools of Clarendon County, South Carolina, in 1954. They found that African American children in segregated schools were more likely to choose the white doll as the "nice" one.

Professor Kenneth Clark was called as a witness in the consolidated legal cases known as *Brown v. Board of Education* that challenged the "separate but equal" ruling in *Plessy v. Ferguson* (1896) which had made segregation legal. When asked in court what conclusion he drew from the experiments, he replied: "The conclusion which I was forced to reach was that these children in Clarendon County, like other human beings who are subjected to an obviously inferior status in the society in which they live, have been definitely harmed in the development of their personalities; that the signs of instability in their personalities are clear, and I think that every psychologist would accept and interpret these signs as such." The Clarks' experiments were cited in a footnote in the Supreme Court decision striking down the concept of "separate but equal" as evidence of the harm segregation caused to African American children, marking the first time a Supreme Court decision included evidence from a study in the social sciences.

Practice: Although Professor Clark said that "every psychologist would accept and interpret these signs" as he did, in fact the science behind the Clarks' doll test has been questioned and criticized by many. With a partner, research the critiques of the Clark doll test experiment. Find critiques based on sample size, methodology, and conclusions. In a brief written report, evaluate those criticisms and the original test and draw a conclusion about the landmark value of the experiment.

Children overwhelmingly chose the white doll as the "nice one" in the Clarks' study. How might observational learning have played a role in their choice?

Social Cognitive Theory

By the 1980s, Bandura had expanded his research and his explanation of human behavior beyond social learning, integrating it into a **social cognitive theory** resting on the idea that part of what people know results from observing others. Bandura's approach to the processes that influence learning identifies four steps.

1. Attention—noticing that something is happening in the environment

2. Retention—recall of what was noticed

3. Reproduction—a producing action that mimics what was noticed

4. Motivation—a consequence from the environment that changes the likelihood of the behavior recurring (reinforcement and punishment)

Additionally, Bandura expanded his cognitive processing with the concept of **self-efficacy**, the degree to which a person believes in his or her own ability to complete tasks or reach goals and influence situations. Self-efficacy can affect virtually every aspect of a person's being, from navigating a social situation such as a party to completing a project for school or finding a fulfilling job. How will an individual respond to a challenge? A person with a weak sense of self-efficacy might ask, "How can I possibly write a 6,000-word essay?" A person with a strong sense of self-efficacy might say, "I think I'll break it down into smaller chunks that are doable." According to Bandura, an individual's level of self-efficacy is the key to successful navigation of goals, tasks, and challenges.

Organisms can store mental representations of learned responses that they may or may not perform depending upon contingencies or consequences. Bandura made the distinction between *acquisition* of a learned behavior and *performance* of that learned behavior. He claimed that reinforcement influences *which* learned behaviors are actually performed. For example, imagine you have two classes, one in which studying usually leads to the reinforcement of good grades and another in which the teacher grades exams in an arbitrary or even random manner. In the second class, even though you study, you are less likely to do well on exams. Your performance in each class is different based on the reinforcement you receive. Bandura agrees with Skinner on this count, except that Bandura maintains that reinforcement influences performance of the behavior but not the actual learning of the behavior.

Implications of Observational Learning

Bandura's numerous studies have attempted to understand the causal factors of aggressive and violent behavior as well as prosocial behavior (e.g., helping and altruistic behaviors). Studies by other researchers have shown that exposing children to aggressive and violent behavior in television, movies, and video games leads them to adopt more aggressive behavior themselves. Social learning theory indicates that children and teens learn aggression by imitating modeled behavior seen in specific media. However, not all aggressive or violent children have learned the behaviors from watching their parents or media sources. Genetics and individual biological factors (such as levels of testosterone) also play a role in determining levels and frequency of aggression.

Desensitization may partially explain a person's response to violence in the media. When graphic horror movies first came out in the 1970s, viewers experienced severe responses, even vomiting, when they saw the decapitation of a monster. Since the Internet is now able to provide virtually any kind of content, viewers can watch any level of horror imaginable. Such access to previously taboo content, including violent treatment of real, live humans, no longer has that shock value. People have become somewhat desensitized to violent content. Many lifelike video games contain so much violence that a rating system like the one used for movies was instituted to protect the youngest players from exposure.

Fighting, guns, and violence of many
kinds are common in video games.

At what point does that desensitization to video content transfer into real-world responses and behavior? What types of cognition and behavior are involved?

Studies of primate species have led to the discovery of **mirror neurons** —nervous system cells that fire both when an organism itself is doing a behavior and also when observing another organism doing the behavior. The neurons "mirror" what is happening in the environment. The presence of mirror neurons can explain the internal "ouch" we feel when witnessing someone else's sudden injury. But after repeated exposures to violence, the mirror neurons show decreased activity, suggesting desensitization. The army puts that phenomenon to work by using a first-person shooter game in virtual reality to desensitize soldiers and prepare them for the violence of combat.

While there is little evidence that playing violent video games leads to real-life violence, there is evidence that exposure to violence affects our brains and behavior in undesirable ways, often making us less willing to help someone injured in an accident and quicker to incorrectly interpret others' behavior as hostile to us.

What learning approach inspired each of these cartoons?

* * *

Learning is a phenomenon shared by all animals that are not completely governed by instinct. Human genetic makeup essentially wires us to learn, whether through classical conditioning, operant conditioning, observational learning, cognition, or some combination of these learning modes.

REFLECT ON THE ESSENTIAL QUESTION

Essential Question: *How do the principles of conditioning work with biological principles to modify human responses, and how does observing others influence behavior?* On separate paper, complete a chart like the one below to gather details to help answer that question.

Biology, Cognition, and Classical Conditioning	Biology, Cognition, and Operant Conditioning	Social Learning

KEY TERMS			KEY PEOPLE
CLASSICAL CONDITIONING	*OPERANT CONDITIONING*	*SOCIAL LEARNING*	Albert Bandura
anxiety hierarchy	abstract learning	mirror neurons	John Garcia
behavior therapy	emotion-focused coping	modeling	Mary Cover Jones
biofeedback		observational learning	David Premack
cognitive map	expectancies		Robert Rescorla
contingency theory	Gestalt psychology	reciprocal determinism	Edward Tolman
desensitization	insight learning	self-efficacy	Joseph Wolpe
latent learning	instinctive drift	social cognitive theory	
phobias	learned helplessness	social learning theory	
reciprocal inhibition	locus of control	vicarious learning	
signal relations	Premack principle	vicarious reinforcement	
systematic desensitization	problem-focused coping		
taste aversion	self-control		

MULTIPLE-CHOICE QUESTIONS

1. After several attempts at escape with no success, the victim in an abusive relationship gives up hope of escape and no longer tries. The best explanation for this is
   (A) latent learning
   (B) intrinsic motivation
   (C) vicarious learning
   (D) learned helplessness
   (E) superstitious behavior

2. Sheldon is refusing to complete his homework on time. After learning about his love of trains, Mr. Khan promises to reward Sheldon with a Thomas the Tank Engine train video after he finishes his next two homework assignments. This is an example of

(A) negative reinforcement

(B) vicarious learning

(C) insight learning

(D) latent learning

(E) the Premack principle

3. In Bandura's studies with the Bobo doll, the children in the group who saw a video of the model punished for being aggressive to the Bobo doll did not imitate the model. They only imitated the model if the model had been given a reward for being aggressive. These children obviously learned the behavior but did not perform it. This is called

(A) the Premack principle

(B) vicarious learning

(C) latent learning

(D) insight learning

(E) learned helplessness

4. A dramatic rise in children's violent play immediately following a viewing of a violent television cartoon demonstrates the role of

(A) latent learning

(B) the Premack principle

(C) insight learning

(D) vicarious learning

(E) learned helplessness

5. After extensive exposure over long periods of time, viewers can become unconcerned with the level or intensity of violence when later viewing a fight, whether on television or in real life. This change best shows the effects of

(A) latent learning

(B) secondary reinforcement

(C) desensitization

(D) observational learning

(E) classical conditioning

6. Ward and June would like to raise their children to be socially aware and helpful people. Social learning psychologists would recommend that the strongest way they can influence their children is to

(A) read prosocial books to their children

(B) avoid reinforcing the aggressive actions of the children

(C) model the desired behaviors

(D) begin the modeling once the children reach puberty

(E) be sure the children view violent behavior on television by the age of ten

7. A laboratory monkey observing a researcher lick an ice cream cone and showing brain activity in the same area as if the monkey himself had licked it is exhibiting the effects of

(A) mirror neurons

(B) instinctive drift

(C) insight learning

(D) the thalamus

(E) the brainstem

8. Monkeys raised in labs showed no fear toward snakes. Monkeys raised in the wild showed strong fear of snakes. Lab-raised monkeys shown a video of wild monkeys responding to snakes began acting fearfully after being exposed to a toy snake. This illustrates the power of

(A) insight learning

(B) prosocial behavior

(C) observational learning

(D) cognitive maps

(E) shaping

9. Which of the following is an example of observational learning?

(A) A hippo allows fish to eat off its skin to clean it.

(B) Students in a classroom have their recess taken away until they are quiet.

(C) A baseball player works in the batting cages until she becomes skilled at hitting.

(D) A worker learns to fear the phone ringing because of a boss who yells over the phone.

(E) Young women wear a clothing style similar to that of a popular singer.

10. In class just before an exam, Brendan is loud and cursing. The teacher kicks Brendan out of class. As a result, Brendan receives an F for that exam. Kaylee sees this and thinks to herself, "I am never going to do that." This is an example of

(A) vicarious reinforcement

(B) prosocial behavior

(C) latent learning

(D) operant conditioning

(E) classical conditioning

FREE-RESPONSE QUESTIONS

1. Human beings learn by watching others. Provide an overview of this topic by explaining each of the of the following. Include both definitions and/or descriptions of the terms, and explain how each concept influences social behavior.

- Observational learning
- Modeling and imitation
- Vicarious reinforcement
- Mirror neurons

2. Create a set of at least four recommendations to assist a parent with a child who is throwing temper tantrums at the most embarrassing times. In your writing, include the following terms in proper context and usage:

- Operant conditioning
- Consequences
- Reinforcement
- Punishment
- Observational learning
- Modeling

UNIT 6: Review

In this unit, you sought answers to these essential questions about learning.

Chapter 9: How do humans learn, and how do experience and association contribute to the learning process?

Chapter 10: How do the principles of conditioning work with biological principles to modify human responses, and how does observing others influence behavior?

Apply what you have learned about learning by answering the free-response question below.

FREE-RESPONSE QUESTION

The Johnson family has just added a new member to their family: Fuzzy, an adorable white Maltese puppy. They are looking forward to using their knowledge of psychology as they implement behavioral techniques in training their new puppy and having him fit into the household.

A) Explain how each of the following classical conditioning techniques could be applied to teach Fuzzy to associate receiving a treat with a desired behavior. Provide an example and identify each of the following components of classical conditioning.
- Conditioned stimulus
- Unconditioned response

B) If the Johnsons want to teach Fuzzy to lie down on command, explain how the following operant conditioning techniques could be used to train him. Give an example of each of the following.
- Shaping
- Negative punishment
- Negative reinforcement

C) Once Fuzzy knows how to lie down on command, explain how the following factors may influence his behavior.
- Stimulus generalization
- Extinction

D) Explain how Mr. and Mrs. Johnson can raise their sometimes boisterous children to be gentle with Fuzzy and take good care of him. Use the following in your explanation.
- Observational learning
- Children's entertainment

UNIT 7: Cognition

Chapter 11 *Memory and Forgetting*

Chapter 12 *Thinking, Problem-Solving, and Language*

Unit Overview

Have you ever thought about your thoughts? Did you ever wonder about how and why you remember some things and people, but other things just do not stick, no matter what strategies you try? This unit will not only examine how memory works, it also will give you some proven strategies to improve your memory for better performance in all your classes and success in later endeavors. It will also examine **cognition**, the activity that occurs in our heads, directed by our brain, that allows us to identify, process, and interpret experiences. The philosopher René Descartes famously said, "I think, therefore I am," meaning, "I think, therefore I have self-awareness, so I must exist." The ability to solve problems, be aware of our own existence, anticipate possibilities, and even ponder our own mortality is the result of a complex series of intellectual activities that most other animals do not possess (as far as we know).

Key Topics

- Similarities and differences among cognitive processes (effortful vs. automatic and deep vs. shallow processing; focused vs. divided attention)
- Psychological and physiological systems of memory (e.g., short-term memory, procedural memory)
- Principles underlying the encoding, storage, and construction of memory
- Strategies for memory improvement
- Convergence of biological, cognitive, and cultural factors in language acquisition, development, and use
- Problem-solving strategies and cognitive biases
- Characteristics of creative thought and thinkers
- Key contributors in cognitive psychology (e.g., Noam Chomsky, Hermann Ebbinghaus, Wolfgang Köhler, Elizabeth Loftus, George A. Miller)

Source: *AP® Psychology Course and Exam Description*

11

Memory and Forgetting

"The memories which lie within us are not carved in stone; not only do they tend to become erased as the years go by, but often they change, or even increase by incorporating extraneous features."

—Primo Levi, chemist, author, and Holocaust survivor

Essential Question: How do humans encode, store, and retrieve information from memory, and how can those processes be improved?

What did you have for dinner yesterday? How about two weeks ago Wednesday? What did you wear three weeks ago Tuesday? Chances are you do not recall details much further in the past than a few days ago. Do you recall your first day of second grade? How about your first kiss? The first time you drove a car? The smell of bread baking or cookies at your grandmother's house? What about the time you were embarrassed by something a friend posted on social media? How accurate are those memories from childhood?

Those last ones you might remember better because we can often remember things that have emotional meaning for us. As we go through life, we begin to evaluate and assign importance to the ideas we encounter, the people we meet, and the things we do. Those things determined to be less important are more easily forgotten. But can you trust your memories? The events you recall—did they really happen? Or happen the way you remember them?

What is Memory?

To build a framework for answering such questions, try these demonstrations. First, read the following words (or listen as your teacher reads them), spending roughly one second on each one: *bed, night, comfort, rest, awake, snore, dream, tired, eat, sound, slumber, wake.* Next, write down your full name, address, phone number, and your parents' full names. When you have finished those, write down the words you recall from the list you read or your teacher read to you without looking back at the book. (Writing your and your parents' names and your address was just for the purpose of putting some mental distance between you and the original list of words.)

Did you recall the word *aardvark*? No? Good. That word was not on the list. Did you recall the word *sleep*? If you did, you are not alone. Many if not most students recall that word when this demonstration is done in class. But go back and read the list now. Do you see the word *sleep*? It's not there. Why did you and so many others recall that word?

Maybe you will explain your response by noting that the words in that list are all connected or related to one another and to the word *sleep*. That is a good explanation and partially correct. Many of those words activated a **schema**, or mental representation of a set of connected ideas. The mind uses schemas (the technically correct form of the plural of *schema* is *schemata*, but most people use *schemas*) to make sense of the world and simplify it. The brain looks for patterns in the environment, whether they exist or not. When you look up at the clouds and see some shapes, your brain is working with your schemas to make sense of randomness. Your brain is trying to make sense of the world by finding patterns.

Try another classroom activity. Write down all the states of the United States you can recall. Then share your lists with your classmates. After sharing, note the patterns that emerge. Some students may list the states in alphabetical order because they learned a song that lists them in that order. Others may start on the West Coast and move east, while still others start east and work westward. Others begin in their home state and move outward. Yet others have a seemingly random list—they have written where they have visited or lived. Our schemas about simple geography and many other concepts can be surprisingly complex.

We all have our own schemas about such characteristics as gender, appearance, and ethnicity; what we see when we are in love; our views as students or children; and our views as teachers or parents. These schemas are influenced by our assumptions, our stereotypes, and our expectations of how things should be and how we expect ourselves and others to act. Schemas can also act as mental filters by allowing some information to pass through so we pay attention to it or blocking other information from our awareness so we ignore it. Schemas, then, influence what we remember and what we forget.

For psychologists, **memory** has a specific meaning: It is learning that has continued over time. The general model of memory psychologists use most often, the **information-processing model**, is a three-step process. The first step is for the brain to receive information in a usable form in order to maintain it in consciousness or prepare it for storage in a process called encoding. The second step is the manipulation and **rehearsal** of information so that it can be stored. The final step is the **retrieval** of the information, recalling stored memories.

As you experience your daily world, your brain operates in **parallel processing,** also called **dual processing,** interpreting numerous events and stimuli at the same time. As you are reading this passage, for example, you are seeing and interpreting the words on the page, but you may also be hearing household sounds around you or smelling your freshly bathed dog. To be able to understand everything, your brain runs all the information through its schemas in an effort to connect new information to older, established information. Making these connections consciously enables a person to improve memory and learning. You filter in the relevant information, and filter out what you do not need.

The Multi-Store Model

The currently accepted model of memory, originally theorized by psychologists Richard Atkinson and Richard Shiffrin, is known as the **multi-store model**. Its three stages are clearly delineated: sensory memory, short-term memory, and long-term memory. The first stage of their multi-store model is **sensory memory** (sensory register), during which we process everything we sense, an activity that takes less than a second to several seconds. Fleeting visual images in sensory memory are called **iconic memory**, and auditory signals are called **echoic memory**. This information will leave our brains unless we attend (pay attention) to it (more on the issue of attention later). If we do not attend to the information, it is lost. If you have ever wondered what your instructions are in class, even though the teacher just explained them, you know that when you don't pay attention, you don't remember.

Selective or **focused attention** occurs when we voluntarily focus on a portion of our sensory input while ignoring other inputs. For example, you might not notice that a parent is talking to you because you are watching (and listening to) TV. This is an example of **selective hearing**. Another type of selective attention occurs when we are in larger gatherings of people, such as a party or a noisy classroom. When, among all the sensory inputs, we hear our name spoken from across the room, our attention suddenly focuses on that. This is called the **cocktail party effect**, by which we are able to filter out nearly everything except that which is most important to us.

Once information is attended to, it can be stored into the next stage—**short-term memory (STM)**. In the Atkinson and Shiffrin model, small amounts of information are stored for up to thirty seconds or so in short-term memory. A newer understanding of STM, however, focuses on the conscious, active processing of auditory as well as visual-spatial information along with information retrieved from long-term memory. This stage of the memory process is a kind of mental "scratch pad." Short-term memory is very sensitive and vulnerable to interruption or interference.

Long-term memory (LTM) is the final stage and the type of memory that can store information indefinitely, often based on its relative importance to the individual. To make it to LTM, stimuli must be encoded. **Encoding** is taking stimuli from the environment and converting it into a form or construct that the brain can understand and use. This conversion takes place by comparing new information to information previously learned. If the stimuli are not encoded, they will be forgotten.

Figure 11.1 represents the stages in the process of moving stimuli into memory or forgetting them. If they are not attended to, they do not make it to short-term memory. If they are not encoded, they do not make it to long-term memory. The key to getting information into LTM is the coding for storage, or rehearsing the information enough so that it sticks.

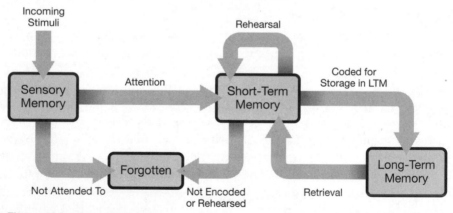

Figure 11.1 Memory Processes

Three Kinds of Long-Term Memories

Within LTM, there are three kinds of memories. **Episodic memories** are the stories of our lives and experiences that we can recall (like episodes of a television show) and tell to someone else. When people recount something that happened to them or someone else, they are using their episodic memories. **Semantic memories** are impersonal memories that are not drawn from personal experiences but rather from everyday, common kinds of knowledge, such as the names of colors, the names of the states, and other basic facts you learn over the course of your life. **Procedural memories** are memories of how to do something, such as ride a bike, bake cookies, create code for a computer, tie your shoes, and all the other tasks you have learned.

Episodic memory of a life event, such as a Bat Mitzvah

Semantic memory of math formulas

Procedural memory of steps in a process

Explicit and Implicit Memories

As the cocktail party effect shows, our brains can process several aspects of sensory input at the same time. This parallel processing is the brain's natural state. (It is not multitasking—that is a different activity.) The brain's ability to handle several different stimuli at once depends on **automatic processing**, information processing of much repeated or well learned activities that occurs without our being aware of it. For example, a basketball player at the free-throw line may have conscious attention focused on the basketball and the hoop. At the same time, however, the player's brain is automatically processing several other inputs without the player's awareness: the flexing of muscles to bend the knees and elbows, the force exerted on the ball, the motion of the arms and hands, the noise of the crowd, the distractors of fans waving behind the basket, and the sounds of the coaches yelling instructions to the other team. A brain deals with all that at once, even though attention is focused on one thing at a time.

This parallel processing uses **implicit memories**, those we retain without conscious effort and often without our awareness. Implicit memories are unconsciously retrieved. This automatic parallel processing contrasts with how computers work. They use serial, or step-by-step, processing. When trying consciously to solve problems, people will also often use a serial process.

How do we retrieve implicit memories from our long-term memories? One way is **priming**, using cues to activate hidden memories. Remember the beginning of the chapter when you read the 12 words and perhaps recalled reading the word *sleep?* That was priming in action. Students will often use priming by quizzing each other verbally right before an exam to make sure all the ideas are reviewed.

Effortful processing, in contrast to automatic processing, is encoding that requires attention and conscious effort. If you were asked to recall basic multiplication facts or what the main perspectives in psychology are, you would be using **explicit memory**, past knowledge that is consciously brought to mind. How did that information get into your brain? You did not learn it automatically but rather had to make an effort to learn it. Compare that process to implicit memories that are operating at the unconscious level; explicit memories are out in the open, recalled clearly in detail. Because explicit memories are the facts and experiences that we consciously know and can declare, they are often called **declarative memory**. We encode explicit memories through conscious, deliberate, effortful processing. By the same reasoning, implicit memories are often called **nondeclarative memory**.

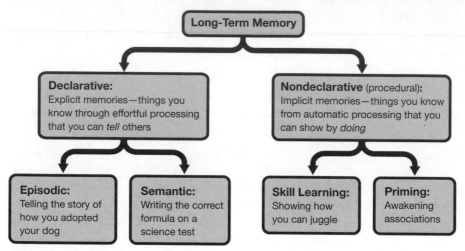

Figure 11.2 Types of Long-Term Memory

Characteristics of Short-Term Memory

Short-term memory, sometimes called **working memory**, has several characteristic features, including the limitation of information it can retain and the limited time frame in which the information can be recalled—about ten to twenty seconds. **Memory span** is the number of items a person can remember and repeat back using attention and short-term memory. It is often tested by measuring **digit span**, the longest list of numbers that can be remembered and repeated back. Subjects are given a string of numbers to recall forward or backward to determine the strength of one's STM. The backward recall is usually harder, and the process is part of intelligence tests.

Just how many items can people remember in tests like these? Psychologist **George Miller** (1920-2012), in his 1950s paper, "The Magical Number Seven, Plus or Minus Two, " gives an answer. This idea of "seven plus or minus two" is what has long been considered to be the amount of meaningful information bits one can hold in short-term memory.

One way to increase the amount of information stored in STM at one time is a process called **chunking**—combining or grouping bits of related information. An easy example is to try to recall this 20-digit number: 1 7 7 6 1 8 1 2 1 8 6 1 1 9 1 4 1 9 4 1. Not so easy. However, if you were to chunk that into five groups, you could recall it more easily: 1776 1812 1861 1914 1941. When chunked, those numbers represent the dates of wars in which the United States was involved.

Or compare how a beginner watches a sporting event with how an expert watches. The beginner typically watches the ball and focuses all his or her energy on following that. The expert, in contrast, already knows where the ball is likely to go, so he or she watches other players during the play to find insights that beginners would miss. Think about American football games, with 22 moving people, each with a role. Experts know the roles and likely outcomes and will be able to use chunking to see not only the running back carrying the ball to a particular spot but also the guard pulling to block as well as the slot receiver crossing over to block the middle linebacker. The more people know, the more they can chunk, and therefore the more information they can hold in their short-term memories.

Another way to keep information in STM is by rehearsing (practicing) the information. Most people will use **maintenance rehearsal**, repeating information to prolong its presence in STM. Some people will use maintenance rehearsal to recall a list of items needed from the store: bread, milk, eggs, paper towels, ice cream; bread, milk, eggs, paper towels, ice cream; bread, milk, eggs, paper towels, ice cream . . . . Maintenance rehearsal can increase the length of time information can be stored in short-term memory to about 30 seconds.

Characteristics of Long-Term Memory

As you read, while short-term memory holds only limited amounts of information for up to thirty seconds, long-term memory can hold an unlimited amount of information for an unlimited amount of time. Critics of the multi-store model, however, say there are more factors involved in creating long-term memories than the model describes. One critique focuses on different levels of processing and their effect on moving information into LTM. When we simply try to memorize something without attaching meaning to it, we use **shallow processing** (trying to learn ideas on a superficial level, only memorizing) and tend to forget the ideas quickly. In contrast, **elaborative rehearsal**, linking new information with existing memories and knowledge in LTM, is a good way to transfer information from STM to LTM. When we make new information meaningful to ourselves, we remember it more effectively.

Deep processing involves elaborative rehearsal along with a meaningful analysis of the ideas and words being learned. For example, when learning a new term or concept, this analysis could include making a list of terms that are related (sometimes called a mind map), examining the term for root-word connections, and relating the new term to specific previously learned ideas (how does this new term connect to what I learned in the previous unit or last semester?). In class, teachers will often have students define a term, rephrase the definition in their own words, come up with at least one example of the term, and create some kind of graphic or visual representation of the term. These activities help students go through a step-by-step formula of a deeper processing of a concept.

This process is especially important in psychology, since nearly all the ideas can be connected to other ones. The more you study psychology, the more interconnectedness you will find among the perspectives, the processes, and the basic understandings. One simple example is the term *schema*. When you examine different psychological perspectives, such as psychoanalytic, behavioral, and humanistic, you will realize that each one uses its own schemas to filter in and filter out information about behavior. Connections among concepts made through deep processing are everywhere in academic study.

Memory Processes, States, and Effects

Memory is a complex phenomenon, as the quote at the beginning of the chapter suggests. Psychologists have organized their understanding of the processes, states, and effects of memory into key concepts.

Recognition and Recall Two key concepts of memory are recognition and recall. **Recognition** is the correct identification of previously learned material. Think of how often recognition occurs while you read. You do not have to look up each word: you have already learned the meanings, so you can quickly identify the meanings and move on. In school, recognition is the process that helps you identify the correct answer on multiple-choice exams. You will see a question stem and four or five possible answers, one correct one and three or four included as distractors (false items included with a correct item). Your ability to recognize the correct response corresponds to how well you learned the material.

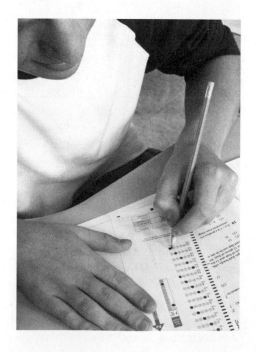

Recall is the direct retrieval of facts or information. In school, you use recall on fill-in-the-blank tests without word banks or possible choices and on essay questions. Students must take all the information from their brains to respond to the prompt for an essay. Recall is more difficult than recognition.

Memory Reconstruction Can we trust our memories completely? Would you risk your life on the accuracy of your memories? In fact, memory errors occur frequently. **Memory reconstruction** is an approach to understanding memory as a cognitive process and the errors that occur within it. People update their memories with logical processes, reasoning, new information, perception, imagination, beliefs, and cultural biases. Though they will view their memories as being honest and correct, research has shown that their recollections are not entirely accurate. During the formation of memories, details are distorted by schemas and perceptions, and people alter their memory of what happened to fit into their interpretation of events. While processing and constructing memories, people can make not only small errors but large ones as well, even to the point of creating **pseudo-memories** (false memories that a person believes to be true). For example, someone might recall that when he was a teen, he bullied another student. Later, he might run into that now grown-up person and learn that actually he was the victim of the bullying, not the aggressor. His reconstruction of his memory may have been influenced by his schema of himself as a person able to take on challenges to his pride. (See page 264 for more on unreliable memories.)

State-Dependent Memory Memory retrieval is most efficient when individuals are in the same state of consciousness, such as under the influence of a mind-altering substance, as they were when the memory was formed.

This phenomenon is called **state-dependent memory.** For example, if you learn information while slightly caffeinated, you theoretically should be able to recall that information while in a similarly caffeinated state. In a similar way, **mood-dependent memory** is the recall of information that can be retrieved while in a mood similar to when it was acquired. Mood-dependent memory applies only when the moods are genuine and authentic, not temporary mood states.

Tip-of-the Tongue State You've no doubt experienced this: "I can almost think of the name of that movie—it's on the tip of my tongue!" Tip-of-the-tongue (TOT) state is the feeling that a memory is available but not quite retrievable. People often experience this when trying to recall a particular word or name. They know they know it, but they cannot bring the word to conscious awareness. It's often frustrating, but it is a normal part of memory and recall.

Sometimes people have the opposite feeling, a feeling that they can predict beforehand whether they'll be able to remember something. Students will use this feeling as a way to judge how much more time to spend studying. This is an example of *metacognition* (thinking about one's own thinking), an idea explored in the next chapter. Sometimes this feeling proves to be accurate, but people are not particularly skilled at predicting their actual ability to recall information. For example, less skilled students will often overestimate how much they think they will remember something.

Serial Position Effect The **serial position effect** is a phenomenon that occurs when people recall the first and last items in a list more easily than the items in the middle. For example, suppose you were asked to name all the presidents. Most students will tend to recall Washington, Adams, and a few other early ones and the more recent ones, like Clinton, Bush, and Obama. Few people recall those in the middle, such Franklin Pierce or John Tyler.

When people recall the early parts of lists, they rely on the **primacy effect**—the tendency of the first item to be remembered best, and when they recall the last parts of lists, they rely on the **recency effect**—the tendency to remember the most recently presented items best. The most recent ones tend to be easiest because they are still in short-term memory.

Relearning When you learn something that you previously learned, you are **relearning**. Relearning measures the memory of prior learning. Learning a concept or skill the first time can be time-consuming, as anyone who has learned to play a musical instrument can attest. However, even after an extended layoff from a skill or idea, the amount of time it takes to relearn that concept or skill is much reduced. This is called a **savings score**, the amount of time saved when relearning information.

Eidetic Memory When a person (usually a child) has visual images clear enough to be retained for at least thirty seconds and realistic in their vividness, that person is experiencing **eidetic memory**. Eidetic memory usually disappears during adolescence and is rare by adulthood. Some adults seem to have a mythical photographic memory, recalling specific dates, times, and other semantic details of events in the past. Real photographic memory has never been demonstrated to actually exist.

Exceptional Memories A number of people have prodigious memories, but the most fascinating belong to those who are considered to have **savant syndrome** (formerly called *autistic savant syndrome*). Kim Peek (1951-2009) was a savant with numbers and dates and inspired the film *Rain Man*. Peek had the ability to count items quickly with only a glance, know days and dates over hundreds of years, and memorize the contents of 12,000 books. Another savant, Stephen Wiltshire, is an artist with an incredible memory. He was flown around London in a helicopter and from that experience alone drew a highly detailed picture of the city with complete accuracy. Highly Superior Autobiographical Memory (HSAM), or hyperthymesia, is a condition that allows those who have it to recall a vast amount of detail about the events in their lives.

Memory and Biology

Stephen Wiltshire was named Member of the Most Excellent Order of the British Empire (MBE) in 2006 for his services to art.

As you may have expected, biology and the brain play a key role in memory formation as well as in forgetting and amnesia. This biological role occurs at the level of both the neuron and the larger structures of the brain. At the neural level, **long-term potentiation (LTP)**, a lasting strengthening of synapses that increases neurotransmissions, is currently believed to be a biological basis for learning and memory in mammals. Much of LTP occurs in the **hippocampus**, the brain structure most associated with emotion and the transfer of information from short-term memory into long-term memory.

Most long-term memories are located in the cerebral cortex, but they are not all in the same location. Different parts of the cerebral cortex have smaller bits of information. For example, when we put "apple" into our brains, different aspects will go to different parts of the cortex. The shape, color, smell, texture, and memories associated with "apple" will all go to different parts of the brain.

The part of the frontal lobe on the inside near the central fissure is thought to be involved in declarative and episodic memory. The **amygdala** is the primary processor of emotional reactions and social and sexual behavior; it also regulates the sense of smell. The **cerebellum** is responsible for procedural memories such as how to tie a shoelace, play the guitar, or touch-type.

Inside the cortex of the frontal lobe is a set of neurons called the **basal ganglia**, which play an important role in memory retrieval and procedural memory. The basal ganglia are key to creating and maintaining habits. Early research showed that when rats were working through a maze for the first time—sniffing, touching, and viewing each part of the maze—their brains were very active. After they were exposed to the maze hundreds and even thousands of times, their overall brain activity decreased, especially in the decision-making parts. The parts of the brain related to smell and touch were also far less active. The rats had internalized the maze with the basal ganglia, which were discovered to store habits by recalling patterns and acting on them. This research formed part of the basis for Charles Duhigg's book *The Power of Habit:* "When people start habitually exercising, even as infrequently as once a week, they start changing other, unrelated patterns in their lives, often unknowingly. . . . [They] becom[e] more productive at work . . . . [They] smoke less and show more patience with colleagues and family." By knowing about this tiny part of our brains, we can make small and large changes in our lives. To establish or change a habit, we just need the desire to change, the cue, the reward, and the routine.

Amnesia

As you read in Unit 3 on the brain and neuroscience (pages 74–125), injury or trauma can create problems with various brain functions. One such problem is **retrograde amnesia**, or forgetting events that occurred before an injury or trauma. You might have seen old television shows in which characters would have coconuts drop on their heads and then forget who they were. Though a silly premise for a television show, that result can actually occur when the impact causes real brain damage. Usually, a brain part other than the hippocampus is affected and the individual loses episodic memories, not basic facts or language abilities.

Anterograde amnesia occurs when the hippocampus is damaged, resulting in the inability to "create" long-term memories and forcing a person to always live in the present. A PBS episode of *NOVA* told the true story of Henry Gustav Molaison, a much-studied man known in scientific journals simply as H.M. In an effort to stop his debilitating epileptic fits, H.M. had an operation to remove medial structures, the hippocampus and the surrounding cortex, on both the left and right sides. The operation succeeded in greatly reducing his seizures, but it permanently prohibited his formation of long-term memories. Long-term memories acquired before the damage remained intact, but no new declarative memories could be created. He was completely dependent on others because he could not remember if he had eaten meals or where he was going or who people were. In popular culture, anterograde amnesia has been represented in the films *50 First Dates* and *Memento,* the latter winning high praise not only from movie critics but also from neuroscientists who appreciated its realistic representation of a devastating condition.

Forgetting

Why do we forget? Psychologist **Hermann Ebbinghaus** (1850-1909) was the first to conduct experimental studies on memory to help answer this question, using himself as the subject. He devised lists of nonsense syllables: meaningless, three-letter combinations such as FEJ and QUF that test learning and forgetting without interference or association with previous knowledge (so syllables such as DOT or BAT were not used). He set about trying to memorize these lists of nonsense syllables and found that the more times he tried to remember the entire list, the better he got at remembering, until finally he had the list mastered. The relationship between the number of repetitions and his success with remembering the syllables was an early demonstration of the **learning curve,** the relationship between the increase of learning and experience.

Ebbinghaus's most famous and enduring idea is known as the **forgetting curve,** or the exponential loss of information shortly after learning it. Though Ebbinghaus focused on very specific aspects of memory and used only himself as a subject, later research confirmed his findings. Other researchers later went on to study procedural and episodic memories as well as the role of meaning in memory.

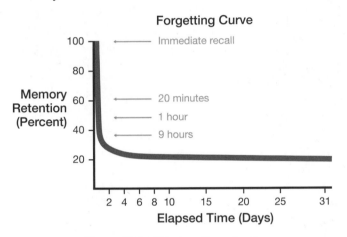

Figure 11.3 Ebbinghaus Forgetting Curve

Ebbinghaus showed that people forget at a predictable rate. But why? One reason is **encoding failure**, which occurs when a memory was never formed in the first place. The phrase "in one ear and out the other" is a great metaphor for encoding failure. We cannot learn or recall what we do not perceive and attend to. If we are focused on checking our phones, we cannot simultaneously be listening to our parents or teachers. This failure to encode leads to frustration and arguments when one person in the communication pair is not focused.

Memory Cues Any stimulus associated with a memory is called a **memory cue;** such cues usually enhance the retrieval of a memory. Often, when we forget something, the problem is that the cues that would help us recall the information are simply missing. If the cue is present, recall increases. The role of memory cues is one reason why it is often helpful to go back over the actions you were taking before entering the room if you forget why you walked into the room. Sometimes the cues are all you need to recall your reason. Memory cues also help explain why priming is a great activity before an exam, since in the process of priming, you are creating cues for yourself to help recall needed information.

Trace Decay Theory Another theory, called **trace decay theory**, addresses the role of **memory traces**, physical changes in nerve cells or brain activity that occur when memories are stored. The more we practice or rehearse a bit of information, the stronger the memory trace becomes (even until it becomes habit). If we do not strengthen the trace, we may experience memory decay, when memory traces become weaker. This theory reflects the phrase "if you don't use it, you'll lose it."

Interference Theory Another theory of forgetting is **interference theory,** which posits that there are two ways to interfere with the creation of new memories. One way is for new memories to impair retrieval of older memories. This process is called **retroactive interference**. This process helps explain why a teacher you had just a few weeks ago may forget your name. Once teachers are introduced to 175 or so new names of students at the beginning of a semester, the names of students they may have had as recently as just two weeks ago get pushed out or interfered with, and teachers have difficulty recalling them. A second kind of interference is **proactive interference**, a process by which prior learning inhibits or interferes with the recall of later learning. Have you ever called a new dog or cat by an old pet's name? If so, you have experienced proactive interference.

You can easily remember the difference between these two ideas with a **mnemonic**: **pr**oactive=**pr**evious; **re**troactive=**re**cent. Proactive interference happens when previous information blocks the new information. Retroactive interference happens when recent information blocks old information. For those who like sports, you could recall the difference with this metaphor: the old pro gets in the way of the rookie's playing time. That is, in proactive interference, the old information interferes with the new.

Repression and Suppression Psychologist Sigmund Freud had a controversial theory of forgetting called **repression**, the pushing of painful, embarrassing, or threatening memories out of awareness or consciousness. In his theory, the ego— the conscious, reality-based part of the mind— represses painful memories to reduce anxiety and emotional pain, and it does so without a person's being aware of it. This process is also sometimes called "motivated forgetting." Freud's repression theory has been extensively examined and researched over the past eighty years, but no research backs it up. (For more on repression, see the discussion on Elizabeth Loftus on the next page.)

In contrast to repression, **suppression** is a conscious process of deliberately trying to forget something that causes distress. One effective way to suppress painful or threatening thoughts is to distract ourselves by keeping busy with anything not related to the emotional pain.

Unreliable and False Memories

Some types of memories are not prone to being forgotten, but they are remembered in a way that makes them unreliable, or they are actually false. The following memory types fall into this category.

Flashbulb Memories

Flashbulb memories are vivid and detailed memories that people create during times of personal tragedy, accident, or emotionally significant world events. Major historical events, such as the assassinations of President John F. Kennedy (1963) and Dr. Martin Luther King Jr. (1968) or the attack on the World Trade Center and Pentagon on 9/11 (2001), leave indelible memories. Flashbulb memories can develop in response to big events in our own lives, but they are more often connected to national and international events. Both positive and negative events can trigger these intense memories. We may have great confidence in our memories from those standout experiences, but the memories may well be inaccurate. Factors affecting these memories are who told us about the events, where we were when we found out, aspects of the event itself, our emotional state during and after the event, the emotional states of others, and the consequences of the events in our own lives.

Eyewitness Memories

Psychologist **Elizabeth Loftus** (b. 1944) has done extensive research on memory construction and false memories and on how memory is malleable, or changeable, how it is not always accurate, and how it can have inaccurate attributions. Early in her career, Loftus did a study on how memory can change after information is shared with eyewitnesses after an event (in the original study, the event was an automobile crash). She built on previous work that found memories were not always accurate like recordings but rather were constructed after the fact. Loftus and her colleague J. C. Palmer showed that the way in which eyewitnesses were asked questions could change their responses and memories. They showed films of car crashes and then asked subjects questions about what they witnessed, using different words in the questions, such as *smashed, collided, bumped, hit,* or *contacted.* Each word prompted different speed estimates from the eyewitnesses. They also discovered that giving witnesses misleading information or asking leading questions altered the memories of witnesses. This process, in which new information alters the way previous information is held in memory, is called the **misinformation effect.** This phenomenon is connected to retroactive interference, since new information alters the way the previous information is held in memory.

The impetus for the research of Elizabeth Loftus came from her own life. She was fourteen when her mother drowned in a swimming pool. Thirty years later, Loftus's uncle told her that she was the one who found her mother's body. She had vivid recollections of the traumatic event. Soon after, her uncle called to let her know he was mistaken, that it was actually her aunt who had found her mother. She realized that misinformation had implanted a false memory.

In an attempt to show how easily memories can be implanted, a student of Loftus's created what has come to be known as the "lost in a mall experiment," in which a person can become convinced that he or she had a childhood experience of being lost in a shopping mall and may even be able to describe various details about the experience. The only problem: It never occurred. It was an implanted memory. The false memory was implanted through leading or suggestive questions.

A related concept is **source amnesia**, the inability to remember the source of a memory while retaining its substance (also called source misattribution). Source amnesia, along with the misinformation effect, is at the heart of many false memories. In the 1980s, false memories were a focus of attention in legal cases because therapists were testifying that their clients had previously forgotten memories that were brought back in a therapeutic setting. These "repressed memories" turned out to be false memories that ruined many lives and put innocent people in jail. Loftus testified in many court cases that memory could be changed and manipulated and showed how the idea of "repressed memories" are likely just ideas implanted during therapy sessions, not recollections of actual events.

Eyewitness testimony, no matter how strongly believed, can simply be wrong. When Jennifer Thompson was raped in July 1984, she told herself she would remember every detail of her rapist so he could be found, arrested, and punished. Thompson worked with a police sketch artist, and a drawing was made. Based on that drawing, a suspect—Ronald Cotton—was detained, identified by Thompson, convicted, and jailed. As it turned out, however, Cotton was the victim of inaccurate eyewitness testimony. After Cotton spent several years in jail, the arrest of the actual rapist on another charge provided DNA evidence that showed Cotton was not guilty of the rape. Thompson and Cotton got to know each other; they collaborated on a book, *Picking Cotton,* that recounts the story; and they now work together and separately on the issues of eyewitness testimony, social justice, innocence of the accused, and forgiveness.

Ways to Improve Memory and Learning

As a student, you are probably always looking for ways to improve your memory so you can do well on tests. Some processes aid your memory automatically. For example, **positive transfer** takes place when mastery of one task aids learning or performing another. One example would be softball players and volleyball players. The arm motion of throwing the softball and serving the volleyball are similar and transfer well from one sport to the other. In a similar way, the skills developed in math class often support the kind of thinking and math required in science classes. Similar transfer can occur between English and social sciences classes. The skills related to studying philosophy transfer to any subject requiring logical thinking and problem-solving.

However, not all transfer is positive. **Negative transfer** can happen as well when the mastery of one task conflicts with learning or performing another. One example of negative transfer is trying to apply the grammar rules of a first-learned language to a second. For example, in English, the conventions of word order shape the way we describe a car: "the blue car." The adjective is first and the noun is second. In Spanish, the phrase is "el coche azul," or "the car blue." In Spanish, the noun is first and the adjective is second. Beginning students of a second language often make transfer mistakes like this one. (See page 293 for more on second languages.)

Learning researchers have begun examining how to make positive transfer work more effectively. For transfer to occur, students need 1) awareness that this new situation is one in which prior knowledge can be useful, 2) successful retrieval of prior knowledge, and 3) successful use and application of the prior knowledge to the new situation. This kind of transfer will be expected of you on the AP® Psychology exam. If you look closely at the questions in this book or on any released exams, you'll see that you will be asked to apply concepts to specific scenarios, especially in the free-response questions. You need to be able to take the old information you've learned, transfer it, and apply it to new situations. That deeper learning is one of the goals for this course.

For deep learning, favorite study habits may work from time to time but not always. Recent research, such as that in books like *Make It Stick: The Science of Successful Learning* by Peter C. Brown et al. and *How We Learn: The Surprising Truth About When, Where, and Why It Happens* by Benedict Carey, offers a variety of other methods for successful learning. The strategies on the next few pages are all research tested. If a method does not work immediately for you, check to make sure you followed the method exactly. Did you go beyond shallow processing? Did you make connections with what you already know? Ultimately, you need to find methods that work for you and your brain. That process takes time, but the effort is worth it.

The Science of Psychology: *Rereading vs. Retrieval in Effective Learning*

How do you study for tests? If you are like most students, you reread the textbook and your notes. In a survey, 84 percent of college students said they used rereading as a study strategy; 55 percent said rereading was the strategy they used most often and consistently. After students reread—with the expectation that rereading will result in the greatest learning—they may test themselves with chapter-ending questions or practice tests to see how well they do. What many do not realize, however, is that the real learning takes place during those self-quizzes, when their brains retrieve information. Indeed, research has repeatedly shown that rereading has little to no effect on learning, while retrieval, especially when it is spaced out, results in solid learning. If the retrieval is done repeatedly but over a short period of time, as a student might do when cramming for an exam, its impact is also negligible.

Design an Experiment on Retrieval: Work with a partner for this activity. First, read the Science Brief from June 2016 on the website of the American Psychological Association titled "A powerful way to improve learning and memory" by Jeffrey Karpicke, Ph.D., for a good summary of the research on this topic. For each study reported in that article, note the authors, title, and date of the study; the research objective; the method of obtaining data; and the results in a chart like the one below. Discuss each study with your partner. When you have completed the chart, design your own experiment for assessing the effectiveness of retrieval for learning. Share your experiment with the rest of the class.

Authors, Title, Date	Objective	Method	Results

Learning How to Learn

Do you remember the first time you played Rock Band® or the first time you played the piano or guitar? When you begin something that is not related to other previously learned activities, you need time, rehearsal, and feedback to become proficient in a skill or knowledge area (such as psychology, history, literature, or chemistry, for example). Probably the best way is to learn how to learn, that is, learn how to be your own teacher.

TIPS FOR IMPROVING LEARNING

- Use **distributed practice**, which is spacing out your practice; **massed practice,** or cramming, is not helpful.

- Use priming to activate associations related to your subject matter. Mind maps or concept maps work well for this.

- Recite: Summarize aloud while you are learning.

- Make the ideas you are studying meaningful. When possible, use deep processing by making connections to ideas you already know. Memory works best when new information is fitted into an already existing mental structure. Explicitly connect new material to other things you know.

- Organize difficult items into chunks.

- Study repeatedly: Take advantage of down time and learn and relearn the material.

- Use available quizzes to test yourself. The **testing effect** is the finding that long-term memory is increased when some of the learning period is devoted to retrieving the to-be-remembered information through testing with proper feedback.

- Know the results of your quizzes, with feedback allowing you to check your progress.

- Minimize distractions to improve encoding. Put away your phone and turn off the television while studying.

- Get enough sleep. Lack of sleep contributes to a lower ability to concentrate and problem-solve, while sufficient sleep aids in consolidation of memory.

- **Overlearn**—continue studying beyond basic mastery.

- Use mnemonics, memory tricks or aids, to help you remember important information or concepts.

Using Mnemonics

  - Form a narrative chain or story: Remember lists in order, forming an exaggerated association connecting item one to two, two to three, and so on.

- Take a mental walk. Mentally walk along a familiar path, placing objects or ideas along the path.
- Form acronyms: **M**y **V**ery **E**arnest **M**other **J**ust **S**erved **U**s **N**ine **P**izzas (the first letters of all our planets, until they demoted Pluto to a dwarf planet in the Kuiper belt).

  - Use the acronym SOHCAHTOA for recalling the sine/cosine/ tangent relationships in trigonometry. You could also use this sentence to help you remember the acronym: **S**tudying **O**ur **H**omework **C**an **A**lways **H**elp **T**o **O**btain **A**chievement.

  - Use the acronym HOMES to recall the five Great Lakes (**H**uron, **O**ntario, **M**ichigan, **E**rie, **S**uperior).

  - Use ROY G BIV for the sequence of colors of the rainbow (**R**ed, **O**range, **Y**ellow, **G**reen, **B**lue, **I**ndigo, **V**iolet).

  - Create your own for any items you need to memorize.

- Use pictures to help you learn. Pick any term or concept and draw it in as many different ways as you can on one piece of paper.

- Practice retrieval with images: Write a term or concept on one side of each note card. Draw a picture or diagram that depicts each term or concept on the other side of the card.

- Practice testing yourself on the pictures and concepts; alternate by using each side of the flash card as a cue to guess the concept/picture on the other side. Explain the concept/picture to yourself during this step to make sure you know how and why they are related.

REFLECT ON THE ESSENTIAL QUESTION

Essential Question: *How do humans encode, store, and retrieve information from memory, and how can those processes be improved?* On separate paper, create a chart like the one below to gather details to answer that question.

How Humans Encode, Store, and Retrieve Information	How Those Processes Can Be Improved
Encode: Store: Retrieve:	

KEY TERMS AND PEOPLE

PHYSIOLOGICAL
amygdala
basal ganglia
cerebellum
hippocampus

THEORETICAL
anterograde amnesia
automatic processing
chunking
cocktail party effect
cognition
deep processing
digit span
distributed practice
dual processing
echoic memory
effortful processing
eidetic memory
elaborative rehearsal
encoding
encoding failure
episodic memory
explicit (declarative) memories
flashbulb memories
focused attention
forgetting curve
iconic memory

implicit (nondeclarative) memories
information-processing model
interference theory
learning curve
long-term memory (LTM)
long-term potentiation (LTP)
maintenance rehearsal
massed practice
memory
memory cue
memory reconstruction
memory span
memory traces
misinformation effect
mnemonic
mood-dependent memory
multi-store model
negative transfer
overlearn
parallel processing
primacy effect
priming
positive transfer
proactive interference
procedural memory
pseudo-memories
recall
recency effect
recognition

rehearsal
relearning
repression
retrieval
retroactive interference
retrograde amnesia
savant syndrome
savings score
schema
selective attention
selective hearing
semantic memory
sensory memory
serial position effect
shallow processing
short-term memory (working memory) (STM)
source amnesia
state-dependent memory
suppression
testing effect
tip-of-the-tongue state
trace decay theory

KEY PEOPLE
Hermann Ebbinghaus
Elizabeth Loftus
George Miller

1. Unlike implicit memories, explicit memories are processed by the
   (A) corpus callosum
   (B) hippocampus
   (C) cerebellum
   (D) hypothalamus
   (E) motor cortex

2. Which of the following best describes explicit memories?
   (A) Accessed without conscious recall
   (B) Nondeclarative
   (C) Processed by the cerebellum
   (D) Acquired through classical conditioning
   (E) The result of effortful processing

3. While reading a novel at a rate of nearly 500 words per minute, Megan effortlessly understands almost every word. This ability highlights the importance of
   (A) implicit memory
   (B) flashbulb memory
   (C) automatic processing
   (D) the spacing effect
   (E) source amnesia

4. Iconic memory is to echoic memory as
   (A) flashbulb memory is to implicit memory
   (B) short-term memory is to long-term memory
   (C) explicit memory is to implicit memory
   (D) visual stimulation is to auditory stimulation
   (E) automatic processing is to effortful processing

5. Students often remember more information from a course that spans an entire semester than from a course that is completed in an intensive three-week learning period. This best illustrates the importance of

(A) the spacing effect

(B) long-term potentiation

(C) the serial position effect

(D) automatic processing

(E) implicit memory

6. Rats given a drug that enhances long-term potentiation (LTP) will learn a maze with half the usual number of mistakes. This suggests that

(A) state-dependent memories are easily retrieved

(B) priming is affected by the release of serotonin into the synapses

(C) proactive interference is minimized by LTP

(D) source amnesia decreases the more the rats run the maze

(E) LTP provides a neural basis for learning and remembering associations

7. Group 1 is asked to write down the names of the seven deadly sins. Group 2 is asked to look at a list of possible names of the sins and circle the correct seven. Why might Group 2 be more likely to recall more sins?

(A) Iconic memory is superior to echoic memory.

(B) Implicit memories are easier to recall than are explicit memories.

(C) Proactive interference is less likely to affect childhood learning.

(D) Source amnesia may interfere with Group 1's ability to recall the names of the sins.

(E) Group 2's list provides more retrieval cues, making this recognition task easier for them.

8. Walking into your bedroom, you think, "I need to get my backpack in the kitchen." When you reach the kitchen, you forget what you came there for. As you return to your bedroom, you suddenly remember, "Backpack!" This sudden recall is best explained by

(A) flashbulb memory formation

(B) the misinformation effect

(C) context effects

(D) source amnesia

(E) semantic encoding

9. Austin can't remember Jack Smith's name because he wasn't paying attention when Jack was formally introduced. Austin's poor memory is best explained in terms of

(A) source amnesia

(B) storage decay

(C) proactive interference

(D) encoding failure

(E) retroactive interference

10. When Loftus and Palmer asked observers of a filmed car accident how fast the vehicles were going when they "smashed" into each other rather than "hit" or "contacted" each other, the observers developed memories of the accident that

(A) demonstrated repression of significant aspects of the accident

(B) omitted some of the most painful aspects of the event

(C) were more accurate than the memories of observers who had not been immediately questioned about what they saw

(D) were influenced by whether Loftus and Palmer identified themselves as police officers

(E) portrayed the event as more serious than it had actually been

1. Memory can be improved by using a variety of techniques. Describe five of the following techniques, and explain how they can help improve memory:
   - Effortful processing
   - Automatic processing
   - Chunking
   - Mnemonics
   - Spacing/distributed practice
   - Deep processing

2. Adina learned multiple languages growing up in Switzerland. When she moved to the United States, her primary language became English, and German, French, and Italian faded into the past. When she had to take a language course in high school, the only course available was Spanish. Her previous language experiences both helped and confused her. Define each of the following concepts, and explain how each could help her recall her previous languages OR interfere with her learning Spanish:
   - Working memory
   - Explicit memory
   - Effortful processing
   - Context-dependent memory
   - Proactive interference
   - Hippocampus

12

Thinking, Problem-Solving, and Language

"Language etches the grooves through which your thoughts must flow."
—Noam Chomsky

Essential Question: How do humans think, and how does thinking solve problems and interact with language?

The opening quotation by linguist **Noam Chomsky** highlights the integral connection between thought and language. While we do some of our thinking in images, much of our cognitive function is performed within the structure of language. That aspect of thinking is a primary focus of psychology.

Cognition—The Act of Thinking

Cognition is the mental activity associated with thinking, knowing, remembering, and communicating. While that definition may seem simple, cognition is a deeply complex set of activities that allows us to process new information, solve problems, create new ways of seeing things, and even think about thinking. Cognition defines much of who we are and how we function as social animals.

Organizing Information: Concepts and Prototypes

One way in which we make sense of our environment and experiences is to form concepts. **Concepts** are mental groupings of similar objects, events, ideas, or people. The concept of "chair," for example, recognizes high chairs, recliners, dentists' chairs, classroom chairs, desk chairs, dining room chairs, and many other types of chairs as fitting the "chair" concept.

We are also able to form *category hierarchies* from concepts. For example, the field of psychology is one discipline within the overarching field of social sciences. You may recall from Chapter 1 that psychology itself is an overarching discipline in which behavior can be viewed from a variety of perspectives and scientific approaches. That hierarchy, reflecting only a few of the perspectives, is represented in the diagram on the next page. The expansion of concepts into hierarchies or subdivisions is an important element of learning.

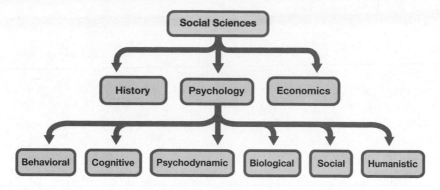

Figure 12.1 Category Hierarchy. There are many more social sciences and many more psychological perspectives than those represented in this category hierarchy.

Another tool we use for organizing and interpreting new information is the **prototype,** a mental image of the best example of a specific concept or category. The prototype contains the essential aspect of the concept. Matching new items to a prototype gives us a quick and easy method by which to sort items into categories. For example, if we encounter an unusual feathered creature, we may draw on our image of a prototypical bird, such as a robin, to categorize it. Our prototypical image of a dog might be the German shepherd, and we might compare all other similar creatures to the shepherd to see if there is a match.

The prototypes we hold in our minds are influenced by our social background, culture, and language. Together, these facets of our lives create a context and set of expectations that we apply to understand our world.

Critical Thinking

When we go beyond acquiring new information using concepts, prototypes, and other cognitive activities and develop opinions and beliefs about that information, we are engaging in **critical thinking**. Critical thinking means different things to different people. Psychologist Jane Halonen writes, "Although there is little agreement about what it means to think critically in psychology, I like the following broad definition: *The propensity and skills to engage in activity with reflective skepticism focused on deciding what to believe or do.* While people have differing definitions of critical thinking, they recognize common themes. One is skepticism, the unwillingness to blindly believe a claim just because someone says it is so. Critical thinkers question everything and everyone, including themselves. Psychology, like other disciplines that use the scientific method, has a "show me" or a "prove it to me" attitude, which leads practitioners to look beyond the conclusions to how the conclusions were reached, assessing claims and making objective judgments. Claims should be assessed based on evidence and strongly supported reasoning, not emotion and stories.

While claims of palm reading, astrology, graphology, numerology, and other forms of parapsychology may draw people in on the carnival circuit, psychologists approach them with extreme skepticism because of the lack of evidence showing any merit to them. Psychologists Carole Wade and Carol Tavris focus on key approaches to critical thinking in order to think scientifically and become wise consumers of psychological claims.

- **Ask questions; be willing to wonder**. Only by using your imagination can you speculate about what might be possible—and impossible. Ask lots of questions and then question all the answers.

- **Define the problem and define your terms**. To solve a problem, first define the terms so you can obtain the correct evidence. If you are asking, "What makes people happy?" first define what *happy* means.

- **Examine the evidence**. As a critical thinker, always be open to the idea of changing your mind after examining the evidence, even if it bruises your ego. If you have ever had an argument with someone who has said, "Nothing you can say will change my mind," you are fighting a losing battle, because that person will never examine the evidence.

- **Analyze assumptions and biases**. Recognize that you may hold unreasonable assumptions and harbor biases. Again, don't let a bruised ego stand in the way of getting at the truth. Being "right" in an inauthentic way helps no one.

- **Avoid emotional reasoning**. "If I feel this way, it must be true." Intuition and gut feelings have their place in decision-making. However, when these emotions replace a clear thought process and make one unable to think through a situation or issue logically, bad decisions are often the result.

- **Don't oversimplify**. A person who thinks critically understands the complex nature of people and issues they face. Go beyond the obvious, resist generalizations, and avoid either-or arguments. Life is complex and our explanations should not be simple.

- **Consider other interpretations**. Often, headlines or news stories reach a simple conclusion based on some new study. Be aware that there could be several possible explanations of reported results. One simple example of the dangers of not considering other interpretations would be concluding that a friend hates you because she ignored you as you passed each other today. Do you know for sure she saw you? What if she just came from an argument with another person? What if she just got out of a challenging class, just got some disturbing news, or had no sleep and was not even aware of anyone outside of her own immediate space? Consider other possible interpretations before you jump to conclusions. Things are not always as they seem—look beyond the obvious.

- **Tolerate uncertainty and ambiguity**. Life can be challenging and we do not always know what is right. Be comfortable with saying "I'm not sure" or "I need more proof," leaving the door open to continue to search for an answer.

Practice: The 2009 book *50 Great Myths of Popular Psychology: Shattering Widespread Misconceptions About Human Behavior* by psychology professors Scott O. Lilienfeld, Steven Jay Lynn, John Ruscio, and Barry L. Beyerstein examines the too-often unchallenged psychological claims that have made their way into popular culture. With a partner, choose one of the following such claims and use each of the bulleted strategies to think critically about it. Gather evidence you need to reach a reasoned conclusion about the claim you have chosen, and present your findings to the class.

1. We use only 10 percent of our brains.

2. Expressing anger is better than holding it in.

3. Full moons cause crimes and insanity.

Creativity and Creative Thinking

Another type of thinking that goes beyond the mere acquisition of information is creative thinking, or creativity. **Creativity** is the ability to produce novel and valuable ideas within any discipline, including art, music, architecture, mathematics, science, and engineering. Any profession that involves solving problems or creating new ideas or new products relies on individual creativity.

What characteristics or components make up creativity? One is expertise—a strong base of knowledge about a topic or a high level of aptitude for certain skills. Another is high intelligence. Imaginative thinking skills and an ability to look at subjects from different perspectives can also contribute to creativity. Some artists are especially skilled in this ability. While some visual artists are exceptionally good at reproducing pictures or images they see, others are able to create new representations of features, traits, or images to create an original work of art that has never before been imagined. An adventurous personality—one comfortable with change, ambiguity, and risk—may also contribute to creativity. The most creative individuals are also known to have high levels of intrinsic motivation and to thrive in environments designed to spark, support, and refine creative ideas. Several companies in Silicon Valley (Google®, Apple®, and Pixar®, for example) have unusual workplaces in which the design and style of work is intended to foster creativity. Pixar, for example, provides a friendly and relaxed atmosphere, including a cereal bar with 14 kinds of cereals, other food and alcohol bars, the Smile Squad to help visitors find their way around, in-house aerobics classes, and improvisation classes. Workers are also encouraged to personalize their own workspaces, as well as to use the pool, play basketball and volleyball, and jog the trails. The company complex is open twenty-four hours a day, and employees can choose to work in whatever time period they prefer. Corporate culture supports the idea that mistakes are not only allowed but actually encouraged as part of the creative process.

Two kinds of thinking also influence creativity. **Convergent thinking**, in which a question invites only one correct answer, limits creativity. One example of convergent thinking is that which is required to answer a multiple-choice question, such as those on the AP® test for this course. Each question is designed to have only one answer, which is known through reading comprehension and interpretation of data and concepts, with no creativity involved. A second kind of thinking is much more compatible with creativity. **Divergent thinking** is required when a question or problem can have several or many possible responses. A standard creativity question is, "How many uses can you think of for a brick (or paperclip)?" Even on weekends when you are bored, you may think divergently when you ask, "What should I do next?" because there may be many possibilities.

Psychologist Mihaly Csikszentmihalyi (pronounced chik-sent-ma-hi-ee) wrote the following about creativity:

> When we're creative, we feel we are living more fully than during the rest of life. The excitement of the artist at the easel or the scientist in the lab comes close to the ideal fulfillment we all hope to get from life, and so rarely do. Perhaps only sex, sports, music, and religious ecstasy—even when these experiences remain fleeting and leave no trace—provide a profound sense of being part of an entity greater than ourselves. But creativity also leaves an outcome that adds to the richness and complexity of the future.

Artists at their easels may feel the excitement and fulfillment of creativity.

Metacognition

When we think about our thinking—whether we are acquiring information or thinking critically or creatively—we are using **metacognition**, the active control and awareness of our own thinking. Metacognition is a complex process during which we examine how we are thinking, the cognitive steps we take, the biases we may have, and our approach to learning a task. We may also use metacognition to test ourselves to see how much we learned, examine our choices, and figure out how to change our thinking in the future.

Solving Problems

The ways humans have put their thinking abilities to use to solve problems is the cornerstone of human progress and a key distinction between humans and other animals. Psychology focuses on three main kinds of problem-solving. One is how people find relationships among numbers, words, symbols, or ideas. A second is how people arrange information to fit a preconceived structure. A third is how people flexibly make a series of changes in order to achieve a goal.

Problem-Solving Methods

How do we solve problems? As you read about the following methods, think of times when you used each one.

Trial and Error The first method is typically **trial and error**, a process by which we try out different solutions until we find one that works. This strategy works best when a problem has relatively few solutions.

Algorithms A second strategy is to use algorithms. An **algorithm** is a methodical, logical rule or procedure that guarantees solving a problem because it explores every possibility. For example, if you wanted to know the sum of all the numbers from 1 to 100, you could add them one by one: 1+2=3; 3+3=6; 4+6=10; and so on for a very long time. Eventually you would get an accurate answer, assuming your math was correct, because you used the algorithm of adding one number to another and then adding that sum to the next number. Or you might know a simpler algorithm for getting the same answer much more quickly. If you add the lowest number and the highest number (1+100), you get 101. If you add the next lowest number and the next highest number (2+99), you also get 101. If you add the next lowest number and the next highest number (3+98), you also get 101. You might by now see the pattern emerging— each "next lowest" and "next highest" number will add up to 101. You can keep going, but once you get to 50+51, all the rest will be duplicates of sums you already did. In other words, there are 50 pairs of numbers whose sums are 101. So you can multiply 101 x 50 and get the sum of all the numbers from 1–100: 5,050. Both methods use an algorithm. Computers, with their blinding speed, handle algorithms well, but for humans, algorithms are often inefficient.

Heuristics A third way to solve problems is to use **heuristics**, which are "rules of thumb." This simple thinking strategy often allows us to make judgments and solve problems efficiently, but the shortcuts involved in heuristics may lead to incorrect outcomes. One example of a heuristic you might use when applying for suitable jobs would be to avoid considering a job if the advertisement for it has spelling and grammar errors—those might suggest a sloppiness that could carry over to other parts of the company. If you cast your vote for candidates on the basis of their party, you are using a heuristic. When choosing a restaurant, you would be using a heuristic if you based your choice on which one had the most cars in its parking lot or the longest wait for a table, since those might suggest the restaurant is very popular. The strategy of using heuristics is usually speedier than using algorithms— imagine reviewing every single restaurant in your area before making a choice, as you would do with an algorithm. Heuristics allow the user to discard more options easily and use fewer data than algorithms. They are often right, but they can lead to error.

Insight The three strategy-based ways to solve problems above are not the only ways. For example, you might solve a problem with **insight**—a sudden and often novel realization of the solution to a problem, such as suddenly seeing a cause and effect relationship. Insight can sometimes occur long after you are first exposed to a problem, sometimes even years later. During all that time, the brain works in the background, unconsciously analyzing information and connections. The larger your base of information (the more you know), the more effective and frequent insight will be as a problem-solving method.

Wolfgang Köhler documented the insight method of solving problems when he studied chimps trying to get bananas that were out of reach. In the room with the chimps and the out-of-reach bananas were several boxes. For most of the time Köhler observed, the chimps were unproductive and upset. They screamed and exhibited behaviors not related to solving the problem of reaching the bananas. Then, suddenly, they placed the boxes on top of one other and climbed on them to reach the bananas. Though other researchers believe the chimps may have used trial and error, in Köhler's view the chimps had sudden insight, an "aha" moment, on how to solve the problem.

These chimps may look like they are talking through a problem, but for the chimps in the experiment, the answer came with insight in an "aha" moment.

Intuition Somewhat akin to the concept of insight is **intuition**—what we know without knowing how we know it. It is an effortless, immediate, automatic feeling or thought that allows us to interpret a situation or problem and quickly reach conclusions. Intuition contrasts with the explicit, conscious reasoning involved in other problem-solving methods. When we use intuition, we are using the automatic processing of our implicit memories to reach conclusions. The mechanisms in our brain do the problem-solving work without our having to focus our attention on it. Intuition allows our experience with the world to work its way through our unconscious mind to assist us in decision-making.

Emotional learning leads to what many of us think of as intuition. We "have a feeling" based on a previously learned fear or other emotional experience. That feeling is different from the conclusions of experts, who are quickly able to deduce something based on very little information because of their previous experience. Psychologist Daniel Kahneman uses the example of a chess master to explain. He says that "after thousands of hours of practice . . . chess masters are able to read a chess situation at a glance." Their minds are already filled with all the possible moves and the consequences of each and can therefore even play many people simultaneously. This expert-level intuition is a far cry from our gut-level intuitions.

In his book *Blink: The Power of Thinking Without Thinking,* Malcolm Gladwell details the process of how experts in any field can use a small segment of information about a topic or issue and come to accurate conclusions without going through the traditional problem-solving steps. This process is called *thin-slicing.* In one chapter, he describes art experts who are able to examine sculptures or paintings briefly and then conclude whether they are originals or excellent forgeries.

We need to use our logical minds to solve problems, but we should not ignore our guts when they tell us something is not right about a situation. For most people, overreliance on either one will not produce as good a result as balancing reason and appropriate attention to a gut reaction.

Mindset—A Mental Stance to Problems

How we approach a problem is another factor in our ability to solve it. Psychologist Carol Dweck has written about this stance, called **mindset**. Mindset is a mental approach to problems and issues, often connected to the psychological construct of intelligence. Do we think that we are able to improve and grow? If so, we have a **growth mindset**. If we conclude that there can never be any change, we have a **fixed mindset** and may be tempted to ask, "Why bother?" Adjusting your mindset can make you more open to finding solutions and fixing mistakes. For example, if you say, "I'm no good at this," chances are you won't get very far toward your goal. Instead, try asking, "What am I missing?" Instead of saying, "It's good enough" as an evaluation of work you have just completed, try adjusting your mindset towards growth by asking, "Is it really my best work?" Replace "I made a mistake and I stink at this" with "mistakes are how I learn." The idea of mindset is to give up the perception of learned helplessness that some students feel and replace it with a more hopeful and corrective way of thinking about learning (and life).

Problems in Problem-Solving: Cognitive Biases

If we know how to solve problems, why is it that we are often so bad at it? One reason is we might be out of practice in the necessary skills. When you were younger, for example, you no doubt had your multiplication tables memorized. Now, you might have to stop, think, and then respond, possibly even needing to reach for your phone or a calculator. Without using our problem-solving muscle—the brain—our skills diminish. Even if we are not out of practice, however, there are predictable ways we fail to solve problems. They involve succumbing to **cognitive biases**—ways of thinking that veer us away from strictly rational conclusions.

Preconceptions, Fixation, and Mental Set

Confirmation bias is the tendency to search for information that supports our preconceptions and to ignore or distort contradictory evidence. The line from the Simon and Garfunkel song "The Boxer" says it well: "A man hears what he wants to hear and disregards the rest." Our confirmation bias is at work when we are in love and ignore all the negatives about our potential lifemate. It is at work when we see others through the filter of stereotypes and prejudice. It is at work when we allow information in that justifies or confirms our bias and ignore or reject information that counters our belief. Confirmation bias is one of the ways we delude ourselves (or, more bluntly, lie to ourselves to stay within our comfort zone). (See page 26 for information on confirmation bias in research.)

A second interference with problem-solving is **fixation**, the inability to see or define a problem from a fresh point of view. If we become fixed on one way of looking at a problem (or even seeing something as a problem rather than something to be ignored), we may be unable to solve or move beyond it. "If all you have is a hammer," the old adage goes, "every problem looks like a nail."

Fixation applied to attempts to solve novel problems is called **functional fixedness**. This cognitive bias is a tendency to think of things only in terms of their usual functions, as if they could have no other functions. The lack of creativity associated with functional fixedness can be an impediment to problem-solving. To avoid it, try thinking of other than the original use for objects. For example, the main use of a credit card is to pay for goods and services. But if you are locked in a room without a key, you could see a new function for a credit card and use it to slide the latch open. Or you could use a high-powered fan as a leaf blower or coffee mugs to hold office supplies.

Mental set, a tendency to approach a problem in one particular way, often a way that has been successful in the past, is also related to fixation. If we studied for a test one way and we scored well, we will tend to stick with that method. If we had to use an out-of-the-way door to enter a twenty-four-hour store after 10 p.m., we might go out of our way to use that same door even before 10 p.m., wasting time and energy.

Problematic Heuristics

While heuristics can be helpful problem-solving tools, a few kinds of heuristics can occasionally lead us astray in problem-solving. One is a **representativeness heuristic,** with which we judge how something represents, or matches, certain prototypes we have. In research by Amos Tversky and Daniel Kahneman, the representativeness heuristic was illustrated with the following example. A former neighbor described Steve this way: "Steve is very shy and withdrawn, invariably helpful, but with little interest in people, or in the world of reality. A meek and tidy soul, he has a need for order and structure, and a passion for detail." Is Steve more likely to be a farmer, physician, salesman, pilot, or librarian? If you use the representativeness heuristic with Steve, he would more likely fit the stereotype of a librarian than the other professions. With the representative heuristic, we make judgments that are based on how well people fit into our preconceived notions of groups they might belong to. Or how about a woman who wears glasses and loves to read? Is she more likely to be a teacher or a biker? That description fits our stereotype of a teacher, but there are only 3.1 million teachers in the United States and about 6 million bikers. The numbers suggest that despite our stereotypes, the woman is more likely to be a biker. Our rule of thumb of how well people fit into our prototype misleads us into reaching the wrong conclusion.

We would also be using a problematic heuristic if we judged that a younger person is more likely to commit suicide than an older person. We often have the prototype (or even stereotype) of a depressed adolescent. However, the reality is that suicide rates are higher in older populations than in younger populations in the United States. Yet another example uses appearances to possibly mislead. When we look at a school with a trimmed lawn, painted and neat classrooms, and a polite and helpful office staff, do these appearances mean the school is well managed? Are appearances reflective of reality? If we conclude the school is well managed based on these outer signs, we are falling to the idea that these traits are connected to good schools. The reality is that some beautiful schools are terrible learning environments, and some schools are amazing despite less than ideal buildings.

A well-trimmed lawn and fresh paint do not make a reliable heuristic about school quality.

The **availability heuristic**, which estimates the likelihood of events based on their availability in memory, is another problematic heuristic. If instances come readily to mind (perhaps because of their vividness), we presume such events are common. The availability heuristic operates on the principle of "if you can think of it, it must be important." Two classic examples follow:

- Are there more words that begin with the letter K or more words with K as the third letter?

- If you were to travel to the Middle East (Southwest Asia), which would you be more concerned with, a terrorist attack or a traffic accident?

We can easily think of many words that begin with the letter K (*koala, kind, kid, kangaroo, kitchen*), but words with K as the third letter are less easily available to our brains (*bake, cake, make,* for example). The same goes for the second question. The news and social media report terror attacks, but we rarely learn of all the traffic accidents that occur.

Related examples of the availability heuristic include fear of planes because of 9/11 or fear of trains because of the bombings in Spain, Britain, France, India, and elsewhere. The availability heuristic can also influence ideas about relationships. If your parents and your friends' parents are all or mostly together (or divorced), you may have a view of relationships based on what is available to your own mind, not what is actually real in the larger picture. Heuristics are usually right, but in these cases we might reach wrong conclusions.

Overconfidence, Perseverance of Belief, and Cognitive Dissonance

Overconfidence is the tendency to overestimate the accuracy of your beliefs and judgments. We often think that we are more correct than we are. We assume we will make few mistakes when attempting to solve new problems, but we actually make many more than we believed we would. On top of that, we may also experience **self-serving bias**, a problem-solving barrier resulting from evaluating ourselves in an overly favorable manner, explaining our success by internal traits and our failure by external factors. If we make only a few mistakes and do well on a test, we tell ourselves, "I did well on this exam because I am smart." If we do poorly, we tell ourselves, "The teacher did not prepare us well." This self-serving bias protects our own interests or self-esteem.

Belief perseverance is the thinking flaw of clinging to our initial conceptions even after the basis on which they were formed has been discredited. In some respects, belief perseverance is a form of denial. Parents who love their son will often continue to believe that he is a "good boy" despite video evidence of his bullying behavior.

Psychiatrist Frantz Fanon wrote, "Sometimes people hold a core belief that is very strong. When they are presented with evidence that works against that belief, the new evidence cannot be accepted. It would create a feeling that is extremely uncomfortable. That uncomfortable feeling is called **cognitive dissonance**. And because it is so important to protect the core belief, they will rationalize, ignore and even deny anything that doesn't fit in with the core belief." This cognitive disconnect is very common and comes into play every time we rationalize, that is, find a seemingly reasonable but actually false explanation for the evidence presented. We may even flat out deny the evidence. If a core belief has become a part of an individual's identity, then that identity is threatened by a challenge to that belief and rationalizing is a common defense.

Additionally, cognitive dissonance is at work whenever we need to justify our struggles (**justification of effort**) in an endeavor. Psychologist Leon Festinger said that people tend to love more the things for which they have to work hardest. Imagine two soldiers, one a volunteer, one a draftee. Both are experiencing the pains of basic training or being a soldier in a war zone. The draftee can easily justify his dislike of the experience—he had no choice in the matter. The volunteer must justify why he or she chose to be in such a dangerous situation. The explanation will often involve loving being a soldier or being in the military. The harder we have to work for something, the more we love it. We must justify to ourselves that the result is worth the effort, whether we are involved in the military, sororities or fraternities, or even relationships. (For more on cognitive dissonance, see page 600.)

Framing

Another cognitive bias is **framing**, the process of presenting or posing an issue or question. How an issue is framed can significantly affect decisions and judgments people make. One version of framing is the *false dichotomy*, the "either you're with us or you're against us" way of thinking. "You are either part of the solution or part of the problem." "Either you love Pokemon® or you hate children." These examples show two extreme positions with no possible middle ground.

False dichotomies can also be built on false premises, as in "all animals are either mammals or fish." Chickens are animals; they are not mammals, so framed this way, chickens must be fish. If the premise is wrong, the conclusion is also wrong.

Psychologists Amos Tversky and Daniel Kahneman studied a concept called **risk or loss aversion**—the tendency of people to prefer avoiding losses to achieving equivalent gains. They looked at how people made decisions and discovered that framing—*how* a question was asked—affected those decisions.

"Your problems are caused by all-or-nothing thinking. It's either that, or you don't have any problems."

They examined a hypothetical life and death situation. Subjects were asked to choose between two treatments for a deadly disease that afflicted 600 people. Treatment A was predicted to result in 400 deaths, and treatment B had a 33 percent chance that none of the ill would die but a 66 percent chance that everyone would die. So the question was framed in a "how many would live" versus "how many would die" format.

- In the positive framing, treatment A will save 200 lives, with treatment B having a 33 percent chance of saving all 600 people and a 66 percent possibility of saving no one.

- In the negative framing, with treatment A, 400 people will die, and with Treatment B, there is a 33 percent chance that no people will die and a 66 percent probability that all 600 will die.

When framed in the positive way, 72 percent of subjects chose treatment A. With the negative framing, only 22 percent chose treatment A, even though the outcome for both treatments is exactly the same. In short, how we frame a question will change people's responses. (As you read in Chapter 11, how we frame questions can actually change our memories of events.) People tend to react differently to choices depending on how the information is framed: loss versus gain and positive versus negative. Is it better to say a medical treatment has a 90 percent chance of success or a 10 percent chance of death? Of course, the answer depends on your objective. Advertisers and politicians carefully frame their statements to affect people's decisions in a way that gets them to buy a product or vote for or against a candidate.

Anchoring

Cognitive bias can also occur through the **anchoring effect**—a cognitive bias favoring the first information offered. When asked a question with a reference point, we will often be biased in favor of the information in that reference point. For example, when asked if the Mississippi River is shorter or longer than 500 miles, most people correctly said longer, but they tended to estimate the length between 1,000 and 2,000 miles. When asked if the Mississippi River is longer or shorter than 5,000 miles, they accurately said shorter, but their guesses were between 3,000 to 6,000 miles. The river is actually 2,320 miles long. In this situation, the anchor pulled the guesses in its own direction.

Here's another example of anchoring. A mom and her daughter are shopping for jeans. The daughter finds a pair she loves for $200, and her mom is flabbergasted at the price. The daughter says the jeans are on sale at 20 percent off—a great deal. To the mother, who paid $20 for regular jeans and maybe $50 for great ones when she was a teenager, even at a great deal these jeans seem way too expensive. Each person has a frame of reference with different anchor points.

Humans, then, are not the rational creatures we often presume to be. We are often irrational—but in predictable ways related to cognitive biases. Knowing how we are irrational can help us understand ourselves and others.

Language: The Basis of Communication

In order to think about thinking, we need language, the primary means through which we communicate our ideas and reflect on our lives. "Humans are so innately hardwired for language," writes psychologist and linguist Steven Pinker, "that they can no more suppress their ability to learn and use language than they can suppress the instinct to pull a hand back from a hot surface."

Language is our spoken, written, or signed words and the ways we combine them to communicate meaning. Our language and its complexity represent one of the greatest differences between humans and other animals.

The Basics of Language

Linguistics is the scientific study of language. Subcategories include phonology, morphology, syntax, grammar, semantics, and pragmatics.

A **phoneme** is the smallest distinctive sound unit in a language. English uses about 40 phonemes. A few of the basic sounds in English are illustrated in Figure 12.2.

Some Basic Sounds (Phonemes) in English	
S as in *sat*	E as in *egg*
T as in *tap*	I as in *ink*
P as in *pan*	O as in *otter*
N as in *nose*	Oa as in *boat*
M as in *mat*	Oo as in *cook*
A as in *ant*	Oo as in *boot*

Figure 12.2 Selected English Phonemes

A **morpheme** is the smallest unit that carries some meaning (semantic interpretation). It may be a word or a part of a word (such as a prefix). Some morphemes are also phonemes, such as *I* or the *s* that indicates a word is plural. The word *unkindness* has three parts: *un-* (the prefix), *kind* (the root word), and *-ness* (the suffix). Each one contributes meaning to the word, so each is a morpheme.

In a language system, **grammar** is a set of rules that enables us to communicate with and understand others. **Syntax** determines the rules for combining or arranging words into grammatically sensible sentences. **Semantics** is the set of rules by which we derive meaning.

How do we know how to shape our language to the situations in which we find ourselves? Pragmatics has the answer. **Pragmatics** in language means knowing when to use certain kinds of language in social situations. One category is purpose: greeting, informing, demanding, promising, and requesting. A second category is responding appropriately to the needs of the situation, such as when speaking with a child or with a person learning one's language or speaking with one's friends outside of school versus in the classroom. A third is following rules for communication, such as taking turns in a conversation, staying on topic, rephrasing a misunderstood message, using verbal and nonverbal signals appropriately, standing appropriately near or far from someone, and using facial expressions and eye contact.

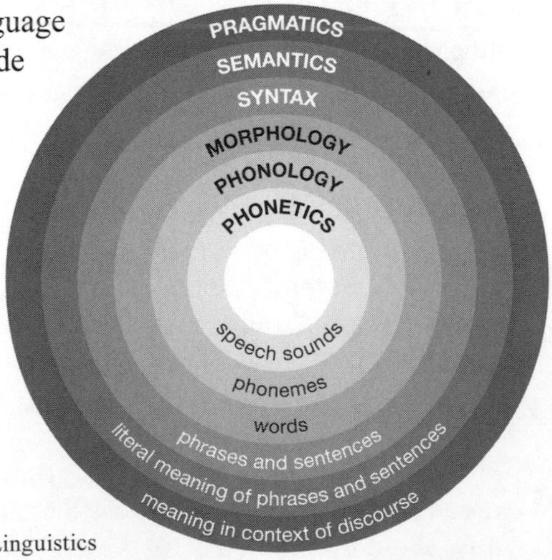

Figure 12.3 Subcategories of Linguistics

Language Development

Humans develop language skills in a predictable series of stages that are universal across cultures. The first is the **babbling stage**, beginning at about four months of age. This is the stage of speech development in which the infant spontaneously vocalizes various sounds at first unrelated to the language spoken in the home. These are essentially nonsense sounds that have no meaning, such as "ba-ba-ba" or "da-da-da."

By the time a child is about ten months old, the sounds take on the sounds of the home language. If children are not exposed to alternate languages, they tend to lose the ability to make and hear the phonemes of other languages. Therefore, an adult English speaker could not "hear" and discriminate among some of the sounds in Mandarin (a tonal language) or languages with clicks, such as Xhosa and Swazi.

Next is the **one-word stage** of language development that typically takes place between ages one and two, during which a child speaks mostly in single words. This is sometimes called the *holophrastic* stage, since a whole idea can be expressed in one word. For example, "Go!" might mean "I want to leave now." "Car" could mean "There is a car."

The **two-word stage** of language development begins at about age two. During this stage, a child speaks mostly two- or three-word statements, such as "car go" or "Daddy fall" or "Mommy silly" or "want cookie." In this stage, known as **telegraphic speech** because a child's speech is like a telegram, a child will use mostly nouns and verbs. **Overgeneralization**—the application of grammar rules in instances to which they do not apply, as in "Daddy buyed me a present"—is common during this stage.

By ages six to ten, children can speak in full **sentences** and master syllable stress patterns to distinguish among words. By this age, they have learned 80 percent of all the language they will ever need. Nearly all the rest is learning complexity, metaphors, irony, puns, simile, allegory, hyperbole, analogy, rhetoric, poetry, rhyme schemes, puns, euphemisms, and other linguistic subtleties. This early language mastery is why it seems like the five-year-old kids you just met speak better Spanish than you do despite the fact you've taken four years of it. They have learned the basics and acquired all the sounds and primary tenses with which you have struggled.

Between the age of five and puberty, language acquisition becomes more difficult than during the first five years of life, but it is still more effective than learning a new language as an adult. Language learned after the age of nine, whether sign language or a verbal/written language, will generally result in communication less fluent than that of native speakers of that language.

How Do We Acquire Language?

MIT linguist Noam Chomsky proposed a nativist theory of language acquisition, positing that people are born with what he termed a **language acquisition device (LAD)**. He proposed that all people have an inborn capacity to learn the language with which they are raised. Healthy children universally are able to learn whatever language they are exposed to regardless of which language it is.

Another approach to understanding how people learn language is called **statistical learning**. In this kind of learning, babies have been observed determining where breaks and pauses would be in speech and what syllables seem to go with other syllables, being able to "extract the structure" of language and determine patterns. Research is continuing on just how babies can do this, though statistical learning does presume that there is enough environmental stimuli for the brain to learn language and that the child and the caregiver are actively engaged with each other.

B. F. Skinner and others with a behavioral perspective proposed that people learn language through conditioning and observational learning. The specific principles of learning are association (seeing/hearing connection between words and actions/things), imitation of sounds (modeling and imitation), and reinforcement of certain kinds of responses. This view has fallen out of favor in light of what researchers have discovered about the brain.

Language and Cognition

Philosopher Ludwig Wittgenstein wrote, "The limits of your language mean the limits of your world." This quote aligns with **linguistic determinism**, the idea articulated by Benjamin Lee Whorf that the language one uses determines the way one thinks and one's view of the world. A softer version of this idea is called **linguistic relativity** (also known as the Sapir-Whorf hypothesis, named after linguists Edward Sapir and Whorf). Linguistic relativity is a hypothesis that assumes that language and thought have *influences* on each other—the language one speaks influences how one thinks, and vice versa—but language doesn't *determine* thought.

Researchers are exploring the mutual influence of language and thought and the correlation between the importance of an idea to a culture and the number of words a language has to describe it. That is, the more vocabulary available to describe different gradations or complex aspects of something, the more subtleties people can explore—and with greater speed. For example, cars are an important part of American culture. There are many slang terms for cars, but there are also different words for different variations of cars: *sedan, coupe, convertible, hatchback, truck, pickup, jeep, 4WD, minivan, van, SUV, compact, midsize, full-size, hybrid,* and *electric*. Does this abundance of vocabulary change the way we understand and think about cars or reflect the importance they hold in our lives?

In the same way, think of all the euphemisms we have for someone who has died. We say people *passed away, expired, ceased to be, went to meet his maker, joined the choir eternal, departed, breathed her last, gave up the ghost, earned his wings, kicked the can, kicked the bucket, met an untimely end, laid down his life, lost her life, reached her journey's end, perished, slipped away, succumbed, terminated, was called home, is six-feet under,* with dozens more expressions beyond these. Do all these euphemisms help soften the way we think about dying? The linguistic relativity hypothesis would say yes.

Grammar also plays a role in how we think about certain social relations. In the Romance languages, for example, there are formal and informal pronouns (*tú/usted; tu/vous*) that reflect a specific relationship with the person addressed. In English, on the other hand, a pronoun is a pronoun, with no markers for the nature of the relationship. The Romance languages also have masculine and feminine forms of nouns. The grammar of a language tells its speakers how to think about gender, a social creation.

Those who speak two languages (bilingual speakers) or more (polyglots) have an advantage both cognitively and socially. The brains of bilingual speakers do a parallel set of processes that enhance the ability to learn new words easily, use information in new ways, put words into categories more easily, come up with solutions to problems more effectively, listen more intently, and make better social connections. Research has also shown that polyglots have increased cognitive control and fewer cognitive issues when aging compared with the monolingual.

REFLECT ON THE ESSENTIAL QUESTION

Essential Question: *How do humans think, and how does thinking solve problems and interact with language?* On separate paper, complete a chart like the one below to gather details to answer that question.

How do we make sense out of and evaluate incoming stimuli, and what kinds of thinking block or open doors to creativity?	How do we solve problems?	What cognitive biases get in the way of solving problems?	How do we acquire language, and how do language and thought interact?

KEY TERMS			KEY PEOPLE
COGNITION AND PROBLEM-SOLVING	*COGNITIVE BIASES*	*LANGUAGE*	Noam Chomsky
	anchoring effect	babbling stage	Wolfgang Köhler
algorithm	availability heuristic	grammar	
cognition		language acqui- sition device (LAD)	
concepts	belief perseverance		
convergent thinking	cognitive biases	linguistic determinism	
creativity	cognitive dissonance	linguistic relativity	
critical thinking		linguistics	
divergent thinking	confirmation bias	morpheme	
fixed mindset	fixation	one-word stage	
growth mindset	framing	overgeneralization	
heuristics	functional fixedness	phoneme	
insight	justification of effort	pragmatics	
intuition		semantics	
metacognition	mental set	sentences	
mindset	overconfidence	statistical learning	
prototype	representativeness heuristic	syntax	
trial and error		telegraphic speech	
	risk or loss aversion	two-word stage	
	self-serving bias		

MULTIPLE-CHOICE QUESTIONS

1. When confronted with the sequence "__N__" at the end of a word in a crossword puzzle, Tony inserts the letters "I" and "G" in the two blanks because that procedure has often led to the correct answer in previous puzzles. This example illustrates the use of

   (A) mental rotation
   (B) elaborative rehearsal
   (C) an algorithm
   (D) a prototype
   (E) a syllogism

2. A researcher asks two different groups their opinion about how much money the president should earn per year. Participants in Group 1 are asked: "Should the president earn more or less than $200,000 per year? How much should he or she earn?" Participants in Group 2 are asked: "Should the president earn more or less than $2 million per year? How much should he or she earn?" The researcher finds that participants in Group 2 are more likely to suggest that the president should make more than $1 million per year. The researcher is investigating the effects of which of the following?

(A) Algorithms

(B) Heuristics

(C) Anchoring effect

(D) Proactive interference

(E) Fixation

3. Two-year-old Mica tells her grandmother that the new couch "costed" too much. The scenario illustrates that children

(A) are not born with an innate language acquisition device

(B) cannot learn grammatical rules during the first two years of life

(C) learn language primarily through operant conditioning

(D) will model only words used by adults in their environment

(E) overgeneralize the use of grammatical rules

4. The Vietnamese language has the sound that goes with the letters "NG" at the beginning of words, including names. Americans have difficulty hearing and speaking that sound. That sound is a kind of

(A) pheromone

(B) semantic unit

(C) syntactic unit

(D) morpheme

(E) phoneme

5. Of the following, which is the best example of divergent thinking in problem-solving?

(A) Focusing on ideas within a category of associated solutions

(B) Devising as many solutions as possible

(C) Arriving at a single, possible solution

(D) Solving a problem with functional fixedness

(E) Developing a personal analogy

6. A teenager was given a new phone as a gift and thought the old phone should be thrown away, not realizing that the old phone could be used as a music player to avoid taking up space on the new phone. This example illustrates

(A) ill-structured problems

(B) insight

(C) divergent thinking

(D) functional fixedness

(E) incubation

7. A teenager believes very strongly that a particular basketball player should not play on his favorite team. Over the course of the season, the teenager focuses on every mistake, turnover, and missed shot the player makes. However, the teen does not notice how well the player passes, helps the other teammates, and rebounds. This teenager's behavior illustrates which of the following?

(A) A mnemonic

(B) Confirmation bias

(C) The availability heuristic

(D) An algorithmic error

(E) Metacognition

8. Noam Chomsky's view of language proposes that

(A) people have an inherent language acquisition device

(B) thinking is merely language of a nonverbal nature

(C) different levels of language ability are determined by heredity

(D) language acquisition can be explained by social modeling

(E) language is learned principally through verbal reinforcement

9. According to Benjamin Whorf's linguistic relativity hypothesis, which of the following is true?

(A) Individuals have a natural predisposition to learn language.

(B) Individuals learn positive instances of concepts faster than they learn negative instances.

(C) Children learn their first language from their relatives and their peer group.

(D) Different languages predispose those individuals who speak them to think about the world in different ways.

(E) Children learn quantifying words such as *more* and *further* sooner than they do absolutes such as *every* and *all*.

10. Which of the following is an example of metacognition?

(A) Memorizing pi to one hundred places

(B) Knowing the effectiveness of different study strategies for different courses for one's own brain

(C) Recognizing the faces of people after meeting them once

(D) Solving a complex problem in a step-by-step, methodical manner

(E) Understanding how the different parts of the brain work during memory formation

FREE-RESPONSE QUESTIONS

1. Explain two primary ways to solve problems: algorithms and heuristics. Also, describe how people can make errors in thinking. Define and explain each of the following in your answer:
   - Confirmation bias
   - Mental set
   - Intuition
   - Availability heuristic
   - Representativeness heuristic
   - Overconfidence
   - Belief perseverance
   - Framing

2. Sophie learned multiple languages growing up in Switzerland. When she moved to the United States, her primary language became English, with German, French, and Italian fading into the past. When she had to take a language course in high school, the only course available was Spanish. Her previous language experiences both helped and confused her. Define each of the following concepts and explain how each concept could help Sophie recall her previous languages OR prevent her from learning Spanish.
   - Explicit memory
   - Effortful processing
   - Context-dependent memory
   - Proactive interference
   - Hippocampus
   - Critical period in language acquisition

Jot down the skeleton of each question so you remember to answer it entirely. For example, as you begin to think about the answer to the first free-response question, you might jot the following on your paper:

- Explain algorithms and heuristics.
- Describe how people make errors in thinking.
- Define and explain each bulleted term.

Then, as you write your answer, you can check off each part of the question and double-check that you are not leaving anything out. For more guidance on answering free-response questions, see pages xxii–xxiii.

UNIT 7: Review

In this unit, you sought answers to these essential questions about memory, forgetting, thinking, problem-solving, and language.

Chapter 11: How do humans encode, store, and retrieve information from memory, and how can those processes be improved?

Chapter 12: How do humans think, and how does thinking solve problems and interact with language?

Apply what you have learned about cognition by answering the free-response question below.

FREE-RESPONSE QUESTION

A prosecutor is trying to solve a robbery case that she has been investigating for several months. The information discovered so far has been vague, but she is confident she can gather enough information to solve the case. The prosecutor has brought in a person of interest for questioning. This person has a previous record of theft and is known to have been in the area at the time of the crime. He claims that he is innocent and that he was blocks away when the crime occurred.

A) Explain how the following terms might relate to this scenario. You may respond from the perspective of either the prosecutor or the accused.
- Belief perseverance
- Representativeness heuristic
- Critical thinking

B) Several people witnessed the events surrounding the crime, and the prosecutor would like to speak with them about what they know. Explain how the following may influence the discussion between the prosecutor and the witnesses:
- Source amnesia
- Retroactive interference
- The framing effect
- The misinformation effect

UNIT 8: Motivation and Emotion

Chapter 13 *Motivation*

Chapter 14 *Emotion*

Unit Overview

Motivation and *emotion*—both words derive from the same Latin root, *movere*, "to move." It's easy enough to see how moving applies to *motivation*—you "move into action" when you are motivated. But what about *emotion?* People often say they are "moved" when they mean their emotions have been stirred and their feelings come out. The prefix *e-* derives from the Latin prefix *ex-*, meaning "out." The movement in emotions is the stirring up and pushing out of feelings.

Of course, their linguistic similarities are not the most important relationship between motivation and emotion. This unit will explore both motivation (the "why" behind behavior) and emotion (the feelings engendered by one's own or another's behavior) and the psychological relationship between them.

Key Topics

- Basic motivational concepts to understand the behavior of humans and other animals (e.g., instincts, incentives, intrinsic versus extrinsic motivation)

- Biological underpinnings of motivation, including needs, drives, and homeostasis

- Similarities and differences among motivational theories (e.g., drive reduction theory, arousal theory, general adaptation theory), including the strengths and weaknesses of each

- Classic research findings in specific motivation systems (e.g., eating, sex, social)

- Theories of stress and the effects of stress on psychological and physical well-being

- Similarities and differences among major theories of emotion (e.g., James–Lange, Cannon–Bard, Schachter's two-factor theory)

- The role of cultural influences in shaping emotional expression, including variations in body language

- Key contributors in the psychology of motivation and emotion (e.g., William James, Alfred Kinsey, Abraham Maslow, Stanley Schachter, Hans Selye)

Source: *AP® Psychology Course and Exam Description*

13

Motivation

*"You may encounter many defeats, but you must not be defeated.
In fact, it may be necessary to encounter the defeats,
so you can know who you are, what you can rise
from, how you can still come out of it."*

—Maya Angelou

Essential Question: What motivates people to behave as they do?

Motives can be divided into three types. **Biological motives** are based on the biological needs for survival—hunger, thirst, pain avoidance, the need for air, and sleep, for example. Biological motives are innate; we are born with them and do not need to learn them. A second type of motives are **stimulus motives.** These express our need for information, learning, and stimulation. Though they appear to be inborn, they are not needed for survival. **Learned motives** are a third type. They are learned needs, drives, and goals. Your learning psychology, pursuing student government office, and auditioning for *The Voice* are examples of learned motives. We often use these to attain power, connection to others, status, approval of others, security, reduction of fear, and achievement. This chapter will examine all three types of motives and the theories that attempt to explain them.

Theories of Motivation

Motivation is the drive that initiates, sustains, directs, and terminates actions—that is, motivation is the force directing a person to behave a certain way. Why do people fall in love, join gangs, eat breakfast, run marathons, and perform a virtually limitless number of other behaviors? Several different theories attempt to explain motivation.

Instinct Theory

In everyday conversation, people often use the word *instinct*—"listen to your instincts," "your first instinct is usually right," "if you want to win, you need to have that killer instinct." It's often used to mean a gut feeling about something, in place of or along with the word *intuition*, and sometimes it's used to mean a behavior that doesn't require any thought (i.e., a *reflex)*. For psychologists, however, *instinct* has a more specific meaning. **Instinct** is an innate and consistent pattern of complex behavior that is performed the same way by every member of the species.

Human instincts include the drives to eat, drink, find shelter, and reproduce, though culture influences the ways in which these instincts play out. The fight-or-flight response, a physiological reaction to threat that directs us to either flee or fight for survival, is another human instinct (see page 110), though it is shared by other species. Other animals have instinctual **fixed action patterns**—behaviors in response to stimuli that, once started, continue to completion. Newly hatched sea turtles moving toward the ocean, honeybees dancing to communicate, baby kangaroos crawling up to get into the mother's pouch, and birds building nests are carrying out fixed action patterns. The turtles are motivated to get to the ocean, but they're not consciously aware of a need; their instinct is the reason they run for the water with all their energy.

This approach to understanding motivation fits into the perspective of **evolutionary psychology**, an approach that tries to explain mental and psychological traits, such as memory, language, perception, and personality, as adaptations to the environment. That is, our traits developed to help us adapt to our surroundings. In this view, the behaviors and traits that people and other animals display today are the result of **natural selection** (see page 119). Instinctual behaviors that increase reproductive success become more frequent, whereas instinctual behaviors that don't help further the species may die out.

The idea that humans are motivated by instincts can be controversial. Instincts can't explain all of the complex behaviors that humans engage in every day. Some scientists argue that our complex behaviors have instinctive components, but humans also have a cerebral cortex for decision-making which may override any instincts or predispositions to behave without thinking.

THINK AS A PSYCHOLOGIST: ANIMAL INSTINCT?

The idea that nonhuman animals are motivated solely by instinct is also increasingly controversial. Instinct is an automatic response, yet many animals behave in ways that seem to show they have made a choice in how to behave. Consider, for example, what two marine ecologists, Robert Pitman and John Durban, witnessed in 2009 near the West Antarctic Peninsula. A pod of killer whales had surrounded a seal on an ice floe when suddenly two humpback whales rushed into the scene, broke up the floe, and when the seal headed toward the humpbacks, one of them turned belly up and with its giant flipper directed the seal onto its belly, clearly protecting it. The seal then swam away to safety.

There are known motivations for nonhuman animals to help others. For example, researcher Hal Markowitz observed that Diana monkeys would help other Diana monkeys even at a cost to themselves. In an experiment in which the monkeys were taught to insert a token in a slot for food, when one monkey saw that an older monkey could not figure out the task, he performed the task for her and gave her the food, even though he could have eaten it himself. His behavior represents *kin selection,* the willingness to take a risk for a member of one's own species. Other animals have been observed to help others because others have helped them in the past, operating on the principle of *reciprocity.*

However, neither kin selection nor reciprocity explains the behavior of the humpback whales. And natural selection would not promote risk-taking for no chance of reward—how could that behavior advance the survival of either the species or the individual? Nor were these whales exceptional—more than 115 such incidents with humpbacks have been recorded and there are countless others involving dolphins, dogs, and apes. Could these examples of interspecies aid be motivated by altruism, the desire to help another with no expectation of a return favor?

Pitman has a possible explanation for this behavior. Killer whales are enemies of humpbacks and pose a serious threat to the calves Pitman wonders if the humpbacks generalize killer whale attacks, so even when they don't threaten humpback calves, the humpbacks rush in to protect the victim. He describes this behavior as "inadvertent altruism."

Practice: Work in teams of four or five students to research studies demonstrating the motives of kin selection and reciprocity behavior in animals, as well as cases of interspecies helping behavior. Prepare a summary of your findings, including a conclusion about the role of instinct and natural selection, and determine the best way to present your findings to the class. Work collaboratively to make your final presentation.

Drive Reduction Theory

Psychologist Clark Hull (1884–1952) argued that people are motivated by needs, drives, responses, and goals. He described the interaction of these four factors as the **drive reduction theory** of motivation. Figure 13.1 shows how Hull believed that this model worked.

A person has a **need** when he or she has an internal deficiency of some sort. The need leads to the creation of a **drive,** an energized emotional state that pushes the person to do something. For example, hunger is an internal need that creates a drive, such as a push to eat. To reduce or eliminate that need, the person responds by trying to find food and stops responding only when the goal is met (i.e., the need has been satisfied; the person is no longer hungry). Drive reduction helps a person (or other animal) maintain a level of **homeostasis**, an internal balance in the body—somewhere between feeling very hungry and feeling overly full, for example.

Drives that are biologically connected to survival, such as drives to fulfill needs for food, water, or warmth, are known as *primary drives*. *Secondary drives* assist us in attaining the goals of a primary drive. For example, people may be driven to earn money (secondary drive) to purchase food (primary drive). This concept is similar to primary and secondary reinforcers, discussed in Chapter 9 (see page 210).

Hull's drive reduction theory does well in explaining basic biological functions and needs, such as hunger and thirst. However, critics of the drive reduction theory believe it is too simple to explain all the varied behaviors of humans and animals. It also does not address topics such as ego, greed, love, commitment, compassion, attachment, and affiliation. By the late 1950s, research headed in a different direction.

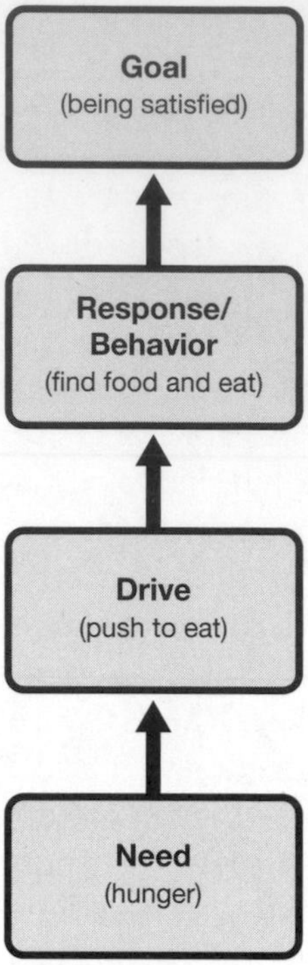

Figure 13.1 Drive Reduction Theory

Incentive Theory

While drives can be seen as pushing behavior, **incentives** can be seen as pulling behavior (see Figure 13.2). In other words, drives are internal stimuli that motivate a behavior, whereas incentives are external stimuli that motivate a behavior—sometimes the same behavior. Consider, for example, an ice cream sundae or a pepperoni pizza or some other food that you find particularly tasty. You may be pushed to eat one of those appealing foods because of an internal drive—hunger, or you might be pulled by an external incentive to eat the food because it's tasty, your friends are also eating and you want to join them, or because there's a contest for how fast or how much you can eat, even if you are not being pushed by the internal drive of hunger.

People are motivated by incentives in all sorts of domains. A good grade is an academic incentive. A cash bonus for finishing a project at work is an economic incentive. A romantic relationship can be a social incentive. In each case, the incentive is something that a person is pulled toward and motivated to achieve. Incentives always have value to the individual striving to achieve them, but that value is based on a variety of factors beyond their ability to satisfy a need. For example, many Americans would find a chocolate sundae to be an incentive, but what about large, fried caterpillars, which are a delicacy in parts of the world? What about balut, a partially developed duck inside its eggshell? For Americans, eating caterpillar or balut probably has low incentive value.

Drives (Internal) and Incentives (External)

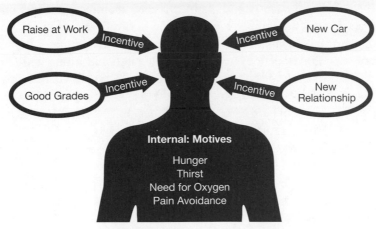

Figure 13.2 Incentive Theory

The incentive theory of motivation is based on the principles established by Edward Thorndike (see page 209), B. F. Skinner (see page 208), and others. It can easily identify external pulls on behavior. However, the incentive model of motivation may not adequately explain altruistic behaviors or compassion.

Arousal Theory

Arousal theory proposes that people and other animals are motivated to perform because they are trying to maintain optimal levels of physiological arousal—the state of being awake and alert. If arousal level is too high, they will be motivated to relax, and if arousal level is too low, they will seek out action or something that stimulates them.

Figure 13.3 shows how arousal influences performance. In general, people are motivated to behave so that they stay moderately aroused all the

The Yerkes-Dodson Law of Arousal

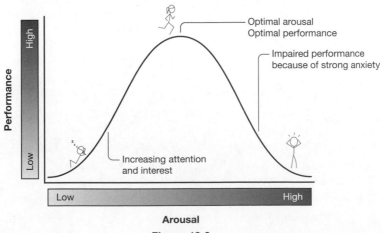

Figure 13.3

time. When arousal is very low, people's performance suffers—they may be inattentive or uninterested (think about a boring lecture when you are tired; you probably won't remember much). When arousal is very high, however, people's performance also suffers—they may be anxious or overwhelmed (people often report that they were overly excited/ambitious and "choked" in this situation). The idea that people need moderate levels of arousal to complete a task successfully is known as the **Yerkes-Dodson law** of arousal or the inverted-U theory of arousal, developed by psychologists Robert M. Yerkes (1876–1956) and John Dillingham Dodson (1879–1955).

Of course, the "best" or optimal level of arousal for each person is determined by a combination of the individual's characteristics and elements of the situation or context. For example, some people prefer quieter environments and time alone to be able to think; they are motivated to find a lower level of arousal than someone who loves to be a regular part of large parties and celebrations. Task difficulty plays a role too. For example, most people need relatively lower levels of arousal to complete difficult tasks that require concentration, such as reading, and relatively higher ones to complete endurance tasks that require stamina, such as swimming.

A weakness of the arousal theory is that it is merely descriptive. It also does not explain complex social needs.

Self-Actualization Theory

Humanistic psychologists believe that all human beings have the capacity to grow and become better humans. **Abraham Maslow** (1908–1970) was a humanistic psychologist who proposed an intuitive understanding of motivation known as the **hierarchy of needs** (sometimes called Maslow's pyramid), which is shown in Figure 13.4. Like many researchers, Maslow believed that behavior was directed toward meeting one's needs, but his theory was innovative because he organized needs by importance and included needs that reflect a more humanistic approach.

Maslow argued that people have basic biological needs for food, water, warmth, and rest, which form the base or foundation of the pyramid. These needs have to be met first because if they aren't met, the person can't survive. Safety needs are next in order

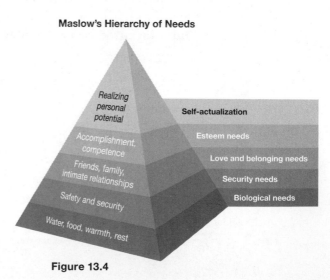

Maslow's Hierarchy of Needs

Realizing personal potential — Self-actualization

Accomplishment, competence — Esteem needs

Friends, family, intimate relationships — Love and belonging needs

Safety and security — Security needs

Water, food, warmth, rest — Biological needs

Figure 13.4

of importance, followed by belongingness and love needs. Most people would regard being ostracized—being left out of a group—as devastating; we need to have friends and to belong, so we are motivated to meet those needs. Maslow argued that once belongingness needs are met, people are motivated to meet esteem needs, the desire to feel competent and good at something—school, video games, skating, sports, music, or some other task. Once all these needs are met, people are motivated toward **self-actualization**, or the need to reach one's full potential. Maslow argued that people were motivated to meet the needs in order—we cannot just jump from meeting our basic needs to focusing on becoming self-actualized.He also felt that through life experiences and reflection, people could grow into stronger, better individuals.

As a humanist, Maslow thought potential and growth were profoundly important in a person's life. He believed that all people are potentially capable of becoming self-actualized and that most people are motivated to try, but he believed few people actually reach this level of existence (fewer than 2 percent, including, he felt, Abraham Lincoln, Mahatma Gandhi, Eleanor Roosevelt, Albert Einstein, and Viktor Frankl). Self-actualized people, in Maslow's view, tended to be relatively free of biases, accepting and trusting of themselves, autonomous, richly appreciative of experience, democratic in their values and attitudes, and creative.

To work toward self-actualization, he argued, a person should try to become less self-centered and focus instead on others. He also believed that being fully absorbed and concentrating on the experience and trying new things rather than staying within the "comfort zone" would develop self-actualization. Maslow

Maslow's Hierarchy of Needs (Extended)

Figure 13.5

suggested that people should listen to their own feelings when evaluating experiences, avoid game playing and pretense, and prepare to be unpopular if their views do not match the majority viewpoints. Self-actualization requires taking responsibility, working hard, identifying one's weaknesses and defenses, and having the courage to give them up. Maslow said there are no perfect humans, and all people have unique paths to reaching their potentials Over the last century, researchers have expanded Maslow's pyramid to differentiate among needs; a recent version includes eight types of needs (see Figure 13.5 on the previous page). Researchers sometimes refer to the lower levels as deficiency needs (i.e., people are motivated when these needs are unmet because they have to be filled to survive) and the upper levels as growth needs (i.e., people are motivated to explore, learn, and reach potential).

Maslow's hierarchy of needs is a wonderfully intuitive approach to understanding human motivation, but it has flaws on several fronts. The biggest issue is lack of empirical/scientific support. There is insufficient research to support Maslow's conclusions. A second criticism is that many people follow advanced levels of needs even though they have not had lower level needs met. Lack of any need for human reproduction has also drawn the criticism of evolutionary psychologists.

Figure 13.6 on the next two pages summarizes the main theories of motivation.

To Maslow, Eleanor Roosevelt exemplified a fully self-actualized person. She was instrumental in developing the Universal Declaration of Human Rights in 1948.

Theory of Motivation	Description	Strength(s)	Weakness(es)
Instinct and Evolutionary Psychology	Instinct drives behavior; behavior that helps preserve the individual and species is passed on	Helps explain behavioral similarities related to adaptations from human past	Explains non-human animal behavior better than human behavior, since humans have few, if any, instincts Does not consider human cognitive capabilities
Drive Reduction Model	Internal deficiencies— drives—push us to behave in such a way that we reduce the drives to maintain homeostasis Primary drives are unlearned, e.g., hunger, thirst, sex Secondary drives are learned, e.g., grades, career success	Does well in explaining basic biological needs such as hunger and thirst	Too simple to explain complex and varied behaviors of humans and some animals Limited to mostly primary biological functioning; lacks ability to explain ego, greed, and commitment
Incentives	Behavior is motivated by the "pull" of external stimuli, or incentives	Based on well-established learning principles Easily identifies external pulls on behavior	Does not take internal stimuli (intrinsic motivators) into account Cannot explain behaviors that have no apparent external worth

Theory of Motivation	Description	Strength(s)	Weakness(es)
Arousal (Yerkes-Dodson)	Proposes that organisms have an optimal level of physiological arousal and behavior is adjusted to either increase or decrease the arousal level	Explains physiological arousal needed for specific tasks	Does not explain motivation for more complex social needs
Hierarchy of Needs (Maslow)	Incorporates the idea that we have various levels of needs, including lower-level physiological and safety needs and higher-level social, self-esteem, actualization, and meaning needs Emphasizes importance of psychological/cognitive factors in motivation	Works well on an intuitive level Recognizes both physiological and psychological needs Recognizes importance of the environment	Lack of empirical support Many people follow advanced levels of needs despite not meeting lower level needs. The order of needs may change in some circumstances. Evolutionary psychologists criticize the absence in the hierarchy of the universal human motives to find a mate and reproduce.

Motivated Behaviors

Theories of motivation present a picture of how motivation works in general, but no single theory is enough to fully explain why people behave as they do. Drives and needs and incentives work together, and sometimes they work in opposition. Psychologists studying motivation, then, often focus on specific behaviors in their attempt to provide a more complete understanding of the factors that influence behaviors in general. This section of the chapter takes such an integrated approach to explain why we engage in two motivated behaviors, eating and sexual behavior, and looks at motivation of social behaviors.

Eating

Why do we eat? Clearly hunger is not the only answer, although hunger plays an important motivational role in eating behaviors. Understanding hunger and **satiety,** the feeling of fullness, is necessary to build a foundation for understanding why we eat.

Biological Bases of Hunger Hunger is often described as a biological drive, probably the most important drive for individual survival. In terms of the drive reduction theory, hunger is a drive that pushes a person to behave in a way that fills a need. Nutrition is the need, and eating is the behavior that allows the person to fill that need. Where does this state of arousal come from?

The nervous and endocrine systems are both active in regulating hunger. The hunger signal has two parts: the "on" signal and the "off" signal. The "on" signal is triggered by something that stimulates the appetite (an **orexigenic**). Two appetite stimulants, the chemicals **ghrelin** and **orexin**, play key roles. In mammals, orexin is produced by neurons in the **lateral hypothalamus (LH)**. (See page 91.) In addition to its role in eating behaviors, orexin has a role in sexual behavior and wakefulness; in each case, it seems to be involved in stimulating the body to "do more"—eat more, engage in more sexual activity, and stay awake longer. Ghrelin is a hormone released by the stomach when the body needs food; it carries the "hungry" signal to the LH. The body produces more ghrelin when it is underweight and less when it is overweight.

The "off" signal occurs when an **anorexigenic**—something that signals satiety—tells the body it feels full and decreases appetite. The satiety system is regulated by the **ventromedial hypothalamus (VMH)**, which receives and responds to satiety hormones such as **leptin** and **peptide YY (PYY)**. For example, leptin is secreted by fat cells in the body, and it travels to the VMH to signal that the body has enough energy to do what it needs to do. Rats with lesions to the VMH don't receive this internal satiety cue. They continue to eat much more than they need to survive and become dramatically overweight. People, too, with low leptin levels (perhaps due to a genetic mutation) may overeat to obesity; they get the "hungry" signal but don't receive the "no-longer-hungry" signal.

According to one theory, these on–off signals help an organism maintain homeostasis, with the balance around a **set point** for each individual, the weight range in which the body performs optimally and in which a person stays without any effort to gain or lose weight. A person with a set point of 135 pounds, for example, will probably weigh between 125 and 150 for most of his or her adult life, as long as no extreme situations are present (e.g., poverty leading to malnourishment, overeating beyond the point of satiety). However, with access to all kinds of foods and cultural encouragement to eat, many people overeat and bypass their body's set point.

An individual's set point is influenced by his or her **basal metabolic rate**, which is the rate of energy expenditure when the body is at rest. Basal metabolic rate seems to have a genetic component—in other words, some people have more fat cells while others have fewer; some people burn calories for energy very quickly while others do so more slowly. But basal metabolism is also influenced by other factors. For example, increasing leptin can lead to an increase in metabolic rate, and extreme dieting can cause a decrease.

Other hormones and chemicals also play a role in hunger signals. **Glucose**, a type of sugar, is an important source of energy that comes from food; food is broken down into sugars that are passed through the blood to cells throughout the body. **Insulin**, a hormone released by the pancreas, regulates the level of glucose in the bloodstream. When people are hypoglycemic (i.e., have low levels of glucose in the blood—*hypo* means "low" or "less than normal"), their body temperature rises, their heart rate increases, and they tend to feel chilled, shaky, and irritable (think about the candy commercial that describes people as "hangry," a combination of hungry/angry that is typical of hypoglycemia). The body is signaling that it needs more glucose, and the person may respond by eating (often something sweet).

Sometimes, though, people eat even without the chemical signals indicating that food is needed for energy. Have you ever looked at the clock, noticed it was close to your regular meal time, and suddenly felt hungry? The clock signaled a hunger response, serving as a cue that you should eat.

External Cues That Influence Eating Behaviors External eating cues are signals and situations that are linked with food. Some examples of eating cues are smells and other sensory experiences, the clock, specific people, and certain emotions.

The taste, smell, texture, and sight of food can lead to eating (and overeating), even when a person isn't hungry. Have you ever eaten a whole container of ice cream, a box of cookies, or too many candy corns? Sweet tastes can stimulate appetite by triggering insulin release, leading to a drop in blood glucose. The opposite can happen too–the smell of something unappealing can suppress feelings of hunger. To a large degree, these responses are inherent in humans and other animals; they are evolutionarily important to encourage eating when energy is low and to discourage eating in situations where the food may be spoiled or poisoned.

Ads for pizza companies are timed to be shown around dinnertime and are external cues triggering a taste for pizza.

Learning plays a role too. Classical conditioning (described in Chapter 9) often leads to otherwise neutral stimuli becoming motivators for eating. For example, the smell of food serves as an unconditioned stimulus—a person feels immediately hungry (the unconditioned response). If the person generally cooks and eats dinner at 6 p.m., the smell of the food will become associated with the time (the conditioned stimulus) and the person will begin to feel hungry as 6 p.m. nears (the conditioned response) even before the food is cooked. Do you eat your meals sitting in front of the television? If so, you may have learned to associate television with food, prompting hunger when watching the screen.

Most people develop associations between food and certain environmental factors. For example, people whose environment contributes to stressful feelings reach for sweet foods. Sugars in the bloodstream provide energy to the body, and people experience a rush of energy after eating food containing sugars. Carbohydrates—foods like candy bars, cookies, pasta, and breads—are among those foods that can lead to the "sugar high" feeling. Other foods, such as eggs, cheese, nuts, salmon, and tofu, trigger a release of serotonin, a chemical (neurotransmitter) in the brain that is involved in feelings of pleasure (see Chapter 5).

Culture, too, is a major motivator of eating behaviors. What one culture considers a delicacy, another might consider disgusting. Would you eat crickets, mealworms, or scorpions? What about that balut mentioned earlier or haggis, a Scottish "pudding" made from organ meat? You're probably more likely to reach for a bag of potato chips or chocolate chip cookies.

Many people in America prefer foods that are salty and sweet, and if they were not raised with spicy foods, they often dislike foods prepared with curries and peppers. In contrast, those flavors are common and preferred in many Latin American and Asian countries. Children raised in multicultural families whose parents like to travel or cook grow up with access to a variety of different cuisines, have more cultural cues motivating them to eat, and are more likely to grow up to be adventurous eaters.

Some cultures have rules about which items are appropriate on certain occasions. For some, a cake is a common high-calorie dessert at celebrations of birthdays, graduations, and engagements. For some, certain foods are to be avoided, such as beef, pork, or insects. Are those delicacies in your household, or are they taboos?

Does your family sit down to a common table, focusing on the food and conversation? If so, how does that affect your eating? Being with others tends to motivate eating, a phenomenon known **social coaction** (an idea related to social facilitation that you will read about in the social psychology unit). People at a party, for example, eat more than they would if they were alone. However, in some circumstances, being with others serves to decrease eating behaviors. In Western cultures in which thin is the ideal, when women eat less in social situations they may be seen as more feminine and therefore more desirable. Family and cultural practices related to parental control of eating and meal customs also exert influence on eating patterns. Many of us were raised with the "you must clean your plate" rule before we could leave the table. This attempt at control by parents over children can carry over into adult eating behavior.

Eating Behaviors Out of Balance: Obesity Over human history, thrifty genes directing us to eat fatty foods have evolved as an adaptation for when food was scarce. Now that high fat, high sugar food is no longer scarce, that gene has become maladaptive. Many genes related to body weight regulation vary among individuals and contribute to obesity. The Pima Indians of Arizona have a high level of obesity within their culture for those following a modern high-fat diet. For those who follow a more traditional low-fat diet, obesity is much less common.

Once fat cells increase in the body, they seldom decrease in number. Early childhood eating patterns as well as adult overeating contribute to the increase in the number of fat cells. Weight-loss diets can usually shrink fat cells, but they do not destroy them. While we may have a set point, it can get reset by the body when it increases in size. A person's metabolism can also have an impact on body weight. The lower the metabolism, the easier it is to gain weight. There is that one friend in just about every group who "has a hollow leg" and "eats like a horse" and never gains weight—that lucky situation shows genetics and metabolism at work. A challenging problem with weight-loss diets is that while they can help a person shed pounds, they can also lower a person's metabolic rate—making it even harder to lose weight.

Some parents will use food to placate children. This practice can create a system that becomes unbalanced very quickly. One child who cried every time he was hungry was given food to calm him. By the time he was twelve, he weighed 300 pounds. Many such children have been in the news over the past few years, and their parents are being held accountable for endangering their health.

In the United States, high-calorie fast foods are available in even the smallest of towns. The documentaries *Fast Food Nation* and *Super Size Me* show just how widespread fast food is and how challenging to health it has become. The media contribute to the problem with ads describing or showing these foods as irresistible. In some places, fast food is the only affordable food.

While genetics and predispositions are factors in weight and health issues, you can also exert control if you are concerned about your own health. For example, try examining your portion size. Rather than use a full dinner plate, use smaller plates and smaller cups and glasses. Resist eating everything you are served in a restaurant: The larger plate size and portion size in American restaurants does lead to increased caloric intake. Another way to keep an eye on your calories and your mix of carbohydrates, fats, and proteins is to use a fitness or weight app on your phone. Simply keeping track of what you eat can reduce overeating. Research shows that obesity can contribute to such health problems as diabetes (blood sugar/insulin issues), joint problems, high blood pressure, and stresses on the heart, so preventing or reducing it is a step toward good health.

One current definition of obesity is based on a measurement of BMI, or body mass index. BMI is a ratio of weight to body size and assumed body fat. Though BMI provides some useful information when examining entire populations, its value for use on an individual person is questionable. Some people who are considered obese—that is, who have a high BMI—can run more than ten miles several times per week or are professional athletes. Other people who are considered too thin can also perform at high levels. In short, do not use BMI scores for finding your appropriate weight for your height. More important indicators of health are physical fitness and underlying measurements of cholesterol levels, blood pressure, insulin resistance, and cardiovascular

Fitness comes in a variety of dimensions.

abilities. Rather than focusing on what the scale or BMI measure says, focus on how you feel. Are you able to go hiking and enjoy the experience, or do you need to stop every hundred yards because you are out of breath? Can you run a mile or more? Are you getting quality sleep, or is severe snoring (possibly a sign of sleep apnea) getting in the way?

You only get one body. What are you going to do with it? Will you take care of it—eat in a healthy way and exercise? Or will you fill it with junk and mistreat it so that it breaks down? If you want to lose weight, avoid falling for diet fads or "cleanses." They are not based in science and only end up hurting your body. Healthy habits are the only way to properly take care of your body.

Sexual Motivation

Sexual motivation is the desire to have erotic experiences that are pleasurable. Sexual desire and romantic love are not always connected with each other. Sexual desire has roots in mating and passing along one's genes, while romantic love has attachment in concert with sexual desire. Each has distinct brain and hormonal mechanisms. Attachment is connected with increased levels of the hormones oxytocin and vasopressin. Sexual desire alone is connected to androgens and estrogens released into the body from the **gonads** (testicles in males, ovaries in females).

Sexual desire ties in to many cognitive and behavioral processes and sociocultural norms. Think back to Chapter 9 on associative learning. Animals seek pleasure and repeat behaviors that lead to pleasure. External and internal stimuli associated with sexual arousal can become rewarding in and of themselves. Sociocultural factors can determine the preferred characteristics of a desirable partner—his or her weight, body type, body size, and body adornment (decoration such as jewelry, hairstyles, and tattoos). Most cultures also tend to have common preferences in hip-to-waist ratios in females. Facial symmetry tends to be highly prized, as does youth, especially in females, since it signals health in parenting.

Evolution has contributed to what we tend to find attractive, since sexual desire was rooted in the ability of our ancestors to reproduce successfully. Though sexuality can be thought of in purely reproductive terms, in humans, sexuality is one part of the complex web of identity, relationships, and social lives.

All cultures have rules about which sexual practices and partners are appropriate. Some cultures avoid cousin-cousin mating, while others encourage it. In virtually all cultures, incest—mating with close family members—is taboo.

The Human Sexual Response Cycle Researchers William Masters (1915–2001) and Virginia Johnson (1925–2013) conducted research in a laboratory where they measured, watched, and/or filmed 10,000 sexual cycles of more than 300 male and 300 female volunteers. Among other findings, they discovered that what people had been told about sex was largely wrong, and their research supported the importance of learning about and improving the sexual experience.

Masters and Johnson identified a four-part series to the **sexual response cycle**—the physiological changes from arousal back to a normal state. This cycle begins with the *excitement stage* when men's and women's genital areas became engorged with blood, a woman's vagina expands, and an internal lubricant is secreted. Her breasts and nipples may enlarge. During the *plateau stage*, breathing becomes more rapid as does the heart rate and blood pressure. For men, the penis will become fully erect and some fluid may appear at the tip of the penis (fluid that contains sperm enough to create conception). For women, vaginal lubrication continues to increase.

Masters and Johnson observed muscle spasms all over the body for both males and females during the *orgasm phase*. There were increased breathing and heart rates, and blood pressure continued to rise. Brain activity appears to be similar for men and women during orgasm, as are their descriptions of the feelings. The female orgasm was found to be an adaptive response as it kept the sperm closer to the uterus in order to increase the possibility of conception.

After the orgasm, the body returns to its normal resting state during the fourth stage, called the *refractory period*. The body needs to reset itself before it can go through the process again and have another orgasm or resolution. One key difference between males and females is that for men the refractory period can last from a few minutes to longer than a day; for women the period lasts from seconds to minutes.

Another pioneering sex researcher was **Alfred Kinsey** (1894–1956) of Indiana University. He gained his data mostly through interviews that culminated in the Kinsey Reports. The books were heavily criticized for their methods, but they did get people talking slightly more openly about sex and nonheterosexuality. He created what became known as the Kinsey Scale, a continuum from heterosexuality to homosexuality. His research, though criticized, allowed people to begin opening their eyes to a possibility that there were more than just straight men and women and the occasional "other." Through his initial work and the work of many other researchers and activists, the notion of straight/gay and masculine/feminine is beginning to be questioned as a social creation (construct) and is not set in stone (Figure 13.7).

Factors Affecting Sexual Motivation During puberty, the development of sexual characteristics begins to change how adolescents view the world around them. More of the world becomes sexualized due to the increase of **androgens** (male hormones, especially testosterone) and **estrogens** (female hormones, such as estradiol). These hormones activate sexual urges and

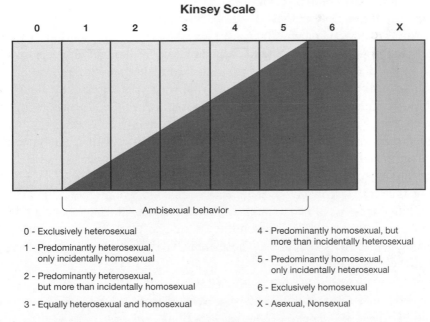

Kinsey Scale

Ambisexual behavior

0 - Exclusively heterosexual

1 - Predominantly heterosexual, only incidentally homosexual

2 - Predominantly heterosexual, but more than incidentally homosexual

3 - Equally heterosexual and homosexual

4 - Predominantly homosexual, but more than incidentally heterosexual

5 - Predominantly homosexual, only incidentally heterosexual

6 - Exclusively homosexual

X - Asexual, Nonsexual

Figure 13.7

behavior in most adolescents. Dreams become more sexual; secondary sex characteristics such as hair, breasts, menarche, and nocturnal emissions change perceptions.

Society contributes to the sexual maturation of adolescents. Depending on the structure and value system of the families, children and adolescents may become exposed to sexual content that is available on television, in movies, and on the Internet. The media, especially advertising, has an obsession with using sexuality to sell.

Though schools and parents have attempted to filter and hide pornography from children, they have been mainly unsuccessful in doing so, since explicit sexual content permeates popular culture. Repeated exposure can have lasting effects, such as believing that a behavior is normal just because it is in explicit material. As you read in Chapter 10 on social learning, people attempt to imitate models to which they are exposed. Teens' exposure to sexual content can contribute to superficial sexual sophistication, which in turn can lead to many problems over time, such as unrealistic expectations about what a potential partner should look like and do.

Adolescent Sexuality Some teenagers will have sex, and although rates of teenage pregnancy are decreasing, it does still occur, partly because of ignorance. In many communities, parents assert control over the information their children are exposed to in schools. Teens then turn to one another—not necessarily the best place to find reliable answers about sex and sexuality— and myths continue to spread. Many schools are unable or unwilling to communicate with teenagers about birth control and how to prevent pregnancy and **sexually transmitted infections (STIs)**. For the most up-to-date rates on STIs, visit the website of the Centers for Disease Control.

Another reason for unwanted teen pregnancies is that many people feel guilty about sexual behavior, and their guilt gets in the way of preparing for it. Also, alcohol reduces people's inhibitions, making them more likely to act on urges that they would not engage in while sober. Popular culture is no help. When was the last time you saw characters in movies or on television about to engage in sex? How many couples discussed condoms? Dental dams? Other birth control or disease prevention actions? Probably very few, maybe none.

One popular form of sex education over the past twenty years or so has been the abstinence-only campaign. However, even those teens who choose abstinence often engage in other risky behaviors that still increase the possibility of STIs. In fact, in areas where there is abstinence-only education, teens do not prepare for the possibility of sex, so they are unprepared when their urges get the best of them. These areas have the highest rates of teenage pregnancy and STIs.

Sexual Dysfunctions and Paraphilias Sexual dysfunctions are problems that consistently interfere with a person's ability to function properly or be aroused for sexual contact. One dysfunction, *premature ejaculation*, is a male's ejaculation before he and his partner want it. A second problem is an *erectile disorder* that occurs when a male is not able to maintain an erection. Female sexual dysfunction occurs persistently over time and may consist of painful intercourse, lack of desire, or inability to attain orgasm (*female orgasmic disorder*). If these conditions interfere with a healthy and enjoyable sex life, they can sometimes be solved through therapy or medication.

Paraphilias are sexual interests that fall outside a societal norm—that is, abnormal sexual desires. The *Diagnostic and Statistical Manual of Mental Disorders*, 5th Edition, states there are eight paraphilias: *exhibitionistic* disorder (desire to perform sexually in front of others), *fetishistic* disorder (experiencing sexual arousal only with objects not considered to be normally erotic), *frotteuristic* disorder (inappropriately touching or rubbing against strangers while in public places, such as on a train or bus), *pedophilic* disorder (sexual desire for children), *sexual masochism* disorder (unhealthy desire to receive pain in connection to sex), *sexual sadism* disorder (unhealthy desire to give pain to others in connection to sex), *transvestic* disorder (becoming sexually aroused by dressing in the other gender but finding the act distressing), and *voyeuristic* disorder (primary sexual arousal from secretly watching others undress, bathe, or engage in sex).

Sexual Orientation One's **sex** is biologically determined—that is, a person's genitalia is the primary marker for one's sex, though some people are born with genetic variations that create multiple genitalia or a lack of genitalia. **Gender,** in comparison, is culturally and socially created. What is considered masculine or feminine in a society is not agreed on worldwide.

Sexual orientation is a sexual identity based on the gender to which one feels enduring sexual attraction. People attracted to the same biological sex as their own are gay or lesbian. People attracted to a different biological sex as

their own are heterosexual, and those attracted to both are bisexual.

The lesbian, gay, bisexual, and transgender (LGBT) population is estimated to be between 1.5 and 5.5 percent. Those who identify as **transgender** (that is, feel as though they were born into a body of the wrong sex) make up approximately 0.3 percent of the population. Areas with greater acceptance of differences in sexual orientation tend to have larger LGBT populations.

Some people extend the identification of sexual orientation to include a nonbinary (not either-or) result. This view proposes that the nonheterosexual population cannot all be labeled simply as LGBT. Proponents of this view add **Q**ueer, **Q**uestioning, **I**ntersex (once called *hermaphrodite*), and **A**sexual, **A**lly, and **P**ansexual—LGBTQQIAAP. Given the relatively recent social construction of "gay" and "straight," activists argue that the additional labels are necessary to give voice to the entire spectrum of human sexuality.

Research on the origins of sexual orientation indicates that fraternal birth order is one factor. The more sons in a family, the increased likelihood the later son(s) will be gay. Other research has found that the hypothalamus size in nonheterosexuals is smaller than in heterosexuals. Serotonin levels may play a role in sexual orientation as well, as might prenatal hormones during development. There is also a genetic component (you will recall that environments can alter how genes are expressed). However, though the exact mechanisms behind sexual orientation cannot be identified, our orientation is not a conscious choice but rather a complex, biologically-created set of phenomena.

Social Motivation: Balance and the Need to Belong

Several theories have attempted to explain what motivates us to interact with others as we do. Fritz Heider (1896–1988) proposed a **balance theory** of social motivation, suggesting that humans have a need for congruence in their social interactions and that social behavior is motivated by a desire for social balance. He illustrated this theory through the use of a triad made up of two people and an object. A triad might be you and your father (the two people) and your dog (the object). A balanced triad would be one in which both you and your father love your dog. Another balanced triad would be one in which both you and your father do not love your dog. But if you love your dog and your father does not, the triad is out of balance, and you will be socially motivated to find a way to balance it. Leon Festinger (1919-1989) also proposed that we are motivated in part by a desire for congruence, that conflicting beliefs or behaviors cause us discomfort and we are motivated to relieve that discomfort by adjusting either our beliefs or our behaviors. (See page 600 for more on cognitive dissonance.) Kurt Lewin (1890-1947), a Gestalt psychologist, developed a theory based on how people see their "life space"—the arena in which they make social decisions. He theorized that people experience psychological tension until they fulfill their intentions, and social behavior is motivated by the desire to resolve that tension.

Both laboratory experiments and social observation have shown that people need each other and need groups in order to survive and thrive. Our need to be with others is partly neurologically based. The hormone oxytocin is released by the pituitary gland whenever humans bond socially. The release of oxytocin triggers the release of the neurotransmitter serotonin (see page 109), which increases the feeling of well-being. In other words, we are biologically motivated to be with others because doing so makes us feel better. Being ostracized or left out has the opposite effect. Studies show the brain's pain center is activated when a person feels left out.

The evolutionary approach asserts that the human need to affiliate aids in survival. People in groups stand a better chance of surviving a battle than does the lone warrior. We have a need to belong—in a romantic relationship, family, team, organization, religion, ethnicity, or nation. Even gang membership fulfills a need for some, especially those for whom other groups—family and neighborhood, for example—do not provide sufficient support to satisfy the affiliation need. Being a part of something bigger than ourselves makes us feel good and avoids the distress associated with being alone.

Motivational Conflicts

There are times in our lives when we are faced with conflicting motives, when we must make a choice between two things that pull us in different directions. If the choice is between two desirable options, it is called an **approach-approach conflict.** Do I go to one concert with my best friends or another concert with my significant other? Should I study abroad in Spain or in Italy? A second conflict is called **avoidance-avoidance conflict**, the choice between two undesirable options. For example, do I want to do unpleasant homework or unpleasant housecleaning?

A conflict in which one event or goal has both attractive and unattractive features is called an **approach-avoidance conflict.** Marriage, for example, has positives and negatives. The positives include togetherness, creating memories together, and companionship, among others. Some potential negatives are challenging finances, arguments, and inevitable compromise. **Multiple approach-avoidance conflict** is a choice between two or more things, each with desirable and undesirable aspects. Suppose that marriage decision, for example, also involves moving to a different city and taking a different job, one with higher pay but also higher stress.

Achievement Motivation

What drives people to achieve goals in their lives? First is the desire for significant accomplishment, as Maslow theorized (see page 307). High achievers are often driven to accomplish goals they themselves have set, such as writing a book or climbing a mountain, rather than goals set by others. They tend to see difficulty as a challenge rather than as an impediment to success. In fact, failure only fuels high achievers. They understand that learning comes with discomfort and mistakes, and they see those as opportunities for growth. The highest achievers tend to want to learn as much as they can and to keep learning.

Low achievers are more interested in performance-oriented goals—that is, goals that are dependent upon the approval of others. Unlike high achievers, low achievers are externally driven. They are often put off by the discomfort of learning something new and adopt an orientation of helplessness.

Parents tend to encourage children to attempt moderately challenging tasks and provide strategies for success. They focus on giving praise for accomplishments and overcoming obstacles, and they give appropriate rewards for success. These parents also encourage children to accept new challenges after previous successes, so the learning never stops.

From a cultural point of view, **collectivistic societies**—those that value the group over the individual, as many Asian cultures do—encourage group success over individual success. **Individualistic societies** such as the United States tend to encourage and reward individual success. There are positives and negatives with each kind of culture; each has an underlying value system that promotes the cultural standards.

Intrinsic and Extrinsic Motivation

In the broadest sense, motivations can be labeled as intrinsic or extrinsic. **Intrinsic motivation** refers to an internal sense of satisfaction and the enjoyment of performing a task. When we operate from intrinsic motivation, we do something because we enjoy it, not because we are getting paid or receiving some other reward. **Extrinsic motivation**, in contrast, is the drive to perform tasks by being pushed or pulled by rewards or punishments.

In the business world (where the psychology subfield of industrial-organizational psychology plays a role), there is a management theory that relates to intrinsic and extrinsic motivation. Theory X asserts that employees are motivated only by the promise of rewards and the threats of punishment, clearly focusing on extrinsic motivation. However, while rewards do help produce some level of work, Theory X, though popular, is not effective in the long term. Theory Y works by encouraging intrinsic motivation by creating comfortable and stimulating working conditions. Author Daniel Pink explores these kinds of motivations in his book, *Drive: The Surprising Truth About What Motivates Us*. He asserts that three factors really motivate us: *autonomy*, the ability to control our work; *mastery*, in which employees become experts as a result of being engaged in their work; and *purpose*, the ability to make contributions and be a part of a cause larger than the individual.

In order to keep their employees fresh and happy and avoid employee burnout, some progressive companies create an environment in which workers are given up to 10 to 20 percent of their time to work on outside projects related to the company's overall goals but not directly related to the day-to-day work for which the employee is responsible. This method has worked with varying success within the corporate culture of the technology companies in Silicon Valley.

REFLECT ON THE ESSENTIAL QUESTION

Essential Question: *What motivates people to behave as they do?* On separate paper, complete a chart like the one below to gather details to help answer that question.

Theories	Motivated Behaviors	Motivational Conflicts	Achievement Motivation

KEY TERMS			KEY PEOPLE
THEORIES	*MOTIVATED BEHAVIORS*	*Social*	Alfred Kinsey
arousal theory		affiliation	Abraham Maslow
biological motive	*Eating*	balance theory	
drive	anorexigenic	*MOTIVATIONAL CONFLICTS*	
drive reduction theory	basal metabolic rate		
	ghrelin	approach-approach conflict	
evolutionary psychology	glucose		
	insulin	approach-avoidance conflict	
fixed action patterns	lateral hypothalamus (LH)		
		avoidance-avoidance conflict	
hierarchy of needs	leptin		
	orexigenic	multiple approach-avoidance conflict	
homeostasis	orexin		
incentives	peptide YY (PYY)		
instinct	satiety	*ACHIEVEMENT MOTIVATION*	
learned motive	set point		
motivation	ventromedial hypothalamus (VMH)	collectivistic societies	
natural selection			
need		extrinsic motivation	
self-actualization	*Sex*		
stimulus motive	androgens	individualistic societies	
Yerkes-Dodson law	estrogens	intrinsic motivation	
	gender		
	gonads		
	sex		
	sexual motivation		
	sexual orientation		
	sexual response cycle		
	sexually transmitted infections (STIs)		
	transgender		

1. Which of the following situations poses an approach-approach conflict for a person who listens only to classical music?

   (A) Having to sit through a good friend's rehearsal for a violin recital

   (B) Choosing to study with one of two friends, both of whom listen to classical music while studying

   (C) Attending a classical music event

   (D) Being offered a cash bonus for ushering at an all-Mozart concert

   (E) Having to choose between an all-Mozart concert and a reggae concert

2. Which best explains the motivation of a student who wants to graduate at the top of her class?

   (A) Belongness need

   (B) Influence of an individualistic culture

   (C) Optimal arousal

   (D) Influence of oxytocin and vasopressin

   (E) Growth needs

3. Individuals who exhibit a strong moral sense, accept themselves as they are, are deeply democratic in nature, and are willing to act independently of social and cultural pressures would be described by Maslow as

   (A) fully functioning

   (B) humanistic

   (C) self-actualized

   (D) real selves

   (E) ideal selves

4. Which of the following concepts explains motivation in terms of an organism seeking to maintain its biological equilibrium?

   (A) Opponent-process

   (B) Plasticity

   (C) Homeostasis

   (D) Incentive

   (E) Natural selection

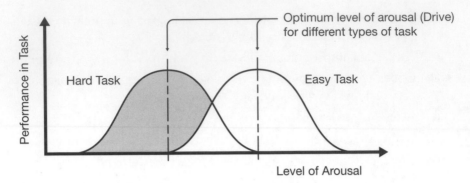

The Yerkes-Dodson Law

Optimum level of arousal (Drive) for different types of task

Performance in Task

Hard Task

Easy Task

Level of Arousal

5. The graph above supports which of the following statements?

(A) Optimal performance is a function of task difficulty and level of arousal.

(B) Difficult tasks require higher than usual levels of arousal for optimal performance.

(C) Difficult tasks become easier when arousal is increased.

(D) Performance level is independent of task difficulty.

(E) Easy tasks require lower than usual levels of arousal for optimal performance.

6. During a psychology experiment, a researcher uses a probe to lesion the ventromedial nucleus of a rat's hypothalamus. After the procedure the rat most likely will

(A) become less aggressive

(B) become more aggressive

(C) eat more and gain weight

(D) stop eating and lose weight

(E) experience a loss of coordination and muscular control

7. Which of the following theories suggests that a physiological need creates a state of tension that motivates an organism to satisfy the need?

(A) Opponent-process

(B) Drive-reduction

(C) Incentive

(D) Arousal

(E) Gate control

8. Recent and current research into human sexuality suggests that
   (A) as people mature they make sexual orientation choices
   (B) gender is binary
   (C) sexuality is a continuum
   (D) sexual orientation and gender align
   (E) first-born sons have a higher likelihood of being non-heterosexual

9. Danielle has a tremendously strong desire for achievement. Based on the research, which of the following statements is most likely true?
   (A) She will seek out tasks that are moderately difficult.
   (B) She is not likely to persist on any task.
   (C) She seeks out tasks that are easy.
   (D) She seeks out tasks that are nearly impossible.
   (E) She is less likely to pursue success in her occupation.

10. The hypothalamus plays a role in the regulation of food intake. Which of the following most accurately characterizes how it does so?
   (A) It produces a sense of satiety to counter hunger feelings that arise from stomach contractions.
   (B) It monitors stomach contractions through the cranial nerves to determine the extent of hunger.
   (C) It primarily responds to such environmental cues as the sight and smell of food.
   (D) It acts with the endocrine system to control hunger and satiety.
   (E) It is effective in triggering, but not in depressing, the sensation of hunger.

1. Androgens and estrogens affect the sexual response cycle.

   A) Explain the four stages of the sexual response cycle.

   B) Explain the role of the hormones in that cycle.

2. As a manager of a manufacturing business you are responsible for increasing profits at least 4 percent each year. Explain how you will attempt to achieve this goal using the following theories or concepts:
   - Incentive theory
   - Arousal theory
   - Maslow's hierarchy of needs theory
   - Theory X and Theory Y
   - Two-factor theory

WRITE AS A PSYCHOLOGIST: USE LOGICAL ORDER

The first free-response question asks you to explain four stages of a cycle. When you encounter a question like this, arrange the stages in the cycle in a logical order—usually sequential order. Transitions will make this order clear: *first, next, then, finally.* For more guidance on answering free-response questions, see pages xxii–xxiii.

14

Emotions

"Stress, in addition to being itself, was also the cause of itself, and the result of itself."

—Hans Selye

Essential Question: Why do people feel as they do?

Robert Plutchik (1927–2006), one of the most influential theorists in the field of emotions, notes in a 2001 article that "the study of emotions is one of the most confused (and still open) chapters in the history of psychology." He points out that more than 90 definitions of emotion have been proposed in the twentieth century alone. With so much disagreement on definition, he writes, "it is no wonder that there is much disagreement among contemporary theorists concerning the best way to conceptualize emotion and interpret its role in life."

Despite the confusion, many psychologists today agree on a few key components of emotion: **Emotion** is a complex experience that begins with a stimulus and includes physiological responses, subjective **emotional feelings**, and **emotional expressions**—the outward signs of what a person is feeling. The physiological responses include changes in heart rate, an increase in blood pressure and perspiration, and other involuntary responses in the autonomic nervous system. Emotional expressions include certain facial expressions and posture as well as such behaviors as crying or stomping one's feet. The ways in which people express emotions are key to understanding them.

Theories of Emotion

Plutchik's **psychoevolutionary theory** of emotions has gained wide acceptance as a way to categorize emotions. It identifies eight emotions that are considered primary or basic: fear, surprise, sadness, disgust, anger, anticipation, joy, and trust. These emotions are considered adaptive for both humans and nonhuman animals because they help to direct attempts to survive and adjust to changing conditions. For example, when people experience fear, they can act to avoid danger; when people experience trust, they can function well in groups.

Figure 14.1 shows how Plutchik believed emotions are arranged. His wheel of emotions includes emotions with the highest intensity in the innermost circle and those with the lowest intensity on the outside. The primary emotions form the middle ring. For example, terror is intense fear and so is in the inner circle, whereas apprehension is a milder form of fear and so is in the outer circle of the wheel. However, emotions often are mixed, as the figure shows: Anticipation and joy, when mixed together, become optimism. Anger and disgust, experienced together, lead to the emotion of contempt.

Early Theories of Emotion

One early explanation of the experience of emotion was that some stimulus in the environment evokes a subjective, emotional feeling, and that feeling leads to arousal of the autonomic nervous system. For example, a person sees a bear (the stimulus) and then experiences the conscious feeling of

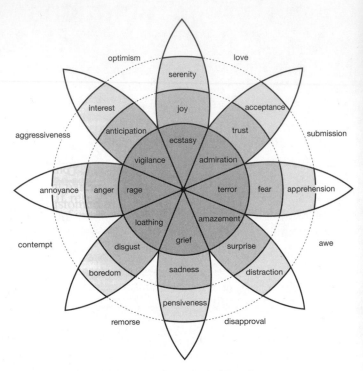

Figure 14.1 Plutchik's Wheel of Emotions

fear and then experiences autonomic arousal (increased heart rate, increased blood pressure, muscle tension). This explanation is called the **common-sense theory** of emotions because it is the explanation many people give as they describe their feelings—"I got scared, so my heart started to beat fast."

An alternative view was proposed, independently, by two psychologists, **William James** (1842–1910) and **Carl Lange** (1834–1900). Both men proposed that a stimulus in the environment leads to a physiological response (arousal of the autonomic nervous system), and that the emotional feeling arises from that response. This explanation, known as the **James-Lange theory**, reflects the idea that feelings are based on physiological arousal. Both the common-sense theory and the James-Lange theory propose a linear order—each step in the chain causes the next step; the difference is whether the arousal causes the feeling or the feeling causes the arousal.

A third view is that physiological arousal and emotional feelings emerge at the same time. This view was originally articulated by psychologist **Walter Cannon** (1871–1945) and his doctoral student **Philip Bard** (1898–1977) and is now known as the **Cannon-Bard theory of emotions**. They asserted that the stimulus (the bear) causes subcortical brain activity (in what we now know as the limbic system—see Chapter 4). This brain activity creates the emotional feeling (fear) and the physiological arousal at the same time. In other words, it's the bear that simultaneously makes the person's heart race and makes the person feel afraid.

The Role of Cognition in Emotion The theories and hypotheses just described include only physiological and emotional responses, not a cognitive component. Other approaches to understanding emotions emphasize the role that people's thoughts play in their emotional feelings and behaviors.

Schachter's two-factor theory of emotions focuses on how people try to understand their states of arousal. Psychologists Jerome Singer (1934–2010) and **Stanley Schachter** (1922–1997) argued that some environmental stimulus causes physiological arousal, but the arousal itself doesn't lead directly to the emotional feeling. Rather, the person recognizes the arousal state and looks to the stimulus to explain it: "That is one big bear! My heart is beating out of my chest! I'm scared!" The person feels the arousal, appraises the situation, and responds based on that appraisal. If you've ever seen a toddler fall down hard, immediately look to the caregiver, and begin to wail if the adult has a look of frozen fear on his or her face—but not if the caregiver laughs and says cheerfully, "You're okay!"—you've seen the two-factor theory in practice. This theory, emphasizing cognitive labeling of the physiology and appraisal of the situation, appears to reflect the complexities of human emotions more accurately than the earlier theories.

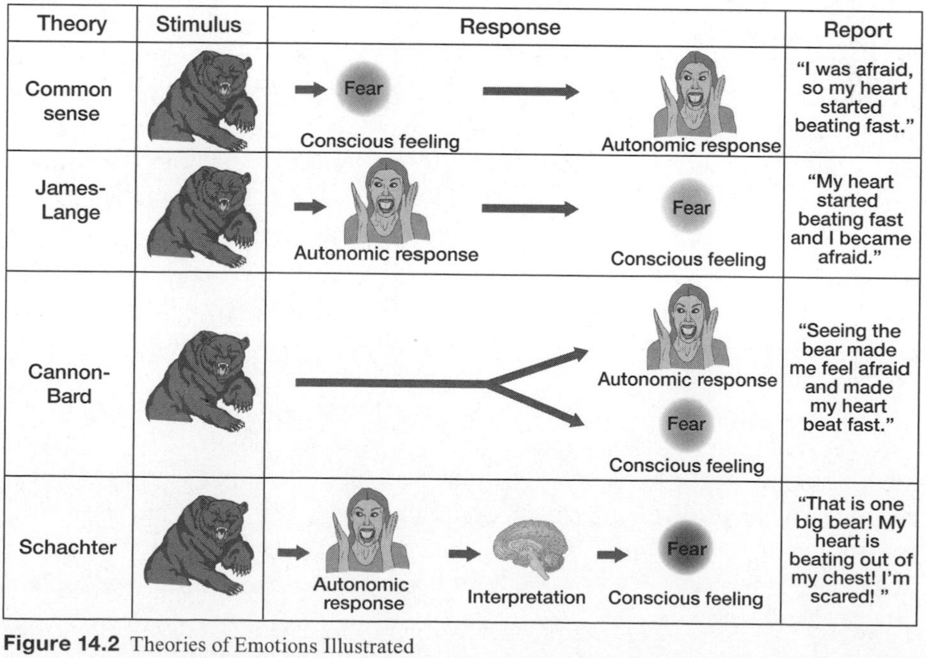

Theory	Stimulus	Response			Report
Common sense		Fear — Conscious feeling	→	Autonomic response	"I was afraid, so my heart started beating fast."
James-Lange		Autonomic response	→	Fear — Conscious feeling	"My heart started beating fast and I became afraid."
Cannon-Bard			Autonomic response	Fear — Conscious feeling	"Seeing the bear made me feel afraid and made my heart beat fast."
Schachter		Autonomic response → Interpretation →	Fear — Conscious feeling		"That is one big bear! My heart is beating out of my chest! I'm scared!"

Figure 14.2 Theories of Emotions Illustrated

Facial Feedback

Parents often tell their unhappy children "Just smile and you will feel better," and some research suggests that the parents may be right. The hypothesis for this practice is that specific facial expressions alter the blood flow to the brain, which in turn gives rise to emotional feelings. This idea, which was introduced in the 1960s but refined in the 1980s by psychologist Robert Zajonc (1923–2008) and others, is known as the **facial feedback hypothesis**. Like the earlier theories, the facial feedback hypothesis focuses on the relationship between a physiological response and subjective feelings.

Imaginative studies have been designed to test the facial feedback hypothesis. In one study, one group of participants held a pencil in their teeth with their lips not touching the pencil. Holding a pencil this way put each participant's face in a position resembling a smile. Another group of participants held the pencil on their upper lip, sandwiched between their lip and the base of their nose. This hold on the pencil put the participants' faces into what is commonly called a "duck face" pose, with lips pressed together in a pout and protruding—picture any number of selfies on social media to understand the duck face. While holding the pencil, each participant rated a series of cartoons based on how funny they were. If facial feedback influenced response, the "smiling" participants should feel happier and rate the cartoons as funnier than the "duck face" participants would. Although early studies did in fact show this difference, more recent work hasn't always supported this idea.

Current Research on Emotion

Theories of emotion have assumed that emotions, whether involuntary responses to stimuli or the result of cognitive appraisal or labeling, are universal and preexist in the brain. For example, from this perspective we feel fear because there is a hard-wired part of the brain in charge of producing the emotion of fear. **Discrete emotion theories**, such Silvan Tomkins' eight core emotions from 1962 or more recently Carroll Izard's twelve discrete emotions, presume that there are a specific number of biologically-determined core emotions that are universally shared. But are emotions actually discrete, identifiable, and universal? Can a distinct neurological signature or "fingerprint" be found in the brain to identify each emotion? Are there certain stimuli that will lead to certain emotional reactions?

We all experience identifiable emotions, such as happiness, sadness, anger, and fear, but researchers have yet to actually discover empirically consistent measurements of the presence or absence of them. In other words, subjects consistently identify their own or someone else's emotions, but empirical measurements of emotions, such as muscle activity and brain imaging, are much less consistent.

Recently, researchers have begun to formulate a more data-driven approach to explaining emotion that uses the latest brain imaging technology and empirical research methods and signals a significant shift from traditional theories about emotion. Starting with James Russell (b. 1947) in 1980 and continuing with the research of Lisa Barrett (b. 1963), an alternative approach that Barrett and Russell call **psychological constructivism** has emerged that views emotions not as discrete elements that can be identified in a particular part or region of the brain but as complex perceptions constructed in the mind from the interaction of sensory input and learned prior associations. Together these create the *conceptualization* of an emotion, identifying and labeling an affective (emotional) state in the context of wide-ranging sensations from the body and external world.

Emotional Intelligence

One contemporary view of emotion involves not just biological responses and labels but also the evaluation of the personal meaning of a stimulus. Psychologist Daniel Goleman (b. 1946) has written extensively on using what he calls **emotional intelligence**—the ability to recognize and label one's own and others' emotions accurately (**emotional appraisal**), to use emotional understanding in problem-solving, and to manage and regulate emotions. Goleman argues that emotional intelligence may be necessary to move children away from egocentrism and toward quality interpersonal relationships (see Chapter 15). In his view, children begin to develop emotional intelligence early in life. By elementary school, children clearly show empathy for others and are able to recognize nonverbal clues that provide evidence for how someone else feels. Middle school children can analyze their own emotions, recognize what creates stress for them, and identify what motivates them to perform at their highest levels. By the end of high school, teens and young adults can use their emotional intelligence to listen and talk in ways that resolve conflicts rather than increase their intensity. Goleman argues that emotional intelligence is a key aspect to being smart and, in fact, may be more important than one's intelligence quotient (IQ).

Emotions and the Body

Emotional response and expression are complicated processes. Internally, complex communication occurs in the brain, often without our conscious awareness of it. Externally, our bodies express emotions in a variety of ways, some of them universal to all cultures, others unique to only certain cultures.

The Neurology of Emotion

Every theory of emotions recognizes that the nervous systems play a critical role in emotional feelings and behaviors. In the **autonomic nervous system (ANS)**, everything occurs automatically without conscious decision-making. One part of the ANS, the **sympathetic nervous system**, arouses the body so it can respond to emergencies. The other part, the **parasympathetic nervous system**, works in a balancing, opposing way to calm the body. All emotions occur somewhere along the continuum of arousal that is created by the autonomic nervous system.

Individual emotions are tied to specific responses in the nervous system, but many emotions are physiologically very similar. Fear and excitement, for example, both involve high arousal, with the person experiencing a high heart rate, dilated pupils, rapid breathing, and sweaty palms. In other words, running for safety when a car is driving off the road onto the sidewalk creates the same physiological responses as riding a roller coaster. Whether people have the subjective experience of fear in either of these situations depends on their appraisal of the situation: Roller coasters are designed for amusement, even if they are sometimes scary, too, but for the most part people know they are safe in a roller coaster. In contrast, a person on the sidewalk with a car careening toward pedestrians is likely to judge the situation as highly unsafe.

Within the **central nervous system (CNS)**, many different parts of the brain are active and involved in processing and responding to emotions. The **reticular formation** at the top of the brain stem is involved in processing the information that comes into awareness. An interconnected set of neural networks within the **limbic system** (see Chapter 4) goes to work processing emotional content. The **amygdala** is involved in the fight-or-flight response that occurs when an animal or person is aroused; it is connected to both the sensorimotor system and the autonomic nervous system. The **hippocampus** is involved in retrieving information from long-term storage and moving it back into working memory; identifying it as dangerous or benign; and regulating memories related to the time, environment, and activities going on in the environment around the person. The **hypothalamus**, as part of its normal, regulatory functions, sends signals (via hormones) to the parts of the autonomic nervous system that can respond to any new situation, emergency or not. The frontal lobe of the cerebral cortex is involved in appraising the situation. The **nucleus accumbens**, for example, is a group of neurons in the frontal lobe that respond to pleasurable situations. A flood of the neurotransmitter **dopamine** to this area signals pleasure or the anticipation of pleasure to the rest of the brain and body (see Chapter 5 for more about neurotransmitters).

Emotional Expression

Crying, smiling, punching a wall, holding hands, punctuating texts with emoticons—all are expressions of emotion. Some emotional expressions develop early in life and may be universal (e.g., smiles), whereas others are specific to a particular culture, age group, or time period. Emotional expression is so important to social interaction that infants become very distressed when their mother models a still face without any expression, and lack of emotion is often a sign of a psychological disorder. Facial expressions, gestures, posture, distance, and nonlinguistic vocal characteristics that express emotional feelings are examples of **nonverbal communication (NVC)**.

All the children in these pictures would understand a smile in the same way.

Facial Expressions You have already read about the facial feedback theory in the context of what causes emotions (see page 332). Facial expressions, of course, also convey emotions. Early in his career, psychologist Paul Ekman (b. 1934) became interested in identifying a set of universal emotions—that is, emotions that are common throughout every culture. Focusing on facial expressions, Ekman identified every muscle in the human face and then every possible combination of facial muscles. Ekman and his colleague Wallace Friesen (b. 1933) developed the **Facial Action Coding System (FACS)**, a tool for measuring movement of these muscles, which led them to create a taxonomy of facial expressions. The FACS can identify more than 5,000 distinct facial expressions.

Ekman found that the emotional expressions of anger, disgust, fear, happiness, sadness, and surprise were universal, present in every culture he studied. Ekman and his colleagues have also identified emotions that are experienced but not expressed by changes in facial muscles.

Although Ekman initially argued that these facial expressions of emotion were universal, research shows that emotions are not always expressed at the same times or in the same ways in every culture. For example, in some cultures it is not okay to smile at a funeral but is okay, even expected, to cry. In other cultures, people are expected to remain generally calm at a funeral, with little emotional expression. Expected or "appropriate" ways of expressing those emotions that vary from culture to culture and situation to situation are known as **display rules**. For example, Japanese people are thought to be less likely than Westerners to show negative feelings such as anger and fear in their facial expressions; instead they may mask them with a smile.

Ekman researched **microexpressions**, momentary and involuntary expressions that often reveal true emotions when a prolonged facial expression conveys a different emotion—the "true" expression behind the display rule. Ekman believed microexpressions occur when people are trying to hide their true feelings from others and also when they repress them (i.e., hide them from themselves; see Chapter 11). Detecting microexpressions works—the government has trained hundreds of investigators in the FBI and Transportation Safety Administration to use this skill.

Indeed, facial expressions aren't always accurate signals of what a person is feeling. Have you ever tried to convince someone that you are happy, but you're miserable inside? Or somebody in the group yells, "Selfie! Say cheeeeeeese!" and everyone in the group turns toward the camera with a frozen and possibly fake smile. Researchers have discovered a distinct difference between a real and a fake smile. A "true" smile, known as a "Duchenne smile" after the 19th century French neurologist who studied the physiology of facial expressions, engages the muscles around the mouth *and* the eyes. Businesswoman and former model Tyra Banks called this expression of emotion "smizing"—smiling with the eyes.

This question of whether emotions can be hidden or whether certain expressions or responses "leak out" into the world relates to the discussion of—and controversy around—the use of **polygraphs**, more popularly known as lie detector machines. A polygraph is a device hooked up to a person to record changes in heart rate, blood pressure, respiration (breathing rate), and **galvanic skin response (GSR)**, a stress-induced change in the skin that affects electrical conduction. The person being tested is asked a series of neutral questions to determine a base level of arousal and a set of questions that could evoke emotional feelings and their accompanying physiological changes. The underlying idea is that a person who lies will feel guilty or bad about lying and that the physical manifestations of this emotion can be detected by the machine. Unfortunately, these machines do not accurately measure emotions, even if they do indicate arousal. Polygraphs often appear in television shows, but they are not considered reliable evidence in a criminal trial.

Other Nonverbal Communication Do you wave your arms when you talk excitedly? Twirl your hair or pull on your beard when you are nervous? Stomp your feet when you are angry? People express emotions through many different gestures and behaviors known as **body language**.

- **Posture and stance** express emotions and emotional states. For example, if you are depressed or sad, you might hunch over slightly and hang your head. If you are confident and happy, in contrast, you are likely to stand straight.

- **Kinesics** is the study of gestures and movements during communication. A number of researchers have found that certain types of movements correspond with certain emotions. For example, an angry person often uses large, fast, and jerky movements; fearful or sad people move more slowly and make smaller movements with lower energy. Anxious people may touch their hair, open and close their fists, and generally fidget.

- **Proxemics** is the study of the space that people place between themselves and others. After examining how people in different cultures use space, anthropologist Edward T. Hall (1914–2009) identified a range of zones in which people feel comfortable interacting (see Figure 14.3). How people feel about each other influences the amount of personal space they need when they interact. For example, people who are close emotionally can interact in the "intimate zone." A person's "intimate space" is the area within about 18 inches of the person, as close as touching and as far away as about an arm's length. Each person also has a personal space, a social space, and a public space, in which close friends, casual friends, and the general public can interact. Different cultures have different zones of comfort. Latin Americans, for example, tend to feel comfortable on the border of personal and intimate space, even with people they do not know well.

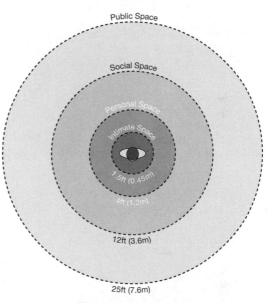

Figure 14.3 Proxemics

- **Paralanguage** refers to the nonlinguistic properties of speech. How high or deep is our voice, and what message does that send? For example, a speaker's voice quality can be smooth, gravelly, nasal, or scratchy, and each quality conveys a different emotion. Changing vocal **pitch**, which is based on the number of sound wave vibrations per second, can turn a high, squeaky voice into a deep, resonant one, reflecting changes in emotions. A rapid **speech rate** can convey the message of excitement, frustration, anger, or stress; a slow rate can indicate boredom. Intonation, rhythm, and emphasis on key words also help to express emotional content in verbal messages.

- **Text or Pictorial Expressions** Pictures—artwork, photographs, drawings—can express the emotions of their creator. A recent addition to pictorial expressions of emotions are emoticons and emojis. Emoticons began as typographic characters that formed images and were added to email and text messages. Early emoticons included :) for happy; :(for sad; and :P for sticking out one's tongue in a playful expression of "nuts to you." As digital communication has evolved, emojis have become popular. Emojis are full-blown graphics that are meant to depict different emotional states. With succeeding versions of operating systems, emojis are becoming more complex and reflective of the emotions in various cultures.

THINK AS A PSYCHOLOGIST: AN ATLAS OF EMOTIONS

In 2016, Paul Ekman and his daughter, a specialist in integrative medicine, helped create an interactive online map called "Atlas of Emotions" that was commissioned by the Dalai Lama. The Tibetan monk wanted a tool people all over the world could use to develop compassion and inner peace, feeling that people have both destructive and constructive emotions and should focus on developing the constructive ones. Ekman surveyed 149 psychologists to try to find areas of agreement on the complex topic of emotions. Based on that survey, he identified five basic categories of human emotion—anger, fear, disgust, sadness, and enjoyment—each with many subsets and levels of intensity. To help people achieve a calm state, the atlas includes triggers of emotional responses and the behaviors that follow so people can learn to avoid the triggers and moderate their responses.

Ekman took the research and the goals of the Dalai Lama to visualization experts who developed the atlas and its "continents" of emotions to reflect the current scientific understanding of emotions.

Practice: Visit the Atlas of Emotions website and work with a partner to answer the following questions. Share your answers with the class.

- Your friend is ruminating on a bad grade he got on his final exam. He says he doesn't see a point in studying if he is always going to get bad grades. His behavior is destructive. On which continent of the Atlas of Emotions is this behavior found, and what state is your friend experiencing? There may be more than one correct answer.
- Find the state "schadenfreude" in the Atlas of Emotions. On what continent is it found? What does *schadenfreude* mean? What negative behaviors might one exhibit in this state? Give an example of when someone might experience this state.

- It has been suggested that the worst acts a person or group can commit against others requires dehumanizing the victim. On what continent is dehumanizing behavior found? According to the Atlas of Emotions, what trigger may cause dehumanization? Is this trigger learned or universal?
- Create two columns of all the triggers of fear listed in the Atlas of Emotion. Separate the triggers into two categories: those that are universal and those that are learned. How might awareness of both types of triggers improve or affect a person's reaction to fear? Can universal triggers be brought to awareness before reaction takes place?

Stress, Health, and Coping

Health psychology is a subfield in psychology that uses psychological and behavioral principles to study health, illness, and health care, including stress and coping. A related field is behavioral medicine, which applies psychology to manage medical problems. For example, asthma and diabetes are diseases that can be treated, in part, with psychological intervention. Together, researchers who study health psychology and behavioral medicine work to prevent illness, reduce stress, and promote health and well-being.

Stress

Stress and emotions are often considered together, because stress is often accompanied by subjective emotional feelings. When people think about stress, images from films and television may come to mind. However, the media portrayal of stress is biased and incomplete. From a psychological point of view, **stress** is a mental and physical condition that occurs when a person encounters some demand or expectation and must adjust or adapt to the environment. Stress can be negative (i.e., **distress**), but it can also be a positive motivating force. **Eustress**, a positive form of stress, pushes people to achieve, to accomplish their daily and life goals. Exercise and travel are both examples of eustress.

A **stressor** is a condition or event in the environment that challenges or threatens a person. Stressors have different intensities and effects on people's lives, and they combine to create an overall stress level for each person. Typical stressors include daily hassles, relationship troubles, and financial problems.

Frustrations, such as those experienced while having difficulty opening a package or not being able to complete a task on time, can be low-intensity stressors. People experience **external frustration**, a negative emotional state, when outside or environmental factors prevent them from reaching a goal. For example, lacking money to pay for a doctor visit or being unable

The prevalence of probable serious mental illness doubled among low-income survivors of Hurricane Katrina, a deadly storm that ravaged the Gulf Coast of the United States in 2005.

to find a job can lead to external frustration. In contrast, people experience **personal frustration** when their own internal characteristics impede their progress toward a goal. Having difficulty getting motivated to start a project or assignment could result in internal frustration.

Less typical, but arguably more stressful, are traumatic or unexpected events that are very intense, such as community flooding, long-term chronic illness, or homelessness. Other examples include experiencing child abuse, witnessing a murder, or having one's home destroyed by fire. **Traumatic stressors** can cause psychological injury or intense emotional pain.

Responding to Stressors How do people react when they encounter a stressor? The first step is usually to conduct a **primary appraisal** of the situation: Is the stressor relevant? Is it threatening? Is the experience positive? The next step is a **secondary appraisal**, during which a person considers the resources that are available to respond to or cope with the stressor: Do I have a course of action I can take? Following appraisal, a person may consider additional factors about the stressor: Is it intense? repeating? unpredictable? uncontrollable? In fact, feeling a lack of control can be a stressor in itself, one that threatens a person's well-being.

People react to frustrations in a variety of ways. Some respond with aggression, intentionally directing behavior toward harming a person, animal, or object. Sometimes the target is the reason for the frustration; in other cases, **displaced aggression** is directed toward some other object (e.g., punching the wall instead of a person who caused the frustration). Another way to cope with frustration is through **escape**, which could include physically removing oneself from the source of frustration (e.g., dropping out of school) or psychologically escaping (e.g., tuning out or becoming apathetic). Escape can also involve **mood-altering behaviors**, including using drugs or alcohol to numb feelings, taking on excessive work, and overexercising. Escape behaviors allow for the appearance of productivity but mask the emotional experiences arising from the stress.

Another consequence of frustration may be **learned helplessness** (see page 235). Psychologist Martin Seligman argues that when events appear to be uncontrollable, people come to believe they cannot overcome the obstacles that stand between them and their goals, no matter how hard they try. Feeling helpless, these people may become passive and withdrawn and in some cases become depressed.

Much of what psychologists know about the ways in which people respond to stress comes from the work of **Hans Selye** (1907–1982). Selye proposed the **general adaptation syndrome (GAS)**, a three-stage process that people go through in response to stressors. The first stage is *alarm*, in which the person appraises the stressor(s) and mobilizes resources to cope. The second stage is *resistance*, during which the person tries to cope with the stressors. *Exhaustion* is the third and last stage, during which the person's energy is depleted. In this last stage, the body essentially shuts down, informing the person that no more energy is available to cope.

Later researchers recognized that if there is long-term, repeated exposure to stressors, **burnout**—physical, mental, and/or emotional exhaustion— may occur. A person with burnout may get sick because the immune system is weakened. Burnout is increasingly common in helping professions, such as human and veterinary medicine, nursing, and social work. Along with emotional exhaustion, in which the person feels "used up" and apathetic toward work, a person experiencing burnout often feels cynical and detached from the job. A burned-out person may also feel very little sense of personal accomplishment.

The Biology of Chronic Stress A **stress response** is the arousal of the autonomic nervous system that occurs in response to the stressor. Often, this arousal leads to the **fight-or-flight response**, which occurs when people encounter something dangerous or even life-threatening and respond physiologically in a way that prepares them to fight or flee. Stress reactions of this sort were highly adaptive when early humans experienced life or death situations on a daily basis as they struggled to survive. Today, however, people often experience stress reactions to more typical daily events, such as seeing someone cut in line in the cafeteria, being stuck in traffic, having someone mispronounce a name, getting a mean text, or getting behind on a deadline. These daily frustrations can alter mood and increase chronic stress levels, especially when the people involved react with the fight-or-flight response.

Road rage, for example, is an emotional response to a stress reaction that occurs in situations that are usually not life-threatening.

Selye was an endocrinologist, and his research informed our understanding of how the body responds to stress via the **hypothalamic-pituitary-adrenal axis (HPA axis)**. The amygdala, which is part of the limbic system and also important for processing emotional feelings, recognizes a threat. The amygdala then signals the hypothalamus, which signals the pituitary gland to signal the adrenal glands to release three hormones: **adrenaline** (epinephrine), **noradrenaline** (norepinephrine), and **cortisol** (sometimes called "the stress hormone"). In combination with noradrenaline, adrenaline prepares the body to fight or flee in response to the possible danger. It causes the pupils to enlarge, increases heart rate, increases blood pressure, enlarges the air passages to the lungs, and increases blood sugar, particularly in the brain. Cortisol plays an important role in altering the body's metabolism during chronic stress, which ultimately takes a toll on people's bodies and minds. Humans are wonderfully adapted to acute stress but poorly adapted to chronic stress. Over time, elevated levels of cortisol can suppress the immune system, increase blood pressure, increase blood sugar, decrease sex drive, produce acne, and contribute to obesity, particularly belly fat.

Coping with Threats and Stressors

Coping is the act of facing and dealing with problems and stressors, especially over the long term. When people have trouble coping with chronic stress, they often show emotional signs such as anxiety, apathy, irritability, excessive worry about illness, and mental fatigue. Behavioral signs that suggest a person is having trouble coping include avoiding responsibilities and relationships, engaging in extreme or self-destructive behavior, and neglecting to wash or eat properly. Some people attempt to cope with stress by self-medicating with alcohol or drugs.

Such cognitive factors as **self-defeating fears and attitudes** can make coping with stress difficult. Examples of statements showing self-defeating fears and attitudes include the following:

- "It would be terrible to be rejected, abandoned, or alone. I must have love and approval before I can feel good about myself."

- "If someone criticizes me, it means there's something wrong with me."

- "I must always please people and live up to everyone's expectations."

- "Other people should always meet my expectations."

- "I am basically defective and inferior to other people."

- "I'm hopeless and bound to feel depressed forever because the problems in my life are impossible to solve."

Psychologist Albert Ellis (1913–2007) argued that when people create an unrealistic view of the world based on this irrational thinking, which he called "awfulizing," stressors seem more severe and are harder to manage.

Varieties of Coping Strategies Successfully coping with stress is important for maintaining both health and a sense of well-being. People have different ways of coping, which vary depending on both the situation and the person. In some situations, a person engages in **emotion-focused coping**, controlling or replacing the negative emotional responses to the stressor (e.g., "Okay, this is upsetting me, but I can stay calm and not lose my temper"). **Problem-focused coping**, as the name suggests, is a strategy for managing or fixing the distressing situation. For example, a person stuck in traffic on the freeway might exit at the next off-ramp and plot a new route on surface streets. A third approach, **appraisal-focused coping**, attempts to reframe the stressors—changing one's perceptions and assumptions about the stressors. "Putting a positive spin on things" is an example of an appraisal-focused coping strategy.

Personality, too, may influence how people respond to and cope with stress. In the 1950s, cardiologists Howard Friedman (1910–2001) and Ray Rosenman (1920–2013) did a multiyear study investigating a possible connection between personality and coronary heart disease. They found that people with what they called a **Type A personality** had a greater risk of heart disease. They defined Type A personality based on a cluster of related characteristics, including being competitive, hard-driving, impatient, verbally aggressive, and easily angered. People with Type A personalities also tend to have high levels of tension and difficulty waiting for appointments; they are pushed by deadlines and hate delays. In contrast, people with **Type B personality** are easygoing and relaxed, very "chill." They have lower stress levels and enjoy games but are comfortable having experiences without focusing on winning. The cartoon in Figure 14.4 uses hyperbole to illustrate the difference.

Subsequent research has shown there are multiple factors that may affect a person's risk of heart disease. Freidman and Rosenman's research, along with that of others who studied Type A and B personalities, has also been somewhat discredited because of its support by the tobacco industry, which was looking for evidence that factors other than smoking could cause health problems.

Figure 14.4

Nonetheless, some people do seem to have a **disease-prone personality**. They tend to have a chronic negative mood and focus on bad things in life. They are typically anxious, hostile, and frequently ill. People with a **self-healing personality**, in contrast, tend to have strong social relationships and to be conscientious, emotionally secure, and enthusiastic about life and all it offers.

Life Changes, Lifestyle, and Health

To provide an objective measure of stress and see its relationship to illness, psychiatrists Thomas Holmes (1919–1989) and Richard Rahe developed a scale based on what they called **Life Change Units**, or **LCUs**. They identified many different life changes and assigned a numerical value to the level of stress that change would typically cause. For example, a person who experiences the death of a spouse has 100 LCUs, a person who experiences divorce has 73 LCUs, and a person going to jail has 71 LCUs. Other life events were given lower LCU values, such as being fired (47 LCUs), having a child leave home (29), and going on vacation (13). The sum of all the events the person has experienced in the previous two years gives a total LCU value, which represents a person's overall stress level. Higher totals indicate more stress, which is associated with greater likelihood of illness. The scale has been revised many times in the last 40 years to reflect events in contemporary life, but the Holmes and Rahe Stress Scale (also known as the Social Readjustment Rating Scale, or SRRS) is still considered a valid measure of life stress.

Events such as those on the scale are usually isolated instances. In contrast, the ways in which people respond to their environments and how they go about their daily lives are collectively known as **lifestyle**. Lifestyle plays an important role in the stressors that affect people and in how they cope with those stressors. Health psychologists suggest that establishing certain lifestyle habits can reduce the likelihood that a person will get sick as a result of stressors. Some of these habits are

- Eating three meals a day

- Getting seven to eight hours of sleep at least four days a week

- Giving and receiving affection regularly

- Exercising to a point of perspiration at least two times per week

- Getting strength from spiritual beliefs

- Confiding in one or more friends

- Doing something fun at least once a week

Confiding in a friend and showing affection are lifestyle habits that can ward off stress-related illness.

In recent years, people have become more aware of the importance of healthy lifestyle habits and are more willing to include them in their lives. Technology, too, has helped foster awareness of healthy habits. For example, fitness devices now can track steps, stairs climbed, distance walked or jogged, heart rate, and other measures of activity. Pairing these devices with apps that allow people to record meals and nutritional information has encouraged many more people to work toward living healthier lives.

On the other hand, **lifestyle diseases** are a big problem in the United States and other countries today. These diseases are related to or caused by health-damaging personal habits. Examples include obesity, type 2 diabetes, heart disease, and diseases related to smoking, alcohol abuse, and drug abuse. Changing bad lifestyle habits is key to controlling lifestyle diseases and reducing the risk of other illnesses. Eating well (see Chapter 13) and exercising can set a person on a more healthy path. In a strange paradox, the more energy a person exerts in exercise, the more energy that person has for other activities.

Individual Strategies for Managing Stress Developing healthy lifestyle habits is only one of many ways to reduce a person's vulnerability to stress. Another important strategy is to develop ways to let go of tension and anxiety. Relaxation allows a person to reduce distracting thoughts while activating the parasympathetic nervous system to produce feelings of calmness. One technique that produces deep relaxation throughout the body is to tighten all muscles in an area of the body and then relax them. People are often instructed to begin with the toes on each side and work up the legs into the torso, arms, and neck. Some people use **guided imagery** to visualize images that are calming, relaxing, or beneficial in other ways. **Stress inoculation** is another strategy, involving positive coping statements to control fear and anxiety. People are encouraged to say or think reassuring, self-enhancing statements and to eliminate negative self-statements and self-critical thoughts. Stress inoculation is analogous to a vaccine for infections—it prepares the mind to handle future stressors by minimizing the severity of reactions a person will experience.

People who find and use a support system also seem to manage stress better than those who don't. They prepare rather than worry—creating choice in their lives rather than reacting to circumstances. Preparing for a variety of possibilities means that a person can be ready if one of them appears.

People can also manage stress by learning to prioritize the important things in life. Spending time on those priorities sometimes means saying no to people who make other demands. Keeping a journal or diary can also reduce stress; people often need to communicate and reflect on thoughts and feelings in a place that holds no judgments. Journaling can help a person develop perspective on life experiences, work out priorities, and come to conclusions about what they or others have said, done, and felt.

Finally, one often-overlooked way to manage stress is to take time to unplug. Being plugged in creates certain brain responses that can be harmful in the long term. People can spend at least a couple of waking hours every week without being tethered to electronics. They might turn off the phone, computer, television, and gaming system and get out into nature. Ultimately, the better people come to know themselves, the more they can make adjustments that lead to managing stress in healthy and effective ways.

Training Programs Promoting Health and Stress Management Many programs have been designed to help people manage stress and improve their health. *Refusal skills training* is a program that teaches young people how to resist pressures to begin smoking and vaping, in part because smoking and vaping may lead to additional addictions. For example, research suggests that tobacco products can change the brains of mice, making them more susceptible to later cocaine addiction. It also shows a significant correlation between early cigarette use to later use of illicit drugs. *Life skills training* focuses on stress reduction, self-protection, decision-making, self-control, and social skills. Though not normally taught as part of the K-12 curriculum, these kinds of skills might be just as valuable as academic skills.

Community health campaigns are community-wide education programs that provide information about how to decrease risk factors and promote health. Given the vast amounts of information and the challenge to keep up with the research, these community health programs may be what many communities need to help people lead healthier lives. People also need mentors and role models, people who serve as positive examples of good and desirable behavior. Regular contact with role models helps people to see and engage in effective strategies for facing the challenges that life has to offer. All this can lead us to a life of **wellness**, a positive state of good health and well-being.

REFLECT ON THE ESSENTIAL QUESTION

Essential Question: *Why do people feel as they do?* On separate paper, complete a chart like the one below to gather details to help answer that question.

Biology of Emotions	Theories of Emotions	Expressions of Emotions	Stress and Coping

---

KEY TERMS AND PEOPLE

BIOLOGICAL TERMS

adrenaline

amygdala

autonomic nervous system (ANS)

central nervous system (CNS)

cortisol

dopamine

galvanic skin response

hippocampus

hypothalamic-pituitary-adrenal axis (HPA axis)

hypothalamus

limbic system

noradrenaline

nucleus accumbens

parasympathetic nervous system

reticular formation

sympathetic nervous system

EMOTIONS

body language

Cannon-Bard theory

common-sense theory

discrete emotion theories

displaced aggression

display rules

emotion

emotional appraisal

emotional expression

emotional feelings

emotional intelligence

facial action coding system (FACS)

facial feedback hypothesis

James-Lange theory

kinesics

microexpressions

nonverbal communication (NVC)

paralanguage

pitch

polygraphs

primary appraisal

proxemics

psychological constructivism

Schachter's two-factor theory

secondary appraisal

speech rate

STRESS AND COPING

appraisal-focused coping

burnout

community health campaigns

disease-prone personality

displaced aggression

distress

emotion-focused coping

escape

eustress

external frustration

fight-or-flight response

frustrations

general adaptation syndrome (GAS)

guided imagery

health psychology

kinesics

learned helplessness

Life Change Units (LCU)

lifestyle

lifestyle disease

mood-altering behaviors

personal frustration

problem-focused coping

scapegoat

self-defeating fears and attitudes

self-healing personality

stress

stress reaction

stressor

traumatic stressor

stress inoculation

Type A personality

Type B personality

wellness

KEY PEOPLE

Philip Bard

Walter Cannon

Albert Ellis

William James

Carl Lange

Stanley Schachter

Hans Selye

1. Which of the following are the stages in Hans Selye's general adaptation syndrome?
   (A) Attack, flight, defense
   (B) Appraisal, stress response, coping
   (C) Alarm, resistance, exhaustion
   (D) Self-control, shock, anger
   (E) Anxiety, fighting, adapting

2. Greg stays up all night during finals week studying for exams. As the week progresses, his muscles tighten and he develops a stiff neck. By the last day of finals, he is taking more frequent breaks, leaning back in the desk chair, and staring off into space. He arrives for the last test with a sore throat and headache. Which of the following best describes Greg's response to stress?
   (A) General adaptation syndrome
   (B) Object relations theory
   (C) Opponent-process theory
   (D) Two-factor theory
   (E) Type B behavior pattern

3. Individuals exhibiting a hostile Type A personality pattern are at an increased risk for
   (A) Alzheimer's disease
   (B) cardiovascular disease
   (C) schizophrenia
   (D) galvanic skin response
   (E) anorexia nervosa

4. Stanley Schachter's explanation of emotions places emphasis on
   (A) simultaneous arousal and emotional experience
   (B) the role of the hypothalamus
   (C) the range of emotions that are genetically inherited
   (D) a cognitive appraisal of physiological arousal
   (E) an optimistic explanatory style

5. Mark, a restaurant host, began his workday in a bad mood. However, by the end of the day, he felt much happier. According to the facial feedback hypothesis, what may have influenced the change in Mark's mood?

(A) The day was so busy that Mark did not have time to reflect on events that were troubling him.

(B) The change in weather during the day helped decrease Mark's stress.

(C) Because it is his job to be courteous to customers, Mark smiled at customers frequently.

(D) Mark helped several customers who then told his supervisor how nice he was.

(E) Mark is good friends with some of the wait staff, and they cheered him up during the shift.

6. Researchers know that autonomic responses such as heart rate, perspiration, and respiration change under stress. Since people usually have stronger autonomic responses when lying than when speaking the truth, it makes sense that the polygraph would be an effective method to detect lies. Which statement best explains why the polygraph is not more widely used in job interviews and in courtrooms?

(A) The polygraph has been shown to be reliable only in highly emotional cases, such as child abuse and spying.

(B) In controlled studies, the polygraph has correctly identified guilty individuals in only a small percentage of cases.

(C) A significant number of people show paradoxical reactions, responding more strongly when telling the truth than when lying.

(D) Most people can avoid detection when they lie.

(E) Physiological arousal is much the same for several emotions, so the polygraph cannot always reliably distinguish guilt from other reactions.

7. Paul Ekman found that when Japanese students watched films that made them feel the emotion of disgust, they masked their expressions of disgust with a smile when an authority figure entered the room. However, when alone, they openly expressed disgust. American students maintained their expressions of disgust both alone and in the presence of an authority figure. Ekman's findings illustrate what he calls

   (A) phi phenomenon

   (B) the two-factor theory

   (C) the facial feedback hypothesis

   (D) display rules

   (E) choleric personalities

8. The James-Lange theory of emotion would describe the experience of emotion in which order?

   (A) Arousal, emotion, stimulus

   (B) Stimulus, arousal, emotion

   (C) Arousal, stimulus, emotion

   (D) Emotion, arousal, stimulus

   (E) Stimulus, emotion, arousal

9. One of the consistent research findings in the area of facial expressions and emotion is the

   (A) way children's facial expressions differ from adults

   (B) way in which individuals' facial expressions change as they get older

   (C) universality of facial expressions across cultures

   (D) vast differences in facial expressions between males and females

   (E) ease with which people can learn to change their facial expressions under differing circumstances

10. When given epinephrine, research participants who were placed in a room with a happy confederate (researcher) described their emotional state as happy, while those placed in a room with an angry confederate described their emotional state as angry. Which theory of emotion best explains these results?

(A) Opponent-process

(B) Schachter-Singer

(C) Cannon-Bard

(D) James-Lange

(E) Ekman's display rules

1. Everyone experiences stress, and some deal with it more effectively than others. Explain what the general adaptation syndrome is and how catastrophes, significant life changes, and daily hassles may affect the phases. Also explain how coping skills can mediate the impact of each.

   Include the following concepts:

   - Alarm
   - Resistance
   - Exhaustion
   - Life Change Units
   - Vulnerability
   - Coping Skills

2. Alexia and Miko were excited about going to the amusement park. Alexia wanted to go on the roller coasters, whereas Miko wanted to eat junk food. On the roller coasters, each had a different experience. Using the theories of emotion, explain how Alexia and Miko could have different emotional responses. Include the following concepts.

   - Schachter two-factor theory
   - Facial feedback
   - Hippocampus
   - Coping skills
   - Dopamine

UNIT 8: Review

In this unit, you sought answers to these essential questions about motivation and emotion.

Chapter 13: Why do people behave as they do?

Chapter 14: Why do people feel as they do?

Apply what you have learned about motivation and emotion by answering the free-response question below.

FREE-RESPONSE QUESTION

Ben trains for months to compete in the upcoming marathon. He often finds himself tired after work and does not want to run, but he forces himself in anticipation for the upcoming event. While he is running, he is often hungry and thirsty, but he finishes his training before he allows himself to eat or drink. He is excited about the opportunity to compete in an event he has considered participating in for the past decade. He is also excited to see his family and friends at the event and receive the medal for completing the race.

Explain how the following factors might contribute to Ben's experience training and competing in the marathon.

- Drive-reduction theory of motivation
- Incentive theory of motivation
- Approach-avoidance conflict
- Motor cortex
- James-Lange theory of emotion
- Schachter two-factor theory of emotion
- Endorphins

UNIT 9: Developmental Psychology

Chapter 15 *Infancy and Childhood*

Chapter 16 *Adolescence Through Adulthood*

Think of the joy a new baby brings to a family. The baby is on a journey that started with nine months in utero and may last up to a century. This unit examines developmental stages through the whole life span. Chapter 15 covers prenatal development—growth during the months before a baby is born—and discusses the motor, cognitive, moral, and social development that occurs from birth to adolescence. Chapter 16 examines development from the adolescent years through older adulthood. Developmental psychologists have shifted their focus in recent years to help our aging population live fulfilling lives into old age. As you read this unit, keep in mind the developmental perspectives of *continuity versus discontinuity (stages), nature versus nurture,* and *stability versus change*—three of the most debated issues in developmental psychology.

Key Topics

- The interaction of nature and nurture
- The process of conception and gestation, including complicating factors
- The maturation of motor skills
- The influence of temperament on attachment and socialization
- The maturation of cognitive abilities
- Similarities and differences in models of moral development.
- Maturational challenges in adolescence, including family conflicts
- The influence of parenting styles on development
- The development of decisions related to intimacy as people mature
- The physical and cognitive changes that emerge as people age
- The influence of sex and gender on socialization and development
- Key contributors in developmental psychology (e.g., Mary Ainsworth, Albert Bandura, Diana Baumrind, Erik Erikson, Sigmund Freud, Carol Gilligan, Harry Harlow, Lawrence Kohlberg, Konrad Lorenz, Jean Piaget, Lev Vygotsky)

Source: *AP® Psychology Course and Exam Description*

15

Infancy and Childhood

"One can choose to go back toward safety or forward toward growth. Growth must be chosen again and again; fear must be overcome again and again."

—Abraham Maslow

Essential Question: How do physical, cognitive, moral, and social development take place from birth through adolescence?

$\mathbf{M}$any developmental theorists have proposed stages of **discontinuous development** that are marked by age-specific periods of time. You can think of these stages like steps in a staircase—when you leave one step, you move to the next but spend little time on two steps at once. The stepwise *discontinuity* approach, however, is viewed by some developmental theorists as being more theoretical than real. As children develop, they may exhibit some aspects of one stage while also exhibiting aspects of the next stage. In contrast, **continuous development** is a relatively even process without distinct stages. The *continuity* approach posits that development is more like riding an escalator than climbing a staircase, with gradual changes over time.

The **nature versus nurture** debate is one of the oldest ongoing arguments among psychologists. Is an individual's development a factor of his or her DNA? Or is it influenced more by environment and life experiences? Psychologists continue to compare the developmental impact of genetics with that of the environment, though they now know that some combination of these factors best explains development, and the combination may be different for each trait and each individual. Researchers also study the heritability of a given characteristic within a specific population. **Heritability** is the extent to which variations of a trait or behavior can be attributed to genetics.

The **stability versus change** debate is related to both of the other debates. It centers on whether the traits an infant displays are enduring or whether they change as the growing person interacts with other people and his or her culture. In other words, to what extent can defining aspects of our lives change over the life span? Early theorists, including **Sigmund Freud**, believed that very little change happened in the adult years. (For Freud's view of psychosexual development, see pages 417–419.)

Prenatal Development

The prenatal period begins with conception and ends at birth. A full-term pregnancy is typically about 40 weeks, with a baby considered full term at 39 weeks. Conception begins when a male sperm joins with a female egg to create a single cell—the beginning of a new life. The fertilized egg, known as a **zygote**, implants itself in the uterine wall, where growth occurs through rapid cell division. The **zygotic period**, also known as the **germinal period**, lasts about two weeks. At the end of the two-week period, the zygote has become an **embryo**.

During the **embryotic stage**, organ development begins as cells continue to divide, replicate, and create new growth. At about one month, the heart begins to beat and the lungs, eyes, ears, palate, and central nervous system develop. The blood vessels of the **placenta** transfer nutrients from the mother to the embryo to foster growth. Basic brain development will also have occurred by the end of the first month, including differentiation of the forebrain, midbrain, and hindbrain. The embryotic stage persists during roughly two months from the time of conception. During embryotic development, the embryo is particularly susceptible to harmful agents called **teratogens**, such as tobacco, certain drugs, and infections, that can damage the cells and tissue of the developing embryo, resulting in physical or functional defects. Harmful exposure may also happen later during fetal development. Exposure to alcohol consumption by the mother during pregnancy may result in the infant's developing **fetal alcohol syndrome (FAS)**. Severe cases of FAS can result in low birth weight, facial deformities, and limited intellectual abilities. Many factors can influence the extent to which exposure to harmful substances during this critical stage of development might affect either the fetus or newborn child, including:

- Duration and dosage of the substance
- Time of exposure during pregnancy (first half of pregnancy is most critical)
- Genetic makeup of the unborn child (some children may be more susceptible)
- Exposure of the mother to environmental factors before or during pregnancy or during nursing after childbirth

The final stage of prenatal development is the **fetal stage**, which lasts from roughly two months gestation until birth. During the fetal stage, the arms and legs continue to develop along with the central nervous system, eyes, and external genitalia. The **fetus** will gain weight and strength, especially in the last few weeks of a term pregnancy. The nervous system begins to build neural networks that will allow transmission of information back and forth between the brain, organ systems, and other parts of the body. The brain will be almost completely formed by the time of birth. Between five months into the pregnancy and birth, most infants will have reached the age of viability, allowing them to

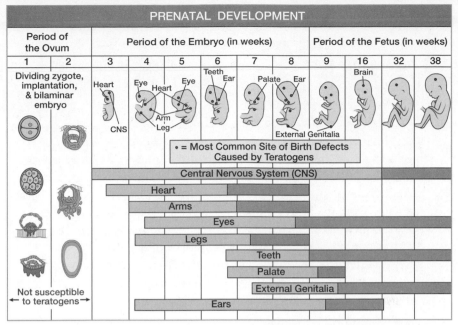

PRENATAL DEVELOPMENT

Period of the Ovum		Period of the Embryo (in weeks)						Period of the Fetus (in weeks)			
1	2	3	4	5	6	7	8	9	16	32	38

Dividing zygote, implantation, & bilaminar embryo

• = Most Common Site of Birth Defects Caused by Teratogens

Central Nervous System (CNS)

Heart

Arms

Eyes

Legs

Teeth

Palate

External Genitalia

Ears

Not susceptible ← to teratogens →

Figure 15.1 The lighter gray indicates periods of high sensitivity to teratogens.

live outside the womb. Depending on development of the lungs, heart, and other organs, the newborn may still need external support until breathing is normal and body temperature is maintained independently.

Infancy

Infancy lasts from birth until about eighteen months of age, a period of great changes in the infant. The order in which an infant's brain, body, and socialization develop involves the interaction of both nature and nurture, although the child's biological development will be determined largely by nature. This orderly, sequential biological growth pattern is called **maturation**. The process of maturation is primarily determined by genetic makeup, but it can also be influenced by extreme environmental factors such as lack of adequate nutrition or exposure to teratogens. Part of maturation is developing memory—most people's earliest memories begin at about age three.

Reflexes

At birth, all healthy newborns will exhibit many remarkable reflexes. A **reflex,** or *reflex action*, is an involuntary (without conscious control) physical response to a stimulus. (See page 77.) It is usually instantaneous upon receiving the stimulus and is established, or fixed, at birth.

- The **grasping reflex** occurs when newborns curl their fingers around objects when their palms are touched. This reflex will disappear at about three or four months but will be replaced by a voluntary grasping action.

- The **rooting reflex** occurs when babies are touched on the cheek and turn their faces towards the stimulus. This generally occurs along with a sucking reflex. It disappears at about five months.

- The **sucking reflex** drives a baby to suck objects placed in the mouth. The rooting reflex and sucking reflex work together to allow infants to receive nourishment. The sucking reflex is permanent but will change through learning and experience.

- The **Moro reflex** is a response to a sudden absence of support, producing a feeling of falling. It is the only unlearned fear in newborn babies. The response may be generated by a sudden loud noise or a change in an infant's body position. The arms and legs will be thrust out away from the body (abduction) and then pulled in closer to the body (adduction), the back may be arched, and the baby will usually cry. It is not the same as a **startle response,** a learned response to unexpected noises that occurs later in development and may replace the Moro reflex. Although the startle response still causes sudden body movements, they are less dramatic than those of the Moro reflex.

- The **stepping reflex** is the appearance of taking steps when the baby's feet touch a flat surface. Although this is not an indication that the baby is ready to walk, it may be a precursor to walking. It generally fades by about eight weeks.

- The **Babinski reflex** is the splaying of the baby's toes when the bottom of a foot is stroked. The toes will then curl inward. It will last through the baby's first year and with the stepping reflex may be beneficial to walking.

Many of these reflexes—because they allow infants to receive food or to cling to a caregiver in the early days of their lives—are considered survival reflexes and may be holdovers from our evolutionary past. Most of these reflexes disappear within the first six months of life, and some will be replaced by learned responses that involve similar behavior.

NEWBORN INFANT REFLEXES			
Infant Reflex	**Stimulation**	**Innate Response**	**Duration**
Grasping	Palms touched	Grasps tightly	Disappears at 3–4 months, replaced with voluntary grasping
Rooting	Cheek stroked or side of mouth touched	Turns toward source, opens mouth, and sucks	Disappears at 5–6 months

NEWBORN INFANT REFLEXES			
Infant Reflex	**Stimulation**	**Innate Response**	**Duration**
Sucking	Mouth touched by object	Sucks the object	Permanent but changes through learning and experience
Moro	Sudden move or loud noise	Startles; thrusts arms out and then pulls them back in	Disappears at 3–4 months
Stepping	Infant held upright with feet touching the ground	Moves feet in walking motion	Fades after about 2 months
Babinski	Sole of foot stroked	Splays toes and twists foot in	Disappears at 9–12 months

Figure 15.2

Motor Development

Eventually, reflexes will be replaced by voluntary behaviors such as sitting, crawling, and walking. Although the timing may vary, most children will begin sitting independently at about five months, crawling at about seven months, and walking near their first birthday. Unlike the timing, the sequence of babies' motor development is consistent. Babies' motor development progresses from the body's midline outward. Children learn to control areas closer to their midsections before they learn to control their arms and legs, which explains why babies sit before they walk. Children will gain the ability to use a simple pincer grasp—holding something between their thumb and index finger or their thumb and middle fingers—at about five months, allowing them to pick up a cookie or hang onto a toy or Daddy's expensive glasses. More specific hand-eye coordination improves dramatically between ages three to five years.

Children also exhibit developmental progression from head to toe. At birth, babies' heads are nearly the same size they will be at adulthood and take up about 30 percent of their total height. Unlike the head, children's extremities grow considerably in the first years of life. Children will be roughly half of their adult height when they become toddlers at about two years old.

The **dynamic systems approach** is one theory explaining how children develop motor behaviors. It posits that children try out various movements and then respond to environmental feedback, which they integrate with thought and biologically dictated actions to determine which movements are successful and which are not. Those that are successful will continue, and those that are not will eventually be discontinued. For example, as a precursor to crawling, a child often rocks back and forth on his hands and knees. However, once crawling is achieved, this behavior fades away because it no longer serves the purpose of helping the child move from place to place. It has been superseded by crawling.

INFANT MOTOR DEVELOPMENT

Average Age Achieved	Gross Motor Skill	Fine Motor Skill
4–8 weeks	Lifts head	Grasps rattle briefly
8–10 weeks	Lifts self by arms; rolls from side to back	Glances from one object to another
16–18 weeks	Sits with support	Carries object to mouth; can hold two objects
5–7 months	Sits without support	Transfers object from hand to hand
7–9 months	Crawls	Pincer grasp
10–12 months	Stands holding on; walks holding on	Pushes car along; hits cup with spoon; shows hand preference; scribbles with crayon
12–18 months	Stands alone; walks alone	Builds up to 3-cube towers; opens book; turns 2–3 pages at a time
2–3 years	Runs; jumps; climbs	Turns single pages in book; cuts with scissors; pours drink

Figure 15.3

Attachment

Newborns demonstrate an early attachment to their caregivers, showing preferences for their faces, scent, and language even a few hours after birth. As the grasping reflex demonstrates, physical attachment to a caregiver is extremely important to a child's early development. Emotional attachment between an infant and caregiver, or the **attachment bond**, is considered to be just as important. Children as young as a few weeks old learn to recognize the facial expressions of their caregivers and may begin to imitate the facial expressions they see in others. Developmental psychologist John Bowlby (1907–1990) was a pioneer in attachment research and the originator of **attachment theory**. He claimed that attachment behavior in infants is innate. After observing infants' behaviors, such as wanting to remain close to a caregiver and raising their arms to be picked up when they were distressed or wanted comfort, Bowlby posited that such behavior aids in survival and initiates nurturing responses from caregivers.

Developmental psychologist **Mary Ainsworth** (1913–1999), noted for her work on patterns of attachment, designed a research method that allowed her to observe the behavior of infants and children covertly through one-way glass. Using this method, Ainsworth observed what she called **strange-situation**

behavior to investigate various forms of attachment and bonding between one-year-old infants and their mothers. In one type of experiment, a child and mother played together in a small room and, at some point, a stranger entered. At first, the child continued to play either independently or with the mother, seeming to be relatively indifferent to the presence of the stranger. However, when the mother exited the room, leaving the child alone with the stranger, the child cried and rebuffed the stranger's efforts to give comfort. Then, when the mother returned, the child made an effort to physically touch the mother and went back to playing independently.

Infants like the one just described have a **secure attachment bond**. Although they show some level of distress when their caregivers leave, they eventually regain comfort knowing, based on their established bond, that the caregivers will return. Infants with an **insecure attachment bond** are more likely to be distressed by the caregivers' departure (**anxious-ambivalent**) and resentful when the caregivers return. Because the caregivers' behavior with these children may be inconsistent, the children's responses may be inconsistent, ranging from inconsolable when the caregivers return to clingy, refusing to leave their sides. Infants with another type of insecure attachment (**avoidant**) may be indifferent to both the caregivers' departure and return. These children may approach the caregivers on their return but then turn away. A child's preference for the mother as caregiver may have biological links but may also result from interactions between the mother and child that meet the child's needs consistently.

STRANGE SITUATION AND ATTACHMENT TYPES		
Attachment Type	Behavior When Caregiver Left Baby With Stranger	Behavior When Caregiver Returns
Secure	Upset; cries and refuses to be comforted by stranger	Makes effort to touch caregiver and returns to playing
Anxious-Ambivalent (Insecure)	Very distressed	Ambivalent and resentful of caregiver
Avoidant (Insecure)	Indifferent	Indifferent; may seek contact but then pull away

Figure 15.4

Another experiment from this line of research examined the mother's form of parenting when the child was given a novel situation that required some problem-solving. Mothers who raise securely attached infants encourage the child to solve the problem, whereas mothers who raise insecurely infants just solve the problems for the infants.

Zoologist and ethologist **Konrad Lorenz** (1903–1989) theorized that if attachment was important in human survival, as John Bowlby had demonstrated, then it may be important in other species as well. Lorenz investigated the attachment of baby geese (goslings) to a mother figure. Birds, including geese, have a critical period for attachment to a mother-type figure. A **critical period** is a specific time in which an emotional or social landmark is developed that will not or cannot occur at a later date. After hatching, goslings have an eighteen-hour critical period during which they will attach themselves to a motherlike figure. As Lorenz discovered, the motherlike figure may even be of a different species. Instinctive bonding to the first moving object seen within hours after birth (or hatching) is described as **imprinting**. Lorenz presented himself shortly after the goslings had hatched, and they imprinted him as a motherlike figure. The goslings followed behind Lorenz in a straight line as he walked, responded to his calls (made through a duck call), and even pecked his face in what appeared to be an affectionate "kissing" behavior. Lorenz raised the goslings and, even as they grew older, they demonstrated a preference for him over others. While cross-species imprinting appears to work, a tendency to prefer to imprint upon one's own species has been demonstrated. Unlike certain animal species, humans seem to have a longer period—a **sensitive period** vs. a critical period—during which attachment forms.

Psychologist **Harry Harlow** (1905–1981) continued the work of Lorenz on attachment in the 1950s, investigating attachment and also maternal separation and dependency. At the time, most psychologists believed that a strong attachment bond formed between infant and mother because mothers provided food in the form of breastfeeding. Providing a child with the basic nourishment required for life created a strong mother/infant bond, they theorized. Harlow challenged this idea, suggesting instead that the strong attachment formed between infant and mother was due to **contact comfort**, or the physical comfort a caregiver provided.

Harlow focused his studies on primates because they are more similar to humans than are rats and pigeons, and their behaviors more closely paralleled human behaviors. In his experiments, controversial for their cruelty to the animal subjects, Harlow separated baby rhesus monkeys from their mothers and gave them two artificial, inanimate surrogate "mothers." One was made of wire and fixed with a bottle that provided milk to the baby monkey. The other was made of cloth-covered wood that would allow for cuddling, but this "mother" provided no food. While the monkeys did go to the wire mother when they needed food, they spent most of their time cuddling and clinging to the cloth mother. When the monkeys were afraid or threatened, they went directly to the cloth mother for protection and comfort. Harlow concluded that milk was not the key to bonding and that contact comfort contributed more to mother/infant bonding and to the health of infants. However, critics point to bias in the results, since the face of the cloth mother was natural looking, while the face of the wire mother was block-shaped and unappealing.

Harlow also conducted isolation experiments (also controversial) and discovered that monkeys raised in isolation without a real or artificial mother did not demonstrate a preference for either mother when afraid. Instead, these isolated monkeys withdrew, turned inward, and rocked back and forth when frightened. They also struck out frequently against other monkeys when they were given opportunities to socialize. Harlow's studies showed that the physical bonds between infants and caregivers may be just as important as the infants' biological dependency on mothers for food, if not more important.

The Science of Psychology: *Longitudinal Study of Attachment*

The Minnesota Longitudinal (long-term) Study of Parents and Children began in 1975 with 267 first-time mothers-to-be and has now followed 180 individuals from three months before they were born until they were in their thirties. In an effort to eliminate variables, researchers focused only on children who were born in poverty. Researchers used a variety of assessments to determine the characteristics and expectations of the mother, the children's temperaments, and parent-child interactions. The mothers and children were assessed six times during the child's first year of life, every six months until the child was two-and-a half years old, and then at increasing intervals throughout the individuals' lives into their late twenties. This long-lasting study is now even looking at the offspring of the people who were children when the study began.

In the 1970s, many professionals doubted that early childhood experiences had much impact on behavior later in life, believing that new experiences "recorded over" old experiences. The Minnesota Longitudinal Study used a different model, summarized in several reports of the study. John Bowlby is quoted in one report: "Development turns at each and every stage of the journey on an interaction between the organism as it has developed up to that moment and the environment in which it then finds itself." Although development grows from cumulative interactions with the child's environment, early experiences determine the framework for those interactions. The study has found strong evidence that early experiences, especially patterns in parent-child attachment, are predictive of certain behaviors later in life.

For example, the study looked at two groups of preschool children who showed poor adaptation on several of the study's assessments. One group had experienced secure attachment and emotional support while they were infants and toddlers; the other had not. Those in the first group bounced back by the time they were in elementary school, while those in the second group continued to have adaptation problems. Similarly, depressed adolescents or those with conduct disorder who had positive early experiences were less likely than those who didn't to show continuing clinical problems as adults.

Practice: Work in small groups to learn more about the Minnesota Longitudinal Study of Parents and Children. Each group should conduct research to answer one of these questions and then report its findings to the rest of the class:

- What kinds of assessments were used to evaluate the parents and children?

- What do specific early attachment patterns predict about behavior later in life?

- How can developments in neuroscience clarify the assessments of temperament?

- How do the findings of the Minnesota study relate to the question of stability versus change?

Cognitive Development

Cognitive development is the process of intellectual growth a child goes through to develop information-processing abilities, perceptual skills, language learning, understanding of concepts, and problem-solving abilities. Swiss psychologist **Jean Piaget** (1896–1980) theorized that what a child is able to do intellectually depends on the development of the brain and on cognition levels.

Piaget spent the early years of his career creating intelligence exams while employed at a school run by Alfred Binet, creator of the first contemporary IQ test. Piaget noticed that children of a given age consistently answered the same questions incorrectly. He also noticed that young children answered some questions incorrectly because their thought process appeared to be different from that of older children, not necessarily because they knew less. Piaget's life's work was inspired by these early observations. He wanted to develop a theory that traced the cognitive development of children in some orderly fashion. He studied his own children and grandchildren to use as references for his theory.

Piaget's Stages of Cognitive Development

According to Piaget, children use their experiences in the world to categorize and judge new events as they occur. They use **assimilation** to make sense of new situations by relating them to prior experience and their existing schemas. For example, if a child sees the big red dog Clifford in a book, he may call him Elmo if he is already familiar with the fuzzy red character from Sesame Street. He assimilates the idea of red fuzzy objects, believing, based on his past experience and schema, that they are all Elmo. However, once the child learns the name for Clifford, a different fuzzy red object, he may no longer confuse the two. At this point, the child has learned the process of **accommodation,** a way to modify his schema to include the new information.

If a child sees the ocean for the first time and calls it a giant pool, she is *assimilating* prior experience. When she no longer makes this mistake and calls the body of water an ocean, she has *accommodated* by differentiating between situations and creating new categories. Children accommodate as they learn language that helps them differentiate among objects.

Even adults experience assimilation and accommodation because people are always facing novel situations or experiencing new foods, new ideas, and new challenges. We try to place these novel experiences into our preexisting schemas, but sometimes we must create new categories because our current classification is inadequate.

To remember the difference between assimilation and accommodation, you might want to use this mnemonic device that focuses on the double letters in each word. In *assimilation*, the double s's stand for the way the schema "stays the same." In *accommodation*, the double c's stand for "**c**reates **c**hange."

The First Stage The **sensorimotor stage** is the first of Piaget's stages of cognitive development. It lasts from birth through roughly the first two years of life. During this stage, children begin to understand that their movements are tied to sensory satisfaction. A child engages in motor activities that bring a desirable result. For example, touching a musical mobile hanging above the crib will make a satisfying noise. If a baby girl cries in her crib, her mother may appear and comfort her.

At about eight months of age, a child begins to understand that objects exist even when hidden. This discovery is known as **object permanence**. Before this discovery, if a child throws his stuffed animal out of the crib out of his sight, he would believe that it no longer exists and would not try to find it. However, the child will come to realize that the thrown object is still there and he just cannot see it.

A similar realization may lead to **stranger anxiety**, fear and distress that develop when children are confronted by individuals who are unknown to them when their parents are not around. Although children may realize at this point that their parents exist but are elsewhere, object permanence may not remove children's distress between ages twelve months and eighteen months, when stranger anxiety appears to be exceptionally strong.

The Second Stage The **preoperational stage** is Piaget's second stage of cognitive development, lasting from roughly ages two through seven. It is called "preoperational" to express the state of mind that cannot yet perform such operations as combining or separating ideas or using logic. Children in this stage can begin to see objects as symbols and often demonstrate this

Until babies develop object permanence, they do not realize that even things they can't see can exist. Peekaboo holds a true fascination for babies.

ability by exhibiting **pretend play**. They may imagine that their play room is a schoolhouse or that a piece of paper represents a plate or a pillow.

During this stage, children also exhibit **animism**, a belief that inanimate objects have feelings and humanlike qualities. For example, a child may become upset if a parent gives the child a kiss good night but does not kiss all of her stuffed animals. She may express to her parent that the stuffed animals' feelings have been hurt, not understanding that the toys are not living beings. Some may argue that such pretense, though false, allows children to develop empathy and understanding for others.

Piaget also proposed the idea of **artificialism,** the belief that anything that exists must have been made by a conscious entity. For example, if a child asks what causes thunder and his mother explains that the noise is "angels bowling," the child will accept this as a reasonable explanation. Animism and artificialism both attribute animation of the natural universe to an unseen, perhaps supernatural, power.

Children in the preoperational stage will also display **egocentrism**—seeing the world only through their own perspective. While adults may explain this as selfish behavior, it reflects the inability of the child at this age to understand a situation from another's point of view. Preoperational children believe others see the world from the same perspective by which *they* see the world. For example, if a family were to go to a carnival and the child had a wonderful time, the child would report that everyone had a great time when asked how

Young children attribute human qualities to toys and therefore see a teddy bear as a perfect guest at a tea party.

the rest of the family enjoyed the carnival. Children at this stage may stand directly in front of the TV, blocking the views of others; because *they* can see the screen, they presume others can as well. At about age four, most children begin to understand that their aunt is also their mother's or father's sister. Earlier, children would only have been able to understand their own connection to their aunt (or other family members) and not the connections with others. They now understand that relationships with others go in more than one direction and they become less egocentric.

Piaget emphasized that children in the preoperational stage exhibit **one-dimensional thinking**. While they understand that a glass is either "tall" or "short," they cannot understand that a tall, thin glass may hold the same amount of juice as a short, fat glass. Such one-dimensional thinking keeps preoperational children from understanding **conservation**, the principle that changing the shape or appearance of an object does not necessarily change the object's mass. If a young boy has a dime in his pocket, he would gladly trade

it for a nickel because the nickel is larger and surely must be more valuable than the dime. Similarly, the same amount of modeling clay rolled out like a snake will appear to children in this stage more than the same amount rolled into a ball, simply because it appears to have more surface area. The preoperational thinker who cannot understand the transformation of shape in relation to mass is demonstrating the principle of **centration**—the act of focusing on only one aspect of a problem when more aspects are relevant.

The Third Stage The **concrete operational stage** is Piaget's third stage of cognitive development, a period lasting roughly from ages seven through eleven. During the concrete operational stage, the child exhibits **two-dimensional thinking** and now understands that changing the shape of an object does not necessarily change the mass. Piaget determined that by the age of eight, children understand that a short, fat glass may hold the same amount of juice as a tall, thin glass, exhibiting the principle of conservation. The boy with the dime in his pocket should now be able to understand that a nickel is not worth more than a dime even though it is larger. Children in the concrete operational stage also become less egocentric; they no longer think that the world revolves around them and understand that their parents and others have separate lives. They recognize that their parents may have jobs that do not involve them, even though they may not fully understand what their parents do in those jobs. Children in this stage begin to think logically about problems and about concrete objects that exist in their environment. However, challenges continue to arise in thinking and reasoning abstractly or thinking in three dimensions.

The Fourth Stage The **formal operational stage** is the fourth and final stage of cognitive development in Piaget's theoretical model. Beginning in early adolescence, children are able to think about constructs and ideas that do not physically exist in the world. They understand abstract concepts like virtue and honesty, even though these are not tangible objects, and they understand sarcasm, which requires the recognition that language used in that way does not convey its literal meaning. They can also reason through hypothetical situations and plan potential solutions for long-term problems. Children in this stage can move between scientific and intuitive thinking and select the appropriate mode of thinking for different tasks. However, even though children now have the ability to think abstractly, they may still benefit from educational instruction that provides concrete examples to make the material more robust and tangible. This mode of thinking allows growing children to create a sense of identity and begin to make plans for their own futures.

PIAGET'S STAGES OF COGNITIVE DEVELOPMENT		
Cognitive Stage	Approximate Age	Description
Sensorimotor	Birth to 2 years	Sensory and motor contact exploration; development of object permanence and separation anxiety
Preoperational	2 to 6 or 7	Symbolic and egocentric thinking; ability to pretend; child does not think logically
Concrete Operational	7 to 11 or 12	Can think logically about concrete objects and do simple math; conservation develops
Formal Operational	12 to adult	Abstract and hypothetical thinking emerges; strategy and planning become possible

Figure 15.5

An easy way to remember Piaget's four stages of cognitive development is to think of the phrase "Students of Psychology Can Fly" (SPCF). The first letters create initials for **s**ensorimotor, **p**reoperational, **c**oncrete operational, and **f**ormal operational stages.

While Piaget's theory is widely known and accepted, it is not without critics and challenges. Many suggest that Piaget underestimated the cognitive abilities of children. Researchers have found that children as young as four months old may have object permanence in certain situations. Many children also develop conservation far earlier than age eight. Others criticize Piaget's stage theory because children can often demonstrate cognitive abilities from more than one stage at the same time. Further, Piaget did not make a clear distinction between competence and performance, and without that distinction, the abilities he ascribes to children in each stage fall into all-or-nothing categories. While most current research supports Piaget's order of childhood cognitive development, his idea that all children move through the cognitive stages at roughly the same age has also been disputed.

Cultural and Biosocial Development

Russian psychologist **Lev Vygotsky** (1896–1934) introduced a theory of cultural and biosocial development commonly known as *cultural-historical psychology*. His **sociocultural perspective** suggests that the social and cultural environment allows children to progress through development stages more quickly or more slowly, depending on the stimuli in that environment. For example, if children are exposed to an enriching environment in which they have access to cognitive stimulation through many resources and much social interaction, they may move through Piaget's stages more quickly than a child with minimal exposure to such stimulating situations. Vygotsky believed that one's culture provided not only language but also problem-solving strategies and other educational tools that would foster children's cognitive development. Because each culture differs, he suggested that universal guidelines for children's cognitive development were misleading. He viewed cognitive development as a social process, disagreeing with Piaget's view that children were independent explorers of their environment. Vygotsky also proposed the **zone of proximal development**—the difference between what a learner can do without help and what a learner can do with help—to suggest the steps to making children more independent. If children need assistance tying their shoes, for example, their parents may initially help them and then coach them as they attempt to tie their own shoes (what they can do with help), but as they become more capable of doing this independently, their parents should provide less and less assistance until the children can complete the task alone (what they can do without help). Some recent work on the interaction of nature and nurture in forming one's level of intelligence seems to support a more eclectic view on the development of children's cognitive abilities.

Development of Perceptual Skills

Developing **perceptual skills**, a facet of cognitive development, involves learning to perceive, organize, and interpret sensory stimuli. Infants use perceptual information to make choices about using their newly acquired motor skills. Developmental researchers Eleanor Gibson (1910–2002) and Richard D. Walk (1920–1999) tested young children's ability to perceive depth by placing them near a **visual cliff**, a table with one half of the top opaque and appearing solid and the other half made of clear Plexiglas®. The meeting of the opaque side with the clear side represented the drop-off of a cliff. (See page 157 for more on this experiment.) Only three of 36 infants tested by Gibson and Walk crawled independently to the "deep" side of the cliff, presumably because they feared the danger posed by the drop-off. The same behavior was seen in infants up to seven months old; however, twelve-month-old infants learned to use their mothers' facial expressions as a guide to behavior. A mother's smile indicated safety and permission to crawl over the cliff, while a frown indicated a mother's fear and the infant avoided the cliff.

The visual cliff experiment has been criticized on several grounds. One is that although the glass made the appearance of a drop off, it was actually solid, so that babies could feel it under them. A second is that infants six-and-a half-months old and younger crossed the "cliff," but infants older than that did not. That difference suggests that the older ones may have had experiences the younger ones did not and that the decision to cross or not cross might have more to do with experience and learning than innate depth perception.

Moral Development

Inspired by the work of Piaget, **Lawrence Kohlberg** (1927–1987), a professor of psychology at Harvard University, explored how children developed the ability to make moral decisions. His theory of the stages of moral development agreed with those of Piaget, but he wanted to take those basic ideas further. About twenty-five years earlier, Piaget had suggested that children develop the ability to tell right from wrong as their cognitive abilities develop. For example, as young children become less egocentric during the concrete operational stage, they begin to sense the impact that their decisions will have on others.

Kohlberg posited that humans tend to explore their environments naturally and that they gradually learn to function in that environment. Socially, humans perceive that certain individuals are competent, and they imitate their behavior to obtain validation from them. Children's moral attitudes develop through regular contact with adult role models. In his studies with children, Kohlberg presented numerous moral dilemmas to his subjects without being concerned whether a child selected the "right" choice or the more moral option. Instead, his main interest was *why* the child made a certain choice. The six stages Kohlberg identified were based on children's underlying reasoning rather than their ultimate decisions. The sequence of his levels and stages of moral development progress in moral reasoning as children's social circles expand.

Kohlberg's Stages of Moral Development

Each of the three levels of Kohlberg's theory comprises two stages: In Kohlberg's model of moral development, each stage builds on the preceding stage, progressing steadily. Their labels refer to their relationship to conventional moral codes.

Kohlberg's First Level At the first **preconventional level** of moral development, children are concerned with how outside forces will judge their behavior and the consequences they will receive for behavior judged either "correct" or "incorrect." If children can get away with behaviors they perceive as "naughty," they will engage in the behavior if it gets them what they want. The **punishment/obedience stage** (first stage) at this level is marked by consequences. A three-year-old may refrain from hitting his little brother not because he believes hitting is morally wrong but because he does not want to be punished by his parents. In this stage, morality is determined by the consequences resulting from a given action, and morality is generally determined by an outside authority figure.

The **satisfying needs stage** (second stage) at this level is based on obtaining satisfaction of a specific need. If children are hungry and can get away with stealing cookies from the kitchen cookie jar, they will do it because it suits their needs. Likewise, if a parent requests that a child be kind to a younger brother, he or she will do so to obtain some end benefit to the perceived "positive" behavior. For example, if a parent says, "Be nice to your brother all day, and we will go for ice cream tonight," the child is likely to comply to get the ice cream. Consistent with Piaget's findings, young children are egocentric and are concerned primarily with themselves—even though we know some adults operate in this stage as well.

Kohlberg's Second Level The second level in Kohlberg's theory is the **conventional level** of moral development. At this level, moral reasoning is still decided by an outside authority, but children and adolescents internalize the expectations of society (parents, grandparents, older siblings, teachers) and attempt to meet the perceived moral expectations. In the **approval-seeking stage** (third stage), social consensus determines individual behavior. Young children and adolescents are especially concerned with the opinions of others and are eager to impress teachers, parents, and peers to gain validation. In some cases, children will do the "right thing" in order to impress certain others, while at other times they will be swayed to engage in negative behavior because it wins the approval of others, especially among peers. Adolescents may report other students who are cheating on an exam so their teachers will view them as honest and upright. They also may be persuaded to let friends "borrow" their completed homework because they want to maintain the friendship.

In the **law and order stage** (fourth stage), an older child or adolescent is not necessarily seeking approval from individuals but is responsible for upholding the laws of society determined by credible authority figures (i.e., parents, teachers, law enforcement).

Kohlberg's Third Level The **postconventional level** of moral development is the only level in which individuals decide for themselves what is right and wrong. Moral decisions are no longer based on fear or punishment or what other people think but on the individual's own sense of morality. Kohlberg thought that most people did not actually attain this level. In the **social contract stage** (fifth stage), laws that an individual deems appropriate are obeyed and those that violate the individual's own moral code are disobeyed. Rosa Parks, for example, knew she would be arrested for sitting in the white section of a bus in Montgomery, Alabama, but she committed an act of civil disobedience to bring awareness to the issue of segregation in busing. She was not concerned that she would be arrested (punishment/obedience) or that some people would think poorly of her (approval-seeking); she acted out of her own moral code regarding right or wrong.

Individuals in the **universal ethics stage** (sixth and final stage) consider the larger question of morality when determining their own moral behavior. Kohlberg believed that this was the "highest" level of moral development. Individuals in this stage consider carefully how a certain moral decision would affect others and which decision would be in the best interest for a larger number of people. In some cases, this decision might mean adhering to accepted laws and guidelines, and in other cases it could require challenging current systems perceived by the individual to be immoral. Mahatma Gandhi engaged in illegal "protest" behavior to secure freedom for the people of India. His goal was greater than a single law or act and was guided by his own moral principles about what was right for his people. Similarly, Nelson Mandela, who served as president of South Africa from 1994 to 1999, violated South African laws of apartheid for the good of the country and to protect the black population from racist segregationists.

KOHLBERG'S STAGES OF MORAL DEVELOPMENT		
Level/Stage	Approximate Age	Description
I: Preconventional	Infancy to 5 years old	External forces dictate behavior; no independent moral judgment
1. Punishment/Obedience		No difference between right and wrong; punishment dictates behavior
2. Satisfying Needs		Obtaining rewards dictates behavior
II: Conventional	5 to 14 years old	External forces influence the internalization of societal moral expectations
3. Approval-Seeking		Social consensus and approval determines behavior
4. Law and Order		Laws of society determine behavior; credible authority figures create laws of society
III: Postconventional	15 years old through adulthood	Individuals decide for themselves what is right or wrong
5. Social Contract		Laws are selectively obeyed based on the individual's own moral code; mutual benefit or social contract determines behavior
6. Universal Ethics		Transcendence of moral code beyond mutual benefit; very few ever achieve this stage

Figure 15.5

Kohlberg's work was based on interviews with males, so men in Western societies were often considered to be at the top of this moral hierarchy, a view that prompted much criticism of Kohlberg's theories. The results also may show a liberal bias, since conservatives are generally less willing to violate the laws of society, even if they personally disagree with them. Morality in collectivist societies is based on going along with the group rather than adhering to what the individual believes is right or wrong.

Kohlberg's colleague and friend, **Carol Gilligan** (b. 1936), was especially critical of Kohlberg, suggesting that for women, moral development was tied to care and relationships with others. Gilligan argued that society encouraged males to be more assertive than females, and therefore females were more likely to forego their own beliefs to benefit the majority. She argued further that women think more about how their moral behavior might affect their relationships with others, a factor that may reduce their willingness to violate societal rules and guidelines as they reach the highest levels of moral development. Subsequent research, however, found little difference in moral decision-making between genders. Other theorists, including **Albert Bandura** (b. 1925), emphasized the social aspects of moral decision-making rather than the cognitive approach used by Kohlberg.

Psychosocial Development

Developmental psychologist and psychoanalyst **Erik Erikson** (1902–1994) introduced a comprehensive psychoanalytic theory consisting of eight stages of **psychosocial development**.

As in Kohlberg's stages of moral development, each stage of psychosocial development builds on the previous stage. The stages may unfold somewhat differently based on an individual's unique environmental influences and sociocultural experiences. An individual may not complete a certain stage, resulting in problems that emerge later in life, but lack of completion does not prevent moving to the next stage. Experiences that occur during any one stage may be modified later, and learned virtues or attributes may also persist through later stages.

Erikson's Theory of Psychosocial Development

Erikson was inspired by the work of Sigmund Freud and worked with his daughter, Anna Freud. Erikson is known as a **Neo-Freudian** because he modified and updated Freud's work to make it his own. Erikson placed less emphasis on the sex drive (libido) and less focus on the unconscious than Freud did; his theory of psychosocial development opposed Freud's psychosexual approach, which you will read more about in the chapter on personality. His stage theory begins at birth and extends into adulthood and old age (unlike Freud's, which ends at puberty), and he was more optimistic about human behavior. Erikson explained each of eight stages of psychosocial development as a "crisis" to be confronted and resolved. The resolution of each stage allows an individual to face the next crisis.

- **Trust versus mistrust** is the first stage of psychosocial development, beginning at birth and continuing through the first year of life. During this stage, the child learns to depend on parents or a caregiver for support, comfort, and responsiveness to needs. Having a responsive caregiver encourages the infant to believe the world is a safe, secure place worthy of trust. Having a rejecting or neglectful caregiver may make a child unable to place trust in others later in life. A successful resolution to this stage is the development of hope.

- **Autonomy versus shame and doubt** is the second stage of psychosocial development. It lasts from ages one through three, defining the child's toddler period. Children in this stage gain a sense of independence from their caregivers and begin to complete activities such as feeding and dressing themselves (*autonomy*). Toddlers begin to demonstrate their own will by asking for items they want, such as "cookie!" They may also deny requests, responding with an adamant "no" to show how they feel about taking a nap. If parents continually interrupt children's independent behaviors, toddlers may question whether or not they can act on their own (*shame and doubt*). The stage resolves with a sense of will.

- **Initiative versus guilt** is the third stage of psychosocial development, which Erikson claimed lasts from ages three through six to define a child's preschool years. Children during this stage begin to take on even more independent activities and can begin to explore activities

that capture their interest. A child may attempt to resolve the crisis of whether or not he can do something successfully. If a young child plans a tea party for her toys and everything goes well, she may engage in more self-initiated activities *(initiative)*. However, if she views the tea party as falling apart, she may question whether she can carry through on such tasks. Morality also begins to develop when children feel guilty for mistakes they have made *(guilt)*. The resolution of this stage is the development of a sense of purpose.

- **Industry (competence) versus inferiority** is stage four. It tracks children from ages six through twelve, defining their primary school years. During this stage, children begin to understand how others view them and how their performance compares to that of others. They also begin to identify tasks at which they excel and those for which they need more practice. If a child is successful at reading out loud in class and does better than his classmates on this task, he or she may begin to develop a sense of industry. If a child falls behind on many tasks in comparison to others of the same age, he or she may develop a sense of *inferiority*. This stage resolves with a sense of competence.

Erikson's stages of psychosocial development continue into adulthood. His last four stages will be presented in the next chapter on adolescence through adulthood.

ERIKSON'S STAGES OF PSYCHOSOCIAL DEVELOPMENT			
Age	Conflict	Resolution	Description
Birth to 1 year	Trust vs. Mistrust	Hope	If infant needs are met, a sense of basic trust develops; if trust is not attained, child becomes fearful of others
1 to 3 years	Autonomy vs. Shame and Doubt	Will	Child develops sense of independence, or self-doubt develops
3 to 6 years	Initiative vs. Guilt	Purpose	Child begins to initiate tasks and plans in play, or initiative is held back by guilt
6 to 12 years	Industry vs. Inferiority	Competence	Child discovers their academic abilities and social relationships or develops feelings of inferiority

Figure 15.6

Sociability and Emotionality

Researchers and psychiatrists Alexander Thomas (1914–2003) and Stella Chess (1914–2007) examined the temperament of young children, suggesting that it was inborn and not learned. **Temperament** is a measure of a child's activity level, sociability, and emotionality. Variables that are measured in studies to evaluate temperament may include the children's activities, levels of irritability, frequency of smiling, and approach and avoidant postures exhibited. Thomas and Chess broke temperament down into three categories: Babies with an **easy temperament** cried little and were easy to calm; they had predictable sleep and wake cycles and were generally happy and cheerful. Those with a **difficult temperament** were less predictable and more irritable; they could be challenging to calm and had unpredictable sleep and wake patterns. Those with a **slow-to-warm-up temperament** were hesitant to interact with new people and shied away from new situations but eventually adapted to the new person/situation. Differences in children's temperaments reflected differences in nervous system functioning and emotions during novel situations. Such differences appear to be innate, resulting in different preferences in social situations as the children develop. Nevertheless, individuals may learn to adapt and modify their behavior in situations that make them feel uncomfortable.

Sociability does not develop equally in all individuals. While some individuals interact happily with others and seek out social interactions (**extroverts**), others need sufficient "alone" time to recharge after social interactions (**introverts**). Individuals with **autism spectrum disorder** are challenged even further by social interactions because they are unable to read other peoples' reactions and facial or body movements intuitively. The presence of these social behaviors in early childhood may directly affect or impair the development of social relationships with others, including parents and family members. Autistic individuals generally also have delays in language usage. They may exhibit cognitive deficits and repetitive and ritualistic behaviors. They may also have trouble developing a clear self-concept, an understanding and evaluation of who they are, and a **theory of mind**—the ability to understand the motives, feelings, and desires of oneself and others.

Parenting Styles

Along with other researchers, clinical psychologist **Diana Baumrind** (b. 1927), noted for her research on parenting, investigated the influence of different parenting styles on children's behavior and developed categories of parenting.

Authoritarian parents are sometimes referred to as *dictatorial* because they enforce their rules without input from their children. They live by the philosophy of "my way or the highway." Authoritarian parents impose their will on their children, often behaving this way to protect the children.

Children of authoritarian parents often cannot make decisions for themselves and, when given some independence, may often make poor decisions. The children's decisions may appear to be especially immature for their age group. In addition, these children often display lower levels of self-esteem and are not well equipped to make independent choices.

Permissive parents may fall under the **rejecting-neglecting parenting** style, in which they are not involved with their children's lives and do not necessarily care to be involved. This style may occur because a parent and child (children) do not live together, the parents work too much and are absent a lot, or parents are simply too concerned with events of their own lives to be interested in their children's lives. Children of rejecting-neglecting parents typically have little self-esteem and often act as adults prematurely because they have had to make decisions for themselves from a young age. Permissive parents may also be **indulgent**. These parents seek friendship with their children and set few boundaries for them. As a result, children of permissive-indulgent parents often are impulsive and demanding because they have become accustomed to getting their way.

Authoritative parents are responsive to the input and needs of their children and set rules and expectations, but they are not as rigid and demanding as authoritarian parents. Children of authoritative parents are well balanced, exhibiting decision-making abilities and high self-esteem. Fortunately, Baumrind's work revealed that most parents fall into the authoritative style of parenting.

Regardless of parenting styles, children's behavior is not entirely determined by parental guidance. Some psychologists have suggested that

Authoritative parents set reasonable rules and expectations and hold their children to living up to them.

a child's temperament is just as important as parenting style in determining parent/child relationships. Parents may also not fall neatly into a single parenting category and may be stricter in some areas and more lenient in others. Genetic factors may also play a role in both parenting behavior and children's behavioral responses. Some children may also be subjected to two different parenting styles, an area needing more research. Baumrind and other researchers conducted their studies primarily in Western societies, so study results may not reflect the parenting styles in different cultures. Future parenting research must therefore address a wider array of parenting styles displayed in other cultures.

Now that you have read the results of research exploring childhood development from birth to adolescence, you may want to review the theories of *discontinuity versus continuity.* Do you believe that children develop according to distinct stages, or do you believe they develop in a more even, continuous pattern? What about *nature versus nurture?* Do you believe that attachment, temperament, and cognitive, moral, and social development are more the result of one's genetic background and biological processes or one's life experiences and environment? You probably understand how early-life experiences have a long-lasting impact on our physical and mental health. In psychology, the field of **epigenetics**, including behavioral epigenetics, studies how nurture shapes nature—that is, how life's experiences and the environment influence the expression of the genes we've inherited. The **epigenetic process** examines how nature and nurture interact to present the traits an individual displays and to influence behavior.

REFLECT ON THE ESSENTIAL QUESTION

Essential Question: *How do physical, cognitive, moral, and social development take place from birth through adolescence?* On separate paper, make a chart like the one below to gather details to answer that question.

Neonatal–Infancy	Attachment	Cognitive	Moral	Psychosocial

KEY TERMS

accommodation

animism

anxious-ambivalent

artificialism

assimilation

attachment bond

attachment theory

authoritative parents

authoritarian parents

autism spectrum disorder

avoidant

centration

conservation

contact comfort

critical period

difficult temperament

easy temperament

egocentrism

extroverts

imprinting

indulgent

insecure attachment bond

introverts

Neo-Freudian

object permanence

one-dimensional thinking

permissive parents

pretend play

rejecting-neglecting parenting

slow-to-warm-up temperament

secure attachment bond

sensitive period

strange situation behavior

stranger anxiety

temperament

two-dimensional thinking

visual cliff

FORMS/ STAGES OF DEVELOPMENT

approval-seeking stage

autonomy versus shame and doubt

cognitive development

concrete operational stage

continuous development (continutiy)

conventional level

discontinuous development (discontinuity)

dynamic systems approach

formal operational stage

industry (competence) versus inferiority

initiative vs. guilt

law and order stage

motor development

nature versus nurture

perceptual skills

postconventional level

preconventional level

preoperational stage

psychosocial development

punishment/ obedience stage

satisfying needs stage

sensorimotor stage

social contract stage

sociocultural perspective

stability versus change

stages of cognitive development

BIOLOGICAL DEVELOP- MENT

Babinski reflex

embryo

embryotic stage

epigenetics

epigenetic process

theory of mind

trust versus mistrust

universal ethics stage

zone of proximal development

fetal alcohol syndrome

fetal stage

fetus

germinal period

grasping reflex

heritability

maturation

Moro reflex

placenta

reflex

rooting reflex

startle response

stepping reflex

sucking reflex

teratogens

zygote

zygotic period

KEY PEOPLE

Mary Ainsworth

Albert Bandura

Diana Baumrind

Erik Erikson

Sigmund Freud

Carol Gilligan

Harry Harlow

Lawrence Kohlberg

Konrad Lorenz

Jean Piaget

Lev Vygotsky

1. Jack, the father of a newborn, gently strokes the bottom of his baby's foot. As he does this, the baby's toes moved outward and then curl in. Which of the following newborn reflexes is Jack's baby demonstrating?

   (A) Rooting

   (B) Moro

   (C) Babinski

   (D) Stepping

   (E) Grasping

2. Baby Erin has learned to crawl and can control her midsection but cannot yet control her legs or walk. Which of the following best explains this?

   (A) Inner to outer development

   (B) Critical period

   (C) Moro reflex

   (D) Head to toe development

   (E) Assimilation

3. Emily, who is two-and-a-half years old, pointed to the ocean and called it a "pool" because she had never seen the ocean before. Which of the following developmental phenomena is Emily experiencing?

   (A) Accommodation

   (B) Object permanence

   (C) Conservation

   (D) Assimilation

   (E) Habituation

4. Andrew, who is four, now understands that even though he loved the new cartoon movie about cars, his sister Alexis did not feel the same way. The ability of Andrew to understand that others may not see the world in the same way he does shows his development of which of the following?

   (A) Accommodation

   (B) Theory of mind

   (C) Assimilation

   (D) Egocentrism

   (E) Preconventional thinking

5. Which of the following children would be considered to have a secure attachment, according to Mary Ainsworth?

   (A) Allen, who cries when his mother leaves but does not seem to care when she returns.

   (B) Sam, who cries when his mother leaves and seeks physical contact from her when she returns before beginning to play independently.

   (C) Bradley, who is indifferent to his mother leaving and returning.

   (D) Szymon, who cries when his mother leaves and clings to her when she returns.

   (E) Ben, who happily plays with the stranger who is present when his mother leaves.

6. Which of the following would Lev Vygotsky have discussed as a limitation of the work of Piaget in regard to children's cognitive development?

   (A) He relied too much on interviews conducted with parents.

   (B) He did not take into consideration the impact that one's social environment may have on cognitive development.

   (C) He relied too heavily on the concepts of sex and aggression as motivating factors for behavior.

   (D) He was wrong about the order in which children develop cognitive skills.

   (E) He focused too heavily on the attachment of children to their mother figure.

7. Julianne tells on her friend Zoe for cheating on an exam because Julianne believes that all students should follow the rules set by the school. In which stage of moral development would Kohlberg place Julianne?

   (A) Conventional

   (B) Preconventional

   (C) Preoperational

   (D) Postconventional

   (E) Concrete operational

8. Which of the following is most consistent with Erikson's psychosocial stage of industry vs. inferiority?

(A) Paul, who is trying to determine which interests and skills he is best at

(B) Logan, who is trying to find a partner he can potentially marry

(C) Tanya, who reflects on her life with satisfaction that she has left something for the next generation

(D) Amelia, who has learned to begin activities with her friends

(E) Rudi, who still relies on her parents for feeding and clothing

9. Which of the following did Harry Harlow contend was the most important factor in forming a strong bond between mother and infant?

(A) Assimilation

(B) Conservation

(C) Contact comfort

(D) Object permanence

(E) Egocentrism

10. Bridget understands that even though her sandwich has been cut in half, she does not have twice as much sandwich as her friend who has an uncut sandwich. Which cognitive landmark has Bridget mastered?

(A) Object permanence

(B) Egocentrism

(C) Animism

(D) Artificialism

(E) Conservation

1. You are opening a new day care center and want to be sure that you are able to meet the needs of all of the children in your care. The day care center will be set up to have children of different ages in separate rooms. As you prepare for the grand opening, you are trying to plan activities for the classrooms listed below. Respond to each concept by recommending an activity based on developmental theories you have studied. Be sure that the activities for the day care match the abilities of the children in each specified group, and explain why the activity would be appropriate for this age.

   A) One-year-olds' classroom
      - Motor abilities
      - Linguistic abilities
      - Attachment

   B) Four-year-olds' classroom
      - Cognitive development
      - Psychosocial development

   C) Eight-year-olds' classroom
      - Cognitive development
      - Psychosocial development

2. Maddie is four years old. She has a large group of friends and has excelled in her performance in beginning ballet classes. She has a good relationship with her family and performs at grade level in school.

   A) Apply the following theories to Maddie's current stages of development. Also, be sure to explain why you have placed Maddie in each respective stage.
      - Cognitive development (stage)
      - Psychosocial development (stage)
      - Moral development (stage)

   B) Explain how Maddie may behave if she demonstrates the following:
      - Theory of mind
      - Result of authoritarian parenting
      - Easy temperament

16

Adolescence Through Adulthood

"People who believe they have the power to exercise some measure of control over their lives are healthier, more effective and more successful than those who lack faith in their ability to effect changes in their lives."

—Albert Bandura

Essential Question: How do the stages of physical, social, and cognitive development contribute to human growth and change from adolescence through adulthood?

In Chapter 15, you read about many developmental milestones from birth to adolescence and the theories of several prominent thought leaders in developmental psychology. Many other developmental psychologists have examined the significant changes that occur during the teen years and how these changes influence life as an adult. Still other psychologists focus on **gerontology,** the study of adulthood and aging. Baby boomers in the United States, those born between 1946 and 1964, have reached retirement age, and they are living longer than ever, even to one hundred and beyond. Many older adults continue to work well into their seventies and eighties and are physically active for just as long. By 2050, more than 20 percent of Americans will be over the age of sixty-five. Focusing on physical and emotional health during this advanced period of the life span is essential to help aging men and women lead productive and healthy lives for as long as possible.

This chapter will examine the physical, emotional, and cognitive changes that occur during the teen years, in midlife, and in older adulthood. While physical strength and sensory abilities hit their peak during the early twenties, they begin a slow decline that becomes clearly noticeable by middle age. An individual's overall intelligence is reported to remain relatively consistent throughout the life span (barring neurocognitive deficits), but the ability to solve new problems and see patterns declines during middle age, while the ability to use already learned knowledge increases. Emotional development, on the other hand, may be quite variable. The impact of turbulent relationships with parents in one's teenage years, a midlife crisis, and depression as one grows older can make a difference in physical and mental health, but these events are not common to all individuals.

As you read through the progression of developmental milestones, remember that individual differences may be significant at any stage. While some individuals may begin a slow decline of health in midlife, others will remain active and cognitively sharp into their nineties. As you read about these phases of the life span, keep in mind the ideas of **nature vs. nurture**—the influence of genetics versus that of the environment and life experiences.

Physical Changes in Adolescence

Adolescence is a time of great physical and biochemical changes. Teenagers and some preteens experience **puberty,** a period during they reach physical and sexual maturity and acquire the ability to reproduce. Puberty begins when the hypothalamus triggers the endocrine system to begin producing different levels of sex hormones.

During the early to mid-teens, a young person may be described as "filling out." Bone and muscle growth increase during this period and dramatic increases usually occur in height and weight. **Primary sex characteristics** develop, including the testes in males and ovaries in females, which allow reproduction. Girls experience their first menstrual period (**menarche**), a monthly cycle during which the uterus sheds its lining if an egg produced by the ovaries has not been fertilized by male sperm to cause pregnancy. During puberty, boys experience **spermarche**, the first ejaculatory experience. While puberty generally occurs in early adolescence, the precise time frame may vary widely between individuals. Genetics and family history often determine whether the onset of puberty is early or late.

Puberty is occurring earlier than ever before, moving from an average age of 14.5 years one hundred years ago to roughly age 12.5 years today. Early onset of puberty has been attributed in part to increased body fat because of the consumption of animal hormones found in many modern foods, especially dairy products and meats. Some girls as young as nine years old experience their first menstrual cycle and a growth spurt as signs of early maturation. Such early development, when their physical development is ahead of their cognitive development, can be a challenging time for girls, who are sometimes teased about their maturing body. Typically, boys experience a growth spurt later than girls; those who experience early growth may be lauded for their strength and physical stature. However, some boys may not experience puberty until their early to mid-teens.

Secondary sex characteristics also develop during puberty, although they are not directly associated with reproduction. Development of body hair in both genders, breast development in females, and changes in voice and facial hair in males are secondary sex characteristics. These developmental changes, just as puberty itself, are influenced by genetics. Chromosomes differentiate genders during prenatal development. Within their body cells, males display a **Y chromosome**, while females display two **X chromosomes**.

Physical and hormonal differences in genders expand during and after puberty. Before puberty, both boys and girls have similar levels of sex hormones, but when sexual maturation is complete, males will have higher levels of **androgens,** the male hormones, while females will have higher levels of the female hormones **estrogen** and **progesterone**. **Testosterone** is the dominant androgen in males and is produced by the testes. It functions in prostate activity to support male reproduction and also helps strengthen muscles and bones. Females also produce testosterone—in the adrenal glands and ovaries—but display lower levels than males. Testosterone has been shown to be associated with aggressive behavior in both genders. Estrogen is produced by the ovaries and influences the menstrual cycle and female sex characteristics. Progesterone is important for conception as well as maintaining pregnancy.

Puberty may also lead to changes in family relationships. Adolescents often become more independent as they mature and may desire more privacy, distancing themselves somewhat from other family members. Hormonal changes may also cause irritability and moodiness and contribute to redefining family social relationships.

Physical Changes During Puberty

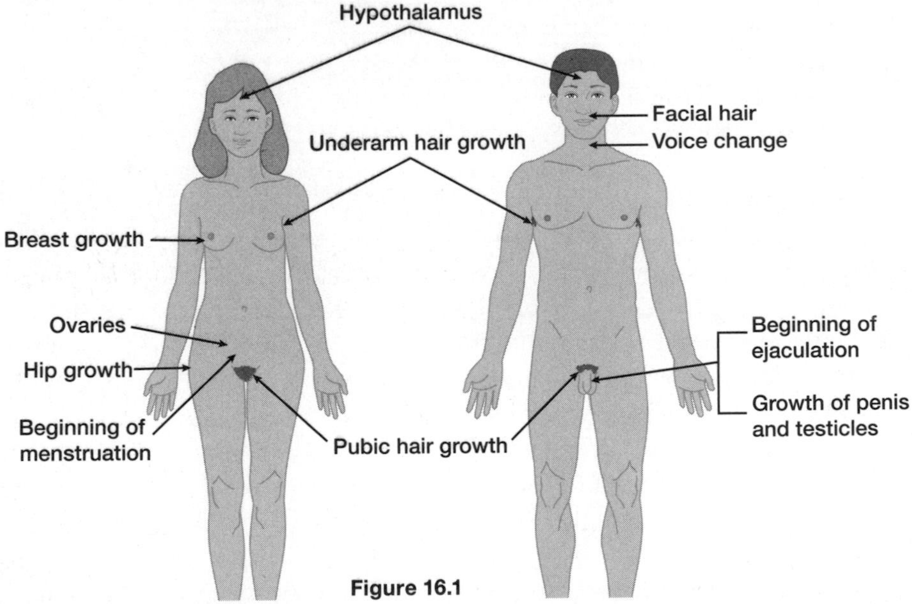

Figure 16.1

Social Changes During Adolescence and Early Adulthood

Adolescents often experience a reemergence of what **Jean Piaget** (see page 366) described as egocentrism—seeing the world from one's own perspective. Teens who experience **adolescent egocentrism** often believe that their experiences are unique and that their parents or others could not possibly understand what they are going through. For example, a teenage girl breaking up with her boyfriend may believe that her parents could never understand the pain of losing one's "first love." In reality, parents will likely recall similar events in their own history and could actually be a source of comfort.

Teens also tend to create **personal fables,** stories of their lives that are idealized and special and that make them feel invincible. Such fantasizing may cause them to engage in risky behaviors and create an overly optimistic sense of the future. For example, if a teenage boy knows the career path he wants to pursue, he may envision himself rising easily to the top of his profession. Teens do not often consider that things may not go as planned. However, such optimism may serve teens well in supporting active pursuit of their interests. Teens may also experience being the center of attention for an **imaginary audience** that listens enthusiastically to their ideas and beliefs. Posts made by teens on social media sites may be expected to attract a lot of interest and agreement by all who read them.

Healthy parent–teen relationships are especially important in support of adolescent development. Overall, while much attention is given to possible conflicts between parents and adolescents, most teens report having relatively positive relationships with their parents. Although these relationships are not entirely without conflict, teens often realize that parents or guardians have their best interests in mind, even when they don't agree with all of their decisions. Positive parent–teen relationships often pay great dividends, providing advantages such as the following:

- Teens who report having a positive relationship with their parents can help peers by giving good advice.

- Parents in healthy parent–teen relationships are more likely to address tough topics such as drug use and sexual activity with their teenage children and guide them when navigating these issues.

- Supportive parents play a larger role than peers in helping teens develop responsibility, gain education, and plan for the future.

- Having a good relationship with parents often carries over to positive relationships with peers.

Healthy friendships between teens often reflect healthy parent-teen relationships.

Peer influence becomes very important during adolescence as teenagers spend more time with peers than parents. Teens often spend most of the day at school, and after school they may be involved in school or community activities with their peers. Parents or adults are not present to direct group behavior, and teens must navigate activities and relationships on their own. Relationships with peers allow children and teens to learn to negotiate with others of their own age to resolve conflicts and make friends. Peer pressure may sometimes persuade teens to engage in behaviors parents would not approve of, but positive peer pressure can also guide teens to engage in more productive behaviors.

The increased influence of technology and social media sites gives teens a larger potential network of friends, but it also exposes them to potential online bullying. **Cyberbullying** is a prevalent problem that allows anonymous bullies to harshly shame other people online. Teens may find criticism or negative comments from an unknown source exceptionally difficult to deal with. Bullied teens may become increasingly self-conscious and self-critical in response to comments from someone they don't even know. Teaching preteens and teens to engage with technology safely has become an important consideration for parents in the information age.

In some societies, teens go through a **rite of passage** that indicates a transition into a new stage of life. The transition may be associated with achieving a significant life event or being recognized for a particular accomplishment—a graduation, christening, or bar or bat mitzvah, for example. Often these rituals coincide with the onset of puberty, at which time teens may be recognized as adults in their communities.

A father congratulates his daughter on her quinceañera, a celebration with Hispanic cultural roots of a girl's fifteenth birthday and passage into adulthood.

The concept of **emerging adulthood** has evolved because teens are no longer jumping into adulthood and achieving complete independence from their parents as they leave their teenage years. Although adolescence is the transition period from childhood to adulthood, traditionally ending as young adults entered their twenties, increasingly young people in their twenties finish college and return home to live with their parents, sometimes depending on their parents to pay health insurance premiums or car payments.

While arrival into adulthood varies considerably by culture and region, true adulthood has been pushed back in Western societies. Young adults are putting marriage and children off until after they establish their careers and adult identities. This delay may require extended support from parents for a period of time, at least until the goals are met.

Some observers have been critical of this transition into adulthood, claiming that it represents a lack of focus and direction; others defend the prolonged process because it allows individuals to decide what they want to do rather than simply comply with what society expects. They argue that taking the time to make thoughtful decisions about a career or marriage may lead to greater success and happiness in the future.

Creating a Sense of Identity

During adolescence, many teens try out different roles to determine the best fit. Dressing differently, changing groups of friends, and engaging in a range of different activities may help them begin to identify who they will become and what they might like to pursue. Developmental psychologist **James Marcia** expanded and refined the theories of **Erik Erikson** (see Chapter 15), the developmental psychologist who identified adolescence as a period of psychosocial crisis between identity and role confusion. Erikson explained that society permitted teenagers and college students to have a period of time in which they were free to explore different activities, interests, and potential career paths to find their identity. Marcia took this idea and proposed four stages in developing a sense of identity based on the criteria of crisis—"who am I?"—and commitment to resolving the identity/role crisis.

Many adolescents experience the first of Marcia's stages, **identity diffusion**, as a time in which they have not yet undergone an identity crisis and have made no commitment about their own identity. In this stage, teens have not truly considered their own beliefs or who they want to become. They do not seem particularly concerned with the outcome of a specific identity, perhaps thinking they will address the issue later. If they have some idea of who they want to become in the future, it is not well considered or perhaps not consistent with their talents and strengths.

Young teens may go on to experience the second stage, **identity foreclosure**, in which they have a sense of their core beliefs (i.e., political, moral, religious), but rather than considering these beliefs seriously and allowing them to shape their lives, they often simply adopt the views of their parents or society, especially about who they should become. For example, if asked which political party they identify with, they may answer "Republican," knowing that their parents are registered Republicans. The young person has made a commitment, it seems, without ever having explored or followed his or her own beliefs.

Adolescents in the third stage, **identity moratorium**, are struggling with their sense of identity. They experience the identity crisis without having made a commitment to its resolution. College students who explore many different possible major subjects or teenagers who make dramatic changes to their looks may be experiencing the identity moratorium while attempting to determine which identity is right for them. They may explore different activities or question long-held religious or political beliefs to determine if they are really committed to the ideals associated with these positions.

Towards the end of adolescence and into early adulthood, young people enter the fourth stage, **identity achievement**, a postcrisis phase during which individuals have identified and acknowledged who they are or want to be. These young people are not struggling with their identity; they have made a commitment. They may still adhere to the religious or political beliefs of their parents, but now it is because they have reflected on what those beliefs mean and have decided that they reflect their own ideals and beliefs as well.

Many factors may contribute to the formation of identity, including cognitive development, relationships with peers and parents, and the expectations of society and family. Even though one's identity is established more or less in the teens and early twenties, many young people have not completed the process and may continue to question their identity into adulthood. Lack of identity may contribute to changes in careers, political affiliations, or divorce later in life. Some adults continue to question who they are and may change course and reevaluate their choices as their lives unfold.

Figure 16.2

Gender Development

Gender identity is an important component of identity development, especially during and after puberty. **Gender identity** is an individual's internalized belief about being male or female, which may or may not be the same as the biological sex exhibited at birth. One's gender identity also involves incorporating **gender roles**—behaviors, traits, and attitudes associated with males and females— into one's self-concept. While gender identity begins to form early in life, adolescents may question whether they fit in with traditional gender roles, which vary by culture and society. Too often, young people are expected to play the part of their respective gender, regardless of how they feel about themselves.

Gender typing is the process children go through to learn the expected roles for boys and girls of all ages. Societies demonstrate these roles both implicitly and explicitly, and gender typing often takes place even before birth. At baby showers, for example, if the parents know they're expecting a boy, shower guests will give gifts of blue clothing and toys. Pink gifts are given for girls and, if the sex of the child is unknown, gifts often are given in yellow or white. Boys are often allowed to cry for longer periods of time before parents pick them up, and they may be described as "tough." On the other hand, girls are often described as "delicate."

The pattern of gender typing continues into childhood as toys and activities are geared toward gender. Girls are often enrolled in ballet or cheerleading, and boys often play football or wrestle. Even the way infant behavior is addressed by parents is a result of gender typing. While physical differences between girls and boys may contribute to differences in gender behavior, the impact of socialization cannot be overlooked. While efforts have been made recently to offer more diverse sports and activities for all genders, gender typing still exerts strong influence.

As teenagers and young adults begin to internalize the gender identity to which they are committed, gender typing may be used as a reference point for evaluating whether their interests are more closely aligned with male or female roles. Someone with an **androgynous personality** may display both male and female characteristics. Dressing in clothes that are ambiguous—not clearly male or female—is dressing in an androgynous fashion.

Some individuals may be unconcerned about whether their gender identity conforms to societal expectations, that is, if they display roles inconsistent with their "expected" gender roles. Others may remain unconcerned even if they experience punishments such as ridicule or lack of acceptance. For example, stay-at-home dads who take care of the house and children while their wives work are often comfortable in that role and not at all concerned about the opinions or expectations of others. Women who choose to be employed as construction workers or plumbers may enjoy this work, even though they face critiques from others about their unconventional choices. Gender roles vary significantly in different cultures and populations, and expectations may also differ.

Ideas of gender roles are evolving slowly as society recognizes that an individual's interests and strengths may not be consistent with those associated with gender. However, while psychologists may suggest that it is healthy for individuals to follow their own interests, society is just warming up to this idea, especially when gender is involved.

Gender identity seems to evolve from a combination of nature *and* nurture. **Social learning theory** posits that gender role behavior is developed through the observation of others and through rewards and punishments. Developmental psychologist **Albert Bandura** (b. 1925) relies on the cognitive and social principles of social learning theory to explain how individuals learn and display gender behavior. He emphasizes that gender role development and functioning in everyday life are the product of social experiences within a specific society (nurture) and that body structure and biological tendencies (nature) allow a range of possibilities rather than a fixed gender differentiation.

A book titled *As Nature Made Him* presents an interesting case study in which a young boy in Canada was raised as a girl after a circumcision went terribly wrong. The author, John Colapinto, addresses the issue of nature and nurture in the development of gender. After the botched circumcision, the parents were encouraged to raise their son like a daughter because their doctor believed that gender was determined exclusively by nurture. At that time, surgery was able to create functioning external female genitalia more easily than male genitalia. The parents were encouraged to dress their (now) daughter in female clothing and encourage her to participate in "female" activities. However, she identified more with males and masculine behaviors and was often ridiculed for her roughness. Even after undergoing hormone therapy in her teens, she struggled emotionally and never "fit in" with other girls. Her family finally told her what had occurred, and she decided to undergo surgery to become male as she had always identified herself. After once again identifying as male, he married and became a stepfather to his wife's children. His story shed much light on gender transitions and the importance of genes in the roles of gender development.

While adolescence can be a challenging time overall, it may be more challenging for those who do not clearly fit into the confines or roles that society has determined suit their gender. Researchers have come to see gender and sexual orientation as less binary and more fluid. Many individuals do not clearly engage in singularly male or female activities. Others cannot clearly identify their sexual orientation as a single gender.

The definitions of *sex* and *gender* are easily confused. *Sex* refers to the physical and biological differences between males and females, while *gender* refers to the social and cultural traits for males and females. Those who differ in gender identity from their biologically defined sex are known as **transgendered**. This is an umbrella term, and the behaviors associated with it may vary considerably. Some transgendered individuals prefer to dress like those of the opposite sex and, at the same time, are sexually attracted to the opposite sex. Others seek gender reassignment surgery and find themselves sexually attracted to those of their birth sex. Still others do not find themselves physically attracted to either sex.

Sexual orientation addresses one's sexual attraction to male or female partners or, in some cases, both or neither. **Heterosexual** individuals are attracted to the opposite sex. **Homosexual** individuals are attracted to the same sex. Those who are attracted to both males and females are said to be **bisexual**, and those attracted to neither are **asexual**.

Evidence from sexual orientation research has established that genetics plays a strong role in sexual orientation. Sexual orientation is also influenced by the prenatal environment (second to fifth months of pregnancy) and sexual differentiation of the brain that occurs during fetal and infant (neonatal) development. Differences in the brain's structure and function, including sex-differentiated activation of the hypothalamus, are thought to contribute to gender identity and sexual orientation. Nevertheless, no definitive conclusions have been reached and research continues. Sexual orientation for some individuals is variable and may change over their life span. However, programs aimed at modifying an individual's sexual orientation have had little success, and the American Psychiatric Association is opposed to them because they rest on the false assumption that non-heterosexuality is a mental disorder.

Happiness and Satisfaction over the Life Span

The teenage years are a time of considerable stress. Recent studies have found that modern teenagers report having more stress and depression than teenagers before them. While this finding may reflect higher levels of reporting than in the past, it remains an area of great concern. Teens report high levels of anxiety and stress stemming from school, family problems, and personal conflicts or generalized anxiety with no particular origin. Between 10 and 15 percent of teens are estimated to report depression at any given time, with females reporting higher levels of depression than males. Teens sleep on average an hour less than their counterparts a decade ago, and this lack of sleep contributes to the high levels of stress and anxiety, especially since the school day begins far earlier than circadian rhythms would dictate. Without nine hours of sleep, teens can experience irritability, reduced reaction time, trouble concentrating, and obesity.

As people age, happiness and satisfaction vary to some degree based on a person's situation. While many individual differences are found in self-reported levels of happiness and well-being, some general themes are also found, including some focused on marriage:

- Individuals who are married tend to live longer and report higher levels of happiness than their unmarried counterparts.

- Adults who report staying in unhappy marriages appear to be at greater risk for physical illnesses. However, as you already know, correlation does not prove causation, and specific illnesses cannot be directly related to an unhappy marriage.

- People are delaying marriage longer today than in years past; the delay may allow both partners to complete their education and obtain a footing in their respective careers.

- Adults with higher levels of education and those who marry later demonstrate lower levels of divorce—a relatively new trend that may be a good sign for lasting and happy marriages.

- People who report the highest levels of satisfaction in their marriages also report that both individuals share decision-making and household and child care responsibilities and feel supported by their partner.

- Just-married individuals report a slightly lower level of happiness, noting that marriage is not living up to their expectations. Some adults appear to be frustrated with the daily hassles and adjustments involved in cohabiting with another person.

Social clocks—cultural timetables for when milestone events should occur—may drive people to have children at a certain time in life, and child-rearing presents certain challenges. While many individuals believe that parenthood leads to great happiness and life satisfaction, young parents report a temporary dip in levels of happiness while they make the initial adjustment to caring for children. Young parents are often juggling careers, childcare, and their own lives and often feel stressed and overwhelmed as life becomes more about their children and less about themselves.

As children get older and more self-sufficient, parental happiness generally returns to levels similar to those before having children. However, many individuals report a dip in well-being between their late thirties and early fifties. The notion of a **midlife crisis**—an emotional or identity-questioning crisis occuring in early middle age—this may be more myth than reality. Some individuals do experience life-changing events such as divorce, dissatisfaction with career, or emotional turmoil in midlife, but the "crisis" does not occur for many individuals. In fact, midlife may offer new freedoms and opportunities, such as trying a new career, moving to a favorite place, or even leaving one's family and setting out alone.

If people do not feel that they are meeting the expectations of society, they may experience lower levels of well-being. Taking life as it comes rather than living up to external expectations has been shown to lead to higher levels of happiness. Contrary to popular belief, financial success does not always lead to higher levels of happiness. However, many people reach middle age before they realize this truth and miss time lost with loved ones while they were striving for financial success and the happiness they thought it would bring. Research has shown that affiliating with a religious community, having a social network, and enjoying good health are associated with higher levels of happiness. However, these characteristics of happy individuals are not restricted to a particular time of life.

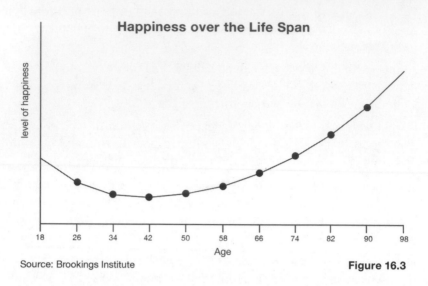

Happiness over the Life Span

Source: Brookings Institute

Figure 16.3

Older adults report high levels of life satisfaction and well-being and suffer from fewer mental health issues than younger individuals. Older adults often spend time and effort on meaningful activities and become less concerned with how they are perceived, increasing their overall level of well-being.

Levels of happiness vary from person to person, as do personality characteristics and emotional states. The trends described here are general trends among the population, and individuals may find their own experiences to be quite different.

Cognitive Development

Just as physical changes occur during and after adolescence, cognition continues to evolve and change over the life span. In Chapter 15, you read about Jean Piaget's theory of cognitive development in children. The last of Piaget's stages is the formal operational stage in which children can think abstractly and in three dimensions.

Teenage Years and Young Adulthood

Cognitive development continues as the brains of teenagers develop into their early twenties. However, by the time young people have reached their mid– to late teens, they have passed the **critical period** for language. Acquiring a new language at that point will be more difficult than it is for younger children, and chances of speaking like a native speaker of a newly acquired language are slim to none.

Researchers have found that **neural pruning**—the process of removing neurons that are no longer necessary—is active in mid– to late adolescence. While having fewer **neural networks** might appear to be a disadvantage, think of the process like pruning a tree: when the dead branches are removed, the rest of the tree can thrive. Neural networks that are well developed and useful are preserved and become more efficient, while those that are not used are eliminated. This process may help the brain become more efficient and consolidate memories more quickly. **Gray matter** in the brain also increases during this period. Gray matter contains the nervous system cells important for sensory and muscle control and also for decision-making and self-control.

Frontal lobe development continues into the early to mid-twenties, possibly even up to the forties. As you read in Unit 3, the **frontal lobe** is the executive control center of the brain. Incomplete development of this area may lead teenagers to engage in risky behavior because their mature **limbic system** (emotional center of the brain) is in conflict with the still-developing frontal lobe. As a result, teens may act without fully considering the implications of their actions. Many survey reports have indicated that teens are more likely than older individuals to engage in risky behaviors such as drinking and driving, having unprotected sex, and experimenting with recreational drugs.

Middle Age and Beyond

Many changes take place in the brain after middle age. For example, levels of neurotransmitters that affect the brain's **fluid intelligence**—the ability to solve problems, see relationships, and think abstractly—decline after middle age, thereby reducing the ability to solve new problems and process new information. Significantly reduced production of the neurotransmitter **dopamine** reduces levels of activity in the frontal lobe of the brain. For this reason, the brain's processing speed, reasoning, response time, and memory capacity may also be reduced. In addition, the weight of the human brain decreases after age sixty, and the brain has fewer active neurons. Neurons atrophy with aging, and older adults may have up to 30 percent fewer functioning neurons than younger adults. The neurons that appear to be most affected by age are those responsible for sensory and motor activities. Blood flow and oxygen to the brain also decrease with age, resulting in the increased time older adults need to process new information. As a result of these gradual changes, older adults may have trouble learning unfamiliar technology, understanding how to set up new programs on their computers or use wireless devices, or responding to changes as quickly as they might have in the past. A general decline in **working memory,** the memory we use to take in information (see page 256), may also make it difficult to remember multiple pieces of information at the same time.

In contrast, crystallized intelligence generally increases with age. **Crystallized intelligence** represents an individual's accumulated intelligence over time and the ability to use skills, knowledge, and experience. Do you know older adults who can name all of the U.S. presidents who occupied the White House during their lifetime? Calling on accumulated knowledge, some older adults may be able to describe historical events in great detail or recall characters and stories from books they read years earlier. Long-term memory does not seem to decline at the same rate as working memory, so older memories can be retrieved more easily than new information. Healthy older adults with active cognitive and physical lives can delay the deterioration of mental capacities. As in other areas of psychosocial development, the intermingling of nature and nurture determines one's cognitive health status. While some individuals with inherited neurocognitive disorders will see a clear decline in cognition after ages sixty-five to seventy, others will remain cognitively astute well into their eighties and nineties.

Some older adults develop a brain condition known as **dementia** in which thinking, memory, and behavior begin to deteriorate. The frontal lobes of the brain begin to deteriorate to some extent in all adults over age fifty. About 14 percent of Americans over the age of seventy-one are diagnosed with a specific form of dementia known as **Alzheimer's disease**, a degenerative disease in which memory loss is progressive and plaques accumulate in nervous system tissues. The age of onset is generally after sixty-five, although some will experience early-onset Alzheimer's disease. Chances of developing Alzheimer's disease doubles every five years until age eighty-five. Lower levels of the biochemical **acetylcholine** have been found to be associated with Alzheimer's disease, as well as the presence of a specific genetic trait (i.e., ApoE4 allele on chromosome 19). Signs of Alzheimer's may include problems speaking or writing, misplacing items, confusion with time or place, and the inability to complete familiar tasks. People with Alzheimer's disease also may experience extreme changes in personality and, in advanced stages, have trouble recognizing family and friends.

Some people who do not have any type of neurocognitive disorder may nonetheless experience a rapid decline of certain cognitive abilities known as the **terminal drop** in the weeks or months prior to death. Older adults may also experience small strokes that obstruct blood flow to the brain and can also reduce cognitive functioning. While some of this decline might be genetic, studies have found that the risk of developing dementia is reduced in those who remain cognitively and physically active. "Use it or lose it" is good advice for anyone who wants to remain cognitively healthy.

The results of **cross-sectional studies** that measured intelligence levels across different age groups indicated that intelligence declines with aging, but results of a **longitudinal study** (long-term study) found that differences between age groups were eliminated when compared over subjects' lifetimes. The researchers concluded that overall intelligence remains steady throughout the life span. Differences between age groups in the cross-sectional research seemed to reflect differences in access to information. The study also demonstrated the **Flynn effect**, a sustained increase since the 1930s in the test scores of both fluid intelligence and crystallized intelligence in people all around the world. The increase in intelligence with each generation, not a decline in intelligence as one ages, no doubt explains why older people's test results were lower than younger people's. These and other aspects of research methods are discussed further in Chapter 19.

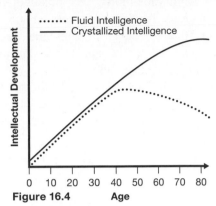

**Cognitive Changes with Age:
Fluid and Crystallized Intelligence**

······· Fluid Intelligence
——— Crystallized Intelligence

Intellectual Development

0   10 20 30 40 50 60 70 80

Figure 16.4   **Age**

Psychosocial Development

Chapter 15 examined the first four stages of Erik Erikson's comprehensive eight-stage psychoanalytic theory, the psychosocial stages of development. (You may wish review pages 374–376.) The remaining four stages represent psychosocial development in adolescents and adults.

You will recall that Erikson was a Neo-Freudian who took the basic premise of Freud's psychosexual theory and updated it by incorporating new ideas. Like other Neo-Freudians, Erikson did not place much emphasis on Freud's ideas of the unconscious, sex, and aggression. He also did not believe that the crises ended at puberty, so he created an eight-stage theory to address the crises people faced from birth through adulthood. Erikson characterized each stage as having a crisis to be resolved. He believed that unless a crisis was properly resolved, it would reappear as a problem later in life.

- **Identity versus role confusion**, Erikson's stage five, is associated with adolescence and represents individuals from ages twelve through eighteen. During this stage, teens (or preteens) begin to discover their own identity, see how it differs from others, and understand what makes them unique and special. As teens attempt to discover how they fit into society and what their role will be, they may try out different types of dress, music, and activities. Teens may adopt the views, opinions, and interests of their peers, parents, or role models, or they may try playing different roles until they find one that best suits their individual needs. Those who do not develop a clear sense of who they are may experience role confusion and an identity crisis. (You may wish to review the information on identity formation on pages 368.) James Marcia (page 391) expanded on this work of Erikson and delved further into how an identity is eventually embraced by the individual.

- **Intimacy versus isolation** is stage six in Erikson's model. It coincides with early adulthood, usually representing the twenties to forties. According to Erikson, the young adult is looking for a potential life partner. While young adults do not necessarily need to get married in order to successfully overcome this crisis, they do need to find and develop emotionally close relationships. If they do not develop close, intimate friendships or relationships, they may feel isolated and alone. As you read earlier in this chapter, emerging adulthood is a challenging time, and many young adults today are not seeking a long-term relationship until later in life.

- **Generativity versus stagnation**, stage seven of Erikson's theory, represents middle adulthood. During this stage, individuals begin to reflect on their life's work and determine whether they are providing something beneficial to younger generations. Individuals who feel productive and sense that they are adding value to society are described by Erikson as experiencing *generativity*. In other words, they are "generating" value and satisfaction. Generativity may be achieved in different ways: by contributing knowledge to the next generation, inventing something useful, creating a safer or more just society, or raising children to carry on one's legacy. If they are not feeling productive or satisfied with the value they are bringing to others, they experience *stagnation*—the feeling that they are not moving forward and are just going through the motions of life. Stagnation is the result of viewing one's work as meaningless or feeling that one has contributed neither talents nor children to benefit society.

- **Integrity versus despair** is the eighth and final stage of Erikson's psychosocial development, and it represents old age (late sixties and older). During this stage of development, older adults reflect on their

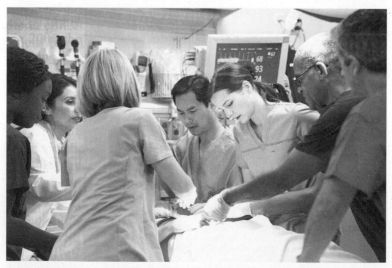

Adults who work in medical fields are likely to experience generativity—the sense of adding value to society.

overall life satisfaction. They evaluate whether their lives have been well lived and whether they have contributed something beneficial to leave as their legacy. Those who possess integrity and see their lives as productive and meaningful may leave the world feeling that they have left it a better place. However, when older adults do not feel they have made a contribution and instead view their lives as having no meaning, they are filled with regret and sadness, leading to despair.

Erikson's research is well known, but it has received criticism for a lack of empirical support. As with other stage theories examined in Chapter 15, questions have been raised about whether these stages can occur simultaneously rather than sequentially, as proposed by Erikson. Feminists have also critiqued Erikson's theory for representing the psychosocial crisis in males more than in females. Another criticism is that changes in societal expectations since Erikson's original theories were introduced may have shifted the ages at which these crises occur.

PSYCHOSOCIAL DEVLOPMENT IN ADOLESCENCE AND ADULTHOOD (See page 369 for the first four stages in Erikson's model.)			
Age	Conflict	Resolution	Description
12 to18 years	Identity vs. Role Confusion	Fidelity	Teenagers develop a sense of identity, or confusion about self occurs
18 to 35	Intimacy vs. Isolation	Love	Young adults develop intimate relationships, or they experience isolation
35 to 65	Generativity vs. Stagnation	Care	Adults seek to generate a legacy that can be passed to future generations, or they struggle with stagnation
65 to death	Integrity vs. Despair	Wisdom	Older adults contemplate their life and either feel a sense of integrity and happiness, or they feel despair and failure

Midlife and Beyond

By the time people enter their forties, muscle mass, bone density, metabolism, eyesight, and hearing have declined to some extent. Generally, people in this age bracket pick up weight around their midsection. Excess abdominal weight in men and women is partly due to changes in hormones, which influence appetite, metabolism, and accumulation of body fat. The expanding waistline is also associated with dietary and exercise habits, lifestyle factors that may need to change. As vision and hearing decline, people may need more light for reading, sewing, or woodworking. Age-related damage to the cilia in the inner ear may mean older people need to increase the volume on the radio or TV and ask people to speak up. By middle age, somewhere between the mid-forties and age sixty, hair may begin to gray and lines show up on the skin.

Women in midlife experience **menopause**, a gradual reduction in hormone levels that ends menstruation and the ability to conceive. Men in middle age also experience hormone changes and a decline in sperm production, but reproduction is still possible. Study results report that people can remain sexually active into their eighties with good overall health. Generally, by middle age, people report having less sexual activity but greater satisfaction in their relationships.

Physical abilities may vary considerably in middle age and are strongly influenced by one's overall health status. Some men and women stay physically active through participation in such sports such as running, tennis, golf, or skiing. They may play softball or baseball on teams sponsored by their employers, or they may walk every morning, do yoga, or work out at a gym regularly on their own. Levels of activity will depend on one's interests, opportunities, and health.

Death and Dying

The ideas of **Elisabeth Kübler-Ross** (1926–2004) provide a foundation for understanding death and dying. Her work focused on interviews conducted with terminally ill patients at a Chicago hospital, and she created a framework regarding death and dying based on those interviews. Kübler-Ross never intended her work to be generalized to all people who have experienced a terminal illness or who know someone with a terminal illness, and when it was, her theory received much criticism. Kübler-Ross recognized that dealing with death could be highly variable and there is no typical response to death.

Kübler-Ross categorized what she learned from her interviews into five stages of coping with dying and death. The first stage is **denial**, the lack of willingness to accept that he or she or a loved one has been diagnosed with a terminal illness. During this stage, second or third opinions of the illness may be sought. Individuals may think a mistake has been made, and the diagnosis is uncertain and not accepted. As you will read in the personality chapter, the ego often employs defense mechanisms such as denial as a way to protect the individual from threatening information.

The second stage is **anger**, a "poor me" reaction in which an individual wonders why he or she has been singled out for this fate. Angry individuals may find themselves upset with friends or relatives who have never faced any health problems. A woman may reason that she is a good person and does not deserve this serious diagnosis. A man who experiences anger over his illness may even be angry with those who are trying to care for him.

Stage three is the **bargaining** stage, during which people attempt to negotiate more time. They may pray to live for another year and may promise to devote the remainder of their lives to finding ways to research the specific illness and help others understand and fight it. Or they may establish a goal like trying to live to see their first grandchild or to see their grown child get married. The bargaining stage may help to give people a reason to live and the energy to devote to recovering.

Stage four is **depression**. During this stage, the people realize that death is inevitable. Depression sets in during this stage because they know that they will not live out the future as they had planned, and they already feel the sense of loss of friends and family. They may also realize that their fate is out of their own hands, and nothing they can do will prevent the inevitable.

The fifth and last stage is **acceptance**, during which the person with a terminal illness comes to terms with the process of dying and says goodbye to loved ones. Some people may shut down and turn inward in this phase, while others may express plans for their funeral or make financial arrangements to take care of family after their death.

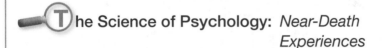

The Science of Psychology: *Near-Death Experiences*

So eager are people to know what awaits beyond death that books about near-death experiences (NDEs) in which people tell their stories of out-of-body experiences or of seeing another dimension—maybe heaven—make their authors millions of dollars and stay on the best-seller list for months. *The Boy Who Came Back from Heaven* (2010) sold ten million copies, though "the boy who came back from heaven" recently admitted he made up the whole story.

Still, most people in the scientific community accept that "experiencers," as they are called, truly have experienced something out of the ordinary, but that what the NDEs experienced might have physiological explanations. Recent research with rats at the University of Michigan documented what researchers called a "death spike," a sudden burst of brain activity right before death, as if different parts of the brain were communicating and trying to make sense out of the stress of dying. Maybe something like the death spike could explain NDEs in humans.

Many people who have been brought back from the brink of death have been in a hospital at the time—they have been resuscitated after a heart attack or other traumatic experience. That setting, with its abundance of technology that can measure brain function and a host of other physiological events, would seem to be an ideal place to carry out experiments to examine NDEs. If people claim to perceive something verifiable after monitors have shown their brain function has flatlined, then there would be some empirical evidence that NDEs could not have been the result of brain activity, a result that would lend credence to the idea that a consciousness separate from the body might exist.

Since many experiencers say they floated out of their bodies and could look down and see what was happening to them on the operating table, researchers devised experiments placing images known only to the researchers on high shelves so that the only way they could be seen was from above. The most recent such experiment was the AWARE study led by Sam Parnia at State University of New York at Stony Brook in which 15 hospitals in the United States, United Kingdom, and Austria participated. During the course of the study, one subject, a 57-year-old man, recounted floating out of his body and seeing the doctors work on and defibrillate him. Researchers determined that what he saw happened three minutes after he flatlined. However, he was not in one of the rooms where an image had been placed, so the results were still inconclusive.

Practice: With a partner, choose one of the following questions to research. Then share the results of your research with your class through a multimedia presentation.

- Who are some of the people researching NDEs? Are their credentials such that their work can be taken seriously in a scientific way?

- In what ways are most reported NDEs similar?

- What seems to be the effect on the experiencers of the NDE?

- What are the biggest problems in designing studies that would produce reliable results?

REFLECT ON THE ESSENTIAL QUESTION

Essential Question: *How do the stages of physical, social, and cognitive development contribute to human growth and change from adolescence through adulthood?* On separate paper, make a chart like the one below to gather details to answer that question.

Physical Development	Social Development	Cognitive Development	Psychosocial Development	Midlife and Beyond

KEY TERMS			KEY PEOPLE
BIOLOGICAL TERMS	*FORMS/ STAGES OF DEVELOPMENT*	identity achievement	Albert Bandura
acetylcholine	acceptance	identity diffusion	Erik Erikson
Alzheimer's disease	adolescent egocentrism	identity foreclosure	Elisabeth Kübler-Ross
androgen	androgynous personality	identity moratorium	Jean Piaget
dementia	anger	identity vs. role confusion	
dopamine	asexual	imaginary audience	
estrogen	bargaining	integrity vs. despair	
frontal lobe	bisexual	intimacy vs. isolation	
gray matter	critical period	longitudinal study	
limbic system	cross-sectional study	midlife crisis	
menarche	crystallized intelligence	nature vs. nurture	
menopause	cyberbullying	personal fable	
neural networks	denial	rite of passage	
neural pruning	depression	social clocks	
neurocognitive disorders	emerging adulthood	social learning theory	
primary sex characteristics	fluid intelligence	terminal drop	
progesterone	Flynn effect	working memory	
puberty	formal operational stage		
secondary sex characteristics	generativity vs. stagnation		
sex	gender identity		
sexual orientation	gender roles		
spermarche	gender typing		
testosterone	gerontology		
transgendered	heterosexual		
x chromosome	homosexual		
y chromosome			

1. Bill is in his mid-forties. He has a job he does not enjoy, but he does not know how to make a change. He recently was divorced and has not found a new relationship. Which of Erikson's stages of psychosocial development is Bill likely experiencing?

   (A) Identity vs. role confusion

   (B) Intimacy vs. isolation

   (C) Formal operational stage

   (D) Generativity vs. stagnation

   (E) Integrity vs. despair

2. Marsha is twenty-six. She has many friends from college. She has just started a job as an accountant, which she enjoys and for which she is well suited. She is living at home with her parents and pays them a small amount of rent. She also has recently taken on her own car and insurance payments. She has plans to look for an apartment in the next few years. Which of the following is Marsha likely experiencing?

   (A) Identity vs. role confusion

   (B) Emerging adulthood

   (C) Gender identity

   (D) Generativity vs. stagnation

   (E) Personal fable

3. Todd is fifteen. He plays baseball and enjoys video games. While he enjoys dancing, he does not practice often or take classes because he does not believe taking dance classes is consistent with how males should behave. Todd is demonstrating which of the following?

   (F) Gender identity

   (G) Gender stability

   (H) Sexual identity

   (I) Imaginary audience

   (J) Sexual orientation

4. Luis is going through puberty. He is growing facial hair and becoming increasingly muscular in his upper body. Which of the following is Luis experiencing?

(A) Primary sex characteristics

(B) Spermarche

(C) Menarche

(D) Secondary sex characteristics

(E) Menopause

5. Charolette is eighty-five. Each morning she successfully completes a crossword puzzle, and she enjoys reading and learning about presidential trivia and American history. She knows more about these topics than ever before. Which of the following is strong for Charolette?

(A) Emotional intelligence

(B) Fluid intelligence

(C) Crystallized intelligence

(D) Accommodation

(E) Preoperational thinking

6. Achad proposed the idea that some teenagers struggle with their sense of identity and, as a result, try out many different roles while they are trying to figure out which best represents their individuality. Achad identified this struggle as which of the following?

(A) Identity foreclosure

(B) Identity moratorium

(C) Identity diffusion

(D) Gender identity

(E) Identity achievement

7. John and Mary have been married for three years. They are considering having children in the next few years and are happy in their relationship with one another. They support each other in their careers and with personal issues. According to Erik Erikson, they are experiencing which of the following?

(A) Identity

(B) Isolation

(C) Industry

(D) Intimacy

(E) Integrity

8. Which of the following individuals is likely to experience the highest levels of happiness?

   (A) Jenna, who has two children under the age of four

   (B) Shreya and Randy, who have just retired

   (C) Ron, who works about eighty hours a week programming computers and cannot see as much of his family as he would like

   (D) Allen, who is eighteen and deciding where to attend college

   (E) Marie, who has just lost her husband of forty years

9. Which of the following is true about brain development during adolescence and early adulthood?

   (A) The myelin sheath is developing along the axons of neurons primarily during adolescence.

   (B) The frontal lobe has completed development by late adolescence.

   (C) New neural networks will not be established after the early twenties.

   (D) All association areas of the brain have been dedicated to particular tasks by late adolescence.

   (E) Neural pruning occurs during mid- to late adolescence.

10. The concept that one's society defines certain points in life in which specific events such as marriage, having children, or establishing a steady career should occur is which of the following?

    (A) Social clock

    (B) Maturation

    (C) Psychosocial development

    (D) Personal fable

    (E) Rites of passage

FREE-RESPONSE QUESTIONS

1. Rodney, an elderly grandfather, does not get as much exercise or cognitive stimulation as he did when he was younger. Although he is healthy and still has his driver's license, he tends to associate only with family and a few friends. In the past, he was busy with many social activities and had a wide circle of friends. He no longer cares how others perceive him and lives life on his own terms. Rodney seems satisfied with his life and is proud of his accomplishments in his career and with his own family, but he has noticed that he has trouble learning and working through new technology.

A) Explain how the following concepts relate to Rodney's current state.
- Erikson's psychosocial development
- Piaget's cognitive development
- Kohlberg's moral development
- Physical well-being
- Social well-being/happiness

B) How might the following affect Rodney's ability to live independently?
- Alzheimer's disease
- Decline in fluid intelligence

2. Meredith is eighteen. She plays in a rock band and often dresses in men's clothing and wears heavy makeup. She is difficult to talk to, and many perceive her as threatening even though she has never been aggressive towards anyone. She thinks everyone in her grade thinks she is odd, and therefore she makes little effort to reach out. Her grades in school are mediocre; her teachers often say that she is not reaching her full potential. She does excel in English and uses her language ability help her songwriting. Meredith often thinks about changing her image and trying harder in school, because she is not sure if her current image is the one she wants to portray or if it is an accurate representation of who she is. When she thinks about the future, she is optimistic about her chances of success, and she believes that if she continues to play music, she will likely be able to "break through" to the professional scene. Use the following concepts to explain Meredith's current state of development and behavior:
- Erikson's stages of psychosocial development
- Identity moratorium
- Gender identity
- Peer influence
- Personal fable
- Imaginary audience

UNIT 9: Review

In this unit, you sought answers to these essential questions about development over the life span.

Chapter 15: How do physical, cognitive, moral, and social development take place from birth through adolescence?

Chapter 16: How do the stages of physical, social, and cognitive development contribute to human growth and change from adolescence through adulthood?

Apply what you have learned about developmental psychology by answering the free-response question below.

FREE-RESPONSE QUESTION

You have a new baby in the house, and you are interested in what to expect during this first year of development. You have been reading quite a bit about development during the early years of childhood.

A) Based on your reading, explain how the following will impact the first few years of your new child's life:
- Rooting reflex
- Trust vs. mistrust
- Sensorimotor stage
- Preconventional level of moral development
- Linguistic development
- Secure attachment

B) Researchers now know more about brain and sensory development than ever before. Explain how the following may develop in the early years of your baby's life:
- Myelin sheath
- Association areas

UNIT 10: Personality

Most people have wondered about personality at some time: Why am I the way I am? What makes that person tick? You have already read about some topics that relate to personality—the biological bases of behavior, consciousness, learning theories, cognition, motivation and emotion, and development. Topics in later units, including intelligence, mental disorders, and social psychology, also have something to say about personality. Though each unit touches on important aspects of human behavior, this unit specifically focuses on key personality theories, such as Freudian, Neo-Freudian, social cognitive, humanistic, trait, and the biological approach, as well as the cultural influences that can help shape personality.

Key Topics

- Similarities and differences among the major theories and approaches to explaining personality (e.g., psychoanalytic, humanist, cognitive, trait, social cognition, behavioral)
- Research methods (e.g., case studies and surveys) that psychologists use to investigate personality
- Frequently used assessment strategies (e.g., the Minnesota Multiphasic Personality Inventory [MMPI], the Thematic Apperception Test [TAT]), and relative test quality based on reliability and validity of the instruments
- Ways in which cultural context can facilitate or constrain personality development, especially as it relates to self-concept (e.g., collectivistic versus individualistic cultures)
- Key contributors to personality theory (e.g., Alfred Adler, Albert Bandura, Paul Costa and Robert McCrae, Sigmund Freud, Carl Jung, Abraham Maslow, Carl Rogers)

Source: *AP® Psychology Course and Exam Description*

17

Personality Theories, Approaches, and Assessment

"I am what is mine. Personality is the original personal property."

— Norman O. Brown

Essential Question: How can understanding personality theories help explain and improve your understanding of yourself and others?

Personality is an individual's unique and relatively stable patterns of behavior, characteristics, thoughts, and emotions. If personality is like a completed puzzle, personality theories try to explain the mystery of the pieces and how they come together. Personality is so complex, however, that no single theory can claim to have all the answers. This complexity explains why there are many theories of personality. Each needs to be assessed on its own merits.

Psychodynamic Theories

Psychodynamic theories are those that assume unconscious forces determine behavior and influence personality. Psychodynamic approaches separate the mind into three levels of consciousness. Figure 17.1 depicts the mind as an iceberg, with **consciousness**, or our sense of reality, above the waterline. It is the smallest part of what goes on in the mind, even though consciousness is what we are most aware of. In the psychodynamic view, the forces that drive a person's personality operate under the surface, either at a **preconscious** level, from which we can bring thoughts to conscious awareness, or an **unconscious** level, beyond our awareness and where most of the action takes place. The Freudian use of the word *unconscious* is therefore different from its common understanding associated with "being knocked unconscious."

Figure 17.1 shows that psychodynamic theory, which includes **psychoanalytic theory**, divides the mind into the id, the superego, and the ego. This theory of the divided mind and how it works as a system to influence personality was developed by Sigmund Freud.

Sigmund Freud and Psychoanalytic Theory

Sigmund Freud is probably the most recognizable name in the field of psychology. In the late 19th and early 20th centuries, he created a body of knowledge so influential that many concepts associated with **psychoanalysis**—Freud's theory of personality, dream interpretation, and psychotherapy—have

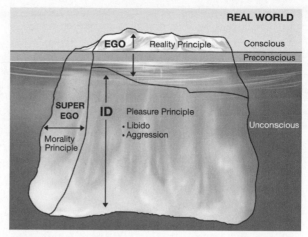

Figure 17.1 In Freud's theory, the conscious mind is just the tip of the iceberg.

become part of our culture. Words such as *ego, denial, repression,* and *sibling rivalry* all owe their existence to Sigmund Freud and psychoanalytic theory. Underpinning Freud's theory is his core idea that humans are highly advanced animals struggling to cope with their animalistic urges. In psychoanalytic theory, all our animalistic biological drives, instincts, and urges—primarily sex and aggression—reside in the unconscious. The unconscious also contains memories of trauma, uncomfortable feelings, and thoughts that we repress, or block from conscious awareness. These repressed feelings, thoughts, and trauma drive our personality and determine our behavior. Freud postulated that slips of the tongue (called "Freudian slips") and dream analysis (see Chapter 8) can reveal the content of the unconscious.

The Structure of Personality Freud also proposed that the personality is composed of the id, ego, and superego, which are mental structures or systems. The **id** exists at birth and contains all the instincts and energy, including sexual energy, necessary for survival. Freud called this instinctual energy **libido**. According to Freud, the id operates exclusively at an unconscious level and has the goal of immediately satisfying instinctual impulses. Freud called this urge toward immediate gratification of impulses the **pleasure principle**.

Freud's focus on sexuality as one source of energy driving human behavior grew out of his training as a medical doctor and a biological researcher. He understood that humans are animals and, like all animals, are hardwired to reproduce. He proposed that human beings' high level of intellectual and social advancement causes adults to repress the basic biological impulse toward sexuality into the unconscious.

Unlike adults, infants have no reason to repress the id's primitive physical urges. Infants are not only unashamed to load their diapers or feed from a breast, but they also derive pleasure from fulfilling the urges that assure the infant's survival.

As an infant grows, the ego emerges. The **ego** is reality-based, residing in both the unconscious and the conscious and existing to take reality into consideration in satisfying the primitive needs of the growing infant. The ego operates by the **reality principle**, a guiding principle in ways to satisfy the id's primitive needs while also negotiating reality.

The third part of the human mind is the superego. The superego develops as a result of the **morality principle**, which is the internalized need to comply with parental and other authority. Operating primarily at the unconscious level but also at the preconscious level, the **superego** is the moral sense of right and wrong, or a person's conscience. When the id expresses a need, the ego tries to address this need and the superego evaluates the success of the ego's expression. If the superego judges the expression to be socially appropriate, then the person is gratified. However, if the superego judges the expression to be socially inappropriate, it punishes the person through depression or anxiety.

Parents' stories about potty training illustrate how growing children internalize their expectations. Parents often describe their little one, while still in diapers, sneaking behind a couch or chair to have a bowel movement. The child hides because the force of shame from the superego competes with the pleasure-seeking impulses of the id. The child has internalized parental and societal expectations that bowel movements are supposed to happen in private. The developing ego must find a way to satisfy both the id's desire for immediate gratification and the superego's shame-provoking sense of right and wrong. So the child enjoys the bowel movement without using the potty but does it privately.

The three parts of the human mind constantly interact with one another. The ego plays the reality-based referee between the libidinal desires of the id and the guilt-provoking ideals of the superego. The ego uses strategies to deal with and reduce the constant threat of anxiety that comes from this struggle between the id and the superego.

The Role of Defense Mechanisms One strategy the reality-based ego uses is **defense mechanisms**, which distort or transform an urge emanating from the unconscious to protect itself from anxiety produced by the competing forces of the id and superego. The following eight defense mechanisms are the most common:

1. **Repression** is the process of reducing anxiety by blocking impulses or memories from consciousness; it underlies all other defense mechanisms.

2. **Regression** occurs when the ego seeks to reduce anxiety by reverting to an earlier period of psychological development. For example, an adult faced with the stress of surgery may begin biting his or her fingernails or sucking on a thumb.

3. **Displacement** occurs when aggressive urges are shifted, or displaced, toward a recipient other than the one who engendered the feelings. For example, when you're angry at your parent or another authority figure but expressing that anger directly at them would cause too much anxiety, you yell at your brother or sister instead.

4. **Projection** occurs when anxiety-producing feelings are repressed and then projected onto another person. For example, a man who is sexually attracted to his wife's sister may repress these desires and believe instead that his wife's sister is trying to seduce him.

5. **Denial** is the refusal of the ego to accept the reality of a situation because doing so would produce unbearable anxiety. For example, a woman who is pregnant may refuse to acknowledge it despite all evidence.

6. **Reaction-formation** defends against anxiety-producing thoughts or impulses by transforming the unacceptable urge into its opposite. For example, a person who has an unacceptable urge to burn things may become a firefighter.

7. **Rationalization** occurs when a person distorts or transforms an anxiety-producing and therefore unacceptable explanation or excuse for an impulse or behavior into an acceptable one. For example, a person may rationalize cheating on a test by thinking, "Everyone else cheats."

8. **Sublimation** occurs when a person redirects an unacceptable urge to something with social value. Someone with an urge for aggressive behavior, for example, may turn it into a creative expression that gives social meaning to an act of aggression, as in a painting of a battle.

Psychosexual Personality Development   Although Freud's psychoanalytic theory of defense mechanisms is generally accepted, many contemporary psychologists criticize his explanation of how the need to satisfy hardwired procreative sexual urges drives personality formation and development. Freud theorized that personality develops during infancy and childhood in a series of five psychosexual stages. During each **psychosexual stage**, the id's urge to seek pleasure becomes associated with specific parts of the child's body that produce pleasurable sensations, which Freud called **erogenous zones**. Core personality traits and characteristics form because of events that occur during the first three stages. When id-based urges are not satisfied or are overindulged, a person becomes **fixated**, or stuck, in a stage and carries the sexual energy from that stage into adulthood. Fixation can also result if a trauma occurred during that stage. The fixation may manifest as an unconscious dynamic in the adult personality.

SUMMARY OF PSYCHOSEXUAL PERSONALITY DEVELOPMENT				
Psychosexual Stage	**Age**	**Erogenous Zone**	**Event or Crisis**	**Outcome of Fixation in Adulthood**
Oral	Birth to 1½ years	Mouth	Transition from breastfeeding to solid food	Overeating, smoking, over-dependence, or sarcasm
Anal	2 to 3 years	Anus	Toilet training, reality-based expectations of behavior	Obsession over neatness and orderliness, messiness, rebellious and hostile personality
Phallic	3 to 6 years	Genitalia	Attachment to opposite-sex parent, identification with same-sex parent	Oedipus complex, castration anxiety, Electra complex, penis envy
(Latency)	6 years to puberty	None, sexual desires are repressed into unconscious	Focus on intellectual and social development	
Genital	Puberty to adulthood	Genitalia	Development of intimate relationships outside the family	Normal sexual desire reemerges

Figure 17.2

During the first eighteen months of life, personality development is centered on the child's need to satisfy sexual pleasure through the mouth during feeding—hence the term **oral stage**. Trauma can occur during the transition from breastfeeding to solid food. If the child is not satisfied or is overgratified during this stage, the child may develop an oral fixation, which may show up in adulthood as overeating, smoking, overdependence, or sarcasm.

During the **anal stage**, which occurs from ages two to three, the child's erogenous zone centers on holding in or expelling feces. The ego emerges during the anal stage when the child is confronted with toilet training and reality-based expectations of behavior. The crisis of toilet training can result in anal fixations that may show up in adulthood in the form of personality characteristics such as obsession over neatness and orderliness or the opposite, like a messy or rebellious and hostile personality.

Freud's third psychosexual stage, the **phallic stage**, is the most controversial aspect of his theory of personality development. During ages three to about six, Freud suggested that children's sexual focus shifts to their genitalia, and an attraction toward the parent of the opposite sex occurs. His description of development is different for young boys and young girls. During the phallic stage, the young boy both sexually longs for his mother and feels fear and hostility toward his father. Freud called this development the **Oedipus complex**, from the Greek story of Oedipus, the king who unknowingly killed his father and married his mother. The boy experiences fear of his father as **castration anxiety**, the fear that the father will damage or remove the boy's penis because of the boy's attempts to seduce his mother. To reduce this profound anxiety, the boy unconsciously employs a defense mechanism called identification. **Identification** is a process by which someone takes on the characteristics of another. Through identification, the boy represses and resolves the anxiety caused by his sexual attraction toward his mother by identifying with his father, incorporating the male-oriented characteristics that his father possesses. Freud proposed that through this process, the boy develops the characteristics of a superior male superego.

During this stage, girls also experience an attraction toward the opposite-sex parent. (Later psychoanalysts called this the **Electra complex**, after the mythological character who plotted to kill her mother and stepfather as revenge for the murder of her father.) Because girls lack penises (which girls blame on the mother), girls are incapable of experiencing castration anxiety. Girls are thought to experience **penis envy** instead. Without castration anxiety, they do not identify with the father and consequently develop a superego that is, according to Freud, inferior.

After the phallic stage, during ages six to puberty, Freud theorized that children pass through a sexually inconsequential stage called the **latency stage** because their sexual desires have been repressed into the unconscious. During this stage, the child focuses on intellectual and social development. According to Freud, during this period children also learn gender roles.

Last, at the start of puberty and continuing through adulthood, normal sexual desire reemerges through the **genital stage**. In the normal course of adulthood, an individual expresses sexuality through the development of intimate relationships outside the family.

Assessing Freud's Theory

Freud developed his theory in the late 19th and early 20th century, when Victorian attitudes supporting sexual repression and a strong social ethic and were widespread. It was also a time when there was minimal scientific understanding of the brain and when the field of psychology was still young; formulating theories of human behavior involved thoughtful speculation based on case studies rather than modern empirical scientific methodology.

Major Criticisms of Psychoanalytic Theory Freud's research method, case studies, and theoretical interpretations of them are one area of major criticism of the psychoanalytic theory. Both the psychosexual theory of personality development and the psychoanalytic theory are based on case studies that Freud developed from clinical therapy sessions with patients who were primarily troubled upper-class Austrian women. These case studies were devoid of scientific methodology. From them, Freud developed biased theoretical explanations that often fail to withstand modern scientific scrutiny using empirically based research methods.

Freud's analyses of case studies were influenced by the accepted belief of male superiority during the Victorian era in which he lived and practiced medicine and psychoanalysis. His views were, in large part, the product of an extremely male-dominated or paternalistic society. This male-centered and misogynistic worldview was the backdrop for the theory that the male superego emerging from the phallic stage is superior to the female superego.

The most controversial example of bias was Freud's decision to interpret his female patients' numerous reports of early childhood sexual abuse as fantasy rather than fact. The strongest critics suggest that the entire theory of psychosexual development rests largely on Freud's decision to interpret post-traumatic memories of early sexual abuse as expressions of infantile fantasies. It is also speculated that Freud wanted his theory to be accepted by the broader medical and male-dominated community and thought it would be more palatable to that audience if sexual abuse was seen as infantile fantasies as opposed to possible reality.

A second major criticism is that the various elements of the mind—the id, ego, and superego—are impossible to verify with empirical research. There are no operational definitions of these concepts and no way to measure them. However, Freud never suggested they were literal. He created and used them as hypothetical ideas to illustrate how the mind works.

A third major criticism is that the proposition that repression and other defense mechanisms prevent awareness of past trauma or current sexual urges is contradicted by current research on posttraumatic stress disorder (PTSD). PTSD exists not because the trauma is repressed but because it is remembered. Repressed memory of trauma is the exception rather than the rule. Nonetheless, recent research does suggest that humans sometimes unconsciously attempt to protect their sense of self by distorting reality, forgetting or misremembering a trauma.

Last, Freud's theory constructs a closed world in which the theory can explain away any apparent counterexamples within itself. It is insulated from criticism from both within that world and without. For example, psychoanalytic theory can attribute a women's obsession with weaving and knitting to an unconscious motivation to conceal a genital deficiency. If the woman rejects this explanation, then according to the theory, she is employing the defense mechanism of denial. Constructed in this way, the psychoanalytic theory allows no explanation to disprove the interpretation. Just as his hypotheses cannot be proved empirically, they can also not be falsified, and they thereby resist scientific scrutiny.

Strengths of Psychoanalytic Theory An unbiased assessment of psychoanalytic theory includes recognizing its positive aspects as well as its failings. Despite its many shortcomings, Freud's body of work has enjoyed a lasting positive legacy. Freud's focus on the importance of early childhood has had a profound impact on how we view these early years. It is to his credit that most of the world recognizes that healthy adulthood stems from a healthy childhood.

In addition, research in both social psychology and attribution theory (see Chapter 24) supports the theory of unconscious defense mechanisms. Some defense mechanisms, such as projection or rationalization, appear to be at work when people unconsciously distort the amount of agreement others share for their own beliefs (known as the false consensus effect). Defense mechanisms also appear to be at work when people attempt to preserve their self-esteem by using rationalization to resolve holding contradictory beliefs (cognitive dissonance).

Last, though some argue that Freud placed too much emphasis on unconscious determinants of behavior, current neuroscientific research seems to validate this emphasis. Although modern neurology and neuroscience were in their infancy during the late 19th and early 20th centuries, Freud's description of the conscious mind as the product of unconscious forces appears to be correct. When it comes to the mind and the physical brain that creates it, what we are aware of is, indeed, just the tip of the iceberg.

Neo-Freudians

While adhering to the psychodynamic premise that personality is influenced by unconscious forces, several of Freud's early followers eventually turned away from his emphasis on biological impulses centered on sex and aggression and focused more on the importance of social factors influencing personality. Collectively, these approaches are termed Neo-Freudian or psychodynamic. The most prominent Neo-Freudian theorists are Carl Jung, Alfred Adler, Karen Horney, and Erik Erikson.

Carl Jung Once a close friend, student, and collaborator of Freud, **Carl Jung** (1875–1961) parted ways with Freud when their thinking about the function of the unconscious and how much emphasis to place on sex as a driving force diverged. Jung saw the unconscious as having two parts. One part, the **personal unconscious**, contained all repressed thoughts, memories, and emotions. The other part, the **collective unconscious**, stored the shared sense of universal experiences common to all human beings. These universal memories within the collective unconscious are organized into **archetypes,** which are universal concepts that influence our behavior and personality.

Archetypes—like the **Shadow**, which represents the evil or dark side of human nature (Dracula, Darth Vader, or Voldemort), and the **Animus**, the masculine archetype in women, or the **Anima**, the feminine archetype in men—can often show up in dreams and influence our behavior at an unconscious level. For example, Jung argued that humans have experienced and retained the concept of motherhood for hundreds of thousands of years. This collective memory of "mother" resides in all of us as the Mother archetype. This archetypal force, stemming from the collective unconscious, shapes our expectations, perceptions, and behavior—our personality—when motherhood affects us in our own lives, whether as a woman who is the mother of a child or an adult influenced by the inherited ideal of the Mother.

In contrast to Freud's negative view that human behavior is primarily a result of sexual and aggressive animalistic impulses, Jung's more positive view emphasized the natural drive toward **individuation**, in which people become fully aware of their true selves through the process of assimilating the personal and collective unconscious into their conscious awareness. Jung coined the term **persona**, which he said was the aspect of personality that a person presents to the world. Though the concept of persona is similar to the Freudian concept of ego, Jung saw the persona as a means of hiding the true self and therefore preventing the positive process of individuation.

Jung's concepts of the collective unconscious and archetypes have not been widely accepted by psychologists but have been embraced in the fields of anthropology, religious studies, philosophy, and the arts. In psychology, Jung made a significant contribution through his theory of personality types. Jung introduced the concepts of **introvert**, the inner-directed personality type, and **extravert**, the outer-directed personality type.

Alfred Adler One of Freud's earliest students and followers was **Alfred Adler** (1870–1937). He, too, disagreed with Freud's emphasis on biological sexual impulses, believing that aggression or "will to power" was the more important drive. Adler developed an approach he called **individual psychology**, which emphasized the drive to reach goals and find purpose. While still adhering to the psychodynamic principle of the unconscious determinants of behavior, Adler proposed that the driving force behind personality development was the need for superiority. When confronted by feelings of inferiority, young children utilize a process Adler called **compensation**, which involves dealing with feelings of inferiority, real or imagined, by developing one's abilities. The perceived inability to resolve feelings of inferiority can lead to an **inferiority complex** and **overcompensation,** hiding feelings of inferiority by flaunting superficial indicators of superiority such as wealth, status, or good looks.

Adler was also a strong proponent of the influence of birth order on personality. He proposed that firstborn children, for example, are most vulnerable to inferiority complexes when the next child enters the picture and bumps the firstborn from primary to a lower status. Although recent studies have shown some validity regarding aspects of Adler's birth order theory, most of his observations have failed to stand up to scientific scrutiny.

Karen Horney Rejecting Freud's emphasis on sex, Karen Horney (1885–1952) also strongly rejected his suggestion that female personality was predicated on the desire to possess a penis. Horney argued that women envied men's superior status in society, not the penis. In other words, culture was the main driver in the formation of personality, not anatomy.

Horney emphasized a child's need for love and security in the formation of a healthy personality and proposed that the lack of love and security in childhood results in personality problems (neurosis) such as hostility and anxiety. Horney's theory involving the childhood causes of psychological problems in adulthood have found confirmation in numerous studies linking a lack of maternal affection in early childhood with increased instances of drug abuse and violence when the child reached adulthood. (See pages 360–364 in Chapter 15 for more on attachment and its role in development.)

You have read about Erik Erikson in Chapters 15 and 16. Erikson worked closely with Freud's daughter Anna Freud, but he, too, broke away from orthodox Freudian psychoanalytic theory. Instead, he proposed that social forces throughout a person's entire life continually influence the development of the personality. Erikson created a theory of personality development based on eight psychosocial stages. (See pages 374–376 and 401–403.) His theory gives a prominent place to adolescence, arguing that during this crucial stage in life, people either establish a sense of adult identity or fail to define themselves. If people fail to establish a sense of adult identity, they either become stuck in adolescent role confusion or become isolated and avoid intimacy.

Critiquing Neo-Freudian Theories All Neo-Freudian approaches reject the sexual pleasure-driven basis of Freud's psychoanalytic theory and its emphasis on the first five or six years of a child's life as the fundamental source of personality. Instead, each emphasizes the important influence of social and environmental forces throughout life. Like Freud, Neo-Freudians argue that unconscious factors play a role in determining personality and behavior, but unlike Freud, they argue that anxiety is socially, not sexually, rooted. Significant criticism of Neo-Freudian theories, as with Freud's theory, centers on a lack of empirical evidence to support them, since their primary research method was case studies. Psychodynamic theories also do not hold up to cross-cultural scrutiny.

Trait Theories

In response to the psychodynamic theorists' focus on the hidden forces behind behavior and personality, trait theorists focus on observable and more measurable **traits**, which are stable personality characteristics of behavior, thought processes, and emotions. Trait theories focus on observable personality characteristics that often determine how we behave across time and across situations. Starting with Gordon Allport's trait research in the 1930s and the categorization of traits by Raymond Cattell, Hans and Sybil Eysenck, and Paul Costa and Robert McCrae, trait theorists have made significant contributions to the empirical study of personality.

Gordon Allport (1897–1967) was the first psychologist to develop a comprehensive theory centered on traits. He rejected psychoanalysis as unscientific and impractical. Allport argued that explanations of behavior require determining a person's unique and enduring traits. He also rejected environmental influences. Instead, Allport proposed that personality is guided by about five to ten central traits with which people are born. In addition, he went through the dictionary and identified thousands of words people commonly use to describe personality and traits.

Raymond Cattell (1905–1998) used a statistical method called factor analysis to identify clusters of traits that are related to each other. **Factor analysis** analyzes multiple variables that are correlated and identifies how those correlations connect with each other. The technique allowed Cattell to find the overarching qualities that connect numerous different traits into clusters and

Raymond Cattel's 16 Source Traits

	1	2	3	4	5	6	7	8	
Reserved									Outgoing
Less intelligent									More intelligent
Affected by feelings									Emotionally stable
Submissive									Dominant
Serious									Happy-go-lucky
Expedient									Conscientious
Timid									Venturesome
Tough-minded									Sensitive
Trusting									Suspicious
Practical									Imaginative
Forthright									Shrewd
Self-assured									Apprehensive
Conservative									Experimenting
Group dependent									Self-sufficient
Uncontrolled									Controlled
Relaxed									Tense

Figure 17.3

thereby reduce the number of traits. The result was a more manageable and measurable way of studying personality traits.

Cattell came up with two overarching types of traits: **surface traits**, which are observable behaviors, and 16 **source traits,** which are more fundamental characteristics that drive personality and result in the observable surface traits (see Figure 17.3). Cattell organized the source traits into 16 pairs, with each pair forming a continuum, and developed a test, called the **16 Personality Factors (PF) Psychometric Questionnaire,** to measure them.

Hans Eysenck (1916–1997) and Sybil Eysenck (b. 1927) also used factor analysis to analyze traits and arrived at three genetically-influenced dimensions of personality that they called temperaments. These three dimensions are as follows:

1. Extraversion/Introversion—needing either more external stimuli or less
2. Neuroticism/Stability—the degree of emotional stability
3. Psychoticism/Socialization—the degree of aggression and nonconformity

The Eysencks developed a representation of their model of personality (see Figure 17.4), with the personality traits around the outside of a circle depicting how combinations of these dimensions can identify most of the dominant personality traits we are accustomed to seeing. They also developed the Eysenck Personality Questionnaire (EPQ), a series of yes-or-no questions, to determine the dimensions of a person's temperament.

Eysenck Model of Personality

Figure 17.4

Paul Costa (b. 1942) and Robert McCrae (b. 1949) developed a list of five traits or factors called the **Five Factor Model**, often referred to as the *Big Five* (see Figure 17.5). These five factors, also organized as pairs of adjectives along a continuum, are Agreeableness, Conscientiousness, Openness, Neuroticism, and Extraversion. (A good mnemonic device for identifying the Big Five is OCEAN—**O**penness, **C**onscientiousness, **E**xtraversion, **A**greeableness, and **N**euroticism.) Costa and McCrea's Big Five model is currently the most widely accepted model of traits. The model is based on responses to various questionnaires and other research methods from a large pool of participants from around the world. The research has demonstrated that the Big Five traits are stable in adulthood, are influenced by genetics, and predict behavior.

Costa and McCrea's Five Factor Model

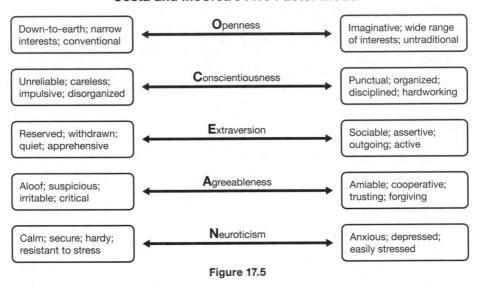

Figure 17.5

Assessing Trait Theories

A strength of trait theories is the high degree of correlation among the traits defined independently by different researchers, no doubt because they were determined by observable behavior. When one aggregates a person's behavior over time and across different situations, patterns emerge. These patterns are what one might call a "personality" or "personality traits."

A criticism of trait theories is that it relies on the research method of self-reporting, which is accurate only to the degree that the subjects know themselves well and can assess themselves with a degree of objectivity. It also does not attempt to explain why certain behaviors and traits have developed. A major criticism of trait theories is that while there are general consistencies across time and situation, situational variables more accurately predict behavior than traits. For example, if cheering for a sports team, an extraverted and an introverted person may both cheer because the situation dictates it, though an extraverted person may cheer more loudly than an introverted person.

Another major criticism of trait theory is that it does not do a good job distinguishing "trait" from "personality." Most people would say that a personality is a constellation of traits, whereas trait theory tends to concentrate on single traits to describe a person.

Behavioral and Social-Cognitive Theories of Personality

As the 20th century progressed, dissatisfaction with psychodynamic theories grew. The **behavioral approach** became an alternative to explaining the development and structure of personality. It rejected unconscious determinants of behavior and valued what can be empirically observed. The behavioral approach focuses on the central role of learning in the development of personality. The contributions of John Watson, Neal Miller, John Dollard, and B. F. Skinner established the behavioral school as an alternative to the more subjective and less scientific approach of Freud and the Neo-Freudians.

Social-cognitive theories share the basic tenets of behaviorism—you are what you learn—but focus on the cognitive aspects of learning and forming behavioral patterns that can be referred to as personality. Major social-cognitive theorists include Albert Bandura, Julian Rotter, George Kelly, and Walter Mischel and Yuichi Shoda. Like behavioral theorists, social-cognitive theorists reject explanations of personality based on unconscious forces that cannot be observed and measured.

Behaviorism

Starting in the early 20th century and continuing through the 1950s, several psychologists focused on observable and measurable causes of behavior rather than on the unobservable structures and causes of personality proposed by psychodynamic theories. John B. Watson and later B. F. Skinner based their work on the idea that psychological research should focus on the mechanics of learning that result in what others might call personality rather than speculate about internal unconscious forces.

The earliest behaviorists to pursue a more scientifically objective approach to explaining behavior were John B. Watson, Neal Miller, and John Dollard. In 1913, John B. Watson introduced the behaviorist view in response to the Freudian psychoanalytic approach to explaining behavior. By the 1940s, Neal Miller (1909–2002) and John Dollard (1900–1980), both originally trained in the psychoanalytic school, attempted to translate the subjective psychoanalytic concept of unconscious forces into more observable phenomenon. Building on the work of earlier behaviorists, they developed **social learning theory**, which explains personality as a system of habits that develop through the acquisition of long-term behavioral patterns.

By far the most recognizable name associated with behaviorism is B. F. Skinner. Skinner's theory, called operant conditioning, argued that what others call personality is the sum of behaviors learned as responses to rewards or through negative reinforcement (see Chapter 9). Skinner's approach, called **environmental determinism**, proposes that all behavior is caused by outside environmental forces and, for this reason, free will is an illusion. Rather than developing a personality theory, Skinner contributed the behaviorist idea that "you are what you learn." For example, a behaviorist would explain that a personality characteristic called "defiant" is the result of rewards for early defiant behavior that were consistent enough for the behavior to become a habit. The behavior continues if reinforced through rewards and will decrease if punished (but see the possible unintended effect of punishments in Chapter 9).

The behaviorist approach to personality proposes that each individual pattern of behavior a person possesses was caused by an environmentally determined event called learning. Since birth, each person experiences countless learning events that consist of a behavior followed by a consequence. Personality is the sum of all those learning events.

Social-Cognitive Theory

The social-cognitive approach to personality suggests that cognitive processes play a role equal to the environment's role to determine the individual's behavior patterns and personality. To social-cognitive theorists, a combination of observational learning and mental processes lead to the long-lasting patterns of behavior called personality. The major social-cognitive theorists include Julian Rotter, George Kelly, Albert Bandura, and Walter Mischel.

Julian Rotter (see pages 236–237) based his approach to personality on two core assumptions. The first is that the choices people make shed light on their personality. The second is that people engage in activities to achieve an outcome that will satisfy their psychological needs. Two concepts are at the center of his theory: cognitive expectancy and locus of control. **Cognitive expectancy** is the belief that one's behavior will yield the desired outcome. **Locus of control** is one's belief about where the forces that determine outcome reside. People with an **internal locus of control** have a strong cognitive expectancy that their own actions will result in the outcome they are seeking. For example, some piano students may believe that if they practice, they will master a piece of music. People with an **external locus of control** have a cognitive expectancy that outcomes they experience are determined more by outside forces like luck or fate. For example, other piano students may think that how much they practice will have little to do with whether they can master a piece of music. A person's locus of control has a profound impact on how they act and thus on their personality.

George Kelly (1905–1967) developed a completely **cognitive theory of personality**. An underlying assumption of his theory is that people have knowledge about the world—how objects work, what is likely to happen in response to different actions or events—that they gain through living. Based on this assumption, Kelly proposed a **fundamental postulate** that states that long-term patterns of behavior are based on how people perceive the world. If people believe most other people are threatening, then they will be cautious in their interactions with others. If people see other people as generally friendly, then their actions will reflect that perception. According to Kelly's **personal-construct theory**, personality is the compilation of all the mental constructs they have when cognitively processing the world around them and the behavior they exhibit based on those constructs.

Albert Bandura (see pages 237–239) proposed that three factors—person, environment, and behavior—interact to determine patterns of behavior and thus personality. Figure 17.6 illustrates Bandura's model of **reciprocal determinism**. In this model, a person's behavior (actions and decisions), environment, and personal factors (cognitive and biological processes, emotions, and competencies) interact to determine behavior. For example, Rachel thinks she is funny and enjoys making people laugh (cognitive, emotional, and competency person factors). These assessments lead her to join her school's improv team (behavior). Being on the improv team (environment) leads to her making people laugh.

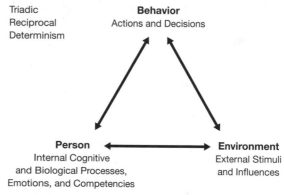

Albert Bandura's Reciprocal Determinism Model

Triadic Reciprocal Determinism

Behavior
Actions and Decisions

Person
Internal Cognitive and Biological Processes, Emotions, and Competencies

Environment
External Stimuli and Influences

Figure 17.6

Bandura rejected Skinner's exclusive emphasis on the environment. Instead, his theory assumes that a person's thinking (cognition), prior learning, and capacity to change the environment influence and determine behavior, not the environment alone.

Bandura also demonstrated that behavior results from **observational learning**, in which people see other people's actions and the consequences of those actions and then incorporate those behaviors into their own behavior. Bandura's most well-known study is the Bobo doll experiment, in which he demonstrated that children's aggressive behavior increased through observation of aggressive behavior. (See pages 238–239.)

Another important influence on behavior is **self-efficacy**, the degree to which a person thinks (cognition) their efforts (behavior) will result in a desired outcome. People with high self-efficacy tend to be persistent and confident. People with low self-efficacy tend to avoid challenges and give up when they encounter challenges. According to the social-cognitive approach, people can develop high self-efficacy by changing their behaviors, thoughts, and social environment.

Walter Mischel (b. 1930) and Yuichi Shoda attempted to address a paradox inherent in many personality theories. Although trait theories assume that people's behavior patterns are consistent, observation of people in varying situations reveals inconsistency. Mischel and Shoda recognized that some patterns of behavior are consistent over time, but they contended that there is insufficient evidence to assert they are consistent across situations. Instead of assuming that fixed patterns of behavior are consistent across different situations, Mischel and Shoda tried to devise a better way to understand personality and analyze people's behavior patterns.

The resulting theory, called **cognitive-affective processing system (CAPS),** proposes that understanding personality involves observing how people use cognitive and affective processes to alter their behavior depending on the situation. How a person adapts to a situation depends on five cognitive-affective units or processes:

1. Encoding strategies—a person's individualized way of processing information from the environment

2. Competencies—a person's cognitive ability to use intelligence to control behavior through self-initiated goals and consequences

3. Beliefs and expectancies—a person's assumption about the consequences of his or her actions

4. Goals and values—cognitive belief systems that tend to increase consistency in behavior

5. Affective responses—how a person reacts emotionally

Mischel and Shoda's cognitive theory emphasizes that various cognitive processes enable people to react differently to varying situations and that the ability to do so is adaptive.

Assessing Behavioral and Social-Cognitive Theories

Although the behavioral theorists never intended to develop personality theories, their theoretical and empirical work on the acquisition of behaviors through learning sheds light on many aspects of personality. In addition, they inspired other personality theorists to take an empirical approach to the subject.

The chief shortcoming of behavioral theories is that they do not take into account mental processes when explaining behavior. To a behaviorist, either a phenomenon is observable or it doesn't exist for scientific study. This position is too extreme for many psychologists to accept.

B. F. Skinner's work is also criticized for its position that free will does not exist. Like the closed world of Freud's psychoanalytic theory, Skinner's theory makes proving the existence of free will impossible. Consider, for example, what would happen if you ask a student to prove he or she has free will by doing a somersault in front of the class. If the student refuses, the class might focus all its attention on the refusal. Skinner's theory would assert that the anticipated reaction of the class will be reinforcing because the attention is rewarding. If the student *does* the roll, then the outcome, pleasing the teacher, will be reinforcing. In both cases, according to behaviorism, environmental determinism explains the student's choice.

Social-cognitive theories have provided valuable contributions, such as recognizing the importance of social factors and mental processes in the development of behavior. Additionally, unlike psychoanalysis, most concepts in social-cognitive theories are testable under scientific conditions. However, social-cognitive theories do not address biological influences on personality. They also seem overly critical of the concept and influence of unconscious aspects of the mind on behavior and personality and dismiss them too easily.

Humanistic Theories

Humanist psychologist Carl Rogers told a story of when he was a child living in an old house with a basement. There was a small window at the top of a basement wall. A bin of potatoes was stored against a basement wall for quite a while. One day his mother asked him to go down in the basement and fetch some potatoes. When he went downstairs, he saw something that stuck with him for life. In the darkness of the basement, the potatoes had begun to sprout, the vines clinging to the basement wall growing ever closer to the light from the small window. Carl Rogers believed the potatoes and their growing vines captured the essence of the humanistic approach to psychology. Those potatoes were growing toward the light despite their desperate condition, and it is in our very nature as human beings to reach for our own light. It is in our very nature, as Rogers expressed it, to *become*. The humanistic approach to personality stresses the positive qualities and potential inherent in all of us.

The humanistic approach emerged in the second half of the 20th century as a "third force" in psychology, contrasting with the negative view of psychodynamic theories and the overly mechanical approach of behaviorism. Additionally, both the psychodynamic and behavioral theories are reactive models: In the psychodynamic model, the ego reacts to the demands of the id; in the behavioral model, a stimulus causes a response. Humanism's contribution was that it emphasized growth, not reaction. The most well-known humanistic theorists are Carl Rogers and Abraham Maslow.

Carl Rogers

Carl Rogers (1902–1987) was first and foremost a psychotherapist. The body of work he produced stemmed largely from case studies from his work with his clients, and it was from his experience first as a minister and then as a psychotherapist that he formed his humanistic views about personality.

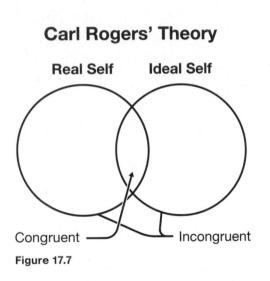

Carl Rogers' Theory

Real Self **Ideal Self**

Congruent —— —— Incongruent

Figure 17.7

Rogers believed that people have an innate drive toward reaching their full potential. He believed that people are naturally good and that a person is born perfectly congruent between the real self and the ideal self. The **real self** is the recognition and acceptance of one's natural self. To see a real self in action, watch a toddler interact with himself or herself in front of a mirror. There's no holding back the love and acceptance he or she has for that person in the mirror.

The **ideal self** emerges as the result of interactions with the significant people in an individual's life, particularly parents. If all went perfectly, parents would have expressed **unconditional positive regard**, acceptance of their children without regard to their behavior. Such unconditional regard rarely happens, and some level of **conditions of worth**, implicit or explicit standards for acceptance and love, are in place in the relationship. These conditions of worth begin to separate the ideal self from the real self, which leads the two selves to become **incongruent**. The more the incongruence or separation, the more severe the impact on individuals' **self-concept**, or image of themselves.

A dysfunctional personality is a symptom of significant incongruence between the ideal self and the real self. For Rogers, this unhealthy state of incongruence could be resolved and a healthier personality achieved through exposure to genuine unconditional positive regard. If a person were provided with genuine unconditional positive regard along with empathy, he or she would begin to become a **fully functioning person**, a person who strives to *become* and accept his or her genuine self.

Abraham Maslow

Abraham Maslow, like Rogers, embraced the basic goodness in human nature. Although Rogers' views were formed from his work as a psychotherapist, Maslow's theory of human behavior developed from his study of healthy personalities. Maslow observed the pessimistic nature of Freud's approach and the mechanistic approach of behaviorists. He took a different approach that looks at human personality as a reflection of the needs a person is striving to satisfy.

As you read in Chapter 13, Maslow created a hierarchy of needs to explain how people's motivations and behaviors reflect physical or psychological needs they are trying to meet. Maslow proposed that all people strive to become **self-actualizing**, fulfilling their natural desire to achieve their full potential. All levels above biological and safety needs are important contributors to personality, as people strive for belongingness, self-esteem, and self-actualization in different manners that relate to their personality.

Maslow saw self-actualization as an ongoing process and becoming fully self-actualized as a rare event. According to Maslow, an unhealthy personality is one in which people are continually frustrated at the inability to satisfy their need to self-actualize.

Assessing Humanistic Theories

As a "third force," the humanistic approach brought a much-needed positive outlook to theories of personality. It provided a new perspective of people as growing organisms rather than simply reactive beings. The humanistic approach has found application beyond psychology in teaching, and Maslow's hierarchy of needs is used throughout international business across many industries and in institutional management to motivate and form more meaningful relationships with employees by recognizing and responding to their needs.

In spite of these contributions, humanistic theories have significant weaknesses. The theories are based on hypotheses that were not developed from empirical data or scientific observation. The concepts are vague and therefore extremely difficult to assess using sound scientific methodology. Additionally, critics point out that the humanistic view is overly optimistic about human nature and naïve in its prescription for a healthy personality. Other critics argue that humanism does not give us a pathway to distinguish a healthy pursuit of self-concept and personal growth from a pathologically narcissistic view of oneself.

Twin studies provide support for a genetic basis to personality.

Biology and Personality

The biological approach to personality focuses on the role of genes and heredity in determining personality. Recent research in behavioral genetics shows increasing evidence that some aspects of personality are inherited.

As you read in Chapter 5, research in behavioral genetics shows that heritability plays a role in behavior and personality. Current biogenetic research suggests that some predispositions and personality traits appear to be inherited. The work of Hans and Sybil Eysenck with trait theory also suggested a genetic link to **temperament**, which is biologically based and determines an individual's responsivity to stimuli and ability to self-regulate. From birth, some babies appear irritable and respond with more stress to environmental stimuli, while others are calmer. Temperament is inborn and unlearned. Personality and child development researchers consider differences in temperament to be determining factors in a child's personality development.

Heritability is the degree to which genes influence psychological characteristics and, in this case, personality. The best way to study heritability of personality traits is through the study of identical twins who are separated at birth and raised in separate environments. These types of studies have shown that extraversion and introversion, agreeableness, and responsiveness to environmental stimuli are temperaments with a genetic basis. The similarities in the personalities of adult identical twins are often remarkable. In one case, identical twins separated at birth and then reunited as older adults had the exact same job, wore the same brand of jeans, and even used the same type of toothpaste.

Assessing the Biological Approach

A balanced assessment of the role biology plays in determining personality recognizes the scientific findings that support the assertion as well as evidence that shows the important role of environment. The results of identical twin studies show a remarkable correlation of personality traits between identical twins raised in separate environments. But those studies also show that genes did not play an exclusive role in determining personality. In twin studies, although the similarity of personality traits and behavior patterns is much higher for identical twins than for fraternal twins, the similarities are still less than 100 percent. The identical twins, though similar, do have some personality differences. Environmental influences explain this difference. One way to think of the relative weights of inheritance and environment is that your genes provide the rough draft and your environment produces the final draft.

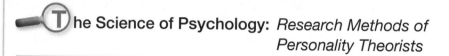 he Science of Psychology: *Research Methods of Personality Theorists*

The chart below compares research methods of personality theorists.

Research Methods	Personality Theories	Strengths	Weaknesses
Case studies	Psychoanalytic, psychodynamic, humanistic	In-depth studies of individuals; good source of hypotheses	Subjects' memories may be inaccurate or incomplete; cannot generalize
Projective tests	Psychodynamic	Taps into unconscious	Lacks validity and has low reliability
Surveys	Trait, social cognitive	Conclusions generalizable if data gathered from random sample	Self-reporting may be inaccurate
Observation	Social-cognitive, behaviorists	Reveals people's interactions with their environment	Observations may be biased and do not show cause and effect
Personality inventories	Trait	More valid and reliable than projective tests	Self-reporting may be inaccurate
Experiment	Social-cognitive, biological	Scientifically sound; can show cause and effect	Can be subject to experimenter bias

Practice: After reading pages 436–438, choose two personality theorists who used different research methods. In an essay, compare their methodology and their conclusions. Find one specific example of a study by each of your chosen theorists, and include those in your essay.

Personality Assessments

The methods for investigating personality vary considerably, and the personality assessments psychologists use depend on the theoretical approach they are researching. The strength of a particular personality assessment depends on its degree of **reliability**, how consistent the results are, and **validity**, whether the assessment measures what it claims to measure. (See Chapter 3 for more on these topics.) There are two broad categories of personality assessments: projective tests and self-report inventories or questionnaires.

Projective Tests

Because psychodynamic theories emphasize the role of unconscious forces in determining personality and behavior, they need tools that can access information that is outside of or beyond a person's conscious awareness. In psychoanalysis sessions, Freud used free association, slips of the tongue, and dreams to gain information about unconscious feelings and influences. Based on these methods of clinical information gathering, researchers developed **projective tests**, which attempt to reveal the contents of the unconscious by getting people to verbally express unconscious issues in response to either an arbitrary or ambiguous shape or image. In projective tests, the person's response to the ambiguous image is assumed to be a *projection* of their unconscious thoughts, feelings, and impulses. Two projective tests are the Rorschach inkblot test and the Thematic Apperception Test (TAT).

The **Rorschach inkblot test** involves asking people to explain what they see in an ambiguous image called an inkblot. An inkblot is formed by placing ink on paper, folding the paper in half, and then separating the halves. A standardized set of ten inkblots is used in assessments, and testers are trained to interpret responses to them. A person's response is scored by examining how many of the ten responses refer to the entire ink blot, major details of the inkblot that do not include the entire blot, minor details to which most people will not generally respond, the shading of the ink, the colors of the ink, and whether or not the figures discerned in the blot are static or moving.

Figure 17.8 Inkblot

Personality theorist Henry Murray (1893–1988), who was strongly influenced by Jung, developed the **Thematic Apperception Test (TAT)**, which involves presenting to people a standardized set of ambiguous photographs or illustrations. Images can show one, two, or more people in a setting. The nature of the setting may not be clear, and the relationship between the people is up to the viewer to decide. Individuals taking the TAT are asked to create a story in response to an image that explains who the people are and what they are doing. They are asked what led up to the situation, what is happening in the picture, and what might happen later.

Both the Rorschach inkblot test and the Thematic Apperception Test are criticized for lacking validity, which means researchers cannot determine that they measure what they are supposed to measure. Although a trained professional interprets the tests, scoring the test results is subjective. Second, because of their subjective nature, the tests have low reliability, which means that the test results are not consistent when the same person repeats the test. Although projective tests can be useful in therapeutic situations and encourage dialogue between psychologist and client, they should not be considered methodologically sound tools for testing hypotheses derived from a personality theory.

Self-Report Personality Inventories

Researchers investigating trait theories use self-report personality inventories. Self-report personality inventories are questionnaires that consist of many closed-ended statements or questions that the test taker responds to with a yes/no or true/false response. The most well-known self-report inventory is the Minnesota Multiphasic Personality Inventory-2 Restructured Form (MMPI-2-RF). It consists of 338 true/false statements that measure a number of personality characteristics and has built-in scales that assess the validity and truthfulness of a person's responses. The MMPI-2-RF is primarily used for diagnostic purposes.

Another well-known personality inventory is the Myers-Briggs Type Indicator (MBTI). The Myers-Briggs is based on four pairs of personality types identified by Carl Jung. These include Extraversion/Introversion, Intuition/Sensing, Feeling/Thinking, and Judging/Perceiving. There are a total of 16 possible combinations of personality types, such as INFP, ESTJ, and so on. The MBTI is used in management, coaching and counseling, and leadership training. However, it has little scientific support, so if you are ever exposed to it, you must not take your results too seriously.

Raymond Cattell's 16 Personality Factor (16PF) Psychometric Questionnaire contains 187 statements that measure the 16 source traits he identified. Unlike the MMPI, Cattell's 16PF was developed to address normal personality factors. Costa and McCrea developed the Neuroticism Extraversion Openness Personality Inventory–Revised (NEO PI-R) to measure the dimensions of the Five Factor Model.

Well-designed self-reporting personality inventories tend to have higher reliability and validity than projective tests, but they also have problems. Participants might want to project a positive image and answer questions with some dishonesty, or they might unknowingly be deceiving themselves. They might also run through the questions quickly and not think carefully about exactly how the question pertains to them.

Observation and Interviews

Behaviorists and social-cognitive theorists rely on observation as the preferred way of measuring behavior and behavior patterns because those methods focus more exclusively on observable behavior. Other methods of measuring observable behavior include rating scales—assessments designed to obtain the judgments of observers in a standardized format. Rating scales are used by teachers or clinicians to measure select types of observable behaviors or traits.

Interviews—one-on-one conversations for the purpose of obtaining research information—are often used by humanistic theorists. While providing a wealth of personal information, the possibility of dishonesty is always a problem. Humanist theorists also use case studies (see Chapter 2) involving in-depth analysis of a single subject. Case studies are also used by psychodynamic theorists.

REFLECT ON THE ESSENTIAL QUESTION

Essential Question: *How can understanding personality theories help explain and improve your understanding of yourself and others?* On separate paper, make a chart like the one below to gather details to answer that question.

Psycho-dynamic	Neo-Freudian	Trait	Behavioral and Social-Cognitive	Humanistic	Biology-based	Assess-ments

KEY TERMS AND PEOPLE

PSYCHOANALYTIC

anal stage

castration anxiety

consciousness

defense
  mechanisms

denial

displacement

ego

Electra complex

erogenous zones

fixated

genital stage

id

identification

latency stage

libido

morality principle

Oedipus complex

oral stage

penis envy

phallic stage

pleasure principle

preconscious

projection

psychoanalysis

psychoanalytic
  theory

psychodynamic
  theories

psychosexual stage

rationalization

reaction-formation

reality principle

regression

repression

sublimation

superego

unconscious

NEO-FREUDIAN (PSYCHODY-NAMIC)

Anima

Animus

archetypes

collective
  unconscious

compensation

extravert

individual
  psychology

individuation

inferiority
  complex

introvert

overcompensa-
  tion

persona

personal
  unconscious

Shadow

TRAIT

16 Personality
  Factors (PF)
  Psychometric
  Questionnaire

factor analysis

Five Factor
  Model

source traits

surface traits

traits

BEHAVIORAL AND SOCIAL-COGNITIVE

behavioral
  approach

cognitive
  affective
  processing
  system (CAPS)

cognitive
  expectancy

cognitive theory
  of personality

environmental
  determinism

external locus of
  control

fundamental
  postulate

internal locus of
  control

locus of control

observational
  learning

personal-con-
  struct theory

reciprocal
  determinism

self-efficacy

social learning
  theory

HUMANISTIC

conditions of worth

fully functioning
  person

ideal self

incongruent

real self

self-concept

self-actualizing

unconditional posi-
  tive regard

BIOLOGY

heritability

temperament

ASSESSMENTS

projective tests

reliability

Rorschach inkblot
  test

Thematic Apper-
  ception Test
  (TAT)

validity

KEY PEOPLE

Alfred Adler

Albert Bandura

Paul Costa

Sigmund Freud

Carl Jung

Abraham Maslow

Robert McCrae

Carl Rogers

"He that has eyes to see and ears to hear may
convince himself that no mortal can keep a secret.
If his lips are silent, he chatters with his fingertips;
betrayal oozes out of him at every pore."

Sigmund Freud

1. To which aspect of psychoanalytic theory was Freud referring?

   (A) Defense mechanisms

   (B) Unconscious

   (C) Superego

   (D) Psychosexual stages

   (E) Libido

2. Rachel is a twenty-five-year-old woman who avoids visiting her mother because doing so causes her a great deal of anxiety. How might Carl Jung interpret this scenario?

   (A) Rachel's mother's parenting style was based on conditions of worth.

   (B) Rachel's mother possesses source traits that intimidate Rachel.

   (C) Rachel is mired in a complex involving her ideation of the Mother archetype.

   (D) Rachel possesses source traits that cause her to be intimidated by her mother.

   (E) Rachel cognitively processes the possible consequences of her mother's behavior as stressful.

3. Lauren was verbally reprimanded by her boss for dressing too casually at work and was told to go home during her lunch break and change into more professional attire. While driving home, Lauren gives the middle finger to a driver as he passes her by. Which defense mechanism is most closely associated with Lauren's behavior?

   (A) Reaction-formation

   (B) Projection

   (C) Rationalization

   (D) Denial

   (E) Displacement

4. One of the more severe criticisms leveled against Freudian psychoanalysis involves

   (A) Freud's overreliance on surface behaviors to infer causality

   (B) Freud's belief that humans are fundamentally animals with advanced intellectual capacities

   (C) Freud's insistence in the anatomically rooted inferiority of women

   (D) Freud's hypothesis about the Oedipus complex

   (E) Freud's assumption that personality characteristics stem from unconscious sources

The following images refer to Question 5.

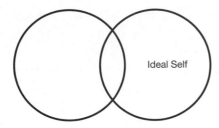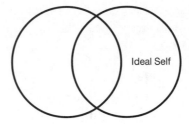

5. Which choice most closely corresponds with these images?

   (A) The image on the left illustrates the impact on the ideal self of conditions of worth.

   (B) Hans Eysenck's theory of source traits includes deviations of the ideal self.

   (C) The left circles for both images are missing the term *congruence*.

   (D) Both images reflect equal degrees of needs.

   (E) Carl Rogers believed in the fundamental dichotomy of human nature as good and evil.

6. Which choice expresses the most similarity between the work of Hans Eysenck and the work of Costa and McCrae?

(A) Both asserted that unconscious processes are a significant factor in determining behavior.

(B) Both observed that extraversion and neuroticism are prominent traits that guide behavior.

(C) Both saw traits as more learned through early childhood conditioning than determined through inheritance.

(D) Both rejected biological factors in determining behavioral traits.

(E) Both tend to focus on situational variations as determining the strengths of source traits.

7. Which theorist is most likely to use identical twin studies as evidence to support his or her theory?

(A) Sigmund Freud

(B) Carl Jung

(C) Karen Horney

(D) Abraham Maslow

(E) Gordon Allport

8. Why would a psychodynamic theorist prefer to use projective tests rather than interviews?

(A) Projective tests have higher validity and are more reliable.

(B) Projective tests like the MMPI-2-RF allow for insight into the underlying causes of a behavior under question.

(C) Interviews fail to take into consideration the cognitive aspect of learning a behavior.

(D) Projective tests like the TAT can reveal insights into unconscious motives.

(E) Interviews are unable to elicit honest responses regarding past events that formed aspects of the core personality.

Question 9 refers to the following quote.

> *"The curious paradox is when I accept myself just as I am, then I can change."*

9. Which choice most closely reflects the statement?

(A) Maslow's hierarchy of needs

(B) Rogers's belief in the importance of congruence

(C) Bandura's reciprocal determinism

(D) Mischel and Shoda's personality paradox

(E) Raymond Cattell's surface vs. source traits

10. Which choice best supports Abraham Maslow's humanistic view?

(A) Humans strive for self-actualization.

(B) The desire for fundamental stability is the need striven for most.

(C) Freud was a pessimist in the assumptions he based on his patients' outcomes.

(D) Humans have an innate need for acceptance that stems from conditions of worth.

(E) No matter how desolate or hopeless the situation, never underestimate the power of positive source traits.

FREE-RESPONSE QUESTIONS

1. Jennifer is twenty-nine and is experiencing a great deal of anxiety in her life. She is recently married and is contemplating divorce.

A) Discuss how each of the following would explain the origins of Jennifer's current state of mind. Be sure to explain each concept in the context of Jennifer's situation.

- Jungian psychodynamic theory
- Reciprocal determinism
- Five Factor Model
- Carl Rogers' humanistic approach

B) Discuss how you would use the following personality tests to support your explanations:

- 16 Personality Factors Psychometric Questionnaire
- Thematic Apperception Test
- Myers-Briggs Type Indicator

2. Thomas and Robert are adopting a baby soon and are familiar with the various theories involving personality development. They are looking forward to applying their understanding of numerous personality theories to promote healthy development of their child.

A) Explain how concepts from each of the following theorists would help Thomas and Robert understand their new baby:
   • Sigmund Freud
   • Alfred Adler
   • Abraham Maslow
   • Hans and Sybil Eysenck

B) Explain how each of the following ideas would lead to a different way for Thomas and Robert to approach their child's frustrations:
   • Reciprocal determinism
   • Phallic stage
   • Archetypes
   • Conditions of worth

WRITE AS A PSYCHOLOGIST: AVOID CONTRADICTIONS

Many free-response questions will have multiple parts, as does the one above. In some cases, the second or third part of a question will refer back to earlier parts or contain some overlap. For example, in the first part of the question above, you are asked to explain how Freud's concepts, among others, would help Thomas and Robert understand their baby. In the second part, you are asked to explain how the idea of phallic stage would lead to a different way from the others to approach frustrations. As you recall, the phallic stage is part of Freud's theory, so you will be discussing Freudian theory twice in this question. Be sure that the different parts of your answer are not contradictory. Check that nothing you write for one part of the question contradicts anything you write for another part of the question. For more guidance on answering free-response questions, see pages xxii–xxiii.

18

Cultural Context of Personality

"[I]t is safe to say that an individual simply cannot be understood with any degree of completeness or precision, without careful consideration of the culture in which he or she lives."

– Harry Triandis

Essential Question: How does culture influence personality?

To some degree, personality is a product of **culture**, a group's shared beliefs, attitudes, standards of behavior, customs, and values that one generation passes to the next. Culture encompasses a shared way of thinking and a shared way of understanding how the world works. For example, American culture contributes to personality traits tied to individualism and expressions of anger, while the culture of Tahiti focuses on the need to be gentle and considerate of others. In Japanese culture, people experience *oime*, which means the feeling of personal or psychological indebtedness to someone else. The ability to experience this emotion is a profound part of Japanese personality. This chapter will explore various influences that culture has on personality.

Research Methods for Studying Cultural Influences on Personality

Cultural psychology is the study of how behavior and personality are both embedded in culture and, at the same time, influential in shaping that culture. In Chapter 17, you read that both biology and the environment play a role in personality. Culture is a powerful environmental influence.

Researchers use two main approaches to study links between culture and personality: the cultural/indigenous approach and the cross-cultural approach. The **cultural/indigenous approach** focuses on studying the unique aspects of a culture without reference to another culture. This approach is sometimes called **emic**, which means from a perspective that is inside the culture. The emic approach looks at a single culture and uses a bottom-up approach to try to understand a cultural phenomenon on its own terms.

The **cross-cultural approach** focuses on understanding human behavior and thought in diverse cultural settings for the purpose of finding universal aspects across all cultures. This approach is referred to as the **etic** approach. While the emic approach looks *within* cultures to gain understanding about that culture and its behavioral norms and personality types, the etic approach uses a top-down approach to look across cultures from the outside to understand general human behaviors and personality types.

Current thinking among social scientists in a variety of related fields embraces **cultural relativism**, the principle that a people's customs, beliefs, and attitudes should be viewed from a neutral, unbiased perspective and that there are no universal standards by which to judge cultures. The cultural/indigenous approach recognizes the legitimacy of cultural relativism. Both the cultural/indigenous and cross-cultural approaches are useful, and the best approach may be to use research techniques from each.

From Anthropology to Cultural Psychology

Before the early 20th century, Western culture (Western Europe and British-influenced countries, including the United States, Australia, and New Zealand) dominated the field of **anthropology**—the study of human societies and cultures—and this dominance reflected a belief that Western culture was superior to all others. In the late 19th century, anthropology relied heavily on the Darwinian perspective that some societies were more evolved than others. The guiding principle in anthropology was that Western cultures were advanced and all others were primitive and inferior. This belief in the superiority of Western culture was a form of scientific racism.

In the early 20th century, through his pioneering anthropological study of cultures, Franz Boas (1858–1942) was the first to reject this scientific racism and became the leading proponent of the idea that human behavior was a product of cultural differences acquired through socialization. Boas coined the term *cultural relativism* and laid the groundwork for cultural psychology and the study of cultural influences on personality.

A student of Boas, Ruth Benedict (1887–1948) continued the research into the links between culture and personality by studying the culturally derived personality characteristics of American Indian groups and the indigenous people near Papua New Guinea (located north of Australia along the southwestern Pacific Rim). Benedict demonstrated that individual personality traits were fundamentally linked to the culture in which the person was socialized.

Ruth Benedict (pictured here) and Margaret Mead were leading anthropologists in their time.

A close associate of Benedict, Margaret Mead (1901–1978) contributed extensively to the study of culture and personality. For example, she rejected the idea that intelligence was a product solely of biology and demonstrated that environmental factors such as family upbringing and socioeconomic factors play a larger role. Mead conducted groundbreaking research in the 1930s on temperamental differences between males and females. Her studies of indigenous cultures in Papua New Guinea revealed gender-specific personality traits that she asserted were not linked to biological differences between the sexes but rather stemmed from cultural differences. For example, among the Biwat people, both males and females were aggressive and competitive and stressed hierarchical status. But among the neighboring Chambri people, gender roles were much more distinct. Females assumed a more dominant social role, and males took on a less dominant role and showed more emotional dependence than their female counterparts. Gender alone cannot account for these differences between the Biwat and Chambri people.

The fields of cultural psychology and cross-cultural psychology began to take shape in the mid to late 20th century. The first conference to facilitate collaboration between Western and non-Western researchers was held in 1967. Following that conference, newsletters and journals were established to foster communication about ongoing research and publicize research findings. Together, prominent researchers developed standards for methodology and ethics appropriate for both etic and emic research.

A number of significant theoretical developments emerged from this scientific activity. One of the most important was the work of Harry Triandis in exploring the influences of individualistic and collectivistic cultures on personality traits. Another is the recent research led by Hazel Markus on the ways in which culture influences our concepts of self.

Margaret Mead studied the peoples of Papua New Guinea. In this photograph, she captured a father and daughter on the island of Manus, with the child resting her hands around her father's neck, a typical position. She wrote, "As soon as children can walk, they become their fathers' constant companions."

Individualistic and Collectivistic Cultural Influences on Personality

Harry Triandis (b. 1926) significantly expanded the understanding of cultural influences by developing a theoretical framework that helped researchers study concepts from social psychology in the context of culture and make comparisons across cultural groups. Triandis's theoretical framework draws on concepts from ecological psychology and anthropology to give a deeper understanding of two main types of cultures: individualistic and collectivistic.

In strong **individualistic cultures**, the needs and desires of the individual take priority over the needs of the group. In strong **collectivistic cultures**, the group takes priority over the individual. Individualistic and collectivistic values exist on a continuum, and there are variations within and among cultures.

CONTRASTS IN EMPHASIS BETWEEN COMMON INDIVIDUALISTIC AND COLLECTIVISTIC VALUES	
Continuum of Values	
Individualistic ⟵——————————————————⟶	**Collectivistic**
Independence ⟵————————————————⟶	Interdependence
Individual rights ⟵————————————⟶	Obligations to others
Self-sufficiency ⟵————————————⟶	Reliance on group
True to own values and beliefs ⟵————⟶	Adhere to traditional values
Continuously improve practices (progress) ⟵⟶	Maintain traditional practices
Pursue individual goals/interests ⟵————⟶	Fulfill roles within group
Individual achievement ⟵——————————⟶	Group achievement
Competition between individuals ⟵————⟶	Competition between groups
Self-determination and individual choice ⟵———⟶	Group or hierarchical decision-making
Shame/guilt due to individual failure ⟵—————⟶	Shame/guilt due to failing the group
Independent living ⟵——————————⟶	Living with kin
Seek help if needed ⟵————————————⟶	Take care of own
Strong individual property rights ⟵————⟶	Property shared within group
Individuals seek knowledge (often textual) ⟵———⟶	Elders transmit knowledge (often oral)
Objects valued for technological uses ⟵———⟶	Objects valued for social uses

Figure 18.1

The Role Ecology Plays in Culture

One of Triandis's early contributions was to recognize the influence ecology has on how cultural characteristics develop. **Ecology**—the physical environment, including natural resources, terrain, and climate—significantly influences the development of culture. If ecology is linked to culture and culture is linked to personality, then ecology eventually influences personality.

Ecological features such as mountains and large bodies of water contribute to cultural isolation. Over time, isolation leads a culture to develop specific rules of conduct and **norms**, which are group-determined standards or expectations of behavior. In a tight, homogeneous culture, people conform strongly to their culture's norms. These norms then manifest themselves in personality traits that are unique to that culture. Examples of tight cultures that developed in isolated conditions include North American Inuit groups and the people of Japan. In contrast, loose cultures, such as the United States and France, have greater tolerance for deviations from cultural norms.

Ecology can play a role in the development of regional cultural characteristics as well. One ecological influence is the mobility of resources needed for survival. For example, a culture that depends on cattle, which have high mobility, as a survival resource tends to develop a culture of honor. A culture of honor is typified by aggression and defensiveness in response to insults and threats. A culture of honor is more common in the southern region of the United States, which has a historically high concentration of cattle ranching, than in the northern region.

Climate also influences culture. Cultures with very cold climates, such as Norway and Iceland, tend to display less violent characteristics, while cultures with warmer climates, such as Afghanistan and Colombia, show more violent characteristics.

When Triandis observed the link between ecology and the need for connection or separation, he inferred something about how common cultural characteristics might emerge. Personality characteristics that are common to a culture develop to some degree as a result of the physical ecology of the area that culture occupies.

Ecologies fostering isolation, such as many in Mongolia, often lead to the development of tight cultures, which in turn influence personality.

Collectivistic and Individualistic Cultures

We know that ecology helps determine the degree to which a culture is tight or loose. Tightness or looseness is a **cultural syndrome**, a pattern of behaviors unique to a specific culture.

Complexity is another cultural syndrome. A culture can be considered less complex if it lacks diversity and social strata and its methods of survival are limited. More complex cultures, such as industrialized or postindustrialized ones, have diverse social strata, socioeconomic diversity, urbanization, and usually advanced technology.

According to Triandis, **collectivism** versus **individualism** is the most significant cultural syndrome. Not all collectivistic cultures are the same, however, and individualistic cultures also vary. For example, India is a collectivistic culture that emphasizes conforming to approved beliefs and behaviors, in-group cohesion, tolerance for authoritarianism, submission to authority, and acceptance of hierarchy and social strata. Japan's collectivistic culture, in contrast, emphasizes cooperation and empathy. Scandinavia, Australia, and New Zealand are individualistic cultures. In those countries, people have a strong appreciation and need for autonomy, independence, and uniqueness. In the individualistic cultures of the United States and Western Europe, competitiveness, hierarchy and social strata, and independence are especially important.

Family structures differ depending on the degree of collectivism or individualism in a culture. Collectivistic cultures emphasize extended family systems, whereas individualistic cultures emphasize the nuclear family system. Additionally, families that allow for easy separation among individuals promote individualism, and individualistic cultures more frequently have people who live further away from and have less frequent contact with grandparents, aunts and uncles, and cousins.

People in collectivistic cultures focus on the group to a great extent. The primary focus in collectivistic cultures is relationships, and individual needs remain in the background. Collectivistic cultural norms tend to focus on equality and cooperation. The opposite is true for individualistic cultures. The individual is the focus and the group remains in the background. Norms in individualistic cultures tend to make equity a priority.

Values are the lasting beliefs in a culture about right and wrong. Values among collectivistic cultures focus on family security, social order, the importance of tradition, harmony, and courtesy. Values in individualistic cultures include competitiveness, independence, self-sufficiency, and broadmindedness.

Assessing Individualistic and Collectivistic Personality Traits

Triandis's research on individualistic and collectivistic cultures has provided insight into the influence of culture on personality development. It is broadly applied to cross-cultural communication, marketing, and international business, and measurement instruments developed to assess these ideas have been shown to accurately predict behavior in many contexts. Critics point out that although culture is a significant environmental influence on personality and leads to shared traits, all cultures have many individual variations within them.

Culture and Two Construals of Self

Most Western cultures assume that each person's core sense of self—self-concept—is shaped by internal attributes and is, by its very nature, separate, unique, and autonomous. Hazel Markus (b. 1949) and her colleague Shinobu Kitayama have shown that this Western-centric concept of self fails to account for the profound influence culture exerts in shaping and reinforcing two different concepts of self.

In social psychology, how people perceive themselves and interpret interactions with others is called a **construal**. Markus and Kitayama assert that cultural factors determine to various degrees whether someone will have an independent construal of the self or an interdependent construal of the self. These two construals strongly shape an individual's sense of self, cognitive processes, motivation, and emotion.

The Independent Construal of Self

In individualistic cultures, the **independent self construal** is the norm. With this construal, people define their identity by looking at qualities they have within them. That is, a sense of personality comes from within the person, not the culture. This independent construal is culturally driven and typical of American and Western European cultures.

In Chapter 17, you read about Abraham Maslow's concept of the self-actualizing person and Carl Rogers's fully-functioning self. Both concepts reveal the cultural norm of the independent construal of the self. Even in the context of social connections and relationships with others, the primary driver is the self and not the relationship or social context. People who hold independent self-construals do have meaningful relationships with others, but their sense of self is what dictates the meaningfulness of the relationships.

The Interdependent Construal of Self

In many non-Western, African, and Latin American cultures, the culturally driven norm is the interdependent construal of the self. For people with an **interdependent self-construal**, social relationships take priority, *not* their selves as individuals. The Japanese culture is strongly associated with the interdependent self. And the sense of self in an interdependent self-construal is only fully complete when it is put in the context of a relevant social relationship. As Markus and Kitayama point out, "The Japanese are most fully human in the context of others."

The interdependent self-construal is always tied to context. In Japanese culture, for example, how one presents the self is a matter of choice based on the social circumstances. For example, if a friend visits, the hosting friend will not ask what drink the friend wants—soft drink, water, juice—but instead would be expected to know what the friend would prefer and offer that. And the visiting friend would not expect to be given a choice. If the context were reversed, the presentation of self would be reversed as well.

The interdependent self has internal characteristics or traits, just as an independent self has, but these personal traits do not influence behavior in a situation. The social situation brings out or elicits expected cultural responses. This relationship between the situation and the self is culturally determined from early childhood socialization. Culturally driven personality characteristics, which lead to opinions, emotional reactions, and internal traits, are subordinate to the situation, and the individual is expected to regulate them.

When the cultural norm is an interdependent self, control of internal attributes indicates maturity. For example, Japanese culture considers the Western-oriented sense of ego and the ideal of self-assertion childish. Furthermore, Japanese culture considers failing to connect with others and subordinate oneself to the group a profound failure. The opposite is true for the independent self. Failure or weakness is bowing to peer pressure or being unable to stand up for oneself. For the interdependent self, cooperation is a self-affirming act. Giving in to the group is a sign of maturity, not a sign of weakness.

You might be tempted to conclude that people with interdependent self-construals are selfless givers who indiscriminately give in to the needs of all groups. However, people with interdependent selves discriminate between ingroup—the social group with which they identify psychologically—and outgroup—social groups with which they do not identify. Interdependent selves show preference to ingroup members, but they treat outgroup members differently. The interdependent characteristics are not expressed with members of outgroups. And given the importance of reciprocal relationships in defining the interdependent self, the distinctions between ingroup and outgroup are much more important than for the typical independent self, for which any group usually plays a secondary role to the autonomous independent self. Figure 18.2 summarizes these comparisons between independent and interdependent self-construals.

INDEPENDENT VERSUS INTERDEPENDENT SELF-CONSTRUALS		
	Independent	**Interdependent**
Self-Concept	Shaped by internal attributes and goals, without social connections	Determined by social relationships
Characteristics of Self	Stable—much the same in all situations	Flexible—varies according to the situation
Values	Personal achievement, self-expression, personal rights	Solidarity, promotion of others' goals, social responsibilities
Devalues	Conformity	Self-promotion
Example Cultures	Western—United States, Canada, and European countries	Asian and developing nations; indigenous populations

Figure 18.2

The work of Markus and Kitayama highlights fundamental personality differences between the independent self and the interdependent self in three areas: cognition, emotion, and motivation. As you read about these culturally derived personality differences, you will begin to realize just how significant a role culture plays in shaping personality.

Cognitive Differences Between Independent and Interdependent Selves

How you think and what you think about reveals a great deal about who you are. In this context, **cognition** has two dimensions. There is content—*what* people think—and there is process—*how* people think. Cognition is a key aspect of your sense of self, and the culturally determined independent or interdependent self-construals affect what you think and how you think.

Three aspects of cognition are affected by self-construal:

1. Self-knowledge and knowledge about others

2. Processing self-knowledge and knowledge about others

3. Thinking in an interpersonal context

Self-Knowledge and Knowledge About Others With an independent self-construal, people's understanding of their self-defining inner attributes form the basis of their knowledge about themselves. Their self-knowledge is more in-depth and is more important to them than their knowledge of others.

In contrast, the interdependent self pays more attention to knowledge about others. If people perceive their selves as integral parts of a larger, important social group, the need to understand others is obviously important.

Maintaining a strong understanding of others—knowing how they are feeling and anticipating their needs and desires—leads to stronger connectedness. For the interdependent self, knowledge about others is more often more elaborate and unique than knowledge about self.

Processing Knowledge About Self and Others Independent and interdependent self-construals also differ in the way an individual processes knowledge about self and others. The independent self tends to process knowledge of self and others in overgeneralizations. The independent self also tends to easily infer that internal attributes cause behaviors. In contrast, the interdependent self is much less likely to overgeneralize knowledge of self and others. Instead, the specific social context dictates how a person organizes knowledge of self and others. With an interdependent self-construal, self-knowledge and knowledge about others is context driven, not inner driven.

For example, in one study, an Asian-Indian group and an American group responded to a hypothetical scenario in which a passenger on a motorcycle was killed in an accident and the driver, a lawyer late to a court date, chose not to tend to the victim. The Indian (interdependent self-construal) group did not attribute negative internal attributes to the motorcycle driver and described obligations to others as influencing his actions. They felt no need to speculate about the inner attributes of the driver because doing so would violate interdependent self-construal. The American (independent self-construal) group, in contrast, consistently identified inner personality attributes to explain the driver's actions. An independent self sees the actions of anyone as independent from the surroundings.

Thinking in an Interpersonal Context How an individual is able to think appears to be connected to interpersonal context. For example, in China, the interdependent self is the cultural norm. When Chinese students were asked to respond to hypothetical "what if" questions, they became frustrated and unable to respond. People with independent self-construals had little difficulty answering hypothetical questions. Why would this be the case?

People with independent self-construals had no problem separating the hypothetical questions from the interviewer asking them. But the Chinese students with interdependent self-construals were raised to be sensitive to the social context in which the questions were asked. To simply answer the hypothetical questions required the students with interdependent selves to ignore the interpersonal context of the interviewer and themselves. They could not do this because of the strong cultural norm of deference to authority—the interviewer—and sensitivity to why the interviewer would be asking such questions. People from China, as well as all Asian cultures, are perfectly capable of thinking hypothetically. In fact, studies show that Chinese, Taiwanese, and Japanese students perform better than American students on hypothetical math questions such as those on the SAT. The difference is that the students understood that answering hypothetical questions that test competence and performance is tied to their reasoning skills and not the social context.

Emotional Differences Between Independent and Interdependent Selves

Are emotions universal, or does culture play a role in emotional experience? In the context of independent and interdependent self-construals, there are two types of emotions. **Ego-focused emotions** are centered on internal independent attributes. These types of emotions help reinforce our independent, autonomous, and self-defining sense of self. Examples include anger, pride, and happiness. **Other-focused emotions** are experienced in a social context or relational situations. These types of emotions serve to reinforce the interdependent needs of the group or relationship. Examples include shame, sympathy, indebtedness, and empathy.

A person with an independent self-construal is culturally influenced to rely on and experience emotions that tend to be ego-focused. These emotional experiences reinforce the autonomous sense of self. In individualistic cultures that foster an independent self, ego-focused emotions reinforce the cultural norms of autonomy and separateness. If you operate from an independent self-construal, others may share your anger or happiness, but these emotions are rooted in your personal sense of self. They are most often caused by threats to or validation of your sense of self.

In collectivistic cultures, emotional experience more often is tied to reinforcing or maintaining relationships. Experiencing other-focused emotions like sympathy or shame reinforces the interdependent sense of self. People with interdependent self-construals are proficient at regulating and expressing their other-focused emotions and equally adept at suppressing their ego-focused emotions. This self-regulation is a natural part of living in a culture in which relationships take priority over the individual.

An experiment that compared how well people could recognize the ego-focused emotion of happiness or joy illustrates the difference between independent and interdependent emotional experience. When people with independent self-construals and people with interdependent self-construals viewed an image of a face expressing happiness, the people with independent selves easily recognized the expression, but the people with interdependent selves had more difficulty. Why? People with independent self-construals see the emotional expression (joy) as an expression of an inner feeling not connected to a social context. In contrast, people from collectivistic cultures had difficulty because they are accustomed to experiencing happiness only in a social or relationship context. The most important thing that gives the facial expression meaning, the social context, is missing.

Japanese culture illustrates several other emotional differences between independent and interdependent self-construals. Figure 18.3 shows several emotions that are central and often intensely important for a culture that fosters connectedness. These emotions may seem foreign to the independent self.

JAPANESE INTERDEPENDENT EMOTIONS	
Amae	Feeling of being unconditionally loved and cared for and of depending on another person
Fureai	Feeling a close connection with somebody else
Shitashimi	Feeling familiar, approachable, friendly
Oime	Feeling psychologically indebted to somebody else
Sonkei	Feeling of respect for someone
Tanomi	Feeling like relying or depending on someone
Sugari	Feeling like leaning on someone

Figure 18.3

The emotion *oime*, which is the feeling of being psychologically indebted to someone else, highlights the power of culture in shaping emotion. This feeling may not seem important for those with independent self-construals. But *oime* is an emotional experience that Japanese people report more frequently and with more intensity than anger or sadness. This feeling of *oime* is extremely unpleasant and indicates the deep psychological importance of fulfilling obligations to others and the negative emotional consequences of not meeting those obligations.

Motivational Differences Between Independent and Interdependent Selves

As you read in Chapter 13, motivation explains the desire or drive to reach a goal as an inner-driven process. But motivation can be culturally determined, and there are significant differences between what motivates an independent and interdependent self. Achievement motivation and the motive toward self-actualization illustrate the differences.

Achievement For the independent self-construal, motivation is usually rooted in inner drives. Motives or needs that enhance a person's individual sense of self, such as the need to achieve, take high priority. The motivation to achieve for the independent self is focused on the need to separate from the pack and further define the self in a more autonomous way. Examples are easy to find in the American individualistic culture. Think about how the valedictorian, the employee of the month, the winner of the Oscar for best actor, or the Nobel Prize winner are all reflections of individual achievement.

For the interdependent self-construal, motivation is not tied to autonomous recognition or focused on separating from others. Individual achievement needs are subordinated to the needs of the group and are centered on affirming an individual's connectedness within a group or relationship. For example, Japanese and Chinese students have a strong need to achieve academically, but their academic achievement is not for the purpose of individual recognition, as is the cultural norm for American and other Western cultures. Their need to achieve academically is directly tied to maintaining or elevating the pride or sense of accomplishment for the family. Japanese and Chinese students are distancing or separating themselves from the pack, but the important difference is the motivation behind their hard work. They are doing so to fulfill their role within the family.

Self-Actualization Self-actualization, the highest level of motivation in Maslow's hierarchy of needs (see pages 306–308), is each person's natural desire to achieve his or her full potential. But according to the independent-interdependent model of self-construal, self-actualization needs are fundamentally different depending on the self-construal.

Self-actualizing needs are framed in terms of an independent self-construal. They stem from the inner drive to fulfill one's unique inner potential. There is an inherent separateness and autonomous quality to self-actualizing. Self-actualizing people are often seen as non conformists and are celebrated as such in individualistic cultures.

By contrast, in collectivistic cultures that promote the interdependent self-construal, the need for fulfillment is focused on the outward qualities of respectability and being the ideal participant in interpersonal or group relationships. The interdependent self is driven to pursue fulfillment needs not from inner drives but from outer drives connected with groups and their relationships within those groups. In fact, the interdependent self-construal does not value self-actualization in the Western sense.

The important work of cultural psychology that began in the 20th century has become more prominent in the 21st century. This field has expanded our understanding of personality to include the important contributions of culture and appreciation for the rich diversity that culture brings to all.

A valedictorian with an independent self-construal (left) is motivated by a sense of personal achievement. Graduates with an interdependent self-construal (right) achieve to raise the pride of their families.

In their book *Psychology of Diversity: Beyond Prejudice and Racism*, James M. Jones and John F. Dovidio define the psychology of diversity as "basic psychological processes that are triggered when we encounter people who are different from us in significant and salient ways, or experience being treated differently by others because of our social status." Psychologists focusing on diversity recognize that interactions at three levels—individual, institutional, and cultural—can pose challenges.

Consider Ramon, whose family recently immigrated from Colombia. He plays first chair trumpet in the high school band, in which he is respected and fully accepted. He has made good friends with other band members. When he is out of the school environment, however, he often feels self-conscious because it seems like people are judging him on his appearance and his accent. Ramon is experiencing a diversity challenge at an individual level.

Molly has been a Catholic all her life. When she grew into young womanhood, however, she began to resent the idea that females in her religion could never become priests. She is experiencing a gender diversity challenge at the institutional level.

In her book *"Why Are All the Black Kids Sitting Together in the Cafeteria? and Other Conversations About Race,"* Beverly Daniel Tatum points out that observers quite often notice that Black kids tend to sit together in cafeterias, but they fail to notice that the White kids tend to sit together also. Kids with similar backgrounds tend to sit and socialize with one another. They are not necessarily intentionally excluding those from other races, but they simply tend to feel more comfortable with those who share similar values or worldviews. However, when observers see this, they tend to "pathologize" the ethnic populations and ignore the majority population's exact same behaviors. This example illustrates a diversity challenge at the cultural level.

Practice: Make an effort, possibly in the school cafeteria, to socialize with students who represent a culture different from your own. Write down your experiences after you do so, and explain them in the context of the definition of the psychology of diversity by Jones and Dovidio. In small group discussions, compare your experiences with those of your classmates.

Essential Question: *How does culture influence personality?* On separate paper, make a chart like the one below to gather details to answer that question.

Research Methods	Cultural Dimensions	Individualistic and Collectivistic	Construals of Self

KEY TERMS		
anthropology	culture	norms
cognition	ecology	other-focused emotions
collectivism	ego-focused emotions	values
collectivistic cultures	emic	
construal	etic	
cross-cultural approach	independent self construal	
cultural psychology	individualism	
cultural relativism	individualistic cultures	
cultural syndrome	interdependent self-construal	
cultural/indigenous approach		

1. If you are an American public school teacher in a diverse American city, which suggestion is most aligned with research in cultural contexts of personality?

   (A) Establish a clear set of cultural rules, and make sure all students abide by them.

   (B) Be aware that some students may come from an individualistic culture, and this will conflict with your collectivistic tendencies.

   (C) If you are sufficiently familiar with the subcultures of your students, use your knowledge of them to better relate to your students and their parents.

   (D) Understand that many of your students will be less motivated to learn because they do not possess American attributes of achievement.

   (E) Communicate to parents in the language they are most comfortable speaking in.

2. According to Harry Triandis,

   (A) a "culture of honor" is ecologically connected to highly mobile sources of survival

   (B) a strong homogeneous culture will tend to have porous and loose borders

   (C) ecology that produces loose culture also produces highly restrictive cultural traits

   (D) violent cultures tend to be cold climates

   (E) the ideal ecology is one that is warmer than average, includes high mountains, and has highly mobile sources of survival

3. Hazel Markus and Shinobu Kitayama asserted that

   (A) collectivistic cultures value extended family systems, while individualistic cultures value the nuclear family

   (B) collectivistic cultures value family security, social order, tradition, and courtesy

   (C) cultural syndromes define individual personalities

   (D) cultural factors influence self-construals

   (E) ego-focused emotions are centered on internal independent attributes

4. The cognitive aspect of an interdependent self-construal is best revealed in which of the following?

(A) Maintaining a high level of knowledge and understanding about others is more important that expressing knowledge about oneself.

(B) How a person organizes knowledge about himself or herself tends to be in a hierarchical and self-defining perspective.

(C) A person's level of motivation is based on inner drives to please others.

(D) Knowledge of self is elaborate and distinctive and frames understanding of others.

(E) People's other-focused emotions serve to reinforce and regulate their own behavior and validate the self.

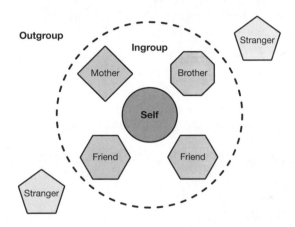

5. Which choice most accurately reflects the image above?

(A) A person with this self-construal comes from a culture that tolerates arranged marriages.

(B) A person with this self-construal has a personality that relies on other-focused emotions and suppresses ego-focused emotions.

(C) A person with this self-construal has a personality that tends to find motivation from within and depends on social context to determine how to relate to others.

(D) A person with this self-construal has a personality that tends to stress self-affirming, ego-focused emotions and is comfortable answering hypothetical questions in a face-to-face session.

(E) A person with this self-construal is deeply troubled by hypothetical questions and tends to have emotional experiences that reinforce the reciprocal needs of a relationship.

6. Which choice most strongly reflects cultural relativism?

   (A) Cultural/indigenous approach and emic

   (B) Cultural/indigenous approach and etic

   (C) Interdependent construal of self and emic

   (D) Cross-cultural approach and etic

   (E) Independent construal of self and etic

7. Which statement is most accurate regarding temperamental differences between males and females?

   (A) Franz Boas insisted that there was a strong degree of universal temperament between men and women across cultures.

   (B) Margaret Mead asserted that temperamental differences between the sexes could to a degree be explained through enculturation.

   (C) Ruth Benedict proved that biological forces lay at the root of temperamental differences between females and males.

   (D) Harry Triandis theorized that males and females have different self-construals.

   (E) Hazel Markus and Shinobu Kitayama demonstrated that temperamental differences between men and women are most influenced by culturally derived construals of the self.

8. Which statement best explains the difference between someone with an independent self-construal and someone with an interdependent self-construal if asked a hypothetical question by an interviewer?

   (A) People with interdependent self-construals have more practice answering "what if" questions and therefore perform better than those with independent self-construals.

   (B) People with independent self-construals have more practice answering "what if" questions and therefore perform better than those with interdependent self-construals.

   (C) People with interdependent self-construals perform well on hypothetical questions that test their reasoning abilities.

   (D) People with interdependent self-construals consider the question in a social context and try to understand why the interviewer is asking the question.

   (E) People with independent self-construals consider the question in a social context and try to understand why the interviewer is asking the question.

9. Which of the following is a value of a collectivistic culture?

(A) Broadmindedness

(B) Courtesy

(C) Self-sufficiency

(D) Equal respect for ingroup and outgroup

(E) Property

10. Which statement best explains why someone with an interdependent self-construal might not recognize an angry expression in a photograph of one person?

(A) People with interdependent self-contruals do not experience anger.

(B) People with interdependent self-construals understand emotional expressions only in a social context.

(C) People with interdependent self-construals feel anger but repress it.

(D) People with interdependent self-construals experience some emotions that people with an independent self-construal do not.

(E) People with interdependent self-construals have trouble recognizing other-focused feelings.

FREE-RESPONSE QUESTIONS

1. You are a marketing manager responsible for increasing sales of a high-definition television set internationally.

A) Discuss how you will shape your marketing based on the following:
   - Triandis's explanations of individualistic and collectivistic cultures
   - Markus and Kitayama's theory of construals of self

B) Develop an experiment that will attempt to test the validity of your marketing approach. Identify and explain the following elements of your experiment:
   - Independent and dependent variables
   - Control group and experimental group
   - Random selection and random assignment

2. You work for a study-abroad program where you place American university students at universities in China. These students need to understand the cultural characteristics related to personality that differ from American culture so that they can avoid conflict and enhance the relationships they will develop in the course of their stay. Discuss how you would address each of the following cultural personality characteristics as part of your orientation program for your study-abroad students:

- Cognitive characteristics
- Emotional characteristics
- Motivational characteristics

Shenzhen University in the Chinese province of Guangdong

UNIT 10: Review

In this unit, you sought answers to these essential questions about personality.

Chapter 17: How can understanding personality theories help explain and improve your understanding of yourself and others?

Chapter 18: How does culture influence personality?

Apply what you have learned about personality by answering the free-response question below.

FREE-RESPONSE QUESTION

Matthew is a hard-working business executive who attempts to meet deadlines and do high-quality work. He leads a team of employees and interacts with them freely. He does occasionally "butt heads" with others because he wants things done his way and will not always listen to the opinions of others. In his free time, he enjoys flying helicopters and traveling to new cities. He has a small group of friends and enjoys going to dinner and having small gatherings with good friends at his home, but he is uncomfortable with large crowds and with people whom he does not know well. Matthew likes things very neat and organized and can become anxious when things are out of place.

A) Using the Five Factor Model of personality, identify how each of the following would apply to Matthew's personality:
- Conscientiousness
- Openness
- Extraversion

B) What tool would trait theorists likely use to assess Matthew's personality, and what would it tell them?

C) Explain how other approaches to personality might explain Matthew's preference for small gatherings over larger crowds using the following psychological concepts:
- Reciprocal determinism
- Vicarious conditioning
- Operant conditioning
- Sensory overload

UNIT 11: Testing and Individual Differences

Chapter 19 Testing and Intelligence

Unit Overview

Smart phones, smart tablets, smart cars, smart thermostats, smart TVs—everywhere you look today, products seem to be operating with a quality once reserved for living beings: intelligence. Many machine intelligence experts believe that by 2050 computers will have human-level intelligence. At the same time, advancements in the "editing" of human genomes make possible the speculation that by the same year, humans will have started the process of dramatically increasing their own IQ, possibly to 1,000.

What is intelligence that it can be bestowed on a machine and developed in a genetic laboratory? This unit explores answers to that question, as well as how intelligence is measured, how its definition is influenced by culture, and how individuals differ in their cognitive abilities.

Key Topics

- Intelligence and characteristics of how psychologists measure intelligence
  — abstract versus verbal measures
  — speed of processing
- Cultural influence on the definition of intelligence
- Similarities and differences between historic and contemporary theories of intelligence (e.g., Charles Spearman, Howard Gardner, Robert Sternberg)
- Test design by psychologists, including standardization strategies and other techniques to establish reliability and validity

- Interpretation of scores in terms of the normal curve
- Relevant labels related to intelligence testing (e.g., *gifted, cognitively disabled*)
- Appropriate testing practices, particularly in relation to culture-fair test uses
- Key contributors in intelligence research and testing (e.g., Alfred Binet, Francis Galton, Howard Gardner, Charles Spearman, Robert Sternberg, Lewis Terman, David Wechsler)

Source*: AP® Psychology Course and Exam Description*

19

Testing and Intelligence

*"I know that I am intelligent, because I know that
I know nothing."*

—Socrates

Essential Question: How have researchers defined and assessed intelligence from the early days of the field through the present?

When you refer to the captain of your school's chess team, you may describe him or her as "smart," but what does this mean? Are smart people conscientious? Do they complete their work on time? Are they good at taking exams? Are they able to quickly come up with answers to questions or think abstractly? This chapter will attempt to answer those questions by examining how researchers have described and measured intelligence over time.

Defining and Measuring Intelligence

While most agree that intelligence exists, just what is it and how can we clearly categorize the skills associated with it? Some consider **intelligence** to be related to success, others believe it reflects one's ability to successfully navigate day-to-day life, and yet others believe that intelligence refers to one's ability to solve novel problems. This section will discuss how individuals have attempted to define the components they believed make up one's intelligence. As you read, consider what factors you believe make up intelligence and which assessment techniques you believe best capture this abstract construct.

Cultural Differences in Defining Intelligence

The qualities believed to make up intelligence differ from culture to culture. What it means to be "smart" can vary considerably depending upon the skills and talents a society values, which can vary over time and place. A culture's definition of intelligence will in many ways also define how intelligence is measured. For this reason, when tests of intelligence are used on cultural groups other than the one for which the test was written, the results may be low scores that are likely to be misleading or inaccurate. For example, tests with inflexible time restrictions are not well received by cultures who take an unrushed approach to problem-solving. Likewise, tests with only a single possible correct response for questions are not well received by cultures who tend to practice divergent thinking (a creative problem-solving approach aimed at coming up with *several* possible good answers). Cultural differences in defining and measuring intelligence provide a challenge in developing culturally fair tests.

Assessment Measures

Two common types of **assessments**—evaluations or tests of ability or other traits, are achievement and aptitude tests. **Achievement tests** identify what individuals know and test their skill levels in different areas. Unit or final exams in your classes are likely to be achievement tests. Your upcoming AP Psychology exam is an achievement test as well, because your test writers want to measure your level of knowledge in the topics you studied and your skill in applying that knowledge to unique situations.

While achievement tests focus on what a person has already learned, **aptitude tests** measure ability in a certain area, such as numerical, verbal, or mechanical reasoning; problem-solving in work-related situations; and spatial awareness. Strength in certain areas can help indicate one's potential vocational or professional direction. For example, those who show high aptitude for spatial awareness may do well as designers, engineers, and architects.

Historical Efforts to Define and Measure Intelligence

Psychometric psychologists focus on measuring and assessing a number of traits, including intelligence. Psychometric psychologists are skilled mathematicians who statistically analyze the results from intelligence and other types of tests, such as personality inventories. Modern intelligence tests are intended to measure individual differences by comparing one's results to those of others who have taken the same exam.

Heritability **Sir Francis Galton** (1822–1911) was one of the first to attempt to measure levels of intelligence. Galton was a statistician who created the concept of *correlation* and coined the name for the now well-known debate of *nature versus nurture*. Galton, a cousin of Charles Darwin, fell decisively on the side of nature, believing that intelligence is inherited rather than influenced by environment. In his 1869 book *Hereditary Genius,* he laid out his thoughts regarding the **heritability**—genetic basis—of intelligence. He even went so far as to suggest ideas that would lead to the field of **eugenics**, promoting reproduction for the highly intelligent and potential sterilization for those with "less desirable traits."

Galton believed that tests of physical and sensory strength would reveal mental capacity. He measured individuals' sensory abilities, bodily proportions, sensitivity to high-pitched sounds, and reaction times. Not surprisingly, given his thoughts about genetics, Galton's test indicated that upper class males scored higher on these intelligence assessments than other groups. His methods of testing and clear bias for white males have been challenged by more recent and empirically sound research. Many modern researchers attribute Galton's findings to *confirmation bias* because he may have unknowingly created tests that would favor subjects who ultimately scored well. (See pages 26 and 284 to review confirmation bias.)

The Binet-Simon intelligence scale was developed by **Alfred Binet** (1857–1911) in partnership with his colleague **Théodore Simon** (1872–1961) in 1905 to identify for the French government those children who would benefit from extra help before the start of their formal education. This assessment is often considered the first modern-day intelligence test. The test provided children with a **mental age**, allowing the assessor to identify if children were ahead of or behind their peers. For example, a five-year-old child of average intelligence should receive a mental age of five, whereas a child who is five years old but does not score as well as peers might receive a mental age of three. The test was fairly successful at identifying those who needed extra help academically and correlated well with teachers' feedback regarding students' progress.

The belief that students would benefit from extra training before enrolling in school to help them catch up with their peers was a move away from Galton's theory that intelligence was entirely genetically inherited. Binet used the term "mental orthopedics" to express the idea that children can improve their attention and self-discipline with practice. This view prompted researchers in the field to recognize the importance of the environment's role in influencing subjects' levels of intelligence and introduced a shift away from the sole focus on genetic influence.

Stanford-Binet Intelligence Test   **Lewis Terman** (1877–1956), a professor at Stanford University, wanted to bring intelligence testing to the United States. Since the Binet-Simon scale had predicted academic success relatively well, Terman was interested in using it. However, the original purpose of that scale was very specific to school-age children. Terman wanted to test intelligence in a wider population, so he modified it to be more appropriate for an American audience of varied ages and a broader range of subjects. Terman identified the new version of the exam as the **Stanford-Binet Intelligence Test**.

Recent research with fMRI technology has shown that a home environment in which children are read to has an impact on children's developing brains.

German psychologist William Stern (1871–1938) then created a formula to compute one's **Intelligence Quotient** (IQ) by taking the mental age (provided by the exam) divided by the **chronological age** (the actual age of the child) multiplied by 100. The results

$$IQ = \frac{\text{mental age}}{\text{chronological age}} \times 100$$

Figure 19.1 IQ Formula

would immediately show if children were ahead of or behind their peers. This formula set the standard for intelligence scores to have a mean (average) of 100. While this formula has since been replaced, a score of 100 still represents an average intelligence score.

Terman believed, like Galton, that intelligence is genetically determined, and he was particularly interested in studying those who had extremely high intelligence scores. Terman began one of the most well-known and longest lasting longitudinal studies in the history of psychology. His hypothesis sought to determine if those with high IQs led lives that were significantly different from others. Terman had a large sample of roughly 1500 individuals with IQs of 150 or above. (Those who Terman studied became known as "Termites.")

Despite some of his subjects perhaps earning slightly better salaries and having above average reports of happiness, they did not report having lives that were significantly different from others, as Terman had expected. They were, however, found to be above average in height, weight, physical strength, and emotional adjustment.

Wechsler Intelligence Scales   **David Wechsler** (1896–1981) believed that the widely used Stanford-Binet assessment did not measure all of a person's intelligence. He created different forms of his own intelligence assessments for children and adults—the **Wechsler Adult Intelligence Scale (WAIS)** and the **Wechsler Intelligence Scale for Children (WISC)**. He believed the Binet and Stanford-Binet tests were too dependent on verbal ability, so he added a **performance scale** which measured perceptual organization and *processing speed*—the time it takes to complete certain cognitive tasks—as well. The specific tasks involved in this new performance measurement included such **abstract tasks** as block design (matching visual patterns), picture completion (recognizing what is missing in a picture of an object), matrix reasoning (visual-spatial problems to solve), digit-symbol coding (remembering symbols and their matching numbers), and symbol searching (finding a designated symbol in a group of symbols). The digit-symbol coding and symbol searching measure processing speed. Wechsler retained the **verbal scale**, which included the more traditional intelligence components such as verbal comprehension and working memory, which he assessed by testing one's understanding of such subjects and skills as vocabulary, arithmetic, and digit span. Today a Wechsler test might be administered when a student is being evaluated for a special education program (e.g., extra services for students performing well below or above their classmates).

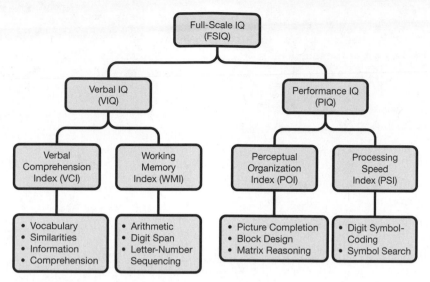

Figure 19.2 Wechsler Intelligence Scale

These types of performance tasks on the Weschler test were very different from what traditional intelligence exams had tested, but Wechsler believed that this assessment represented a more complete view of intelligence. (See Figure 19.2.) Wechsler also modified the way in which intelligence scores were reported. Instead of using the traditional formula created by William Stern, he proposed that, through the use of norming, an individual's scores be compared to others' using a percentile rank. The normal distribution that Wechsler used to compare intelligence scores is still used today and will be discussed further on page 478. (See also pages 59–62 in Chapter 3.)

Factor Analysis **Charles Spearman** (1863–1945) discovered that individuals who score high on one measure of intelligence (vocabulary, for example) often also score well on other measures of intelligence (such as arithmetic). This positive correlation was the impetus for Spearman's idea that all the specific skills (*s*) that comprised intelligence come together to make up one's overall intelligence, which Spearman described as general intelligence (*g*). The statistical procedure Spearman created to analyze correlations between different measures is known as **factor analysis**. If various measures of intelligence correlated positively, they likely were all related to some other variable that was not measured, the **factor**. For example, you may find that some people in your class who do well in math are the same people who do well in English or social studies. The factor to which these students are all related is general intelligence.

Primary Mental Abilities Psychometric psychologist L. L. Thurstone (1887–1955) had a different perspective. Rather than focusing on the underlying characteristics that tied intelligence together, Thurstone identified seven primary factors that compose intelligence, although he did not necessarily see them as related to one another. The factors he identified as **primary mental abilities** included memory, numerical ability, word fluency, verbal comprehension, spatial ability, perceptual speed, and inductive reasoning. He was beginning to recognize that strong ability in a wide variety of characteristics is likely related to one's overall intelligence.

Fluid and Crystallized Intelligence   Raymond Cattell, who studied under Spearman, primarily focused his research on personality (see pages 424–425) but also added to Spearman's idea about general intelligence. Cattell did not believe intelligence could be easily identified by a single concept such as Spearman's *g*-factor. Rather, he believed that there were actually two distinct types of intelligence that combine to create *g*-factor. The first was **fluid intelligence**, which is demonstrated by recognizing patterns, seeing relationships, and using logic to solve novel problems without a connection to past knowledge. An example of fluid intelligence in action would be the quick thinking of an attorney as she presents a counter-argument to a piece of evidence that has just been presented by the opposing side. This ability to quickly and logically respond to new information tends to decrease with age, generally beginning a slow decline about middle age (although there are large individual differences).

According to Cattell, the second type of overall intelligence is known as **crystallized intelligence**, which represents one's accumulated knowledge. If you were asked for the definition of a rarely used word or who the president of the United States was during World War I, you would have to call on your accumulated knowledge (crystallized intelligence) to respond correctly. Crystallized intelligence generally increases with age, even old age, as one's accumulated knowledge and experiences expand. Even though older people might take longer to respond to a question than people half their age, their knowledge

Trial attorneys use fluid intelligence to respond to new information.

base is often larger. Cattell believed that fluid intelligence, which represents reasoning ability, and crystallized intelligence, which represents what one already knows, combine to make up intelligence. This hypothesis may explain why one's overall intelligence remains relatively constant throughout life—reductions in fluid intelligence are balanced out by increases in crystallized intelligence.

Test Construction

Just as defining intelligence can be tricky, constructing tests that can accurately measure intelligence poses its own challenges. How can we be sure that we are measuring what we intend to measure? How can we be sure the same test will work for all subjects in all situations time and again? This section explores measures that researchers take to deal with such challenges.

Standardization and Norms

You have likely taken many standardized tests in your life. The AP Psychology exam you are preparing for in this course will be yet another example of this type of exam. The standardization process makes comparisons between test results from different test takers easier and more accurate.

Standardization refers to the procedures by which an exam is created, administered, and scored. For standardized tests, all factors regarding timing, directions, setting, seating, and monitoring should be the same for all test takers. It would be unfair if the proctor for your AP exam never gave you a time limit for completing the exam, but test takers at all other schools had to complete the 100 multiple-choice questions in 70 minutes. If you could review answers and take all of the time you wanted, your results would likely be higher than those with time restrictions, and for this reason, it would not be appropriate to compare your score to those of others who experienced different test conditions.

If you have taken a college entrance exam such as the ACT or SAT, you may have noticed that the proctor reads very specific directions and even tells you when you can open your test booklets. Once you complete a section of the exam, you are not permitted to go back and work on that section. All of these measures have been put in place to standardize the exam and make sure your score can be compared with those of thousands of others who take the exam on the same day, with the same guidelines, and under the same conditions.

Standardized tests also use test **norms**—the distribution of scores of a clearly defined group. The group from which norms are determined must be carefully identified by age, gender, and any other relevant factor to accurately serve as a sample for the entire population taking the test. A **norm-referenced test** is one that allows you to be compared to this sample group of test takers and determine your relative position in the testing group. If you received an ACT score of 28, you could not gauge how well you did on the exam until you knew that the highest possible score was 36, the state average was 21, and the school average was 24.

To further describe one's score in comparison to others, **percentile rank** is used to indicate the percentage of people in a population who scored at or below an individual's score. Using the example above, in 2016 an ACT score of 28 translated to a percentile rank of 88. That percentile would indicate that you scored better than 88 percent of the students taking the same form of the test on previous test dates.

Validity

Validity is the degree to which assessments succeed in measuring what they are designed to measure. There are several different kinds of validity.

Content Validity When a test measures the content or subject of what it was designed to measure, it has **content validity**. If a test in your English class on *Beowulf*, which your class just finished reading, included questions related to *Beowulf*, it would have a high degree of content validity. If it had instead included questions on geometry, you could rightly challenge the content validity of the exam. The exam would not have a high degree of content validity for *Beowulf*.

The above examples are exaggerated, and content validity is usually more challenging to determine. In order to properly assess whether or not a measure contains content validity, an expert should carefully examine all aspects of the concept the test developers are attempting to measure. For example, intelligence tests are strictly timed and, as a result, may be a good measure of speed of processing. However, if researchers do not believe that processing speed is an important component of intelligence, they may question the content validity of that intelligence test.

Face Validity The degree to which a test appears valid *to the test taker* is called **face validity**. A test has face validity if it appears at first glance to measure what it sets out to measure. For example, because you now know that psychology involves the analysis of data and thus involves statistics, you could see a normal distribution on a unit exam in psychology and determine that at least that part of the test has face validity. However, a friend who has not taken psychology might take a quick look at the exam and claim that it is not a psychology test but is instead a math test. Your friend, a nonexpert who did not look at the exam closely, is questioning the face validity of the exam when the exam actually has both face and content validity.

Construct Validity Almost everyone would agree that people have personalities and intelligence. Personality, intelligence, and other hypothetical concepts, such as self-esteem, are **constructs**. Although we cannot pinpoint where in the brain or person these traits reside, we acknowledge their existence and try to assess and measure them. Constructs are more difficult to define operationally than concepts such as height and weight, which exist in the physical world and can be seen and touched. Researchers need to be very clear about how they plan to measure a given construct because others may have very different perspectives regarding what comprises that characteristic. For example, Wechsler believed that a good intelligence test must include both performance and verbal measures. For this reason, he questioned the construct validity of the Stanford-Binet test, which did not include any performance measures. **Construct validity** requires an assessment to be based on the entire range of theoretical concepts that underlie the subject.

Concurrent Validity Occasionally, an individual will take more than one assessment to measure a personality characteristic or other trait. In these cases, the individual should expect that all tests that claim to measure the same concept will give a similar result. For example, if a student took three tests that claim to measure her level of extraversion, she would expect that all three would be consistent in their findings. If they are, these assessments are high in **concurrent validity**, a quality of tests given at the same time whose results matches the results of other assessments that claim to measure the same characteristic. Note that this type of validity looks outside of the test itself to compare the results to other tests, establishing *external validity*. Measures of *internal validity* address the validity within a single assessment. (See pages 30–31 for a refresher on internal and external validity.)

TYPES OF VALIDITY	
INTERNAL VALIDITY (content-related)	
Content Validity	Test measures all aspects of what it is designed to measure
Face Validity	Test appears to a test taker or other nonexpert to measure what it is designed to measure
Construct Validity	Test is based on entire range of theoretical concepts underlying subject
EXTERNAL VALIDITY (criteria-related)	
Concurrent Validity	Test results match others that are designed to measure the same characteristics
Predictive	Test accurately forecasts performance on a future measure

Figure 19.3

On occasion, an individual may get a different result on two (or more) assessments that claim to measure the same construct. For example, if you took five different assessments, all of which claimed to measure intelligence, and four reported that you had an IQ between 115 and 120 but the fifth test claimed your IQ was 85, we would question the concurrent validity of the fifth test. Only a highly positive correlation between assessments that claim to measure the same component can establish criterion validity for those tests.

Predictive Validity If an assessment accurately forecasts performance on a future measure, it has **predictive validity**. For example, thousands of high school students take the EXPLORE and PLAN aptitude tests to predict how they will perform on the ACT. The ACT, in turn, claims to predict one's success in college. Other tests that claim predictive validity are assessments for careers and those that focus on the ability to problem-solve in the future, using questions the test takers have not seen before rather than ones on the extent of the knowledge they already have.

Reliability

Reliability is an assessment's consistency and stability of results. Like validity, reliability has several different types. Following are those that are often found in standardized assessments (see Figure 19.4).

Repeating Tests   The degree to which an assessment yields similar individual results each time it is taken is called **test-retest reliability**. For example, you may know people who took the ACT or SAT multiple times trying to improve their scores, only to receive the same scores each time or improve by a single point. This example demonstrates high test-retest reliability.

If an instructor allows you to take a make-up exam on a chapter to improve your grade and you do not study or review in between tests, you are likely to receive nearly the same score. However, if you study the concepts from the questions that you had incorrect on the first test, you might find that your score improves considerably. This test-retest reliability issue is called *practice effects*. In these cases, we would not question the test-retest reliability of the exam, because a confounding variable (time spent studying) is the explanation for the inconsistent result rather than a poorly constructed test.

Different Test Versions   The degree to which different versions of the assessment yield similar results is called **alternate-forms reliability**. For someone retaking the ACT or taking the make-up version of an exam, the same material is covered but with different questions. If there is a strong positive correlation between the scores of all versions of an assessment, it would be said to have high alternate form reliability.

Two Parts of a Test   A less well-known type of reliability, **split-half reliability**, is the degree to which two halves of an exam have equal difficulty. In one sitting, test takers are told to answer only the odd-numbered questions. In another sitting, they would be instructed to answer the even-numbered questions. If the scores from both halves of the test are comparable, the exam has internal consistency and a high degree of split-half reliability.

The Role of Assessors   Finally, **interrater reliability** is the degree to which raters of an exam agree on the score. Individuals should receive a similar score no matter which assessment expert administers and scores the test. For example, if two different instructors grade your free-response question, they would have high interrater reliability if they gave you the same grade. High interrater reliability depends on both the strength of the assessment and the expertise and training of the rater.

TYPES OF RELIABILITY	EXPLANATION
Test-Retest Reliability	An individual receives a similar score after taking the same exam two or more times
Alternate-Forms Reliability	An individual who has taken two or more different versions of the test should receive the same score
Split-Half Reliability	Two groups of test takers should receive similar scores when given different halves of the assessment that cover the same material
Interrater Reliability	A measure of the test scorers—those with high inter-rater reliability will give similar scores

Figure 19.4

Reliability and Validity of Intelligence Testing

Do IQ tests actually measure what they are designed to measure? The validity of intelligence tests is up for debate. When evaluating intelligence tests on the basis of their ability to predict school performance, they stand up fairly well. IQ scores and school grades generally correlate well. However, they do not correlate as well to careers that involve physical strength or endurance. In fact, it is estimated that as much as 75 percent of one's performance—physical or otherwise—is unrelated to IQ. For example, a worker may have great intellectual ability but not much conscientiousness (work ethic and ability to follow through on tasks). That worker may arrive late to work and meetings and not complete assigned projects. This performance is not related to the worker's level of intelligence but will most certainly have an impact on job success.

Some correlations regarding the consistency (test-retest reliability) of IQ test results over time are as high as 0.90 (remember that the highest positive correlational coefficient that can exist is 1.0). For test takers distracted by a personal matter or unusually tired on testing day, there will likely be lower levels of reliability from one test to the next. Those who are in a testing environment they find comfortable may score higher than if they are in a setting in which they are nervous or distracted. It is important to take both environmental and personal factors into account when examining the results of assessments of intelligence. All these variables help to explain why the validity of intelligence tests is open to debate.

Assessing the Range of Intelligence

What does it mean to be of "normal" intelligence? What is the cutoff for having an intellectual disability, and why should that matter? Who is gifted? Does everyone fall neatly into one of these categories? Understanding some of the basics of intelligence standards and extremes requires an understanding of psychological statistics. Review Chapter 3 if you feel the need.

Normal Distribution

The application of intelligence tests to the normal distribution (see pages 59–62) has all three components needed to work with any normal distribution. First, and most important, we always know that the scores of an IQ test will result in a normal distribution. Second, we know that the mean (the average score in a population) is 100. And, third, we know that the **standard deviation** (the average distance from the mean) is 15.

With a normal distribution, approximately 68 percent of the population will fall within one standard deviation of the mean (covering IQ scores between 85 and 115), about 95 percent of the population will score within two standard deviations of the mean (covering IQ scores between 70 and 130), and 99.7 percent of the population will score within three standard deviations of the mean (covering IQ scores between 55 and 145). Only 0.15 percent of the population will have an IQ score of below 55 and 0.15 percent of the population will have an IQ score above 145. (See Figure 19.5.) We will discuss these outliers in the next section.

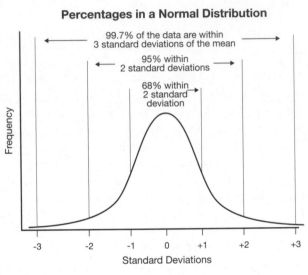

Percentages in a Normal Distribution

Figure 19.5

Percentile Rank Once you know how the percentage of the population is distributed in the normal distribution, you can start to compute the percentile rank for a given IQ score. Remember that percentile rank indicates the percentage of people that scored at or above a given score. If a person has an IQ score of 100, his score falls directly in the middle of the population, giving him a percentile rank of 50 because he scored better than 50 percent of the population. (For a review of how to compute percentile rank for three standard deviations above and below the mean, see pages 60–61.)

When working with a normal distribution, remember that **z-scores** represent how many standard deviations a score is away from the mean. For example, if an individual had an IQ score of 130, her z-score would be +2 because her score is 2 standard deviations above the mean. If her IQ score was 100, the z-score would be 0 because she is directly at the mean. Z-scores are useful because they provide a succinct method of describing where a person's score falls in comparison to others in the normal distribution.

The Flynn Effect Results of modern-day intelligence tests are displayed as a normal distribution. Each year, the test is renormed to keep the mean (average) numerical value of intelligence at 100. If these tests were not renormed each year, those who took intelligence tests years ago might appear less intelligent than those who take intelligence tests today. The **Flynn effect**, named after the New Zealand psychologist James Flynn who identified the phenomenon, claims that people are getting "smarter" or at least getting better at taking standardized tests. (See page 400 for more on the Flynn effect.)

There are many possible explanations for the Flynn effect, such as better nutrition early in life, which may allow for early brain development and development of neural networks. Students today also take far more standardized tests to quantify what they know than did students in the past, so perhaps students are just getting better at taking these types of tests. In addition, the wealth of information available on the Internet and through personal devices today allows younger people access to far more information than their counterparts had even a generation earlier. All of these factors may contribute in their own way to the improved scores. While the origins of the effect are not yet definitively understood, it is clear that the results are changing and, for this reason, one's results can be compared only to those of the group who took the exam at the same time. Comparing one's score to those who took the exam many years ago would provide misleading results and would be a misrepresented comparison if the tests were not continually renormed.

Gender and Intelligence

Many studies have examined gender differences in intelligence, and a great deal of debate remains to be resolved. Males tend to perform better on tests of visuospatial ability, and females tend to perform better on tests of verbal ability. Females tend to score lower on the the ACT and SAT tests, which are supposed to predict performance in college, yet women earn higher undergraduate grades than men. However, most researchers have found that there is no difference in the overall intelligence of males and females, although there is more variability in the scores of males—more males than females score at the very low or very high end of the intelligence range.

Extremes of Intelligence

Normal distribution tells us that most people (95 percent) will score within two standard deviations from the mean on intelligence tests. Those with scores below 70 (more than two standard deviations below the mean) are considered intellectually disabled; those with scores above 130 (more than two standard deviations above the mean) are considered gifted. Still others do not neatly fit into any particular category. And IQ is only one factor in determining giftedness or intellectual disabilities. Consider, for example, people with **savant syndrome**—a condition characterized by generally low scores on traditional intelligence tests but one or more extraordinary abilities. (See page 260.)

Intellectual Disability Those who score two or more standard deviations below the norm on a traditional IQ test are said to have an **intellectual disability**. This group of individuals was historically known as "mentally retarded." However, the negative connotations associated with this term inspired groups to campaign for a change to the name in an effort to reduce stigma. To be identified as a person with intellectual disabilities, one needs to demonstrate before the age of eighteen that he or she has challenges in three broad areas of adaptive skills. For one, people with intellectual disabilities may face challenges in *social skills*—skills in communicating and interacting with others. They may find they have difficulty making friends or knowing how to appropriately interact with others. They may also have trouble with *conceptual skills* that involve thinking through abstract concepts, such as planning for the future or providing proper change for a bill in a monetary transaction. Or they may spend all of their monthly budget in the first week, leaving little or nothing for the next three weeks. Finally, a person with an intellectual disability may have difficulty with *practical tasks,* the necessary skills for day-to-day living, such as following the instructions in a recipe or making the necessary train or bus connections to get to or from work.

Down Syndrome and Other Organic Disabilities Occasionally, an organic condition causes intellectual disability. **Down syndrome** is a disorder characterized by an extra chromosome 21. It is displayed by a round, flat face and slanted eyes. Brain size and weight are below average and muscle movements are slow and clumsy. *Phenylketonuria (PKU)* is an inherited disorder in which an enzyme defect causes phenylalanine, an amino acid, to build up in the body.

Recent dramatic breakthroughs in Down syndrome research point to the possibility of drugs that can restore brain size and repair disabled chemical pathways.

The sufferer often demonstrates an IQ score of 20 or below if the disorder is not treated in infancy. Because of that extraordinarily low IQ score, communication will be nearly impossible for some with that disorder. *Hydrocephaly* occurs when cerebrospinal fluid accumulates in the skull, destroying brain tissue and possibly causing intellectual disability. There are other causes of intellectual disabilities as well, including the zika virus. Many of the causes are still unknown.

Giftedness On the other end of the intelligence spectrum are those who score two or more standard deviations above the mean. Generally, about two to three percent of individuals receive the **gifted** label, and there are other factors besides intelligence that are associated with that label. **Lewis Terman** (see page 470) found from his longitudinal study on the gifted that those who score extremely well on IQ tests do not align with many of the typical stereotypes people tend to have of highly intelligent people. They do not necessarily have lives that are extraordinarily different from others. They may experience more stability because of higher paying jobs, report slightly higher than average levels of happiness in marriage, and be above average in their health when compared to the general population. However, as you have learned, it is impossible to determine causation from correlation.

Joseph Renzulli (b. 1936) proposed that giftedness comprises three factors—intelligence, creativity, and motivation. Much research has confirmed that giftedness is not solely determined by genetics but rather a combination of talents. However, it is difficult to determine if those with advanced talents are inclined to work harder and that the hard work, not necessarily the high IQ, causes the increased levels of success.

THINK AS A PSYCHOLOGIST: GRIT AND THE GIFTED

Most experts agree that traditional intelligence assessments do not accurately identify those who are most likely to be successful. Research by Angela Duckworth (b. 1970) at the University of Pennsylvania suggests that grit may be a better predictor of success than IQ scores. **Grit** can be described as the ability to pick oneself up and try again in the face of setbacks. Everyone fails at some point. Duckworth believes that people define themselves in these times of failure rather than in times of success. Those who give up in the face of setbacks lack grit and, according to Duckworth, eventually will find themselves stagnating if they do not continue to press forward. Duckworth developed the Grit Scale, a self-reporting survey to assess one's grit.

In his book *How Children Succeed,* Paul Tough offers an example of a "gritty" high school student from a blighted neighborhood on the south side of Chicago. She was determined to go to college but had little family support, and her educational experience left much to be desired. Through studying and receiving assistance, she was admitted to Western Illinois University, where she took advantage of her professor's office hours to seek additional help and used other resources on campus to ensure her success in college. Clearly, she was driven to succeed by determination and commitment to her goals.

Critics of the grit theory argue that it offers little beyond the conscientiousness factor in the Big Five Model (see page 426) and that, after accounting for intelligence and personality, especially conscientiousness, grit had a very small effect on success.

Practice: Duckworth's Grit Scale is available online for you to test yourself if you are interested in getting a sense of your level of grit. The Big Five personality model also has a self-test online. You may want to complete these surveys to get an idea of how grit compares to conscientiousness. Then work with several other classmates to find out more about grit, focusing on these questions:

- How did Duckworth come up with the idea of grit?

- Based on your experience taking the self-tests for both grit and the Big Five, how would you describe the similarities and differences between grit and conscientiousness?

- What empirical evidence backs up the idea of grit?

- What kinds of studies have been done that attempt to disprove Duckworth's hypothesis? (You may want to look specifically into the recent work of Marcus Credé, Michael Tynan, and Peter Harms.)

- What are your conclusions about the value of grit over IQ in predicting future success?

Challenges to Intelligence Testing

While intelligence testing is still commonly used today to identify those who may need extra assistance or more challenging work in school—or even just for those who are curious about intelligence—the widespread use of intelligence testing has received much criticism. One reason is because individuals from minority groups (in particular, Hispanics and African Americans) are far more likely to be identified as having lower intellectual scores than Caucasians. This finding could potentially be caused by something called **stereotype threat**: If a member of a group believes that the group tends to do poorly on an assessment, this knowledge may cause anxiety, and the person may fulfill the poor expectation by scoring poorly on the assessment. Stereotype threat is not an issue when one does not know that the group tends to score poorly on a given assessment. (See page 634 for more on stereotype threat.)

Stereotype threat has also been demonstrated with gender. A number of studies have shown that when females are told that as a group they perform less well than males on math tests, test results reflect that. However, when no sterotype threat is activated, females perform equally to males on average.

If any assessment is to be objective, it must be free of bias and **culture-fair**—independent of knowledge from any specific culture. Often, however, bias in the design of an assessment does not show up until a certain group has scored significantly differently on it (usually lower) than other groups. Questions using regional language or references to events or objects with which one may not be familiar put some groups at a distinct disadvantage. An intelligence test should be an aptitude test, which assesses one's ability to solve problems, rather than an achievement test, which emphasizes what one already knows. Good tests of intelligence must provide all test takers, no matter their racial, ethnic, or socioeconomic background, an equal chance to demonstrate their problem-solving abilities. While intelligence tests have improved in this area, it is unlikely that bias has been eliminated entirely, so test makers continue to work on making these assessments fairer.

The single number provided by an intelligence test may also be problematic. Because there is a margin of error for all exams, scores reported in a range may be more useful. Genes provide a person with a range of intelligence, and the environment helps to determine whether a person falls at the low or high end of that range. This concept is known as *reaction range* and has moved the discussion of intelligence away from the single-number approach.

Contemporary Intelligence Research and Theories

Most researchers have moved considerably from Galton's view that intelligence is purely genetic. They question the idea that those who score high on intellectual assessments owe their success primarily to the genes they inherited. While there is general agreement that intelligence includes both genetics and the environment (nature and nurture), researchers continue to disagree on how much of each component contributes to one's intelligence. This percentage becomes more difficult to identify because it may also differ between individuals.

The challenge in determining the heritability of intelligence is that it can explain a characteristic only in a group and not in an individual. In other words, even if a researcher were to determine that in a certain group the heritability of intelligence was 70 percent, we could say this is only true for the group and not for any one individual in the group.

Twin Studies

One way the contributions of genes and environment on intelligence can be studied is by investigating the similarity of intelligence scores between identical twins raised apart. Thomas Bouchard (b. 1937) is known for his ongoing work with twin studies in which he attempts to identify the similarities in intelligence for those who share the same DNA yet have had different home environments. Positive correlations have been found between identical twins raised apart, which suggests a strong genetic link. However, the strong positive correlation is not enough to say that this correlation reflects only genetics, because other factors cannot be ruled out.

Studies have found that adopted children have intelligence scores more similar to their biological parents than their adoptive parents, a finding that again demonstrates a strong link to biology in intelligence. Recent research has also found that as one ages, the similarities to biological relatives in intelligence increase.

Multiple Intelligences

Howard Gardner (b. 1943) of Harvard University expanded on the idea that intelligence is made up of more than a single factor. He criticized traditional intelligence tests for placing too much emphasis on those skills which are generally associated with school success, such as verbal and mathematical abilities. He believed that there are **multiple intelligences** which are relatively independent of one another and combine to identify intelligence in numerous different settings. Gardner's theory identified eight different types of intelligence:

- *Logical-mathematical* individuals thrive when working with numbers and can identify logical patterns in novel number sets. They reason sequentially and would do well in science- or math-related careers.

- *Linguistic intelligence* most closely resembles those skills that have been assessed by intelligence exams in the past. Individuals who score well on the linguistic scale enjoy working with words and know the rules for organizing words into meaningful passages. They may also be good at public speaking, using words to convince their audience of an argument. Law and journalism are examples of career fields that correlate with high levels of linguistic intelligence.

- *Spatial intelligence* may involve the ability to rotate objects in space. An architect or an interior designer may need good spatial intelligence to imagine a completed building or a redecorated room. Athletes often also demonstrate strong spatial abilities. For example, a pitcher or quarterback must know precisely where to throw a pitch or a pass to be successful.

- *Bodily-kinesthetic intelligence* may also be found in athletes or dancers who can move their bodies to convey meaning and emotion. Actors also must use body language, voice, and facial expressions to convey the feelings of their characters.

- *Musical intelligence* can be seen in those who can detect small differences between notes and the pitch of the music they hear. They may be able to match the voice or rhythm of music. Clearly, those who compose music or play musical instruments would likely be strong in this area.

- *Interpersonal intelligence* refers to those who are skilled in interacting with others. These individuals are good at "reading" others and can appropriately respond to different moods, personalities, or temperaments. Those who work as politicians should be (but are not always) good at this skill, and those who work in sales, teaching, or public speaking should know how to "read the room" and respond accordingly.

- *Intrapersonal intelligence* refers to the ability to know and acknowledge one's own feelings and moods. Those who are strong in this area are very self-aware and know their own strengths and weaknesses. Public figures should be high in intrapersonal intelligence so they can accurately know and communicate their positions on issues.

- *Naturalistic intelligence* refers to those who excel at identifying different types of flora and fauna. They can easily categorize different types of trees or birds and enjoy being out in nature. Careers that might suit a naturalist would include biology or park management.

Gardner's theory has received much attention in the past thirty years. However, it also has contributed to the mistaken idea that there are different "learning styles" and that educators should teach according to each individual's learning style. While people may have ways in which they are more comfortable learning, their education may be better served by attempting to identify areas of weakness in individuals' learning and having those individuals practice these areas so that they can become more capable of learning in all ways.

Gardner's theory has also received criticism for its lack of empirical support. It is very difficult to test these different proposed intelligences in a standardized format, and since Gardner does not believe in standardized testing, it does not appear that empirical support is forthcoming from his research. Many also have questioned whether his categories are actual intelligences or simply talents, and this further begs the question of whether there is truly a difference between the two. Still others question whether spreading the concept of intelligence too far will dilute the concept and reduce the significance of what we take intelligence to mean.

Triarchic Theory of Intelligence **Robert Sternberg** (b. 1949) agrees with the basic premise of Gardner's theory—that traditional intelligence tests are not particularly good at assessing overall intelligence and that intelligence is made up of multiple factors. However, he disagrees with the division of intelligence Gardner proposed, because he believes the categories are too specific. Sternberg proposed three larger categories under which different types of intelligence could be categorized, and this is known as the **triarchic theory**:

- *Practical intelligence* represents a person's ability to solve everyday problems and navigate daily routines and responsibilities and has generally not been covered by traditional IQ tests. Those who score high in practical intelligence can prioritize work and personal tasks well and delegate tasks that fit others' talents.

- *Analytical intelligence*, the type of intelligence that can be tested by traditional intelligence tests, also sometimes known as problem-solving, is generally associated with performance in school or on academic tasks.

- *Creative intelligence* may be demonstrated when someone comes up with a novel solution to a problem. Divergent thinking tasks in which there are multiple correct and workable answers to a problem fall under the domain of creative intelligence.

Emotional Intelligence While intelligence assessments may provide a relatively accurate snapshot of who will be successful in school, some argue that success in work and with family or peer relationships may be more important. For example, some individuals may score well on traditional intelligence tests but not interact well with people. Perhaps those who are better able to interact with others and communicate their ideas and beliefs will be more "successful" and satisfied with their lives. Emotional intelligence represents this strong social ability.

Emotional intelligence refers to a battery of social skills, from the ability to read emotions in others to managing and expressing appropriate emotional responses in oneself. Just as one may have a genetic predisposition for ability in an intellectual area, emotional intelligence can come easily for some while others have to work at it. It is also possible for those who score very high on traditional intelligence exams to score well on assessments of emotional intelligence, although many argue that this is not a trait that should be labeled with a number. And some researchers have suggested that emotional intelligence can be taught, especially to young children.

One aspect of emotional intelligence is the ability to recognize and respond appropriately to emotions in others.

Modern intelligence researchers and psychometric psychologists continue to debate the definition of intelligence and how to properly and fairly assess it. Some argue that the identification of intelligence as a single number cannot provide a complete summary of one's intelligence and that what it means to be smart is too diversified to carry a single label.

REFLECT ON THE ESSENTIAL QUESTION:

Essential Question: *How have researchers defined and assessed intelligence from the early days of the field through the present?* On separate paper, make a chart like the one below to gather details to answer that question.

Defining and Measuring Intelligence	Test Construction	Assessing The Range	Contemporary Intelligence Research and Theories

KEY TERMS			KEY PEOPLE
DEFINING AND MEASURING INTELLIGENCE	*TEST CONSTRUCTION*	*ASSESSING THE RANGE*	Alfred Binet
abstract tasks	alternate-forms reliability	Down syndrome	Sir Francis Galton
achievement tests	concurrent validity	emotional intelligence	Howard Gardner
aptitude tests	constructs	Flynn effect	Charles Spearman
Binet-Simon intelligence scale	construct validity	gifted	William Stern
chronological age	content validity	grit	Robert Sternberg
crystallized intelligence	culture-fair test	heritability	Lewis Terman
eugenics	face validity	intellectual disability	David Wechsler
factor	interrater reliability	multiple intelligences	
factor analysis	norm-referenced test	savant syndrome	
fluid intelligence	norms	standard deviation	
heritability	percentile rank	stereotype threat	
intelligence	performance scale	triarchic theory	
Intelligence Quotient	predictive validity	z-scores	
intelligence tests	reliability		
mental age	split-half reliability		
primary mental abilities	standardization		
psychometric psychologists	test-retest reliability		
Stanford-Binet intelligence test	validity		
Wechsler Adult Intelligence Scale (WAIS)	verbal scale		
Wechsler Intelligence Scale for Children (WISC)			

1. Rachel is taking the ACT for the third time in the hopes of improving her score by five points so that she can attend the school of her choice. When she receives her test result, she finds she has received exactly the same score as the first two times she took the ACT. Which of the following best explains Rachel's score?

    (A) Construct validity

    (B) Content validity

    (C) Concurrent validity

    (D) Test-retest reliability

    (E) Interrater reliability

2. Which of the following researchers conducted a longitudinal study on gifted individuals to determine if their lives were more satisfying than others?

    (A) Alfred Binet

    (B) Sir Francis Galton

    (C) Lewis Terman

    (D) Raymond Cattell

    (E) Robert Sternberg

3. Marie has just celebrated her ninety-second birthday. She is physically healthy and walks two miles each day. She lives on her own and still drives short distances, but she is starting to forget where she leaves her glasses and cannot figure out how to work her new security system. Based on this information only, which of the following may be declining in Marie?

    (A) Fluid intelligence

    (B) Crystallized intelligence

    (C) Emotional intelligence

    (D) Linguistic intelligence

    (E) Interpersonal intelligence

4. Edward has gathered research on 200 sets of identical twins raised apart. Those studies have led him to believe that intelligence is 75 percent genetics. While he cannot say for a single individual the percentage of intelligence which is attributable to genetics, Edward is trying to identify the _____ of intelligence.

(A) alternate-forms reliability

(B) split-half reliability

(C) heritability

(D) norms

(E) standardization

5. When Paula takes her AP Psychology exam, the proctor reads from a set of instructions, which all students are told to follow precisely. Her friend taking the same exam at the same time in a different location was given the same instructions. Which of the following is best described in this scenario?

(A) Validity

(B) Cultural fairness

(C) Interrater reliability

(D) Heritability

(E) Standardization

6. Which of the following represents the percentile rank on the results of a score of 85 on an IQ test?

(A) 130

(B) 50

(C) 84

(D) 16

(E) 68

7. Which statement best describes the research consensus on intelligence scores of males and females?

(A) Differences in overall intelligence are explained by the stereotype threat.

(B) Gender bias in testing disadvantages females.

(C) Males and females have about equal intelligence.

(D) Males tend to be more intelligent than females.

(E) Females tend to be more intelligent than males.

8. The work of Alfred Binet challenged which approach to intelligence?

(A) Sir Francis Galton's heritability theory

(B) Raymond Cattell's fluid and crystallized intelligence theory

(C) L. L. Thurstone's primary mental abilities approach

(D) William Stern's intelligent quotient formua

(E) Charles Spearman's factor analysis

9. Which of the following categories did Sternberg propose that contributed to intelligence?

(A) Verbal ability, performance skill, vocabulary

(B) Analytical skills, interpersonal intelligence, mathematical intelligence

(C) Intrapersonal skills, verbal skills, kinesthetic ability

(D) Fluid intelligence, crystallized intelligence, mathematical ability

(E) Practical intelligence, creative intelligence, verbal skills

10. Which of the following is credited with creating the formula below to determine IQ?

$$\frac{\text{mental age}}{\text{chronological age}} \times 100$$

(A) David Wechsler

(B) Alfred Binet

(C) Théodore Simon

(D) Sir Francis Galton

(E) William Stern

1. Intelligence tests that are reliable, valid, and culture-fair have often proved elusive. Psychologists even differ on how to define intelligence properly. Intelligence tests have changed considerably over the years and continue to change as psychologists refine what intelligence is and how it can be most accurately assessed.

   A) Briefly explain the contributions of the following people to the concept of intelligence testing:
   - Sir Francis Galton
   - Alfred Binet
   - David Wechsler

   B) Please provide a definition for each of the following terms and an example showing how each can contribute to better results on intelligence tests:
   - Construct validity
   - Interrater reliability
   - Standardization

   C) What evidence could you provide that an intelligence test was culture-fair?

2. Jim is a sophomore in high school and is being evaluated for a gifted program at his school. He has just received the results from his third try at the IQ test. Jim's result on the assessment reveals that his IQ score is 130. This matches well with the earlier two scores on the same assessment, which reported that Jim's IQ score was 134 and 132, respectively. Jim's father claims he received the same score when he was in high school and took an IQ test and feels proud that his son inherited his intelligence genes. He even wonders if he and his son got the same questions right.

   A) Explain how the following concepts relate to Jim's experience with IQ tests:
   - Test-retest reliability
   - Alternate-forms reliability
   - Concurrent validity

B) Assess the results of Jim's IQ test. If Jim's third score (130) is accurate, identify the following about Jim's score based on a normal distribution with a mean of 100 and a standard deviation of 15:
- Percentile rank
- Z-score
- What type of IQ tests did Jim take?

C) Explain three ways in which Jim's father's statement reveals misunderstandings.

WRITE AS A PSYCHOLOGIST: ANALYZE AND SYNTHESIZE

When you analyze, you find the separate ideas or concepts within a whole. For example, to answer part C of the second question, you need to analyze the parts of Jim's father's response to his son's scores. What exactly is he saying? An analysis would reveal these ideas within his statement: 1) He claims he received the same score, 2) he feels proud of passing his genes on to his son, and 3) he wonders if they got the same questions right. A strong answer would address all of the parts of Jim's father's statement and synthesize them—bring them together—into a coherent whole that draws on all your knowledge of intelligence testing over generations, the heritability of intelligence, and the evolving nature of intelligence tests. For more guidance on answering free-response questions, see pages xxii–xxiii.

UNIT 11: Review

In this unit, you sought answers to this essential question about testing and individual differences.

Chapter 19: How have researchers defined and assessed intelligence from the early days of the field through the present?

Apply what you have learned about testing and intelligence by answering the free-response question below.

FREE-RESPONSE QUESTION

Ms. Ottman wants to create assessments for her AP Psychology class that are both reliable and valid and that prepare her students well for their upcoming Advanced Placement Psychology examination. She works with other instructors on the exams to make sure that the exams cover all of the learning objectives in the course and align with the information taught in class. She wants the exams to be cumulative and will proctor these three exams, one each week leading up to the AP exam. She and the other instructors use the same rubric to grade the free-response questions on the exam and, after grading is complete, find that in 98 percent of the cases they issue students the same grade. After the students have taken their actual AP exam, the instructors find that their exam scores and the results from the actual AP exam are almost identical.

Explain how, if at all, the following types of reliability and validity are addressed in this situation:

- Test-retest reliability
- Interrater reliability
- Concurrent reliability
- Content reliability

UNIT 12: Abnormal Behavior

Unit Overview

What exactly does *abnormal* mean, and when does abnormal behavior constitute a psychological disorder? Consider these examples—all of them true.

Marilyn, a sixty-four-year-old woman, claims that she is being set up in a government conspiracy to get her incarcerated. She states that she feels an overwhelming "need to get on a plane and go away."

A seventeen-year-old named Susanna is anxious when she is not the center of attention. She often responds to minor events with explosive and prolonged emotional reactions. Despite the drama, Susanna earns decent grades in school, participates in a number of extra-curricular activities, and has a number of friends.

Twenty-four-year-old Syd says he hears the voice of an angel guiding him to touch the head of all the children he encounters to anoint them with the spirit of God. He has a part-time job at a fast food restaurant owned by his uncle but is strictly forbidden to enter the dining area. Syd's mother recently found him in his bedroom eating pages from a Bible.

Are these behaviors abnormal—or simply odd? Do any of these individuals have a diagnosable psychological disorder? This unit will explore those questions and the ways mental heath professionals address them.

Key Topics

- Contemporary and historical conceptions of psychological disorders

- Use of the most recent Diagnostic and Statistical Manual of Mental Disorders (DSM-5) as the primary reference for diagnostis

- The major diagnostic categories, including the following disorders: anxiety, bipolar, depressive, dissociative, feeding and eating, neurodevelopmental, neurocognitive, obsessive-compulsive, personality, schizophrenia spectrum, somatic symptom, and trauma- and stressor-related

- The strengths and limitations of various approaches to explaining psychological disorders: medical model, psychoanalytic, humanistic, cognitive, biological, and sociocultural

- The consequences of diagnostic labels (e.g., the Rosenhan study)

- The intersection between psychology and the legal system (e.g., confidentiality, insanity defense)

Source: *AP® Psychology Course and Exam Description*

20

Theories and Diagnosis of Psychological Disorders

*"Mental illness... is not a thing, or physical object . . .
hence it can exist only in the same sort of way
in which other theoretical concepts exist."*

— Thomas Szasz

Essential Question: How do practitioners determine whether or not someone is mentally ill?

Psychopathology is the scientific study of mental disorders and different types of maladaptive behaviors associated with various disorders. A number of terms, such as **mental illness**, **mental disorder**, and **psychological disorder**, have similar meanings and will often be used interchangeably. On the other hand, **psychiatric disorder** is aligned with medical definitions and clinical conditions. You may recall from earlier units that both a psychologist and a psychiatrist will diagnose and treat people with mental illness. However, a psychiatrist as a medical doctor will use a medical/clinical approach to diagnosis and treatment more than behavioral or cognitive approaches.

Abnormal Behavior vs. Psychological Disorder

Determining if behavior is abnormal requires situational and cultural contexts. If a person from the United States were to defecate off the side of a bridge, the police would most likely become involved, and the person would be arrested for indecent exposure and possibly other charges. Such behavior in American culture would be considered deviant, criminal, and highly abnormal.

However, the same behavior is not considered deviant or abnormal in other cultures, such as those in rural parts of India or Asian countries. Additionally, public urination by men in many areas of India, China, and Japan is simply a part of everyday life witnessed on the streets, even in major cities.

American psychiatrist Thomas Szasz (1920–2012) argued in his 1961 book, *The Myth of Mental Illness*, that the field of psychology made a fundamental error when using a **medical model** to identify and classify mental illness. The medical model assumes that psychological disorders stem from disturbances in biological processes, such as reduced levels of seratonin in depression or enlarged brain ventricles in schizophrenia. Szasz argued instead that what many consider psychological disorders are really "problems in living." Although his views are often considered radical, he posed an important set of questions: What determines mental illness? Who decides what is and what is not mental illness?

Abnormal Psychology

The field of **abnormal psychology** is dedicated to the study and treatment of psychological disorders or mental illness. However, the controversy inherent in the use of the term *abnormal psychology* is the implication that abnormal behavior alone may constitute a psychological disorder. Psychologists use a number of criteria when trying to determine whether a person has a definitive psychological disorder. Abnormal behavior may be characterized as odd, eccentric, annoying, or even illegal, but it does not automatically translate as mental illness. In fact, most people who exhibit abnormal behavior are not diagnosed with a disorder.

The criteria for psychological disorders include:

- **Maladaptive behavior**–Behavior that causes harm by making it difficult to fulfill the normal functions of everyday life. A teenager may be unable to function normally at school or maintain friendships; an adult may not be able to hold onto a job or maintain close relationships.

- **Personal distress**–A person's individual perception of his or her own emotional distress. The person reports feeling pain and discomfort associated with the abnormality.

- **Atypical behavior**–Behavior that deviates from what is considered socially or culturally normal. For example, someone may feel the need to check to make sure a door is locked over and over again, count cracks in a sidewalk, or eat hair and other non-nutritive substances.

- **Violation of cultural norms**–Behavior that so deviates from what is culturally accepted that it is considered unacceptable and intolerable. For example, although the vast majority of people with psychological disorders are not violent, anger associated with delusions of being victimized can lead to violence against others.

Insanity

Insanity is a legal term and is used to determine whether an individual is to be held accountable or liable for criminal behavior. Insanity is not a mental health or psychological term and is not defined or classified as such by the American Psychiatric Association. It refers to the inability to know right from wrong or the inability to control one's actions during a criminal event. The criminal court system is confronted with people who, because of mental illness, have committed crimes they had no idea they committed or no way to prevent. Such people are protected from full criminal punishment by being judged *not guilty by reason of insanity.* They will likely be sentenced to a treatment facility rather than prison.

A second form of protection against criminal prosecution is a declaration of **mental incompetence,** a legal term applied when criminal suspects are deemed mentally ill and unable to understand the criminal proceedings or aid in their own defense. Such persons are usually placed in a mental health facility until they are deemed mentally competent to stand trial.

One of the most startling examples of the intersection of crime, insanity, and mental illness is the story of Andrea Yates, who in 2001 confessed to drowning her five children in a bathtub. The jury was told that she had a history of depression following childbirth and had episodes of **psychosis**—a mental disorder so severe that she lost touch with reality. Jurors were also told that her psychiatrist had discontinued her antipsychotic medication, instructing the family that she be monitored continuously and not left alone with the children. In the hour between the time when her husband left for work and her mother-in-law arrived, Andrea Yates drowned her children. She was charged with capital murder and convicted. The prosecutor asked for the death penalty, and the jury rejected her insanity defense. But because of testimony by a psychiatrist who has admitted he mixed up some of the facts, she escaped the death penalty and was sentenced to life in prison. Her conviction was later overturned, and after a new trial in 2006 she was found not guilty by reason of insanity.

The insanity defense is rarely used and even more rarely results in an acquittal. In the Andrea Yates case, however, a second jury recognized that Yates was in every sense of the definition legally insane when she committed the crime. Finding her legally insane was based on overwhelming evidence of her having a severe psychological disorder.

Defining Psychological Disorders

The **American Psychiatric Association (APA)** defines a **psychological disorder** as "a syndrome characterized by clinically significant disturbance in an individual's cognition, emotion regulation, or behavior that reflects a dysfunction in the psychological, biological, or developmental processes underlying mental functioning." In other words, a psychological disorder, also called a mental disorder, is a dysfunctional and maladaptive pattern of behavior.

Throughout the history of psychology, different definitions have been used to describe psychological or mental disorders. Archeologists have found evidence from the beginnings of human civilization that appears to show how early humans dealt with psychopathology. Human skulls from as far back as 5,000 years ago show a treatment called trephining, in which holes are drilled into a living person's skull in order to release demonic spirits thought to be causing the person's disordered behaviors. This early theoretical approach is called **demonology**.

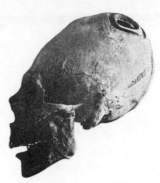

Figure 20.1 Trephining

During the height of Ancient Greek civilization, the highly acclaimed physician Hippocrates, considered "the father of medicine," first suggested that mental illness stemmed not from demonic possession but from an imbalance in one or more of the **four humors** (i.e., body fluids, including blood, black bile, yellow bile, and phlegm). Hippocrates laid the intellectual groundwork for the idea that psychological disorders arose from physical sources and not demons or supernatural sources, though the physical sources he identified had no basis in scientific fact.

During the Middle Ages in Europe, also referred to as the intellectual Dark Ages, the cultural dominance of the Roman Catholic Church led to a common belief that psychological disorders were caused by evil spirits. In a way, this position was a regression back to demonology, and it included the practice of exorcism—a ritualistic practice attempting to drive evil spirits out of a body—believed to be the best way to help affected people.

In the 18th century's Age of Enlightenment, as scientific reasoning tried to find its place in Western society, French physician Philippe Pinel (1745–1826) introduced moral therapy, which supported more humane treatment of the mentally ill in an effort to change the practice of locking away the insane in institutions with horrible conditions and no opportunities for recovery. However, Pinel's work by no means ended the now much-discredited theories of the causes of mental illness. In the 1800s, it was still commonly believed that mental illness was caused by various abnormalities in the organs of the body or imbalances in the four humors of the body. For this reason, treatment was brutal by current standards even though considered more humane at that time. Attempts to treat or cure mental illnesses included bloodletting, douching, dousing in cold or hot water, shaking, restraining, spinning, and even castration. (See Figure 20.2.)

In the early 20th century, the field of psychopathology embraced a new method for treating mental illness, the **lobotomy**—a surgical procedure to damage or remove the frontal lobe (Figure 20.3). Based on behavioral changes seen in an 1840s railroad worker named Phineas Gage, who survived a tamping iron going through his skull and removing much of his frontal lobe

Figure 20.2 Early Treatment for Mental Illness

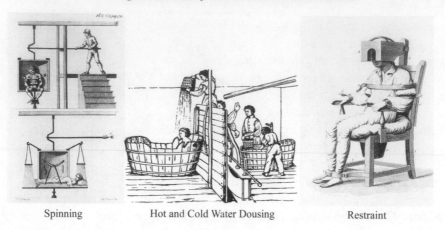

Spinning   Hot and Cold Water Dousing   Restraint

(see page 78), the cause of severe mental illness was hypothesized to be a dysfunction of the brain, primarily the frontal lobe. Consequently, the solution was to remove the lobe—or at least to destroy it. In 1936, Portuguese neurologist Egas Moniz (1874–1955) introduced lobotomy as a way to treat schizophrenia, and he won the Nobel Prize in medicine for his work. Lobotomies were often successful in reducing aggression associated with schizophrenia, but the costs were often severe emotional and intellectual deficits.

The procedure was simple and in time was even performed as a ten-minute outpatient procedure. A surgeon would insert an instrument that resembled an icepick through the eye sockets and move it back and forth to sever the nerves connecting the frontal lobes to areas of the brain that control emotion. Because the procedure was performed "blind," with no way to know exactly where the instrument was, results were inconsistent. The popularity of lobotomies declined in

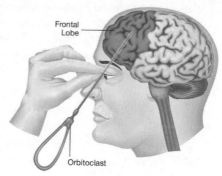

Figure 20.3 Lobotomy

the mid- to late 1950s as opposition to the technique became widespread and antipsychotic drugs became available. Over the next sixty years, psychological research expanded greatly and the field of psychological diagnosis advanced as new understandings of mental illness emerged.

The Diagnostic and Statistical Manual of Mental Disorders (DSM-5)

Today, one manual is used as the source of criteria for defining psychological disorders, the *Diagnostic and Statistical Manual of Mental Disorders, 5th Edition* (commonly referred to as the **DSM-5**). In the course of sixty years, the mental health field has come to rely on the DSM-5 as the "bible" of psychiatric diagnosis. The first edition was published in 1952. It included a listing of 106 psychological disorders and emphasized the Freudian psychodynamic approach. In 1968, the DSM-II was published and included 182 disorders. When the DSM-III was published in 1980, the psychodynamic approach was replaced by the more empirical biomedical approach. The number of disorders expanded to 265, and a five multi-axial (5 axes) system of diagnosis was introduced that focused more on biological, psychological, and social dimensions of mental disorders. In 1994, the DSM-IV was published with a list of 297 disorders. A revised DSM IV-TR (Text Revision) was published in 2000. Each new edition introduced improved definitions and diagnostic criteria for psychological disorders.

Changes in the DSM-5

The current DSM-5 was published in 2013, and like the previous editions, it introduced new and improved diagnostic criteria. Although it removed some disorders and added others, those changes were not made without serious discussion and debate. For example, the issue of Internet addiction was hotly debated in pre-publication discussions and was pushed by many to be included as an official disorder. In the end it was not included, although Internet Gaming Disorder is listed in the DSM-5, Section 3, under "Conditions of Further Study." However, in a number of Asian countries, especially China, families send their sons to inpatient treatment centers in hopes of curing them of Internet gaming addiction, which wreaks havoc in their daily lives. Is it abnormal to spend eighteen hours a day on the Internet? Yes, say psychologists. Is it harmful? Probably. Is it an official psychological disorder? Not until the DSM writers and publishers say it is.

The DSM-5 considers environmental events, medical conditions, and potential genetic links for behavior as part of the diagnostic criteria. In contrast to earlier editions, the DSM-5 does not require that all criteria be met before a diagnosis is made. Altogether, twenty categories of disorders are identified, with symptom descriptions and diagnostic criteria for a professional diagnosis. An overview of all categories and specific psychological disorders will be presented and discussed in the next chapter.

Assessing the DSM-5

The history of mental illness, psychology, and psychiatry is filled with failed efforts to help those suffering from mental illness. One hundred years ago, homosexuality was considered a mental illness (it was formally declassified by the American Psychiatric Association in 1973); the cause of schizophrenia was not known, and the treatment was often institutionalization in an asylum. Seventy years ago, lobotomies and electroconvulsive "shock" therapy were commonly used for people diagnosed with schizophrenia or severe depression.

Today, treating psychological disorders focuses on the use of medications. The most common treatments for childhood ADD/ADHD, anxiety, and depression are pharmaceutical. We can look back at the practices of treating mental illness a hundred years ago and see them as primitive and in some cases even cruel. How will the field of psychology assess our current methods of diagnosis and treatment a hundred years from today?

Critics of the DSM-5 express concern that lowering the threshold for diagnosis of some disorders could result in an increase in "false positives"—people being diagnosed with mental illness—and treated—where no illness exists. For example, critics wonder about the newly introduced childhood psychological disorder called disruptive mood dysregulation disorder (DMDD), characterized by extreme, frequent outbursts of temper and an enduring irritability. Will the child who has temper tantrums now be labeled with a psychological disorder and treated with a strong medication? Another concern is that the criteria used to determine whether someone has a psychological disorder too often relies on subjective judgment rather than biological evidence.

However, continuing research into mental illness and treatment of people with mental illness, despite former discredited theories and approaches, have freed countless people from the straitjacket of debilitating attempts at treatment. The DSM-5 is a manifestation of the best intentions of the field of psychiatry and the field of mental health as a whole and is dedicated to helping those struggling with mental illness to lead happier and more productive lives.

THINK AS A PSYCHOLOGIST: WHAT CAUSES MENTAL ILLNESS?

What causes mental illness? The consensus among many psychologists, psychiatrists, and neuroscientists is: we don't know.

Nonetheless, researchers have made progress in assembling some of the clues. Some lines of research have identified biological markers for schizophrenia and depression. Genetic studies have identified potential genes that set the stage for different mental illnesses. And various brain imaging techniques have documented differences between the brains of individuals who have a mental illness and those who don't.

Biology doesn't tell the whole story, though. For example, not everyone who has a genetic marker for cancer develops the disease. Some factor in the environment also plays a role. With mental illnesses, some factor from the interaction of brain, mind, and environment might be the trigger. The problem could be anywhere in the system—genes, cellular function, neurochemical processes, or communication between different brain structures and processes.

The interplay of biology, individual neurobiology, and environment makes it difficult, if not impossible, to separate the brain and the human social environment. The feedback loop involving the environment, the brain, and the mind is just as active for abnormal development as it is for normal development.

Although current thinking is that problems that result in mental illnesses occur in the brain, experts believe that too much emphasis on biology makes us miss the role that the physical environment, social environment, and individual behavior play in how mental illnesses develop and progress.

Practice: With several other classmates, choose one of the questions below to find out more about what causes mental disorders. Report your findings to the class.

- Watch Thomas Insel's TED talk, "Toward a New Understanding of Mental Illness," or read the interactive transcript. What approach to understanding mental illness is he talking about? Describe what you think the short-term and long-term results will be.

- Visit the National Institute of Mental Health's (NIMH) website at https://www.nimh.nih.gov. List three types of research into the causes of mental illness that the institute has recently funded. What research areas or theories do they seem to be focusing on? How will the NIMH approach impact future developments in how we understand mental illness?

- Do the fields of psychiatry, neuroscience, and clinical psychology share an approach to understanding the nature of mental illness? What impact is a shared approach likely to have on understanding the causes of mental illness? What impact is a lack of shared approach likely to have?

- Are we likely to find one or more treatments for mental illnesses that work quickly—within one to a few weeks? Why or why not? Support your opinion with three references. What are the benefits of treatments that work quickly? If there are any costs, discuss one of them.

Theories of Psychopathology

During the last hundred years, a number of models or theoretical approaches have been introduced that attempt to explain the causes, or **etiology**, of psychological disorders. Most mental health professionals today do not rely exclusively on one approach. Instead, they use an **eclectic** or broad-based approach, trusting a combination of established approaches to diagnose and treat individuals with psychological disorders.

The Medical Model vs. Psychological Models

The **medical model**, also referred to as the **biological approach**, presupposes that psychological disorders have a biological cause. These models see such disorders as anxiety, depression, obsessive-compulsive disorder (OCD), and schizophrenia as being caused by genetics, brain damage, dysfunction of the brain's neurotransmitter system, or a combination of these neurobiological factors. The medical/biological model has become the predominant model, as evidenced by the common language used to describe psychological disorders: mental *illness*, *patient*, mental *hospital*, *therapy*, and *symptoms*.

Another indication of the growing reliance on this approach is the increasing acceptance and use of pharmaceutical drugs for the treatment of increasing numbers of psychological disorders. Prescription drugs are often the first and primary methods of treatment for such disorders as anxiety, depression, OCD, and post-traumatic stress disorder (PTSD), among others.

Psychological models, on the other hand, incorporate a number of different approaches to explain psychological disorders, including psychodynamic, psychosocial, behavioral, cognitive, and humanistic models. The various psychological models not only help explain the formation of personality—they also provide different perspectives on the possible causes of psychological disorders.

Psychological disorders in adulthood may be evaluated using either biologically-based trait theories or social learning theories such as those introduced by Bandura and Freud. Early childhood influences are especially important, and adult mental disorders are often found to be associated with events in an individual's first five years of life.

Psychodynamic Model The **psychodynamic model** for explaining mental disorders is based on the Freudian belief that all psychological problems or disorders stem from repressing past trauma, memories, or thoughts in the unconscious mind to avoid anxiety. When these anxiety-producing thoughts try to break through to conscious awareness, they may cause mental distress and maladaptive behavior. To see the psychoanalytic approach in action, imagine a woman who has been diagnosed with the disorder once known as multiple personalities. She is repressing the anxiety-producing traumatic memories of prolonged childhood abuse by developing alternate personalities that keep those memories in her unconscious, even though her alternate personalities are maladaptive and disruptive to daily life.

The psychodynamic approach tries to get into the minds of individuals to understand how they view the world and their relationships within it. The psychodynamic approach, therefore, sees all human functioning as stemming from forces within the individuals themselves, particularly in their unconscious.

Behavioral Model In contrast, the **behavioral model** of psychological disorders is based wholly on the theory that all behavior, whether adaptive or maladaptive, is learned. (See Chapters 9 and 10.) These useful theories explain how behaviors are acquired and maintained. For example, behaviorists explain the development of a fear of buttons based on classical conditioning. Seven-year-old Natalie, for example, had a loose button on her sweater, put it in her mouth, and soon it became lodged in her throat and she began to choke. Unable to breathe, she began to panic. Her mother found her just as Natalie was falling to her knees, and her mother was able to remove the button. Soon after the incident, Natalie began to cry and hyperventilate when she was putting on a shirt with buttons. At seventeen years old, she still cannot have any article of clothing with buttons and starts to panic if she just touches a button.

Classical Conditioning's Influence on Psychopathology

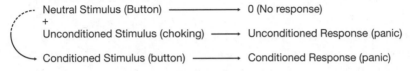

Figure 20.4 Classical Conditioning's Influence on Psychopathology

Similarly, operant conditioning can be used to explain illness anxiety disorder (IAD), a condition previously known as hypochondriasis or hypochondria. As a child, the person with IAD may have experienced prolonged periods of emotional isolation from parents. Then, when the child became seriously ill, the parents provided a good deal of attention. The child learned that experiencing illness was positively reinforced by receiving much needed, even craved, love and attention. As an adult, the learned association between stress (the trigger) and the feeling of being seriously ill is reinforced by receiving medical attention.

Cognitive Model   The **cognitive approach** sees psychological disorders as illogical, irrational, or maladaptive thought processes. For example, when applying the cognitive approach to explain intermittent explosive disorder, which is characterized by intense outbursts of rage out of proportion to a provocation, the cause will likely be attributed to maladaptive thought processes: The affected person's cognitive process views a minor incident or situation in such an irrational way that he or she feels seriously threatened or insulted. The illogical belief (thought) is so strong that it triggers the *fight-or-flight response* of the limbic system and suddenly the person explodes into a rage.

The cognitive model focuses on examining someone's way of thinking to understand his or her behavior. The person's perceptions, attitudes, areas of focus or directed attention, memories, and information processing are evaluated in order to make an accurate diagnosis of a mental disorder.

Humanistic Model The **humanistic approach** to explaining psychological disorders is based on the belief that mental illness stems predominantly from issues involving low self-esteem, a poor self-concept, and the feelings and maladaptive behaviors that result from the inability to be one's authentic self. The humanist school of psychology believes that each individual has a natural drive toward growth of the authentic self. When this natural tendency is blocked, a person may experience stress, which in turn may distort his or her perception of reality.

For example, Ana's greatest desire is to pursue an acting career, but her family and cultural factors pressure her to abandon her authentic passion and pursue a more practical career as an accountant. This divergence between her authentic needs for personal growth and the **conditions of worth**—the conditions Ana believes she has to meet to be worthy of her family's love—makes her feel incongruence between her real and ideal self and can lead to depression.

Assessing the Psychological Models While the psychological models presented above may explain the causes of certain psychological disorders, they cannot and should not be used to explain more serious psychological disorders such as major depression and schizophrenia. The medical model/ biological approach is prevalent for a very important reason. As a result of a great deal of empirical research into the brain and its neurological processes, studies show a direct link between a number of psychological disorders and neurological dysfunction. However, overreliance on the biological approach has come at the cost of virtually abandoning sound psychological theories that do not view human behavior and emotions as simply a product of chemical processes.

Diathesis-Stress Model

The **diathesis-stress model** was developed in the 1960s by David Rosenthal, professor of psychiatry at Columbia University, when he was studying quadruplets who had all developed schizophrenia by their early twenties. The diathesis-stress approach recognizes a combination of biological and environmental causes of psychological disorders. Individuals who are genetically or neurobiologically predisposed to a psychological disorder may exhibit the disorder when exposed to environmental stressors that trigger characteristic symptoms of the disorder. This model assumes that people's genes put them at risk of developing a psychological disorder. For example, schizophrenia and clinical depression are viewed as biologically-based disorders, but certain environmental events must occur in order for the disorder to manifest as symptoms.

When applied together, three specific concepts help to explain this approach. First, **diathesis** refers to the predisposition or biologically-based vulnerability to a particular mental illness. This vulnerability may occur in various degrees. Some people may be highly vulnerable while others are less susceptible. The amount of environmental stress required to trigger the mental illness will vary depending on the level of biological vulnerability.

Second, **stressors** are those environmental events that can trigger the onset of a biologically-based disorder. If the diathesis potential is high and the individual's environment, including family, relationships, and social circumstances, presents a high enough level of stress, symptoms of the disorder are likely to show up.

The third concept, **protective factors**, refers to steps that can be taken to decrease the likelihood that a specific disorder will present itself. Protection involves modifying the environment to reduce exposure to stressors or teaching the vulnerable person adaptive coping skills to help reduce or eliminate symptoms of the disorder.

The Diathesis-Stress Model

Diathesis
Genes
Neurotransmitters dysfunction
Brain dysfunction

Stressors
Culture-related
Trauma
Work environment
Life event
Physical stressor, illness
Social stressor

Vulnerability to mental disorder

Protective Factors
Avoid/eliminate stress triggers
Improve coping skills
Temperamental resiliency
Cultural resiliency

Risk Factors
Poor coping skills
Extreme stress over time
Poverty
Temperament/attachment difficulties

Lower probability of mental disorder

Higher probability of mental disorder

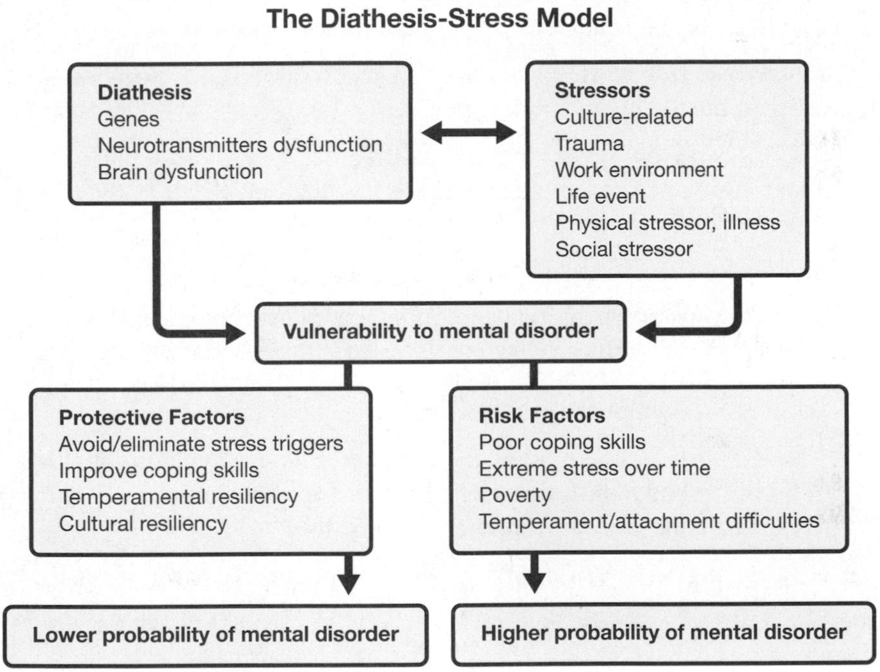

Figure 20.5 The Diathesis-Stress Model

Sociocultural Model

In recent years, mental health professionals have been looking more closely at the role culture plays in the causes and variations of psychological disorders. Culture is a significant factor in the development and structure of personality. (See Chapter 18.) Culture also exerts a strong influence on the development of unique variations of defined psychological disorders. While the medical model and other psychological models focus more on the individual, the sociocultural model emphasizes societal and cultural influences in the individual's environment.

The DSM-5 reflects greater awareness and sensitivity to cultural influences in the area of psychological disorders than earlier diagnostic manuals. Three culture-specific concepts have been added to its appendix, as follows:

- **Cultural syndromes** are categories of similar symptoms and explanations of causes that occur in a culturally-specific context and are recognized within the culture.

- **Cultural idioms of distress** involve expressions of distress that do not necessarily involve specific symptoms or disorders but provide shared ways of experiencing and expressing personal and social concerns within a culture.

- **Cultural explanations of distress or perceived causes** refer to labels, attributions, or explanations that point to culturally agreed upon meanings for and causes of symptoms, illness, or distress.

Cultural syndromes are psychological disorders specific to a particular culture. Some interesting examples include:

- **Taijin Kyofusho** – A social anxiety disorder specific to Japan in which a man or woman experiences intense fear that his or her body, a bodily function, or appearance will embarrass others.

- **Susto** – Specific to areas of Latin America, this psychological condition includes severe anxiety along with physical symptoms caused by what is believed to be a religious-magic traumatic event that separates the soul from the body. Symptoms may include apathy, insomnia, irritability, and physical symptoms such as diarrhea.

- **Amok** – Originating in Southeast Asia, this condition begins as a period of brooding and manifests as a sudden and possibly homicidal explosion of rage usually caused by a perceived insult.

- **Hwabyeong** – Specific to the Korean peninsula, hwabyeong is an overwhelming feeling of anger related to perceived unfairness. It is often caused by the buildup of unresolved anger that has been suppressed for a long time. The trigger is usually a family-related event, and symptoms include heat sensation, respiratory symptoms, and heart palpitations.

Cultural relativism is a concept that explains the intersection between psychopathology and culture. In this model, psychological disorders can only be fully understood within the context of the culture in which they occur. Sociocultural factors include gender, socioeconomic conditions, age, and the values, traditions, and societal expectations that contribute to the cultural context. The sociocultural context can help determine what is and is not considered abnormal. Such context can also determine how psychologists may handle universal psychological disorders such as depression, anxiety, and schizophrenia.

Cultural factors can influence not only the dimensions and severity of the disorder but also the treatment strategy. For example, in most Western cultures, depression is more accepted or tolerated among women than men and is therefore more frequently seen in women. Another factor is the educational level and socioeconomic status of the individual. Poverty can be a key element in the development of depression or anxiety disorders and also limit access to treatment, so the disorders are often undiagnosed. Additionally, cultural stressors such as violence are also highly correlated with stress-related disorders.

Sociocultural factors play a role in the frequency with which disorders appear in a given society. For example, anorexia nervosa and bulimia tend to appear primarily in Western cultures such as in the United States, Europe, and other cultures that hold thin, often unrealistic models as icons of beauty. Additionally, depression and anxiety disorders are much less common in Asian cultures such as in China and Japan. Cultural norms for specific disorders vary widely between countries. In Japan, for example, mental illness, particularly depression, is considered a taboo condition that can bring disgrace and dishonor to the family and extended family. For this reason, Japanese men, women, and children who experience depression will more often report physical illness or bodily ailments.

Assessing the Sociocultural Model Assuming that your perception of the world, reactions to situations, triggers for certain emotions, and perceptions of psychological disorders are universally shared is a stabilizing coping mechanism. Although the field of psychology has been dominated by Western culture since its origins, it has finally begun to recognize more fully the powerful influence of culture on human behavior, personality, and psychological disorders.

Psychiatrist George L. Engel (1913–1999) developed the **biopsychosocial approach**, an integrated model that combines the biological (medical), psychological, and sociocultural models and is believed by most professionals to be a more thorough approach to use when explaining, diagnosing, and treating psychological disorders.

All three approaches are helpful to consider in order to best understand the etiology of psychological disorders and to improve treatment. (See Figure 20.6 on the next page.) For example, a young man, Robert, presents himself to a clinical psychologist with symptoms that indicate **bipolar disorder**, a psychological mood-related disorder characterized by fluctuations between depressed and excited mood swings. The clinical psychologist working from a biopsychosocial approach recognizes that Robert's condition potentially has a biological component, that is, a genetic or neurological predisposition. The psychologist would also explore psychological factors that contribute to the illness and identify possible etiological factors such as maladaptive thought patterns, learned maladaptive behavioral patterns or habits, and possible issues involving low self-esteem and a negative self-concept. Finally, the psychologist will take into account the sociocultural component and look for any societal or cultural factors that could be contributing to the disorder. Societal/cultural factors may include gender issues, cultural expectations, work environment, education, and socioeconomic conditions.

Prevalence of Psychological Disorders

Prevalence refers to the proportion of a specific population that is estimated to have a certain condition within a given year. The U.S. National Institutes of Mental Health, part of the National Institutes for Health and Prevention (NIH), and the World Health Organization (WHO) revealed significant trends regarding the prevalence of psychological disorders in 2014. In the United States, the estimated prevalence of mental disorders of all kinds accounted for 43.6 million individuals or 18 per-

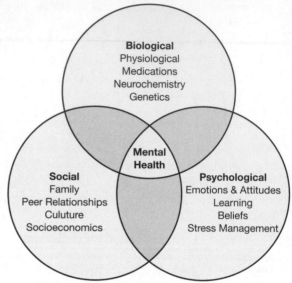

The Biopychosocial Model of Health

Figure 20.6 Biopsychosocial Model of Health

cent of adults (18 years or older) who reported **any mental illness (AMI)**. AMI is defined as mental, behavioral, or emotional disorders diagnosed according to specific DSM-5 criteria. Females represented 21.8 percent and males 14.1 percent of all reported cases. These statistics exclude substance abuse. **Serious mental illness (SMI)** refers to mental, behavioral, or emotional disorders as defined above but that result in serious functional impairment that substantially interferes with major life activities. A total of 9.8 million American adults or 4.2 percent of the population were diagnosed with serious mental illness in 2014 based on DSM-5 diagnostic criteria. Among U.S. children ages eight to fifteen, AMI prevalence is estimated to be 13.1 percent. Attention deficit hyperactivity disorder (ADHD) alone has an overall prevalence rate of 8.6 percent in the United States, with significant differences shown between girls and boys. Boys are almost three times more likely (12.9 percent) than girls (4.9 percent) to be diagnosed with ADHD.

Figure 20.7 shows a more detailed breakdown of the lifetime prevalence of selected psychological disorders in the United States. **Lifetime prevalence** refers to the percentage of the population that at some point in their lives will have experienced the condition.

Psychological Disorder	Lifetime Prevalence Percentage
Schizophrenia	1.1
All Mood Disorders	20.8
Bipolar Disorder	3.9
Any Anxiety Disorder	28.8
Obsessive-Compulsive Disorder	1.6
Panic Disorder	4.7
Anorexia-Nervosa	0.6
Binge-Eating Disorder	2.8
Autism Spectrum Disorder	1.8

Figure 20.7 Adult Prevalence of Psychological Disorders in the United States (2014)

Mental illness is found throughout the world. The most prevalent psychological disorders are depressive disorders and anxiety disorders. Additionally, the global prevalence of substance abuse is significant.

As statistics indicate, the high prevalence of depressive disorders around the world is significant. Why would depression be so prevalent in all societies? Rollo May (1909–1994), an American child psychologist in the 1940s, defined depression quite simply: "Depression is the inability to construct a future." His definition implies that, to the depressed individual, all has been lost and he or she cannot see a way to move forward. A number of correlational studies (i.e., studies that compare various factors to understand relationships between them) have shown a relationship between geographic areas of high poverty and violence and higher incidence of depression. A higher frequency of depression in certain impoverished areas could also result from limited access to mental health care in those areas. In addition, the relatively consistent reporting of schizophrenia worldwide confirms that schizophrenia is at least in part biologically based and

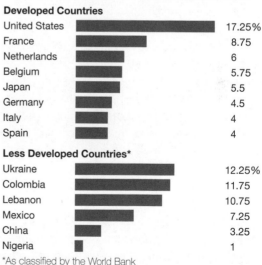

Percentage Prevalence of All Mental Disorders for Selected Countries

Developed Countries

United States	17.25%
France	8.75
Netherlands	6
Belgium	5.75
Japan	5.5
Germany	4.5
Italy	4
Spain	4

Less Developed Countries*

Ukraine	12.25%
Colombia	11.75
Lebanon	10.75
Mexico	7.25
China	3.25
Nigeria	1

*As classified by the World Bank

Figure 20.8 Prevalence of All Mental Disorders for Selected Countries

not triggered environmentally. Lastly, the highest prevalence of overall mental illness is found in the United States. This finding can be the result of increased reporting of mental illnesses and better access to mental healthcare, but it also suggests the effects of socioeconomic factors such as poverty and violence, which are pervasive in many areas of the country.

Consequences of Diagnostic Labels

The DSM-5 provides the most up-to-date list and descriptions of more than 250 psychological disorders. Each one has a label—a name—and the DSM-5 helps psychologists determine which disorder or disorders are potential diagnoses for a given patient by evaluating patients' symptoms and matching them to characteristics, or criteria, of a labeled disorder. Labels are convenient and efficient, but they can also be dangerous.

The benefits of labels include targeted treatment—certain therapies are known to work better with some disorders than others. Labels can also help people struggling with mental illness and their families to achieve greater understanding of and patience with troubling symptoms and to feel optimism that a known and named condition can be treated and managed.

The controversy surrounding labels arises when the label itself becomes a predominant or prejudicial factor. In a now-famous 1973 study conducted by Stanford University's **David Rosenhan** (1929–2012), he and seven other men and women whom Rosenhan called "pseudopatients" presented themselves to numerous psychiatric hospitals across the United States. The only symptom they reported when attempting to gain admission to the hospitals was auditory hallucinations. They all reported that they heard a voice inside their heads repeating the words *empty, hollow,* and *thud.* No other symptoms were reported. After being admitted (and all were admitted), the "pseudopatients" were instructed to act normally and report that they no longer heard voices. Each was diagnosed or labeled with schizophrenia. The longest hospitalization was fifty-two days; the average was nineteen days. All were discharged with a diagnosis of "schizophrenia in remission."

The illustrative example here is how normal behavior in eight individuals was interpreted as abnormal by the professional staff of various institutions. By simply recognizing the label *schizophrenic*, the staff demonstrated a consistent prejudicial view or interpretation of perfectly normal behavior. For example, during interviews, note-taking behavior of the "pseudopatients" was deemed a symptom of psychopathological behavior, which further confirmed the diagnosis (the "label") of schizophrenia. Rosenhan and his fellow "pseudopatients" all reported feeling extremely dehumanized by the hospital staff. For example, their personal possessions were randomly searched and they were observed while using the toilet. Denying that they had any illness to a staff member was considered confirmation that they, indeed, had an illness.

It was only when they agreed with their diagnosis that they progressed toward being discharged.

The power of labels is aptly demonstrated by the Rosenhan experiment and similar published studies. Rosenhan demonstrated that, once labeled, the label itself can determine not only how professionals perceive and react to a person but also how the labeled persons themselves will begin to act differently—perhaps displaying a "self-fulfilling prophecy." All too often, a person who is labeled with a psychological disorder, or simply labeled as "different" or "difficult," begins to act in ways that fulfill the stereotype of the label.

Stigmatization of Labels

Labels are needed, but they can become stigmatized and in turn stigmatize the psychological disorder they name, making the label a symbol of disgrace or dishonor for those who are labeled. A powerful example of stigmatizing labels is the terminology once used for what is now called **intellectual developmental disorder**—a label introduced in the DSM-5 to refer to impairments of general mental (or cognitive) abilities. These labels are not yet stigmatized, but the newer terms replaced "mental retardation," which imparted a stigma on those patients who received the label. The term *retarded,* which now is considered an inappropriate and derogatory term, was used to replace the terms *idiot, moron, imbecile*, and *feeble-minded* when those terms, once considered a way to identify those who scored lower on cognitive assessments, eventually became stigmatized and derogatory. The medical term Down syndrome is another example. It is named after John Langdon Down who was the first medical professional to describe the condition that later would be associated with individuals born with an extra 21st chromosome. In 1965, the term Down syndrome officially replaced the terms *mongolism, mongoloid,* and *mongolian idiocy.* As with mental retardation, these terms came to have a negative connotation.

Last, society and culture contribute to the stigmatization of psychological disorders. Although Western culture, particularly in the United States, has made great strides in destigmatizing mental illness and its labels, movies and other popular culture perpetuate unfair stereotypes and long-held popular beliefs about poor intellectual abilities. Reinforcing false stereotypes of people with mental illness may imply that they are more prone to violence. The truth is that individuals with mental illness, ranging from anxiety disorders to depression to schizophrenia, are much less likely to exhibit violence than the average person. In fact, people with mental illness are much more likely to be *victims* of violence than those without mental illness.

ADD/ADHD: Who Has the Problem?

Consider attention deficit disorder/attention hyperactivity disorder. The common behavioral symptoms of ADD/ADHD are a persistent pattern of inattentiveness and/or hyperactivity and impulsiveness. To what degree is ADD/ADHD a neurodevelopmental disorder? How accurate is the diagnosis process? And what are the implications of diagnosis? The disorder is a legitimate psychological disorder categorized by the DSM-5 as a neurodevelopmental disorder that predominantly affects children but is also found in adults. The DSM-5 lists nine behavioral symptoms for inattentiveness and nine behavioral symptoms for hyperactive/impulsive tendencies which will be discussed in Chapter 21. Confirmation of diagnosis requires the presence of six or more of the symptoms in children and at least five symptoms in teens and adults.

The controversy surrounding ADD/ADHD involves a number of issues. One issue is the frequency and accuracy of diagnosis. A person will be

diagnosed with diabetes through an empirical and medically reliable set of diagnostic tests. However, when it comes to diagnosing children with ADD/ADHD, critics argue that, all too often, the diagnostic threshold is achieved through subjective assessments completed by teachers. A teacher's observations of inattentiveness and difficulty engaging in quiet activities might also be a result of poor classroom management skills on the part of the teacher or a lack of discipline and control in parenting.

Another issue involves defining ADD/ADHD as a disability to begin with. Some take the controversial position that children with ADD/ADHD do not have a disorder; they are actually gifted with much higher cognitive processing speed. Simply put, these children are placed in an environment that delivers information at such a slow rate that they become bored and restless, and the resulting behavior is assessed as a disorder. Another concern is that such children are unnecessarily put on prescription medications such as methylphenidate (trade name: Ritalin®) or amphetamine/dextroamphetamine (trade name: Adderall®) when a better solution may be to modify the child's learning environment to better fit his or her learning style and abilities which may alleviate the symptoms without the use of medication for some children. However, the parents of children who are diagnosed with ADD/ADHD are often encouraged to put their child on strong pharmaceutical drugs. Some alternative or complementary therapies treat the underlying neurological disorder directly rather than hiding the core clinical problem by giving symptom-relieving drugs. For example, one therapy shown to be effective is neurofeedback (or biofeedback) therapy in which the child with ADD/ADHD is taught to control their brainwaves that are associated with alertness. Children receiving this treatment are better able to pay attention without the use of drugs.

* * *

The people you read about on page 495—Marilyn, Susanna, and Syd—all were diagnosed with mental illness: Marilyn Hartman with major depressive disorder, Susanna Keysen (the subject of the movie *Girl, Interrupted*) with borderline personality disorder, and Syd Barrett (founding member of the band Pink Floyd), with schizophrenia. You will read more about these and other disorders in the next chapter.

REFLECT ON THE ESSENTIAL QUESTION

Essential Question: *How do practitioners determine whether or not someone is mentally ill?* On separate paper, make a chart like the one below to gather details to answer that question.

Historical Conceptions of Disorders	Contemporary Conceptions of Disorders/DSM-5	Strengths and Weaknesses of Different Models

KEY TERMS			KEY PEOPLE
abnormal psychology	four humors	*MODELS*	David Rosenhan
American Psychiatric Association	intellectual disability	any mental illness (AMI)	
atypical behavior	lifetime prevalence	behavioral model	
conditions of worth	lobotomy	biological approach	
cultural idioms of distress	maladaptive behavior	biopsychosocial model	
cultural syndromes	mental disorder	cognitive model	
cultural relativism	mental illness	diathesis-stress model	
demonology	mental incompetence	harmful dysfunction theory	
deviance	prevalence	humanistic model	
Diagnostic and Statistical Manual of Mental Disorders, 5th edition (DSM–5)	protective factors	insanity	
	psychiatric disorder	medical model	
	psychological disorder	psychodynamic model	
diathesis	psychopathology	psychological model	
dysfunction	psychosis	serious mental illness (SMI)	
eclectic	statistical abnormality	sociocultural model	
etiology	stressors		

1. What distinguishing symptom or factor is needed to identify someone as possibly suffering from a mental disorder as opposed to just acting in an abnormal way?

   (A) The individual's behavior does not conform to certain social standards.

   (B) The person cannot keep a steady job.

   (C) The behavior displayed causes others within the culture group embarrassment.

   (D) The individual's behavior is observed in the context of his or her culture.

   (E) The individual perceives his or her own behavior with emotional distress and discomfort.

2. A key difference between the medical model and psychological models is

   (A) the medical model does not recognize the influence of the environment

   (B) the medical model uses the term *patient* instead of *client*

   (C) the medical model treats all conditions with medications

   (D) psychological models focus on disordered thinking and emotional regulation and recognize the impact of the environment

   (E) psychological models disregard the physiological factors in disorders

3. Kevin drove his car into a crowd, killing one person and injuring many others. His attorney was able to convince the jury that he had a history of delusions and was unable to discern that his actions were wrong during the incident. What was the verdict of the jury?

   (A) Not guilty by reason of mental disability

   (B) Guilty by reason of psychiatric illness

   (C) Not guilty by reason of insanity

   (D) Guilty

   (E) The jury was not required to reach a verdict because of the defendant's mental illness

4. Philippe Pinel's contribution to the advancement of psychopathology included:

(A) the "four humors" theory of mental illness

(B) advocacy for the more humane treatment of the mentally ill using moral therapy

(C) the procedure of cutting or sectioning the prefrontal cortex to reduce symptoms of severe mental illness

(D) advocacy for the more humane treatment of psychologically disordered patients by developing the process of trephining

(E) a three-tiered approach to determining the presence of mental illness

5. Sophie's psychiatrist attempts to treat Sophie's generalized anxiety disorder by prescribing an anti-anxiety medication, working with her to help her change her irrational thoughts that trigger increased anxiety, and working with her family to try to reduce environmental factors that have been causing more frequent panic attacks. This approach is best described as

(A) biopsychosocial

(B) humanistic

(C) psychoanalytic

(D) behavioral

(E) medical

Refer to the diagram below to answer the following question.

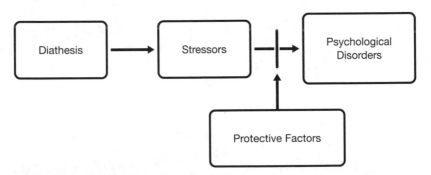

6. Which choice would most closely correspond with the diagram above?

(A) Rick's depression is caused by a combination of early childhood trauma and a neurological chemical imbalance.

(B) Rick has a predisposed vulnerability to depression and when confronted with the death of his father, he experiences a depressive episode.

(C) Depression runs in Rick's family, and the family dynamics as well as cultural expectations regarding his own self-worth have led to a prolonged bout with severe depression.

(D) Rick has been diagnosed with depressive disorder as a result of blood tests and patient interviews that confirmed both a neurological anomaly and cognitive dysfunctions.

(E) The depression Rick is dealing with is a product of environmental factors centered on operant conditioning.

7. Yana is experiencing a profound and debilitating sense of anxiety centered on her fear that her physical appearance will cause embarrassment to others around her. What she is experiencing can best be described as a

(A) social anxiety disorder

(B) cultural idiom of distress

(C) cultural syndrome

(D) psychogenic disorder

(E) derived biopsychosocial condition

Refer to the diagram below when answering the following question.

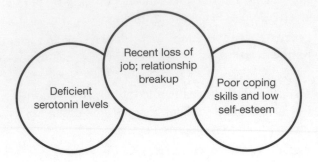

8. Ali's diagnosis of panic disorder as reflected in the diagram above is most associated with the

(A) biological model

(B) harmful dysfunction model

(C) psychodynamic model

(D) humanistic model

(E) biopsychosocial model

9. According to the humanistic model, psychological disorders are predominantly the result of

(A) cultural factors

(B) irrational belief systems

(C) inability to express authentic self

(D) early childhood trauma

(E) psychological distress

10. The Rosenhan study

(A) demonstrated a positive correlation between predispositions of illness and stress factors

(B) confirmed the connection between physical vulnerabilities and sociocultural stressors in eliciting symptoms of psychological disorders

(C) provided evidence that men are diagnosed at higher rates than women for depression and anxiety-related disorders

(D) provided insight into the enigmatic causes of schizophrenia

(E) illustrated the negative influence psychological labels can have on the perception and treatment of people with mental disorders

1. George Engel developed the biopsychosocial model, which integrates the biological (medical), psychological, and sociocultural models. Discuss three factors a therapist working in the biopsychosocial model would address in each of the following domains in order to come up with an integrated understanding of a disorder. Give an example to demonstrate the impact of each factor.
   - Biological
   - Psychological
   - Sociocultural

2. You are a clinical psychologist and your client is Kimberly, who has persistent sadness. Explain how you would diagnose Kimberly's symptom and look for its causes using three of the following approaches:
   - Medical model
   - Psychodynamic model
   - Behavioral model
   - Cognitive model
   - Humanistic model

WRITE AS A PSYCHOLOGIST: CHOOSE STRONG EXAMPLES

The first free-response question calls on you to identify three factors within each domain of the biopsychosocial model *and* provide an example to demonstrate the impact of each factor. When planning your response, try to think of strong, specific examples for each factor. For example, one factor in the biological model a therapist would consider is genetics. Instead of providing a general example of the impact of genetics, such as "family histories," provide a specific example, such as "a family history of depression and anxiety that pervaded family interactions." For more guidance on answering free-response questions, see pages xxii–xxiii.

Types of Psychological Disorders

21

*"I started to see crypto-communists everywhere . . . I started to think
I was a man of great religious importance, and to hear
voices all the time . . . I began to hear something like
telephone calls in my head, from people opposed
to my ideas . . . The delirium was like a dream,
from which I seemed never to awake."*

—John Nash, Nobel Prize winner and
subject of the film "A Beautiful Mind"

Essential Question: What are the different types of psychological
disorders, and what are the symptoms that determine if someone has a
specific disorder?

The Diagnostic and Statistical Manual of Mental Disorders, 5th Edition
(DSM-5) is the standard classification system of psychological disorders
used in the United States. Symptom descriptions and diagnostic criteria are
presented for each disorder. In addition, this latest edition of the DSM has
attempted to harmonize with another classification tool—the **International
Classification of Diseases (ICD)**. The ICD is published by the World Health
Organization (WHO) and classifies an extensive range of medical conditions
and also includes a comprehensive classification system for mental disorders.

The experts who compiled the DSM-5 considered another aspect of
psychological diagnosis: **comorbidity**, or the presence of two or more disorders
at the same time. Some controversy surrounds comorbidity, because symptoms
of some disorders overlap with symptoms of other disorders, potentially
confusing treatment plans. Decisions about resolving the controversy will no
doubt be discussed in the next round of revisions.

Neurodevelopmental Disorders

Neurodevelopmental disorders—conditions associated with central nervous
system functioning—begin in early childhood. These disorders usually include
developmental deficits that affect social, intellectual, academic, and/or personal

functioning. The symptoms can be very specific, such as mispronunciation and articulation problems associated with speech sound disorder, or more global, such as the learning and adaptive behavior problems common to severe intellectual disability (formerly referred to as mental retardation). Neurological developmental disorders include *intellectual developmental disorder, autism spectrum disorder, attention-deficit/hyperactivity disorder,* and *tic disorder,* among others.

Intellectual developmental disorder refers to deficits of general mental abilities such as intellectual functioning and adaptive behaviors. **Intellectual functioning** refers to learning ability, problem-solving, and reasoning. **Adaptive behavior** refers to social, practical, and conceptual skills such as the ability to follow rules and/or avoid being victimized (social), upkeep of personal hygiene and use of money or a telephone (practical), and the ability to apply literacy, number concepts, and self-direction (conceptual). An important change in diagnostic criteria in the DSM-5 is the removal of traditional IQ scores, replacing them with descriptions of adaptive functioning to evaluate the degree of severity of a specific neurodevelopment disorder.

Autism spectrum disorder (ASD) is a developmental disorder that centers on repetitive behaviors and impairments of social communication and interaction. A person diagnosed with **autism** will show impairment of abilities in the following ways:

- social and emotional interaction or exchange, including an inability to participate in typical give-and-take conversations and an inability to understand and respond to normal social cues

- understanding and using nonverbal communication such as body language and eye contact and understanding facial expressions

- development and/or maintenance of social relationships

Autistic behaviors may include repetitive motion and speech, use of objects, and ritualized patterns of behavior. Additionally, individuals with autism may exhibit extreme sensitivity to sensory stimulation from the environment. All symptoms can range from mild to profound.

As you read in Chapter 20, **attention deficit hyperactivity disorder (ADHD)** is a neurodevelopmental disorder marked by persistent inattention and/or persistent display of impulsive behavior that interferes with basic functioning and development. Most often diagnosed during childhood, and disproportionately among boys, this disorder can be apparent in a young child's inattention, chronic disorganization, lack of focus, and inability to stay on task. Hyperactive behaviors may include constant fidgeting, running around, and general restlessness. Impulsive behaviors may include a wide range of actions that take place without forethought, including sudden hitting, interrupting, or throwing objects. For a definitive diagnosis of ADHD, all behavioral symptoms must take place in more than one setting. In other words, the behavioral symptoms must manifest themselves across various situations such as at school, at home, and in other settings. As you read in Chapter 20, the diagnosis of ADHD can be controversial, because some of the diagnostic criteria describe young children generally.

Anxiety Disorders

Nearly everyone has experienced a feeling of nervousness from time to time— maybe about relationships, health, work, or financial issues. **Anxiety**, a feeling of unease, fear, or worry that something bad is about to happen, is a part of everyday life. However, what elevates common nervousness to an anxiety disorder is the intensity and persistence of symptoms and their interference with daily life. The DSM-5 lists twelve specific types of anxiety disorders. The most prevalent are *generalized anxiety disorder, panic disorder, specific phobia*, and *social anxiety disorder*.

   Generalized anxiety disorder (GAD) is defined as prolonged (six months or longer) feelings of unspecified worry and unease. Individuals with GAD are unable to stop the constant feelings of dread without a clear cause, and these feelings disrupt their daily lives. Other specific symptoms may include fatigue, restlessness, irritability, sleep disturbances, and muscle tension. Physical symptoms associated with heightened levels of distress, including headache, gastrointestinal problems, or diarrhea, are common in people with GAD.

Panic disorder is described as an acute, or sudden and severe feeling of extreme anxiety or fear that something terrible will happen at any minute. A panic episode can come on quickly and reach its peak within minutes. The trauma involved in a panic attack can be exacerbated by the concurrent worry that the panic is associated with a life-threatening condition, such as a heart attack. Symptoms associated with panic disorder may include accelerated heart rate, chest pains, tremors, feelings of choking, shortness of breath, nausea, or numbness. The individual may also experience **derealization**, a feeling of unreality, or **depersonalization**, a feeling of being detached from oneself.

Specific phobia disorder is an anxiety disorder encompassing an overwhelming, unreasonable, and persistent sense of fear of a *phobic stimulus*, which can be an object or situation that provokes the fear response and sometimes a panic attack. Any contact with the phobic stimulus may produce immediate fear, and usually the person will actively avoid the stimulus. Sometimes even the thought of the object or situation may result in an unreasonable fear response. The individual may recognize that the fear is excessive and even unwarranted but is still unable to control it. The DSM-5 reports that about 6 to 8 percent of all people have specific phobias and the rate is higher (about 16 percent) among teens. Women are diagnosed with specific phobia disorder more often than men. The specific phobias among women are predominantly animal phobias, natural environment phobias such as lightning, and situation-specific (situational) phobias such as a fear of falling, driving a car, or using an elevator (Figure 21.1).

Prevalence Rates of Specific Phobias, 2007

Specific Phobia	Total Prevalence
Animal	4.7%
Natural environment	8.9%
Heights	4.5%
Water	2.4%
Storms	2.0%
Blood-injection-injury	2.1%
Situational	12.2%
Closed spaces	3.2%
Going to dentist	2.4%
Being in a crowd	1.6%
Traveling by car, bus, or train	0.7%
Hospitals	1.4%
Other	1.0%

Figure 21.1 Prevalence of Specific Phobia

Agoraphobia, a fear of open, crowded, or enclosed spaces such as shops or movie theaters, is another common phobia. Agoraphobia may also include a fear of being outside the safety of one's home or standing in line in a crowd. Many people diagnosed with agoraphobia have a history of panic attacks. The frequent panic attacks of agoraphobic individuals are often associated with specific places in which such panic attacks occurred in the past. In extreme cases, even leaving their homes for the uncertain space outside can bring on a panic attack.

Social anxiety disorder (social phobia) causes some people to become overwhelmed with anxiety and fear when in social situations. They have an intense fear of being criticized or embarrassed so they avoid such social situations as large events or parties, public speaking, being on stage, or using public restrooms.

Obsessive-Compulsive and Related Disorders

All of us have experienced symptoms associated with **obsessive-compulsive and related disorders (OCRDs),** possibly including checking a wristwatch constantly to verify the time, washing hands frequently to avoid germs, holding on to useless material things too long, or having a recurring dream. However, as with anxiety disorder, the difference between having a few compulsive habits and having a disorder is the persistence and intensity of those symptoms. This category of disorders includes the general **obsessive-compulsive disorder (OCD)** as well as disorders with specific obsessions, including hoarding, obsessive skin picking, obsessive hair pulling, a preoccupation with one's appearance, and others. Brain imaging has revealed damage to the basal ganglia in people with OCRDs, though whether it is a cause or effect is not yet certain.

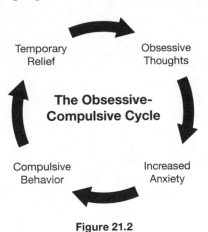

Temporary Relief

Obsessive Thoughts

The Obsessive-Compulsive Cycle

Compulsive Behavior

Increased Anxiety

Figure 21.2

People with disorders in this category are troubled by repetitive thoughts, distress, and compulsive behaviors. For example, someone with obsessive-compulsive disorder might have an obsession with even numbers, feeling the need to adjust the volume on a car radio to an even number if it was set at an odd number. Or someone with OCD might insist on standing or sitting only on the right of someone at the dinner table or in a theater or almost anywhere because not doing so would cause anxiety to spike to an uncomfortable level.

A simple and efficient way to understand compulsion is to think about how the intense anxiety correlates with the obsession and compulsion (Figure 21.2). Simply put, the obsession increases the anxiety and the compulsion reduces it. The obsession may be rooted in a neurochemical imbalance, most often either over- or under-production of the neurotransmitter **serotonin,** or it may have psychological origins.

In severe cases, OCD behavioral patterns can be burdensome. For example, a man was constantly obsessed with the idea or image that he had hit a small child while driving his car. Any bump felt while driving would spike the obsessive anxiety-producing thoughts, and then he would begin compulsively checking and rechecking his route. He would drive around the block to the place where he thought he might have hit someone, checking repeatedly to make sure no one had been hit. He might repeat the compulsive behavior dozens of times in an effort to reduce his anxiety. Once, he was stopped by the police for exhibiting suspicious behavior. His OCD cycle was so severe that he eventually gave up driving.

People suffering from severe OCD may express thoughts of suicide or fantasize about contracting a fatal disease. Thoughts of death stem from the individual's awareness of the irrational nature of the obsession and compulsive behavior and inability to stop it, and they may see no other way out.

A woman with **hoarding disorder**, for example, knows it is ridiculous to refuse to throw away used bandages, but inside her mind is the obsessive thought that something profoundly important is connected to that used bandage and throwing it away could lead to tragedy. The thought of throwing it away sends her anxiety soaring. So, she saves it, along with everything else—used teabags, price tags from purchased items, and shoes beyond repair. One woman saved all the hair that accumulated in her hairbrush.

Body dysmorphic disorder is a condition related to OCD in which the affected person has an obsessive preoccupation with his or her physical appearance. In this disorder, the anxiety-reducing compulsive behavior may include compulsive grooming or frequent checking of one's appearance in mirrors or window reflections. As with OCD in general, most people with body dysmorphic disorder are aware of the illogical nature of their obsession and compulsive rituals, and know their anxiety disrupts their ability to function normally in everyday life.

Trauma and Stress-Related Disorders

Imagine being in lower Manhattan on September 11, 2001, and seeing people jumping out of windows a hundred stories above you. Or imagine parents waiting outside a hospital room for word about whether their child who had been hit by a car would live or die. Or imagine surviving when all the other members of a platoon died in a bomb explosion. The DSM-5 includes a chapter focused on trauma and stress-related disorders, exploring the cause of psychological symptoms that result from exposure to such traumatic events. Symptoms such as *anhedonia* (the inability to experience any pleasure), *dysphoria (*an intense state of unease), externalized anger, and aggression may arise from experiencing such trauma. Two common trauma and stress-related disorders are *acute stress disorder* and *post-traumatic stress disorder.*

Acute stress disorder (ASD) is characterized by symptoms that begin to develop shortly after people experience or witness a traumatic event. They may include uncontrollable flashback memories and nightmares, dissociative symptoms, sleep disturbances, hypervigilance, and problems processing the traumatic event. Traumatic events are often violent: Common examples include sexual or physical assault, kidnapping, violent crime, military combat, and natural disasters such as earthquakes, hurricanes, or tornadoes. Children who are victims of inappropriate sexual contact or sexual assault with or without violence, or who experience a traumatic medical event are also susceptible to ASD.

When ASD symptoms persist for more than a month or develop six or more months after the traumatic event, the individual may be diagnosed with **post-traumatic stress disorder (PTSD)**, which was once known as "shell shock." PTSD became a familiar topic in the media after the Vietnam war and again after the war in Iraq, as returning veterans, mostly men, were diagnosed with the disorder in veterans' hospitals around the United States. Yet women are actually reported to be affected by PTSD at a higher rate than men and across a wide range of traumatic events.

The DSM-5 also distinguishes between diagnoses of PTSD for adults and children. Children suffering from PTSD may experience developmental regression, such as the loss of language ability, and their symptoms may manifest in play behavior.

Roughly 9–16 percent of veterans of the wars in Afghanistan and Iraq are estimated to have PTSD..

In adults, the common symptoms of PTSD include re-experiencing the traumatic event through flashbacks and nightmares. Such memories are frighteningly intense and include the quality of actually reliving the traumatic experience. Environmental triggers, such as viewing a similar event on TV, seeing a person in uniform, or perceiving certain sounds and smells, can cause intense psychological distress. As a result, sufferers of PTSD may often avoid certain individuals or activities associated with these triggers.

Cognitive distortions and the avoidance mechanism of amnesia may also be symptoms of PTSD. Sufferers may develop negative thoughts, including irrational levels of distrust. They may also blame themselves for the traumatic event. Some individuals with PTSD may become highly aggressive with little or no provocation; they may also startle easily and have trouble concentrating.

Fortunately, the majority of people who experience traumatic events do not develop PTSD. Researchers continue to evaluate individuals who have experienced traumatic events, those with PTSD and those without, hoping to discover why some individuals are affected and some are not and identify those at risk. Understanding the underlying differences may lead to better treatment for people who do develop PTSD. Research suggests that people may be genetically or psychologically predisposed to having more debilitating responses to traumatic events, but no definitive conclusions have yet been reached.

Dissociative Disorders

Dissociative disorders are characterized by defense mechanisms, including disruptions in memory and identity, in response to trauma. The two most common dissociative disorders are *dissociative amnesia* and *dissociative identity disorder (DID)*. **Dissociative amnesia** is the inability to remember parts of the past as a result of trauma. The loss of these memories is triggered psychologically rather than by physical damage and is often associated with traumatic events such as rape or child abuse. *Localized amnesia*—the inability to remember events during a specific stretch of time, such as the period of childhood from age five to age seven—is the most common type of memory loss. *Selective amnesia* involves the loss of only certain specific memories. For example, a soldier may remember what he was doing before and after an explosive device blew up near him and killed his fellow soldier and friend, but he cannot remember the actual event. *Generalized amnesia*—the total loss of memory of one's life, including learned skills and acquired knowledge—is rare. People with generalized amnesia are often referred to law enforcement and psychiatric care because they are found to wander aimlessly. This behavior is also characteristic of a *dissociative fugue* experience. *Fugue* refers to the complete loss of awareness of one's identity and the assumption or development of another identity.

Dissociative identity disorder or **DID**, formerly called multiple personality disorder, is the presence of at least two distinct identities (alters) that appear in a host's behavior along with impaired memory beyond mere forgetfulness. For example, Clara walks with her husband and three young daughters in the aisles of a grocery store. When they get to the children's cereal section, Clara the wife and mother is no longer there. In her place is a six-year-old child named Bridgette. Her speech is that of a little girl and she quickly takes off the glasses that Clara had been wearing because the little girl has no vision problems and sees better without the glasses. She whines about the choice of cereal. At dinner time, while the father and three daughters are at the dinner table, a twenty-two-year-old single woman named Hannah sits in the living room rolling her eyes and muttering that she feels like she is in prison and just wants to go out and party. Hannah, Bridgette, and Clara are the same person but are different personalities, different alters. Seven other personalities appear as well. Clara is the core identity, but when any of the other identities take over, they live the life that Clara has disappeared from, at least temporarily. Clara has dissociative identity disorder and like others with the disorder experienced prolonged physical and/or sexual abuse at an early age, in her case between the ages of seven and fifteen.

In DID, the two or more separate identities or alters are completely different—they may be different ages, have different mannerisms, and display unique brain functioning when traced. For example, some individuals diagnosed with DID display different evoked potentials (responses to stimulus) for each alter. Using an electroencephalograph (EEG) to measure the brain wave response to a common stimulus, the evoked potential for each alter is shown as a different pattern on the EEG graph.

Disparity between diagnoses of DID in different regions and cultures around the world is a controversial topic among psychology and psychiatry professionals. Although many psychological disorders are found relatively consistently throughout the world, DID seems to be specific to Western cultures. More than 80 percent of DID cases are concentrated in Western cultures. The inconsistent rate of diagnosis has raised questions about the prevalence and validity of the disorder. While the rate of schizophrenia diagnoses has remained relatively consistent, DID diagnoses peaked in the early 21st century and have decreased since then.

Treatment for DID is complex and focuses mainly on dealing with the specific trauma in a therapeutic setting and reintegrating the various alters. Reintegration can be difficult because each alter has developed a specific role or function in coping with stress and events. The core personality must not only confront the traumatic memories from his or her past but must also learn to deal with the challenges of everyday life that are different for each alter.

Somatic Symptom Disorder and Related Disorders

Somatic symptom disorder and related disorders are physical disorders caused by psychological stress. In other words, an individual with a somatic symptom disorder presents a psychological problem in bodily (*somatic*) form. Following are among the somatic symptom and related disorders the DSM-5 lists.

Somatic symptom disorder is characterized by extreme anxiety about physical symptoms that are interpreted as evidence of illness. The thoughts, feelings, and behaviors of individuals with somatic symptom disorder, formerly called *hypochondriasis*, focus on such symptoms as various pains (local or generalized) and fatigue that disrupt their daily lives. The symptoms are real, not imagined. For example, a man might feel some chest pain, a common symptom of a non-life-threatening condition called acid reflux. However, he may be so consumed with worry that he sees the pain as life-threatening—a sign of a heart attack or a form of cancer. In extreme cases, somatic symptoms can become totally debilitating.

Illness anxiety disorder (IAD) is a severe obsession with having or getting a serious illness despite no indication of illness following a medical exam. Individuals with IAD will often check their bodies for any signs of illness. The absence of actual physical symptoms distinguishes illness anxiety disorder from somatic symptom disorder. Two types of this disorder are encountered clinically: the care-seeking type in which the person frequently seeks medical care such as tests and medical procedures, and the care-avoidant type in which the individual rarely seeks any type of medical care but still believes he or she is very ill.

Conversion disorder (functional neurological symptom disorder) is "conversion" of extreme anxiety into a physical disorder. The physical symptoms are real but no neurological or medical cause can be identified clinically. Conversion disorders are characterized by motor symptoms such as weakness or paralysis, abnormal movements, limp, and tremors. Sensory symptoms include reduced or absent sense of touch, vision, or hearing. In extreme cases, non-epileptic (psychogenic) seizures may occur, as well as inability to speak and even coma.

If a person falsely reports, or deliberately creates or exaggerates symptoms to get medical attention, that person is exhibiting symptoms of *factitious disorder.* Some individuals may even induce symptoms or injure themselves just to receive medical attention. People who display these behaviors

The headache is real, but this woman with somatic symptom disorder fears it signals a life-threatening problem.

are found to have significant emotional illness. They have a deep need to be seen as "sick" and receive sympathy for being ill; they are not seeking financial gain. Another more harmful type of factitious disorder is called *factitious disorder imposed on another* (previously known as Munchausen syndrome by proxy), which involves the deliberate falsification of physical or psychological symptoms or actually inducing these symptoms in someone else in order to gain emotional attention and sympathy.

Feeding and Eating Disorders

Feeding and eating disorders are maladaptive behaviors centered on food intake or avoidance. The most commonly diagnosed and treated eating disorders listed in the DSM-5 are *anorexia nervosa, bulimia nervosa*, and *binge-eating disorder.*

Anorexia nervosa (often referred to as *anorexia*) is a life-threatening eating disorder that involves intense fear of weight gain or becoming overweight, a distorted perception of one's weight or body shape, and persistent restriction of caloric intake leading to extreme weight loss and increasing damage to physical health. It affects more females than males and occurs more frequently in young adults.

Typical symptoms of anorexia include abrupt and profound weight loss coupled with exercise and constant weighing, compulsive and covert checking of one's body in mirrors or reflective surfaces, and increased verbalization of the fear of weight gain or being fat. Many individuals diagnosed with anorexia will also exhibit *body dysmorphia* (page 528)—an increasing cognitive misperception of being overweight despite evidence to the contrary (Figure 21.3). These individuals will usually have a strict daily calorie-counting regimen, develop phobias to certain foods, hoard food, and become preoccupied with images of food and recipes. They may also develop an obsessive interest in preparing food for others but refuse to eat with them, have ritualistic eating behaviors, and increased social isolation, depression, and anxiety.

Of all the mental disorders, anorexia poses the greatest risk of death. The risk of suicide is significantly higher among those struggling with anorexia than that of the general population. The short- and long-term medical consequences of the disorder can be life-threatening as a result of damage to the cardiovascular system (heart and blood vessels), which may include irregular heart rhythms, congestive heart failure, or acute heart failure. Other medical complications associated with anorexia include renal (kidney) damage, gastrointestinal damage, cessation of the menstrual cycle leading to infertility, osteoporosis (bone damage), tooth damage or loss, and skin complications.

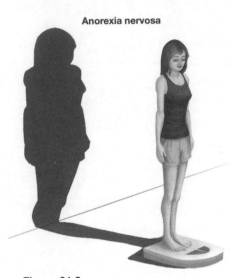

Anorexia nervosa

Figure 21.3

Treatment often involves immediate medical care, including hospitalization for those who are significantly underweight or experiencing severe complications of anorexia. Inpatient care is often the preferred treatment because it offers a combination of medical supervision, dietary and nutrition education, and group and individual psychotherapy to address the underlying psychological issues that led to the anorexia.

Bulimia nervosa (commonly referred to as *bulimia*) is a potentially life-threatening eating disorder that involves secretive **binging**—eating large or excessive amounts of food in a short period of time. Binging is usually accompanied by a feeling of lack of control, followed by some form of compensatory behavior such as **purging**—self-induced vomiting, misuse of laxatives or diuretics (medications that increase urination to remove excess fluid from the body), and fasting or excessive exercise to compensate for the high calorie intake. Signs of bulimia include relieving one's bowels with the use of laxatives immediately after eating, callouses or wounds on the knuckles or hands resulting from frequent self-induced vomiting, discolored or damaged teeth, and major fluctuations in weight. Medical issues associated with bulimia are similar to those for anorexia—cardiovascular and gastrointestinal problems, cessation or irregularity of the menstrual cycle, and osteoporosis. Like anorexia, bulimia affects mostly females, though its incidence among males is increasing, and it occurs more frequently in young adults.

Some individuals with bulimia have exceptionally low self-esteem, which is responsible for their preoccupation with weight and body image. Bulimic individuals usually present maladaptive cognitive distortions such as **awfulizing** (cognitive perceptions that things are much worse than they really are) and rigid thinking. Binge-purge episodes may be followed by a sense of shame and increased feelings of depression and anxiety. Individuals with bulimia usually follow a binge-purge episode with dieting, a process described clinically as the "**bulimic cycle**" (Figure 21.4). Treatment focuses on the underlying self-esteem issues and emotion management of bulimia and behavioral therapy, addressing issues that perpetuate the bulimic cycle. Immediate attention is typically given to any medical problems that have developed as a result of the disorder.

Binge-eating disorder is the most common eating disorder and involves recurrent episodes of eating excessive amounts of food in a short period of time accompanied by an intense sense of lack of control over the eating behavior. It is similar to bulimia but does not involve purging, and many people with the disorder are overweight. A binge episode is often preceded

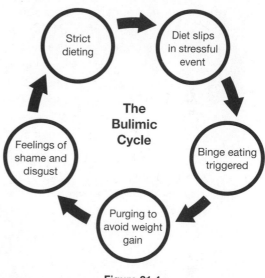

Figure 21.4

by emotional distress associated with anger, depression, or shame. The disorder is often linked to uncontrolled emotions, social isolation, and depression.

Schizophrenia Spectrum and Other Psychotic Disorders

Many consider **schizophrenia** the most profound and devastating of all mental disorders, and it is the most prevalent disorder among all psychoses. **Psychosis** refers to any disorder in which the affected person has lost contact with reality. The range of psychotic disorders includes *delusional disorder, brief psychotic disorder*, and *schizophreniform disorder* (essentially, short-duration schizophrenia).

Five symptoms are commonly associated with all psychotic disorders. These symptoms are often separated into those considered positive (additions) or negative (reductions) in relation to normal behavior. **Positive symptoms** not present in normal behavior include delusions and hallucinations. **Negative symptoms** refer to those with a marked decrease of normal functions; the most typical negative symptom is *diminished emotional expression*. A diagnosis of schizophrenia requires at least two of the symptoms outlined below, and one of them must be delusions, hallucinations, or disorganized speech.

The five symptoms of psychosis include:

- **Delusions**—the persistence of false beliefs, usually held by affected individuals as ideas about themselves in relation to the world around them. A wide variety of delusions include *persecution*, the idea of being harassed or spied on; *referential*, the belief that comments or gestures are directed toward the affected individual; *grandiose delusions*, an image of having great abilities or being important or famous; and *nihilistic delusions*, a belief that a disastrous event is going to happen. Delusions are defined as bizarre if they are clearly beyond the realm of possibility. One common bizarre delusion is the belief of being in communication with God or Jesus; another is that the individual is missing an essential body organ. One schizophrenic patient reported that he had an x-ray showing that he had no heart. Another diagnosed schizophrenic was convinced that he was under surveillance by the Department of Defense, the FBI, and the CIA.

- **Hallucinations**—sensory experiences without any external sensory stimuli. An authentic hallucination is involuntary and cannot be controlled by the individual. However, it is experienced as though it is as real as any other normal sensory perception. The most common type of hallucination is an auditory hallucination—hearing a voice that is totally separate from the individual. Imagine having an invisible person talking harshly straight into your ear, harassing you, or  telling you to do something, and you will get a sense of what a person with schizophrenia experiences.

- **Disorganized speech**—combining thoughts or switching from one thought to another. A good way to explain this type of thinking is to imagine your train of thought expressed in speech as a highway with on- and off-ramps. A nonpsychotic person has the ability to remain focused on one thought while keeping the on- and off-ramps closed. In contrast, in a psychotic person or someone with diagnosed schizophrenia, the on- and off-ramps are wide open, and unrelated thoughts can suddenly intrude. The person can switch from one topic to a totally unrelated one—sometimes linking words together because they rhyme (called *clang association*), or spewing out an almost completely nonsensical jumble of words (often referred to as *word salad*).

- **Grossly disorganized/abnormal motor behavior**—a variety of abnormal or bizarre physical behaviors, which may include childlike mannerisms. During interviews, one schizophrenic patient twirled her hair throughout the entire conversation. Catatonic (stupor-like) behavior may also be exhibited, including bizarre postures and utter lack of mobility. Catatonia may also include aimless and repeated movements, including facial expressions or constant repeating of certain words.

- **Negative symptoms (diminished emotional expression and avolition)**— the withholding of emotions and exhibiting diminished emotional expression. The experience of diminished emotions is described as the **flat affect** (**affect** here is a noun describing subjective mood or emotional state). Sometimes, however, expressed emotions are highly inappropriate, such as laughing when others are sad or displaying anger or tears during a joyful event. More typically, emotions will be entirely absent. **Avolition** refers to a significant decrease in or absence of any purposeful activity. The individual may simply sit or stand for hours without showing interest in participating in any activities.

In order to distinguish schizophrenia from a depressive or bipolar disorder with psychotic features, delusions or hallucinations must be evident for at least two weeks even if a major mood disorder is absent.

Schizophrenia is a brain disease whose exact cause is not yet known, although studies have suggested that a combination of genetics and environmental factors may contribute to its development. Abnormally elevated levels of the neurotransmitter **dopamine** have been linked to schizophrenia, and enlarged fluid-filled ventricles of the brain are also associated with neurological aspects of the disorder. Schizophrenia is more prevalent among individuals whose fathers are older, at the time of their birth and those with autoimmune diseases and exposure to viruses and malnutrition during the second trimester of fetal development. Schizophrenia affects about 1 percent of people worldwide and is slightly more frequent among males. The risk of developing the disease is greater (10 percent) in someone who has a sibling or close relative with schizophrenia. The presence of schizophrenia in one identical twin increases the risk to 50 percent in the other twin, which demonstrates a strong genetic link as well as the role of environmental factors in the development of the disorder.

The onset of schizophrenia usually occurs in the late teens to early twenties, and the severity of the symptoms varies with individuals. The spectrum of severity is described as the "rule of quarters." A quarter of those who develop schizophrenia will have one psychotic episode but will then recover and lead a relatively normal life. Another quarter will respond well to medication and be able to live relatively independently. The third quarter will need to live with supervision in a supportive facility. The last quarter will have the most severe symptoms and will require permanent care; 15 percent are unresponsive to medication.

Schizoaffective disorder is essentially schizophrenia plus periodic symptoms of disordered affect or mood. An individual diagnosed with schizoaffective disorder will not only display two or more of the five psychosis-related symptoms described above but will also present a major mood episode of either pervasive depression or mania.

Bipolar and Related Disorders

Undoubtedly, at some point you have experienced a sad day. You had "the blues." You may also remember a time when you had a really "up" day. Everything was clicking; you were really happy and excited to be alive. You did not have a mood disorder, obviously, but if your depressed or excited moods were so extreme and prolonged that they led to disruptions in your daily life, then they could be an indication of a bipolar disorder. (See Figure 21.5)

The American Psychiatric Association clearly differentiates among schizophrenia, bipolar disorders, and depressive disorders. The importance of these distinctions is explained in the DSM-5 as follows:

> Bipolar and related disorders are separated from
> the depressive disorders in the DSM-5 and placed
> between the chapters on schizophrenia spectrum and
> other psychotic disorders and depressive disorders in
> recognition of their place as a bridge between the two
> diagnostic classes in terms of symptomatology, family
> history, and genetics.
>
> –DSM-5 p. 123

The overlap in symptoms among these diseases does not mean that someone with bipolar or depressive disorder will develop schizophrenia or vice versa. Instead, it means:

1. The spectrum of symptoms can overlap in certain cases of schizophrenia, bipolar disorders, and depressive disorders.

2. The etiology or origins of these disorders may also overlap. Genetic links have been demonstrated for all three diseases.

Bipolar and related disorders include the following subcategories of disorders: *bipolar I disorder, bipolar II disorder, cyclothymic disorder, substance/medication-induced bipolar and related disorder, bipolar and related disorder due to another medical condition, other specified bipolar and related disorder,* and *unspecified bipolar and related disorder.*

Bipolar I is a mood (or affective) disorder in which an individual has experienced at least one manic episode (mania) as well as episodes of **major depression**. **Mania** is a state of abnormally elevated mood and intensely high energy that disrupts daily life. Mood in a manic episode is often characterized as either excessively euphoric, like "feeling on top of the world," or extremely irritable and dysphoric, experiencing profound unease. During a **manic episode**, people may also experience feelings of grandiosity and begin many projects that are often beyond their skills or talents. They may also require significantly less sleep. People with bipolar I may display *flight of ideas* speech because their thoughts may race faster than they can express coherently. Read the following passage aloud very fast and you will get a sense of what flight of ideas is like:

> *My husband drove me here today, a sweet but angry man. I know I married the right man. His car is the same color as my sister's car. She believes in global warming and that's why she drives a small car with good miles on it that allows her to drive wherever she wants. My husband won't vote unless there's someone worth voting for and I don't vote because politicians drive me crazy. Crazy drivers drive me crazy like my sister's husband, but I won't drive with him.*

An individual with bipolar I may also experience **hypomania**, a condition that is similar to mania but less severe. It is characterized by a pattern of episodes alternating between hypomania and major depression. To be diagnosed with bipolar I, however, the individual must also have experienced a full manic episode. For a diagnosis of **bipolar II**, an individual would have experienced a hypomanic episode but never a manic one (Figure 21.5).

Bipolar I and II

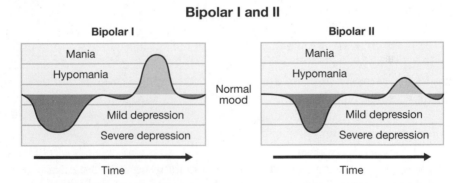

Figure 21.5 In between mood swings, people with bipolar disorders experience normal states.

The severity of depression for both bipolar I and bipolar II is classified as major depression (sometimes referred to as clinical depression). Major depression includes severe symptoms such as fatigue, sustained depressed mood, diminished interest or pleasure in activities, decreased appetite, weight loss, sleep disturbances, feelings of worthlessness, guilt, diminished ability to concentrate, and persistent thoughts of death or suicide.

Cyclothymic disorder is a mood disorder that involves elevated moods similar to hypomania but not as severe. The depressive episodes in this disorder are are also not as severe. The key characteristic of cyclothymia is its chronic nature. The alternating mood swings must be present for at least two years.

To summarize, the bipolar and related disorders are a class of mood disorders that involve both poles of moods—ups and downs. Bipolar I is the most severe, and bipolar II is less severe. Cyclothymic disorder is the milder of the three mood disorders, but it is the most chronic.

Depressive Disorders

The most common features of **depressive disorders** are significant feelings of sadness, emptiness, or irritability that are accompanied by somatic and cognitive disruptions that significantly affect daily function. The DSM-5 describes eight types of depressive disorders. The three most common disorders are *disruptive mood dysregulation disorder, major depressive disorder,* and *persistent depressive disorder.*

Disruptive mood dysregulation disorder (DMDD) is a childhood psychological condition characterized by extreme irritability, anger, and intense and sometimes frequent temper outbursts. It is a new addition to the DSM-5, added because many children under the age of ten were being diagnosed with bipolar disorder when their symptomatic behaviors did not accurately fit the bipolar definition. DMDD describes children whose behavior far exceeds the normal temperamental characteristics of children. Temper tantrums are so severe and persistent they may require clinical care. Emotional outbursts can occur three or more times a week, and between outbursts the child manifests a constant angry or irritable mood. Confirmation of a DMDD diagnosis requires that symptoms are present in at least two different settings (home, school, daycare) for twelve or more months, and the child must be at least six years old.

Major depressive disorder, also known as unipolar depression, involves severe symptoms such as fatigue, sustained depressed mood, diminished interest or pleasure in activities, decreased appetite, weight loss, sleep disturbances, feelings of worthlessness, guilt, diminished ability to concentrate, and persistent thoughts of death or suicide. A diagnosis of major depressive disorder requires the presence of at least five symptoms in a two-week period. At least one of the symptoms needs to be depressed mood or loss of pleasure or interest. Depression runs in families, demonstrating a genetic predisposition to develop the condition. However, the condition will usually only manifest if environmental factors trigger it. A high degree of **comorbidity** is also associated with major depression, including comorbid non-mood disorders and physical illnesses. If the depression is severe enough, psychotic symptoms such as delusions or hallucinations may be present.

Persistent depressive disorder is a depressed mood that has lasted for at least two years. It is considered a milder form of depression with no suicidal thoughts. Someone with persistent depressive disorder may experience two or more of the characteristic symptoms: poor appetite or overeating, sleep disturbances, fatigue, low self-esteem, poor concentration, feelings of hopelessness, and a lack of interest in activities they had previously found interesting. The causes of persistent depressive disorder vary from person to person, but neurological factors may be involved, including deficits in the production of one or more of the neurotransmitters in the brain—serotonin, dopamine, and norepinephrine. Antidepressant drugs that affect levels of these neurotransmitters are frequently prescribed. Genetic links are also suggested; if one parent has depression, the risk for their child to develop it as a teen or adult is increased significantly. Environmental factors may also increase the risk of developing persistent depressive disorder. Intense and prolonged stress, traumatic events, and the loss of a close family member can trigger the onset of the disorder.

Personality Disorders

People with personality issues that are so problematic, abnormal, and enduring that they lead to distress or impaired interactions with others suffer from *personality disorders*. Personality disorders differ from other disorders in their absence of delusions and depression. The diagnosis of personality disorder is somewhat controversial because of the subjectivity in determining symptoms, but four defining features seem to be common to all personality disorders:

1. Distorted thinking

2. Interpersonal difficulties

3. Problems with impulse control

4. Problems with emotional responses

Confirming a diagnosis of personality disorder requires that these features be evident to a significant degree and be persistent in at least two of the four categories. A diagnosis is made only if the symptoms cause significant functional impairment or distress for the individual.

Personality disorders can be grouped into three clusters based on common attributes.

Cluster A: "Odd, Suspicious, and Eccentric" disorders include disorders that show patterns of paranoia, social isolation, cognitive or perceptual distortions, and eccentric behaviors. **Paranoid personality disorder**, for example, is just what the name implies. It is a pattern of distrust and suspiciousness about other people's motives, and usually those motives are considered malevolent. It is different from paranoid schizophrenia because it does not present any of the five psychotic features characteristic of that disease or loss of touch with reality.

Cluster B: "Dramatic, Emotional, Erratic" disorders, as their name implies, are disorders that cause signficant disruption and even harm to self and others. **Borderline personality disorder** is marked by a significant and disruptive pattern of instability in interpersonal relationships, mood, self-image, and impulse control. Attention-seeking and self-centeredness are characteristic of both **histrionic personality disorder** and **narcissistic personality disorder**.

Antisocial personality disorder (APD) is most frequently associated with criminal behavior. A person with APD often is unable to feel any empathy or guilt, and that inability leads to a pattern of disregard for the rights and well-being of others and rampant manipulative behavior. Although people with APD may not ever commit a crime, about 50 percent of serious crimes are committed by people with APD. People with APD are predominantly male, and with their ability to put a facade on their lack of empathy and even appear charming, people with antisocial personality disorder may use their ruthlessness to land themselves in powerful positions in business.

Research suggests that APD has a significant biological basis. People with APD have a weaker autonomic response to fear and show less recognition of emotion in facial expressions. Twin studies have confirmed a genetic basis for a tendency to APD, and when that is combined with environmental stressors, the disorder is more likely to develop.

Some studies have found that about 21 percent of top business executives likely have antisocial personality disorder.

Cluster C: "Anxious, and Fearful" disorders include *avoidant, dependent,* and *obsessive-compulsive personality disorders.* In contrast to some of the self-aggrandizing symptoms in Cluster B disorders, disorders in this category include symptoms of inadequacy, submission, clinginess, hypersensitivity, and orderliness. **Obsessive-compulsive personality disorder** involves a disruptive preoccupation with orderliness, perfectionism, and personal and interpersonal control but should not be confused with obsessive-compulsive disorder (OCD) with its obsessive urge and a compulsive behavior to relieve the anxiety the urge produces.

"Can you tell me a little about yourself and what brings you to see me?" This is how a clinical interview begins. It's a simple question that helps a clinician develop a diagnosis, but the clinical interview is not a simple process. At the heart of a clinical interview is a search for clues that will help a clinician develop and test a hypothesis about a diagnosis.

The search for clues involves looking for information about psychological symptoms, patterns of maladjusted behavior, stressors, and interpersonal conflicts. The history of a person's problem also provides clues, including how long the problem has been present, how severe the problem is, and whether stressors were involved in the onset of the problem.

There are two styles of clinical interviews: structured and unstructured. The setting of the interview often determines which style a clinician uses. Structured interviews are used more often in hospitals, whereas unstructured interviews are used more often in private practice.

A structured interview is organized around scripted questions. Clinicians might record a patient's responses on a form or take notes. The scripted questions help make sure that the clinical interview is standardized and systematic.

Clinicians in private practice tend to use unstructured interviews. The clinician organizes an unstructured interview around themes such as the presenting problem, the history of the problem, family history, relationship history, developmental history, educational history, work history, medical history, substance use, legal history, previous counseling, and mental status. The unstructured interview relies heavily on the clinician's knowledge of the DSM and ability to recognize diagnostic symptoms.

The purpose of the interview is the same in both cases: looking for symptoms that map to DSM-5 diagnostic criteria. Clinicians take notes during the interview, recording the patient's verbal responses and their observations about nonverbal information. To make the diagnosis, clinicians compare the patient's responses to the DSM-5 diagnostic criteria.

Even when using scripted questions, the clinician has room to improvise. Clinicians know that they need to approach a patient with empathy and establish a rapport. If a person is in the hospital, his or her problems are serious, and the individual may be suicidal or psychotic. Clinicians are aware that a patient is telling his or her life story and asks questions to make sure they understand the narrative. While they are listening empathically to the story, they are gathering clues that will lead to a diagnosis.

If you ask an experienced clinician how they go about making a diagnosis, their answer is likely to be, "Ask lots of really good questions."

Practice: Work with several other classmates to find out more about how mental disorders are diagnosed, focusing on these questions:

- Why are interviews the primary method for diagnosing a mental disorder?

- Why are brain scans and genetic testing not a part of diagnosing mental disorders?

- What empirical evidence backs up using structured interviewing?

Neurocognitive Disorders

Neurocognitive disorders (NCD) refer to a group of disorders in which the primary problem is in cognitive function, but it is an acquired disorder rather than a developmental one. Delirium and cognitive impairment related to **Alzheimer's disease** are the main disorders in this category. A number of other NCDs listed in the DSM-5 are identified by brain diseases that can cause cognitive impairment. For example, **Lewy body-related dementia** causes neurocognitive impairment but also includes hallucinations as a symptom. The central features of **delirium** include cognitive dysfunction in attention or awareness, limited attention span, and confusion. Additionally, memory deficit, disorientation, and perceptual disturbance may be caused by a direct physiological or medical condition. Delirium tends to be transient—it comes and goes.

* * *

This chapter has introduced many psychological disorders, but the list is far from complete. If you can read the DSM-5, you will discover dozens of other disorders that you are not required to learn for AP Psychology—such as gender dysphoria; disruptive, impulse control, and conduct disorders; substance-related and addictive disorders; and paraphilic disorders. There's even a condition called "psychology student syndrome." If certain symptoms hit home as you were reading, you may have wondered whether you might actually have a particular disorder. We might all experience a few key symptoms—down days, strange thoughts, and an occasional battle with anxiety. But don't hesitate to talk to someone if you have any real concerns.

REFLECT ON THE ESSENTIAL QUESTION

Essential Question: *What are the different types of psychological disorders, and what are the symptoms that determine if someone has a disorder?* On separate paper, make a chart like the one below and gather details to answer that question. Using the KEY TERMS list and the material in the chapter, choose two disorders from each category and identify their symptoms. Add more rows so that all the categories are included.

DISORDERS	SYMPTOMS
Anxiety Disorders	
1)	1)
2)	2)
Bipolar and Related Disorders	
1)	1)
2)	2)
Traumatic and Stress Disorders	
1)	1)
2)	2)

KEY TERMS

adaptive behavior	*DEPRESSIVE DISORDERS*	OCRDs	*SCHIZOPHRENIA DISORDERS*
affect	depressive disorders	body dysmorphic disorder	avolition
awfulizing	disruptive mood dysregulation disorder (DMDD)	hoarding disorder	delusions
comorbidity	major depression	obsessive-compulsive disorder (OCD)	diminished emotional expression
dopamine	major depressive disorder	*PERSONALITY DISORDERS*	disorganized thinking
intellectual functioning	persistent depressive disorder	antisocial personality disorder	flat affect
International Classification of Diseases (ICD)	*DISSOCIATIVE DISORDERS*	borderline personality disorder	grossly disorganized/abnormal motor behavior
serotonin	dissociative amnesia	histrionic personality disorder	hallucinations
ANXIETY DISORDERS	dissociative identity disorder	narcissistic personality disorder	negative symptoms
agoraphobia	*EATING DISORDERS*	obsessive-compulsive personality disorder	positive symptoms
anxiety	anorexia nervosa	paranoid personality disorder	psychosis
depersonalization	binge-eating disorder		schizoaffective disorder
derealization	binging	*BIPOLAR DISORDERS*	*SOMATIC DISORDERS*
generalized anxiety disorder (GAD)	bulimia nervosa	bipolar I disorder	illness anxiety disorder (IAD)
panic disorder	bulimic cycle	bipolar II disorder	somatic symptom disorder
social anxiety disorder	purging	cyclothymic disorder	*NEURODEVEL-OPMENTAL DISORDERS*
specific phobia disorder	*TRAUMA DISORDERS*	hypomania	attention deficit hyperactivity disorder (ADHD)
NEURO-COGNITIVE DISORDERS	acute stress disorder (ASD)	mania	autism
Alzheimer's disease	post-traumatic stress disorder (PTSD)	manic episode	autism spectrum disorder (ASD)
delirium			
Lewy body-related dementia			
neurocognitive disorders (NCD			

1. Adam suffers from major depression. The biological cause most closely linked is

   (A) damage to Adam's prefrontal cortex after birth

   (B) insufficient levels of the neurotransmitters serotonin and norepinephrine in Adam's brain

   (C) enlarged gaps around his hippocampus

   (D) the recent divorce of Adam's parents and his suffering from the loss of his mother

   (E) a negative "learned helplessness" pattern of coping Adam has developed in his interactions with others

2. Which disorder is most closely linked to an excess of the neurotransmitter dopamine?

   (A) Attention deficit/hyperactivity disorder

   (B) Bipolar II disorder

   (C) Schizophrenia spectrum disorder

   (D) Autism spectrum disorder

   (E) Obsessive-compulsive disorder

3. Persistent depressive disorder is to major depression disorder as _____ is to bipolar I.

   (A) schizoaffective disorder

   (B) hypomania

   (C) cyclothymic disorder

   (D) bipolar II

   (E) mania

4. Anhedonia, dysphoria, externalized anger, and dissociative symptoms are all related to

   (A) schizophrenia disorder

   (B) anorexia nervosa

   (C) bulimia nervosa

   (D) disruptive mood dysregulation disorder

   (E) trauma and stress-related disorders

5. What evidence exists that suggests the scientific legitimacy of dissociative identity disorder (DID)?

(A) Evoked potentials for each alter are different.

(B) Localized personality traits are different between each alter.

(C) The diagnoses of people with DID peaked in the mid-1990s and then began to decrease.

(D) Western cultures and Asian cultures show a similar rate of diagnosis.

(E) Psychotherapists who specialize in treating DID confirm its existence.

6. Somatoform disorders share a common symptom which involves

(A) physical symptoms with no apparent physical cause

(B) peculiar personality characteristics that have become disruptive to daily life

(C) intermittent bouts of delusions and hallucinations

(D) at least one episode of hypomania

(E) anxiety related to past trauma

7. Bulimia nervosa involves a cyclical behavior pattern in which:

(A) extreme exercise is used to reduce weight

(B) obsessive thought is followed by compulsive behavior

(C) explosive emotional outburst is followed by irritability and non-targeted anger

(D) purging is followed by feelings of shame and disgust

(E) binging is preceded by extreme weight gain

8. Which of the following pairs of personality disorders are in the same cluster?

(A) Paranoid and histrionic

(B) Antisocial and narcissistic

(C) Obsessive-compulsive and schizoid

(D) Antisocial and paranoid

(E) Borderline and obsessive-compulsive

Use the following chart to answer question 9.

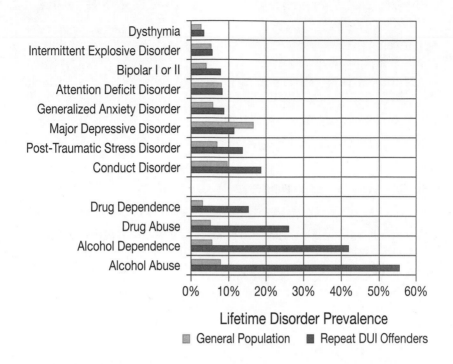

Lifetime Disorder Prevalence

▨ General Population   ■ Repeat DUI Offenders

9. Which is the most accurate conclusion that can be made based on the chart?

(A) Non-substance abuse psychological disorders pose the greatest risk of repeated DUIs.

(B) Repeat DUI offenders had significantly higher rates of bipolar disorder, anxiety, PTSD, and conduct disorder than the general population.

(C) Repeat DUI offenders had significantly lower rates of bipolar disorder, anxiety, PTSD, and conduct disorder than the general population

(D) Those with major depression had a higher rate of repeat DUI than the general population.

(E) Attention deficit disorder and conduct disorder have the most similar rate of repeated DUIs.

10. What is the primary difference between Bipolar I and Bipolar II disorders?

(A) Bipolar I involves major depression while Bipolar II involves dysthymia.

(B) Bipolar I exhibits only hypomania while Bipolar II exhibits mania symptoms.

(C) Bipolar II is transient in its presenting symptoms while Bipolar I is recurrent.

(D) Bipolar I includes psychotic symptoms and Bipolar II does not.

(E) Bipolar II involves only hypomania while Bipolar I involves mania.

FREE-RESPONSE QUESTIONS

1. Schizophrenia is considered by many to be the most severe mental disorder. Explain each of the following symptoms of schizophrenia and give an example of how each might be expressed in a person with the disorder:

   • Delusions
   • Hallucinations
   • Disorganized speech
   • Grossly disorganized/abnormal motor behavior
   • Negative symptoms

2. Personality disorders are grouped into three categories according to the characteristics the disorders share. Choose one disorder from each of the following clusters and describe it and its symptoms.

   • **Cluster A:** "Odd, Suspicious, and Eccentric"
   • **Cluster B:** "Dramatic, Emotional, Erratic"
   • **Cluster C:** "Anxious and Fearful"

UNIT 12: Review

In this unit, you sought answers to these essential questions about abnormal behavior.

Chapter 20: How do practitioners determine whether or not someone is mentally ill?

Chapter 21: What are the different types of psychological disorders, and what are the symptoms that determine if someone has a disorder?

Apply what you have learned about abnormal psychology by answering the free-response question below.

FREE-RESPONSE QUESTION

Ravvi is a freshman in high school; she gets good grades and has a large circle of friends. She is involved in school activities and loves singing. Lately, Ravvi finds herself gasping for breath and feeling like she is having a heart attack. She has been seeing a therapist for a few months, but the therapist cannot yet determine what is making Ravvi anxious. She has been losing sleep and interacts less often with her friends than before. She is constantly worried about the next time an attack might occur and interacts with people less because of this concern.

A) Identify the specific disorder Ravvi is likely experiencing and the category of disorders that contains it.

B) Using what you have learned in previous chapters about different approaches to explaining human behavior, identify how each of the following approaches would explain the etiology of Ravvi's illness.
   - Behavioral approach
   - Humanistic approach
   - Psychoanalytic approach
   - Cognitive approach

C) A researcher found a link between anxiety and depression.
   - Describe the type of study the researcher has likely conducted.
   - Predict the type of relationship one might expect between the variables in the study and explain why you make that prediction.

UNIT 13: Treatment of Abnormal Behavior

Chapter 22 *Treatment Approaches and Modes*

Chapter 23 *Cultural, Ethnic, and Gender Influences on Treatment and Prevention*

Unit Overview

If Kathy had a cut on her arm and it became infected, she would go to the doctor who would prescribe antibiotics. If Javier broke his wrist, the doctor would x-ray it and put it in a cast so it could heal properly. Unlike the standard medical treatment for an infected cut or a broken wrist, however, there are numerous approaches for treating mental health problems and disorders, and no single approach has proven to be the best and most effective.

This unit explores many of those approaches, including similarities and differences among them and their effectiveness in addressing psychological problems. It also considers the importance of the cultural and ethnic context as treatment methods and plans are put into effect.

Key Topics

- The central characteristics of psychotherapeutic intervention
- Major treatment orientations used in therapy (e.g., behavioral, cognitive, humanistic) and how those orientations influence therapeutic planning
- Similarities and differences in treatment formats (e.g., individual, group)
- The effectiveness of specific treatments used to address specific problems
- How cultural and ethnic context influence the choice and success of treatment (e.g., factors that lead to premature termination of treatment)
- Prevention strategies that build resilience and promote competence
- Major figures in psychological treatment (e.g., Aaron Beck, Albert Ellis, Sigmund Freud, Mary Cover Jones, Carl Rogers, B. F. Skinner, Joseph Wolpe)

Source: *AP® Psychology Course and Exam Description*

22

Treatment Approaches and Modes

"When we are no longer able to change a situation, we are challenged to change ourselves."

—Viktor Frankl

Essential Question: To what degree are psychotherapeutic approaches similar and different regarding philosophy, techniques, and effectiveness?

Psychotherapy is a general term for the treatment of mental health problems through interaction between trained psychologists and those seeking help. As you will see, one approach to psychotherapy may be better for treating depression, while another may be more effective for treating anxiety issues such as social phobia. Many mental health professionals use an **eclectic approach**, taking ideas from a variety of approaches to best serve the client. These approaches include both psychological and biomedical models, because psychological problems may stem from neurological abnormalities or from learning, childhood trauma, destructive habits of thinking, or even sociocultural factors.

Psychological Therapies

Therapy for mental illness can be divided into two general categories: the biomedical approach, with its primary focus on biological causes and medical treatment, and the psychological approach. The **psychological approach** is separated into four categories that are based on the main theories for the causes of mental illness: psychodynamic, humanistic, behavioral, and cognitive.

Psychodynamic Approaches

Psychodynamic and humanistic therapies are often referred to as **insight therapies** because the central goal is to help the patients or clients gain insight into the underlying causes of their mental distress or illness and use that insight and improved self-awareness to resolve psychological problems. The **psychodynamic approach** aims to help patients gain insight into these underlying causes by tapping into the unconscious.

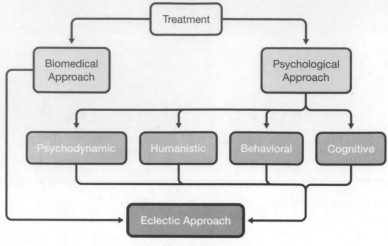

Figure 22.1

Psychoanalysis The original psychodynamic approach, called **psychoanalysis**, was developed by **Sigmund Freud** in the 1890s. Its central goal was to create a trusting environment so that a patient would more easily reveal repressed unconscious conflicts causing emotional turmoil. Freud's psychoanalytic approach was based on the theoretical assumption that **neurosis**, mental problems in one's conscious life, stems from long-repressed childhood memories, trauma, feelings, or libidinal urges involving the id. (See Chapter 17.)

In traditional psychoanalysis, often requiring two or three sessions a week for up to seven years, the patient reclines on a couch while the psychoanalyst sits out of direct view, listening carefully to what the patient says and taking notes. It is an unequal partnership with the psychoanalyst in a superior "expert" role.

The two main techniques Freud developed to help reveal the inner conflicts of the patient's unconscious were free association and dream analysis. During **free association**, the patient is encouraged to say whatever comes to mind. As the patient's trust in the psychoanalyst increases, the patient's ego will lower its guard so that the true nature of the unconscious will begin bubbling up to the surface for the psychoanalyst to interpret.

"HAVE A COUPLE OF DREAMS, AND CALL ME IN THE MORNING."

Dream analysis was another significant aspect of psychoanalysis and, for the few that still practice strict Freudian psychoanalysis, it still is. Freudian analysis of dreams is based on the theory that what is consciously remembered in a dream (**manifest content**) are the symbolic representations of the unconscious forces, urges, or conflicts (**latent**

content). The job of the patient is to report the manifest content and the job of the psychoanalyst is to analyze this content to determine its latent meaning and provide insight for the patient into the unconscious roots of problems.

Freud's psychoanalysis has resulted in a number of terms and techniques that continue to be recognized as integral aspects of many other forms of psychotherapy. Freud realized that **therapeutic rapport** (a trusting relationship with the therapist) was essential in overcoming **resistance**, the unwillingness of the patient to reveal anxiety-provoking conflicts hidden in the unconscious. Freud also coined the term **transference** to describe the natural consequence of the therapeutic relationship when the patient *transfers* his or her emotional issues unconsciously onto the therapist and develops strong positive or negative feelings for the therapist. A typical example of transference is when the patient begins to emotionally relate to the therapist as a parent figure. The job of the therapist is to detect when transference is happening and in an emotionally neutral manner communicate to the patient that it is taking place and then help the patient understand what it reveals. **Countertransference**, in which the therapist experiences an unconscious emotional response to the patient as a result of the therapeutic process is also possible. Last, Freud can also be credited for introducing the concept of **catharsis** to the therapeutic process, which refers to the often intense emotional release a person can experience in therapy.

Psychodynamic Therapies Traditional Freudian psychoanalysis is not often used now for a number of reasons. Psychodynamic therapies evolved from Freud's original approach but today have much less emphasis on the id or superego and even less reliance on the central idea of sex or animalistic aggression as an underlying unconscious impulse. Instead, a psychodynamic therapist, though still believing strongly in the unconscious influences of the mind, will conduct therapy face-to-face, focusing more on current relationships. Psychodynamic therapy usually only requires once-per-week sessions with a total length measured in months, not years.

One type of psychodynamic therapy is **interpersonal psychotherapy** (or IPT). As the name suggests, the focus is on helping the client improve existing relationships rather than delving into deep-seated trauma from early childhood. The primary mental health issue that IPT addresses is depression. It also borrows from the humanistic approach.

Another type of psychodynamic therapy, **object relations therapy**, is based on the social psychoanalytic perspective that social relationships in early childhood lie at the heart of mental problems in adulthood.

The *object* refers to the significant person in the client's life and the emotional problems stemming from that relationship. Therapists who use this approach will develop a very intense and nurturing relationship with the client to help heal the damage from the earlier relationships that lacked the necessary nurturing.

Assessing Psychoanalysis and Psychodynamic Therapies Freudian psychoanalysis is not used much today because for many disorders it does not work as well as other approaches. It also lacks empirical research supporting its efficacy, so justifying many years of expensive psychoanalytic treatment is hard to do. Also, psychoanalysts' interpretations of patients' free associations or dream analysis are significantly subjective.

Additionally, traditional psychoanalysis runs the risk of fostering patient-dependency because it takes so long and the therapist holds a very authoritative position. Modern psychotherapy emphasizes helping the client develop autonomous coping skills, an emphasis that runs counter to traditional psychoanalysis.

Psychodynamic therapies have moved away from the more controversial aspects of Freud's original theories and therapeutic approach. Interpersonal psychotherapy (IPT) has been shown to help alleviate depression and anxiety, but cognitive-behavioral therapy (CBT) is slightly more effective. Also, IPT's effectiveness is only slightly better than no therapy at all, but when combined with pharmacotherapy (antidepressive or antianxiety medicine) IPT shows more effectiveness.

Humanistic Therapies

Another branch of insight therapy is the humanistic approach. As you read in Chapter 17, the **humanistic perspective** sees humans as fundamentally good. The central goal of humanistic therapy is to help people accept themselves through self-awareness and self-fulfillment. Though both psychodynamic and humanistic approaches are considered insight therapies, humanistic therapy focuses on the present and future rather than the past and on conscious experiences rather than unconscious thoughts. The humanistic school of psychology has developed a number of influential approaches, including person-centered or Rogerian therapy, Gestalt therapy, and existential therapy.

Person-Centered or Rogerian Therapy A widely used form of humanistic psychotherapy developed by **Carl Rogers** was an outgrowth of his unwavering belief that all humans possess a fundamental drive to fulfill their unique and positive potential. Rogers believed a person's psychologically troubled life was caused by the divergence of the real self from the ideal self. If a child's upbringing is consumed by conditions of worth, the child will lose the sense of his or her real self and become emotionally troubled in the ideal self as an adult. The end result is a person who suffers emotionally from the loss of self, and this suffering can take many forms.

In **person-centered therapy** (also called client-centered or *Rogerian therapy*), the therapist honors the inherent human potential of the client by acting as a nonjudgmental facilitator of the therapeutic process. The therapist does not give advice or interpret the meanings of the client's thoughts or behaviors.

Four principles are central to the Rogerian client-centered approach: unconditional positive regard, empathy, congruence, and active listening.

- **Unconditional positive regard** is intended to reinforce for clients that they have value (without conditions) for who they really are. Directly emanating from unconditional positive regard is the practice of allowing the client to steer the direction of the therapy. For this reason, this form of therapy is sometimes called **nondirective**.

- A Rogerian therapist must show the deepest level of understanding through **empathy**, the ability to truly see, feel, and understand what the client is experiencing.

- **Congruence** (sometimes referred to as authenticity or genuineness) refers to the therapist's willingness to foster an honest and open relationship with the person. Rogers believed it is essential to model an authentic and genuine relationship so that the person will be more comfortable striving for congruence in other relationships.

- **Active listening** (sometimes referred to as *reflection*) by the therapist reinforces the principles of unconditional positive regard, empathy, and congruence through intensely and empathically listening to the client and paraphrasing what the client says, focusing on the specific emotions and feelings expressed. Active listening prevents the therapist from offering advice or judgments, which implicitly conflicts with the potential for clients to gain insight for themselves. Active listening enables the therapist to create a sort of nonjudging mirror in which the client *sees* what he or she is saying and feeling and then gains insight, self-acceptance, and ultimately an empowering sense of self-awareness and the ability to change and grow.

Client: I just got so sick of his constant criticism, especially when he told me to "man up." It was like no matter how well I did in school or my career choices I was never good enough.

Therapist: M-hm. He kept putting you down. Even when you excelled.

Client: Yeah, and that's why I gave up on sharing my success with him. But I still love him, I mean - he's my dad. How can I not? But I also feel like I hate him too, which make me feel so guilty. (begins to cry)

Therapist: Your father's criticism hurt you terribly, and yet you never gave up on trying to share your success with him. You feel conflicted by your strong feelings, even now. I can see how painful this is for you.

Client: Yes, and I know I'm an adult now so it shouldn't matter. But somehow I kept expecting him to be different.

Therapist: No matter how old you are, he's still your father. And now that he's sick, you feel guilty that you haven't reached out to him.

Client: Yeah, the guilt is killing me, but I still can't seem to make myself reach out. I just know I'll be rejected again.

Therapist: Maybe you will be. But what hurts more—right now? The guilt of the fear of being rejected?

Client: The guilt. Definitely... I think I should give him a call. Maybe just ask how's he doing and let him know I'm here for him.

Figure 22.1 Example of Active Listening

Gestalt Therapy Frederick (Fritz) Perls and his wife Laura Perls developed another type of humanistic therapy—Gestalt therapy. The term *gestalt* (from the German word for shape or form) refers to the ability to perceive that the whole is greater than the sum of its parts. Gestalt therapy is based on the belief that troubled people have lost a sense of their own wholeness and become strangers to aspects of their personality.

Gestalt therapy focuses on a person's perceptions of his or her own feelings and own sense of reality in the present moment. When people lose awareness of aspects of themselves, they lose their ability to grow; they've become trapped behind a mask. Unlike client-centered therapy which emphasizes a nondirective approach to therapy, Gestalt therapy is much more experiential and therapist-directed. The Gestalt therapist will often challenge clients to become more aware of what they are feeling in the *here and now*. The therapist pays close attention to any nonverbal gestures and challenges the client to probe such gestures to find the feelings they express.

One technique used in Gestalt therapy is to have the client engage in a dialog with a feeling they are experiencing or with an aspect of their personality (sometimes called the **empty-chair technique**). Another technique is **exaggeration**. The client is encouraged to dramatically exaggerate a specific feeling or nonverbal gesture or movement to become better aware of the feelings or emotions behind it. These techniques are intended to help clients become more familiar and comfortable with their true feelings and enhance their self-awareness. Last, the Gestalt therapist models the idea of self-awareness in the present moment by expressing what he or she is feeling or experiencing. Gestalt therapists do not interpret or judge their client's feelings; they simply express them as a way to encourage the client to trust their own feelings.

Assessing Humanistic Therapy The most significant challenge when assessing the effectiveness of humanistic therapies is the lack of empirical research. Most research is qualitative and derived from either client or therapist feedback, which tends to be positive but inherently subjective and therefore biased. The positive attributes shared by all effective therapeutic approaches are those factors that are strongly linked to the outcomes of any form of psychotherapy. This **common factors theory** will be addressed later. (See page 563.) The common factors are central to all humanistic therapies and therefore it is very difficult to isolate the unique techniques of a particular humanistic therapy in order to measure effectiveness.

Behavior Therapies

Insight therapies assume that with improved self-awareness comes a resolution of psychological problems. In contrast, **action therapies** focus on providing practical solutions and teaching coping skills to help resolve psychological problems. Behavioral therapy and cognitive therapy are the most widely used action therapies.

As you have read, behavioral psychology— behaviorism— is based on the theory that all human behavior, healthy or unhealthy, is learned. So **behavioral therapy** uses classical conditioning or operant conditioning to help clients unlearn maladaptive behaviors and replace them with more adaptive or healthy behaviors. Behavioral therapists are not concerned with unconscious or repressed memories and do not believe that they hold the key to improving mental health. They see the problematic behaviors not as a symptom of underlying psychological issues but as the problems themselves—change the behavior and you've solved the psychological problem. Behavioral therapy offers a number of methods of solving behavior problems, including exposure therapies, aversion therapy, operant conditioning, and modeling.

Exposure Therapies Classical conditioning is a learning theory that explains how involuntary (automatic) responses such as feelings of fear or disgust become associated (connected) with new stimuli. (See pages 202–208.) That person you know who is deeply afraid of heights got that way because at some point the neutral stimulus (being in a high place) became associated with a natural or unconditioned stimulus (falling from a height), which caused a great deal of fear. Behavior therapies that use classical conditioning to reduce anxiety are called exposure therapies. **Mary Cover Jones**, often called "the mother of behavioral therapy," developed the earliest form of exposure therapy in 1924 when she demonstrated the principles of desensitization (or counterconditioning) by eliminating a little boy's fear of rabbits by associating a pleasant stimulus (food) with the unpleasant stimulus (a rabbit). As the little boy was given yummy food to eat, Jones slowly moved the caged rabbit closer and closer to the little boy until eventually the boy was eating and petting the rabbit at the same time. Fear gone; psychological problem solved!

Years later, after giving up on the psychoanalytic approach to treating anxiety disorders, **Joseph Wolpe** developed an exposure therapy for reducing anxiety, primarily phobias, called **systematic desensitization**. Wolpe continued where Mary Cover Jones left off. His method includes three steps:

1. The client learns to practice deep relaxation.

2. The client creates a **hierarchy of anxieties** from lowest anxiety-producing stimulus to highest.

3. Led by the therapist, the client is introduced to the least feared object or situation while practicing deep relaxation. When able to deal with this first stimulus without experiencing anxiety, the client is introduced to the next fear-producing object or situation while practicing relaxation until the client is successfully able to deal with the object or situation at the top of the hierarchy.

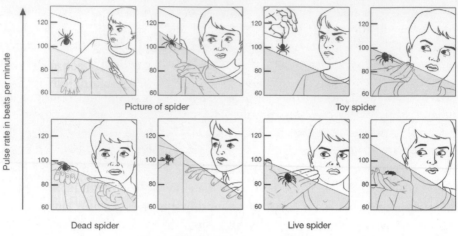

Figure 22.3 Systematic Desensitization

Today, with the introduction of computer technology, a form of systematic desensitization called **virtual reality graded** (or *gradual*) **exposure**, is used. The client wears virtual reality goggles that provide a visual experience of the feared object or situation. This approach is obviously more practical than providing real life exposure to situations such as airplanes or heights. This technology has been used successfully to treat anxiety disorders including social phobia and post-traumatic stress disorder (PTSD).

Another form of exposure therapy is called flooding. **Flooding** requires the client to be fully exposed to the anxiety-producing stimulus in a harmless and controlled situation from which he or she cannot escape. Operant conditioning is at work since the client is unable to experience the reinforcement of escaping the fearful situation and must confront the fear until it is extinguished.

Aversion Therapy Combining the principles of both classical conditioning and operant conditioning is aversion therapy. **Aversion therapy**, as the name suggests, is a form of behavioral therapy in which an unwanted behavior is associated with a stimulus to which the client has a great aversion. Aversion therapy is based on classical conditioning—when the unwanted behavior, such as drinking alcohol, is associated with an unpleasant stimulus (vomiting, for example), a newly learned (conditioned) response (fear/disgust) is elicited.

This use of operant conditioning in aversion therapy is essentially punishment. If you experience an unpleasant consequence when behaving a certain way, you will eventually stop the behavior. For example, if you fail to put your seatbelt on, the car starts an annoying beep. To avoid the unpleasant beeping, you will put your seatbelt on right away.

Operant Conditioning Behavior therapists use **behavior modification** based on operant conditioning principles developed by **B. F. Skinner** by which learning (or unlearning) voluntary behaviors results from positive or negative reinforcement or punishment. For example, intellectually disabled children, children with autism spectrum disorder (ASD), or institutionalized adults can learn more appropriate social behaviors and life skills by being positively reinforced each time they display an approximate behavior or by being punished when they display undesirable behaviors. If the ethical punishment is effective, **extinction** will occur and the undesirable behavior will be replaced by a more appropriate one.

Token economy systems are often used with this approach in such institutional settings as prisons, psychiatric hospitals, or schools. Tokens are earned for desired behaviors and exchanged for rewards like using the computer, playing video games, or eating desirable food.

Modeling In some situations, the most practical behavioral therapy method is modeling, in which the therapist demonstrates the desired behavior to help clients learn the behavior themselves. An excellent way to extinguish irrational fears is for the client to observe the therapist or some other person handling the feared object without any bad consequence. Modeling can also be used in the same way to help clients overcome anxiety over social situations.

Assessing Behavioral Therapy Behavioral therapy can be a quick and efficient way to deal with certain behavior problems. For example, behavioral therapies are effective in treating anxiety disorders, such as social phobia and many specific phobias. They also show positive results for children diagnosed with attention deficit hyperactivity disorder (ADHD) when coupled with medication or biofeedback therapy.

Certain behavioral therapies should be used with caution. Aversion therapy and flooding could be harmful if done carelessly, because the client is subjected to negative situations that may backfire and reinforce the very undesirable behaviors intended to be removed. And behavioral therapy is not effective in eliminating the symptoms of major depression, bipolar disorder, or schizophrenia. These psychological disorders emanate from neurological chemical imbalances and the biomedical approach using medicine is the first line of treatment.

Cognitive-Behavioral Therapy

A type of action therapy closely related to behavioral therapy is **cognitive-behavioral therapy (CBT)**. Cognitive psychology emerged from the behaviorist school, because behavior is almost always linked to cognition (thinking). Cognitive-behavioral therapists approach psychological problems based on the assumption that cognition leads to emotional responses and behavior.

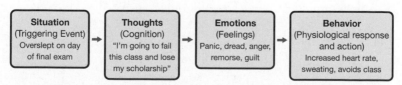

Figure 22.4 Cognitive-Behavioral Therapy

The guiding principle of CBT is that depression, anxiety, or any other psychological problems are caused by maladaptive or illogical thinking. To solve these problems, the cognitive-behavioral therapist helps the client fix the maladaptive thought processes. Within the general CBT approach are two main types of therapies. Albert Ellis's rational-emotive behavioral therapy and Aaron Beck's cognitive therapy share a number of similarities but also distinguish themselves in key ways.

Rational-Emotive Behavior Therapy In the early 1950s, **Albert Ellis** rejected Freudian psychoanalysis and developed **rational-emotive behavior therapy (REBT)** based on his belief that the reason behind most psychological problems was irrational thoughts. Ellis believed that people cognitively perceive themselves and their world in their own particular way, and those perceptions (cognitions) guide reactions to events and people. Psychological problems arise when those thoughts are irrational and lead to behavioral consequences that are distressful. Ellis thought that the therapist should be more of a teacher, challenging the client's irrational thoughts in a straightforward and rather impersonal way.

The key challenge confronting a client in REBT is understanding that the activating event does *not* cause the emotional and behavioral consequences—the client's irrational way of thinking does. Ellis coined the term **awfulizing** to refer to the tendency to irrationally overestimate or exaggerate a situation or event. So during a typical REBT session, the therapist will carefully observe the client's thought processes and emotional reactions and then directly challenge the absurdity of those thoughts.

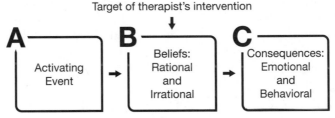

Figure 22.5 Albert Ellis's ABC Technique Ellis believed that the cause of emotional and behavioral problems was not an **A**ctivating event but rather the **B**eliefs and thoughts of the person interpreting it. The **C**onsequences could be healthy if the interpretation is rational.

Aaron Beck's Cognitive Therapy After extensive research into the causes of depression, psychiatrist **Aaron Beck** (b. 1921) concluded that the symptoms of depression grew as result of cognitive dysfunctions. By the early 1960s, Beck's **cognitive therapy** was introduced as an effective way for treating depression by helping the client recognize dysfunctional cognitive distortions. The *Beck Depression Inventory,* a self-reporting inventory, helped therapists assess the severity of depression. Cognitive therapy is now considered effective for other disorders, including anxiety, eating, and personality disorders.

Central to cognitive therapy is Beck's **cognitive triad**, which comprises three interrelated and dysfunctional types of automatic thinking: 1) negative thoughts about self, 2) negative thoughts about the world, and 3) negative thoughts about the future (Figure 22.6). Each of these **cognitive distortions** or errors in logic feed off each other in a self-reinforcing negative cycle. A cognitive therapist's goal is to help clients recognize their negative thoughts

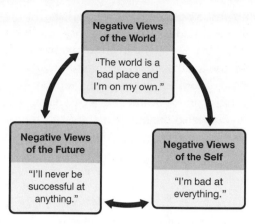

Figure 22.6 Cognitive Triad

as unrealistic, reject them, and replace them with more realistic functional thoughts. Some cognitive distortions coined by Beck include **catastrophizing** (*If I don't earn a 5 on my AP Psychology exam, my life will be ruined*), **all-or-none thinking** (*He never called me back; I must be a total loser*), and **personalization** (*The teacher didn't call on me because she hates me*).

Assessing Cognitive Therapy Cognitive-behavioral therapy is considered an effective and cost-efficient approach for treating a number of psychological disorders, including bipolar disorders, depression, and anxiety (especially when used in combination with pharmacotherapy). Various personality disorders, drug dependency, smoking cessation, and even certain symptoms of schizophrenia, such as delusional thinking and hallucinations, have been reduced using CBT.

Modes of Therapy

The term *modes of therapy* refers not to the various psychotherapeutic approaches, such as psychodynamic, humanistic, behavioral, or cognitive, but to the differing ways to deliver these therapeutic approaches. The most recognizable mode is individual psychotherapy. Other modes include group, self-help groups, family, and couples/marriage counseling. Therapists who practice these other modes of therapy still use one or more of the psychotherapeutic approaches, depending on what best serves their clients.

Group Therapy

Group therapy provides what can be a vital element to mental healing: knowing you are not alone. In a small group, usually around six to twelve, persons with similar problems come together under the direction or facilitation of a trained therapist or counselor to discuss their psychological issues.

Group therapy offers a number of benefits that individual therapy lacks. First, group therapy provides members with the beneficial realization that they are not alone in their suffering and struggles, and that knowledge reduces the sense of isolation and hopelessness. Second, the counselor can monitor the interactions between group members and encourage healthy interpersonal behaviors. Third, with proper guidance by a trained therapist, the dynamics of the group itself can serve to address healthier coping skills such as problem-solving, self-confidence, assertiveness, listening skills, and empathy. Group therapy also enables a therapist to treat more clients at the same time and is less expensive for the clients than individual therapy.

Self-Help Groups

Self-help groups come in many forms but share a common goal of providing support in each person's road to healing. Self-help groups may have a facilitator who organizes meetings, but such groups are characterized by the absence of a trained psychotherapist directing the process of the group. The most recognizable self-help group is Alcoholics Anonymous, in which group members follow a 12-step program to stop drinking and remain sober. Beyond the meetings, each group member has a sponsor, a fellow recovering alcoholic, who often provides twenty-four-hour support for his or her fellow recovering alcoholic. The recovering alcoholic is only a phone call away from the support of the sponsor. This template has been duplicated for other substance abuse disorders, such as Narcotics Anonymous, Gamblers Anonymous, and Overeaters Anonymous, and also for other eating disorders. Other self-help groups include survivors of specific traumas, Alzheimer's support, depression, anxiety, anger management, and families with ADD/ADHD children.

Family Therapy

What brings a family into family therapy? It starts with the recognition of the importance of the family itself and a desire to address problems causing distress within the family. Though mental health issues of a particular family member may be the catalyst, when a family enters therapy, the whole family becomes the primary focus. A family therapist approaches treatment based on **family systems theory**, which holds that each family member affects every other family member. The function of family therapy is to help each member understand that the family works as an interrelated system of relationships and then to identify the dysfunctional aspects of those relationship dynamics and replace them with healthier relationship skills.

Couples/Marriage Counseling

People enter into marriage with the intention of forging a lifelong bond, but sometimes that relationship can become broken. The two most important ingredients to a successful marriage are good communication and mutual respect. **Marriage or couples counseling** focuses on improving the communication between couples. One popular approach is called **transactional analysis (TA)**, which is based on the theory that each adult operates from three possible ego states: parent, adult, and child. When two adults are in a committed yet dysfunctional relationship, it is because the couple is transacting, or communicating, from ego states other than adult to adult. The goal of TA is to help a couple improve their relationship by understanding the three ego states and how each one presents itself through communication. Then they learn how to better relate to each other via healthy *adult to adult* transactions.

Assessing Psychotherapeutic Effectiveness

Does psychotherapy work, and which approaches are more effective than others? The earliest attempt to determine the effectiveness of psychotherapies came in the 1950s when Hans Eysenck published research concluding that existing psychotherapies, especially psychoanalysis, were not any more effective than no treatment at all. Though controversial, Eysenck's work began a vital conversation about the effectiveness of psychotherapy that continues to this day. The field of psychology is stronger when it willingly subjects itself to the rigor of sound empirical research.

In the more than sixty years since Eysenck's eye-opening publication, thousands of studies have been conducted to answer the fundamental question: Does psychotherapy work? The current answer, based on empirical research, is a qualified yes. What has been determined through a research process called **meta-analysis**, in which multiple studies are statistically analyzed to determine a common result, is that most psychotherapeutic approaches seem to show effectiveness because they all share what are called **common factors**:

- **Therapeutic alliance:** A relationship between client and therapist that is caring, genuine, understanding, and empathetic. This bond must be established first.

- **Positive expectations:** The client begins to believe that the therapeutic process will result in positive outcomes. The client and therapist agree on goals and the tasks needed to achieve them.

- **Specific action plan:** The therapist prescribes a plan of action and the client uses it and begins to form a sense of self-efficacy based on the new coping behaviors.

If a therapeutic approach includes the three factors above, the meta-analysis shows that it will be more effective in helping a person than no therapy at all. However, the meta-analysis shows some therapeutic approaches to be slightly more effective for specific psychological disorders than others. Behavioral therapy appears to be effective for ADD/ADHD behavior problems, bedwetting, marital dysfunctions, and phobias. Cognitive-behavioral therapy appears to be effective for anxiety disorders such as generalized anxiety disorder, phobias, panic disorders, PTSD, and depression. Psychodynamic interpersonal therapy is also effective for depression. Many anxiety and depressive disorders have the best long-term results when both psychotherapy and psychotropic drugs are part of the therapeutic plan.

To examine the empirical research yourself, you can visit two excellent sources: the American Psychological Association's (APA) PsychINFO site and the National Center for Biotechnology Information's (NCBI) PubMed site. Be wary of approaches that do not have empirical research to back them up. If you want to find out if equine therapy, adventure therapy, or rebirthing therapies are truly effective, find the empirical research that proves it.

THINK AS A PSYCHOLOGIST: CYBERTHERAPY

As you read, virtual reality is already helping people overcome their phobias in a practical way and without putting anyone in a risky or embarrassing situation. Advances in technology have made it possible to virtually re-create social gatherings for people with social anxiety, encounters with spiders for people who fear them, rides on airplanes or in cars for people with phobias of those experiences, and realistic battle situations for veterans who have PTSD. Now researchers at the Institute for Creative Technologies at the University of Southern California and the Dan Marino Foundation are developing a virtual reality tool for young adults with autism spectrum disorder (ASD) who are capable of succeeding in a number of jobs but have great anxiety about the job interview. The tool, Virtual Interactive Training Agent (VITA), provides a safe virtual environment in which people with ASD and developmental disabilities can practice job interviews repeatedly. The researchers have created six different virtual interviewers—three male and three female—with a range of personalities, from the soft-spoken to the brash. There are also different, common scenarios in which clients can practice their interviewing skills. The exchanges between the client and the very humanlike virtual job interviewer on the screen are video recorded, reviewed, and analyzed by a vocational expert and the client so they can work on specific areas of improvement.

The same institution has developed SimCoach, a "virtual human support agent," to screen veterans who might need help. Many veterans and their family members are either reluctant to seek professional help for PTSD and other disorders or lack the information to find a professional. As a gentle questioner, SimCoach asks people at the other end of the screen certain questions in a nonjudgmental way. It does not diagnose, but it does point users to information and resources to help with their problems and sometimes puts them on the road to face-to-face therapy.

Biomedical Approach

Advances in medicine and psychiatry and knowledge of how the brain functions have made profound strides in the last half of the 20th and first part of the 21st centuries. Unlike psychologists, who are not medically trained, physicians and psychiatrists, whose training focuses on biology, are inclined to view biological abnormalities as the cause of mental illness, and they therefore offer treatment using a **biomedical** or **biological approach**. Biomedical therapy involves the use of pharmaceutical medications to treat psychological disorders and is ideally used in combination with psychotherapy. **Psychopharmacology** is the study of how drugs affect the mind and behavior. Medications used to treat psychological disorders are called **psychotropic** medications. There are also other biomedical treatments that are much less frequently used and much more controversial, including electroconvulsive therapy and psychosurgery.

Psychopharmaceutical Drugs or Pharmacotherapy

Many types of psychopharmaceutical drugs treat the symptoms of different psychological disorders. They do not cure the disorders; they only treat the symptoms. The drugs are divided into classes: antianxiety, antidepressant, mood stabilizers, stimulants, and antipsychotics (Figure 22.7). All these psychotropic drugs are more effective when used in conjunction with psychotherapy.

Antianxiety drugs (also called anxiolytic drugs) are drugs that reduce symptoms related to anxiety, such as tension, fear, apprehension, and nervousness. There are two common approaches to treating anxiety using drugs—short-term and long-term. For acute anxiety, such as that associated with phobias or panic disorders, anxiolytic drugs called benzodiazepines are often used. **Benzodiazepines** are tranquilizing drugs that depress the central nervous system by increasing the effects of a brain chemical called **gamma-aminobutryric acid (GABA)**, which depresses neural activity in the brain. The most frequently prescribed benzodiazepines are Xanax, Librium, lorazepam, and Valium. For more long-term treatment of anxiety, antidepressant drugs called **selective serotonin reuptake inhibitors (SSRI)** are often prescribed. (Reuptake means absorption.) Common SSRI drugs are Prozac, Zoloft, Paxil, and Lexapro.

PSYCHOPHARMACEUTICAL DRUGS

Psychotropic Drug	Used for	Brand Names	Effects	Side Effects
Antianxiety	PTSD, Panic Disorder, Social Phobia, OCD	Xanax, Librium, Ativan, Valium	Depresses central nervous system; reduces apprehension and nervousness	Sleepiness, dizziness, fatigue, headaches, slurred speech
Antidepressants	Depression (recently, for long-term treatment of anxiety disorders)	Prozac, Zoloft, Paxil, Lexapro, Wellbutrin	Improves mood by reducing absorption of neurotransmitters serotonin and norepinephrine	Depending on class of antidepressant: Nausea, weight gain, dry mouth, reduced sex drive, blurred vision, suicidal ideation
Mood Stabilizers	Bipolar disorders	Lithium, Lamotrigine	Reduces manic episodes and depressive episodes	Dry mouth, heart arrhythmia, swelling, nausea, loss of appetite
Stimulants	ADD/ADHD	Ritalin, Adderall, Dexedrine	Improves focus and attention by preventing absorption of dopamine and norepinephrine	Decreased appetite, difficulty sleeping, headache, stomachache
Antipsychotics	Schizophrenia	Haldol, Prolixin, Thorazine	Reduces positive psychotic symptoms such as delusions and hallucinations through inhibiting the neurotransmitter dopamine	Tardive dyskinesia, Parkinson-like tremors
Atypical Antipsychotics	Schizophrenia	Clozaril, Abilify	Reduces positive and negative symptoms such as apathy and withdrawal	Overeating, diabetes, high cholesterol, constipation, dry mouth, drowsiness, dizziness, blurred vision

Figure 22.7

Antidepressant drugs elevate mood by affecting neurotransmitters such as serotonin that are linked to depression. Recently, antidepressants have been found to reduce the symptoms associated with anxiety disorders, PTSD, and obsessive-compulsive disorder.

Different types of antidepressant drugs have different effects on certain neurotransmitters. As you read, SSRIs affect the neurotransmitter serotonin. Other types of antidepressants include **serotonin and norepinephrine reuptake inhibitors (SNRI)** and **norepinephrine and dopamine reuptake inhibitors (NDRI)**. Wellbutrin is a NDRI antidepressant and is also used to help people stop smoking.

Mood stabilizers are drugs prescribed for people diagnosed with bipolar disorders because they reduce dramatic mood swings. They are also used for mood problems related to schizophrenia and schizoaffective disorder. The best-known mood stabilizers are lithium and Lamotrigine.

Stimulants are psychotropic drugs that do what the name implies: they stimulate the central nervous system. Stimulants are *not* antidepressants. The most common use for stimulants is for the treatment of attention deficit disorder (ADD) and attention deficit hyperactivity disorder (ADHD). The brain of a child with ADD/ADHD is unable to fully utilize two particular neurotransmitters—dopamine and norepinephrine. These two neurotransmitters get absorbed back into the neurons before they can do their stimulating work. Essentially, a child with ADD/ADHD lacks the neurological ability to stimulate, so the child will self-stimulate if his or her external environment is not stimulating enough. That's why the ADD/ADHD child fidgets, talks out of turn, darts about, and seems unfocused. Children with ADD/ADHD need stimulation that the brain is not providing, and that's why stimulants reduce the symptoms of ADD/ADHD. The most common stimulants prescribed for ADD/ADHD are Ritalin, Adderall, and Dexedrine, all of which are reuptake inhibitors. They stop the absorption of dopamine and norepinephrine and allow the brain to experience more stimulation. The child then is able to stay more focused and pay attention for longer periods of time.

Antipsychotic drugs (also referred to as first-generation antipsychotics or FGA) are used to reduce positive symptoms of schizophrenia and, in extreme circumstances, of bipolar disorder. As you read in Chapter 21, schizophrenia includes positive symptoms (behaviors that are introduced), such as delusions of paranoia and auditory hallucinations, and negative symptoms (behaviors that stop happening), such as normal emotional reactions and social interaction. Examples of common antipsychotic drugs are Haldol, Prolixin, and Thorazine. **Atypical antipsychotic drugs** not only reduce positive symptoms but also target such negative symptoms as withdrawal and apathy. Atypical antipsychotics are referred to as second-generation antipsychotics (SGA) because they were developed a few decades after the original antipsychotic drugs. Atypical antipsychotics include Clozaril and Abilify.

Assessing Psychotropic Drugs Psychotropic drugs are only prescribed after a careful diagnosis by a medical doctor. They all carry the possibility of serious side effects. Negative side effects can be very serious. Tardive dyskinesia (TD) is a neurological disorder caused by long-term use of antipsychotic drugs. TD is characterized by uncontrolled facial and tongue movements or uncontrolled arm or leg movements. The condition may go away if the antipsychotic drug is removed soon enough, but too often the condition is permanent.

A great deal of research indicates that a psychotropic drug used in conjunction with psychotherapy is more effective in treating psychological disorders than is a drug alone. These drugs reduce the symptoms of a disorder, but they do not treat the underlying causes.

Electroconvulsive Therapy

Electroconvulsive therapy (ECT) is used in the most serious cases of depression. ECT involves the administration of a short-duration electric current between the temples that causes a seizure. (The patient is anesthetized so the seizure does not cause physical convulsions.) The seizure in turn causes the brain to release a significant amount of neurotransmitters that immediately improve mood. ECT is used when medications have failed to alleviate the symptoms. It is also used in serious cases of schizophrenia when medication has failed to show improvement.

ECT was first introduced in the 1930s and became widely used, but by the 1950s, its popularity waned. Recently, its use has not only increased, but some psychiatrists are employing a repetitive or frequent-application process based on the idea that the convulsions not only produce a flood of neurotransmitters but also stimulate neuron growth that appears to permanently relieve the symptoms of depression. ECT has a number of side effects, with memory loss being the most concerning. ECT not only causes retrograde amnesia (forgetting events prior to the treatments) but also anterograde amnesia, which is the inability to remember new material.

Psychosurgery

Psychosurgery is the intentional surgical destruction of part of the brain in order to reduce symptoms of mental illness. Psychosurgery was first used in the 1930s in a procedure called a **prefrontal lobotomy** (see page 500). This brutal procedure is fortunately a relic of the past. Modern neurology has introduced a much more selective method of destroying brain tissue in order to treat the most severe forms of depression and obsessive-compulsive disorder. The procedure is called a bilateral anterior cingulotomy. It involves inserting an electrode into the brain and carefully guiding it to specific neurons that connect the frontal lobe to the limbic system, the seat of basic emotional responses. With a controlled electric current, small areas of selected brain cells are destroyed.

Deep Brain Stimulation and Repetitive Transcranial Magnetic Stimulation

Neuropsychiatrists have recently begun treating severe cases of depression through **deep brain stimulation** in which a thin wire is surgically implanted in the area of the brain associated with depression. The wire is connected to a battery and supplies a slight electric current that stimulates neuronal growth that appears to reduce the symptoms of depression.

Another neurological technique that avoids destruction of brain tissue or inducing convulsions through electric shock is the use of noninvasive magnets called **repetitive transcranial magnetic stimulation (rTMS)**. An electrified coil placed very near the skull delivers an electromagnetic pulse to a specific area of the brain. Research seems to indicate that after repeated exposure to the electromagnetic stimulation, specific neurons appear to grow in such a way that reduces the symptoms of depression.

Assessing the Biomedical Approach

The discovery in the mid-20th century that drugs could reduce the symptoms of severe psychological disorders is rightly considered one of the most important turning points in the treatment of mental illness. No longer was a person with schizophrenia destined to suffer from the psychotic symptoms in an institution, nor was a person with severe depression doomed to perpetual sadness. Additionally, as more and more psychotropic drugs have been developed, more and more people who suffer from anxiety, obsessive-compulsive disorder, PTSD, or other disorders have been able to find relief from their symptoms.

But there are important caveats. Psychotropic drugs reduce the symptoms but do not cure the illness, and they can also produce serious side effects. Another important concern is the increasing reliance upon such drugs as the first or only treatment. People diagnosed with bipolar disorder, depression, or anxiety and prescribed antidepressant or antianxiety drugs should get psychotherapeutic treatment as well. Unfortunately, too many people take the medications without undertaking psychotherapy. They become dependent on the drug to relieve the symptoms but miss the opportunity that psychotherapy affords to treat the underlying psychological causes of the disorder. Research has shown that a combination of psychopharmacological drugs and psychotherapy produces the best long-term results.

Confidentiality and the Law

No matter what type of treatment they offer, psychotherapists and psychiatrists are required by law to protect the confidentiality of their clients. A federal law, the Health Insurance Portability and Accountability Act (HIPAA), sets national limits on the way patient or client information can be shared. State laws are often stricter than HIPAA. In general, information can be shared only with the consent of the person in treatment, usually for the purpose of coordinating care or facilitating insurance coverage. A psychotherapist who does not follow these confidentiality laws may be subject to fine.

There are a few instances, however, when therapists are allowed to break confidentiality: when people pose a threat to themselves or others or when a court orders the records be released. Further, therapists are required by law to report ongoing domestic abuse or neglect of children, people with disabilities, and the elderly.

* * *

The fields of psychology and psychiatry have produced a variety of treatment approaches to help alleviate the suffering that comes with mental illness. Mental health professionals are increasingly embracing **evidence-based practice**, in which the treatment method chosen for a client or specific disorder is based on empirical research that provides scientific evidence of its effectiveness.

REFLECT ON THE ESSENTIAL QUESTION

Essential Question: *To what degree are psychotherapeutic approaches similar and different regarding philosophy, techniques, and effectiveness?* On separate paper, make a chart like the one below to gather details to answer that question. In the top part of the chart, identify the different approaches within the two broad categories with notes about what each approach might be especially good at treating. In the bottom part of the chart, briefly describe how the approaches are similar and different.

Psychological	Biomedical

Similarities and Differences

KEY TERMS AND PEOPLE

PSYCHOLOGICAL

action therapies

active listening

all-or-none-thinking

aversion therapy

awfulizing

behavior modification

behavioral therapy

catastrophizing

catharsis

cognitive-behavioral therapy (CBT)

cognitive distortions

cognitive therapy

cognitive triad

common factors theory

congruence

countertransference

dream analysis

eclectic approach

empathy

empty-chair technique

exaggeration

exposure therapies

extinction

flooding

free association

Gestalt therapy

hierarchy of anxieties

humanistic perspective

insight therapies

interpersonal psychotherapy (IPT)

latent content

manifest content

modeling

nondirective

object relations therapy

person-centered therapy

personalization

psychoanalysis

psychodynamic approach

psychological approach

psychotherapy

rational-emotive behavior therapy

resistance

systematic desensitization

therapeutic rapport

token economy systems

transference

unconditional positive regard

virtual reality graded exposure

BIOMEDICAL

antianxiety drugs

antidepressant drugs

antipsychotic drugs

atypical antipsychotic drugs

benzodiazepines

biological approach

biomedical approach

deep brain stimulation

electroconvulsive therapy (ECT)

evidence-based practice

gamma-aminobutyric acid (GABA)

mood stabilizer

norepinephrine and dopamine reuptake inhibitor (NDRI)

prefrontal lobotomy

psychopharmacology

psychosurgery

psychotropic

repetitive transcranial magnetic stimulation (rTMS)

selective serotonin reuptake inhibitor (SSRI)

serotoin and norepinephrine reuptake inhibitor (SNRI)

stimulant

MODES

common factors

family systems theory

group therapy

marriage or couples counseling

meta-analysis

modes of therapy

self-help groups

transactional analysis (TA)

KEY PEOPLE

Aaron Beck

Albert Ellis

Sigmund Freud

Mary Cover Jones

Carl Rogers

B.F. Skinner

Joseph Wolpe

1. Which statement best describes the difference between psychodynamic therapy and behavioral therapies?

   (A) Psychodynamic therapy assumes that inner drives rather than environmental learning explain human behavior.

   (B) Behavioral therapies focus on realizing one's full potential, while pychodynamic therapy stresses dream analysis.

   (C) Behavioral therapies help clients develop insights, while psychodynamic theories help clients change behaviors.

   (D) The main tool in psychodynamic therapy is dream analysis, while the main tool in behavior therapies is understanding the whole picture.

   (E) Behavioral therapies focus on past behavior, while psychodynamic therapy focuses on the present and future.

2. Which choice best reflects an eclectic approach?

   (A) A psychoanalyst interprets the latent content of a patient's dream and analyzes transference taking place between the patient and the therapist.

   (B) A therapist instructs the client to speak to his shame in the empty chair and encourages the client to focus on the here and now.

   (C) A therapist uses systematic desensitization to treat a phobia and active listening to emphatically reinforce unconditional positive regard.

   (D) A therapist challenges the client to consider the illogical premise of a belief and educates the client regarding the cognitive triad.

   (E) A therapist encourages a client to take authentic responsibility for the decisions made and explores with the client the benefits of fostering an authentic relationship.

3. A therapist using object relations therapy
   (A) approaches psychological issues based on the belief that neuroses stems from unconscious conflicts between the ego and the id
   (B) believes the client's psychological problems stem from dysfunctional transactions with aversive objects through negative reinforcement and punishment
   (C) will pay close attention to the client's early childhood relationship with the mother and/or father and form a close and nurturing relationship with the client
   (D) will assign homework in which the client will be asked to write in a journal describing any distressful emotion and connect it with the thoughts that accompany them
   (E) focuses on the meaningfulness of significant objects in the client's life and encourages the client to prioritize those items as a way to increase positive meaningfulness

4. Which choice most accurately reflects a difference between two specific humanistic therapies?
   (A) Person-centered therapy is nondirective and focuses on the worth of the client, while Gestalt therapy tends to be more therapist-directed and challenges the client to own his or her feelings.
   (B) Existential therapy will more often confront the client's fear of freedom and death, while person-centered therapy tends to foster dependency in an empathic therapeutic setting.
   (C) A Gestalt therapist will actively listen to the client in a nondirective therapeutic setting, while a person-centered therapist will act more as a coach, encouraging the client to accept his or her limitations.
   (D) An existential therapist will help the client learn more rational ways of thinking in order to reduce anxiety or depression, while a Gestalt therapist will employ techniques such as the empty-chair and exaggeration to help the client become more self-aware.
   (E) One therapist will focus on aversive therapy in order to reduce dysfunctional behaviors, while another therapist will utilize positive reinforcement to encourage the acquisition of more functionally desirable behaviors.

5. The biomedical approach considered the *least* neurologically invasive would be

(A) prefrontal lobotomy

(B) electroconvulsive therapy

(C) deep brain stimulation

(D) repetitive Transcranial Magnetic Stimulation (rTMS)

(E) tardive dyskinesia

6. A patient presents symptoms associated with PTSD. Which choice represents the best psychopharmacological drug treatment?

(A) Xanax and Librium

(B) Clozaril and Abilify

(C) Adderall and Dexedrine

(D) Lithium and Lamotrigine

(E) Haldol and Thorazine

7. Which of the following is a mode of therapy?

(A) behavioral therapy

(B) psychodynamic therapy

(C) cognitive-behavioral therapy

(D) self-help group

(E) cultural and gender sensitivity

8. Behavioral therapy shows the most effectiveness in the treatment of

(A) severe depression and PTSD

(B) schizophrenia and schizotypal disorder

(C) phobias and social phobias

(D) child deviant behavior

(E) dissociative identity disorder

Refer to the diagram to answer the following question.

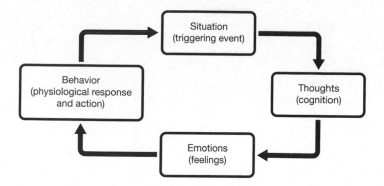

9. Based on the diagram, one can most reasonably conclude that
   (A) the unconscious is a key driver of stress
   (B) cognitive processes affect emotions and behavior
   (C) the cognitive triad stresses the role of the triggering event as the primary cause of distress
   (D) the terms *awfulizing* and *catastrophizing* are unrelated
   (E) a warm and supportive therapeutic environment is more conducive to therapeutic insight

10. Which would be most efficient when researching the effectiveness of different therapeutic approaches?
    (A) Evidence-based practice
    (B) Placebo effect
    (C) Regression to the mean
    (D) Common factors
    (E) Meta-analysis

1. Emilia wants to choose a therapist based on the therapeutic approach used. She knows that the most effective therapies share three common factors. Explain how the three factors are expressed in each of the following types of therapy.
   - Cognitive-behavioral therapy
   - Humanistic therapy
   - Psychodynamic therapy

2. A friend has told you that he has been fighting a losing battle with depression. He worries that if his family finds out, the tension in his household would get even worse. He is very hesitant about seeing a psychotherapist and has come to you for advice about what would be the best thing for him to do.

   A) Using the following, how would you encourage your friend to seek help from a psychotherapist?
      - Ethical guidelines
      - Eclectic approach

   B) Having discussed the merits of psychotherapy in general, your friend asks you what specific approach would be best. To help him choose the right treatment, explain the pros and cons of each of the following approaches based on the mental issues he is dealing with.
      - Biomedical approach
      - Psychoanalysis
      - Cognitive therapy
      - Existential therapy

WRITE AS A PSYCHOLOGIST: REVISE AND EDIT

Leave time for reviewing your answers to the free-response questions so you can revise them if necessary to make the wording as clear and strong as possible. Double-check that you have answered all parts of the question. Although you won't lose points for mistakes in grammar, usage, or mechanics, a response that is free from those is the ideal, so leave time for editing your work as well. For more guidance on answering free-response questions, see pages xxii–xxiii.

23

Cultural, Ethnic, and Gender Influences on Treatment and Prevention

*"If we are interested in the prevention of
mental-emotional disorders, we must change
those social conditions that produce these disorders."*

—George Albee

Essential Question: How can cultural and gender competence enhance psychotherapy, and to what degree can community mental health and preventive programs reduce the prevalence of mental illness?

The Western Eurocentric view of psychotherapy tends to focus almost exclusively on a male-oriented individualistic cultural perspective, as you read in Chapter 18. However, in a society that is growing more ethnically and racially diverse, modern therapists are attempting to recognize and embrace the challenge of cultural and gender diversity. This chapter examines the role of cultural and gender issues as well as community mental health and preventive programs in the effectiveness of treatment and prevention.

Cultural and Gender Competence in Psychotherapy

It is human nature to make assumptions based on previous experience as we fit new experience into our existing schemas, those frameworks of thought that help us organize the information and sensations we take in. Assumptions are efficient though not always reliable decision-making shortcuts. Psychotherapists acknowledge this human characteristic and commit themselves to resisting cultural and gender assumptions or stereotypes about their clients and to becoming as culturally and gender competent as they can so they can effectively serve clients who are different from themselves.

Cultural Issues

A carpenter is not measured only by the use of her hammer. A psychotherapist too may be highly competent in one or more therapeutic approaches, but if she is unable to adequately honor and adapt to the cultural context and background of clients, then she may as well be using a hammer to screw in a light bulb.

A vital tool in an increasingly culturally diverse society is **cultural competence**, the ability to provide effective treatment by recognizing the influence of cultural factors in the context of the individual and striving for outcomes that honor the client's cultural needs (Figure 23.1). But cultural competence goes beyond mere understanding and requires a good therapist to honor cultural differences, adapt the therapeutic process accordingly, and advocate for cultural diversity (Figure 23.2). Ethical therapy requires those practices.

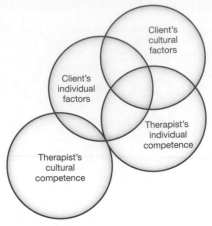

Figure 23.1 Cultural Competency in Psychotherapy

Even though society is becoming more culturally diverse, ethnic and racial groups that represent that diversity do not benefit equally from mental health services. One factor is barriers to access. Ethnic and racial minorities are disproportionately poorer and unable to afford services. Another factor is cultural bias in the psychotherapeutic approaches. The theoretical and philosophical basis of the most widely used psychotherapeutic approaches is rooted in a Western Eurocentric cultural perspective. A third factor is that ethnic and racial minorities avoid therapy or end treatment too early, frustrated by the lack of cultural competence on the part of psychotherapists and mental health organizations. Anyone of lower socioeconomic status may also have to discontinue treatment because of cost. Increasing ethnic and racial diversity among staff and encouraging therapists to improve cultural competence are key to improving these problems.

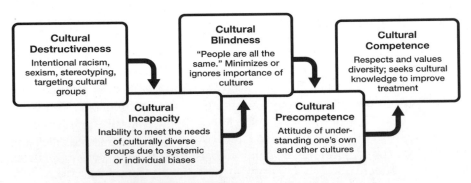

Figure 23.2 Cultural Competency Continuum

The American Psychological Association (APA) includes specific guidelines to promote better cultural competence in the field. Cultural competence in therapy includes four key components: 1) therapist cultural self-awareness, 2) knowledge of the client's cultural context, 3) knowledge of personal factors unique to the client, and 4) culturally appropriate interventions to bridge the gap between the therapist and the client's cultural perspective.

A culturally competent psychotherapist will be aware of his or her own cultural biases. Suppose, for example, that a young client from a *collectivistic* culture in East Asia that values interdependence enters therapy for depression and divulges that he is gay. He is concerned about how his family will react if he tells them. If not also from a collectivistic culture, the culturally competent therapist should be aware of his or her own cultural assumptions and recognize the culturally different context that the young man must face.

This individualistic-collectivistic cultural divide can manifest itself in both verbal and nonverbal communication differences. Some cultures consider eye contact a sign of disrespect and will avoid it, especially with strangers. In a first session, if the client constantly refuses to make eye contact, the therapist must be culturally competent enough to avoid attributing this to a negative psychological symptom. It's not a sign of guilt or anxiety; it could simply be culture.

Last, culturally competent therapists will be aware of the moral perspective from which *they* operate and recognize that the client's perspective may not be the same. If a therapist is morally opposed to sex outside of marriage, then what is her ethical responsibility as a therapist to handle a family in crisis because a sixteen-year-old family member is in a sexual relationship against her parents' wishes? Or if a therapist is morally comfortable or indifferent about sex outside of marriage, how does that attitude affect the therapy she provides? Should a therapist be morally neutral? A competent therapist must confront all these questions and deal with them in a culturally competent and ethical manner to best serve the client.

Gender Issues

An integral aspect of cultural issues related to psychotherapy is gender. **Gender** refers to the psychosocial experiences related to being female or male. Do therapeutic outcomes differ depending on the gender of the therapist and the gender of the client? What are the gender issues with which competent and ethical psychotherapists should be familiar? Like cultural competence, **gender competence** refers to the ability to provide effective treatment by recognizing and effectively responding to the influence of gender factors in the therapeutic relationship. Studies indicate that it is not the gender of the therapist that is at issue but the gender *competence* of the therapist. More research is needed to fully understand this issue, but therapeutic outcomes do improve with gender-competent therapists.

For example, in Western cultures such as the United States, females are culturally trained to express such emotions as sadness and fear, while males are taught to repress such emotions. Consequently, how people emotionalize their symptoms of depression may be quite different depending on gender.

A gender competent therapist will be aware of this difference and approach diagnosis and the therapeutic process accordingly.

Some believe that clients with certain mental health issues, such as sexual trauma or eating disorders, should have a therapist of the same gender. Most professionals agree that people entering psychotherapy should let their preference be known. If a female person requests a female therapist, that request should be honored. Women who suffered abuse by a male, for example, may have trouble trusting a male therapist, and trust is imperative to achieve therapeutic goals.

Psychotherapists participate in a high-stakes profession in which their clients' very lives could be in the balance. A gender and culturally competent therapist must recognize and respect cultural and gender differences, acknowledge their own cultural and gender blind spots, understand the socioeconomic factors that impact the emotional well-being of their clients, and actively engage in multicultural experiences to improve their cultural competence.

he Science of Psychology: *Therapy in a Pluralistic Society*

Unfortunately, funding for research in cultural and gender competence and methods is very small—most funding goes to research with a biological focus. However, there have been some studies that have looked at very specific culturally adapted treatments, and in most cases, the results have been positive. For example

- Ceremonies that reflect cultural traditions, such as African-based rituals of the drum call and the blessing of the day, have been included in therapy.

- Interventions with African American girls incorporated principles that are part of African American culture, such as spirituality, collective responsibility, and experiences with racial discrimination.

- In substance abuse programs with American Indians, leaders modeled ways to turn down offers of substances without offending Indian or non-Indian friends.

- When working with Puerto Rican children whose tradition is rich in storytelling, therapists, leaders, and mothers incorporated *cuentos*, Puerto Rican folktales, in part as a way to model good relations with parents.

The big question is: Do these culturally adapted therapies increase positive outcomes? Most evidence, especially in meta-analyses, shows that they do. The more targeted the adaptation, the more successful the outcomes.

Practice: Despite those findings, cultural competence and cultural adaptations have been controversial. Working with three or four other students, conduct research to learn the reasons for the controversies. After clearly articulating the views of the skeptics, develop your own position on the value or drawbacks of culturally adapted therapy and share your views with your class.

Community Mental Health

Today, mental health care is primarily community-based and outpatient, as opposed to inpatient hospitalization. Long-term psychiatric hospitalization is now much more rare than it was a half a century ago. The **1963 Community Mental Health Act** marked a national shift toward establishing community mental health centers across the nation. A number of programs and approaches to community mental health care developed, including the case-management model, community teams, support groups, assertive community treatment, outpatient commitment laws/programs, and community support programs.

By the mid-1950s, long-term institutionalization of people with mental illness peaked. When it became clear that long-term psychiatric hospitalization was doing more harm than good, a major shift called **deinstitutionalization** began in which treatment shifted from inpatient psychiatric hospitalization to outpatient community mental health programs. Deinstitutionalization was propelled by forces that included the development of psychotropic drugs, the introduction of federally funded welfare programs, and recognition that the poor care and mistreatment of the people with mental illness in psychiatric institutions was seen as a denial of basic civil rights.

Community-Based Treatment

Starting in the 1960s, care for people with mental illness has been influenced most by the **community mental health movement**. With the 1963 Community Mental Health Act and the introduction of psychotropic drugs to reduce the symptoms of severe psychological disorders, the custodial care model (or *warehousing*) of people with mental illness was replaced by a model that brought people with severe mental illness back to their communities where they could be given psychiatric rehabilitation locally, at a lower cost, and on an outpatient basis. **Psychiatric rehabilitation** (sometimes referred to as *psychosocial rehabilitation*) refers to the many services provided to persons with psychiatric disabilities (severe mental illness) so that they can function in their community.

Since the 1990s, community-based mental health care has been driven by two movements—evidence-based practice and the recovery model. **Evidence-based practice** is the use of research-based and outcomes-oriented data and other information to determine what works best. The **recovery model** is seen as an alternative to the long-term care model that emphasizes stabilization. Many suffering from mental illness don't want to simply get stabilized; they want to get well. The recovery model constitutes a new paradigm that stresses healing, social support, empowerment, and hope. From these two movements, improved mental health care has focused on a number of programs and treatment models to enhance care for people with mental illness at the community level.

Community Support Programs Starting in the 1960s, community support programs were established throughout the nation to provide psychiatric rehabilitation for those who had previously been institutionalized. **Community support programs** comprise a system of treatment of the severely mentally ill using a **case manager** who coordinates the services and treatments that each client needs to achieve or maintain healthy functioning in their community. Those who provide mental health services in these programs understand that severe mental illness often requires multidimensional care that includes services that go beyond the clinical setting (Figure 23.3 on the next page). By the 1980s, problems appeared that challenged the effectiveness of community support programs. Decreased state and federal housing subsidies, substance abuse and addiction, unemployment, poverty, and crime led to the need for a more intensive approach.

Assertive Community Treatment One such intensive approach is **assertive community treatment**. It was developed to address the weaknesses of community support programs and is a much more comprehensive and intensive approach to providing mental health services to those with severe mental illness as well such additional problems as substance abuse and lack of family support. Assertive community treatment teams provide specialized support, treatment, and whatever else is needed to enable the person to achieve and maintain **community integration** and to prevent homelessness or rehospitalization. By the late 1990s, it was determined that consistent implementation of six evidence-based practices significantly improved the effectiveness of community mental health treatment:

- Psychotropic drug management
- Assertive community treatment
- Employment support
- Family support
- Treatment for co-occurring disorders
- Recovery orientation

Assisted Outpatient Treatment From 1955 to today, the number of psychiatric hospital beds in the U.S. has shrunk by 95 percent. This represents a profound change in the way our society views the treatment of those with severe mental illness. During the height of institutionalized psychiatric care, all states could, through a judge's order, commit a person involuntarily to one of the many large mental institutions in existence.

By the 1980s, it became clear that in the absence of involuntary

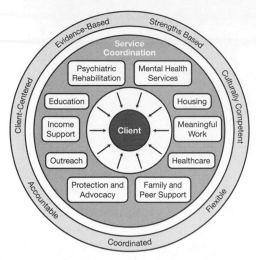

Figure 23.3 Components of Community Support

psychiatric hospitalization, a new approach was needed for those suffering severe mental illness who were unable or unwilling to get treatment. In those cases, most states have passed assisted outpatient treatment laws that allow a judge to order specific treatment. **Assisted outpatient treatment (AOT)** is a civil court order requiring community-based mental health services. Such a court-ordered treatment plan usually includes psychiatric medication and/or attending treatment sessions but may also require abstinence of other drugs as well as the avoidance of certain places or people. When used by community courts, AOT enables the community to ensure that treatment is provided when the alternative could endanger the individual or the community. The most recognizable AOT law is New York State's *Kendra's Law*. A man with schizophrenia who was not medicated for the disorder killed a woman named Kendra by pushing her onto the path of a subway train. The state of New York passed Kendra's Law to require psychiatric treatment for people with severe mental illness as a condition for living in their community.

Assessing Community Mental Health

Community-based treatment has shown mixed results. On one hand, meta-analyses of studies looking at the effectiveness of deinstitutionalization and community mental health programs show that evidence-based programs provide effective treatment. However, although treatment using the community mental health model is also much

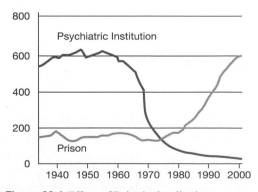

Figure 23.4 Effects of Deinstitutionalization

more cost-effective, the availability for that treatment has not kept up with demand. While emptying the huge psychiatric institutions is considered a success, many people suffering from severe mental illness, without the support necessary to cope beyond the gates of those institutions, have become homeless or incarcerated. The current estimate is that between 20 and 25 percent of homeless people suffer severe mental illness. Some people have argued that, in too many cases, life in psychiatric institutions was replaced by life on the streets or in a jail cell.

Severe mental illness often includes **comorbidity**, the diagnosis of two or more psychological disorders at once. Substance abuse is often the comorbid disorder among people with severe mental illness and this factor has contributed to the dramatic increase in incarceration. As the rate of long-term psychiatric hospitalization decreased, by the late 1970s, the rate of criminal incarceration began to climb (Figure 23.4). Community mental health works, but only for those who have access to it. Most agree that more needs to be done to increase access to community mental health so that those suffering severe mental illness don't find themselves trapped in homelessness or incarceration.

Preventive Approaches for Mental Illness

An individual's mental health and numerous psychological disorders, including anorexia nervosa, anxiety disorders, and depression, are influenced by **social determinants**—factors such as poverty, violence, economic and political inequality, and even social media that are associated with increased risk of mental illness. The field of preventive care looks to stop mental illness before it starts by recognizing the links between society and mental illness and then trying to change those societal factors that can lead to psychological disorders.

Imagine you and your family live in a large town where many live below the poverty line. Unemployment and crime are much higher than the national average. Also, the city water supply is full of toxic lead, which is particularly devastating for young children. Could these circumstances increase the incidences of mental illness? The scenario describes some of the socio-demographic factors of Flint, Michigan, and there has been a significant increase in depression, anxiety, guilt, and overall distress as a result of the Flint lead contamination crisis, which began in 2014. Local, state, and federal governments are attempting to provide mental health services for the psychological consequences of the lead contamination. While much needed, it is intervention *after* the fact. Could things have been done to prevent the mental illness in the first place? The short answer is yes. Mental illness should never be seen as isolated from the social context.

Resilience refers to the ability of individuals or communities to absorb the trauma associated with an event or crisis and essentially bounce back. Preventive approaches for mental illness recognize the importance of resilience in coping with events that could otherwise lead to mental illness. Most people possess enough resilience to recover from and cope with even profoundly traumatic events. When events are so traumatic or stresses are so prolonged, however, people may find that they need help to cope. Community mental health professionals provide such services as **crisis centers** and **crisis hotlines** to help with immediate mental health problems and also attempt to address societal stressors such as poverty, substandard housing, violence, and discrimination. **Community psychology** involves the relationship between individuals and the community and addresses social, economic, and political factors that lead to mental illness and identifies steps to take to reduce or prevent mental illness.

An excellent although tragic example of this interrelationship between the individual and the community would be the serious opioid and heroin epidemic that has recently hit some regions of the United States—especially New Hampshire—very hard. As the use of heroin spiked in local New Hampshire communities, so too did overdose deaths. The suffering of the addicts and their families is also the community's suffering. Ending the epidemic requires a community psychology approach. It involves addressing the problem in homes, schools, churches, and town halls. Family doctors have to adapt their practices to address the crisis directly. Reducing opioid abuse requires preventive measures that address the root causes, which can be very complex, difficult to fully identify, and difficult to remove.

Social and Environmental Factors

If social and environmental factors can be effectively addressed, many mental health problems can be not only resolved but also prevented in the future. Community preventive programs use the Institute of Medicine's **continuum of care model**, which focuses on three preventive interventions (Figure 23.5).

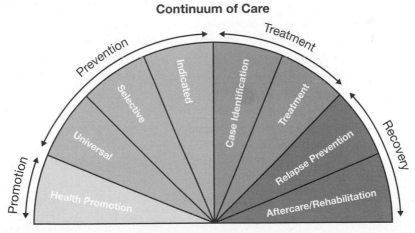

Figure 23.5 Continuum of Care

First, universal interventions are those that address an entire population; no particular group is targeted. Examples include drinking-age laws and education mandates. Second, selective interventions are targeted to specific vulnerable or high-risk groups, such as young mothers or children and young adults. Third, indicated interventions are intended for high-risk individuals who are showing early signs of psychological disorders. Most agree that preventive programs to address social determinants should begin at the earliest possible time.

Parenting and Family Support

Many studies have shown that the strongest indicators of mental illness in adulthood are stressors that occur during childhood. The significant factor most associated with adult mental illness is poor parenting during the earliest years of childhood. Therefore, one of the most effective ways to prevent mental illness is to provide services for young adults who need help being better parents. Promoting healthy parenting and preventing child abuse and neglect through education and support services are the best preventive actions that communities can take to reduce the chances that those children will become adults dealing with drug abuse or other psychological disorders.

Assessing Preventive Programs

Societies and cultures are complex, and trying to reduce or prevent mental illness by changing society and culture can be very difficult. Nonetheless, numerous public-health preventive programs clearly work. Fluoride in water and mandatory immunizations against certain diseases have proven effective. Educating children about the health risks of smoking has also worked. Preventive programs in the area of mental illness are most effective when they address high-risk populations as early as possible. Parenting classes for young parents, Head Start for preschool-aged children from poor families, and anti-bullying policies in schools all show effectiveness at reducing the prevalence of mental illness among vulnerable populations. Finally, using evidence-based practice as a community mental health professional will yield interventions that are more likely to work than other approaches.

REFLECT ON THE ESSENTIAL QUESTION

Essential Question: *How can cultural and gender competence enhance psychotherapy, and to what degree can community mental health and preventive programs reduce the prevalence of mental illness?* On separate paper, make a chart like the one below to gather details to answer that question.

Cultural Competence	Gender Competence	Community Mental Health	Preventive Approaches

KEY TERMS		
1963 Community Mental Health Act	community psychology	deinstitutionalization
assertive community treatment	community support programs	evidence-based practice
assisted outpatient treatment (AOT)	comorbidity	gender
	continuum of care model	gender competence
case manager	crisis centers	psychiatric rehabilitation
community integration	crisis hotlines	recovery model
community mental health movement	cultural competence	resilience
	culture	social determinants

MULTIPLE-CHOICE QUESTIONS

Use the diagram when answering the following question.

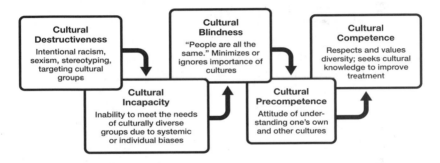

1. When a psychotherapist tries to teach her client to show more eye contact when talking to her, she is demonstrating cultural

    (A) destructiveness

    (B) incapacity

    (C) blindness

    (D) precompetence

    (E) competence

2. Ethnic and racial minorities avoid therapy or end it early because

    (A) they have better support systems within their own communities

    (B) they tend to be uninsured

    (C) their problems resolve more quickly because of their cultural attitudes

    (D) they have to travel a long distance to a mental health facility

    (E) they are frustrated by the therapist's lack of cultural competence

3. The psychosocial experience and cultural construct used to identify behaviors as male or female is

(A) sex

(B) race

(C) denomination

(D) gender

(E) masculinity

4. A male therapist who recognizes, respects, and adapts his therapeutic approach for a female client who is dealing with depression is showing

(A) feminism

(B) cultural neutrality

(C) feminine-masculine neutrality

(D) nonsexism

(E) gender competence

Refer to the graph below when answering the following question.

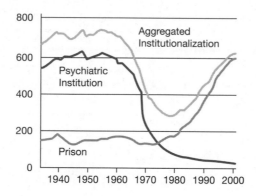

5. The graph illustrates the

(A) positive effects of community mental health programs

(B) unintended consequence of deinstitutionalization

(C) significant decrease in the prevalence of schizophrenia in the United States from 1960–1990

(D) growing need for more judges and prison cells in the United States

(E) environmental factors associated with increased diversification of the U.S. population

6. Community psychology emphasizes

(A) group as opposed to individual therapy

(B) the relationship between individuals and their communities

(C) after-hours use of community buildings for therapy sessions

(D) the importance of group housing

(E) prenatal care to prevent mental health problems

7. What is the purpose of assisted outpatient treatment?

(A) To require specific mental health treatment through a civil court order

(B) To provide help relocating homeless individuals with mental illness to suitable housing

(C) To implement clinical treatment to prevent the onset of severe mental illness

(D) To involuntarily commit severely mentally ill patients to receive psychiatric hospitalization

(E) To prevent the effects of comorbidity among the severely mentally ill

8. A young mother is diagnosed with generalized anxiety disorder a few months after her husband lost his job and her family was evicted from their apartment. This scenario may reflect what concept?

(A) Resilience

(B) Social determinants

(C) Continuum of care

(D) Community psychology

(E) Cultural indifference

9. Which choice best represents the field of community psychology?

(A) A therapist adapts his therapeutic approach to the client's age.

(B) A psychiatric hospital confirms diagnosis through peer review.

(C) A community mental health professional sets up a youth center.

(D) A psychologist practices eclectic therapy among indigenous people.

(E) A school counselor provides career counseling.

10. Which best indicates an effective preventive mental health program?
   (A) Survey results from diverse clients show high satisfaction when compared to a culturally homogeneous group of clients.
   (B) The rate of teen alcoholics of single parents who went through healthy parenting classes is 30 percent lower than a control group who did not participate in classes.
   (C) The amount of funding for a *Say No To Drugs* education program has increased by 50 percent to hire more staff.
   (D) The number of homeless schizophrenics in an urban area has decreased by 80 percent compared to a rural area of similar size.
   (E) The incidence of gun violence among rural white people is 50 percent lower than among urban minorities.

FREE-RESPONSE QUESTIONS

1. As the head of a community mental health organization, you have been asked to justify public funding for your organization.
   A) Provide a cogent and compelling justification for continued public funding by discussing the following:
      - Deinstitutionalization
      - Assertive community treatment
      - Social determinants
      - Single-parent parenting classes

   B) To present an even more compelling justification for your organization, explain how you would incorporate the following into your presentation.
      - Meta-analysis
      - Random sampling
      - Evidence-based practice

2. As the lead psychotherapist for a mental health clinic located in a large city, you want to ensure your staff of psychotherapists provides the best service possible. Discuss how you would convince your staff of the vital importance of the following.
      - Cultural competence
      - Cultural competence continuum
      - Gender competence
      - Continuum of care model
      - Recovery model

UNIT 13: Review

In this unit, you sought answers to these essential questions about treatment of abnormal behavior and community support and prevention.

Chapter 22: To what degree are psychotherapeutic approaches similar and different regarding philosophy, techniques, and effectiveness?

Chapter 23: How can cultural and gender competence enhance psychotherapy, and to what degree can community mental health and preventive programs reduce the prevalence of mental illness?

Apply what you have learned about treatment of abnormal behavior by answering the free-response question below.

FREE-RESPONSE QUESTION

Dr. Dahlin has been working with his client Itamar for three weeks as the result of a court order. Itamar has complained that he hears voices talking to him when he thinks he is alone in his house. He also believes that the government has been spying on him and listening in on his phone conversations. As Dr. Dahlin meets with Itamar, sometimes Itamar will have laughing fits and other times he will lack any kind of emotional response at all. Occasionally, Itamar will speak in phrases such as "wood is hard, problems large, my mother's Marge." Based on this information, respond to the questions below.

A) What type of practitioner is Dr. Dahlin likely to be?

B) From which type of mental illness may Itamar be suffering? Explain at least two symptoms that led you to this conclusion. Be sure to connect these directly with the diagnosis.

C) Explain how psychologists from the following perspectives would treat Itamar.
- Biological
- Behavioral
- Cognitive

D) What type of court order is involved in the treatment of Itamar? Explain why such a court order became necessary in the 1980s and after.

UNIT 14: Social Psychology

Chapter 24 Social Cognition and Influence

Chapter 25 Social Behavior: Our Public Selves

Unit Overview

Imagine yourself at a school dance. You hang out with a few close friends and wonder what everyone else is thinking of you. You get some punch and immediately spill a little, making you even more self-conscious. You hear people laughing and are sure they are laughing at you. But you look around and see that no one is paying attention to you. You relax and "people watch." Football players are hanging out together, talking and laughing. Janice and Pedro are holding hands, deep in conversation. On the dance floor, Yolanda is teaching friends a new dance, and her followers are laughing at their mistakes.

A social psychologist would look at this scene and identify different elements of **social psychology**—a branch of psychology that uses a scientific approach to understand how and why social groups influence individual behavior and attitudes and how, in turn, individual attitudes and behaviors affect social groups. This unit explores how we see ourselves and others in social situations and what factors help explain our behavior toward others.

Key Topics

- Application of attribution theory to explain motives
- The structure and function of different kinds of group behavior
- How individuals respond to expectations of others, including groupthink, conformity, and obedience to authority
- Attitudes and how they change (e.g., central route to persuasion)
- Predictions about the impact of others on individual behavior
- Processes that contribute to differential treatment of group members
- The impact of social and cultural categories (e.g., gender, race, ethnicity) on self-concept and relations with others
- Anticipation of the impact of behavior on a self-fulfilling prophecy
- The variables that contribute to altruism, aggression, and attraction
- Attitude formation and change, including persuasion strategies and cognitive dissonance
- Important figures in social psychology (e.g., Solomon Asch, Leon Festinger, Stanley Milgram, Philip Zimbardo)

Source*: AP® Psychology Course and Exam Description*

Social Cognition and Influence

"If you put good apples into a bad situation, you'll get bad apples."
—Phillip Zimbardo

Essential Question: How do we perceive ourselves and others in social situations, given various influences that can affect our behaviors?

The school dance scenario at the beginning of the unit is fairly typical in high schools all over the country. First, we worry about what others think of us, and then we begin to make assumptions about others around us. Social psychologists call this **social cognition**, because it involves how we think about ourselves and others in social situations. The term *social situations* refers to a group of two or more people or may also describe an individual alone who *thinks* that others are observing him or her. For example, you may be driving on a highway and come across a sign that says "Speed Controlled by Radar." You immediately take your foot off of the accelerator and look at the speedometer whether you are or are not driving over the speed limit. You want to make sure that you do not get a ticket. So, even if no one is *actually* observing your speed, and in reality you are alone, you adjust your behavior because you *think* you are in a social situation.

Social psychology also addresses **social influence**— how we are influenced by others in a social situation. Think back to the group dancing in the gym. Perhaps one or two people in Yolanda's group did not really want to dance, but they went along with the dance lessons—partly because they did not want to stand out, but also because learning dance moves is often more fun with others. For one thing, there's safety in numbers—more people will make mistakes, so a person's individual mistake will not stand out.

Social influence might encourage people to find safety in numbers.

A third aspect of social psychology is **social behavior**—how we behave in social situations. Getting up to dance in Yolanda's group when you did not really want to is *social influence*, while actually dancing in Yolanda's group is *social behavior*. The public display of affection between Janice and Pedro is also *social behavior*, performed to let others know that they are a couple. Rick also exhibits social behavior by being the center of attention in his group, telling jokes and entertaining his friends. Football players talking and laughing about their last game is also an example of social behavior.

The football players' behavior is actually a good illustration of a fundamental tenet of social psychology: *the social situation influences or even controls behavior.* On the football field, football players are expected to behave aggressively toward the other team to win the game. A defensive lineman runs over the player in front of him, anyone on defense tackles an opposing player with the ball, and offensive players elude defensive players, to name only a few behaviors both expected and accepted in a football game. However, though it's fine to *talk* about a game, obviously the actual football game behaviors would be inappropriate at a school dance.

Schemas: The Building Blocks of Social Cognition

Have you ever viewed an event with a friend and later discussed it, finding that the two of you had wildly different interpretations of what happened? Consider Chris, for example, the newly installed director of an office handling ethnic minority issues in psychology. She is a petite biracial woman who had moved to Washington, DC and did not yet know her way around. One day, as she was walking to her car, a large man with a menacing goatee started to approach her. She panicked and began running toward her car. The man quickened his pace and Chris panicked even more, getting into her car and slamming the door. Later she found out that the man, Phil, simply wanted to find out more about ethnic minority psychology research. His perspective was that he only wanted her to feel good about her new position. Her perspective was that she felt her life was in danger. In psychology, the different perspectives are called schemas, a term you no doubt remember from earlier chapters. A **schema** is a cognitive filter through which we view the world and interpret information.

Chris's behavior was consistent with a personal safety schema. Phil, being less sensitive to this safety schema, had a **self-schema**—a construct about himself and his experiences—that he was a good man with good intentions. He had no idea he would be perceived as a threat within another person's schema.

The contemporary concept of schemas has its roots in the work of British psychologist, Frederic C. Bartlett (1886–1969), who investigated how cultural schemas guide us to recall certain events. In his book *Remembering* (1932), he reports what happened when he asked nonnative research subjects to recall an Alaska Native folktale called "The War of the Ghosts" both immediately after reading it and then after several periods of delay. The legend structure differed markedly from the structure of Western fairy tales, and subjects' recollections were influenced by their Western schemas of fairy tales; they even changed details to align with Western activities. (Seal hunting became fishing, for example.)

Schemas come from personal experience and are so numerous that we cannot count how many we each might hold. For example, Chris's schemas (the biracial women who worked with minorities), include all of these schemas: Black, Asian, biracial, administrator, newcomer, daughter—many different facets of herself. However, Chris also has schemas about other people, objects, and concepts. These will be discussed later.

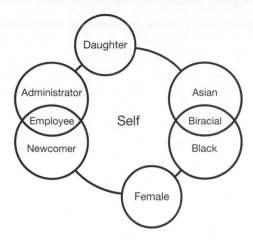

Figure 24.1 Chris's Self-Schemas

Self-Schemas: How We Perceive Ourselves and Maintain Our Thoughts about Ourselves

Hazel Markus (b. 1942) is a social psychologist who has contributed extensively to the notion of self-schemas. Self-schemas are the most important elements of our concepts of ourselves. Markus investigated the stability and malleability of self-schemas and also people's "possible selves." In general, our most central self-schemas are more stable, and newer or more peripheral self-schemas are more malleable. Because Chris's self-schema as an ethnic minority was so central to her identity, she would be more sensitive to racial injustices, such as the shooting of an unarmed Black youth, than someone whose central self-schemas are not as attuned to racial issues. However, even central self-schemas can be transformed. Chris's self-schema about race may have been profoundly modified when Barack Obama became president of the United States.

Central self-schemas filter our perceptions. For example, when a talk-show host asked a dentist on his show to review a new movie, the dentist only commented on how good the actors' teeth were. You and your friends may have different

President Barack Obama no doubt modified the self-schemas of many African Americans about race.

perspectives of an event because you are using different self-schemas to perceive these events. Your self-schema as an outgoing, fun person might view a party as a fun event and a good time, but your more reserved mother might think your "fun" is making a spectacle of yourself. Your behavior may be the same for all who view it ("he's having a great time"), but it doesn't fit your mother's self-schema of how people should behave.

Another form of self-schema Markus and her colleagues studied was **possible selves**—aspects of ourselves that we either aspire to be or could conceivably be. For example, if you want to be a psychologist, whenever you are studying or even just interacting with the world, your future-psychologist self might influence your perceptions. When you were very young, you may have wanted to be an engineer, and everything you did may have been with that in mind until it was replaced by wanting to be a psychologist. Possible selves may also include negative outcomes, such as fearing becoming homeless as a result of risky financial decisions—a negative self-schema that might influence choices later in life.

A graduate contemplates possible selves.

Self-Serving Biases Most people like to think of themselves as being good, moral individuals and will not have self-schemas with evil intent or lack of caring about others. Positive self-schemas are maintained through **self-serving biases**—tendencies to perceive ourselves in a positive light. Many studies investigating this phenomenon have found that people see themselves as having above average intelligence and high moral standards and as being more helpful than they are in reality. When a student does well on a test, for example, the student will likely attribute the success to his or her intelligence or hard work (an internal cause). If a student does not do well, that student may blame an unfair test or unfair grading system (external cause). People ascribe such schemas to favorite teams and celebrities as well.

Assessing the Behavior of Others

If you have a friend who tries all the scariest roller-coaster rides, you might think, "I wonder why he likes roller coasters?" You might conclude that he is a sensation seeker. In psychology, such a conclusion is called an attribution. An **attribution** is the way in which we explain the cause or causes of behavior. You attributed your friend's fondness of roller coasters to his tendency to be a sensation-seeker rather than to some other explanation.

Attributing his roller-coaster riding behavior to his being a sensation-seeker is an **internal attribution**—an assumption that behavior is driven by such internal characteristics as traits or feelings. If you attributed his behavior as responding to a friend's dare, you would be inferring an **external attribution**. If a fellow student gets an A on an exam, you might think she is smart, and if she gets an F on an exam, you might think she is dumb. These are both internal attributions. They are also **stable attributions** because qualities like smartness are internal and stable within a given individual. A temporary or **unstable attribution** would be attributing the student's A to studying hard for the exam rather than being smart—that is, attributing her performance to an internal and unstable factor.

Attribution theory was first developed by Fritz Heider (1896–1988) and was later expanded by other researchers who, even into the 21st century, have used attribution theory as an investigative tool to determine the causes of behavior. Attribution theory suggests that causes of behaviors comprise two dimensions: 1) internal vs. external and 2) stable vs. unstable. For example, if a fellow student gets an A on an exam, you can say that the person is smart (internal, stable characteristic), studied hard (internal, unstable characteristic), took an easy test (external, stable characteristic), or the teacher was in a good mood (external, unstable characteristic).

DIMENSIONS OF BEHAVIOR		
	Stable	**Unstable**
Internal	The student must be smart.	The student must have studied hard.
External	The test must have been easy.	The teacher must have been in a good mood.

Figure 24.2

Other factors also influence how we assess the causes of behavior. For example, social psychologist Harold Kelley (1967–2003) identified three factors that contribute to our assessments of internal versus external causes of behaviors: 1) consensus, 2) distinctiveness, and 3) consistency.

Consensus   Let's say Tom, a fellow student, raves about how good your school's boys' basketball team is. If consensus is high and mostly everyone thinks the basketball team is good, then you are more likely to attribute Tom's comments to external factors; however, if consensus is low and only a few people besides Tom think the team is good, then you are more likely to attribute Tom's comments to internal factors.

Distinctiveness   If Tom does not usually rave about sports teams, suggesting the presence of high distinctiveness, you will be more likely to attribute his comments to external factors (like the basketball team is especially good this year). However, the presence of low distinctiveness—if

Tom always raves about your school's sports teams—will make you more likely to attribute Tom's comments to internal factors (such as that Tom is generally an enthusiastic sports fan).

Consistency   If Tom tends to rave about many things in addition to the sports team, he would be showing high consistency, which would suggest that his comments about the sports team can be attributed to internal factors. If Tom is not one to rave about things but raves about the sports team, demonstrating low consistency, his comments can be attributed to external factors (this year's team is outstanding).

Actor–Observer Differences

In the 1960s, social psychologists Edward E. Jones (1926–1993) and Keith Davis of Duke University introduced the idea of *correspondent inference theory* to explain why people make internal or external attributions. These researchers found that we have a tendency to attribute internal, stable (also known as dispositional) explanations of behaviors when we observe other people's behaviors, but we attribute external or temporary explanations of behaviors when we explain our own behaviors. This concept is called the **actor-observer bias**. Later, Stanford University professor Lee Ross (b. 1942) termed this tendency the **fundamental attribution error**—the tendency to attribute behaviors of others to dispositional (internal, stable) factors and to ignore other explanations such as external factors. For example, if you observed a man hitting another man, you might tend to believe that the hitter was an aggressive person rather than consider that the other man may have struck the first blow or insulted the hitter. Then when we observe the behavior of individuals from a minority group or underrecognized group (e.g., ethnic, sexual, and religious minorities), we tend to apply the fundamental attribution error to the entire group. Social psychologist Thomas Pettigrew (b. 1931) termed this tendency the **ultimate attribution error**. For example, if we witness a member of a minority hitting someone, we may believe that everyone from that ethnic group is aggressive. This will be discussed later when reviewing issues of racism, prejudice, and stereotyping.

Attitude Change

How do you feel about the field of psychology? How do you feel about the person who sits to your right in your psychology class? To your left? How do you feel about your psychology teacher? All of these questions relate to attitudes. Attitudes are formed about everything we encounter—a presidential candidate, Niagara Falls, global warming, or even something as seemingly insignificant as the color green. Positive, negative, or neutral attitudes may arise toward any of these objects identified; we cannot help but to feel *something* about them. **Attitudes** represent how you feel toward various objects.

Kurt Lewin (1890–1947), often called "the father of social psychology," felt that attitude was social psychology's most indispensable concept. Lewin and other social psychologists essentially agreed that the three components of attitudes are 1) affects (feelings), 2) behaviors, and 3) cognitions. However, while Lewin originally felt that attitudes closely predicted behaviors, subsequent research indicated that affects, behaviors, and cognitions about objects are merely components of attitudes toward those objects. Also, while Lewin originally believed that attitudes correlated with behaviors, modern psychologists have proposed that this is not the case.

In 1934, a classic study by Richard LaPiere (1899–1986), as well as later research it inspired, reveals this schism. During a time of tremendous racism toward Asian individuals, LaPiere traveled around the United States with a couple of Chinese descent. Among 184 restaurants they visited, they were refused service by only one. Six months later, LaPiere wrote back to all 184 restaurants, asking them if they served Asian individuals. Owners of 129 restaurants replied and 117, a full 91 percent, said they would never serve

Asians. Of course, LaPiere knew that all but one restaurant had indeed served Asian customers just six months earlier.

Results of the LaPiere study suggest that a very weak link exists between attitudes and behaviors. Three general ways have been suggested to forge a stronger link between attitudes and behaviors.

1. Eliminating or minimizing other influences on behavior strengthens the connection between attitudes and behavior. For example, if you want to eat a healthy diet but a friend does not, you may be influenced by your friend to eat junk food, acting against your beliefs. However, if you see less of your friend, that influence may be minimized and you would be more likely to eat a healthy diet.

2. Attitudes associated with a *specific* behavior predict behavior more than attitudes that are only *generally* related to a behavior. For example, if you decide in the morning that you will eat a salad for lunch, you are more likely to actually do so than if you had only decided you would eat a healthy meal.

3. Firming up attitudes aligns the connection between attitudes and behaviors. One way to strengthen the connection between attitudes and behavior is to base an attitude on personal experience. The restaurant owners in LaPiere's study lived in the Midwest in the 1930s and had

few opportunities to meet Asian people. Accordingly, their attitudes were weak because they were not based on personal experience. However, when they actually encountered the Chinese couple traveling with LaPiere, they may have felt that these nice, quiet people were exceptions to their generally prejudicial attitudes and it was okay for them to serve the couple.

Cognitive dissonance, a theory introduced by **Leon Festinger** (1919– 1989) in 1957, identifies the discomfort felt when we hold two contradictory views simultaneously or act in a way that conflicts with our beliefs. To reduce this discomfort, we might change either our actions or beliefs so the two positions align. For example, someone exaggerating qualifications on a resume might feel cognitive dissonance about lying. That person could resolve the dissonance by removing the exaggerations from the resume or by concluding that "everybody does it anyway" and stop feeling guilty.

To demonstrate support for his theory, Festinger had research participants engage in a boring task, such as turning a set of wooden knobs a quarter turn over and over for an hour or transferring a jar of beebees by a pair of tweezers to another jar one by one. After this task, the experimenter asked the participants to tell a person in the waiting room (who was actually a "confederate" working with the researcher) that the task was very interesting. For their trouble, the researcher offered the participant either $1 or $20 to essentially lie to the confederate. Who do you think felt that the task was more interesting? Believe it or not, the group that was paid only $1 changed their minds about the experiment more than the group that was paid $20 did when asked later how interesting the experiment really was. This is what Festinger called "underjustification"; the research participants were underjustified to lie, so in order to believe they really did not lie to the confederates, they had to change their minds about the experiment and feel that it really was interesting. The participants who were given $20 to lie to the confederates still felt that the study was not very interesting. At the end of the study, Festinger told the participants that giving them either $1 or $20 was part of the study and he asked all of them to give the money back, and all of them did!

Numerous studies have been conducted since Festinger's original study. Most have concluded that, while psychologists originally felt that attitudes "caused" behaviors and people needed to change their attitudes in order to effect positive behaviors, the more effective way to handle cognitive dissonance is to first change the behaviors, and attitude change will follow.

Role-playing is an aspect of cognitive dissonance as people assume the characteristics of the roles they play. For example, in a 2010 study by researchers Carney, Cuddy, and Yap, research subjects were asked to assume a high- or low-power pose and found physiological differences the poses elicited. For the high-power pose, study subjects were asked to sit at a desk, lean back, put their feet up on the desk, and place their hands behind their heads. Blood tests revealed that the subjects had higher levels of testosterone compared to those of a control group that did not hold this "power pose." For the low-power pose, study subjects were asked to contract their arms and legs, holding a sort of fetal position. Blood tests revealed that these subjects had increased levels of cortisol, an adrenal hormone associated with stress.

The "high-power pose" increased testosterone levels. The "low- power pose" increased levels.of cortisol.

Philip Zimbardo (b. 1933), a renowned social psychologist, revealed the nature and importance of roles in his Stanford Prison Experiment, an experiment that was made into a movie in 2015. In the study, Zimbardo randomly divided student volunteers who had been screened for stability and psychological health into prisoner and guard groups. A mock prison was set up in the basement of a university building, complete with an unlit closet used for solitary confinement. With the help of the local Palo Alto police, the students assigned to the prisoner roles were rounded up at their homes and brought to the police station where they underwent the usual booking procedures, including a strip search. They were then delivered to the mock prison. They were given ill-fitting smocks to wear marked with their prisoner number and had to wear chains around one ankle. The guards, meanwhile, were given uniforms and wooden batons to represent their authority. They were told they could not physically hurt the prisoners, but they could abuse them psychologically to convey the idea that the guards had all the power and the prisoners had none. They could refer to prisoners only by their number, and they wore sunglasses to avoid eye contact.

Within a few days in these roles, the would-be prisoners became docile and defeated, though one tried a hunger strike to gain some leverage, but he was placed in solitary confinement as a result. Other prisoners were ordered to bang on the door of the dark closet to harass the prisoner in solitary confinement. The guards became rough and aggressive. They demanded that the prisoners do humiliating acts, such as using a bucket in their cell instead of a toilet for elimination and not being able to empty the bucket. One-third of the guards were later judged to have carried out sadistic acts. The experiment was terminated after six days when a graduate student who came to the "prison" to conduct interviews strongly objected to the unethical treatment of the young men in the study.

Results of the study had implications for modern prison reform just by showing how roles can be assumed. Based on his study, and also on events in the infamous Abu Ghraib Prison in Iraq, a military prison known for its heinous and unlawful torture of inmates, Zimbardo wrote *The Lucifer Effect* (2007), discussing how roles shape people's behaviors. He testified in front of the U.S. Congress about how the Abu Ghraib Prison environment and the absence of any authority figure to reinforce proper conduct affected prison guards negatively, turning normal, nonsadistic individuals into aggressive tormentors.

Persuasion

Have you ever gone into a store to buy a certain kind of cell phone but ended up being convinced to buy a more expensive model with more features? Sales people are knowledgeable in the art of persuasion. Why can we be persuaded to do something in one situation but resist persuasive attempts in another situation?

Carl Hovland (1912–1961) and fellow researchers at Yale University investigated the elements of persuasion. The elements are represented by the question "Who says what by how to whom?" and are broken down as follows: 1) the communicator's qualities (who), 2) aspects of the message (what), 3) how the message was communicated (by how), and 4) who the target audience was (to whom). The first element ("Who says?") is the most important aspect of persuasion. If the speaker is perceived to have credibility, people will generally believe that person; if the speaker is not so perceived, people will generally not believe that person. For example, when Barack Obama became president, supporters perceived him as credible and believed what he said; those who did not support him disbelieved what he said.

The second element, the communicated message, has a number of variables. Rational messages and emotional messages are both often persuasive. Also, when a message differs significantly from your existing knowledge, it may be persuasive because it arouses interest in how something so different can possibly be correct.

If the audience you are addressing generally agrees with you, you can be more persuasive by presenting a one-sided argument that affirms your audience's beliefs. However, if the audience is neutral and you present a one-sided argument, they may discount your argument. Presenting a two-sided argument, carefully discussing both sides of the issue before concluding that the side you want them to believe is more reasonable, may be the more persuasive route.

Two different effects are possible in the sequence of presenting information. The **primacy effect** (see page 260) explains that information that comes early has greater persuasive power than information that comes later. This effect occurs when all information is presented and a judgment is made later. The **recency effect** explains that information that comes later (more recently) than information that comes earlier has greater persuasive power. This effect occurs when the later information comes just before a judgment must be made.

The third element, how a message is communicated, is also called the *channel of communication*. If a message is communicated in an active manner, it is more persuasive than if it is communicated passively. For example, if you were interested in buying a new app for your cell phone and were actively clicking links to explanations of the qualities of the app, you would be more convinced by the information you found than if you were simply watching a commercial for it on your computer that you had to sit through. Another finding by researchers is that personal messages are more persuasive than messages delivered by the media.

The final component of persuasion deals with personal aspects of the audience, including their average age, how they are feeling, the size and diversity of the audience, and what they are thinking. For example, if a speaker is addressing high school or college students, referring to popular songs or artists when delivering the message would help the message connect with the audience. However, if a speaker is addressing retired people, discussing senior social opportunities, travel, investments, and interaction with grandchildren would be a better strategy.

Reason vs. emotion is an important distinction in persuasion. Two routes to persuasion, part of a model of attitudes and persuasion, were introduced in the mid-1980s by Richard Petty and John Cacciopo (b. 1951): the central route and the peripheral route. The **central route** involves reason and logic and an audience highly motivated to think and make decisions about the topic at hand. The **peripheral route** to persuasion relies on emotion or other superficial factors, which can be effective if the audience is not especially motivated to think about the topic or to make good decisions.

To understand the central route vs. the peripheral route of persuasion, consider this scenario. If Mikayla is in the market for a new car, she might look at *Consumer Reports* to read up on positive and negative features of various cars and talk with many people about the cars they have. When viewing a commercial for a certain car, she might compare the message of the commercial with the various elements that she has examined. If the commercial resonated closely with positive aspects she studied, she might say that the commercial was very persuasive, but if the commercial did not match what she studied, she might say that the commercial was weak. Her thinking followed the central route. On the other hand, if Mikayla's friend Carly is not in the market for a new car and hadn't really thought about cars very much, she might like the car because Mikayla likes it. She is persuaded via the peripheral route.

Studies have shown that people who apply the central route of persuasion are more strongly persuaded for a longer period of time. People who use the peripheral route to persuasion might be convinced temporarily by the communication, but the persuasion might not last. Thus, in the example above, although Carly was convinced because Mikayla liked the car, another friend might like a different car, and Carly could be persuaded to like that car. She may even prefer that car to the car Carly likes. She used the peripheral route to persuasion because she was not really interested in buying a new car.

Researchers have reexamined the central and peripheral routes through the lens of cognitive psychology. Cognitive psychology identifies controlled vs. automatic processing, where controlled processing is intentional, explicit processing, and automatic processing is unintentional, implicit processing. (See pages 255–256.) The central route can be likened to controlled processing, where a thoughtful evaluation can take place. However, if certain emotions are continually associated with a particular object over an extended period of time, this peripheral route may become an automatic process.

Two other methods of persuasion have also been found effective. One, known as the **foot-in-the-door approach** (using the metaphor of a door-to-door solicitor), is based on the idea that if you ask people to do a small thing first, they are much more likely to comply with a larger request later. For example, if you ask for a $1.00 donation to a charity, people will likely comply, because the amount is small. If you later ask them for a $10.00 donation or even more, they will also likely comply. Refusing the larger request would lead to cognitive dissonance—if they did it once, why wouldn't they do it again? The opposite strategy, known as the **door-in-the-face approach**, is also effective. With this approach, you begin by asking people for a very large request—a $100 donation, for example—a request that most people will not only likely refuse but that also might make them slam the door in your face. However, if you later ask them for a much smaller request, a $10.00 donation, for example, they are likely to comply. Refusing to comply would challenge their sense of reciprocity—you adjusted your request, so it seems only fair that they should adjust their response.

Group Influence

So far, the discussion of persuasion has been focused primarily on a single person trying to persuade someone to buy something or to vote for someone, or it involved media influence on persuading individuals to like a certain product. However, most of the time we are persuaded to do something or to adopt a certain position because we are influenced by a group of people or by society in general. For example, the influence of social media in shaping group opinion and behavior with posts and tweets is strong. The prevailing response or opinion can be very persuasive to masses of people.

Normative vs. Informational Social Influence

Most social influence is good, helping people behave in ways that are acceptable. Have you ever visited another country and not known how to behave in a manner considered to be polite? For example, in the United States, we are taught as children to eat quietly, without mouth noises and with our mouths closed. However, if you are eating noodles in Japan, it's polite to slurp the noodles noisily with gusto to show your appreciation. Eating your noodles quietly might suggest you didn't like them and might insult your host. Another norm in Japanese society is giving compliments three times because your host will refuse to accept your compliments the first two times. If you don't express the third compliment, you are considered impolite and insincere. When your behavior is influenced by social norms in this way, the process is called **normative social influence**.

Informational social influence provides noncoercive information that helps solve a problem or make a decision. It does not have a persuasive purpose. For example, consider the following problem. Take six toothpicks and try to make four triangles out of these toothpicks without breaking the toothpicks. Suppose you are working on this toothpick problem by yourself and cannot solve the problem. Now, suppose instead that you are in a group and someone in the group asks, "Is it okay if we don't keep the toothpicks flat on the table?" and another person asks, "How many toothpicks will it take to make a pyramid?" You will immediately solve the toothpick problem! None of the members of the group is trying to coerce you into believing something you don't already believe; they are merely providing information to solve the problem.

Figure 24.3

Informational social influence may also apply to social situations. Let's say that you see a friend and say "hello." However, your friend just passes you by without even acknowledging your presence. You get very upset with your friend and may even think bad thoughts about him. However, another friend lets you know that your first friend was in a complete daze because he had just lost his dog. You know immediately why your friend walked past you without acknowledging you and you no longer feel angry toward him because your other friend exerted informational social influence.

Conformity

Conformity is behavior that is in accord with accepted group standards. Are you your own person, or do you follow the crowd? Most people say they are their own persons, and their own opinions will not be swayed by those of others who think differently. Polish Gestalt psychologist **Solomon Asch** (1907–1996) set out to determine to what degree other people influence our opinions—or the external expression of our opinions. In his social pressure conformity experiments at Bryn Mawr College, Asch measured differences in research subjects' visual judgments by asking groups of eight males to view sets of two cards, the first displaying one vertical line and the second displaying three vertical lines of different heights (Figure 24.4). When asked in separate experiments which one of three lines on the second card matched the height of the single line on the first card, seven subjects chose the "wrong" line unanimously. The eighth participant, always set up to go last, knew the answer was wrong and chose the real matching line at first. Eventually, however, he shifted his answer and went along with those who chose the wrong answer.

Unbeknownst to the "real" participant, the other participants in the group were confederates working with the experimenter. At first they gave correct answers and then began making "mistakes" uniformly. Although the real participant gave the correct answer initially, he began agreeing with the confederates and answering with the incorrect answer. Three-quarters of the subjects answered incorrectly at least once, and 37 percent conformed to the group judgment. The same results occurred in other groups.

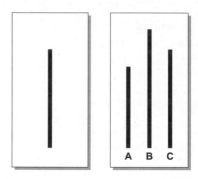

Figure 24.4 Asch experiment

When later interviewed about their answers, the real subjects said they knew that the others had chosen the wrong answers, but they didn't want to be different from the group. The real subjects had conformed to the group without any overt pressure at all—no disapproving looks from the others. However, the majority of the participants did not conform, sticking to what they knew was correct.

Obedience to Authority

The Asch studies make a statement about some people's willingness to "go with the crowd," but judging the lengths of different lines has no significant consequences. It is different when direct pressure from an authority figure urges individuals to conform to a group. In a landmark series of studies in the 1960s, **Stanley Milgram** (1933–1984) randomly assigned one of two subjects to be the "teacher" and the other to be the "learner." In these experiments, the "real" subject was always the teacher and Milgram's confederate was always

Figure 24.5 Participants in Milgram's experiment did not know that the shocks they were administering were fake. Two-thirds of the participants obeyed instructions.

the learner. The teacher and learner were shown a panel with different levels of electrical shock (mild, moderate, severe—all the way up to 450 volts) that would be delivered to the learner for incorrect answers. The learner was in a separate room and strapped to a chair from which he could reach four buttons to indicate his answer, one to four. The teacher was told that the learner was strapped down so he could not escape. The teacher read a series of word pairs for the learner to remember. Later, when the teacher read the first word of each pair, the learner was to press the button for the correct paired word from the list. If the answer was correct, the teacher said, "Correct," and moved to the next word. However, if the answer was incorrect, the teacher said, "Incorrect," gave the correct answer, "shocked" the learner, and then moved to the next word. Levels of shock increased with each wrong answer. Although the learner was not really being shocked, the teacher heard recorded responses associated with the various levels of shock. These recordings started with mild "ouch" responses at the beginning and proceeded to horrible screams in the middle. Near the highest level of shock, the recorded voice yelled that his heart was hurting, and at the very end, there was nothing but silence and no responses to the words. While most of the real subjects protested that they did not want to continue the study, nearly two-thirds of the subjects complied with the researcher's demands and proceeded all the way to 450 fake volts. After all, the experimenter was the "authority." A similar experiment from 2009 found about the same percentage of people willing to comply with the researcher's demands.

Certain conditions are shown to make people less obedient, however. One is the emotional distance of the victim. In variations of Milgram's study, compliance remained high in two-thirds of subjects when teachers could hear the learners through the wall; however, if the teacher was able to see the agony of the learner, compliance went down and decreased even further if the learner was right next to the teacher. Obedience went up when learners were in a soundproof room, and the teacher could not hear any protests.

Closeness and legitimacy of the authority figure also influence obedience. For example, if the experimenter communicated with the participant only by telephone and was not seen in a white lab coat, compliance went down.

Obedience went down even further if 1) the teacher never met the experimenter and only received instructions through a recording, or 2) the experimenter left the room and someone who appeared to be a janitor felt that the shock level was too low and wanted to increase the level.

Institutional authority increases obedience to authority even further. Milgram's first experiments were conducted at Yale, a highly respected institution where legitimate research is conducted, but subjects' obedience decreased when Milgram moved his experiments to an undistinguished storefront near the campus.

Finally, remember the Asch studies on conformity? When Asch's participants were in a situation where all of the other confederates gave incorrect answers, most of the participants conformed to the group answers at least once. However, Asch also found out that if one of the confederates gave the correct answer, the real participants almost never gave incorrect answers and stuck with their own perceptions. Similarly, in conditions where the teacher was part of a group of people delivering shocks to the learner, if all of the other participants obeyed the authority's demands, the real participants also obeyed. However, if even one of the other group members refused to deliver shocks at the upper levels of the scale, the real participants also refused to go to the higher levels.

Why Do We Obey?

Milgram's studies showed *that* we obey; they do not explain *why* we obey, but Milgram had speculations about that. Recent studies, informed by Milgram's speculations, have shown there are several reasons why people might obey an authority figure. First, from an evolutionary perspective, we seem to have given up our responsibility to engage in a risky or dangerous activity if there is an authority figure to take on this responsibility. *We* are not shocking the learner; *the experimenter* is taking responsibility for the shocks. Second, we have been socialized from childhood to obey authority figures, such as our parents, our teachers, and the police. Third, the shocks were delivered incrementally by only 15-volt jumps. The difference between a 15-volt shock and a 30-volt shock is not that large, and the difference between a 165-volt shock and a 180-volt shock is less than 10 percent greater. As you read in the chapters on sensation and perception, we tend not to notice stimuli that are less than 10 percent different from other stimuli. Finally, although all participants had a choice to continue with the experiment or not, they may not have *perceived* that they had the choice to discontinue. When they expressed concern about the experiment, the script of the experimenter was something like "The experiment requires that you continue." Thus, even though a participant could have said, "Well, I don't care what the experiment requires, I am not going to continue to torture the learner," most of them did not refuse to go to the highest level of voltage.

You might not be surprised that the Milgram study and the Zimbardo Stanford Prison Experiment study were very controversial studies. In the Milgram study, research participants *thought* they were injuring or even killing the learners. Milgram made sure to reintroduce the learner to the teachers after the study and **debrief** the teachers so they knew they did not really harm the learner. Even though they actually did not really hurt anyone, the teachers (participants) still had to live with the knowledge that they *could* have killed someone merely because the researcher asked them to do so. In follow-up interviews a year later, none of the participants reported lasting ill effects. In the Stanford Prison Experiment, some of the guards really did physically harm the prisoners, and some of the prisoners in follow-up interviews had long-term negative effects from the study.

Because of the potential harm done by these and many other studies in psychology and outside of psychology (e.g., medical research), researchers must have their research proposals evaluated by review boards at their home institutions to determine if participants will be properly protected. These review boards are called Institutional Review Boards (IRB), and every institution conducting research with human participants must have their research vetted through these IRBs. Zimbardo's experiments were approved by the Stanford IRB, but the deception involved in Milgram's experiment led to the tightening of ethical standards for experiments with human subjects.

 ## he Science of Psychology: *Just Following Orders?*

When prominent military and political leaders of defeated Nazi Germany faced military tribunals in Nuremberg, Germany, for their war crimes in 1945 and 1946, many invoked the "superior orders" defense—"I was given an order and had to obey it." However, the Nuremberg trials were the first cases in which such a defense could not be used to relieve someone from the responsibility of war crimes, although it could be used to reduce sentences. The superior orders defense, like the Milgram and Zimbardo studies, cast participants as unthinking conformists who bowed to authority and simply "followed orders." The Milgram and Zimbardo experiments seemed to explain or at least confirm the notion highlighted at the trials that Nazis committed atrocities in part because they were told to by an authority—that they were diligent servants of their superiors with little mind of their own. Political theorist Hannah Arendt coined the term "banality of evil" to express the idea that acts of evil do not require psychopaths—they can be carried out in the normal, boring course of a job, all in a day's work.

Hermann Göring (far left, first row) was the second-highest Nazi official to be tried and convicted at the Nuremberg trials. He was sentenced to death by hanging but committed suicide the night before he was to be hung.

Researchers S.A. Haslam and S.D. Richter dispute this idea. They have studied the behavior of Adolf Eichmann, a major organizer of the Holocaust, and found evidence that he was energetic, creative, and actively committed to carrying out the ideals of the Nazis, not an automaton mindlessly following orders. Haslam and Richter conclude that tyranny is not caused by blind obedience but rather by strong identification with authority, by "buying in" to the principles and goals of authority figures. Eichmann said his one regret was that he didn't kill more Jews. In a similar way, some of the participants in the Milgram study, when told that their participation helped advance scientific knowledge, saw their actions in the study as a contribution to a worthwhile cause, identifying with the authority. Haslam and Richter conducted their own televised prison experiment in conjunction with the BBC, often referred to as the BBC prison study. That 2002 experiment, which had to be terminated early because of potential psychological harm to participants, gave them the ideas to further explore the issues of authority, obedience, and identification.

Practice: With a partner, find out more about the critiques Haslam and Richter had of the Zimbardo and Milgram studies as well as the critiques Zimbardo and others had of the methodology and findings of the BBC prison study. Develop an argument supporting one side, the other side, or another related position and gather evidence to support it. Present your argument and evidence to the rest of the class.

Group Behavior

Have you ever performed in athletics, music, dance, or theater? If so, is your performance better when people are watching you, or is it poorer? When your performance is enhanced by the presence of others watching you perform, the effect is known as **social facilitation**; if your performance is poorer when you are watched by others, the effect is called **social inhibition**. The question is, why does the presence of others sometimes facilitate and at other times inhibit performance?

When does the presence of others enhance your performance and when does it detract? The answer depends on the difficulty of the task and your level of preparedness.

Social Facilitation vs. Social Inhibition

A wealth of research found support for *both* the social facilitation *and* the social inhibition positions. Social psychologist Robert Zajonc (1923–2008) figured out why we were finding differences in the effect that the presence of others has on performance.

For a long time, it had been known from the work of Yerkes and Dodson (see pages 305–306) that extremely low levels of arousal and extremely high levels of arousal led to a decreased level of performance, but there are optimal levels of arousal that led to an increase in performance. Yerkes and Dodson also discovered that easy tasks require very little arousal for maximum performance and an almost unreasonable amount of arousal to decrease this performance. The same can be said for well-learned tasks. However, for difficult tasks or poorly learned tasks, just a small amount of arousal can cause a decline in performance. Have you ever tried to perform a musical piece you did not practice much or take a test for which you had not studied very hard and "choked" on the performance? You suffered from the Yerkes–Dodson Law.

Zajonc concluded that the presence of others increased arousal. Therefore, in applying the Yerkes–Dodson law, an easy or well-learned task is enhanced by the presence of others (social facilitation), while a difficult or poorly learned task is inhibited by the presence of others (social inhibition). This solved the seeming contradiction between social facilitation and social inhibition.

Social Loafing

If you've ever been on the losing side of a tug of war contest and thought, "If only we had pulled just a little bit harder, we would have won," your thought is actually close to the truth. A study conducted by Ingham, Levinger, Graves, and Peckham (1974) demonstrated that people pull harder on a rope simulating a tug of war contest when they believe they are alone than when they are in a group. Other researchers have called this phenomenon **social loafing**, referring to the tendency to exert less effort when working in a group if individual effort cannot be measured independently. In other words, not "the more, the merrier," but "the more, the lazier."

The key to social loafing is that a person's individual effort cannot be measured or detected. Whenever you buy new clothing, you may find a number on a little slip of paper in the pocket or somewhere on the clothing designating the person who inspected the piece. Before the inspectors were identified, however, many articles of clothing had defects that got past an inspector. Then, when inspectors were assigned numbers to place in each article of clothing they inspected, the inspectors became identifiable, which reduced the number of defective clothes dramatically. Making the inspectors individually identifiable nearly eliminated the effects of social loafing.

Deindividuation

While social loafing deals with issues of effort, deindividuation deals with issues of how we behave toward others and their property. **Deindividuation** is the loss of identity as a result of participation in a larger group, which lessens the sense of personal responsibility for one's actions and can lead to a higher degree of aggression. In the Stanford Prison Experiment, for example, one of the reasons the guards behaved aggressively toward prisoners was that the guards lost their personal identities and became deindividuated. To further illustrate this point, Philip Zimbardo conducted a study in 1970 in which research subjects were divided into groups of individuals who either gave shocks or

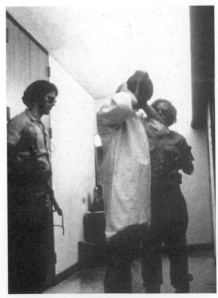

Guards in the Stanford Prison Experiment forced prisoners to wear pillowcases over their heads to depersonalize and demean them.

received shocks. Subjects in the shocker group wore either pillowcases with eye holes over their heads or their own clothes with name tags to identify themselves. Those with executioner-style pillowcases over their heads gave shocks of higher intensity and for longer periods of time than those who wore their regular clothes and name tags; the shock receivers were confederates of the experimenter and pretended that they were receiving painful shocks.

This was also the case with those "receiving" the shocks. When they had pillowcases with eye holes over their heads, they received shocks of higher intensity and for longer periods of time than when they wore their regular clothes and name tags. Thus, deindividuation can occur with either the victim or the aggressor.

Deindividuation can also occur as a result of group behavior. If everyone else is rioting or stealing or throwing rocks, individuals can lose themselves in the crowd and follow the crowd's behaviors.

Interestingly, higher aggression toward a victim can be counteracted under conditions of deindividuation. When researchers dressed up some of the "shockers" in nurse's uniforms, the level of intensity and duration of the shock decreased. Since nurses are generally thought of as compassionate caregivers, losing oneself to a compassionate character leads one to act more humanely.

Group Polarization

Let's say a football game with your school's biggest rival is coming up. You had a plan to paint graffiti on the statue of your rival's mascot, even with the chance that you would get caught because of the increased security during the week of this historic rivalry game. If you were to get caught, you would likely be suspended from school and possibly endanger your future college plans. However, if you were successful, you would be a hero among your classmates and just might impress the classmate you wanted to date. Should you go ahead with your plan or not? Would it help to discuss this with some friends or not?

Most people would say that you should discuss this plan with your friends to really determine the positives and negatives and make a better final decision. However, research shows that a group discussion will almost always lead to a riskier decision. Group discussion does not lead to a straightforward 50/50 "do it or don't do it" result. Instead, the action the group discussion leads to is a riskier one than the original. This shift from a 50/50 decision to a riskier decision has become known as a **risky shift**. In other words, a risky shift is the tendency to shift from uncertainty about performing a task or not to making a decision with greater risk.

The risky shift phenomenon over time has been subsumed under what social psychologists call **group polarization**—the tendency for people to hold even more extreme views on topics after a group discussion of like-minded people. Social psychology researchers noticed that when people discussed things in a group, their opinions ended up being more extreme. In 1969, researchers identified some people in France who were minimally supportive of their president, Charles de Galle, who was in a dispute with the United States at the time. Those people also felt slightly negative toward Americans. However, when the researchers got these people together to discuss the positives and negatives of Franco–U.S. relations, at the end of the discussion they were even more supportive of President de Galle and even more negative toward Americans. The same phenomenon—holding even more extreme views on a topic after group discussion—tends to be true across a number of different issues such as feminism and racial attitudes.

You may not be surprised that the Internet has increased group polarization. Chat rooms or exclusive groups allow like-minded individuals to exchange ideas and radicalize one another's opinions. Moreover, because people may have screen names that are not their own, the Internet also gives individuals the opportunity to hide their true identities. Both group polarization and deindividuation can increase extreme and aggressive views. Even the cultivation of terrorism and terrorists has been attributed to group polarization principles.

Groupthink

You may have heard of an especially disastrous decision made by a supposedly intelligent group of people, and you may have found yourself wondering, "How could such intelligent people make such a shortsighted mistake?" Social psychologist Irving Janis (1918–1990) wondered the same thing after President John F. Kennedy's decision to invade Cuba early in his administration, historically known as The Bay of Pigs. Janis labeled this phenomenon **groupthink**—referring to the tendency to make bad decisions because of the illusion that the plan of action is a good one and is supported by all members of the group. Janis described certain conditions under which groupthink may occur. These include:

- A respected and directive leader
- High cohesion among group members
- Isolation of the group from others
- Lack of procedures to seek information other than what is currently available to the group and to externally evaluate the group's information and decisions
- A highly stressful situation with perceived limited solutions

While deliberating the proposed plan of action, the group focuses in on the "correctness" of this plan because of certain other elements:

- An illusion of invulnerability
- Rationalization
- Unquestioned belief in the morality of the group

- Stereotyped view of opponents
- Pressure to conform to the group
- Self-censorship
- An illusion of unanimity
- Mindguards—those who provide filtered or limited information to the group

President Kennedy was from the Boston area, home to Harvard University, and brought to the White House a number of Harvard-educated advisors he called "the best and the brightest." Therefore, the group had an *illusion of invulnerability.* How could such smart people ever make any bad decisions? They also rationalized that because they were so bright, their decisions were the best that could be made and that other decisions were flawed. Because their self-view included the position that they were working for the American people, who are basically moral, they had an *unquestioned belief in their own morality* in working toward decisions for the country. Their objective was to overthrow the Fidel Castro government in Cuba, a newly installed Communist government that took over the reigns of power by force, and by so doing fulfilled a *stereotypical view* of the Castro regime in the minds of the group. In their deliberations about the invasion, if anyone questioned whether or not the group's strategy should be pursued, the questioner was under *pressure to conform* to the rest of the group. Interviews after the ultimate failure of the invasion revealed that some group members had doubts but had engaged in *self-censorship,* feeling it would be out of line to express these doubts. Because no one overtly expressed these doubts, an *illusion of unanimity* was created around the plan to invade. If anyone had actually expressed doubts, that person would have been intercepted by *mindguards* to protect the leader, President Kennedy, from these views. While there did not appear to be any mindguards in the Bay of Pigs fiasco, there are such individuals in other cases of groupthink that Janis examined.

John F. Kennedy's "best and brightest" cabinet may have used groupthink to make important decisions.

Many people have found groupthink to be a useful explanation for a number of decisions made since the Kennedy era. An analysis of the U.S. invasion of Iraq in 2003 concluded that groupthink was a major contributor to this decision. Groupthink also may have been a factor in financial fraud cases, certain forms of terrorism, and "pack journalism," a situation in which most journalists reach the same conclusions.

Nevertheless, groupthink and poor decision-making can be avoided. Strategies to avoid groupthink include a general diversity of the group, which improves decisions by bringing in fresh, new perspectives to force the group to examine different perspectives before proceeding. You may recall that participants in the Asch conformity studies tended to go along with the rest of the group, but if even one other member expressed the participant's views, the participants stuck with their own perceptions. Two other formal methods of avoiding groupthink are the devil's advocate method and the dialectical inquiry method. In the **devil's advocate method**, an individual is assigned to be the "outsider" by questioning all group decisions and to consider an alternative view of the information or propose a different plan of action for the group to consider. In the **dialectical inquiry method**, two subgroups work on different plans of action, and the leader of the entire group does not express his/her preference before the plans are presented. Research results have indicated that decisions made using these methods are better than those reached by a standard consensus method.

Minority Influence

Most people remember the shock and disbelief experienced after the Sandy Hook Elementary School shootings in Newtown, Connecticut. A 20-year-old shooter with mental health problems killed twenty elementary school children and six school administrators with an assault rifle after he had also killed his mother, who owned the weapons he carried. However, even though this event occurred in December 2012, and even though polls still show that the vast majority of the American public—both gun owners and nonowners—favors background checks for those seeking to purchase guns, no national legislation has addressed this issue.

Social psychologists might explain this situation as the result of **minority influence**—a disproportionate influence of the minority opinion over a majority opinion under certain conditions. First, if the minority is consistent in its opinions, it will exert such influence; if the minority wavers from its opinion at all, it will lose its influence. Second, the group with the minority opinion must be self-confident. Third, when a majority group member "defects" to the minority opinion, this change exerts strong influence on the majority opinion. Finally, if the minority includes a perceived leader, more people will be won over to the minority opinion.

Nevertheless, if all attributes of the minority opinion are also attributable to the majority opinion, the majority opinion will prevail. In other words, if the majority is consistent, self-confident, and has a perceived or respected leader, opinions or actions prescribed by the majority group will be the result.

If you were to look at the first three aspects of group behavior (social facilitation vs. social inhibition, social loafing, and deindividuation) versus the second three aspects (group polarization, groupthink, and minority influence), do you notice the difference between these two clusters? In the first cluster, group influence is due only to the mere presence of others, whereas in the second cluster, people within the groups must interact with one another to exert influence. In other words, groups can have an influence on our behaviors by both passive and active interactions.

* * *

This chapter has presented various aspects of social perception and influence. The perceptions that we use to perceive ourselves and others can be used, in turn, to perceive *us*. These perceptions may influence us to behave in certain ways or to change our attitudes. When we encounter others, we may feel compelled to go along with the crowd or to obey authority figures.

Similarly, when we are part of a group or groups, we may perceive the groups to hold authority over our behaviors and thus be influenced by the group. In understanding these influences, we may behave in a more conscious manner that truly reflects our own beliefs.

REFLECT ON THE ESSENTIAL QUESTION

Essential Question: *How do we perceive ourselves and others in social situations, given various influences that can affect our behaviors?* On separate paper, make a chart like the one below to gather details to answer that question.

Schemas	Attitudes	Persuasion	Group Influence	Group Behavior

KEY TERMS			KEY PEOPLE
GENERAL	*ATTITUDE*	*GROUP INFLUENCE*	Solomon Asch
social behavior	attitude	conformity	Leon Festinger
social cognition	cognitive dissonance	informational social influence	Stanley Milgram
social influence	debrief	normative social influence	Philip Zimbardo
social psychology	role-playing		
SCHEMAS	*PERSUASION*	*GROUP BEHAVIOR*	
actor-observer bias	central route	deindividuation	
attribution	door-in-the-face approach	devil's advocate method	
attribution theory	foot-in-the-door approach	dialectical inquiry method	
external attribution	peripheral route	group polarization	
fundamental attribution error	primacy effect	groupthink	
internal attribution	reason vs. emotion	minority influence	
possible selves	recency effect	risky shift	
schemas		social facilitation	
self-schemas		social inhibition	
self-serving biases		social loafing	
stable attribution			
ultimate attribution error			
unstable attribution			

MULTIPLE-CHOICE QUESTIONS

1. Which best explains why nonnatives retold the Native Alaska folktale "The War of the Ghosts" with changes?

   (A) Nonnatives had trouble remembering the story, which was from the oral tradition.

   (B) Nonnatives are less spiritual than native Alaskans.

   (C) The story was very complicated and much time elapsed before they were asked to retell the story.

   (D) Nonnatives have a different schema for fairy tales.

   (E) The story used words that were not part of the nonnative vocabulary.

2. A self-schema can be conceived of as a

(A) cognitive filter we use to understand information and situations

(B) way to give the best impression of ourselves to others

(C) tool for self-understanding

(D) method of investigating forgotten material about ourselves

(E) way to maintain our self-esteems when we are given negative feedback

3. Whereas the _____ route to persuasion uses logic and reason, the _____ route to persuasion uses emotion.

(A) prime; subprime

(B) undisputed; disputed

(C) primary; secondary

(D) boring; exciting

(E) central; peripheral

4. In Festinger's classic study on cognitive dissonance, participants were more likely to change their attitudes about a boring experiment when they were

(A) engaged

(B) unengaged

(C) overjustified

(D) underjustified

(E) coerced

5. In Asch's classic study on conformity, when all but one of the confederates gave obviously wrong answers, the true research participant was more likely to

(A) conform to what most of the group was saying

(B) conform to the confederate to whom he was most attracted

(C) want to be unconventional

(D) stick with his own perception of the correct answer

(E) ask to be able to terminate participation in the study

6. In Milgram's study on obedience to authority, approximately how many of the participants "shocked" the victim at the highest level?

(A) None

(B) A very low percentage

(C) About half

(D) Most

(E) All

7. Let's say that you are performing a very easy task. Under what condition would your performance on the task be enhanced?

(A) When you were alone

(B) When you were with your family

(C) When you were with your best friend

(D) When you were with a stranger

(E) When you were in the presence of a large crowd

8. If an anonymous person on the Internet disagrees with a position on someone's blog, the anonymous person will be more likely to

(A) be intelligent in evaluating the blogger's position than in person

(B) be more truthful than in person

(C) invite others to add different perspectives than in person

(D) be more supportive of the blogger's position than in person

(E) be more cruel or offensive toward the blogger than in person

9. You are debating comprehensive immigration policy. One group is leaning in favor of this policy and another group is leaning against this policy. You decide to divide yourselves into those in favor and those who oppose this policy to discuss your positions and then come back together as a whole group. What do you predict will happen?

(A) The two groups will have the same positions but there will be some subtle nuances to their positions.

(B) The two groups will change to the opposite positions.

(C) The two groups will feel even more strongly toward their original positions.

(D) The two groups will feel more confused about which position to support.

(E) The two groups will feel it was a waste of time because they feel exactly the same as before their discussions.

10. In groupthink, the purpose of a mindguard is to

(A) make sure the decisions of the group are fully rational

(B) filter information to the group

(C) question the group's morality

(D) support stereotyped view of opponents

(E) guard the leader of the group from opposition

FREE-RESPONSE QUESTIONS

1. Marina has been pressing her parents to get a dog. Explain how she can use the central route and the peripheral route to persuasion. Discuss these points in your answer.
- The differences between central and peripheral routes to persuasion
- The quality of the outcome when each is used
- The duration of the outcome when each is used

2. A student at a community college is conducting an experiment. Participants who have not heard of Milgram's study are told that the purpose of the study is to evaluate the effectiveness of a new approach to pain relief that could greatly benefit people with chronic pain. The student sits next to the participant, instructing him to administer increasing degrees of electrical shock to a cat he cannot see. If the participant administers the shocks, he will hear sounds of the cat's reaction to it. (In reality, there is no shock and there is no cat.)
- Which of the above conditions, if any, would predict that the participant will obey the researcher?
- Which of the above conditions, if any, would predict that the participant will resist the researcher?
- How would obedience or resistance change if another participant is resisting the researcher?

Behavior Toward Others

"No one is born hating another person because of the color of his skin, or his background, or his religion . . . if they can learn to hate, they can be taught to love."

—Nelson Mandela

Essential Question: What factors help explain our behavior to others?

Human beings engage with one another in many ways. We love; we hate. We flirt. We argue, fight, bully, and go to war. We join groups and exclude others from groups. We play games with one another, sometimes unintentionally. We help one another. The threads that tie together these different ways of engaging are behaviors toward others as individuals and as groups. This chapter covers four major ways we interact with others: aggression, conflict, attraction, and altruism.

Aggression

Aggression is hostile behavior with the intent of harming someone physically or mentally. We usually think of war as the ultimate form of aggression, but aggression outside of war is actually more frequent. For example, in 2011, Anders Behring Breivik, a thirty-two-year-old Norwegian man, was upset that Norway was becoming more and more tolerant of immigrants. He first set off a bomb in central Oslo that killed eight people. Then he went on an island that hosted a summer camp and killed 69 youths in their early- to mid-teens as well as camp counselors.

Mass shootings like the one in Norway have become almost commonplace in the United States. Between 1966 and 2012 there were 90 mass shootings, more than in any other country. From 1984 through 2015, 400 people were killed, and an additional 432 were injured in 46 different mass shootings. These figures are for gun violence only and do not count bombings such as the Boston Marathon bombing in April 2013, which killed three people and injured more than 100 more, or the Oklahoma City car bombing in April 1995, which killed 168 people, including 19 children, and injured more than 500.

Aggression is not limited to killing, shooting, or maiming. Some of you may have experienced fistfights, shouting matches, and aggressive drivers. People report being bullied at work by managers and coworkers.

Cyberbullying, a more recent form of aggression, occurs among school children, college-age adults, and even coworkers. Such forms of bullying can have tragic consequences. For

Data collected in 2016 show that about 34 percent of students between the ages of twelve and seventeen have been cyberbullied.

example, a fourteen-year-old girl committed suicide because of the bullying she suffered over social media. Other negative effects of cyberbullying are anxiety, depression, and low self-esteem.

How do psychologists explain such aggression? Social psychologists identify two forms of aggression: hostile aggression and instrumental aggression. **Hostile aggression** is based on anger and occurs when someone becomes upset with someone else and responds emotionally with the intent to harm the other. **Instrumental aggression** also is an intent to harm another person, but in instrumental aggression, the motivation is not emotional; rather, it is to advance a cause or to achieve something. For example, a hit man paid to murder someone may not be angry at the target, but he intends to harm the target to get paid. Experts on terrorism think that acts of terrorism are acts of instrumental aggression. The terrorists are not angry at their victims, but they perpetrate their terrorist acts to make a political statement.

What causes aggression? Two broad sources of aggression are biological factors and psychological factors.

Biological Factors

Biological factors include genetic and biochemical influences that set the stage for aggression. In addition, substances such as alcohol can influence whether aggressive behavior occurs.

The Role of Genetics in Aggression There is good evidence for a genetic role in aggressiveness. For example, pit bulls, Doberman pinschers, and German shepherds are sometimes bred to be aggressive. In 1979, Kirsti Lagerspetz (1932–2001) demonstrated a similar effect on white rats. She bred a group of more aggressive white rats together and a group of more docile white rats together. After 26 generations, she had a group of identifiably more aggressive rats and a group of identifiably more docile rats.

Among humans, the degree of aggressiveness is more similar between identical twins than between fraternal twins, showing a strong genetic basis for aggression. Among convicted criminals who are identical twins, half of their twins have also been convicted of crimes. In comparison, only one-fifth of fraternal twins have both been convicted of crimes. Although the environment has an influence on aggressiveness, genetic influences seem to predispose people to aggressiveness or passivity.

Biochemical Influences You may have noticed that men tend to be more aggressive than women. Some believe this difference is due to socialization. However, hormonal differences may account for the difference in aggressiveness. Men have higher levels of the hormone testosterone than women have, and testosterone is linked to aggression. James Dabbs (1937–2004) and his colleagues have reported that men who are imprisoned for aggressive crimes (for example, sex crimes and violent crimes) have higher testosterone levels than men who are imprisoned for nonaggressive crimes (such as burglary, theft, or drugs). Dan Olweus (b. 1931) and his colleagues found that adolescent boys who engaged in bullying and other forms of aggressive behavior had higher levels of testosterone than boys who did not engage in these behaviors. In addition, use of anabolic steroids—a synthetic version of the male hormone testosterone that can build muscle and enhance athletic performance—has been associated with increases in aggression.

Alcohol's Disinhibiting Effects Alcohol makes aggression more likely because it produces a **disinhibition of aggression**, turning off our normal ability to control unacceptable responses such as aggression by depressing activity in the frontal lobes, impairing judgment, planning, and restraint. Instead of ignoring a slight or offense, under the influence of alcohol we may act on an impulse to yell at or even hit a person who has offended us. Many researchers have found this connection between alcohol and aggression. Most statistics about crime and alcohol use report that alcohol is involved in 40 percent of violent crimes.

Psychological Factors

A number of psychological theories have been developed to explain the nonbiological variables that contribute to aggression. They address environment, cognition, and emotion and the roles they play in evoking aggressive behavior.

The Frustration–Aggression Hypothesis Have you ever been driving and had someone cut you off? You most likely got angry and either yelled at the driver, blasted your horn, or made a gesture to display your anger (or at least thought about doing one of these behaviors). If you have engaged in such actions, you have exhibited aggression caused by frustration.

In 1939, John Dollard (1900–1980) and colleagues first proposed the frustration-aggression hypothesis this way: An organism that is prevented or inhibited from reaching a goal will experience frustration and react with aggression. They defined *frustration* as the prevention of goal-directed behavior. When you are driving, your goal is to reach your destination without hindrance. When someone cuts you off, that person is hindering you from reaching your goal. According to the frustration-aggression hypothesis first proposed in 1939, your reaction is likely to be aggression.

Dollard and his colleagues studied their hypothesis by conducting experiments on rats. They first taught a rat to press a bar to receive food, and then they withheld food so that the rat was very hungry. Then they electrified the floor between the rat and the bar. When the rat tried to cross the electrified floor but could not, it began fighting with another rat in the box that was not hungry. Based on what Dollard and his associates observed in studies with rats, they initially contended that frustration leads to aggression, and that if aggression is observed, it was preceded by a form of frustration.

Updated Hypothesis When the frustration-aggression hypothesis was tested with humans, however, a different pattern emerged. Although frustration frequently led to aggression, it did not *always* lead to aggression. For example, studies with children found that frustration did not necessarily lead to aggression, but it often led to less creative play or other forms of regression.

Leonard Berkowitz (1926–2016) successively expanded and updated the frustration–aggression hypothesis. He reasoned that frustration leads to anger rather than directly to aggression. Anger is an emotion, not a behavior, while aggression is a behavior, such as yelling, gesturing, and hitting. Some other factors had to be involved to explain why frustration does not always lead to aggression. Subsequent studies found that for frustration to lead to aggression, at least two conditions need to be met. First, the frustration needs to be intentionally caused—a driver cutting you off, for example. Second, there needs to be a cue for aggression, some object that triggers the change from anger to aggression, such as the driver giving you an insulting hand gesture.

People react differently to frustration when they know it is not intentional. A 1962 experiment found that when a group working on a problem was interrupted because of a hearing aid malfunction of one of the participants (a confederate of the experimenter), no one in the group aggressed against the individual, because the group members believed the interruption and resulting frustration were unintentional.

Even if frustration is intentional, a person might not act on angry feelings without a cue for aggression. In 1967, Berkowitz and Anthony LePage told research participants that they would be given anywhere between one and seven shocks, depending on how another person judged the quality of their ideas. One shock meant that the judge felt the participant's idea was good, and seven shocks meant the judge felt the idea was very poor. All the participants received seven shocks regardless of the quality of their ideas, which gave the participants the feedback that their ideas were judged to be poor. They were frustrated in their goal of generating a good idea. In another phase of the study, the researchers gave participants the opportunity to shock the judge. In the room where the participants could deliver the shock, there were various items that the participants were told were left over from a previous study. Among the items were either neutral objects—a broom, for example—or an object of aggression, such as a shotgun. When the participants were in the presence of the cue for aggression, they aggressed more by delivering more shocks to the judge.

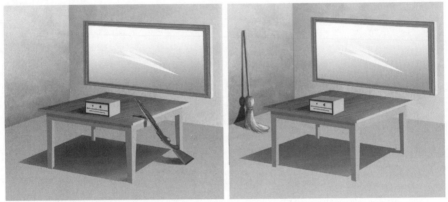

Figure 25.1 Aggression requires two conditions: being intentionally frustrated and being exposed to a cue for aggression.

Aggression and Social Learning Social learning occurs through observing others, called models, engaging in activities. **Albert Bandura** and Richard Walters conducted the most famous study demonstrating the role of social learning in aggression. (See pages 238–239.) Bandura and Walters had eight-year-old boys observe a child in another room through a one-way mirror. The child in the other room was attacking a Bobo doll—a blow-up clown doll that is weighted at the bottom so that when it is hit, it falls but then pops back up. This child performed many forms of aggression against the Bobo doll, punching it, kicking it, hitting it with a baseball bat, and throwing blocks at it. Later, an adult came into the room and either reprimanded the aggressive child or praised him for being strong. Later, the child who had been observing behind the mirror was placed in the room with the Bobo doll. If he had seen the first child being reprimanded, he did not aggress against the Bobo doll, but if he had seen the first child being praised for his behavior, he performed the kinds of aggression that the first child did. Subsequent studies by Bandura and his associates supported the original research findings.

Bandura and Walters believed that if aggression is reinforced, it will increase, just as Skinner's operant conditioning model predicts. However, they also thought that reinforcement could be vicarious. That is, observing someone else receive reinforcement would work just as well as direct reinforcement in the same situation.

The Bandura studies on social learning have broad implications. Everyone around us is a potential model of behavior to imitate. Parents, siblings, classmates, coworkers, and people in the media are all models of behavior. In an ongoing research program that began in the 1980s, Leonard Eron (1920–2007) and his associates have demonstrated that parents and violence on television can be models for subsequent child and adult aggression.

Conflict and Peaceful Resolutions

When people interact with one another, **conflict**—opposing actions, ideas, or goals between individuals or groups—can arise. Have you ever had a disagreement with one of your siblings or your parents? Married couples, romantic partners, committee members, Boy Scout and Girl Scout troops, sports teams, musicians, professional athletes and their general managers, and countries within the United Nations all experience conflict at some point. This section explores conflicts among people and ways to address these conflicts.

Conflicts between labor and management have been enduring. Garment workers strike in New York in 1913 for 8-hour workdays.

Fast food workers strike in Minneapolis in 2016 for $15 an hour pay and benefits, including sick days.

Social Dilemmas

A **social dilemma** is a situation that places the desires of the individual into conflict with the good of the group. Because people within a group have different motivations for their respective behaviors, social dilemmas are also known as *mixed motive interactions*. Social psychologists have studied two types of social dilemmas through hypothetical scenarios: the Prisoner's Dilemma and the Tragedy of the Commons dilemma.

The Prisoner's Dilemma In the **Prisoner's Dilemma,** a police officer interrogates two suspicious men in separate rooms. The officer has enough information to put each of them in prison for one year but knows that one of them committed the major part of the crime and the other was an accomplice. The officer tells each of them individually that if he confesses to being the accomplice and provides evidence that the other person committed the major part of the crime, the other person will receive ten years in prison and the confessor will receive only probation. If they both confess to the crime, they both will receive five years in prison. Neither potential prisoner knows that the other is getting the same deal. Figure 25.2 shows their dilemma: If they don't confess, they might receive only one year in prison, but there is a potential to receive ten years in prison; if they do confess, they might receive no years in prison, but there is a potential to receive five years in prison. What should each of them do?

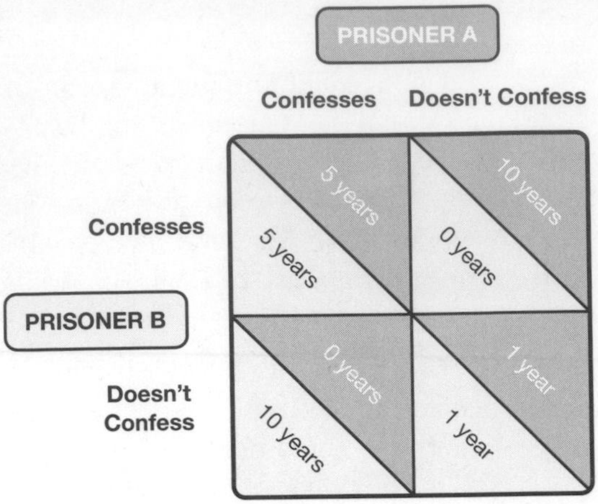

Figure 25.2 Prisoner's Dilemma

Researchers have generally found that when put in the position of a potential prisoner, research participants confess to the crime. People confess because they are willing to gamble that they might not have to serve any time in prison. However, if you consider Prisoner A and Prisoner B to be partners in a group rather than separate individuals, you can see from Figure 25.2 that all the cells add up to a collective ten years in prison except for the cell in which neither prisoner confesses. If neither prisoner confesses, the collective years in prison are only two. The best strategy for the group is to not confess, but because most people act in selfish or self-serving ways for the *chance* of not serving any time, they confess. If they saw themselves as part of a group, they might recognize that even as individuals they would get more benefit from not confessing.

The Tragedy of the Commons In 1968, ecologist Garrett Hardin (1915–2003) analyzed a scenario of 100 farms surrounding a common feeding ground for cows, called "the commons." The commons was just large enough to sustain one cow per farm. As the cows grazed in one area of the commons, they would eventually eat the grass down to the dirt, so they would have to move to a different area of the commons. By the time they got back to the first area, enough time had passed for the grass to regrow, and they could graze there again. If a farmer got greedy and placed an extra cow on the commons, that farmer could earn twice as much as other farmers. No one would notice one extra cow, and the commons could still sustain all the cows. However, if all 100 farmers placed an extra cow on the commons, the larger herd would eat the grass too fast. The cows would get back to the first area before the grass had enough time to regrow, and the cows would starve to death. This scenario is known as the **Tragedy of the Commons**—a situation in which shared resources are depleted if individuals act in their own self-interest instead of for the common good. As with the Prisoner's Dilemma, personal greed leads to a loss for the collective.

Demonstrating a similar theme, Julian Edney, a leading researcher in social and environmental psychology, devised a clever experiment around a game he called "Nuts." In this game, three participants sat around a table with a bowl in the middle. The bowl contained ten nuts (the kind that go around a threaded bolt). Every ten seconds, the contents of the bowl would be doubled. The goal of the game was for participants to accumulate as many nuts as they could. When the participants were told to begin the game, most of the groups dove right into the bowl to try to grab as many nuts as possible. Edney reported that 65 percent of the groups failed to make it to the ten-second mark for the first round of doubling. After the study, Edney pointed out that if participants had waited for several rounds of doubling, each of the three participants could have accumulated dozens of nuts, but even if they had pushed all the other participants out of the way and gathered all the nuts at the beginning of the study, the most they could have accumulated was ten nuts.

In a study related to the Tragedy of the Commons, Jeffery Mio (b. 1954), Suzanne Thompson, and Geoffrey Givens handed out fliers to movie-going patrons. Half of the fliers explained the Tragedy of the Commons and discussed how important it was to take care of our environment. The other half of the fliers explained the importance of everyone voting. The bottom of all the fliers included a request to dispose of the fliers in the nearest trash can. At the end of the movie, the researchers searched the lobby, bathroom floors, and theater floors to see how many fliers were littered instead of thrown away. As it turned out, 43 percent more voting fliers were littered than environmental fliers. Thus, the story of the Tragedy of the Commons seemed to have resonated with participants and encouraged them to take socially responsible action.

Peaceful Resolutions

How do we resolve the kinds of destructive competition that social dilemmas can cause? Mio and his colleagues have suggested that specific interventions can be implemented to reduce this kind of destructive competition.

Regulation As Mio and his colleagues observed, at first Edney's line of research seemed to suggest that merely informing participants of destructive competition and its consequences would eliminate the problems it caused. However, the data from a variety of studies revealed that the best way to eliminate (or at least control) destructive competition was to regulate behavior.

In the original Tragedy of the Commons, farmers were asked to be considerate and place only one cow on the commons to save the commons from destruction. Unfortunately, as soon as one person broke this pact among the farmers, other farmers began breaking the pact until the commons was destroyed. Therefore, it seems that strong regulation is needed to control selfish behavior.

Mio and colleagues connected a lack of strong regulation to the destruction of the savings and loan industry in the 1980s. A lack of strong regulation also played a role in the 2008 financial collapse because regulation and oversight of the investment banking industry had been weakened; the result was the deepest global recession since the Great Depression. Thus, while some feel we need less regulation of industries, regulation seems essential to maintain our social pact. More recently, George Lakoff pointed out that the purpose of a regulation is to protect a person, the environment, or the community, so a response to those who want to get rid of regulations can be that they therefore want to get rid of protections. How many people would be in favor of allowing policies that would lead to a more dangerous environment?

Small is Beautiful In the Tragedy of the Commons scenario, no one would notice the difference between 100 cows and 101 cows grazing on the commons. However, if we divided the commons into 25 sections, one section for four farms with four cows each, it would be obvious if there were five cows on the commons section rather than four. Also, if all four farmers wanted to be selfish and place an extra cow on their section of commons, only their four farms would be destroyed and not all 100. Therefore, reducing the size of the social dilemma can limit the damage that destructive competition does.

Acid rain was reduced by changing the payoffs for polluting.

Changing the Payoffs One way of getting people to cooperate with one another is to change the cost of not cooperating. For example, if a person (or company) was fined or had to give up something of value for not complying, there would be more compliance. In 1989, G. "Anand" Anandalingam examined the issue of acid rain, which was a major problem in the 1980s. Many "smokestack" industries were discharging pollutants into the air that reacted with oxygen, water, and other substances to form sulfuric and nitric acids, which returned to the ground during precipitation or even as dust particles. The acidity damaged ecosystems, and the particles posed a health threat to humans in the form of asthma and emphysema. In a game model, Anandalingam had participants assume the positions of owners of these industries, allowing them to "carbon trade" with other owners. Owners could decide to use scrubbers and other kinds of cleanup techniques to markedly reduce the pollution that their companies were emitting, or they could buy credits from other companies who were emitting fewer pollutants to avoid heavy fines. This trade situation ended up resulting in a tremendous drop in pollution levels. This model of intervention was tried in the real world, and the amount of acid rain was drastically reduced.

Communication While not effective for the truly selfish, communication is effective in increasing cooperation for the majority of individuals. Recall in the Prisoner's Dilemma, the two prisoners were not allowed to communicate with one another. If they could communicate with one another, chances are that neither of them would confess to the crime (thus, they would have acted in a cooperative manner), and combined they would have served less time than if either or both of them had confessed. Robyn Dawes (1936–2010) discovered that when placed in a social dilemma, participants cooperated with one another more than twice as much when they could communicate with one another than when they could not communicate with one another.

Appeals to Social Norms Altruism is the concept or practice of selfless behavior out of concern for the well-being of others. Appeals to **altruistic norms**—expectations of acting on behalf of the group rather than in self-interest—are perhaps the least effective method of overcoming destructive competition and selfishness. However, appealing to altruistic norms can convince some people to cooperate with others in the community. Moreover, such appeals can begin to create an atmosphere of cooperation. Over time, people will conform to those cooperative norms.

How events are framed and labeled can reinforce cooperation. For example, Lee Ross (b. 1942) and his colleagues found that when the Prisoner's Dilemma was labeled a "community game" as opposed to a "Wall Street game," participants cooperated with one another at a much greater rate.

Other social norms also counteract competitiveness and selfishness. The **social responsibility norm**—the expectation that people, especially those in positions of authority, help others even at a cost to themselves—puts the good of others above self-interest. And the **reciprocity norm**—the expectation that if an individual or group has helped you, you should help them in return—also helps reduce conflicts. The reciprocity norm is consistent with The Golden Rule of "Do unto others as you would wish them to do unto you." Those who violate The Golden Rule are often chastised or shunned by the broader community, bringing the violator back into community standards.

Conflicts Beyond Social Dilemmas

In social dilemmas, people are generally part of a community, so they are competing against those in their own community. What happens in conflicts beyond one's own community, such as rivalries, opposing teams, or even international enemies? **Muzafer Sherif** (1906–1988) was among the first social psychologists to study this kind of conflict. In his 1966 study, Sherif studied competition between two boys' summer camps in Robber's Cave State Park in Oklahoma. During the first week, each camp was unaware of the other, so each group of campers spent the time getting to know one another and forming a group identity.

After the first week, Sherif had the camp counselors slowly introduce the two camps and engage them in a competition against one another, with the winner receiving medals or other desired prizes. The competition degenerated into bad behavior, such as one group stealing the flag of the other group and throwing trash into the other's camp. Even fistfights took place in the second week.

In the third week, Sherif introduced **superordinate goals**—challenges that would benefit both groups and that required the two groups to cooperate with one another. For example, Sherif sabotaged their water system by clogging the pipes. The two groups had to work together to fix this problem so that they would both have water. Sherif observed that the two groups, who had outwardly disliked one another during the second week of camp, ended up liking each other more during the third week.

During the second week (the week of competition), each group of campers perceived the other group as bad. They had negative stereotypes of each other, thinking the other group was selfish and uncivilized, for example. Each group thought nearly the same thing about the other group. When members of opposing groups have the same negative perceptions of each other, they are engaged in **mirror image perceptions.** Mirror image perceptions have been observed in real world conflicts. For example, during the Cold War, Soviet Union citizens had negative perceptions about Americans and vice versa. More recently, researchers have identified that Arabs and Israelis and Northern Irish Catholics and Northern Irish Protestants experience mirror image perceptions.

Racism

Racism has many facets, from dramatic and large-scale acts of violence to everyday discrimination However, ascribing racism to small groups like the Ku Klux Klan (KKK) absolves the general population from the racism in everyday life that is embedded in American culture. At its root, **racism** is the categorization of a person or group of people based on their race or ethnicity and the systematic mistreatment of people in the targeted group. Typically, the groups that engage in these categorizations are the groups in power. Elements of racism include stereotypes, prejudice, and discrimination.

A number of studies have also shown that racism and other kinds of prejudice are strongly tied to ingroup or outgroup membership. An **ingroup** is a group with which one identifies; an **outgroup** is a group with which one feels no identification. While racism is often thought of as negative feelings toward an outgroup, it is also a result of a strong bias toward an ingroup and the reservation of positive feelings such as admiration and trust only for other members of the ingroup. These strong positive feelings toward one's ingroup are generally based upon the assumption that the ingroup is superior to or more deserving than outgroups.

While ingroup/outgroup bias operates at the level of relatively small social circles, **ethnocentrism**—judging other cultures based only on the values and characteristics of one's own culture—operates on larger social and cultural levels. William Sumner (1840–1910) coined the term, which reflects the idea that one's

The Ku Klux Klan marches in Washington in 1926.

own culture is the center of everything and all other cultures are seen only in relation to the central culture. Ethnocentrism can lead to negative attitudes toward cultures other than one's own. For example, people in Western cultures generally judge arranged marriages as oppressive because they limit personal choice, something Westerners value. But for people in cultures in which arranged marriages are common, choice may be undesirable, and arranged marriages may present a favorable, orderly way to make a match and strengthen social bonds.

Stereotypes

Stereotypes are overgeneralized attitudes about a group of people—African Americans, women, gays, Whites, Asians, people with disabilities—based only on their membership in a group, not on any individual characteristics. These attitudes can be false or can contain an element of truth. Often stereotypes about a group are false and serve the purpose of controlling or putting down the stereotyped group. For example, in the days of slavery, cotton plantation owners would call their slaves "lazy," because the owners wanted to make more money from their slaves' labor and wanted to give them a reason to feel they had to work harder.

However, sometimes stereotypes can contain an element of truth. For example, White Americans may see Asians as being quiet and passive. Many Asians *may* be quiet and passive, and on average, Asians may be quieter than other ethnic groups. However, *all* Asians are not quiet and passive. Thus, this form of stereotype either "demands" that all members of a group fit the image (there is no allowance for individual variation within the groups) or exaggerates the differences among groups.

Stereotype threat—a situation in which people feel at risk of performing as their group is expected to perform—is one of the many effects of stereotyping. The elements of stereotype threat include 1) that there is a strong negative stereotype about one's group; 2) one excels in this area, going against the stereotype; 3) this area is important to one's sense of self; 4) one is placed in a situation that challenges the limits of one's abilities; and 5) the negative stereotype is triggered. Studies in the 1990s showed that when African American and White college freshmen were asked to take portions of the Graduate Record Exam—years before they or their White counterparts would be ready for it—and they had to identify their race at the top of the test so the scores of African Americans and Whites could be compared, at least two elements of the negative stereotypes were in place: the students were asked to perform beyond the limits of their capabilities, and the negative stereotype was triggered by having to indicate their race on the exam. These elements created anxiety in the African Americans that affected their working memories (see page 256), which in turn affected their performance on the test. The stereotype threat became a **self-fulfilling prophecy**—a prediction that causes itself to become true. When they were tested without the elements of negative stereotype present, White and Black students performed at the same level.

Prejudice

Prejudice is unjustified, usually negative judgments about a group of people based on their membership in a group. Prejudice usually involves bias or stereotypes. For example, the perception of some predominantly White police officers when stopping African American males is that they have a potential for violent behavior, and this assumption has led to a higher use of deadly force by the police.

Scapegoating occurs when members of a group in power hold members of a less powerful group responsible for their problems. For example, in 1940, Carl Hovland (1912–1961) and Robert Sears analyzed economic data and discovered that when economic conditions in the South deteriorated, lynching of African Americans increased. After terrorist attacks in New York in 2001 and in Paris in 2016, Muslims were the target of scapegoating in the United States and European Union. In the United States, immigrants have been scapegoated as the cause of the decline in wages.

In 1954, Gordon Allport connected scapegoating with feelings of prejudice. His theory has received continuing research support since then. More recently, studies have shown that scapegoating serves two functions. First, it gives people a target to blame for their problems, and second, it gives people more of a sense of control over their lives.

Discrimination

Discrimination is negative behavior toward members of a target group based on their race, ethnicity, or other shared characteristic. Stereotypes and prejudices occur strictly in your head. Even though they may be bad, they don't hurt others. Because discrimination involves behavior toward others, however, it does or can hurt them. You might have a stereotype about nerds (they study a lot), and you might have a prejudice against nerds (you resent them), but your attitudes and feelings don't hurt them until you call them names, hit them, steal their notebooks, exclude them from activities, and bully them online. These negative behaviors discriminate against them.

Why is it important for us to know about the effects of negative categorization and discrimination? If you have ever been called a name or been discriminated against because of your membership in a group, you know it doesn't feel good. But the effects of discrimination go beyond feelings. Discrimination can lower a person's self-esteem and create stress that leads to mental and physical health problems for both adults and children.

Racism: Discrimination Plus the Power to Discriminate

Although discrimination is negative behavior, it may be expressed only at the individual level, not institutionally. For example, if a bully harms a nerd, teachers and administrators at your school might punish the bully. The bully's discrimination was not backed by the power of the school administration.

In contrast, racism is discrimination plus the power to discriminate. Thus, in the days of legal segregation, discriminating against People of Color was supported by the law. For example, Southern states used the power of the state to require People of Color to use separate water fountains and beaches, attend separate schools, and sit in the back of the bus. Some Northern cities also had segregated schools and other institutions.

The power to discriminate can be applied to any categorization of people, not just those based on race or ethnicity. Marginalized groups—those with little social, cultural, and political power—include women, who encounter sexism; people who are disabled, who encounter ableism; sexual minorities, who encounter heterosexism; and people who belong to religious minorities, who encounter negative categorization based on religion.

Although people who are members of marginalized groups can negatively categorize those who have power and discriminate, their discrimination isn't an "-ism" because they generally have no power to enact or institutionalize negative behaviors against those who hold the power.

Attraction

So far in this chapter, you've read about people in conflict and how they behave at their worst. In this section, you'll learn about what brings people together What attracts people to one another? What makes us fall in love?

According to social psychologists, four factors contribute to being attracted to another person: proximity, physical attractiveness, similarity, and reciprocity.

Proximity

One of the most important factors influencing whether one person likes another is how close they are to each other physically. This factor is called the **proximity** or **propinquity effect** and occurs when you like another person. The saying "love the one you're with" touches on this idea. Mitja Back, Stefan Schmukle, and Boris Egloff confirmed this long-held belief in 2008 when they randomly assigned people to sit next to each other at the beginning of a college term. When they were contacted one year later, most of these students said they had remained friends with students who sat next to or very near them that very first class meeting. Why would simply being physically close to one another increase the probability of two people liking each other? Interaction, anticipation of interaction, and exposure are three related factors.

Interaction Have you been in a new situation where you did not know anyone in the room with you? If someone introduced himself or herself to you, you probably ended up liking that person more than most other people in the room. Proximity affects people's liking of other people because when they are near one another, there is a higher likelihood that people will interact. When people do interact, they end up liking one another more than they like others with whom they do not interact.

In a classic study, Chester Insko and Midge Wilson demonstrated this effect when they had people interact in groups of three. In each group, Person A interacted with Person B while Person C observed the interaction, and Person B interacted with Person C while Person A observed the interaction. Thus, all three people were exposed to the same experience. However, at the end of the study on average, Person A liked Person B better than Person C, and Person C liked Person B better than Person A. The only difference among participants was that Person A and Person C never directly interacted with one another.

Anticipation of Interaction You don't even have to interact with people to like them. Studies by John Darley and Ellen Berscheid show that if you have *anticipated* that you will interact with others, you will like them better. People seem to have a personal bias to like someone with whom they are going to be interacting. For example, when going out on a date, most people hope that they will like their date. People rarely anticipate that they will dislike each other.

Mere Exposure Effect Another reason that proximity promotes liking another person is the **mere exposure effect**, through which liking someone or something occurs merely because of repeatedly seeing that person or thing. The mere exposure effect was documented by Robert Zajonc in 1968 and has been documented in a host of studies since. Advertisers use this effect to make consumers like their products by repeating commercials one after another or by establishing characters used repeatedly in commercials.

Physical Attractiveness

People tend to like those whom they find physically attractive. Researchers have demonstrated this phenomenon in experiments at least since 1966. In their classic experiment, Elaine Hatfield, Vera Aronson, Darcy Abrahams, and Leon Rottman hosted a "welcome week" get-together for freshmen at a university. The freshmen had to fill out a survey that measured numerous personality characteristics and personal likes and dislikes and submit a picture of themselves. Independent judges rated these pictures on attractiveness. The researchers told participants that a new computer program matched them with five people they might find very compatible. In reality, the researchers gave each participant five randomly assigned names. They gave participants the task of meeting and interacting with all five of their "matched" partners before they left the get-together for the night. Even though participants—particularly men—had said in the survey that physical attractiveness was not as important to them as a warm character or similar interests, the only factor consistently related to whether someone was asked out on a date was physical attractiveness.

Many studies have confirmed these findings, but Alan Feingold went one better in 1990 and 1991. He discovered that while men were more willing to admit that physical beauty was a very important factor in being attracted to a mate than women were, women were equally affected by the physical beauty of a potential mate.

Matching People don't just go after the most beautiful person they can find. Instead, many people are attracted to those whom they feel are about as physically attractive as they are, which is called the **matching phenomenon**. You can imagine how people might think: "That person is way out of my league. However, that other person is about as attractive as me so I might have a chance."

People match themselves on many characteristics, not just physical attractiveness. That is, they measure attractiveness in different ways, including age, economic status, or professional or social status.

Physical Attractiveness Stereotype Are attractive people better than nonattractive people? Most of you would say no. However, evidence shows that there is a **physical attractiveness stereotype**, through which people ascribe more positive characteristics to attractive people than to nonattractive people. For example, in a 1972 study, Karen Dion described a little boy's transgression, such as throwing a rock through a window of an abandoned house, and attached a picture of a boy to the description of the transgression. Research participants who saw a picture of an attractive young boy made comments like "Boys will be boys." But those who saw a picture of an unattractive boy said things like "Now that is a juvenile delinquent in the making."

The physical attractiveness stereotype is related to a cognitive bias known as the **halo effect** (using the metaphor of a saint's adornment), through which overall positive feelings for a person or object carry over to specific qualities. For example, the halo effect would lead observers to conclude an attractive person is also smart, creative, or trustworthy even when no evidence is available to support those judgments.

Attractiveness is defined by culture and era. In the 1880s western United States, larger, heavier women were considered more attractive than thinner women because they were seen as able to endure the hardships of settling the West. Today, thinner women are seen as more attractive. Other cultures view different characteristics as more attractive. Women in Bakossiland, Cameroon, prefer men with chest hair, but women in many other parts of the world prefer men with relatively hairless chests.

Similarity

We have a lot of old sayings about relationships. You've already encountered "love the one you're with"—that's the proximity effect. Another is "birds of a feather flock together." People interpret it to mean that people who are similar will be attracted to each other. Research bears this out: People like others who are more like them than different. *Perceived* similarity may be as important as actual similarity, if not more important.

Part of the reason we may like those who are similar is that they validate our beliefs, whereas those who are different challenge our beliefs. Those who are culturally similar may have the same kinds of experiences as we do, and therefore their world views may be more like ours. For example, African American students may share the experience of being followed in a department store by a security guard—and the world view that reflects that experience—but White classmates not used to that experience may challenge African Americans, suggesting they might be misinterpreting the event.

Liking Those Who Like Us

Has a friend of yours ever told you that another classmate likes you? Chances are that you will like the classmate who likes you more than if you didn't know this. Various researchers have confirmed that we like people who like us. Part of the reason we may like those who like us is **reciprocity**, the feeling of being somewhat obligated to give something to someone who has given something to us. Another part of the reason is that people who like us raise our self-esteem by perceiving us as someone worthy of affection.

Loving

Psychology has a lot to say about what attracts people to one another and what promotes liking. What does it have to say about love? How are attraction and liking transformed into love? Are there different kinds of love?

The Triangular Theory of Love

Robert Sternberg (b. 1949) developed the **triangular theory of love,** which says that love has three components (see Figure 25.3)—intimacy, passion, and commitment. **Intimacy** is a feeling of closeness and attachment and is associated with privacy. **Passion** is sexual or romantic feelings and excitement. **Commitment** is a promise to sustain the relationship. These three components, in different combinations, lead to eight kinds of love, as follows.

- Nonlove: no components of love
- Liking: only intimacy
- Infatuation: only passion
- Empty love: only commitment
- Romantic love: combined intimacy and passion
- **Fatuous love** (a whirlwind, short-lived relationship): combined passion and commitment
- **Companionate love** (deep love such as that between long-married couples for whom passion may no longer be active): combined intimacy and commitment
- **Consummate love** (the most complete and ideal form of love, combining consummate love and passion): intimacy, passion, and commitment

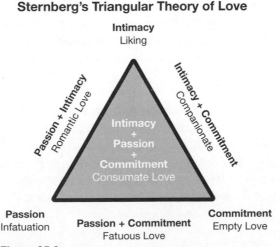

Sternberg's Triangular Theory of Love

Figure 25.3

The type of love in a relationship can change over time. The balance or relative emphasis of one component to another can also change over time, even if the type of love remains stable.

Because it is difficult to research kinds of love that involve sexual intimacy, the most studied kind of love is companionate love. Researchers in this area typically use self-reports from both married and dating couples. Responses show that companionate love is generally a positive experience for both men and women characterized by trust, loyalty, respect, and friendship. In fact, companionate love is used to describe lifelong friendships, so it is not restricted to romantic involvement. Its ability to endure—even strengthen—over time sets it apart from the other kinds of love. Some researchers are looking into the biochemistry of companionate love to see what role the attachment hormones oxytocin and vasopressin (see page 91) might play in the development of companionate love.

Attachment

Recall from Chapter 15 that the love most people feel for their mothers is based on attachment. Mary Ainsworth and her colleagues identified three attachment styles: secure attachment, anxious-ambivalent attachment, and avoidant attachment. (See pages 360–361.) Social psychologists have examined whether these styles of attachment to parents carry over to adult romantic relationships. In general, researchers have found that if you are securely attached as an infant, chances are you will have a secure, loving adult relationship. If you had an anxious-ambivalent or avoidant attachment as an infant, you may have troubled adult relationships.

For example, Cindy Hazan and Phil Shaver conducted a series of studies examining how attachment styles can relate to adult romantic relationships. Consistent with the general attachment styles identified with children, when describing their adult relationships, many reported that their approach to adult relations were secure (e.g., "I find it relatively easy to get close to others," "I am comfortable depending on them and having them depend on me," and "I don't worry about being abandoned"); many fewer reported an avoidant style (e.g., "I am somewhat uncomfortable being close to others," "I find it difficult to trust others completely," and "I am nervous when anyone gets too close or wants me to be more intimate"); and slightly fewer than the avoidant style reported an anxious-ambivalent style (e.g., "I find that others are reluctant to get as close as I would like," "I often worry that my partner doesn't really love me," and "I want to get very close, which sometimes scares people away"). The two components related to difficult or troubled relationships are attachment-related anxiety and attachment-related avoidance. Those who have secure relationships are low in both anxiety and avoidance, whereas those who have troubled relationships are low in avoidance but high in anxiety (preoccupied with their own negative characteristics), low in anxiety but high in avoidance (dismissive of their partners), and high in both anxiety and avoidance (fearful of relationships).

Helping Behavior

In 1964, a woman named Kitty Genovese was attacked multiple times late at night near her apartment building. She screamed when she was attacked by a man who stabbed her with a knife. Her screams scared him away, but he waited nearby in his car until he saw that no police were coming. Then he came back, stabbed and raped her, and stole $49 from her. One of her neighbors called the police nearly a half hour after the initial attack. She died at the hospital from 13 stab wounds. A report of the murder in the *New York Times* inaccurately said that 38 witnesses stood by and did nothing to help Genovese. Later reports said that neighbors did try to help her. Although the reports were sensationalized, the case of Genovese led to the creation of the 911 emergency call system and spurred social psychologists to study helping behavior and altruism.

Helping Behavior and the Bystander Effect

Early psychologists to study the phenomenon of people not helping others in distress included **John Darley** (b. 1938) and **Bibb Latané** (b. 1937) in 1968. They observed that people are less likely to help someone in need if there are other people watching the distress. They called this phenomenon the **bystander effect.** Through a series of experiments, Darley and Latané found that a person was less likely to help another person if others were around.

In their classic 1968 experiment, Darley and Latané placed a research participant in a separate room and had the participant interact with another person through a communication system. The researchers led participants to believe that they were 1) the only person participating with one other person, 2) participating in a three-person group, or 3) one of six participants. Participants were to initially take two-minute turns discussing typical college student problems they faced. One of the participants, a research confederate, revealed that he sometimes has problems with seizures. When his turn to talk came again, the confederate started talking but then eventually stuttered and said that he was having a seizure. The only way participants could help the supposed victim was by leaving their room. Every one of the participants who believed they were the only one aware of the victim's seizure reported it right away, but only 62 percent who thought they were part of the group of six reported it.

Darley and Latané initially believed that people were frozen by the bystander effect because of the **diffusion of responsibility**—the phenomenon in which someone witnessing a problem is less likely to take action when others are also present because they assume that others are taking on the responsibility. However, social psychologists have identified other factors that explain people's inaction in emergency situations. These other factors include:

1. Noticing the emergency

2. Interpreting the situation as an emergency

3. Determining whether you have the ability to intervene

4. Determining if helping exceeds risks that might be present

Helping in an emergency despite the presence of others is called **bystander intervention**. To do so, you first need to break the cycle of inaction (i.e., the bystander effect). Your helping actions, such as calling 911, will give onlookers the information needed to also overcome the bystander effect and turn it into bystander intervention by helping in whatever way they can.

Prosocial Behavior

Whenever people help others, their motives are often questioned. Did they help because they wanted public recognition, a reward, or good feelings? How would you answer that question in relation to the following examples?

- Following the terrorist attacks on September 11, 2001, more than 100 individuals, not rescue or safety professionals, stayed inside the World Trade Center buildings to help coworkers and strangers get to safety. They lost their lives as a consequence.

- Two former marines—one on Long Island, the other in Connecticut— put on their uniforms, drove to the site, and helped search the debris for survivors, saving two police officers who had been in the buildings. One of these men did not give his name to officials or reporters.

- Sometimes people who lose a child create a foundation in the child's memory. Carlos Arredondo lives his life to honor the memory of the sons he lost—one in the Iraq war, the other to suicide because of survivor's guilt. Immediately following the Boston Marathon bombing in 2013, Arredondo, thinking of his sons, rushed into the chaos and cleared debris so that emergency responders could help victims. He saved the life of Jeffrey Bauman Jr., who lost both legs in the bombing.

Regardless of the reason for or motivation behind the behavior, when people help one another, they are engaging in **prosocial behavior**.

A common belief is that the helper is a good person whose motivation is **altruism**, the desire to help another person strictly for that person's benefit without expecting any personal benefit. Significant research has focused on altruism as a reason underlying prosocial behavior. A second major explanation for prosocial behavior is the social exchange theory.

Altruism Daniel Batson and his colleagues reasoned that if our motivations are truly to help another person without regard for our own benefit—a concept that Batson calls *true altruism*—we must be able to empathize with the other person. To test this hypothesis, Batson and his colleagues set up a game similar to the Prisoner's Dilemma, in which participants competed for tickets for a drawing to receive desirable objects (like a department store gift card). You may recall from earlier in this chapter, the best strategy in a Prisoner's Dilemma is for both people to cooperate. When both people cooperate, both benefit.

Batson set up his experiment so that research participants knew in advance that their partner (a confederate of Batson's) would not cooperate with them. Nearly every participant decided not to cooperate with the partner, so, as in the standard Prisoner's Dilemma, they were both penalized a moderate amount— they lost some drawing tickets for the gift card.

In another condition, the confederate first told a horrible story about how her fiancé just broke off their relationship days before they were to be married. In this condition, research participants often cooperated with the confederate, even knowing that the confederate had not cooperated with them. They knew that they were losing some of their own chances to win the gift card to give the confederate more chances to win the gift card. Batson and his colleagues reasoned that the story about calling off the wedding was heartbreaking enough to cause the participants to empathize with the confederate and to motivate them to act altruistically toward her.

Social Exchange Theory Despite Batson's evidence, you might wonder: Does altruism really exist? In 1959, well before Batson conducted his research, John Thibaut (1917–1986) and Harold Kelley (1921–2003) examined the psychological aspects of the **social exchange theory**, which suggests that people engage in a cost-benefit analysis and help others only because they get some benefit from providing assistance or because doing so relieves a negative feeling they might have.

Helping others provides benefits to the helpers.

Among the researchers in this area are Irving Piliavin and Jane Piliavin, who reason that people help others because they feel distressed, and helping others will relieve their own discomfort. Whereas Batson concludes that true altruism explains why research participants helped the confederate by giving up chances to win a gift card, social exchange theory argues that participants helped the confederate because they felt bad for her, and helping her relieved some of their bad feelings.

The Science of Psychology: *The Helper's High*

There is abundant evidence that helping others not only relieves the negative feeling resulting from seeing others in need but actually promotes a positive feeling so strong that it has been compared to the "runner's high" with its euphoric release of endorphins. The "helper's high," a phenomenon named by Allan Luks in 1988 but identified in 1965 by Frank Riessman as "helper therapy," is so powerful that it can have dramatic positive impact on both a person's happiness and physical well-being. Numerous self-reports and other studies have confirmed the health benefits of volunteering. People who give their time to help others experience less depression, greater self-esteem, and even less physical pain than those who do not.

Is behavior with such positive personal reward really altruistic? Or, since it helps both the giver and receiver, is it really cooperation? Do the helper's high and other benefits that giving bestows to the giver contradict the definition of altruism?

Practice: With a small group, research how psychologists have answered this question. Look into the work of Douglas G. Mook ("Why Can't Altruism Be Selfish?"), the work of Dennis L. Krebs and Frank Van Hesteren ("The Development of Altruism: Toward an Integrative Model") and the findings of the psychologists mentioned in this chapter. In your group, arrive at a conclusion about the relationship between personal reward and altruistic behavior. Develop a creative way to present your conclusion and the research that supports it, and make your presentation to the rest of the class.

REFLECT ON THE ESSENTIAL QUESTION

Essential Question: *What factors help explain our behavior to others?* On separate paper, make a chart like the one below to gather details to answer that question.

Aggression	Conflict and Resolution	Attraction	Loving	Helping Behavior

KEY TERMS			KEY PEOPLE
AGGRESSION aggression disinhibition of aggression frustration-aggression hypothesis hostile aggression instrumental aggression social learning *CONFLICT AND RESOLUTION* altruism altruistic norm conflict mirror image perceptions Prisoner's Dilemma reciprocity norm social dilemma social responsibility norm superordinate goal Tragedy of the Commons	*RACISM* discrimination ethnocentrism ingroup outgroup prejudice racism scapegoating self-fulfilling prophecy stereotype threat stereotypes *ATTRACTION* commitment companionate love consummate love fatuous love halo effect intimacy matching phenomenon mere exposure effect passion physical attractiveness stereotype proximity or propinquity effect reciprocity triangular theory of love	*HELPING BEHAVIOR* altruism bystander effect bystander intervention diffusion of responsibility prosocial behavior social exchange theory	Albert Bandura John Darley Bibb Latané Muzafer Sherif Robert Sternberg

1. Whereas _____ aggression is based on emotion, _____ aggression is goal-based.

   (A) hostile; symbolic

   (B) instrumental; hostile

   (C) symbolic; sanctioned

   (D) hostile; instrumental

   (E) sanctioned; symbolic

2. One reason why consumption of alcohol can contribute to aggression is that alcohol can act as a(n)

   (A) stimulant

   (B) disinhibitor

   (C) hallucinogen

   (D) anxiety reducer

   (E) intensifier

3. According to Berkowitz's modernization of the frustration-aggression hypothesis, aggression will only be evidenced once someone is frustrated if _____ and _____ are present.

   (A) intentionality; cues for aggression

   (B) a target; a source

   (C) a model; a victim

   (D) anger; a target

   (E) a trigger; dissatisfaction

4. A result of social dilemmas is that short-term gains lead to

   (A) inequities among participants

   (B) unpredictable outcomes

   (C) outside intrusions

   (D) upheavals among participants

   (E) long-term losses

5. Peaceful resolutions of social dilemmas include

(A) lifting regulations

(B) increasing the size of the group

(C) upholding personal freedom

(D) lowering the cost of noncompliance

(E) appealing to altruistic norms

6. Let's say that you have a hated opponent about whom you have many negative stereotypes. According to the notion of mirror image perceptions, your opponents

(A) will try to undermine your perceptions of them

(B) will intensify their behaviors to try to defeat you

(C) have the same negative stereotypes about your group

(D) surprisingly will be forgiving of your perceptions

(E) might try to prove that they are not as bad as you think

7. According to the physical attractiveness stereotype, physically attractive people

(A) are perceived as unintelligent

(B) try to prove that they are good people

(C) will start dressing in a more provocative manner

(D) have more problems than average looking people

(E) are assumed to have other positive qualities

8. Research indicates that one aspect of our attraction to certain other people is best explained by the idea that

(A) opposites attract

(B) we care more about inner qualities than outward appearances

(C) we like people whose attractiveness matches our own

(D) we like people we rarely see because they do not become overly familiar

(E) we like people who play hard to get

9. According to Robert Sternberg, consummate love is composed of intimacy, passion, and

(A) infatuation

(B) commitment

(C) compassion

(D) romance

(E) fatuousness

10. Research has found that a key component of altruism is
    (A) charity
    (B) happiness
    (C) empathy
    (D) cognitive evaluation
    (E) personal skills

WRITE AS A PSYCHOLOGIST: A FINAL READ

Journalist and presidential speechwriter William Safire joked, "If you re-read your work, you can find on re-reading a great deal of repetition can be avoided by re-reading and editing." Obviously when you answer the free-response questions you are not writing for publication, as Safire did. But leaving time for a final read through of your responses is a good practice, not only to catch repetition that might muddy your answers, but also to try to see them through the eyes of those who will be evaluating your exam. Based on rubrics you have used throughout this course, imagine the rubric the test readers will be using. Stand back from your responses, evaluate them yourself, and make last-minute improvements to show what you know in the best light possible. For more guidance on answering free-response questions, see pages xxii–xxiii.

UNIT 14: Review

In this unit, you sought answers to these essential questions about social psychology.

Chapter 24: How do we perceive ourselves and others in social situations, given various influences that can affect our behaviors?

Chapter 25: What factors help explain our behavior to others?

Apply what you have learned about social psychology by answering the free-response question below.

FREE-RESPONSE QUESTION

You are very excited about your new job as a salesperson in the household goods section of a large department store. You want to impress your boss and make as many sales as possible to be sure that you keep your job and perhaps even earn a promotion in the future.

A) Give specific examples of how you can use the following methods of persuasion/compliance to increase your sales of coffee makers.

- Foot-in-the-door
- Peripheral route to persuasion
- Reciprocity
- Door-in-the-face
- Framing effect

B) How might the following components of attribution play a role in explaining your sales and those of other salespeople (either good or bad) by yourself and your supervisor?

- Fundamental attribution error
- Self-serving bias
- Locus of control

C) You find yourself attracted to another salesperson who works in the department next to houshold goods. You see this person every day, and you have been picking up signals that the other person may like you, too. Explain your attraction to this person using these concepts:

- Matching
- Mere exposure effect
- Proximity
- Reciprocity

MULTIPLE-CHOICE

Identify the choice that best completes the statement or answers the question.

1. The field of psychology became a science in its own right when
   (A) Aristotle focused on observable nature and data
   (B) William James, influenced by Charles Darwin, focused on the function of consciousness
   (C) Sigmund Freud developed a comprehensive theory of personality development
   (D) Wilhelm Wundt opened the first laboratory to study human behavior
   (E) Brain imaging techniques became available in the early 20th century

2. After questioning the religious beliefs of his upbringing, a young man came to embrace them as he became an independent adult. He now refuses to engage in combat because he believes in the Golden Rule: "Do unto others as you would have them do unto you." His reasoning best illustrates which stage in Lawrence Kohlberg's theory of moral development?
   (A) Postconventional
   (B) Conventional
   (C) Egocentric
   (D) Preconventional
   (E) Concrete operational

3. Only one method can allow researchers to determine cause and effect. Which is it?
   (A) A psychological test
   (B) A case study
   (C) A survey
   (D) Naturalistic observation
   (E) An experiment

4. When children under two years of age see a ball go under the couch and out of sight, they think it no longer exists. The children have yet to establish which concept?

(A) Mental representation

(B) A schema

(C) Object permanence

(D) Assimilation

(E) Deep structure

5. According to Erik Erikson's theory of development, the key concern of adolescence is

(A) establishing an identity

(B) establishing a career

(C) sharing intimacy with another

(D) leaving the parents' world

(E) raising children

6. After seeing her parents give his sister a quarter for taking her dishes from the table, rinsing them, and putting them in the dishwasher, Bishesh begins cleaning his own dishes. According to social-learning theorists, Bishesh's behavior is an example of which of the following?

(A) Spontaneous recovery

(B) Discrimination training

(C) Observational learning

(D) Stimulus generalization

(E) Classical conditioning

7. A dog retrieves the slippers every day because in the past he received a food reward for this behavior. The dog's behavior is an example of which concept?

(A) A classically conditioned response

(B) An operantly conditioned response

(C) A discriminative stimulus

(D) An unconditioned response

(E) An unconditioned stimulus

8. In the diagram, which letter identifies the part of the eye that responds to brightness by letting more or less light in?

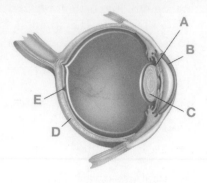

(A) A

(B) B

(C) C

(D) D

(E) E

9. A researcher is training laboratory rats to complete a complex series of rope runs, ladder steps, tunnel runs, and tower climbs. Each time the rats learn a new part of the course, they are rewarded with a food pellet. Within a few days, the rats learned the entire course. Which of the following did the researcher use to teach the rats the course?

(A) Spontaneous recovery

(B) Negative reinforcement

(C) A fixed-interval schedule of reinforcement

(D) Generalization

(E) Shaping

10. A researcher randomly assigned child participants to one of two groups. One group viewed a television program with violent content. The second group watched a program with nonviolent content. The children were then observed on a playground where researchers counted the number of actions considered to be aggressive. What is the dependent variable in this study?

(A) Sex of the children

(B) Type of television program viewed

(C) Duration of free play

(D) Acts of aggressive behavior

(E) Level of televised violence

11. People with schizophrenia tend to experience which of the following?

(A) They typically have a history of being maltreated as children.

(B) They typically experience onset in late adolescence or early adulthood.

(C) They have multiple personalities.

(D) They are typically afraid to go outside.

(E) They typically experience body dysmorphia.

12. A researcher surveyed coping skills in the same group of 50 people from early in their childhood through their middle adulthood. In this example, the group of 50 people surveyed represents which concept?

(A) Randomization

(B) Sample

(C) Operational definition

(D) Control group

(E) Population

13. Eleanor Gibson and Richard Walk created a table called a visual cliff that used a glass surface to give the appearance of a drop-off to examine behavior in crawling infants. Even when persuaded by their mothers to crawl out onto the glass covering, most infants refused to crawl onto the glass. This illustrated that the infants had gained which idea?

(A) Sensory adaptation

(B) Selective attention

(C) Perceptual constancy

(D) Depth perception

(E) Procedural memory

14. Which part of the nervous system is most immediately activated by sudden loud thunder?

(A) Somatic

(B) Parasympathetic

(C) Neostriatum

(D) Cortical

(E) Sympathetic

15. Which of the following sets of scores has the greatest standard deviation?

(A) 24, 26, 28, 31

(B) 60, 61, 62, 63

(C) 200, 201, 201, 202, 203

(D) 6, 7, 10, 13

(E) 3, 8, 10, 24

16. According to Albert Bandura, if people believe their efforts will result in success and they have control of events in their life, they have a high level of

(A) social responsibility

(B) self-efficacy

(C) reciprocal determinism

(D) insight

(E) self-monitoring skill

17. In part one of a study, a dog is conditioned to salivate at the sound of a bell ringing. In part two, a flashing light is paired with the sound of the bell ringing. After several pairings of the sound of the bell and the light, what will the dog do?

(A) Salivate when the researcher comes into the room

(B) Salivate when the light is flashed

(C) Stop salivating when the bell is rung

(D) Only salivate when the bell is rung

(E) Stop salivating when the light is flashed

18. Humans are motivated to do which of the following according to cognitive dissonance theory?

(A) Reduce tension produced by inconsistent behaviors and thoughts

(B) Maintain an optimal level of arousal

(C) Satisfy needs resulting from tissue deficits

(D) Respond to an inborn need to pass their genes to the next generation

(E) Satisfy basic needs such as hunger before proceeding to higher needs such as self-actualization

19. Freud claimed that the mind can protect the organism from anxiety by pushing painful memories into the unconscious where they are impossible to access. Which Freudian concept does this describe?

(A) Repression

(B) Morality principle

(C) Pleasure principle

(D) Primary-process thinking

(E) Id

20. A child has learned that her teachers ignore rather than reward her tantrums with the hope the behavior will eventually stop. Which of the following operant principles are the teachers attempting to use to control the child's behavior?

(A) Stimulus substitution

(B) Negative reinforcement

(C) Delayed reinforcement

(D) Positive reinforcement

(E) Extinction

21. An individual who gossips but accuses peers of being gossips is exhibiting which of the following defense mechanisms?

(A) Reaction formation

(B) Projection

(C) Sublimation

(D) Identification

(E) Denial

22. A researcher shows a series of pictures to a volunteer. The volunteer then tells a story about each of the pictures. The researcher assumes that the volunteer will project her own unconscious feelings into the stories she tells. This is an example of which of the following tests?

(A) Thematic Apperception Test (TAT)

(B) Wechsler Intelligence Scale for Children (WISC)

(C) Minnesota Multiphasic Personality Inventory (MMPI)

(D) Stanford-Binet Test

(E) Rorschach Inkblot Test

23. According to Erik Erikson, a person in late adulthood will reach the final stage of psychosocial development in which one reflects, reviews, and evaluates one's life and the choices one has made. Erikson labeled this stage

(A) identity versus role confusion

(B) generativity versus stagnation

(C) intimacy versus isolation

(D) integrity versus despair

(E) initiative versus guilt

24. A schema can be described as

(A) a fixed response to a particular stimulus

(B) a fissure between the lobes of the brain

(C) an optical illusion

(D) an outer fold of the ear

(E) a mental construct

25. Organisms are motivated by trying to maintain a biological balance. Which concept does this describe?

(A) Plasticity

(B) Natural selection

(C) Homeostasis

(D) Opponent-process

(E) Incentive

26. The section of the brain considered most important to the initiation of feeding behaviors is the

(A) suprachiasmatic nucleus

(B) hypothalamus

(C) superior olive

(D) hippocampus

(E) substantia nigra

27. Which research protocol can reduce problems connected to the intentional deceit of subjects of an experiment by a research team?

(A) Random assignment

(B) Using only single-blind studies

(C) Using only double-blind studies

(D) Debriefing

(E) Random sampling

28. Which of the following are the stages in Hans Selyes' general adaptation syndrome?

(A) Alarm, resistance, exhaustion

(B) Attack, flight, defense

(C) Anxiety, fighting, adapting

(D) Appraisal, stress response, coping

(E) Shock, resistance, self-control

29. Cordell has blue eyes and brown hair and is tall. These characteristics are best described as

(A) dominant genes

(B) recessive genes

(C) phenotypic traits

(D) genotypic traits

(E) mutations

30. Which of the following variables refers to what is measured when two groups are compared in an experiment?

(A) Random

(B) Control

(C) Stimulus

(D) Dependent

(E) Independent

31. Using a statistical technique called factor analysis, Raymond Cattell created a personality test called the 16PF. Which perspective did he use?

(A) Cognitive

(B) Psychoanalytic

(C) Trait

(D) Humanistic

(E) Behavioral

32. The more people present at a scene, the less likely it is that anyone will help a person in need. This phenomenon is a demonstration of

(A) social facilitation

(B) reciprocity

(C) a social norm

(D) situational ambiguity

(E) diffusion of responsibility

33. Learned helplessness is more likely to occur when

(A) a response is reinforced independently

(B) an organism receives negative reinforcement

(C) reinforcement occurs on an intermittent schedule

(D) actions have no effect on the environment

(E) young organisms fail to imprint at the critical period

34. In experimental psychology, a significant difference refers to a
    (A) difference not likely due to faulty design
    (B) result that departs from previous findings
    (C) result that indicates a correlation equal to 1.0
    (D) result that proves a new theory
    (E) difference not likely due to chance

35. In a normal distribution, roughly what percent of the scores occur within one standard deviation above and below the mean?
    (A) 16 percent
    (B) 68 percent
    (C) 5 percent
    (D) 97 percent
    (E) 34 percent

36. Which of the following best describes the Flynn effect?
    (A) Fluid intelligence declines as people age, but crystallized intelligence increases.
    (B) Each generation appears to be getting smarter than previous generations or at least better at taking tests.
    (C) Test scores can be compared only with those from the previous twenty-five years.
    (D) Crystallized intelligence declines as people age, but fluid intelligence increases.
    (E) Test scores can be compared only with those from the previous five years.

37. Jazmine has to assemble a dresser but cannot find her screwdriver. Which of the following terms best expresses her ability to find an alternative way to finish the dresser?
    (A) Mental set
    (B) Divergent thought
    (C) Rigidity
    (D) Confirmation bias
    (E) Functional fixedness

38. Despite its unpleasant side effects, electroconvulsive therapy (ECT) has recently been shown to be most effective in the treatment of which disorder?

(A) Schizophrenia

(B) Dissociative identity disorder

(C) Depression

(D) Psychogenic amnesia

(E) Panic disorder

39. A key difference between acute stress disorder (ASD) and post-traumatic stress disorder (PTSD) is

(A) the intensity of the flashbacks is great in ASD

(B) more women than men are diagnosed with ASD

(C) PTSD has symptoms that persist for more than a month

(D) children can experience ASD but not PTSD

(E) people may be genetically predisposed to PTSD but not to ASD

40. Mina works hard in school because her parents give her 100 dollars for every "A" she receives. Mina's parents are attempting to influence her academic efforts by taking advantage of

(A) reactance

(B) intrinsic motivation

(C) instinctive needs

(D) extrinsic motivation

(E) primary needs

41. Classical conditioning is most effective when the neutral stimulus (NS)

(A) precedes the conditioned stimulus (CS) by a few minutes

(B) immediately precedes the conditioned stimulus (CS)

(C) is presented at the same time as the conditioned stimulus (CS)

(D) immediately precedes the unconditioned stimulus (US)

(E) follows the conditioned stimulus (CS) by a few minutes

42. Substances produced by the brain that reduce pain are known as

(A) cortisols

(B) glucocorticoids

(C) hormones

(D) endorphins

(E) pheromones

43. In Piaget's cognitive development theory, which of the following cognitive growth indicators tends to be acquired last?

(A) Object permanence

(B) Use of schemas

(C) Assimilation

(D) Telegraphic speech

(E) Hypothetical thinking

44. When a person commits the fundamental attribution error, he or she tends to explain failures of others by underestimating the importance of

(A) motivational factors

(B) dispositional factors

(C) support systems

(D) inherited traits

(E) external situational factors

45. Which of the following terms refers to the body's tendency to maintain a level of body fat that remains relatively fixed and impervious to change?

(A) Set point

(B) Hyperphagia

(C) Glucagon theory

(D) Hypophagia

(E) Metabolic conversion

46. Which of the following statements best illustrates the humanistic perspective?

(A) Most behavior can be explained by operant conditioning principles.

(B) All humans have peak experiences.

(C) Self-actualization can happen only through therapy.

(D) All humans are by nature good.

(E) Humans are doomed to a life of neurosis and suffering.

47. Psychoanalytic theory is criticized for which two weaknesses, among others?

(A) Lack of empirical support and discounting the effect of environment

(B) Its focus on early childhood and defense mechanisms

(C) Gender bias against women and lack of empirical support

(D) Insistence that the id, ego, and superego were verifiable and focus on parent-child relationships

(E) The need for lengthy therapy and the lack of boundaries between patient and therapist

48. Where in neurons are neurotransmitters normally stored?

(A) The terminal buttons

(B) The axon

(C) The nodes of Ranvier

(D) The soma

(E) The myelin sheath

49. John Locke's proposition that people are born with a mind that is like a blank slate (*tabula rasa*) laid the groundwork for which of the following modern theories of psychology?

(A) psychoanalysis

(B) epigenetics

(C) behaviorism

(D) biopsychosocial theory

(E) twin studies

50. Ethologist Konrad Lorenz showed that imprinting occurs at a specific age for certain organisms. He demonstrated the existence of

(A) an unconscious inference

(B) a reflex

(C) a critical period

(D) an archetype

(E) a schema

51. Shimon sometimes experiences periods of major depression. At other times, he is extremely talkative and active, appears to be in a euphoric mood, goes days without sleeping, and reports that his thoughts are racing. The most likely diagnosis of Shimon's condition is

(A) schizophrenia

(B) major depressive disorder

(C) delusional disorder

(D) dissociative identity disorder

(E) bipolar disorder

52. Carol Gilligan criticized Lawrence Kohlberg's theory of moral development based on the premise that Kohlberg's theory or stages

(A) underestimates the capabilities of infants and children

(B) do not apply equally well to all racial and ethnic groups

(C) are too limited in their critical period parameters

(D) fails to account adequately for differences between males and females

(E) has been invalidated by changes in the structure of families in the United States

53. When you can focus on a specific conversation in a noisy and crowded room, you are exhibiting

(A) dichotic listening

(B) auditory localization

(C) deep processing

(D) divided attention

(E) selective attention

54. As you watch a friend walk toward you, your retinal image of your friend gets larger. Despite this, you do not perceive him to be growing larger. This is an example of

(A) retinal disparity

(B) continuity

(C) motion parallax

(D) size constancy

(E) common fate

55. In the image to the right, we see three sets of parallel lines rather than six unrelated lines. The perceptual organizing principle that explains this is

(A) similarity

(B) connectedness

(C) continuity

(D) proximity

(E) closure

56. A monkey's choosing a circle from among several geometric shapes in order to be rewarded with a banana is an example of

(A) stimulus discrimination

(B) positive transference

(C) latent learning

(D) stimulus habituation

(E) disinhibition

57. Which explains the effect of certain antidepressant medications?

(A) They reduce GABA, preventing a controlled release of dopamine.

(B) They intensify the effects of GABA and reduce glutamate.

(C) They reduce absorption of seratonin.

(D) They prevent the absorption of dopamine.

(E) They speed up the body's functions.

58. A group of friends watched an episode of a crime investigation show. After discussing the show, they determined that they would have been able to solve the crime more expertly than did the television investigators. The friends' overestimation of their ability to determine who committed the crime is most likely due to a reasoning error known as

(A) confirmation bias

(B) cognitive dissonance

(C) the availability heuristic

(D) actor-observer bias

(E) hindsight bias

59. Which of the following would be used to measure the relationship between age and reaction time?

(A) Standard deviation

(B) A t test

(C) Central tendency

(D) A histogram

(E) Correlation

60. Following a series of hardships, Mr. Gaith disappeared and was discovered two years later in another state working as a prep cook at a fine dining restaurant. When questioned, he responded that he had found himself in a strange city and could not remember any personal information. Mr. Gaith most likely would be diagnosed with

(A) dementia

(B) dissociative amnesia with fugue symptoms

(C) dissociative identity disorder

(D) bipolar disorder

(E) retrograde amnesia

61. A young child shown a nine-inch round plate and a six-inch round plate containing equal amounts of candy corn says he is certain the smaller bowl has more candy corn than the larger bowl. Piaget would say that this child has yet to acquire what concept?

(A) Equilibrium

(B) Circular reactions

(C) Functional fixedness

(D) Conservation

(E) Object permanence

62. Which type of psychological therapy uses free association, dream interpretation, and analysis of transference?

(A) Psychoanalysis

(B) Cognitive-behavioral

(C) Humanistic

(D) Client-centered

(E) Behavioral

63. Metacognition refers to

(A) artificial intelligence

(B) amnesia

(C) mental disability

(D) thinking about thinking

(E) thinking without thinking

64. Two-year-old Reem tells her grandmother that "she swept the floor" yesterday. The scenario demonstrates that children often

(A) overgeneralize the use of grammatical rules

(B) learn language primarily through operant conditioning

(C) will model only words used by adults in their environment

(D) cannot learn grammatical rules during the first two years of life

(E) are not born with an innate language acquisition device

65. The primary content of the *Diagnostic and Statistical Manual of Mental Disorders* (DSM-5) includes which of the following?

(A) Discussions of the pros and cons of various treatment approaches for each type of mental disorder

(B) A history of and treatments for mental disorders through time

(C) Tables of biological abnormalities responsible for each type of mental disorder

(D) Classification and diagnosis of each type of mental disorder

(E) Discussions of insurance coverage for each type of mental disorder

66. A therapist using systematic desensitization to help a client overcome a fear of big dogs would probably begin treatment by asking the client to

(A) walk into a room where there is a small dog

(B) walk into a room where there is a large dog on a leash

(C) look at pictures of dogs

(D) identify the stimuli that trigger fear in an anxiety hierarchy

(E) buy a puppy

67. Different people will have different experiences after drinking the same amount of alcohol. These effects are different as a result of the _____ of the users.

(A) expectations

(B) cognitive biases

(C) intelligence quotient (IQ)

(D) success in developing a social network

(E) agility

68. Alexia accidentally touched a hot iron. She immediately pulled her hand back. Which of the following is true about the withdrawal of her hand?

(A) It was due to instructions from the brain.

(B) It was a voluntary behavior.

(C) It was initiated in the spinal cord.

(D) It was an operantly conditioned response.

(E) It was initiated in the motor cortex.

69. A stereotype is defined as which of the following?

   (A) An adjustment of one's behavior in response to peer pressure

   (B) An action performed in response to experts

   (C) A harmful action taken against someone who is a member of a social group

   (D) An overgeneralization about a social group

   (E) A certainty that one's own culture is superior to all others

70. Danush and Rada had planned to take a flight for their vacation. After news of a plane crash, they drove more than 1,000 miles to their destination despite knowing that fatal car crashes are far more common than airplane crashes. The couple's decision mainly involves

   (A) the overconfidence effect

   (B) belief bias

   (C) the availability heuristic

   (D) the representativeness heuristic

   (E) confirmation bias

71. Benjamin Whorf's linguistic relativity hypothesis proposes which of the following?

   (A) Languages with many words to describe certain phenomena lack deep structure.

   (B) People of cultures with few words to describe certain phenomena are more precise in their descriptions.

   (C) The number of phonemes used in spoken language is universal across cultures.

   (D) Speakers of different languages think differently due to the differences in their languages.

   (E) People of different cultures use similar words for common objects.

72. Hypnosis has empirical support for its effectiveness in which of the following areas?

   (A) retrieving repressed memories

   (B) allowing age regression to revisit the mind at a younger age

   (C) reducing pain

   (D) treating phobias

   (E) helping people perform tasks they would not otherwise be capable of doing

73. A researcher tests the same group of participants at two, five, and eight years of age. Which method was used?
   (A) Cross-cultural
   (B) Cross-sectional
   (C) Projective
   (D) Correlational
   (E) Longitudinal

74. Omotoyosi has a brain injury and is having difficulty with vision and audition. These symptoms indicate that damage has occurred in the
   (A) frontal and temporal lobes
   (B) frontal lobe only
   (C) temporal lobe only
   (D) parietal and occipital lobes
   (E) occipital and temporal lobes

75. Which of the following is a binocular cue for depth perception?
   (A) Interposition
   (B) Motion parallax
   (C) Linear perspective
   (D) Retinal disparity
   (E) Texture gradient

76. If students who take the SAT obtain roughly the same score the second time they took the test as the first time, the test likely has
   (A) standardization
   (B) test-retest reliability
   (C) objectivity
   (D) validity
   (E) norms

77. Curare is a poison that causes paralysis by blocking acetylcholine from entering the receptor sites of the adjacent neuron. This drug is an example of an
   (A) inhibitory postsynaptic potential (IPSP)
   (B) agonist
   (C) antagonist
   (D) excitatory neurotransmitter
   (E) excitatory postsynaptic potential (EPSP)

78. Visual sharpness is best in the
    (A) cornea
    (B) pupil
    (C) lens
    (D) iris
    (E) fovea

79. If a neuron is in a resting state, which of the following is true?
    (A) Both the sodium and the potassium channels are open.
    (B) The outside of the cell membrane is negative compared to the inside.
    (C) The concentration of sodium ions is equal inside and outside the cell membrane.
    (D) The neuron is not polarized.
    (E) The inside of the cell membrane is negative compared to the outside.

80. Many therapists will make a formal diagnosis, give advice, or interpret the unconscious motivations of patients. Who among the following did not treat patients that way, focusing instead on examining irrational thoughts?
    (A) Aaron Beck
    (B) Sigmund Freud
    (C) Albert Ellis
    (D) Carl Rogers
    (E) Carl Jung

81. Xenevian exhibits a strong moral sense, accepts himself as he is, is deeply democratic in nature, and is willing to act unconventionally in the face of social and cultural pressures. Maslow would likely describe him as
    (A) his ideal self
    (B) his real self
    (C) humanistic
    (D) self-actualized
    (E) fully functioning

82. Wolfgang Köhler considered a chimpanzee's sudden solving of a problem evidence of

(A) spontaneous recovery

(B) instinct

(C) modeling

(D) learning set

(E) insight

83. Even when she doesn't feel like it, Melinda studies carefully for every test because she is very proud when she gets a report card with all As. Which type of theorist would best explain Melinda's motivation?

(A) Sociobiological theorist

(B) Humanistic theorist

(C) Incentive theorist

(D) Arousal theorist

(E) Drive-reduction theorist

84. A student who obtained a percentile rank of 85 on an achievement test is best characterized as having

(A) ranked 85th from the top in a group of 100 test takers

(B) answered 85 percent of the test questions correctly

(C) scored higher than 85 percent of the test takers

(D) scored 85 percent higher than the average test taker

(E) scored 85 percent of the highest score

85. Stanley Milgram's and Solomon Asch's studies both showed that

(A) people obey authority without thinking of the consequences

(B) the behavior of others in a group strongly influences individual behaviors

(C) experiments held outside of prestigious institution reduce the authority's legitimacy

(D) people are driven by the need for praise and acceptance

(E) people were unaffected by the discomfort of others

86. While grocery shopping, Nishal heard voices that seemed to be narrating his every action. The voices made statements such as "Now he is reaching for the butter" and "Now he is placing the butter in his shopping cart." No one else heard the voices. Nishal has heard voices narrating his behavior on several other occasions. What is Nishal experiencing?

(A) Hypnosis

(B) Hallucinations

(C) Grandiosity

(D) Delusions

(E) Illusions

87. Stimuli will move into long-term memory if

(A) they are attended to and not rehearsed

(B) they are attended to, rehearsed, and not retrieved

(C) they move directly from sensory memory into long-term memory

(D) they move through short-term memory and are coded for storage

(E) they are episodic, semantic, or procedural

88. As a child, Grant often skipped school and engaged in repeated acts of vandalism and petty theft. As an adult, he has been arrested for corrupt business practices. The most likely diagnosis for Grant's current behavior is

(A) borderline personality disorder

(B) dissociative identity disorder

(C) narcissistic personality disorder

(D) oppositional defiant disorder

(E) antisocial personality disorder

89. Simran has a sleep disorder for which she takes medically prescribed amphetamines. For which of the following sleep disorders is Simran most likely being treated?

(A) Narcolepsy

(B) Somnambulism

(C) Sleep apnea

(D) Circadian rhythm sleep disorder

(E) Insomnia

90. Stanley Schachter and Jerome Singer view emotion as resulting from
    (A) a need for affiliation
    (B) biochemical changes in the hypothalamic-pituitary axis
    (C) cognitive labels of physiological changes
    (D) instinctual behavior
    (E) the level of physiological arousal

91. Tardive dyskinesia is a side effect of which kind of medication?
    (A) Antidepressants
    (B) Antipsychotics
    (C) Neuroleptics
    (D) Anxiolytics
    (E) Benzodiazepines

92. Most people in the United States tend to rate themselves as better than the average person on a number of different skills and traits. This is an example of
    (A) the fundamental attribution error
    (B) self-serving bias
    (C) enlightened self-schema
    (D) objective self-awareness
    (E) self-actualization

93. The primary purpose of the myelin sheath is to
    (A) reduce the amount of unused neurotransmitter in the synaptic cleft
    (B) facilitate the incoming stimulus signals as sensory receptors
    (C) increase the speed of conduction of the action potential along the axon
    (D) protect the terminal buttons of the neuron from damage by enzymes
    (E) increase the speed of passage of the action potential across the synapse

94. Unquestioned belief in the morality of the group is a feature of
    (A) groupthink
    (B) blaming the victim
    (C) cognitive dissonance
    (D) bystander apathy
    (E) the need for power

95. The primary reason people have psychological difficulties according some humanistic therapists is that people have
    (A) repression of unpleasant emotions
    (B) conflicts between the real and the ideal self
    (C) inadequate reinforcement
    (D) malfunctions of the body
    (E) irrational beliefs or assumptions

96. Howard Gardner and Robert Sternberg agreed on which of the following about intelligence?
    (A) Emotional intelligence is more important than IQ.
    (B) There are three broad categories of intelligence.
    (C) There are eight specific categories of intelligence.
    (D) Traditional intelligence tests are limited to assessing analytical intelligence and disregard practical intelligence.
    (E) Analytic intelligence is the most useful of the intelligence types.

97. After staring at a green, black, and orange "American flag" for about a minute, an individual will see a red, white, and blue flag afterimage. Which of the following explains this phenomenon?
    (A) Opponent-process theory
    (B) Convergence
    (C) Color constancy
    (D) Retinex theory
    (E) Trichromatic theory

98. Anthony is working on a group project and knows he will be away on vacation just before the assignment's due date. At the start of the project, he bakes cookies for everyone in his group hoping that they will return the favor by doing his part of the project while he is gone. Which of the following methods of persuasion has Anthony employed?

(A) Central route to persuasion

(B) Peripheral route to persuasion

(C) Primacy effect

(D) Foot-in-the-door approach

(E) Reciprocity

99. REM sleep, generally an "active" state of sleep, is accompanied by which of the following contradictory characteristics?

(A) Slowed respiration rate

(B) Lowered muscle tone

(C) Reduced eye movements

(D) Slowed heart rate

(E) Lowered blood pressure

100. Which of the following is a partial reinforcement schedule that is most resistant to extinction?

(A) Shaping

(B) Variable ratio

(C) Non-contingent

(D) Fixed interval

(E) Fixed ratio

1. On an online forum, a teacher posts an article she believes will be helpful for her colleagues. Almost immediately, a heated discussion breaks out about both the content of the article and the appropriateness of the post for the forum. The teacher is hurt and confused by the response, but she chooses to focus on the comments that support her sharing of the article and discount the critics. She begins to fear, though, that her professional reputation might be damaged. She leaves the conversation after a while, angry at the unprofessional jerks "out there," and goes to the gym for a kickboxing workout. After lengthy consideration about the response to her original post and receiving a private message praising her post, she rejoins the conversation and adds the reasons why she shared to the group.

   Explain the teacher's responses using the following concepts.

   - Cognitive dissonance
   - Sympathetic nervous system
   - Confirmation bias
   - Group norms
   - Self-concept
   - Metacognition
   - Catharsis
   - Fundamental attribution error

2. Lily often has very intense responses to situations when others do not, and she wants to understand why. For example, Lily often cries when she receives her report card even though it is usually good, and she is intensely frightened of roller coasters even though she knows they are relatively safe.

   A) Explain how the following concepts relate to how people process and regulate their emotions.
   - Two-factor theory of emotion
   - Confirmation bias
   - Neuroticism

   B) How might the following concepts help Lily manage her emotions more easily?
   - Internal locus of control
   - Rational-emotive behavioral therapy
   - Biofeedback

Index

A

ablation, 79
abnormal behavior, 496–498
abnormal psychology, 497
Abrahams, Darcy, 637
absolute thresholds, 151
abstinence in sex education, 318
abstract learning, 233
acceptance, 405
accommodation, 365
acetylcholine (ach), 108, 400
acetylcholine receptor (achr), 190
achievement, 456–457
    motivation and, 321–323
achievement tests, 468
acid rain, 630–631
Ackerman, Diane, 140
acquisition, 202
acromegaly, 84
action potential, 106
action therapies, 556
activation-synthesis theory, 185
active listening, 555
actor-observer bias, 598
acute depression, 80
acute stress disorder (asd), 527–528
adaptation, 118, 141–142
    perceptual, 155
    sensory, 141–142, 155
adaptive behavior, 523
adaptive traits, 118
adderall®, 515
adenosine, 179, 190
adenosine triphosphate (atp), 106
Adler, Alfred, 421, 422–423
adolescence
    cognitive development in, 398–399
    egocentrism in, 388
    physical changes in, 387–388
    sexuality in, 318
    social changes during, 388–391
adrenal glands, 84
adrenaline, 110, 342
adulthood, 391
    cognitive development during youth, 398–399
    emerging, 391
    social changes during early, 388–391
afferent neurons, 103
afterimage, 132
aggression, 622–632

biological factors in, 623–624
disinhibition of, 624
hostile, 623
instrumental, 623
psychological factors in, 624–627
social learning and, 626–627
agnosia, 88
agonists, 110–111, 188
agoraphobia, 525
Ainsworth, Mary, 360–361, 640
alarm, 341
Albee, George, 577
alcohol, 189
    disinhibiting effects of, 624
    fetal, syndrome, 356
Alcoholics Anonymous (AA), 562
alcoholism, treatment of, 205
Alexander, Bruce, 193
algorithms, 281–282
all-or-none principle, 106, 561
Allport, Gordon, 424, 634
alpha waves, 176
alternate-forms reliability, 476
altruism, 631, 642
Alzheimer's disease, 108, 400
ambiguity, tolerating, 279
ambiguous figures, 156
American Psychiatric Association (APA), definition
    of psychological disorders and, 498–500
American Psychological Association (APA), 42–43
    Animal Care and Use Committee of, 44
    code of conduct, 14–15
    Committee on Animal Research and Ethics of,
    44–45
    ethical principles of psychologists, 14–15
    guidelines to promote cultural competence,
    578–579
    psychinfo site, 564
Ames room, 162, 163
amnesia
    anterograde, 262
    dissociative, 529
    generalized, 529
    localized, 529
    retrograde, 262
    source, 266
amok, 508
amphetamines, 190–191, 515
amplitude, 134
amygdala, 90–91, 96, 188, 334
anal stage, 418, 419

B

babbling stage, 291
Babinski reflex, 358, 359
Back, Mitja, 636
balance theory, 320
Bandura, Albert, 228, 386
    influences of, 237–238
    moral decision-making and, 374
    psychological models and, 504
    reciprocal determinism and, 429
    social cognitive theory and, 241, 427, 428
    social learning theory and, 394, 626–627
Bard, Philip, 331
bargaining, 405
Barger, William, 207
bar graph, 56
Barrett, Lisa, 333
Barrett, Syd, 515
Bartlett, Frederic c., 594
Bartoshuk, Linda, 140–141
basal forebrain, 188
basal ganglia, 261–262
basal metabolic rate, 311–312
basal metabolism, 312
basic fields, 13–14
basic psychologists, 12
basilar membrane, 135
Batson, Daniel, 642–643
Baumrind, Diana, 377
Beck, Aaron, 560
Beck Depression Inventory, 560
behavior
    abnormal versus psychological disorder,
    496–498
    adaptive, 523
    assessing, of others, 596–598
    atypical, 497
    endocrine system and, 83–85
    group, 611–617
    helping, 641–643
    maladaptive, 497
    observable, 6
    prosocial, 642
    social, 593–594
    toward others, 622–644
behavioral approach, 6–7, 10, 427
behavioral genetics, 75, 113–118, 434
behavioral perspective, 201, 504–505
assessing, 559
behavioral psychology, observational learning and,
    237–239
behaviorism, 3, 201, 427–428
behavior modification, 558
behaviors
    hyperactive, 523
    impulsive, 523–524
    mood-altering, 341

    motivated, 310–312
behavior theories
    assessing, 430–431
    of personality, 427–431
behavior therapies, 228, 556–559
belief perseverance, 287
bell curve, 59
belongingness, 307, 320–321
Benedict, Ruth, 446
benzodiazepines, 189, 565
Berkowitz, Leonard, 625
Berscheid, Ellen, 636
beta-endorphins, 143
beta waves, 176, 177
Beyerstein, Barry L., 279
bias
    analyzing your, 278
    confirmation, 26, 284
    cultural, 578
    experimenter, 31
    hindsight, 45
    sampling, 29
    self-serving, 287, 596
    social desirability, 39
bilateral anterior cingulotomy, 568
Binet, Alfred, 364, 469
Binet-Simon intelligence scale, 469
binge-eating disorder, 531, 533
binging, 532
binocular cues, 158
biochemical influences, 624
biofeedback, 230, 515
biological approach, 9, 11, 504
    assessing, 435
biological bases of hunger, 311
biological factors in aggression, 623–624
biological motives, 301
biological needs, 306
biological psychologists, 13
biological rhythms, sleep and, 175–183
biology
    in classical conditioning, 228–232
    memory and, 261–262
    mental illness and, 502–503
    in operant conditioning, 232–234
    personality and, 434–435
biomedical approach, 565–570
    assessing, 569–570
deep brain stimulation, 569
electroconvulsive therapy, 568
psychopharmaceutical drugs or pharmacotherapy,
    565, 567–568
psychosurgery, 568
repetitive transcranial magnetic stimulation (rtms),
    569
biopsychosocial approach, 9–10, 11, 509, 510
bipolar cells, 129
bipolar disorders, 509, 536–538

clinical interviews, styles of, 541
clinical psychologists, 12
closure, 157
cocaine, 190
cochlea, 135
cochlear implants, 137
cocktail party effect, 154, 253, 255
codeine, 190
coercion, 43
cognition, 276, 453
    aspects of, 453
    in classical conditioning, 228–232
    creativity and creative thinking in, 279–280
    critical thinking in, 277
    language and, 292–293
    in operant conditioning, 232–234
    organizing information in, 276–277
    problem-solving in, 281–284
    role of, in emotion, 331
cognitive affective processing systems (CAPS), 430
cognitive approach, 7–8, 10, 505
cognitive-behavioral therapy (CBT), 111, 554,
    559–561, 563
cognitive biases, 284–289
    anchoring and, 289
    belief perseverance and, 287
    cognitive dissonance and, 287
    confirmation and, 284
    fixation and, 285
    framing and, 288–289
    functional fixedness and, 285
    justification of effort and, 287
    mental set and, 285
    overconfidence and, 287
    problematic heuristics and, 285–286
    self-serving, 287
cognitive development, 364–370, 398–401
    cultural and biosocial development, 369–370
    middle age and beyond, 399–401
    of perceptual skills, 370
    Piaget's stages of, 364–369
    teenage years and young adulthood, 398–399
cognitive differences, 453–454
cognitive dissonance, 287, 421, 600
cognitive distortions, 561
cognitive expectancy, 428
cognitive map, 231
cognitive psychology, 13, 505, 604
cognitive theory of personality, 428
cognitive therapy, 560
    assessing, 561
cognitive triad, 561
cohort effects, 42
Colapinto, John, 394
collective unconscious, 422
collectivism, 450
collectivistic cultural influence, on personality,
    448–451

collectivistic cultures, 322, 448, 450, 579
color blindness, 133
color constancy, 162
color vision, theories of, 132–133
color weakness, 133
commitment, 639
common factors, 563
common-sense theory of emotions, 330
communication, 631
    channel of, 603
    language as basis of, 289–293
    nonverbal, 334–338
community-based treatment, 581–583
community health campaigns, 346
community integration, 582
community mental health, 581–584
    assessing, 583–584
Community Mental Health Act (1963), 581
community psychology, 585
community support programs, 582
comorbidity, 522, 538, 584
companionate love, 639, 640
compensation, 422–423
complex cells, 153
complexity, 450
complex sleep apnea syndrome, 183
computerized axial tomography (CT or CAT scans),
    82
conception, 356
concepts, 276
conceptual skills, 480
concrete operational stage, 368, 369
concurrent validity, 475
concussion, 112
conditioned reinforcement, 210
conditioned response, 203
conditioned stimulus, 202–203, 206
conditioning
    avoidance, 215
    classical, 202–208, 313
    in classroom, 221
    escape, 214–215
    higher order, 207–208
    instrumental, 209
    second order, 207–208
conditions of worth, 432, 506
conduction, 135
conductive hearing loss, 137
cones, 129
confidentiality, 44, 569
confirmation bias, 26, 284, 469
conflict, 627
    motivational, 321
    peaceful resolutions and, 627–632
conformity, 606
confounding variables, 31
congruence, 555
conjunctivitis, 133

drive(s), 303, 310
   primary, 304
   secondary, 304
Drive: The Surprising Truth About What Motivates Us (Pink), 323
drive-reduction theory, 309, 311
drugs
   antianxiety, 565
   antidepressant, 539, 566, 567
   antipsychotic, 566, 567
   psychoactive, 187–192
   psychotropic, 565, 568
   synthetic, 187
dualism, 3, 173–174
dual processing, 253
Duckworth, Angela, 481
Duhigg, Charles, 262
dura mater, 76
Durban, John, 302–303
dwarfism, pituitary, 84
Dweck, Carol, 284
dynamic systems approach, 359–360
dysfunctional personality, 432–433
dysphoria, 527

E

Eagleman, David, 102
ear, anatomy of, 135
eardrum, 135
early adulthood, social changes during, 388–391
easy temperament, 377
eating, 311–315
   external cues that influence, 312–314
Ebbinghaus, Herman, 262–263
echoic memory, 253
echolocation, 127, 135, 138
eclectic approach, 503, 551
ecology, role of, in culture, 449
ecstasy, 191
Edney, Julian, 629
educational psychologists, 14
efferent neurons, 103
effortful processing, 255
Egloff, Boris, 636
ego, 6, 415, 416, 420
egocentrism, 366
   adolescent, 388
ego-focused emotions, 455
Eichmann, Adolf, 610
eidetic memory, 260
Einstein, Albert, 201, 307
Ekman, Paul, 335–336, 338–339
elaborative rehearsal, 257
Electra complex, 419
electrochemical communication, 104
electroconvulsive "shock" therapy (ECT), 501, 568
electrode, 80
electroencephalogram, 81

electroencephalography, 81, 176
electromagnetic spectrum, 127–128
Ellis, Albert, 343, 560
embryonic stage, 356
emerging adulthood, 391
emotion(s), 300, 329–346
   body and, 333–338
   current research on, 332–333
   ego-focused, 455
   neurology of, 333–334
   other-focused, 455
   reason versus, 603
   role of cognition in, 331
   theories of, 329–333
emotional appraisal, 333
emotional expressions, 329, 334–338
emotional feelings, 329
emotional intelligence, 333, 486
emotionality, 377
emotional learning, 283
emotional reasoning, avoiding, 278
emotion-focused coping, 236, 343
empathy, 555
empirical data, 24
empiricism, 3
empty-chair technique, 556
empty love, 639
encephalogram, 176
encoding, 254
   failure in, 263
endocrine system, behavior and, 83–85
endorphins, 110, 190
Engel, George l., 9–10, 509
enkephalins, 110
environmental determinism, 201, 428
epigenetics, 119, 379
epilepsy, 80, 92
epinephrine, 110
episodic memories, 254
erectile disorder, 319
Erikson, Erik, 391, 401, 421, 423
   on psychosocial development, 374–377
erogenous zones, 417
Eron, Leonard, 627
escape, 215, 341
escape conditioning, 214–215
estrogens, 317, 388
ethics guidelines for conducting psychological research, 42–45
ethnocentrism, 633, 633
etic approach, 446
etiology, 503
eugenics, 468
eustress, 339
evidence, examining, 278
evidence-based practice, 570, 582
evolution, 4, 316
evolutionary psychology, 9, 11, 118, 118–120, 302, 309

criticisms of, 120
exaggeration, 556
exceptional memories, 260
excitatory neurotransmitters, 108
exhaustion, 341
exhibitionistic disorder, 319
exorcism, 499
expectancies, 235
expectations, 165
experimental design, 30, 32
experimental groups, 30–31
experimental method, 27–32
experimental psychologists, 14
experimenter bias, 31
explicit memory, 255–256
exposure hierarchy, 230
exposure therapies, 557–559
external attribution, 597
external frustration, 339–340
external locus of control, 237, 428
external validity, 30, 475
extinction, 208, 559
extrasensory perception (ESP), 166
extraversion, 425
extraverts, 422
extrinsic motivation, 322–323
extroverts, 377
eye, structure of, 128–130
eyewitness memories, 265–266
Eysenck, Hans, 424, 425, 434, 563
Eysenck, Sybil, 424, 425, 434
Eysenck Personality Questionnaire (EPQ), 425

F

fables, personal, 389
face-blindness, 88
face validity, 474
facial action coding system (FACS), 335
facial expressions, 335
facial feedback, 332
factitious disorder, 531
factor, 471
factor analysis, 424, 471
false consensus, 421
false dichotomy, 288
family support, 586
family systems theory, 562
family therapy, 562
Fanon, Franz, 287
farsightedness, 133
Fast Food Nation (documentary), 314
fatuous love, 639
feature detectors, 131, 153
Fechner, Gustav, 151
feedback, facial, 332
feeding and eating disorders, 531–533
    anorexia nervosa, 531–532
    binge-eating, 533

bulimia nervosa, 532–533
feelings, emotional, 329
Feingold, Alan, 637
female orgasmic disorder, 319
Festinger, Leon, 320, 600
fetal alcohol syndrome (fas), 356
fetal stage, 356
fetishistic disorder, 319
fetus, 356
fibers, 102
50 Great Myths of Popular Psychology: Shattering Widespread Misconceptions About Human Nature (Lilienfeld et al.), 279
fight-or-flight response, 119, 302, 334, 341, 505
figure-ground pattern, 155–156
fine motor skills, 360
five factor model, 426, 437
fixation, 285, 418
fixed action patterns, 302
fixed interval schedule, 216, 218
fixed mindsets, 284
    growth mindsets versus, 236
fixed ratio, 218
fixed ratio schedule of reinforcement, 217
fixed reinforcement, 216
flashbulb memories, 265
flat affect, 535
flight of ideas, 537
flooding, 558
fluid intelligence, 399, 472
Flynn, James, 479
Flynn effect, 400, 479
focusing, 130–131
food, using, as reinforcement, 232
foot-in-the-door approach, 604
Forever Today: A True Story of Lost Memory and Never-Ending Love (Wearing), 90
forgetting, 262–264
memory and, 251–270
forgetting curve, 263
formal operational stage, 368, 369
fovea, 129
Fox, Michael J., 109
framing, 288–289
Frankl, Viktor, 307, 551
free association, 552
Freeman, Walter, 80
free-response questions, 444
frequency, 134
frequency distributions, 53
frequency polygon, 57
frequency theory, 136
Freud, Anna, 423
Freud, Sigmund, 111
    assessing theory of, 420–421
    discontinuous developments and, 355
    dream interpretation by, 184–185
    humanistic approach and, 8

psychoanalysis and, 414–419, 552–553
psychological models and, 504
repression and, 264
suppression and, 264
unconsciousness and, 175, 201
Freudian slips, 415
Friedman, Howard, 343
Friesen, Wallace, 335
frontal lobe, 86–87, 94, 399
frotteuristic disorder, 319
frustration-aggression hypothesis, 624–625
frustrations, 339–340
personal, 340
fully-functioning person, 433
functional fixedness, 285
functionalism, 4
functional magnetic resonance imaging (fMRI), 82
fundamental attribution error, 598
fundamental postulate, 429

G

Gage, Phineas, 78–79, 499–500
Galton, Francis, 468–469
galvanic skin response (GSR), 336
Gamblers Anonymous, 562
gambling, 217
gamma aminobutyric acid (GABA), 110, 189, 565
Gandhi, Mahatma, 307, 373
Garcia, John, 204, 230
Garcia effect, 204
Gardner, Howard, 484–485
gate-control theory of pain, 143
Gazzaniga, Michael, 93–94
gender, 319
definition of, 395
development of, 393–395
intelligence and, 479
as issue in psychotherapy, 579–581
gender competence, 579–580
gender identity, 393
gender roles, 393
gender typing, 393–394
gene-environment interactions, 115–116
general adaptation syndrome (GAS), 341
generalizations, 28–29
generalized amnesia, 529
generalized anxiety disorder (GAD), 524
generativity, stagnation versus, 402
genes, 114–115, 118
genetic mutations, 118
genetics, role of, in aggression, 623–624
genetic studies on causes of mental illness, 502
genital stage, 418, 419
genome, 113
genotype, 113
Genovese, Kitty, 641
germinal period, 356
gerontology, 386

gestalt, 155
principles of, 159
gestalt psychology, 5, 233
gestalt therapy, 556
ghrelin, 311
Gibson, Eleanor, 157, 370
gifted, 481
gigantism, 84
Gilligan, Carol, 374
Girl, Interrupted (movie), 495, 515
Givens, Geoffrey, 629
Gladwell, Malcolm, 283
glaucoma, 133
glial cells, 102
glucose, 312
glutamate, 110
golden rule, 631
Goleman, Daniel, 333
gonads, 84, 91, 316
Göring, Hermann, 610
grammar, 290, 293
grandiose delusions, 534
graphs, 55
grasping, 357, 358
gray matter, 399
grit, 481
grit scale, 481–482
grossly disorganized/abnormal motor behavior, 535
gross motor skill, 360
group behavior, 611–617
group influence, 604–609
grouping, 156–157
group polarization, 613–614
groups, marginalized, 635
group therapy, 561–562
groupthink, 614
growth mindset, 284
fixed mindsets versus, 236
guided imagery, 345
guilt, initiative versus, 375–376
gustation, 139, 140
gyri, 85

H

habituation, 155
hair cells, 135
Hall, Edward T., 337
Hall, G. Stanley, 5
hallucinations, 534
hallucinogens, 189, 191
halo effect, 638
Halonen, Jane, 277
happiness over life span, 396–398
Hardin, Garrett, 628
Harlow, Harry, 7, 362–363
Haslam, S. A., 610
Hatfield, Elaine, 637
Hazan, Cindy, 640

independent variable, 27–28
individualism, 450
individualistic cultures, 448, 450
individualistic influence on personality, 448–451
individualistic societies, 322
individual psychology, 422
individuation, 422
inductive reasoning, 152
indulgent, 378
industrial-organizational psychology, 13, 322
industry, inferiority versus, 376
infancy, 357–359
    motor development in, 359–360
    reflexes in, 357
infatuation, 639
inferential statistics, 64–65, 66
inferiority, industry versus, 376
inferiority complex, 423
information
    organizing, 276
    processing incoming, 152–155
informational social influence, 605
information-processing model, 253
information processing theory, 185, 253
informed consent, 43
infradian rhythms, 176
infrared light, 128
infrasound, 135
ingroup, 632
inhalants, 189
inhibitory neurotransmitters, 108
initiative, guilt versus, 375–376
inner ear, 135
insanity, 498
insanity defense, 498
insecure attachment bond, 361
insight, 282
insight learning, 233–234
insight therapies, 551
Insko, Chester, 636
insomnia, 182
instinct, 302
    animal, 302–303
instinctive drift, 232
instinct psychology, 309
instinct theory, 301–303
Institute for Creative Technologies, 564
Institute of Medicine's Continuum of Care Model, 585–586
Institutional Review Board (IRB), 42, 44
instrumental aggression, 623
instrumental conditioning, 209
insulin, 312
integrity, despair versus, 402–403
intellectual developmental disorder, 513, 523
intellectual disability, 480
intellectual functioning, 523
intelligence, 467

analytical, 486
assessing range of, 477–481
bodily-kinesthetic, 484
contemporary research and theories on, 483–487
creative, 486
crystallized, 399, 472
cultural differences in defining, 467–468
defining and measuring, 467–472
extremes of, 479–480
fluid, 472
gender and, 479
historical efforts to define and measure, 468–472
interpersonal, 485
intrapersonal, 485
linguistic, 484
logical-mathematical, 484
musical, 484
naturalistic, 485
practical, 485
spatial, 484
triarchic theory of, 485
intelligence quotient (IQ), 470
intelligence testing
    challenges to, 482–483
    construction of, 473–477
    validity and, 477
intensity, 127
interaction, 636
    anticipation of, 636
interdependent self, 452
    cognitive differences between independent selves and, 453–454
interdependent self-construal, 451–452
interference
    proactive, 264
    retroactive, 264
interference theory, 264
internal attribution, 597
internal locus of control, 237, 428
internal validity, 31, 475
International Classification of Diseases (ICD), 522
Internet addiction, 501
Internet gaming disorder, 501
interneurons, 103
interpersonal context, thinking in, 454
interpersonal intelligence, 485
interpersonal psychotherapy (IPT), 553, 554
interposition, 158
interpretation, considering, 279
interrater reliability, 476
interval scale, 55
interval schedules, 216
interviews, 38–39, 40, 438
intimacy, 639
    isolation versus, 402
intonation, 337

intrapersonal intelligence, 485
intrinsic motivation, 322–323
introspection, 4
introversion, 425
introverts, 377, 422
intuition, 283
iris, 128
Ishihara test, 133
isolation, intimacy versus, 402
Izard, Carroll, 332

J

James, William, 4, 173, 330
James-Lange theory, 330
Janis, Irving, 614
jet lag, 180
Johnson, Virginia, 316–317
Jones, Edward E., 598
Jones, James M., 458
Jones, Mary Cover, 228, 229, 557
journaling, 345
journalism, pack, 616
Jung, Carl, 2, 421, 422
justification of effort, 287
just noticeable difference (JND), 150–151

K

Kahneman, Daniel, 283, 285, 288
Kaku, Michio, 24
Kant, Immanual, 127
k-complexes, 178
Kelley, Harold, 597, 643
Kelly, George, 427, 428–429
Kendra's Law, 583
Kennedy, John F., 265, 614, 615
Keysen, Susanna, 495, 515
Kiel, Richard, 84
kinesics, 337
kinesis, 166
kinesthesis, 141
kinesthetic sense, 139
King, Martin Luther Jr., 265
kin selection, 303
Kinsey, Alfred, 317
Kish, Daniel, 127
Kitayama, Shinobu, 451–452, 453
knowledge, processing, about self and others, 454
Koffka, Kurt, 155
Kohlberg, Lawrence, 371–374
Köhler, Wolfgang, 233, 234, 282
Kübler-Ross, Elizabeth, 404
Ku Klux Klan (KKK), 632

L

labels, stigmatization of, 513–514
Lagerspetz, Kirsti, 623
Lakoff, George, 630

Langdon, John, 513
Lange, Carl, 330
language, 289–293
    acquisition of, 292
    basics of, 289–290
    body, 336
    cognition and, 292–293
    development of, 291
language acquisition device (lad), 292
Lapiere, Richard, 599–600
Latané, Bibb, 641
latency stage, 418, 419
latent, 6
latent content, 184, 552–553
latent learning, 231
lateral hypothalamus, 91, 311
law and order stage, 372, 373
law of effect, 7, 209
learned helplessness, 232, 341
learned motives, 301
Learned Optimism: How to Change Your Mind and Your Life (Seligman), 235
learning, 201, 428
    abstract, 233
    associative, 202
    emotional, 283
    improving, 266–267, 269–270
    insight, 233–234
    latent, 231
    observational, 429
    statistical, 292
    stimulus-response, 202
    styles of, 485
    vicarious, 238
learning curve, 263
Ledoux, Joseph, 93–94
left brain interpreter, 93–94
lens, 128
Lepage, Anthony, 625
leptin, 311
lesbians, gays, bisexuals, and transgendered (lgbt) population, 319
lesions, 79
Levi, Primo, 251
Levinson, Stephen C., 165–166
Lewin, Kurt, 320, 598–599
libido, 6, 374, 415
Life Change Units, 344
life skills training, 346
life span, happiness and satisfaction over, 396–398
lifestyle, 344–345
lifestyle diseases, 345
lifetime prevalence, 510
light and shadow, 159
lightness constancy, 163
liking, 639
Lilienfeld, Scott O., 279
limbic system, 89–91, 334, 399

state-dependent, 259
unreliable and false, 264–266
working, 399
memory cues, 263
memory reconstruction, 258–259
memory span, 256
memory traces, 263–264
menarche, 387
meninges, 76
menopause, 404
mental age, 469
mental disorder, 496, 498
mental health, community, 581–584
mental illness, 496
causes of, 502–503
global occurrence of, 511, 512
preventive approaches for, 584–586
mental incompetence, 498
mental set, 285
mere exposure effect, 637
Merritte, Douglas, 207
Mesmer, Franz, 186
mesmerism, 186
meta-analysis, 65, 563
metacognition, 260, 281
methadone, 110
methamphetamine, 191
methodology, 26–27
methylphenidate, 515
microexpressions, 336
microsleep, 180
midbrain, 89
middle ear, 135
midlife and beyond, 403–405
midlife crisis, 397
Milgram, Stanley, 43, 44, 606–608, 609
Miller, George, 256
Miller, Jodi, 80
Miller, Neal, 427
mindguards, 615
mindset, 284
fixed, 284
fixed versus growth, 236
growth, 284
Minnesota Longitudinal (Long-Term) Study of
Parents and Children, 362–363
Minnesota Multiphasic Personality Inventory-2
Restructured Form (MMPI-2-RF), 437
minority influence, 616–617
Mio, Jeffery, 629–630
mirror image perceptions, 632
mirror neurons, 243
Mischel, Walter, 427, 428, 430
misinformation effect, 265
mistrust, trust versus, 375
mixed motive interactions, 627
mnemonics, 269–270
mode, 58

modeling, 237, 559
modes of therapy, 561–564
couples/marriage counseling, 562–563
family, 562
group, 561–562
self-help groups, 562
Molaison, Henry Gustav, 262
mongolism, 513
monism, 3
Moniz, Egas, 500
monocular cues, 158, 159
monozygotic (MZ) twins, 116
monuclear cue, 160
mood-altering behaviors, 341
mood-dependent memory, 259
mood stabilizers, 566, 567
moon illusion, 164
moral development, 371–374
morality principle, 416
moral therapy, 499
moro reflex, 358, 359
morpheme, 290
morphine, 111, 190
motion parallax, 159–160
motion perception, 160
motion sickness, 141
motivated behaviors, 310–312
eating as, 311–315
sex as, 315-321
social balance and belonging as, 320-321
motivation, 241, 300, 301–323
achievement, 321–323
extrinsic, 322–323
intrinsic, 322–323
sexual, 315–321
theories of, 301–310
motivational conflicts, 321
motivational differences, between independent and
interdependent selves, 456–457
motives
biological, 301
learned, 301
stimulus, 301
motor cortex, 87
motor development in infancy, 359–360
motor neurons, 103
Muhammad Ali, 109
Müller-Lyer illusion, 164
multimodal perception, 144
multiple approach-avoidance conflict, 321
multiple intelligence, 484–487
bodily-kinesthetic, 484
interpersonal, 485
intrapersonal, 485
linguistic, 484
logical-mathematical, 484
musical, 484
naturalistic, 485

practical, 485
spatial, 484
triarchic theory of, 485
multiple personality disorder, 529
multiple sclerosis (MS), 104
multi-store model of memory, 253–254
multitasking, 153
Murray, Henry, 437
musical intelligence, 484
mutations, genetic, 118
myelin, 104
Myers-Briggs Type Indicator (MBTI), 437
myopia, 133

N

narcissistic personality disorder, 540
narcolepsy, 182, 190
Narcotics Anonymous, 562
Nash, John, 522
National Center for Biotechnology Information
(NCBI) Pubmed Site, 564
National Institutes for Health and Prevention (NIH),
510
National Institutes of Mental Health, U.S., 510
A Natural History of the Senses (Ackerman), 140
naturalistic intelligence, 485
naturalistic observation, 35–36, 40
natural selection, 9, 118–120, 302
As Nature Made Him (Colapinto), 394
nature versus nurture debate, 3, 355, 468
near-death experiences, 405–406
nearsightedness, 133
needs, 303, 310
belongingness, 307, 320–321
biological, 306
hierarchy of, 8
love, 307
safety, 306–307
negative correlation, 33
negative punishment, 213–214
negative reinforcement, 212–213
negative symptoms, 534, 535
negative transfer, 266–267
Neo-Freudians, 374, 421–423
critiquing theories of, 423
nerve deafness, 137
nerves
auditory, 135
cranial, 102
optic, 129
sensory, 94
nerve synapses, 187
nervous systems, neuroanatomy and organization of,
75–78
neural adaptation, 155
neural diversity, 103
neural firing, 105

neural metabolic crisis, 112–113
neural networks, 398–399
neural pruning, 398
neural structure, 103–104
neurilemma, 104
neuroadaptation, 188
neuroanatomy, 75, 102–104
neurocognitive disorders, 400, 542
neurodevelopmental disorders, 522–524
attention deficit/hyperactivity disorder (ADHD),
523–524
intellectual developmental disorder, 523
neurofeedback therapy, 515
neurofibromatosis, 115
neurology of emotion, 333–334
neurons, 102, 399
afferent, 103
communication among, 105–113
efferent, 103
life and death of, 112–113
mirror, 243
motor, 103
sensory, 103
neuropharmacology, 111
neuroplasticity, 138
neurosis, 423, 552
Neuroticism Extraversion Openness Personality
Inventory-Revised (NEO PI-R), 437
neuroticism/introversion, 425
neuroticism/stability, 425
neurotransmitters, 104, 107–111, 187
neutral stimulus, 202
nicotine, 190
nicotinic receptor, 190
nightmares, 183
night terrors, 183
night vision, 128
nihilistic delusions, 534
nociceptors, 142
nocturnal, 176
nominal scale, 54, 55
nonconscious, 174, 175
nondeclarative memory, 256
nondirective, 555
nonlove, 639
nonverbal communication (NVC), 334–338
noradrenaline, 342
norepinephrine, 110
norepinephrine and dopamine reuptake inhibitors
(NDRI), 567
normal distributions, 59–62, 478
normative social influence, 605
norm-referenced test, 473
norms, 449, 473
nucleus, 91
nucleus accumbens, 91, 188, 334
nurture, nature versus, 3

O

obedience
 to authority, 606–608
 reasons for, 608–609
obesity, 314–315
object permanence, 365
object relations therapy, 553–554
observable behavior, 6
observation, 438
observational learning, 237, 429
 behavioral psychology and, 237–239
 implications of, 242–244
obsessive-compulsive disorder (ocd), 526, 540
occipital lobe, 88
Oedipus complex, 419
olfaction, 139
Olweus, Dan, 624
one-dimensional thinking, 367
one-word stage of language development, 291
operant conditioning, 7, 208–220, 428, 505
 avoidance, 215
 biology in, 232–234
 characteristics of, 220
 classical and operant conditioning together, 220
 cognition in, 232–234
 escape, 214–215
 flow chart of, 213
 reinforcement and punishments, 210–214
 schedules of reinforcement, 215–218
 shaping, 219
 Thorndike and law of effect, 209–210
operant conditioning chamber, 7, 215
operational definitions, 26
opiates, 189–190
opium, 111, 190
opponent-process theory, 132
optical illusions, 164
optic disc, 129
optic nerves, 129
oral stage, 418
orders, following, 609
ordinal scale, 54–55
orexigenic, 311
orexin, 311
organ of corti, 135
Oster, Emily, 52
other-focused emotions, 455
others, behavior toward, 622–644
otolith organs, 141
outgroup, 632
outliers, 61–62
oval window, 135
overcompensation, 423
overconfidence, 287
overeaters anonymous, 562
overgeneralization, 291

oversimplification, 278
oxycodone, 110
oxycontin, 190

P

pack journalism, 616
pain, 142–143
 gate-control theory of, 143
 referred, 142
 somatic, 142
 visceral, 142
panic disorder, 525
papillae, 140
paradoxical stage, 178
paralanguage, 337
parallel processing, 132, 253
paranoid personality disorder, 539
paraphilias, 318–319
parapsychology, 166
parasympathetic nervous system, 77, 333–334
parenting, 586
 styles of, 377–379
parents
 authoritarian, 377
 authoritative, 378
 permissive, 378
parietal lobe, 87
Parkinson's disease, 80, 109
Parks, Rosa, 372
Parnia, Sam, 406
partial (intermittent) reinforcement, 216
passion, 639
Pavlov, Ivan, 7, 23, 202–204, 232
payoffs, changing, 630–631
peaceful resolutions, 629–631
pedophilic disorder, 319
Peek, Kim, 260
peer influence, 390
penis envy, 419
peptide yy (PYY), 311
percentile rank, 60, 473, 478–479
perception, 126, 150–166
 defined, 150
 depth, 157–160
 effect of cultures on, 165–166
 general properties of perceptual systems,
 150–151
 motion, 160
 multimodal, 144
 parapsychology, 166
perceptual organization, 155–166
 processing incoming information, 152–155
 subliminal, 151
 virtual reality in, 161
perceptual adaptation, 155
perceptual constancy, 162–163
perceptual organization, 155–166

posture, 336–337
The Power of Habit (Duhigg), 262
practical intelligence, 485
practical tasks, 480
practice effects, 476
pragmatics, 290
precognition, 166
preconscious, 174, 175, 414
preconventional level, 371, 373
predictive validity, 475
prefrontal cortex, 192
prefrontal lobotomy, 79–80, 568
prejudice, 634
Premack, David, 234
Premack principle, 232, 234
premature ejaculation, 319
prenatal development, 356–357
preoperational stage, 365–366, 369
presbyopia, 133
pretend play, 366
prevalence, 510
preventive approaches for mental illness, 584–586
primacy effect, 603
primary appraisal, 340
primary drives, 304
primary effect, 260
primary mental abilities, 472
primary reinforcement, 210
primary sex characteristics, 387
priming, 255, 269
Prisoner's Dilemma, 627–628, 631, 642–643
proactive interference, 264
problem, defining, 278
problematic heuristics, 285–286
problem-focused coping, 236, 343
problem-solving, 281–284
     cognitive biases in, 284–289
procedural memories, 254
processing, deep, 257–258
progesterone, 388
projection, 417, 421
projective tests, 436–437
propinquity effect, 636
proportion, 151
proprioception, 141
prosocial behavior, 642
prosopagnosia, 88, 153
protective factors, 507
proxemics, 337
proximity, 156, 636
pseudo-memories, 259
psychedelics, 191
psychiatric disorder, 496
psychiatric rehabilitation, 581
psychiatrists, 12
psychoactive drugs, 187–192
psychoanalysis, 6, 10, 111, 415, 552
     assessing, 554

psychoanalytic theory, 414
     criticisms of, 420–421
     Freud, Sigmund and, 415–419
     strengths of, 421
psychodynamic approach, 551–554
psychodynamic interpersonal therapy, 563–564
psychodynamic model, 504
psychodynamics, 6
psychodynamic theories, 414–423
use of case studies and, 438
psychodynamic therapies, 553
     assessing, 554
psychokinesis, 166
psychological claims, challenging, 278–279
psychological constructivism, 333
psychological disorder, 496, 498
     abnormal behavior versus, 496–498
     criteria for, 497
     defining, 498–500
     prevalence of, 510
psychological factors in aggression, 624–627
psychological models, 504, 506
psychological research, ethics guidelines for
     conducting, 42–45
psychological therapies, 551–561
     behavior, 556–559
     cognitive-behavioral, 559–561
     humanistic, 554–556
     psychodynamic approaches, 551–554
psychologists
     applied, 12
     basic, 12
     biological, 13
     clinical, 12
     cognitive, 13
     counseling, 13
     developmental, 13
     educational, 14
     evolutionary, 9
     experimental, 14
     human factors, 13
     industrial-organizational, 13
     personality, 14
     psychometric, 14
     school, 13
     social, 14
psychology, 2
     abnormal, 497
     birth of, as a science, 3–5
     cognitive, 604
     cultural, 457
     cultural-historical, 369
     defined, 1
     evolutionary, 118–120, 302
     Gestalt, 233
     health, 339
     historical origins of, 2–5
     individual, 422

modern approaches to, 6–12
roots of, 3
social, 593–594
subfields and careers in, 12–15
Psychology of Diversity: Beyond Prejudice and Racism (Jones And Dovidio), 458
psychometric psychologists, 14, 468, 468
psychopathology, 496
    abnormal behavior versus psychological disorder, 496–498
    consequences of diagnostic labels, 512–515
    defining psychological disorders, 498–500
    DSM-5 and, 500–503
    theories of, 503–512
    behavioral model, 504–505
    cognitive model, 505
    diathesis-stress model, 506–507
    humanistic model, 505–506
    medical model, 504
    psychodynamic model, 504
    psychological models, 504
    sociocultural model, 507–512
psychopharmacology, 187, 565
psychophysics, 150–151
psychosexual personality development, 417–419
psychosexual stage, 417
psychosis, 498, 533
    symptoms of, 534–535
psychosocial development, 374–377, 401–403
    Erikson's theory of, 374–377
psychosocial rehabilitation, 581
psychosurgery, 79, 568
psychotherapeutic effectiveness, assessing, 563–564
psychotherapy, 551
    cultural and gender competence in, 577–581
    gender issues in, 579–581
    Western Eurocentric view of, 577
psychoticism/socialization, 425
psychotropic drugs, 565
    assessment of, 568
puberty, 387, 387–388
punishing stimulus, 210
punishment, 7, 210
    negative, 213–214
    positive, 212–213
punishment/obedience stage, 371, 373
pupil, 128
purging, 532
puzzle boxes, 6–7
p-value, 64

Q

qualitative research, 435
quantitative research, 435
questions
    asking, 278

R

racism, 632–635
radical behaviorism, 7
Rahe, Richard, 344
Rain Man (film), 260
random assignment, 30
random sample, 29
random selection, 37–38
range, 58–59
rapid eye movement (rem) sleep, 178, 179, 182, 183
Rasmussen's syndrome, 80
rating scales, 438
rational-emotive behavior therapy (REBT), 560
rationalization, 417, 421
ratio scale, 55
ratio schedules, 216, 217
Rat Park, 193
Rayner, Rosalie, 206, 228
reaction-formation, 417
reality principle, 416
real self, 432
reason, emotion versus, 603
reasoning
    deductive, 152
    inductive, 152
recall, 258
recency effect, 260, 603
receptors, 107
reciprocal determinism, 116, 238, 429
reciprocal inhibition, 229
reciprocity, 303, 631, 638
recognition, 258
recovery, spontaneous, 208
recovery model, 582
referred pain, 142
reflection, 555
reflex, 357
    Babinski, 358
    grasping, 357
    in infancy, 357
    moro, 358
    rooting, 358
    stepping, 358
    sucking, 358
reflex arc, 77
refusal skills training, 346
regression, 417
regulation, 629–630
rehearsal
    elaborative, 257
    maintenance, 257
reinforcement, 210
    conditioned, 210
    continuous, 216
    fixed, 216
    food as, 232

sleep apnea, 182–183
sleep deprivation, 179, 180, 181
sleep spindles, 178
sleepwalking, 183
slow-to-warm-up temperament, 377
slow-wave sleep, 178
small is beautiful, 630
smell, 139–140
    absolute thresholds in, 151
Snellen test, 133
sociability, 377
social anxiety disorder, 526
social behavior, 593–594
social clocks, 397
social coaction, 313
social cognition, 593
    schemas in, 594–598
social-cognitive theory, 241–242, 427, 428–430,
    430–431
    assessing, 430–431
social contract stage, 372, 373
social desirability bias, 39
social determinants, 584–585
social dilemmas, 627–629
    conflicts beyond, 631–632
social exchange theory, 643
social facilitation, 611
    social inhibition versus, 611–612
social influence, 593, 594
    informational, 605
    normative, 605
social influence theory, 186
social inhibition, 611
    social facilitation versus, 611–612
social learning, aggression and, 626–627
social learning theory, 237, 394, 427
social loafing, 612
social norms, appeals to, 631
social psychology, 14, 592, 593–594, 598–599
    group behavior, 611–617
    group influence, 604–609
    persuasion and, 602–604
    research in, 421
social readjustment rating scale (srrs), 344
social responsibility norm, 631
social situations, 593
social skills, 480
sociocultural approach, 9, 11, 369, 507–512
    assessing, 509
Socrates, 467
Solomon, Richard, 235
soma, 103
somatic nervous system, 77
somatic pain, 142
somatic symptom disorders, 530–531
    conversion disorders, 531
    illness anxiety disorder, 530
somatic symptom disorder, 530

somatosensory cortex, 87, 95
somesthetic senses, 139, 141
somnambulism, 183
sonar, 135
sound
    locating, 137
    theory of, 136
sound waves, 134–135
source amnesia, 266
source traits, 425
Spanos, Joseph, 186
spatial intelligence, 484
Spearman, Charles, 471
specific action plan, 563
specific phobia disorder, 525
speech, telegraphic, 291
speech rate, 337
spermarche, 387
Sperry, Roger, 93
spinal cord, 75, 76, 102
split brain, 92
    research on, 92–94
split-half reliability, 476
spontaneous recovery, 208
stability versus change debate, 355
stable attributions, 597
stagnation, generativity versus, 402
stance, 336–337
standard deviation (SD), 59, 478
standardization, 473
Stanford-Binet Intelligence Test, 469–470, 474
Stanford Hypnotic Susceptibility Scales, 187
Stanford Prison Experiment, 601–602, 612
stapes, 135
startle response, 358
state-dependent memory, 259
state of suggestibility, 186
statistical learning, 292
statistical significance, 64
statistics, 52
    descriptive, 53–63, 66
    inferential, 64–65, 66
    thinking critically about, 52–53
stepping reflex, 358, 359
stereotypes, 633–634
stereotype threat, 482–483, 634
Stern, William, 470, 471
Sternberg, Robert, 485, 639
stigmatization of labels, 513–514
stimulants, 189, 190, 566, 567
stimulus
    conditioned, 202–203
    reinforcing, 210
    unconditioned, 202
stimulus discrimination, 204–206
stimulus generalization, 204–206
stimulus motives, 301
stimulus-response learning, 202

Tragedy of the Commons, 628–629
traits, 424
  adaptive, 118
trait theories, 424–427
  assessing, 426–427
tranquilizers, 189
transactional analysis (TA), 562–563
transcranial magnetic stimulation (TMS), 80, 138
transduction, 127
transference, 553
transgender, 319, 395
transorbital lobotomy, 80
transvestic disorder, 319
trauma and stress-related disorders, 527–528
  acute stress disorder (ASD), 527–528
  post-traumatic stress disorder (PTSD), 528
traumatic stressors, 340
tremors, 80
trephining, 499
trial and error, 209, 281
Triandis, Harry, 455
  collectivism versus individualism and, 449
  cultural influences on personality and, 448
  research of, 451
  role of ecology in culture and, 449
triangular theory of love, 639–640
triarchic theory of intelligence, 485
trichromatic theory, 132
true altruism, 642
trust, mistrust versus, 375
tunnel vision, 130
Tversky, Amos, 285, 288
twin studies, 116–117, 483–484
two-dimensional thinking, 368
two-word stage of language development, 291
tympanic membrane, 135
Type A personality, 343
Type B personality, 343

U

ultimate attribution error, 598
ultradian rhythm, 175
ultrasound, 135
ultraviolet light, 128
uncertainty, tolerating, 279
unconditional positive regard, 432, 555
unconditioned response, 202
unconditioned stimulus, 202
unconscious, 6, 175, 414, 415
universe ethics stage, 372–373
unstable attribution, 597
unstructured interviews, 541
updated hypothesis, 625

V

validity, 436, 474–475
  concurrent, 475
  construct, 474
  content, 474
  external, 30, 475
  face, 474
  of intelligence testing, 477
  internal, 475
  predictive, 475
values, 450
variability, 58–59
variable(s), 25
  confounding, 31
  dependent, 28
  independent, 27–28
variable interval, 218
variable interval reinforcement, 216–217
variable ratio, 218
variable ratio reinforcement schedule, 217
variable reinforcements, 216
variance, 59
ventromedial hypothalamus (vmh), 91, 311
verbal scale, 470
vestibular sense, 139
vicarious learning, 238
vicarious reinforcement, 238
violation of cultural norms, 497
virtual interactive training agent (VITA), 564
virtual reality graded exposure, 558
virtual reality in perception research, 161
visceral pain, 142
visible spectrum, 128
vision, 127–133
  absolute thresholds in, 151
  focusing in, 130–131
  peripheral, 130
  problems in, 133
visual accommodation, 128
visual acuity, 133
visual association cortex, 88
visual cliff, 370
  depth perception and, 157
visual information processing, 131–132
vitreous humor, 128
vomeronasal organ, 140
Vygotsky, Lev, 369

W

Wade, Carole, 278
wake/sleep cycle, 177–179
Walk, Richard D., 157, 370
Walters, Richard, 626–627

warehousing, 581
Washburn, Margaret Floy, 5
Watson, John B., 208, 427
    behaviorism and, 201
    classical conditioning and, 206
    "Little Albert" and, 7, 206–207, 228
    observable behavior and, 6, 7
wavelength, 127
Wearing, Clive, 90
Weber, Ernst, 150
Weber's law, 151
Wechsler, David, 470–471
Wechsler Adult Intelligence Scale (WAIS), 470
Wechsler Intelligence Scale for Children (WISC), 470
Wechsler Intelligence Scales, 470–471
weight loss, 190
Weisel, Torsten, 153
Weitzenhoffer, Andre Muller, 187
wellness, 346
Wernicke, Carl, 79
Wernicke's area, 79, 88
Wertheimer, Max, 5
Whorf, Benjamin Lee, 292
Why Are All the Black Kids Sitting Together in the Cafeteria? And Other Conversations About Race (Tatum), 458
Wilson, Midge, 636
Wiltshire, Stephen, 260
withdrawal, 188
Wittgenstein, Ludwig, 292
Wolpe, Joseph, 229, 557
working memory, 256, 399
World Health Organization (WHO), 510, 522
Wundt, Wilhelm, 1, 3–4, 6

X

x chromosome, 387
x-rays, 80

Y

Yates, Andrea, 498
y chromosome, 387
Yerkes, Robert M., 306, 611
Yerkes-Dodson law of arousal, 305, 306, 611–612
young adulthood, cognitive development in, 398–399
Young-Helmholtz theory, 132

Z

Zajonc, Robert, 332, 611–612, 637
Zimbardo, Philip, 593, 601–602, 612–613
    Stanford Prison Experiment of, 609
zone of proximal development, 370
z-scores, 59, 478–479
zygote, 116, 356
zygotic period, 356

Image Credits

page 5: Thinkstock; page 10: Thinkstock; page 11: Thinkstock, Contentra, Biodiversity Heritage Library; page 21: Thinkstock; page 26: Thinkstock; page 28: Thinkstock; page 36: Thinkstock; page 39: Aaron Bacall / Cartoonstock; page 45: Thinkstock; page 78: (top) Chris Hope, (bottom) iStock; page 82: © 2011 Ovaysikia, Tahir, Chan and DeSouza; page 83: United States Department of Health and Human Services; page 85: Bruce Blaus; page 107: Thinkstock; page 114: Thinkstock; page 117: Thinkstock; page 137: Thinkstock; page 139: Thinkstock; page 142: iStock; page 155: Thinkstock; page 157: Science Source / Getty ; page 162: Science Source / Getty; page 163: Thinkstock; page 167: Thinkstock; page 181: Thinkstock; page 182: Thinkstock; page 184: (top) Thinkstock, (bottom); page 187: Thinkstock; page 193: Thinkstock; page 206: Thinkstock; page 207: Wikimedia; page 212: Thinkstock; page 214: Thinkstock; page 219: S. Harris / Cartoonstock; page 221: Thinkstock; page 229: Thinkstock; page 233: Thinkstock; page 234: The Mentality of Apes by Wolfgang Köhler; page 241: Photograph by Gordon Parks, Courtesy of The Gordon Parks Foundation / Library of Congress; page 243: Thinkstock; page 244: Tom Prisk / Cartoonstock, John McPherson / Cartoonstock, Betsy Streeter / Cartoonstock; page 251: Thinkstock; page 255: Thinkstock; page 258: Thinkstock; page 259: Thinkstock; page 261: © The Stephen Wiltshire Gallery, www.stephenwilshire.co.uk; page 267: Thinkstock; page 281: Thinkstock; page 283: Thinkstock; page 286: Thinkstock; page 288: © Mike Baldwin / Cartoonstock; page 298: Thinkstock; page 308: National Archives; page 312: Thinkstock; page 315: Thinkstock; page 319: Thinkstock; page 320: Thinkstock; page 322: Thinkstock; page 335: Thinkstock; page 340: Thinkstock; page 343: OWLTURD.COM; page 344: Thinkstock; page 351: Thinkstock; page 366: Thinkstock; page 367: Thinkstock; page 368: Thinkstock; page 375: Thinkstock; page 378: Thinkstock; page 385: Thinkstock; page 389: Thinkstock; page 390: Thinkstock; page 393: Thinkstock; page 396: Thinkstock; page 402: Thinkstock; page 416: Thinkstock; page 431: Thinkstock; page 434: Thinkstock; page 436: Hermann Rorschach / Wikimedia Commons; page 446: Library of Congress; page 447: Reproduced by permission of the American Anthropological Association. Not for sale to further reproduction. / Library of Congress; page 449: Thinkstock; page 457: Thinkstock; page 464: Thinkstock; page 469: Thinkstock; page 472: Thinkstock; page 480: Thinkstock; page 486: Thinkstock; page 496: Thinkstock; page 499: Wellcome Images; page 500: (top) Everett Collection Historical / Alamy Stock Photo, INTERFOTO / Alamy Stock Photo, Everett Collection Historical / Alamy Stock Photo, (bottom) Reprinted with permission from the American Psychiatric Journal of Psychiatry, (Copyright ©1949). American Psychiatric Association. All Rights Reserved.; page 513: Thinkstock; page 514: Thinkstock; page 524: Thinkstock; page 528: Thinkstock; page 531: Thinkstock; page 534: Thinkstock; page 540: Thinkstock; page 542: Thinkstock; page 552: S Harris / Cartoonstock; page 553: Thinkstock; page 562: Thinkstock; page 594: Thinkstock; page 596: Official White House Photo by Pete Souza; page 597: Thinkstock; page 600: Thinkstock; page 601: Thinkstock; page 607: Milgram Collection, Archives of the History of American Psychology, The Drs. Nicholas and Dorothy Cummings Center for the History of Psychology, The University of Akron, (right) Stanley Milgram papers, 1927-1993 (inclusive). Manuscripts & Archives, Yale University; page 609: National Archive; page 610: Thinkstock; page 612: Philip G. Zimbardo, Inc; page 615: Library of Congress; page 622: Thinkstock; page 623: Thinkstock; page 626: ILGWU Archives, Kheel Center, Cornell University; page 627: Thinkstock; page 629: Thinkstock; page 631: Thinkstock; page 632: National Photo Company, Library of Congress; page 635: Thinkstock; page 642: Thinkstock